Pelican Books

A History of the People's Democracies: Eastern Europe since Stalin

François Fejtö was born in Hungary in 1909 and became one of the country's leading journalists. He joined the circle of anti-fascists who opposed the alliance with Hitler's Germany, and became co-editor of the socialist journal *Nepszava* and the literary review *Szep Szo*. Eventually he was forced to leave Hungary, and he took refuge in France where for the last twenty years he has been correspondent in charge of foreign affairs for Agence France-Presse. He is one of Europe's leading analysts of Communist affairs and is the author of several books on Eastern Europe.

François Fejtö

A History of the
People's Democracies

Eastern Europe since Stalin

Translated from the French by
Daniel Weissbort

Penguin Books

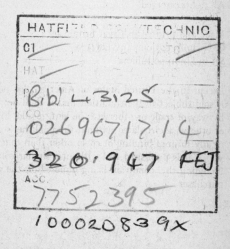

Penguin Books Ltd, Harmondsworth,
Middlesex, England
Penguin Books, 625 Madison Avenue,
New York, New York 10022, U.S.A.
Penguin Books Australia Ltd, Ringwood,
Victoria, Australia
Penguin Books Canada Ltd, 2801 John Street,
Markham, Ontario, Canada
Penguin Books (N.Z.) Ltd, 182–190 Wairau Road,
Auckland 10, New Zealand

Histoire des démocraties populaires: après Staline first
published 1969
This translation first published by Pall Mall Press 1971
Published in Pelican Books with a new second epilogue 1974
Reprinted 1977
Copyright © Éditions du Seuil, Paris, 1969
Translation copyright © Pall Mall Press Ltd, 1971
Second epilogue copyright © François Fejtö, 1974
All rights reserved

Made and printed in Great Britain by
C. Nicholls & Company Ltd
Set in Linotype Juliana

Contents

Introduction:

Stalinism at its Apogee and in Decline

The Nineteenth Congress of the Communist Party of the Soviet Union

On 5 October 1952, in the great hall of the Kremlin Palace, Stalin inaugurated the Nineteenth Congress of the Communist Party of the Soviet Union. Twelve hundred delegates, representing six million party militants, gave their seventy-three-year-old leader, the party's Secretary General, an ovation that seemed never to come to an end.

A few weeks later, Prague witnessed the opening of one of the most startling trials of the century, with Rudolf Slansky, former Secretary General of the Czechoslovak Communist Party and Stalin's erstwhile lieutenant, appearing as the principal defendant.

These two events, a few months before Stalin's death, exemplified some of the principal features of what his successors called 'the period of the cult of personality' – the dictator's hegemony; the tendency to envelop everything (including oneself) in mystery, to bluff and dissemble: and the use of purges to settle personal differences and resolve tensions.

The Congress aroused considerable interest in a divided world. It was the first Congress of the C.P.S.U. since March 1939, though party statutes laid down that one was to be convened every three years. In the meantime the U.S.S.R. had suffered vast human and material losses – seventeen million people – but had emerged victorious from a world war. She had extended her frontiers, and had surrounded herself with a chain of friendly, allied countries, now represented at the Congress, of which the newest, the People's Republic of China, was only two years old. The socialist camp now consisted of eleven countries: Albania, Bulgaria, China, Czechoslovakia, the German Democratic Republic, Hungary, North Korea, Mongolia, Poland, Rumania and the U.S.S.R. (Yugoslavia was expelled from the alliance in 1948; North Vietnam and Cuba joined it later).

After the 1948 crisis and the secession of Tito's Yugoslavia, unity seemed to have been achieved. No one contested the leading role of the Soviet Union, the Soviet party and Stalin, and the need for a unified stategy of the socialist camp and the international Communist party, in order to withstand the pressure of the capitalist world and the nuclear diplomacy of the United States, was acknowledged by all the leaders and militants. Thus the Nineteenth Congress was to legislate for the international Communist movement.

A few days before the opening of the Congress, Stalin published an essay in Pravda,[1] The Economic Problems of Socialism in the U.S.S.R.', which his sycophantic followers immediately hailed as a revelation. It was, in fact, a somewhat tortuous attempt to justify an economic (especially agricultural) policy whose paralysing effects were beginning to worry even the most orthodox Soviet and East European economists. Four years later Khrushchev, in his secret speech, described the situation in 1952 as critical for the rural population especially in connection with animal husbandry and meat production; 'Stalin', he said, 'had rejected every proposal to give the peasants a material incentive to increase livestock production by raising the price of agricultural products.' While Stalin made use of the thesis that, in contrast to capitalism, 'the aim of socialist production is not to make a profit but to benefit man and secure his material and cultural welfare', his policy had little to do with this theory. Indeed, Stalin himself implied as much when, in the same article, he rejected the argument that 'there is no contradiction under socialism between productivity and the forces of production in a society'. On the contrary there are and will continue to be contradictions, but if the leading organs 'apply the right policy, these contradictions cannot degenerate into conflicts ... This will not be the case if our policy is incorrect ... A conflict will then become unavoidable and

our production yields may seriously impede the development of
the forces of production.' Thus the possibility of internal conflict
was being held in abeyance. Stalin was convinced of the sound-
ness of his policy, and the Nineteenth Congress brought no
change in the economic sphere.[2]

Nor was the dictator prepared to abandon the language of the
cold war. The most one could say was that in his closing speech
he was comparatively optimistic about the establishment of a
modus vivendi with the West, whose internal contradictions and
divisions were, in his view, bound to worsen. Did he really believe this? It seems that at the beginning of the fifties Stalin had
told his closest associates that 'the final showdown would come
in 1953'.[3]

In spring 1952, ten weeks before the German Federal Republic
joined NATO, he had proposed to the three Western powers that
steps be taken towards the reunification of Germany by means of
free elections. In return, he asked for recognition of the frontiers
established at Potsdam and the neutralization of Germany. When
these proposals were turned down by the West, Stalin, having
probably foreseen as much, quickly withdrew them, and began
expediting the integration of East Germany into the Soviet bloc.
His action emphasized the division of Europe. At the Nineteenth
Congress, he urged the Western Communist parties to raise the
banner of national independence that the bourgeoisie had abandoned 'in pursuit of dollars'. He imagined he could preach with
impunity a kind of one-way nationalism, exclusively directed
against American hegemony but passive before his own imperialistic designs, though the rebuff he had suffered at the hands of Tito
not long before should have taught him better.

The most significant result of the Nineteenth Congress, not
properly appreciated at the time, was the reorganization of the
leading organs of the Soviet party. The Politburo (eleven members) was replaced by a Presidium (twenty-five full and eleven
deputy members). The size of the secretariat was doubled.
Khrushchev was given the task of proposing this measure and,
together with Malenkov and Beria, played a prominent part in
the proceedings. Was Stalin taking sadistic delight in forcing the
man he knew to be most opposed to his policy publicly to defend

the project? This is what Khrushchev suggested later, when he revealed that the main object of the reorganization was to get rid of the old members of the Politburo and replace them by new men whom Stalin believed he could manipulate as he liked.

In other words, the calm outward unity of the Congress was an illusion. The internecine conflict that had brought about so many changes since the death of Zhdanov (1948) and the disgrace and execution of Voznesensky (1949) continued behind the scenes and became increasingly acute. An 'atmosphere of distrust and general suspicion' prevailed in the Kremlin, and spread to the other Communist capitals.[4]

The public image projected by Stalin was paternal and serene. Three years before, the celebration of his seventieth birthday had seen him at the height of his fame and power. Few men since Napoleon had been the object of such widespread and passionate adulation, which between 1949 and 1952 had intensified into religious veneration. In Gomulka's words, its object 'was an expert in everything, knew everything, decided everything, ran everything . . . Whatever his actual knowledge, his talents, his personal qualities might be, he was the wisest of men.' Stalin was the incarnation of the eternal truth of Marxism-Leninism, the dream of terrestrial salvation.

But this superman was treating his colleagues – as they were to reveal a few years later – more and more suspiciously, arbitrarily and despotically. Like the tsars before him, he suffered from a kind of persecution mania. He no longer trusted even the most devoted and obsequious of his servants. 'He toyed with the absurd and ridiculous idea that Voroshilov was a British agent', and had a device installed in his home to enable him to hear everything he was saying. At the first meeting of the central committee elected by the Nineteenth Congress, Stalin attacked Molotov and Mikoyan, 'accusing them of imaginary misdeeds'. His plan was 'to get rid of all the members of the old Politburo'. On one occasion Bulganin, returning home in the same car as Khrushchev, confided 'Sometimes, when one visits Stalin at his gracious invitation and is sitting in his presence, one doesn't know if one will be sleeping at home or in prison'.

Since Stalinism involved the concentration of power in the

hands of a limited number of people, and ultimately in the dictator, Stalin's mental imbalance had extremely serious political consequences both for the U.S.S.R. and the People's Democracies. The East European Communist leaders imitated his every move and gesture. They made themselves the object of personality cults, and employed all the police methods appropriate to this oriental brand of despotism.[5]

But the delegates to the Nineteenth Congress were quite unaware of these negative aspects of the system. The militants were treated to a wonderful display of bright revolutionary optimism. The building of socialism had been achieved; now it was a question of moving gradually into the higher phase – Communism. Stalin's genius pointed the way. Of course, as Stalin stressed in his closing speech, the interests of the Soviet party were synonymous with those of the other peace-loving peoples: he addressed a fraternal greeting to the 'new shock brigades, from China and Korea, to Czechoslovakia, and to Hungary'; Matyas Rakosi and Klement Gottwald in particular were flattered, and they felt their position had been endorsed when they received the same treatment as Mao Tse-tung. In his report, Malenkov expressed satisfaction over the establishment of relations of an unprecedented kind between the 'democratic states' (as they were still called).

Mikoyan, who concentrated on economic relations, emphasized Stalin's daily concern for the strengthening of the ties of friendship between the U.S.S.R. and the fraternal peoples of the democratic camp. He tried to justify the severance of the Eastern countries from their traditional Western partners by claiming that 'the market of the democratic camp possesses sufficient resources for each country to find in it all it needs for its economic development'. Czechoslovakia provides a good example of the economic reorientation of the bloc countries: in 1947, the year when the U.S.S.R. forced her partners to reject Marshall Aid, the Soviet Union accounted for 6 per cent of that country's foreign trade; in 1950, 27.5 per cent; in 1955, 34.5 per cent; and in 1963, 38.9 per cent. According to Mikoyan, the U.S.S.R. was contributing in no small measure to the industrialization of the People's Democracies. Her supplies of modern machinery and equipment to these countries had increased tenfold between 1948 and 1952.

As a striking example of the kind of aid the Soviet Union was furnishing, he cited Rumania, which, as a result, 'now produced herself nearly all the oil-mining equipment she needed'.

For the present there was cause for satisfaction, while the future was positively resplendent. The leaders of the People's Democracies who spoke at the Congress all agreed about this. One after another, they paid tribute to the disinterested aid from Stalin, the Soviet people and the Soviet party. 'The Polish workers', announced Boleslaw Bierut, leader of the Polish Workers' (Communist) Party, 'owe everything they hold most dear to the C.P. of the U.S.S.R.: their liberty, independence, the rapid development of industry and national culture and the growth of internal strength ... Fraternal aid, friendship and the example of the Soviet people are playing a decisive part in these epoch-making transformations. The U.S.S.R. is setting the world a new example in international relations between peoples ... based on alliance, brotherly friendship and mutual aid.'

The Hungarian Workers' (Communist) Party was represented by Matyas Rakosi. 'For the first time in history, the Hungarian people are enjoying freedom', he claimed. 'They have realized that they belong to the 800-million strong peace-loving camp headed by the Soviet Union.' The same theme was echoed in more or less identical terms by the Rumanian Gheorghiu Dej (who ten years later was to spurn the Soviet economic *diktat*, mild as it then was): 'For the first time in their history, the Rumanian people have acquired real freedom, independence and sovereignty as a state.' The Bulgarian Vulko Chervenkov, Dimitrov's successor and a cunning and ruthless politician, spoke of 'the gratitude, love and boundless devotion felt by the Bulgarian party and the entire Bulgarian people for the fraternal Soviet peoples, the party of Lenin and Stalin, great in wisdom and strength – and the teacher and inspired leader, Comrade Stalin'. The leader of the Albanian party, Enver Hoxha, referring to the construction of a hydro-electric power station, with Soviet aid, exclaimed: 'The light of Stalin shines on Albanian soil.' He also took the opportunity to fulminate against the common enemies of Stalin and Albania, 'the fascist gangsters of Belgrade who aimed to turn our country into their colony by destroying our party'.

Throughout the Congress not a single discordant note was struck: there was no halt in proceedings, nor were any reservations expressed. The high-flown style of the oratory was in accord with the tenets of 'socialist realism' as applied to literature and the arts, a sort of idealizing, declamatory classicism that soared high above the dreary grey reality. This was a period of real ideological inflation.

It was two years before the truth was told about the relations between the U.S.S.R. and the People's Democracies. In May 1955 Khrushchev, Bulganin and Mikoyan went to Belgrade and publicly admitted that 'grave errors' had been committed with regard to Yugoslavia and that Beria principally was to blame for them. In July of the same year, a report presented by Mikoyan was the subject of discussion in the Soviet Central Committee on Relations with the People's Democracies. Mikoyan talked above all of the mixed companies formed after the war in the Eastern countries, a model subsequently challenged by Mao Tse-tung. Molotov found himself being upbraided for having 'interfered', notably in Poland, 'in an unwarranted and crude fashion', and it was alleged that Popov, the Soviet ambassador in Warsaw, had behaved like a colonial governor.

In 1956 many East European public figures denounced the U.S.S.R.'s domination, 'the inequality between the People's Democracies and the Soviet Union, the limitation on the sovereignty of the former in the atmosphere of international tension produced by the cold war'.[6] Yielding to popular pressure, the Soviet government itself admitted in a solemn declaration on 31 October 1956 that 'errors have been committed in the relations between socialist countries', and that 'these violations and errors have devalued the principles of legal equality between the socialist states in their relations with each other'.

The abuses were no accident, but were inherent in the centralized Communist control system, operated from 1947 mainly through the Communist Information Bureau (Cominform). Deprivation of national sovereignty was preceded by the elimination of parliamentary democracy and by monopolization of political power by the Communist parties, helped and pressurized by the U.S.S.R. In Slovakia, for example, the Communists, who were in a minority, used the security police to eliminate their democratic rivals in October 1947. This victory, however, left them completely dependent on the Stalin-backed Prague centralists. In 1950, the 'victors' of 1947 were in their turn ousted and accused of 'nationalist deviationism', while Slovakia lost every vestige of autonomy.[7] Similar tactics were used in each East European country; Tito's Yugoslavia alone did not conform to this pattern.

The Slansky Trial: An Example of 'Total Stalinization'

The Slansky trial opened in Prague on 22 November 1952. It showed how far Stalin's Russia – or, more precisely, Beria's secret-police apparatus, which was superimposed on the Soviet state – had infiltrated the East European Communist parties and governments, robbing them of their sovereignty, paralysing their nerve centres, and producing a kind of collective pathological condition, compounded of fear, mistrust, apathy and self-destructiveness, from which it was to take the leaders and their peoples much time and trouble to recover.

The truth about the trial and successive purges emerged only gradually. It was finally manifest, if not in every detail, at the time of the tremendous Czechoslovak liberalizing, emancipatory movement that began to take effect from January 1968.

The affair can be traced back to 1949, to the aftermath of the trial of Laszlo Rajk, the Hungarian Foreign Minister sentenced to death and executed for 'Titoism', treason and espionage on behalf of the imperialists. The trial enabled its Soviet organizers – there again one recognizes Beria's hand – to show how American intelligence, in collusion with Tito, had managed to penetrate the top echelons of a ruling Communist party. What held good for Hungary must do so equally for the other People's Democracies, especially Czechoslovakia, 'socialism's westernmost bastion', whose leaders, and particularly President Gottwald, had dreamed, prior at least to the 'Prague coup' of February 1948, of following an independent, Czechoslovakian path to socialism. However, since Yugoslavia's expulsion from the Cominform, the slightest hint of independence or expression of doubt regarding the Soviet ideal had become suspect, and was regarded as a 'deviation' in itself. The atmosphere was poisoned and a witch-hunt was soon afoot, enabling Soviet secret agents to manipulate the country's leadership. Rudolf Slansky, Secretary General of the Czechoslovak party, a veteran 'leftist' Communist, rough but honest, was the first one to fall into the trap. At a meeting of party activists after the Rajk trial, he declared 'We need a Czechoslovak Rajk'.[8] The security services, strengthened by 'Soviet experts', were alerted to the task of unmasking the imperialist agents who had infiltrated the upper echelons. Just as in Hungary, these were sought above all among those Communists who had escaped to the West during the war or had once been members of the international brigades.

The Hungarian party leader, Matyas Rakosi, who was already committed entirely to the Soviet secret police, willingly did all he could to facilitate their activities in Czechoslovakia. Certain of the defendants in the Rajk trial had been in contact with Czech and Slovak Communists in the West during the war. On the basis of their disclosures Rakosi supplied Gottwald with a list of suspects. The first to be arrested on the strength of this information were G. Pavlik, director of Cedok (the tourist office); Eugen Loebl, Deputy Minister of Foreign Trade; and Vilem Novy, editor of *Rude Pravo*. In autumn 1950, Otto Sling, First Secretary of the Regional Committee of Brno, the country's second most important industrial town, was arrested on a charge of espionage and treason. His arrest was followed by that of his friend Marie Svermova, the widow of a hero of the Slovak rebellion, and very popular in workers' circles. Suddenly, after some behind-the-scenes bargaining between the different secret services, the purge was extended to Slovakia, where the entire party élite – V. Clementis, Jan Masaryk's successor in the Foreign Office; G. Husak, chairman of the Council of Commissars; the poet L. Novomesky, Commissar of Culture; L. Holdos, Commissar of Religious Cults – was first denounced for its 'bourgeois nationalism', and then thrown into prison.

The inquisition struck at its own ranks. Late in 1950 one of the original organizers of the purge, K. Svab, Deputy Minister of Security and one of Slansky's trustees, was arrested on a charge of having protected class enemies.[9] In spring 1951, a secret-service report presented to Gottwald implicated Slansky himself, describing him as a 'dangerous agent of imperialism', and accusing him of 'having planted nationalist-bourgeois elements and Zionists in various important posts in the party and state apparatus'. Gottwald, dumbfounded it seems, consulted Stalin, who at this time advised him not to attach to much credence to the report but to remain vigilant. Nevertheless, 'political errors' were attributed to Slansky and at the September 1951 session of the Central Committee he was relieved of his duties as Secretary General of the party and appointed vice-chairman of the Council. This was only the beginning. In November 1951, the security services, on the basis of a letter they themselves had forged, informed Gottwald that Slansky 'had been urged by American espionage to defect to the West'. They called for the arrest of the traitor. Gottwald again consulted Stalin, who sent Mikoyan to Prague to 'investigate'. Mikoyan was convinced of Slansky's guilt, and Slansky was arrested on 24 November 1951.

His fall brought a large number of his associates with him: B. Geminder; the economist L. Frejka, who had drawn up the first Czechoslovak five-year plan; the journalist A. Simone; Mrs Jarmila Taussigova, who presided over the party's Committee of Inspection, one of the bodies responsible for carrying out the purge in the preceding years. The entire party apparatus and state administration were screened and decimated. The great trial that was to bring the country and the world irrefutable proof of the treason of the accused was being prepared.

Loebl has published a detailed account of the circumstances surrounding his arrest and the interrogation and torture he suffered. His testimony, which is of exeptional importance, like that of Slansky's brother, Richard,[10] his widow, the prosecutor, Josef Urvalek, and the then Minister of Security, Bacilek,[11] clearly reveals the crucial role of Soviet agents, and especially Beria's henchman, General Likhachev (who was 'liquidated' in the U.S.S.R. shortly after his chief's execution), in the preparation of the trial. The indictment was drawn up by the Czechoslovak Politburo, but with Beria's agents dominating the proceedings.

The technique developed in the thirties for the sensational

Moscow trials was refined at the time of the Rajk trial and used again now. The defendants were subjected to all kinds of moral pressure and physical torture in order to convince them that there was no escaping their fate. They were informed by the police that the party had complete knowledge of their actions and demanded a full confession of guilt. They were promised that the court would deal leniently with them if they made complete confessions. They were bullied and maltreated to such an extent that several of them believed they had fallen into the hands of fascist torturers. Richard Slansky describes how, when he remarked during his interrogation that his wife had been an associate of Klara Zetkin (one of the founders of the German Communist party and Lenin's friend), the police interrogator jumped down his throat: 'Who is that filthy Jewish ...? What's her racket?' The prison doctor, Sommer (who was to take his own life in spring 1968), used various drugs on the accused, such as mescaline and *actébrone*, which induced a state of euphoric indifference, blurring thought and weakening resistance.[12] Turned into puppets and deprived of all their dignity as human beings, the defendants were forced to memorize the confessions drawn up by the Czech police under expert Russian supervision. They had to run through their absurd confessions in a kind of dress rehearsal attended by the prosecutor and chairman of the court which was to find them guilty the next day. They were 'conditioned' in such a way as to eliminate any possibility of their retracting before the court.

Thus the trial passed off without a hitch. Eleven of the main defendants, after having duly confessed in full, were sentenced to death for treason, espionage, sabotage and military desertion, and executed on 3 December 1952. Three – E. Loebl, Artur London and V. Hadju – were sentenced to solitary confinement for life. These men lived to tell the tale.

The main trial was followed by other less spectacular but similarly contrived judicial farces, such as the trials of Marie Svermova and her group; of G. Husak and other Slovak leaders; of the economists of the so-called Great Trotskyist Council; and of a group of officials in the security services who had worked on Slansky's behalf. After the Communists, prominent people in the former political parties and the clergy were attacked. In 1968 it was calculated that the purges had claimed some 136,000 victims through death, imprisonment and internment[13] – a large number for a country with a total population of fourteen million unused to such practices.

The anti-Semitic bias of the Slansky trial is notable. Eleven of the fourteen defendants were Jews. The organizers tried to show that this was no accident, and that the Jewish prisoners were predisposed by birth, character or education to become instruments of American espionage. One of them, the journalist A. Simone, quoted the words allegedly spoken to him by an American colleague, David Schoenbrun: 'It is the duty of every Jew to support the Americans, even if he does not agree with every aspect of their policy.' The defendants of Jewish origin were called Zionists despite the fact that they had played a leading part – as had Slansky – in the liquidation of the Zionist organizations in Czechoslovakia after 1949. The confessions and testimonies at the trial provided the material for a sort of new 'protocol of the elders of Zion'; the Jews, an international people rooted in the young state of Israel, were playing a key role in the vast American conspiracy against the Soviet Union, of which one aim was precisely defined by Gottwald at a conference in 1952 as 'to destroy the ties of friendship between Czechoslovakia and the Soviet Union, and to turn the country into a new Yugoslavia'. 'There is nothing surprising in the fact that the trial of the ringleaders of the conspiracy in Czechoslovakia against the State should have revealed the absolute accord, both on an ideological level and as regards criminal action, between the two arrant traitors Tito and Slansky', wrote the Cominform paper. 'The traitors and enemies of the Czechoslovak people – Trotskyists, Titoists, Zionists, bourgeois nationalists in the service of the American imperialists – strove to weaken the alliance and ties of friendship between the Czechoslovak people and the peoples of the great Soviet Union and of the People's Democracies, to push the country on to the path of Titoist Yugoslavia.'[14]

The entire world Communist press took up the proclamation of the editorial in *Rude Pravo* of 24 November 1952, that Zionism was the 'number-one enemy' of the working class. From then on, one of the aims of the trial organizers seemed to be to justify the anti-Israeli, pro-Arab switch in the foreign policy of the Soviets, who in 1948 had still been supporting Israel's cause. Czechoslovakia, with Russian approval, had supplied the Israeli army with small arms and ammunition as well as fighter planes.[15] However, as from 1949 the U.S.S.R. realized that the influence of American Jews, and through them the United States government, had prevailed in Israel over that of pro-Soviet elements. In so far as it was possible to exploit the deterioration in relations with Israel and the Jews by a rapprochement with the Arabs, the Soviet Union found it easy enough to accept this state of affairs. Hence the eagerness of the Slansky trial protagonists, prosecutors and prosecuted alike, to show that the Arabs and the Communist countries had common enemies. (This attitude survived Stalinism, and was to become constant in Soviet policy.)

But the anti-Zionism of the Slansky trial was not stirred up solely, or even principally, to justify the pro-Arab switch in Soviet diplomacy. It soon became clear – and only people blinded by fanaticism could be under any illusion about it – that anti-Zionism served as a cover for unacknowledged anti-Semitism. It is one of the strange paradoxes of history, flowing directly from totalitarian and repressive attitudes, that the tradition of pogroms and the myth of the elders of Zion were reborn in the minds of the Kremlin leaders who, by stimulating and exploiting latent anti-Semitism, tried to turn national social and economic discontent first against highly placed Jews and then against Jews in general, the survivors of the Nazi holocaust. Several factors made the process easier : the presence of numerous Jews, former party militants, former deportees, or members of the Spanish international brigades, in the top echelons of the parties, economic apparatus and, above all, political police of the People's Democracies; the more or less open sympathy of the Jews for Israel; family and cultural links between East European Jews and Western Jewry; etc.[16] In these countries, where Jewish left-wing intellectuals had played an important part in the creation of Communist parties and workers' movements, certain sections of the population tended to associate Communism with the Jews. Hence the effectiveness of the Nazi slogan linking Judaism and Bolshevism. By delivering the Jews up to popular wrath as scapegoats, the Kremlin leaders and their stooges, such as Kopecky and Bacilek in Czechoslovakia and Gheorghiu Dej in Rumania, could dissociate themselves from Jewry and at the same time appeal to nationalist sentiments. Besides, many of the veteran Jewish Communists, either because they found it hard to adapt themselves to totalitarian methods or because they overcompensated for their doubts by an excess of zeal, were becoming an encumbrance to the leaders, who were anxious to win over younger, more easily manipulated elements from the party ranks.

In any case, it is clear that the impulse for the campaign came from Stalin's entourage. The connection between the Prague trial and the 'white-coated murderers' scandal seems obvious. Soon after the Nineteenth Congress, Stalin received a letter from a certain lady doctor named Timachuk, who was associated with the state security service, accusing several Kremlin doctors of 'deliberately using treatments that were contra-indicated'. According to the informer, these doctors had already caused the death of one Politburo member, Cherbatov, in 1945, and of another, the celebrated Zhdanov, in 1948; they were alleged to have tried and to be still trying to shorten the lives of other political and military leaders. Stalin at once ordered the arrest of the doctors. According to Khrushchev, he summoned 'the examining magistrate personally, giving him instructions on the methods to be used. These methods were simple: beatings, beatings and more beatings.' The doctors, most of whom were Jews, ended by making the requisite confession, that it was on the instigation of the American intelligence service, and especially the Joint Distribution Committee set up to aid Jews in the U.S.S.R. and the Eastern countries, that they had undertaken their odious activities on behalf of Israel and the United States. Their arrest and indictment were made public on 13 January 1953 in a press communiqué that caused panic among the three million or so Jews in the U.S.S.R. Rumours were rife in Moscow of the deportation of the entire Jewish community.

Despite Khrushchev's subsequent revelations, the affair was never entirely explained. Khrushchev shifted all the responsibility for it on to Stalin and Beria, and it is possible that the latter did exploit his master's obsessive fear of plots against himself. In all events, Stalin allowed the anti-Jewish purges. In the spring of 1952, the Secretary General of the Rumanian party, Gheorghiu Dej, took advantage of the atmosphere of the Kremlin to eliminate from the party leadership Anna Pauker and Vasile Luca, two prominent personalities of Jewish origin who were passionately attached to the U.S.S.R. This enabled Dej, a man of limited intelligence but a remarkably cold-blooded and astute tactician, to gain control over the entire party and state organization. From 29 June 1952 Dej combined the offices of head of the party and Prime Minister. (This appointment, no doubt approved by Stalin, marked the first stage in a development that led this outright Stalinist, through the consolidation of his personal power, finally to assert himself as a national Communist leader resisting the overlordship of a weakened Kremlin.[17])

In Poland, the Jewish members of the Politburo, Jakob Berman and Roman Zambrowski, were able to keep themselves out of trouble by sacrificing a certain number of less important Jewish officials and officers.[18] In fact, in this country where anti-Semitism has particularly deep roots, the anti-Jewish movement affected the party only later during the struggles for succession to Bierut in 1956 and Gomulka in 1967–8.

In Hungary, Matyas Rakosi, who as a Jew himself was in danger, arrested in December 1952 Gabor Peter, head of the political police, who had received Soviet assistance in arranging the Rajk trial, together with a certain number of Jewish doctors and high officials. In East Germany, the 'revelations of the Slansky trial' allowed Ulbricht to arrest Paul Merker, the Jewish Politburo member, and to commit his main rival, Franz Dahlem, for trial.[19]

No doubt there are still many gaps in our knowledge of the turbulent events of 1951–2 in the People's Democracies. The main difficulty arises from the fact that Soviet policy as a whole was inconsistent. Each of the rival cliques in the Kremlin was trying to place and protect its own protégés among the satellites. Thus, in Hungary, Beria and Malenkov supported Imre Nagy, dismissed in 1948 but then vice-chairman of the Council and logical successor to the Jew Rakosi.[20] In Czechoslovakia, Malenkov's man seems to have been Zapotocky, while Antonin Novotny was tied to his Soviet counterpart Khrushchev, whose position at the end of 1952 was by no means settled. One of Czechoslovakia's main inquisitors, Bacilek, paid tribute to Novotny after his promotion, in a speech in December 1952, for 'his important contribution to drawing up the case against Slansky'. He maintained this compromisingly respectful attitude in 1968, when, after Novotny's departure, the Prague trial was subjected to a close scrutiny. What is evident is that Novotny did not immediately gain by the great purge. In early 1953 Gottwald removed him from the secretariat and appointed him vice-chairman of the Council – a doubtful honour in view of the fact that Slansky had been appointed to the same post after his removal from the secretariat and shortly before his arrest. It was only after Stalin's death that Novotny, backed by Khrushchev, was able to recover lost ground and finally to reach the top.

There were individuals within the various Communist parties, even among the leaders, who, in what looked like the heyday of Stalinism – though it was in fact already in decline – disapproved of the methods used. Some had compromised themselves less than others, and were subsequently to try to save the party's honour, in so far as they were allowed to do so. Nevertheless, the next generation would never cease wondering how an undeniably able working-class leader not without courage, like Gottwald, could bring himself, 'in his declining years, to deny, dismantle and condemn his entire life's work, to confirm the death sentence not only of his friends and comrades, but also of the movement he represented'.[21] Is the 'taste for power', the inevitable corruption that corrodes whoever possesses absolute, unlimited power, sufficient explanation of the abysmal moral degradation into which this man fell, like Stalin, Rakosi, Ulbricht and so many others? His case can also be seen as expressing the contradictions inherent in the Communist system, between the theory (which is humanistic and progressive) and the practice (which is oppressive and repressive); as springing from the tension created by the stubborn refusal of social and economic facts to bend before the will of Utopian ideologists, and as a direct result of the considerable fear that uncontrollable social, national, intellectual and economic forces inspired in the Communist leaders. In Stalin's case, the fear became an obsession towards the end of his life, and this led him to rely on the instruments of repression, to transform Marxism-Leninism – as the distinguished novelist and political analyst Manes Sperber has put it – into a 'police concept of history', to justify repression by raising bogies, first Trotskyism, then the Zionist plot. The anti-Semitism of 1951–3 was to break out again in the U.S.S.R., Czechoslovakia and Poland immediately after the 1967 Arab-Israeli conflict, at a time of increasing internal and external tension in the movement, and when – just as towards the end of Stalin's rule – certain elements in the machine (especially in the police) felt that only the strengthening of the repressive and demagogic character of the régime through the creation of ideological diversions could save the party dictatorship.

However, from 1952, and even in 1948, there was at least in theory an alternative to the Stalinism that a great Hungarian poet, Attila Jozsef, had once called 'fascist Communism' – namely the democratization of Communism, the strengthening of socialist structures through real concessions to the national and liberal aspirations of the people, a realization of the 'democratic potentialities' of socialism. It was this trend that characterized the successive onslaughts of revisionism and rehabilitation in Communist parties and public opinion in the post-Stalinist period. One has only to recall the prominent part played by a number of rehabilitated Communists in the liberalization of Czechoslovakia: Professor Goldstuecker, the economist Loebl, the former leader of the Prague rebellion Smrkovsky, the Slovak leaders Husak, Novomesky and Holdos, among others.

Seen in this perspective, the Slansky trial and the subsequent purges in the People's Democracies look like the first moves in a huge offensive undertaken by the most reactionary and imperialistic forces in the Soviet bureaucracy against the autochthonous reformist and nationalist tendencies that had already begun to stir under the surface. One of the aims of this offensive was to absorb the Eastern countries, so various in language, tradition, development and aspirations, into the Soviet Union. The Slansky trial did not simply mean the 'Stalinization' of Czechoslovakia and the other Communist countries; it also marked the final stage in their 'satellization'.

The disappearance of the father figure cut short this apparently irreversible process of integration into the totalitarian system, though it only later became clear that the repression and integration had, in fact, reached their climax at the beginning of 1953. They could only have been carried further at the risk of violent explosions. The repression was already turning on itself. None of the pre- or post-war anti-Communist governments executed or imprisoned so many Communists as the Stalinists between 1949 and 1953, nor did any of them succeed in arousing so much hatred of the Soviet Union as the Stalinist governments. Even from the strictly hegemonistic Soviet point of view, the view of the Communist organizations, the terrorist methods employed during the years 1949–53 turned out to be absurd and ineffective, creating a sense of what was 'intolerable' and having serious economic repercussions. Even in Stalin's immediate entourage, some realized that arbitrary rule, the negation of normality, the destruction of personal and national values, the suppression of initiative had been taken too far. If the basic legacy – the predominance of the U.S.S.R. and the dictatorship of the party in the various Communist countries – was to be saved, there would have to be some retrenchment, some concessions, and a return to common sense; and a type of N.E.P.[22] would have to be put into practice. The problem was how to control the movement of regeneration in nations that had suffered on both moral and physical levels from Stalinism to the point that their consciousness, their very sense of identity, was obscured, and their political, economic and social institutions dislocated. ('We are a sick people', I was told by the Czechoslovak historian K. Bartosek in April 1968. But all the peoples of the Eastern countries are sick as a result of the oppression.) The history of the People's Democracies after Stalin is largely an account of the various solutions that the governments and peoples, at first at the Kremlin's instigation, then under the guidance of their own leaders, tried to apply, the various therapies they used to treat if not cure the disease.

The objective – consolidation through normalization – led logically to the triumph of realism over ideology, to adjustments being made to the Soviet model, itself in process of modification, and to a return to national traditions. Thus after integration came diversification and self-determination; after the terror, a gradual relaxation, even if with pauses and temporary set-backs; after the great trials, the great rehabilitations; after unquestioning obedience, resistance; after isolation, the opening of doors. And all this in cycles of ebb and flow, freezing and thaw.

Whatever the circumstances of Stalin's death, whether hastened by his associates or not, the tyrant already had had his day by the beginning of 1953. He had impressed on the Eastern countries a medieval pogrom atmosphere – a wave of savage, arbitrary terror. The Czechoslovak writer Jan Prochazka was to speak of Stalinotsarism that swept over one of the most civilized countries in Europe and spared none of the other People's Democracies. 'The dictatorship of the proletariat' established in 1948 degenerated, as the Hungarian writer Gyula Illyes put it, into 'the reign of a gory King Ubu'.

Part I

The Events

From Monolithism to Polycentrism

1

The New Course

Collective Leadership and the Fall of Beria

On 6 March 1953 a communiqué issued by the Central Committee of the Soviet party, the Council of Ministers and the Presidium of the Supreme Soviet announced that Stalin had died on 5 March at 21.50 hours. The news caused general dismay in the U.S.S.R. as well as in the People's Democracies. Men and women wept in the streets of Budapest and Prague. Had the dictator been so beloved? Old people recalled how on Francis Joseph's death in 1916 men also wept in Prague, Vienna and Budapest. Had the emperor been so beloved? Two years after his passing the Austro-Hungarian monarchy collapsed.

Men seem to grow attached even to despotic rulers who, owing to their long reigns, come to symbolize authority, order and continuity. In a sense, Stalin was an incarnation of the archetypal father. Certainly he was a terrifying father – his close associates must have been relieved at his death, and may even have precipitated it; but their initial behaviour betrayed a fear of the vacuum left by the Generalissimo. His successors talked of the 'irreparable loss'; they called 'for the greatest unity in leadership, so that there should be no confusion or panic,' It was as if they had been hypnotized by the colossus who had terrorized them, and were not prepared for his removal.

For a few days it seemed that Malenkov, as expected, would succeed Stalin at the head of the party as well as the government. It was he who delivered the first oration, followed by Molotov and Beria, at the funeral on 9 March. One of the first steps taken after Stalin's death was the appointment of Malenkov as chairman of the Council of Ministers, with four vice-chairmen: Beria,

Molotov, Bulganin and Kaganovich. Voroshilov was appointed chairman of the Presidium of the Supreme Soviet (i.e. President of the U.S.S.R.). The party leadership was reorganized; the Politburo kept the name Presidium, but it was reduced to ten members. Khrushchev resigned as First Secretary of the Moscow Committee 'to concentrate on his work in the Central Committee of the party', i.e. in the secretariat. This was a promotion.

For several days after Stalin's death, only Malenkov's name was mentioned in *Pravda*. On 10 March it reproduced a faked photograph showing Malenkov in the company of Stalin and Mao Tse-tung. But on 21 March, the Central Committee published its decision to release Malenkov from his post as secretary of the Central Committee; and a secretariat of five was elected: Khrushchev, Suslov, Pospelov, Shatalin and S. D. Ignatiev. This was a first step towards a diversification of power. Thenceforth Malenkov's name was no longer mentioned in isolation; generally the reference was to the Malenkov–Beria–Molotov *troika*.

Thus began the transitional period of collective leadership in the U.S.S.R., a hard struggle for power which had a profound and lasting effect on the People's Democracies. Three basic forces were discernible at the time at the top of the Soviet hierarchy (and in the leadership of the satellite countries). The first, led by Molotov and Kaganovich, was represented by the leaders who aimed at preserving the Stalinist model with only a few modifications. The second trend was represented by Malenkov and, before his removal in late June 1953, by Beria; its proponents advocated far-ranging economic reforms and a degree of liberalization in political life – a change-over from terroristic to a more benevolent and enlightened paternalism. The third trend, which might be described as 'centrist', was associated with Khrushchev who also supported de-Stalinization, but insisted on the primacy of party control.[1]

In the first few months after Stalin's death the three groups in the Kremlin seemed to be in agreement on a number of pacificatory measures that would open a new chapter in the history of Soviet Communism. The most important were an amnesty and the announcement of an alleviation of the penal code, 27 March; substantial price reductions, 31 March; rehabilitation of the

Kremlin doctors, with an acknowledgement that 'the statements made by those arrested had been obtained by members of the investigation section of the Ministry of State Security through the use of methods strictly forbidden under Soviet law', 4 April. Professor Vovsi and his fourteen colleagues were immediately freed; Ignatiev, Minister of the Interior at the time of their arrest, was removed from his post, and his assistant Riumin was arrested, to be executed after the Beria trial.

From now on there was increasingly less mention of Stalin in the press and this was clearly due to instructions from the Kremlin. On 16 April *Pravda* published an editorial condemning leaders who 'violate the principle of collective leadership' by deciding on important matters independently. However, it was easier to preach collective leadership than to practise it and the *troika* in fact finally broke down at the end of June 1953. On 10 July *Pravda* published a Central Committee communiqué accusing Beria of 'criminal actions ... directed against party and state and intended to undermine the Soviet state in the interest of foreign capital'. It announced Beria's dismissal from his posts in the party and government, and his arrest. In December 1953 the news was released of Beria's sentence after a secret trial and his execution with a number of associates. 'On becoming the U.S.S.R.'s Minister of the Interior in March 1953, Beria', according to the Kremlin, 'made preparations to seize power; he exerted considerable pressure to get members of his group of plotters into leading positions in the central machinery of the Ministry of the Interior, as well as in local organizations.'

After Beria's arrest those who had come out on top in this initial phase of the struggle convened a secret Cominform meeting in the Kremlin to reassure the somewhat shaken Eastern and Western Communist leaders. Malenkov, Molotov and Khrushchev informed the leaders of the fraternal parties that Beria had instructed the bodyguards of the other members of the Presidium to spy on their masters, and that he had kept files on the private lives of these men, and had tapped their telephones, in addition to other checks on their movements. Furthermore, he had advocated an East German policy tantamount to abandoning the building of socialism and the transformation of the German Democratic Republic (G.D.R.) into a bourgeois state. They also claimed to have uncovered 'criminal plans of Beria to establish personal contact through his agents with Tito and Rankovic'. A letter addressed to the latter, who was the Yugoslav Minister of the Interior, was allegedly found on Beria at the time of his arrest. When questioned by representatives of the Italian party, who pointed out that on Stalin's death the Soviet press had abruptly dropped all attacks on the country, the Soviet leaders announced that they had taken a joint decision to normalize diplomatic relations with Yugoslavia.[2] 'As we have diplomatic relations with Tito's masters [the Americans], why should we not have them with Tito himself?', they argued. It seems, however, that Beria wanted to go even further.[3]

Malenkov, Molotov and Khrushchev did not confine themselves to justifying Beria's removal (in a manner which, as it happens, closely followed the Stalinist pattern of exaggerated and unverifiable allegations), but also initiated a secret trial of Stalin and Stalinism that was only made public three years later. They emphasized that the party rules laid down by Lenin had long been violated by Stalin. The party congress had not been called for thirteen years, and even the Central Committee had not met for a considerable time, and decisions on fundamental administrative and economic questions had often been taken by Stalin personally, without consulting even the leading party bodies. Finally, the propaganda put out over the previous few years 'reflected a deviation from the Marxist-Leninist concept of the role of personality in history'; a 'cult of personality' had been erected, an error that must now be corrected.[4]

This very moderate self-criticism came as no surprise to the representatives of the fraternal parties. Several, notably Ulbricht, Rakosi and Zapotocky, since Stalin's death had already had occasion to note the change in Kremlin policy, with all it entailed for them personally. The new Soviet leaders criticized Stalin's practices, but they preserved his concept of centralism, and the direction they now gave Soviet policy was to be binding on all ruling parties. In making known their will that the fraternal parties in power were to introduce collective leadership, they were undermining the interests of the 'little Stalins' in the Eastern countries.

Only one of them, the Czechoslovak President Gottwald, had involuntarily facilitated the introduction of the new order by contracting pneumonia at Stalin's funeral in Moscow and dying a few days after his return to Prague. On 14 March 1953 Antonin Zapotocky succeeded him as President of the Republic, while Antonin Novotny took over the secretariat of the Central Committee. Thus the change-over to collective leadership in Czechoslovakia went smoothly, and the 'cult of personality', as in Moscow, could be laid at a dead man's door.

This was not the case, however, in the other People's Democracies. Criticism of Stalinist practices had necessarily to take the form of self-criticism, which Ulbricht, Rakosi, Bierut, Gheorghiu Dej, and Hoxha all found humiliating. Certain Soviet leaders wondered if it might not be better, for the good of the cause, to replace these by men less divided in their loyalties; but they were saved by lack of unity in the Soviet leadership and the continued presence of Stalinists. Thenceforth, all five put their faith in the Molotov group, which protected them and carried on a running defensive battle with the reformers in the Soviet Union. It was chiefly thanks to the Stalinists in the Kremlin that the Stalinists in the People's Democracies survived so long in the face of the pressure of public opinion.

Even so the Kremlin's support was limited. Molotov and Kaganovich were in no position to approve the use of the coercive measures that had formerly been available against rivals or opponents. They warned their protégés to remember the delicate balance of power in the Kremlin, and to obey the rules of collective leadership. This, however, opened the door to pluralism and breached the party's monolithic façade. Other countries were to become increasingly out of line with the Soviet Union from 1953. Such were the German Democratic Republic, Czechoslovakia, Rumania and Albania, where the Stalinist leaders succeeded in circumventing Kremlin orders and keeping their power more or less intact (often by convincing the Russians that a strong government was the only possible one in the circumstances and that they were the best defenders of Soviet interests). This is one of the main causes of the increasing tensions that were to alienate Albania in 1960 and come between the U.S.S.R. and Rumania later on. Paradoxically enough, it was the resistance of the ruling Stalinist cliques to de-Stalinization that was to lead some European Communist countries, following China's example, to the brink of desatellization. Rather than let themselves be drawn into the quicksands of liberalism, these leaders would deck themselves out in national colours and come forward as anti-Soviet Stalinists.

Two Cases of Soviet Intervention

1. *East Germany: Ulbricht saved by insurrection.* In the summer of 1952 the leadership of the East German party, the S.E.D. (Sozialistische Einheitspartei Deutschlands), embarked on a course of all-out Bolshevization with Stalin's blessing, and probably at his instigation. It was resolved to increase the tempo of socialist construction by eliminating the artisan class and small tradespeople and collectivizing agriculture. The initial result of collectivization measures was an increase in the number of refugees flooding into West Berlin: 14 per cent were peasants, and over 50 per cent skilled workers and their families.[5] In the early spring of 1953 the food crisis worsened. For several months the authorities were unable to distribute the amount of fats allowed in the rations, and there was also a shortage of potatoes, meat and coal.[6] Incidents and protests among workers were reported.

In April 1953 Ulbricht asked the Soviet Union for urgent economic aid, but on 15 April Moscow informed him that it was in no position to assist, and suggested that the S.E.D. modify its policy, reduce the tempo of socialization, and relax pressure on the various social strata. It was probably at this time that Ulbricht met Beria, who explained 'his' German policy – which Ulbricht later claimed before the Central Committee he had rejected.[7] But the fact of the matter is that Ulbricht, for the first time in his long career as an *apparatchik*, disobeyed Kremlin orders.

No sooner had he received a negative response from the Soviet leadership than he made a speech before an assembly of senior party and state officials in which – referring to that 'wise pilot of socialist construction, Joseph Vissarionovich Stalin' – he appealed for vigilance, and advocated that industrial work output be raised by at least 10 per cent, so as to increase production and thereby resolve the crisis. The decree was published on 28 May 1953. It was the last straw, and the attempt to implement it met with fierce resistance from the workers.

The Soviet leadership, however, was not prepared to tolerate Ulbricht's outbursts. On 5 June the new Soviet chief commissar, V. Semionov, arrived in East Berlin with a self-critical statement for Ulbricht to sign. This time the tone of the command was peremptory. Ulbricht gave in readily, especially as he had got wind of approaches made by the Soviets (notably Beria and Malenkov) to his Minister of Security, Zaisser (General Gomez of the International Brigade in Spain), and to Rudolf Herrnstadt, editor of the official party organ *Neues Deutschland*, who were both plotting against him and were then working on a radically revised political programme.

On 11 June *Neues Deutschland* published without comment the official statement promising to 'correct mistakes made in widely different fields by the government and state administrative organs', and to raise 'the standards of living of the workers and intellectuals, peasants, artisans and other sections of the middle class'. It admitted that 'mistakes had been made with regard to wealthy and even average peasants'. Forced deliveries of agricultural products were to be reduced, and peasants who had fled to West Berlin were invited to return and promised restitution of their former goods. Middle- and upper-class children were again to be admitted to institutions of higher education. Discrimination in the distribution of food cards was abolished. Nevertheless, the decree of 28 May on the raising of output remained in force. The trades union newspaper indicated that the decree would be implemented from 16 June to take effect retrospectively from 30 May.

The same day, the Politburo met to arbitrate on the conflict between Ulbricht and his 'liberal' opponents. Most of the Politburo seemed to favour the arguments advanced by Zaisser and Herrnstadt, who were believed to be in favour with the new Soviet leadership. But providence came to Ulbricht's aid. Discontented with the increased output and decrease in real wages, the workers on the Stalin Allee construction project downed tools on the morning of 16 June, and came out on the streets. About a hundred appeared initially; their numbers quickly grew, and the first police cordons in their path were swiftly breached. A member of the Berlin party committee reported to the Politburo, suggesting that concessions be made to the workers, but was kept waiting. Semionov, who was at the meeting, came to see him, made some inquiries, and disappeared. Valuable time was lost. Finally, Ulbricht appeared, and informed the party committee's representative of the Politburo's decision to revoke the demand for increased output. In the meantime, however, the demonstrators had already spread through the city, making political demands in addition to the economic and social ones. Placards appeared calling for the abolition of output demands, lowering of prices, resignation of the government, and free elections with a secret ballot. Apparently Ulbricht did not take the movement too seriously; he thought he knew 'his' Berliners. 'It's raining', he said. 'People will go home.'[8] Nevertheless, in the evening, at an urgently called meeting of party activists, Ulbricht announced: 'The party is abandoning the false path it has pursued up to now, and is setting out on a new course.' It was too late.

The next day, 17 June 1953, processions formed in the outer suburbs of East Berlin to march towards the centre. The strike had become general, and the entire population was on the streets. Several thousand demonstrators tried to occupy government buildings. The red flag was torn down from the Brandenburg Gate and burnt. At midday, General Dybrova, the commandant of the Soviet sector of Berlin, declared a state of siege, and two motorized Soviet divisions occupied the city. Rebels taken prisoner were tried by special tribunals and executed. By 9 p.m. order had been restored in East Berlin.

The disturbance in the capital was followed by an almost general rising: in Leipzig the workers called a strike, and occupied the Youth Movement headquarters and the prison, burning all the portraits on the walls except Karl Marx's. Similar demonstrations occurred at Merseburg, Rostock, Halle, Dresden, Jena, Bitterfeld, and elsewhere, to be put down quickly by Soviet military intervention. Repression followed: forty-two people were executed, and there were 25,000 arrests. This recalled the Kronstadt rebellion of February 1921. Once again the dictatorship of the proletariat was suppressing a proletarian movement.[9] 'We want to be free men and not slaves', cried the Berlin workers.

The forty-eight-hour rebellion had demonstrated both the régime's unpopularity and Ulbricht's clumsiness. The Soviets had every reason to be exasperated with him for having delayed so long and for his reluctance to implement their instructions. Ulbricht, however, did his utmost to see that the opposition bore all the blame for the upheaval. The workers, he claimed, would never have marched against the régime had they not felt that the leadership was weakening, and if fresh prospects for the future had not raised hopes of a Russian withdrawal and the fall of the dictatorship.

But, only a few days after the Berlin uprising, Beria was overthrown on the pretext of having pursued 'a capitulatory policy' in East Germany. The Kremlin claimed that his policy called for the abandonment of socialist construction in the German Democratic Republic as well as the dissolution of the agricultural co-operatives, which would have led to a betrayal of East Germany. The Soviets accused Beria alone. At the first post-crisis meeting of the East German Central Committee, in late July 1953, Ulbricht substantiated their version of the events, alleging that Zaisser had acted in collusion with Beria without informing the Politburo. In 1961 the Committee was to include Malenkov – then no longer in power – in its denunciations, and in March 1963 Khrushchev claimed that Beria and Malenkov had urged the East German party to abandon the G.D.R. as a socialist state, and to renounce the building of socialism as an aim.[10]

At all events, the sudden change in the Kremlin and the ousting of Beria allowed Ulbricht to rid himself of his opposition leaders. The Soviet leaders decided to lend him their support, provided he honestly tried to follow the new course and acknowledged his mistakes through self-criticism. Ulbricht hastened to satisfy them and withdrew with some grace. The victory he had just won against his opponents enabled him to put a good face on it, especially as he had succeeded in obtaining considerable Soviet financial aid to implement the new economic policy pledging the party to raise the standard of living of the workers.[11]

2. *Hungary: The Rakosi–Nagy duel.* The economic and social

situation in Hungary in the spring following Stalin's death was no less serious than in Germany. It had been a particularly hard winter and the succeeding period was difficult. The exactions – especially in the great Hungarian plain, the country's granary – led to peasant demonstrations.

From May onwards the Russian leaders began taking notice of the disturbing news from Budapest. Matyas Rakosi, who was both General Secretary of the party and Prime Minister, was summoned to the Kremlin, where he too was urged to follow the Soviet lead, announce a 'new course', and make a division between party and government leadership. When the Soviets asked him to suggest someone who could replace him at the head of the government, Rakosi apparently 'raised objections to all those that were put forward . . . Everyone was suspect, with the exception of himself.' 'It staggered us', Malenkov was to declare later.[12]

Rakosi returned to Hungary without having settled the question of the division of power. He seemed to be in no hurry. Had he been encouraged by the Molotov clique to resist orders from Khrushchev, Malenkov and Beria? He even went so far as to elaborate a new five-year plan with his deputy Ernoe Geroe, which, broadly speaking, gave expression to the same unrestrained ambitions as its predecessor, making not the slightest concession to consumer interests.

However, the Kremlin, stirred by the rising in East Berlin, summoned the top men in Budapest – Rakosi, Geroe, Farkas, and the chairman of the Presidium Dobi – to Moscow. Imre Nagy, stubbornly opposed to the economic policy of Rakosi and Geroe, was requested to join them. At the meeting, Mikoyan severely criticized the Rakosi government's economic policy, apparently ignoring the fact that it had been approved in Stalin's time by the Soviet leadership, to which he had belonged. 'The disproportionate development of iron-smelting', he declared, 'indicates a somewhat rash attitude. Hungary has neither iron mines nor coke. She must import all her raw materials.' This was precisely what Nagy had been saying repeatedly since 1948. Rakosi bowed his head and admitted 'having gone too far'. Krushchev then intervened: 'If Rakosi is so quick to criticize himself, it is to avoid being criticized further.' Molotov, for his part, tried to outdo his colleagues in condemning Rakosi's agricultural policy: 'There must be no systematic dissolution of the co-operatives', he said, 'but do not restrain those peasants who are indicating their desire to leave.'[13]

The Hungarian delegation returned to Budapest with a mandate to initiate a new political and economic course immediately. A Central Committee meeting was called for 28 June 1953. 'The comrades listened in astonishment and with bated breath to Rakosi's self-criticism and his admission to having substituted his personal leadership for collective leadership.' He castigated himself for having lacked Communist humility, for having ignored his comrades' warnings and impatiently and arrogantly rejected the slightest attempt to question him. He admitted that there had been 'arbitrary interference in judicial inquiries and in certain political trials' and tendered his resignation. Geroe and Farkas followed him.

Knowing that Rakosi and his friends were acting on orders from Moscow, the Central Committee approved everything submitted to it. However, even before it had had time to select the new leadership, word came from Khrushchev that Beria had fallen and that Rakosi should remain as head of the party. Thereupon Rakosi altered proposals already agreed. He resigned only from the post of Prime Minister, in which Imre Nagy was to succeed him, and remained as First Secretary of the party. Furthermore, it was decided not to publish the resolution which, according to our fragmentary information, harshly condemned Rakosi's policy as one that 'bankrupted production, destroyed the worker-peasant alliance, sapped the strength of Popular Democracy, trampled legality underfoot, set the masses against the party and government and, in short, led the country to the brink of disaster'. It completely rehabilitated Imre Nagy and gave him his due for having opposed the over-rapid rate of collectivization since 1949, which led to his being 'incorrectly described as an opportunist and forced to submit to disciplinary action'.

On 4 July 1953, as chairman of the Council, Nagy appeared before Parliament. Since the Central Committee deliberations had taken place in private, his inaugural speech created a sensation. He announced that the five-year plan was to be revised, and excessive industrialization would be discarded. Priority was to be given to the development of light industry and food production, and agricultural investments would be increased. Collectivization would be slowed down, and collective farms could be dissolved at the end of the year where the majority of the members so wished. Nagy envisaged the rebirth of the artisan class; he promised an improvement in the food situation, a revision of the labour code, liberalization of intellectual life, religious toleration, abolition of Stalinist internment camps (holding some 150,000 people at the time), reduction in police powers and democratization of political life.

All these measures, conforming to the enlightened Communism Nagy had always preached and which was now approved by the Soviets, were sensible; radical treatment was needed to cure the disease that was destroying Hungary. Nevertheless, the change-over was too abrupt. Not only were the people psychologically unprepared for reform; the party organization as well was taken by surprise and alarmed. Accustomed to ruling over a terrorized population, the organization was afraid to let go of the reins, fearing that the masses might take the concessions as a sign of weakness, and sweep it away.

Rakosi skilfully exploited the anxiety of the *apparatchiks* in his struggle with Nagy. He delivered a speech to the Budapest activists which, in essence if not in form, amounted to a disavowal of the policy of the new head of government. He deprecated the radical nature of the new measures, and let it be known that the party organization would maintain its grip, that the old policy would be pursued with a few modifications. The most significant passage in his speech was addressed to officials in the rural districts, who were in an especially difficult position because the peasants in many places were taking Nagy's speech as permission for the immediate breaking up of the collective farms, and were beginning to redistribute the land. Rakosi ordered the officials to stop this process at all costs, and to impress on the peasants that the disintegration of the collective sector would not be tolerated. Hundreds of political officers were dispatched to the countryside to help the local secretaries control the peasants.

From then until March 1955 when, taking advantage of Khrushchev's dismissal of Malenkov, Rakosi succeeded in overthrowing Imre Nagy, the entire political, economic and cultural life of Hungary reflected the conflict of reformism and Stalinist conservatism in the government. The new economic policy was deliberately sabotaged by Rakosi and Geroe, and could not, therefore, achieve the results Nagy hoped for. On several occasions, notably before the party Congress in May 1954, Nagy appealed to the Soviets to neutralize the schemes of Rakosi, who had gone so far as to push a resolution through the Politburo in Nagy's absence.

According to Nagy, the Soviets again gave him their support; Khrushchev attacked Rakosi, reproaching him for 'ignoring collective work'. They all ordered him 'to discard this policy of malice and contempt for others, the signs of mania for power, all offensive and vexatious attitudes'. On the same occasion, the liberation and rehabilitation of innocent victims of the Stalin trials were discussed, and Khrushchev told Rakosi to speed up the process. 'You are the one chiefly responsible for the arrests', he declared. 'You do not want to let the prisoners go because you know you are guilty and will be challenged.'

Under the circumstances, the Soviets might have done better to dismiss Rakosi. Khrushchev apparently wanted to do so, but he was far from being all-powerful within the Soviet Presidium. Furthermore, in spite of their criticism, the Soviet leaders stressed that 'the party leadership needed Comrade Rakosi' and that 'his authority must be preserved as long as it did not prejudice the party's authority'. They admitted that 'Rakosi's position was difficult' while advising him to 'make a clean breast of it', as 'neither silence nor subterfuge would raise the party's prestige, but rather frank speech'. This was probably asking the impossible of Rakosi. Had he scourged himself over the execution of Laszlo Rajk and a thousand militants (not to mention the Communists and non-Communists in prison), he would have contributed to the more rapid and complete extinction of his own and the party's authority. The compromise solution reached by the Kremlin, consisting in support for both Rakosi and Nagy – the coexistence of two diametrically opposed policies – created an uncertainty and spiritual malaise in Hungary that culminated in the explosion of 1956.

In October 1954 Imre Nagy, exasperated by the 'duplicity' of those who verbally approved of his policy but acted in contradiction to it, made a final effort. He called a meeting of the Central Committee and asked it 'to take a clear and unequivocal stand, reaffirming the principles and aims established in the June resolutions and the resolutions of the Third Congress (May 1954), as constituting the only correct path for the building of socialism'. 'The old economic policy', he declared, 'was a completely erroneous concept of socialism, equating it with maximum production of iron and steel, and with over-industrialization. That was not socialism, comrades!' The Central Committee, which took Nagy's firmness and confidence as evidence of a complete victory in Moscow over Rakosi (who was absent from the meeting), came out in favour of his policy by a large majority – a miscalculation rectified several months later, after Malenkov's fall, by Nagy's expulsion and the unanimous condemnation of his policy by this same Committee at the instigation of a triumphant Rakosi.[14]

Czechoslovakia: Collective Leadership under the Sign of Stalinism

In Czechoslovakia the 'collective leadership' that followed the personal rule of Gottwald (who died on 14 March 1953) consisted of three men[15]: Zapotocky, elected President of the Republic on 21 March, known for his connections with Malenkov; Antonin Novotny, in charge of the secretariat of the Central Committee and officially First Secretary of the party from the time his sponsor Khrushchev became First Secretary of the Soviet party in September 1953; and Viliam Siroky, the Slovak leader, who had been greatly helped by the purge of his 'nationalist bourgeois' compatriots, appointed head of the government.

Of these three, Novotny was the most dynamic and astute. Born in 1904, he had joined the party at seventeen. In 1935 he represented his party at the Comintern congress. He was arrested in 1941 as a prominent member of the underground resistance, and interned in Mauthausen until 1945. After the war he was appointed First Secretary for the Prague district, a common stepping-stone to the top. We have already mentioned his role in the preparations for the Slansky trial and that his relations with

President Gottwald towards the end were not exceptionally good. Novotny was typical of the new generation of bosses who were totally identified with the Czechoslovak party organization, one of the oldest, strongest and most fundamentally Bolshevik in the Communist world. In the following years he displayed quite remarkable tactical skill in preserving his personal power; it needed a tidal wave of public opinion at the beginning of 1968 to sweep him from office as First Secretary and then as chief of state.

The economic and political situation at the time of the new team's installation, without being disastrous, was difficult. In order to halt the rising inflation resulting from the policy of all-out industrialization, the decline of the consumer industry, and the fall in agricultural production, the new leadership had recourse to the dangerous expedient of monetary reform. Proclaimed simultaneously with the abolition of rationing of foodstuffs and industrial products on 30 May and put into practice on 1 June 1953, it rated the new Czechoslovak crown at 1.40 the rouble.

As *Rude Pravo* admitted on 1 June, the reform naturally entailed considerable financial loss for a large part of the population, especially if they had not placed their savings in the savings bank. The Czechoslovak government, however, did its utmost to convince the workers that a 'healthy prices policy required the absorption of the excess money in circulation', this being 'the indispensable prerequisite for the suppression of the black market'.

The decree of 30 May came as a great shock. The country was expecting some relaxation rather than a new austerity programme and coercion. The next day a violent protest movement got under way in several large industrial centres, notably in the Lenin works (formerly Skoda) at Plzen, the steel works and mines of Ostrava, the large Prague machine factory, C.K.D.-Vysocany, etc.[16] At Plzen a crowd of 5,000 workers coming from the Lenin factories occupied the premises of the local branch of the National Committee (the town hall) by force and, with the help of improvised loud-speakers, demanded free elections. The demonstrators trampled portraits of Stalin and Gottwald under foot, destroyed Soviet flags, set fire to the municipal archives, and hung a large portrait of President Benes (the last President of the

Democratic Republic) in the conference chamber. Militiamen, instead of resisting or driving back the rioters, fraternized with them, and it was some time before the demonstrators were dispersed. At about 7 p.m. the Communists organized a counter-demonstration in favour of the party and Comrade Zapotocky, carrying banners and portraits of Malenkov. Official propaganda attributed these disturbances to 'bourgeois and social-democrat provocateurs'. The entire organization of the party and trade unions was mobilized to restore discipline. The speed and decisiveness of the repression,[17] the appeal to the workers' patriotism, the forceful restoration of control, undertakings to secure a rise in the standard of living through wage increases – all helped the leaders to impose their policy and establish their own authority. Gottwald's successors showed that they intended to keep the initiative and that they would continue to govern, after the Stalinist manner, despite a formal condemnation of the cult of personality. Most of the Czechoslovak leaders were suspicious of what was happening in Hungary under Nagy's government. While preparations were going ahead in Budapest for the rehabilitation of Rakosi's victims, in Czechoslovakia the purge initiated by the Slansky trial was under way.[18]

Not that there was any question of Zapotocky, Novotny and their friends defying the Soviet hierarchy. Each of them continually protested his loyalty to the U.S.S.R. using every opportunity to produce evidence to back their assertions. Their attitude was similar to that of Maurice Thorez and the French Communist leaders; they were devoted to Stalin's person, his ideas and his practices, which they had elevated into a cult among the militants of their country.[19] They saw no need to repudiate a system that they wanted to preserve with as few changes as possible. As for Krushchev, Novotny tried to convince him – not without success – that he, Novotny, was the best man to determine how Soviet practice should be adapted to Czechoslovak conditions.

It was precisely over the question of the application of Soviet methods in agriculture that the first serious disagreement within the Czechoslovak leadership took place, after the Plzen disturbances. President Zapotocky, Malenkov's protégé, advocated a policy very similar to Imre Nagy's in Hungary. On 1 August 1953, in a widely reported speech to the workers of the Klicava dam (near Kladno), he criticized forced collectivization, and promised the peasants that he would allow them to leave the collective farms and engage in private farming if they so desired. A few months later, speaking at Brno, Zapotocky admitted that most of the production co-operatives established by force had failed and were hovering on the edge of bankruptcy.[20] Although he repeatedly emphasized that the reorganization would neeed careful and controlled introduction, in many parts of the country – as also in Hungary after Nagy's speech of 4 July 1953 – the peasants began redistributing the land without waiting for permission. Novotny reacted vigorously, ordering the party machine to oppose every untimely division. In the Politburo, he defended the view that problems in the co-operatives (J.Z.D.) should be resolved through an improvement in their organization and not their abolition. He called Zapotocky's ideas 'petit bourgeois', and asked the Soviets to come to the rescue. In April 1954, a joint meeting of the Soviet and Czechoslovak leaderships, attended by Khrushchev, took place in the utmost secrecy. The Soviet leaders, while reiterating Zapotocky's criticism on certain details of agricultural policy, decided in favour of Novotny.

After this episode of arbitration, Zapotocky's part in the Ninth Czechoslovak Party Congress (June 1954) was unobtrusive. The star role fell to Novotny, who announced authoritatively: 'The party is the controlling force, and cannot be put on the same level as the state administrative machine.' Novotny's victory, gained with Khrushchev's help, foreshadowed Khrushchev's own. All the leaders were equal in the collective leadership, but from now on the First Secretary of the party was first among them.

The 'New Course' in the Other People's Democracies

The leaders of the other People's Democracies were less than enthusiastic about fulfilling Moscow's demands; their main concern was to safeguard the basic Stalinist political and economic structure, while carrying out some formal modifications (e.g. collective leadership), and employing less severe methods.

In Rumania, Gheorghiu Dej waited until April 1954 before surrendering the party leadership to an old friend from his railway days, Gheorghe Apostol, keeping the chairmanship of the Council for himself. Later, when he saw that Malenkov's influence was waning like Khrushchev's was waxing, Dej set matters right. In December 1955 he again assumed the post of First Secretary of the party, appointing Chivu Stoica, a former trade unionist and one of the few Rumanian Communists nationally known before 1945, chairman of the Council.

In the economic field, Dej was more prompt about carrying out Soviet orders, especially those of Malenkov. On 23 August 1953 he announced the 'new course' to the Central Committee and condemned his own previous policy, which consisted of giving absolute priority to heavy industry in preference to agriculture and the consumer industries. Dej gave notice that considerable sums were being allocated to the private sector of agriculture which, at the time, still supplied the country with 75 per cent of its cereals. He announced that the party's historic mission was to realize the ideals of the Rumanian nation; but he took no steps to ease the internal political situation.

In Bulgaria, where Stalinism was no less rigid than in Rumania, the party leadership felt able to loosen the screws a little. In September 1953, on the occasion of the anniversary of the Communist party's assumption of power, political prisoners serving sentences of up to five years who had already completed a half or a third of their time were set free. In November of the same year, the measures approved in February 1953, just before Stalin's death, were repealed. One prescribed the death sentence for anyone who tried to leave the country without permission, allowing the prosecution of close relatives, even if they were minors; the other forbade workers to change their place of work.

In January 1954 Chervenkov dutifully carried out his self-criticism before the Central Committee. 'The cult of personality', he said, not without a trace of humour, 'is harmful, even when it concerns exceptionally powerful and eminent individuals.' He censured his subordinates for having been excessively adulatory, and ordered the removal of all the portraits and busts of himself. Then in February 1954, at the carefully prepared Party Congress, the separation of powers was introduced. Chervenkov (like Gheorghiu Dej in Rumania) made the mistake of staying on as chairman of the Council and having a protégé of Khrushchev's appointed First Secretary – Todor Zhivkov, who was to rob him of power. The new Central Committee elected by the Congress included a few supporters of Kostov, who had been executed in 1949 and very quietly rehabilitated in 1953.[21]

In Albania, Enver Hoxha displayed greater cunning: when the separation came, he held on to the party leadership. Mehmet Shehu (who had organized the great anti-Titoist purge after 1948), appointed chairman of the Council in July 1954, was completely loyal to him.

The most cautious and the slowest country to follow this path was Poland. The dictator Bierut's motto seemed at first to be *quiete non movere*. The few concessions he made in the economic field were accompanied by a strengthening of police organization. However, the party Congress of March 1954 divided powers there as well: Bierut was appointed First Secretary, but the running of the state was entrusted to Zawadski, who became chairman of the State Council (President of the Republic), and the former socialist Cyrankiewicz, who became chairman of the Council of Ministers (Prime Minister).

Quite a stir was caused in the upper echelons of the Polish hierarchy, however, when a high security official, Joseph Swiatlo, defected in autumn 1953, and published a series of well-document-ed articles in the United States which revealed the extent to which all branches of the administration, even members of the Politburo and Central Committee, were controlled by the security services. Swiatlo also revealed the background of some political trials. The cadres were roused. Poland began looking for its Beria. On 7 December 1954 the Ministry of Public Safety under Stanislaw Radkiewicz was dissolved, and its departments were divided be-tween the Ministry of the Interior and the newly created Commit-tee of Public Safety, responsible to the chairman of the Council. Radkiewicz was appointed Minister of State Farms. He and his acts of cruelty were much discussed in 1955–6.

But from the end of 1954 thousands of political prisoners were set free. The party's ideological organ declared that 'the party intends to rehabilitate all members who have been unjustly accused'.[22] At the beginning of 1955 four high security officials and several army intelligence officers (counter-espionage) were expelled from the party and prosecuted for having 'violated revolutionary legality' and carried out a *Beriovshchina* (Beria-type purge). The party intellectuals were restless; at the Writers' Congress in June 1954 several speakers attacked the censorship.[23] In the economic field, there being a great shortage of foodstuffs and ordinary consumer goods, in October 1953 the Central Committee decided to slacken the pace of industrialization, and to lower the investment rate (from 25.1 per cent of the national income in 1953 to 19 or 20 per cent in 1954); it also ordered a reduction in prices. Nevertheless, it became clear over the following years that all these measures were inadequate: productivity and the standard of living remained stagnant. The current of 'relative liberalization' set in motion by the Third Plenum of the Central Committee was soon brought to a standstill by the Stalinists. There followed 'a long period of waiting and observation'.[24]

2

Relations between the U.S.S.R. and the Socialist Countries

The Policy of Détente

After Stalin's death the new Soviet leadership reconsidered all aspects of the U.S.S.R.'s foreign policy. It seemed the right moment to try, if not to terminate the cold war which had culminated in the Korean war, at least to prevent it from growing and to soften its effects. Overtures came from the West; President Eisenhower, who entered office in January 1953, announced on 16 April: 'The world knows that a whole era has ended with the death of Stalin.' He proposed that a peace plan be discussed. Unprecedentedly, *Pravda* published on 25 April the words of the President of the United States. Churchill, too, welcomed the 'fresh opportunity for the world provided by the coming of new men to power in the U.S.S.R.', and suggested a summit conference.

The Soviets responded to these advances with further acts of courtesy and goodwill. Restrictions on the movements of foreign diplomats in the U.S.S.R. were reduced. The peace negotiations in Korea, which had been at a standstill for several months, ended in agreement in late July. The war in Indo-China was still raging, but in November 1953 Ho Chi Minh intimated that he was prepared to negotiate an armistice. Meanwhile the Soviet government regularized its relations with Turkey, solemnly renouncing all its former claims on Turkish territory; and diplomatic contacts, severed a few months previously by Stalin, were re-established. On 8 August Malenkov in a triumphant speech to the Supreme Soviet announced that the U.S.S.R. now possessed the hydrogen bomb, and declared at the same time: 'There are today no contentious or outstanding issues that cannot be resolved peacefully, on the basis of mutual understanding between the interested parties. This applies equally to disagreements between the United States and the Soviet Union. We have been, and are, for peaceful coexistence of the two ideologies.'

Was this a mere tactical move, or did it indicate a profound change in Soviet views? Tito, on his return from an official visit to London in March, cautiously predicted: 'Once a military equilibrium has been established (now almost accomplished), Stalin's successors will try to find a way out of their dilemma.' He was right. Differences arose in the Kremlin on how far concessions should go. Beria seems to have wanted to go further than his colleagues, in order at the eleventh hour to prevent the integration of the German Federal Republic into NATO. Molotov remained the 'hawk' he always had been. But all were agreed to resume the discussions with the West that had been broken off in 1949. Diplomacy was called on to repair the damage caused by an excess of ideology. An element of pessimism, of fear, had lain under Stalin's aggressiveness. His successors, armed with the H-bomb, seemed to have greater confidence in the power of the U.S.S.R.; they hoped also, by means of more flexible tactics, to be able to exploit the differences existing between the Western nations of which Stalin had already been aware in 1952. Economic interest, the need to ease the pressure on the population and raise the standard of living, prompted the Soviet leaders to seek a *détente*, if only to gain a little time; hence the more open foreign policy initiated by Malenkov and pursued by Bulganin and Khrushchev after his removal, which led to the signing of the Austrian treaty in May 1955 and to the Geneva summit conference in July of the same year. First in the U.S.S.R. and then in the People's Democracies, the siege mentality of 1948–53 gradually gave way to a more relaxed attitude towards the West. Fear of war receded, and propaganda became less strident. The expression 'peaceful coexistence' took on a real if still ambiguous meaning. This change-over was not entirely smooth. The external threat of war was after all one of the major justifications for dictatorship, and the East German, Polish, Hungarian and Rumanian leaders had other reasons to fear a *détente*: the U.S.S.R. might be persuaded to reach an agreement with the United States at their expense. But for the people – and for a few exceptional leaders such as Nagy – the international *détente* held out a promise, and justified the 'new course' of liberalization.

China Appears on the Scene

One of the chief concerns of the new Soviet leadership was to make sure that the improvement in relations with the West did not affect the unity of the bloc. The leading role of the U.S.S.R. was now unequivocally accepted; but would it continue to be? Some Soviet leaders thought that the methods used in Stalin's time to ensure unity in the socialist camp had to be made more flexible, that relations between the socialist countries must be reshaped.

Their views on this point coincided with those of Mao Tsetung, who wanted to see Soviet policy shed what had been its most offensive aspect under Stalin: the attitude that other countries and parties were inferior. Since 1949 Mao had been largely autonomous in his handling of Chinese affairs, and had never accepted the status of satellite; after Stalin's death he sought nothing less than an active part in planning the unified strategy of the Communist world. Moreover, he seems not only to have defended the rights and privileges of his own country and party, but also to have demanded the same for the other socialist countries.

In October 1954 Khrushchev, Mikoyan and Bulganin visited Peking. Relations between the socialist countries were the main subject of their discussions with Mao and his colleagues. A perusal of the documents signed at the end of these talks will show how Chinese pressure was applied. The agreement was preceded by a joint declaration, according to which 'friendly relations between the U.S.S.R. and China form the basis for collaboration between the two states in accordance with the principles of equality of rights, reciprocal advantages, mutual respect, national sovereignty and territorial integrity'. The two governments undertook to 'consult with each other on every occasion when a matter of mutual concern arose ... that there may be concerted action to ensure the security of the two countries and preserve the peace'.[1]

The Sino-Soviet agreement created a precedent. The terms in which it was couched were almost identical to those formulated by the Yugoslavs in 1948 when rejecting the idea of Soviet hegemony. 'The socialist states', they had said, '... must be natural allies and learn from each other, basing their relations on complete equality.'[2] Now the Sino-Soviet agreement, condemning hegemony by implication, prepared the way for a Moscow–Belgrade reconciliation.

The agreement between Khrushchev and Mao Tse-tung provided, among other things, for the transfer to China of all Soviet shares in the 'mixed companies' created in 1950. Later on it became known that at that time Mao had criticized the mixed companies sharply, denouncing them as 'a form of Russian interference in Chinese economic life'.[3] Here again he followed the Yugoslavs, who as early as 1947 had refused to set up mixed companies after the model of those already established in Rumania, Bulgaria and Hungary, regarding them as 'a special form of Russian exploitation of the natural wealth of the People's Democracies'. One of the best-known Yugoslav economic experts, Milentije Popovic, pointed out that the conditions imposed by the Soviets on the socialist countries in the establishment of these companies were substantially more stringent than those on capitalist neighbours, for example Iran.[4] Indeed, the mixed companies functioned in such an obviously iniquitous fashion that Stalin's successors could find no defence for them. During the course of 1954 most of them were liquidated.

In the great Politburo debate on foreign policy with Molotov in 1955, Khrushchev and Mikoyan referred to Mao in affirming that the methods used in dealing with the People's Democracies were 'contrary to the spirit of proletarian internationalism' and 'reflected great-power chauvinism'.

There is also reason to believe that Mao played some part in Malenkov's dismissal. He had been won by Krushchev and Mikoyan to the view that Malenkov's economic policy (and that of his protégés such as Nagy) might lead to a reduction in the output of heavy industry in the U.S.S.R. and the People's Democracies. This clearly was not in the interest of China, which was counting on an increase in aid and supplies of equipment from the other socialist countries. Thus, at the end of 1954 and the beginning of 1955, Khrushchev's and Mao Tse-tung's ideas on bloc reorganization seemed to coincide. In Mao's mind, increased independence of the Communist countries and parties was not to stand in the way of greater unity and strength, but on the contrary to establish them on surer foundations. For this reason he gave Khrushchev – his future principal opponent – moral support, standing by him (though not, as we shall see, wholeheartedly) when he overruled Molotov's objections and tried to remedy Stalin's mistakes over Yugoslavia by bringing that country back into the socialist fold.

The Rehabilitation of Tito and Yugoslav Socialism

Few events after Stalin's death had a more profound effect on the development of the Eastern countries or more strongly encouraged centrifugal tendencies than the reconciliation between the Soviet leaders and Tito and his colleagues.

Khrushchev, the prime mover of the Moscow–Belgrade rapprochement, was undoubtedly aware of the repercussions of his action in the U.S.S.R. and among the fraternal parties. Since 1948 the whole of Communist propaganda had hinged on the struggle against 'Tito's fascist clique', and provided the justification for the Cominform. The Eastern leaders, from Gheorghiu Dej and Rakosi to Ulbricht – not to mention the most vehement of them all, Enver Hoxha – had for years been competing with each other in denouncing Tito's betrayal of socialism, his involvement with imperialism, his subversive interventions in the People's Democracies. The campaign against Tito's Yugoslavia really did constitute 'the most massive case of provocation . . . in the history of the international revolutionary workers' movement',[5] and to repair the damage was not an easy task in view of the number of vested interests involved.

Why, therefore, did Khrushchev apply himself with such vigour to the task? As he himself explained in Prague in June 1954 at a meeting of party representatives from Italy, France and other countries, he was convinced that the break in 1948 had been a serious political error for which Stalin must bear the principal blame. 'The old man's mind wasn't functioning so well any more', he told d'Onofrio, the Italian delegate to the Prague congress.[6] No doubt Khrushchev, like most of his colleagues, did not regard Tito as having been entirely guiltless in this affair; he had behaved like a nationalist, deserving therefore some measure of blame. But, in his opinion, differences could and should have been settled by diplomatic means, by persuasion, and by negotiations, rather than by wielding the big stick.

The effort to correct this error was an integral and vital part of the new policy aiming to rid Soviet foreign relations of all Stalinist traces. Khrushchev knew that the other powers regarded his attitude to Tito's Yugoslavia as a 'test case'. Reconciliation would encourage belief in the Kremlin's peaceful intentions. Furthermore, Khrushchev seems personally to have admired Tito, who, in spite of the difficult position in which he had been placed, the blockade and pressures from every side, had succeeded in preserving his country's independence and its Communist régime. Finally, Khrushchev hoped that once the error had been corrected and apologies and material reparations made, he would be able to bring Yugoslavia back into the socialist community, which of course would be reorganized and made more flexible.

Not everyone in the socialist camp believed that this was feasible. Mao Tse-tung, consulted by the Soviets in June 1954 before contact was established with Belgrade, agreed that 'Yugoslavia should be regarded as a fraternal socialist country in order to facilitate its return'; but at the same time he gave vent to a certain scepticism: 'One must remember that the Yugoslav leaders have already gone very far in their relations with imperialism', he wrote to Khrushchev.[7]

In spite of the similar origin of the two régimes, in a victorious civil war without any appreciable Soviet aid, the Chinese regarded the Yugoslavs with suspicion. They were annoyed by their claims to be the great theoreticians of guerrilla warfare; they also feared competition in India, Burma and Egypt, which Tito had visited at the end of 1954 and the beginning of 1955.

Within the Soviet leadership reconciliation was violently opposed by Molotov, who defended the merits of the 1948 policy. 'Tito was and remains anti-Soviet', the former head of the Soviet foreign service declared. 'His views bear no relation to Communism.' Molotov was only voicing what the Stalinists in the People's Democracies thought but dared not say. Nevertheless, Khrushchev, with a majority in the Presidium, overruled his objections and those of the Albanians.[8]

The Soviet delegation, headed by Khrushchev as party leader and including Prime Minister Bulganin and the First Deputy Prime Minister, Mikoyan, arrived at Belgrade airport on 27 May 1955. Khrushchev immediately stepped up to the microphone to make a statement that evidently surprised the Yugoslav leaders, including Tito, who became very thoughtful. Passing over Stalin's work in silence, he blamed the break with Yugoslavia entirely on Beria and his deputy Abakumov (sentenced and executed at the end of 1954). He went on to declare that the Yugoslav party had remained Marxist-Leninist, thereby minimizing the ideological differences that the Yugoslavs themselves were by no means prepared to ignore. His idea was to face the Yugoslavs with the following dilemma : 'You claim to be Marxists and Communists. If that is so, there is no reason why we should not find ourselves on common ideological ground. If, on the other hand, you refuse to come to terms, then you are admitting that those who accuse you of abandoning the Marxist-Leninist path are justified.' But the Yugoslavs, on the lookout, did not fall for this. 'We have remained Marxist-Leninists', they replied in effect, 'but Marxist-Leninist in our own individual way.'

All the journalists and observers who came to Belgrade for the Soviet-Yugoslav meeting found a pamphlet by the Yugoslav Edvard Kardelj in their mail entitled 'Socialist Democracy in Yugoslav Practice', the text of a lecture given in autumn 1954 in Oslo. Kardelj rejected 'classical bourgeois democracy'; but he also rejected centralized, bureaucratic, state socialism, the 'socialism of the apparatus' that prevailed in the Soviet bloc (and in Yugoslavia up to 1950). Yugoslav socialism, he explained, is based on 'direct democracy, guaranteeing the maximum amount of democratic workers' self-government through managerial bodies'.

He pointed out the theoretical and practical importance of the workers' councils set up in his country in 1950, thanks to which the Yugoslav leaders were gradually able to shake the workers out of their lethargy, and interest them in the running of their enterprises. The League of Communists, as the party was called from 1952 to distinguish it from the other, Stalinist Communist parties, set itself the task of developing the initiative of the masses, in order to secure maximum participation in the economic, social and political life of the country, in the management of social organizations and institutions, and economic and state bodies.[9]

It is quite true that between 1950 and 1955 the situation in Yugoslavia changed considerably, thanks to the systematic reform of the leaders. The excessive powers enjoyed by Rankovic's security police (U.D.B.A.) and its extension, the public prosecutor's office, were restricted, although this did not hamper Rankovic's influence on public policy. Many artisans were allowed to reopen their workshops (there were over 150,000 in 1954); and finally, in March 1953 the government authorized the dissolution of the agricultural co-operatives, and this succeeded in ending all but one fifth of those enterprises.

But these reforms still did not go further than the tactical concessions that Communists of a 'rightist', opportunistic, Bukharinist strain might feel able to make without relinquishing effective control of the party. Despite its change of name, the party retained its monopoly of political power. Referring to Marx and Lenin, Tito and Kardelj talked about the 'withering-away of the state' as of a process that had already begun in Yugoslavia, and yet the army, police force and foreign policy remained as highly centralized as before, and entirely outside democratic control. Central economic planning also survived more or less disguised, and the independence of enterprises was more apparent than real.[10] If Yugoslavia in the period of the reconciliation was enjoying greater freedom than any other Communist country, if internal commerce and the production of consumer goods had been stimulated and the press enlivened, the Djilas affair at the beginning of 1954 showed just how far liberalization was to be allowed to go.

One of the régime's principal figures, Tito's friend and close associate Milovan Djilas, who had had differences with the Soviets since 1944, had taken the lead in the struggle against Stalinism for effective democracy after 1949. As long as he confined himself to theoretical discussions, he was acclaimed. But in October 1953 this *enfant terrible* of Yugoslav Communism began publishing articles in *Borba* (the régime's main organ) demanding real democratization, and expressing the opinion that the Leninist type of party and state was obsolete. He condemned the privileges, unscrupulous ambition, pride, ostentation and stupidity of the new ruling class, composed of 'formerly heroic men and women'. Stung to the quick, the party rose as one man to silence him.

Tito abandoned Djilas not without regret. Opening the Central Committee meeting that was to condemn and expel him, he restated the issue. 'I was the first', he said, 'to speak of the withering-away of the party, and of the League. However, I did not say that this should take place in six months or in a year or two, but that it was a long-term process. There can be no question of the withering-away of the League or of its liquidation before the last class enemy has been neutralized, before the vast majority of citizens have been imbued with socialist consciousness. The League of Communists is responsible for the realization of revolutionary aims ... It must exist, it must even grow stronger ideologically, fully aware of the huge task incumbent upon it.'

This was an ultra-Leninist profession of faith which showed that Tito intended keeping within the limits of authoritarian if enlightened paternalism that had typified the government's procedures since 1950. Djilas had to surrender all his party and state posts, and was then sentenced to a number of years in prison for having published abroad articles critical of the Communist régime. While he was serving his term in the Sremska Mitrovica prison, his book *The New Class* appeared in 1957 in New York and then in Paris.[11] The book deserved the world-wide acclaim it received as the first systematic sociological analysis of the Stalinist régimes and of their governmental machines. For its illicit transmission abroad and for his anti-Communist propaganda, Djilas received a further seven-year sentence, from which he was released in 1961 on the condition that he refrained from such activities. The following year he was again sentenced for five years for publishing his

Conversations with Stalin in New York, but was pardoned in 1966.

A number of writers and observers commented on the coincidence of the punitive measures taken against Djilas and the Soviet-Yugoslav rapprochement. By clamping down on revisionism in his own country, it was claimed, Tito was trying to persuade the Kremlin of his orthodoxy. This hypothesis is highly suspect. In his negotiations with Khrushchev and the other Soviet leaders, Tito had always stressed the originality of the Yugoslav experiment, not its orthodox nature, the right of each Communist party and country to work out its own salvation, and also to avoid belonging to any military bloc. On all these points his view had prevailed. The joint declaration issued on 3 June 1955 included the following passages, literally destroying the whole basis of Marxist-Leninist solidarity and opening the way to pluralism or, as it was later called, socialist polycentrism:

Faithfulness to the principles of mutual respect and non-intervention in internal affairs for whatever reason, economic, political or ideological, because matters of internal organization, of different social systems, and different forms of socialist development remain solely the concern of each country individually.

Acknowledgement of the principle that military blocs heighten international tension, sap the mutual confidence of nations and increase the danger of war.

Either these are mere words or one must assume that for the first time the U.S.S.R. explicitly admitted the possibility of different forms of socialism, and condemned in theory her own policy of blocs.

Tito in return implicitly acknowledged his solidarity with the other 'socialist' countries (although it should be noted that the Yugoslavs generously applied this term to India, Egypt, and even to the Scandinavian countries with their social democratic régimes), supported China's claims on Formosa and the Soviet views on European security. The Soviets now felt themselves shielded from the damaging barbs of their implacable critics in Belgrade. On the other hand, the reconciliation with the U.S.S.R. enabled the Yugoslavs to keep aloof from the Atlantic bloc and to play down the militaristic aspects of the Balkan alliance concluded shortly before with Turkey and Greece.

But it was Tito who gained most from the meeting. Not only was he completely cleared of charges of treachery and complicity with the imperialists, but his basic ideas were legitimized, opening the way for Yugoslavia's ideological penetration of the other Communist countries.

The Effects of Reconciliation

A close associate of Tito's, Veljko Vlahovic, in an article on 7 July 1955 in the party organ *Komunist*, condemned all hegemonic trends in the workers' movement, and outlined plans for a huge International to bring together Communists of various tendencies and democratic socialists on the basis of mutual tolerance. But in Tito's view, tolerance did not apply to the intolerant, the dogmatists. In a speech at Karlovac on 27 July he attacked 'certain leaders of neighbouring countries' who continued to repress those militants calling for a rapprochement with Yugoslavia. In particular he picked on the Hungarian and Czechoslovak leaders who 'had shed the blood of innocent Communists' (an allusion to the Rajk and Slansky trials) and lacked the courage to admit their mistakes.

Thus Tito openly encouraged the forces of opposition wherever anti-Stalinist trends had been halted after Malenkov's fall.

In Hungary and Poland supporters of Imre Nagy and Gomulka lost no time in pointing out the paradox between the pluralistic spirit of the Belgrade declaration and the ideological condemnation of 'deviations', inspired largely by the Yugoslav example. 'The ideological and political platform of those who . . . attack the slightest deviation from fixed dogmas is at base no more than the continuation of the campaign against Titoism in a disguised form', wrote Imre Nagy.[12] In his view, Hungarian socialism was simply the legitimate Hungarian form or, in other words, 'the application of Marxism-Leninism to the specific conditions of Hungary'. And Rakosi bore 'a heavy responsibility before the whole international revolutionary movement for the part he had played in the anti-Yugoslav campaign of provocation'. In Poland too, the similarities were quickly observed between Tito's 'rehabilitated' ideas and the 'right-wing nationalist deviation' of Gomulka and his friend Spychalski, which led in 1949 to their expulsion from the party and subsequent arrest.

Thus the Belgrade declaration put the East European Stalinist leaders in an embarrassing position. By following the Soviets (who had nothing to lose by it) in the rehabilitation of Tito, they would undermine the Stalinist, centralist bases of their own power. By refusing to come to terms with Tito, they would lag behind the Kremlin, which would go against Stalinist tradition, and also would stimulate an opposition that could appeal to both Tito and Khrushchev. Most of the Eastern leaders caught in this dilemma adopted delaying tactics in the hope that the rapprochement with the Yugoslavs would turn out to be merely a 'temporary, tactical manoeuvre'. Thus Matyas Rakosi, in a speech delivered in August, spelt out the limits of the concessions he felt obliged to make: he cast the entire blame for the deterioration in Hungarian-Yugoslav relations on the former security chief, Gabor Peter, the 'Hungarian Beria' who had been arrested at the end of 1952 and so could not defend himself. He avoided any reference to the Rajk trial or the rehabilitation of victims of the anti-Titoist purges which Tito had demanded, and confined himself to advocating the re-establishment of normal relations with Belgrade. This did not satisfy Nagy's resurgent supporters. At a meeting of journalists, a former editor of *Szabad Nep*, Miklos Gimes, raised the question of the review of the Rajk trial – and was immediately expelled from the party. Then economic negotiations, begun in the autumn with Yugoslavia to settle claims arising out of the 1949 break, were cut short, according to Budapest, because of 'the excessive demands of the Yugoslavs'.

At the ceremony commemorating the Russian Revolution on 6 November 1955, one of Rakosi's associates, Istvan Kovacs, acclaimed Stalin 'Lenin's best disciple and his successor in his work'. It sounded like a challenge to Khrushchev. Indignant Nagyist writers grouped around *Irodalmi Ujsag* began a campaign for the liberalization of the press that Rakosi dared not put down in his usual fashion.

In Rumania, Gheorghiu Dej cautiously expressed satisfaction at the improvement in Soviet-Yugoslav relations. He strengthened his position at the Second Party Congress in December 1955 by drafting his friends Nicolae Ceausescu and Alexandru Draghia into the Politburo and establishing close ties with Peking to lessen his dependence on Moscow.

Prague kept silent. In the utmost secrecy the Central Committee appointed a special board, similar to the one set up in the U.S.S.R., to study 'the legal and juridical conditions' of the 1952–4 trials.

In Poland a crisis was brewing. At the end of 1954 Gomulka was unobtrusively released, and the party leadership entered into tortuous negotiations with him about his rehabilitation, which it wanted to be partial and gradual so that 'the party should not lose face'. However, in contradistinction to this, two ministers who had been dismissed at the time of the anti-Titoist purges were tried and convicted. Was this an attempt at intimidation, or a last fling on the part of the police? The backwash of Tito's rehabilitation was already being felt in the party organizations, the University, the Warsaw Committee, and in several pilot factories such as the one in Zeran. People were beginning to find their tongues; following the Central Committee meeting of autumn 1955, the economic regression and Poland's future prospects began to be discussed in the party cells. Before this, on 25 August, the highly respected poet Adam Wazyk had published his 'Poem for Adults' in *Nowa Kultura*, a poem of disillusionment, of the collapse of Utopia, but also of hope that the path to people's hearts would be found again. 'We call for simple truths, the bread of freedom, the flame of reason.' The issue of the magazine was sold out rapidly. The party leadership reproached the poet for his 'petit bourgeois' tendencies, but when the workers on the great Nowa Huta site – whose hardships he had described – were asked to condemn him, they sided with him instead.

In Budapest and Warsaw it seemed history had taken a step forward, that the days of ultra-conservatism were numbered. The leaders watched each other warily; everyone was wondering what was going on in the Kremlin, where there was undeniably an eve-of-battle atmosphere at the approach of the Twentieth Congress of the C.P.S.U., called for February 1956. The Stalinist old guard put up a sharp resistance, but Khrushchev the innovator – and this is what puzzled the leaders of the People's Democracies – seemed to be gaining an increasingly strong hold over the machine, which was known to be orthodox and conservative. Could a heretic become Pope of the Communist church?

The Warsaw Pact

Khrushchev the unpredictable had shown, however, after his journey to Peking in 1954, that he had no intention of surrendering the essentials of Stalin's legacy, nor of abandoning Soviet hegemony. A meeting of Eastern heads of government in Moscow during November 1954 took a very firm line against the remilitarization of West Germany, and assured NATO that drastic counter-measures would be taken if Bonn became a member of the Atlantic Alliance. When this occurred, in March 1955, representatives of the Eastern countries, including the U.S.S.R., signed a pact 'of friendship, co-operation and mutual aid' in Warsaw on 14 May 1955 in the presence of the Peking envoy, Marshal Peng Teh-huai, who pledged China's support.

This Warsaw Treaty was at once a general political agreement and a military pact. It was conceived from the start as a response to the integration of the Federal German Republic into the Atlantic Alliance. But, above all, it represented an attempt to legalize a de facto situation (the subordination of the armed forces of the People's Democracies to the Soviet high command),[13] and to supply the bloc under the U.S.S.R. with a more solid political and organizational framework than had hitherto existed with the bilateral treaties between the People's Democracies and the Soviet Union. In addition, it provided a legal basis for the maintenance of Soviet occupation troops in Hungary and Rumania, whence according to the terms of the 1946 peace treaty they were due to be withdrawn after the impending conclusion of a peace treaty with Austria.[14]

Albania was one of the principal beneficiaries of the treaty, as up till then it had had no formal ties with the U.S.S.R. and the People's Democracies, and its leaders, who since 1947 had feared absorption by Yugoslavia, were in great need of reassurance on the eve of the Soviet-Yugoslav reconciliation.

The Soviet leaders, on the whole, showed foresight. Having

agreed to relax their relations with the People's Democracies by restoring certain formal attributes of independence and sovereignty, they wrote into the pact a pledge of 'mutual fraternal aid'. It was this clause that the Kremlin used in autumn 1956 to justify its repressive intervention in Hungary, describing it as fulfilling 'the U.S.S.R.'s internationalist obligations towards the Hungarian People's Democracy'.

The pact was and still is regarded by its signatories as the expression of an ideological community rather than as an alliance based on common national interests. Ten years after it was concluded a zealous upholder of the Warsaw Treaty, Czechoslovak Minister of Defence General Bohumil Lomsky, said: 'The strengthening of unity on the basis of socialist internationalism is for each socialist country a necessary condition for its further development, for the carrying out of its internal and external tasks.'[15]

3

The Twentieth Congress
of the C.P.S.U.

A Psychological Shock and the Admission of Facts

The Twentieth Congress of the C.P.S.U. met in Moscow from 17
to 24 February 1956. Two months later the Polish leaders, after
thoroughly weighing the pros and cons, decided to inform their
party activists, the élite militants, of what had taken place. They
let them read Khrushchev's famous secret report on Stalin's
crimes presented to the Congress at the evening session of 24
February. Four people fainted at one of the briefings in the Warsaw radio centre; the rest listened dumbfounded. The impact was
immediate; but the revelations were to have even more far-
reaching effects in the future, and it is no exaggeration to say that
they marked a turning-point in the history of the Communist
movement.

The Soviet party chief launched himself into a violently icono-
clastic attack on the man or superman who, despite all the
rumours circulating since his death, still symbolized for most
Communists the power of the Soviet party, the U.S.S.R., and the
revolutionary idea. Pope and Caesar rolled into one – a divine,
omnipotent, infallible figure for the militants, the personification
of the devil for the enemies of Communism – Stalin was used by
his former lieutenant as a scapegoat for all the acts of violence,
terror and oriental and medieval despotism perpetrated by the
régime under his rule. Khrushchev accused him of having in-
vented the monstrous concept of 'enemy of the people', a term
which 'automatically rendered superfluous any attempt to establish proof of the ideological mistakes of the man or men engaged

in a controversy'; it 'justified the use of the cruellest methods of repression, violating every norm of revolutionary legality, against anyone who disagreed with him in any way whatsoever'. Under Stalin's iron rule, he said, 'arrest and deportation on a massive scale ... executions without trial or explanation, created conditions of insecurity, fear and even despair'. Khrushchev thus confirmed everything Trotsky had written of Stalin's machinations and underhand dealings, his cruelty, and the part he had played in setting up the great trials of 1937–8. 'Several thousand honest and innocent Communists', he said, 'died as a result of gross distortion of the facts.' He informed the Congress that many of the Stalinist trials had now been reviewed and declared null and void. Between 1954 and the beginning of 1956, the Military Chamber of the Supreme Court of the U.S.S.R. alone rehabilitated 7,679 people, many of them posthumously.[1] Khrushchev spoke of the mass deportation of 'whole peoples', including Communists and Komsomol (Communist Youth Organization) members. The Ukrainians escaped this fate only 'because there were too many of them and there was nowhere to send them'. With regard to Yugoslavia, Khrushchev showed how megalomaniac Stalin had been. When Tito refused to obey him, Stalin said contemptuously to his closest associates, Khrushchev among them : 'I have only to raise my little finger, and it will be the end of Tito. He'll collapse.' 'We have paid dearly for that movement of his little finger', exclaimed Khrushchev.

This indictment (which must be read in its entirety for its full impact to be appreciated[1]) was not, of course, to reach a world public, at least initially. In his first speech to the plenary session, Khrushchev confined himself to condemning 'the cult of personality' in the general terms that had become familiar since 1954.

His second report, devoted solely to Stalin, was delivered at a private session from which even the representatives of the fraternal parties were excluded. Moreover, Khrushchev instructed those present to be as discreet as possible: 'We must not supply the enemy with ammunition; we must not wash our dirty linen in public.' After the Congress, the document was gradually made known to different levels of the party, and, in spite of all precautions, there were some leaks. The Moscow correspondent of the New York Times was able to publish an article summarizing the speech as early as 16 March. The Moscow office of the Agence France-Presse confirmed the news on 19 March. The following day the Yugoslav paper Borba reported the basic points in detail, and soon the text was communicated to the leaders of the other Communist parties. However, the Poles felt able to take the risk of informing activists of the contents in full; but Rakosi, Novotny, Gheorghiu Dej, and Enver Hoxha thought it wiser to communicate only toned-down and generalized versions. Nevertheless, late in May American intelligence managed to get hold of the document, and the State Department published it on 4 June. The Voice of America and Radio Free Europe finished the job.

Communist prestige suffered a grievous blow, and the Chinese were not unjustified in blaming Khrushchev later on for having severely undermined the authority and prestige of the Soviet Union and world Communism by his repudiation of the late dictator.[2]

Most probably Khrushchev had not foreseen all the consequences of this course of action determined by the vicissitudes of internal Soviet political life. The Twentieth Congress represented a stage in Khrushchev's and Mikoyan's struggle with the conservatives in the Presidium who 'rejected everything new and opposed all the propositions the Central Committee was to submit to the Twentieth Congress'.

The conservatives, headed by Molotov, kept trying to thwart Khrushchev's internal and foreign policy plans, and on the eve of the Twentieth Congress an academic battle was raging which was incomprehensible to non-initiates.

In 1955 Molotov had darkly hinted to the Supreme Soviet that only the 'bases' of a socialist society had been constructed in the Soviet Union, and that in the People's Democracies, 'only the first steps towards socialism had been taken'. If Molotov was right and socialism in the U.S.S.R. was still in a precarious and weak state, then the optimism that underlay Khrushchev's policy of détente constituted a monumental error. These points were restated by Mao Tse-tung seven years later.

At Khrushchev's instigation, the Central Committee forced Molotov to publish a self-critical statement in Komunist,[3] but, although he admitted that he had expressed himself unfortunately, he did not capitulate. In the Presidium he continued to challenge the effectiveness of the personal diplomacy of Khrushchev, who, constantly harassed and in danger of finding himself in a minority in the Central Committee and the Presidium, staked everything on one throw : he took the dispute on to the floor of the Congress itself.

This explains the snarling, vengeful tone of his report on Stalin. Its main object was to vindicate his own policy and to confound his opponents, who were defending Stalin and wanted to go on governing in the same way, whereas he, Khrushchev, was convinced that the U.S.S.R. would be able both to strengthen its international position and make socialism more attractive by introducing greater flexibility, justice and tolerance into its methods of government.

Khrushchev and his Stalinist opponents came from the same background of the party, state or economic bureaucracy that flourished under Stalin's iron protection. But while Stalinist dogma provided the theoretical justification for his bureaucracy, it also revealed its sense of guilt and insecurity, and gave expression to its doctrinal obsessions. The cadres enjoyed undoubted political and material advantages – but at the cost of blind obedience, police surveillance and the permanent fear that they might fail to satisfy and so lose their positions. The bureaucracy was now anxious to preserve the advantages while removing the 'conditions of insecurity, fear and despair' described by Khrushchev in his report. This was the 'class' source of the 'liberal' trend represented by Khrushchev.

The conflict between Stalinists and anti-Stalinists recalls the break-up of the nineteenth-century French bourgeoisie into conservative and liberal monarchist, Carlist, Orléanist and republican factions, and Khrushchev took the part of Louis-Philippe in Russian Communism; like him he had to wage a war on two fronts – against those who accused him of sounding the knell of established authority, and those who regarded his liberalism as a mere half-way house, a first step at best. In any case, Khrushchevism implied a high degree of confidence in the stability of the organization, in its capacity to survive transformation and the maintenance of its basic power in spite or because of the abandonment of despotic methods. The future vindicated this confidence within the U.S.S.R. But in the People's Democracies, the transformation turned out to be more dangerous; it was harder to draw a line between Stalinism and the foundations inherited from Stalin, which were not supposed to be substantially modified.

The End of Monolithism

The proceedings of the Twentieth Congress on the whole vindicated the principles of Khrushchevism: the condemnation of the cult of personality, the restoration of collective leadership and the rejection of historical and economic dogmatism.[4]

A number of points in the 'new course' propounded and ratified by the Congress particularly concerned the People's Democracies: firstly the confirmation of the rapprochement with socialist Yugoslavia, with whom it was decided 'to strengthen the bonds of friendship and co-operation as much as possible'; secondly, in respect to Tito's rehabilitation, the acknowledgement of socialist pluralism – that is, each Communist country's right to work out its own method of building socialism, in relation to its own historical, economic and social conditions.

It is true that Khrushchev was somewhat equivocal here, treating the form of socialism in the People's Democracies as distinct from the Soviet model and adapted from the outset to the conditions obtaining in each country. With this pragmatic turn of mind and comparative indifference to doctrinal consistency, he was no doubt trying to convince the Eastern Stalinist leaders that as regards the originality and independence of their régimes they had no call to envy Belgrade.

But the public in the People's Democracies was not deceived. Referring to the 'ideas of the Twentieth Congress', Gomulkists and Nagyists in particular accused their governments of submitting to the Kremlin and automatically adopting the Soviet model. 'A basic reason for political tension in Hungary', wrote Nagy, 'lies in the fact that a body of leaders remote from the Hungarian people is resisting ideas of national independence, sovereignty and equality of rights – the feeling of nationality and the progressive traditions.' Even after the suppression of the Hungarian rebellion, the ideas of 'nationalized' Communism, of a multiplicity of socialist models and of the independence of the parties, continued to stir people. The People's Democracies' loss of self-determination is said to have arisen from the 1948 Cominform resolution against Yugoslavia. After this resolution creative activity distinct from the implementation of the revolution had become the most heinous of crimes.[5] Hence it was a question of taking up the threads broken in June 1948.

A further impetus came from the rehabilitation of the East European victims of the great pre-war purges. The Polish party had been most affected by purges carried out in the Communist International. In 1938, on the initiative of Stalin and his inquisitors, the Executive Committee of the Comintern ordered the dissolution of that party on the pretext that its leadership had been infiltrated by 'enemy agents'. Nearly all the Polish leaders exiled in the U.S.S.R. were then either 'liquidated' or deported. When Khrushchev visited Warsaw in March 1954, the Poles, when they were told of the rehabilitation taking place in the U.S.S.R., asked about the fate of their 'old comrades' who had disappeared in the storm. Khrushchev promised them that he would initiate an inquiry into this. The Polish leaders drew up a list of some twenty-five individuals, among the best known of whom were Adolf Warski-Waresarski, a friend of Lenin's from the days of Zimmerwald, and Kiental, one of the founders of the Comintern, who had fled to the Soviet Union in 1929; Wladyslaw Bronski, who brought Lenin the news of the February Revolution; Maksymilian Walecki and Wern Kostromus. At the beginning of 1955 Khrushchev informed Warsaw that all the leaders in question had been sentenced to death or given terms of penal servitude after bogus trials.

The work of the investigation committees proceeded. In May Khrushchev promised the Poles that the pre-war party would be solemnly rehabilitated, and pictures of the 'annihilated' leaders appeared in the Warsaw papers. Then on 19 February 1956, during the Twentieth Congress itself, a communiqué issued simultaneously in Warsaw and Moscow cleared the names of the vanished leaders. Thus the Polish party had its history, denied it by Stalin, returned to it. But until then, not even the bravest party members had dared to protest.[6]

The Kremlin also made a gesture towards the Hungarian party. It rehabilitated its founder, Bela Kun, former head of the Commune of 1919 who had been arrested and executed in Moscow in 1937 as an 'enemy of the people', despite his services to the Communist International.[7] News of this rehabilitation was received in Hungary with mixed feelings. Rakosi, for his part, had no interest in lifting the veil of secrecy from the struggle of cliques and the purges that had helped him; nor was the Nagyist opposition devoted to Kun. However, the rehabilitation of Bela Kun and the Polish and Yugoslav leaders caused Eastern militants and chroniclers to reappraise the Communist International, which, dominated by the Soviet police, became a willing tool of the Kremlin in the thirties. The Rumanian leaders' questioning of the Comintern's Rumanian policy and the Soviet annexation of Bessarabia and Northern Bukovina[8] may be regarded as a delayed effect of the revelations of the Twentieth Congress, as may also the doubts expressed by Polish historians regarding the validity of the Comintern's instructions to the fraternal parties on the morrow of the Russo-German pact denying war support to 'bourgeois Poland which, with France and England, belongs to the imperialist bloc'.[9]

In rectifying some of the falsifications of history occasioned by proletarian internationalism, Stalin's successors were aiming at improving relations between themselves and the various national parties. But at the same time, whether they liked it or not, they could not help undermining the foundations of Soviet hegemony and stimulating nationalist and anti-Soviet tendencies.

The policy of coexistence required the Western Communist parties, isolated as a result of the cold war and Stalinist sectarianism, to revive the tactics of the popular front. But the reconciliation with the socialists wanted by Khrushchev necessitated certain theoretical concessions. The bridge between revolutionary Communism and the reformism of the Second International had to be rebuilt,[10] and the proposition that effected this bridge was that socialism might also be achieved by parliamentary means. Without renouncing the principle of revolutionary conquest of power, Khrushchev admitted that in certain circumstances it would be possible 'for the working class, with the support of the working peasantry, the intellectuals, and all patriotic forces ... to gain a large majority in Parliament, and to transform this organ of bourgeois democracy into an instrument of the people's real will'. This would create 'conditions guaranteeing radical social changes ... the transfer of the principal means of production into the hands of the people'. In actual fact, the absorption of the old social democratic parties by the Communist parties of the People's Democracies, and the persecution of even left-wing socialists (in Czechoslovakia a group of ex-socialists were tried as late as 1954) were serious obstacles to a socialist-Communist rapprochement. Khrushchev, however, was vague on this point, fearing he might be accused of revisionism. His comrade-in-arms Mikoyan was also apprehensive. In support of the proposal to seize power without force, he was clumsy (or clever?) enough to remind the Congress of Prague, where the February 1948 revolution 'had been carried out by peaceful means: the Communists came to power by concluding an alliance not only with the socialists, but also with the bourgeois parties that supported the United National Front'. The Chinese were less hypocritical than Khrushchev and Mikoyan when they described the events in Prague as 'an example of a bourgeois counter-revolutionary coup crushed by the working class by means of its state apparatus and mainly its armed forces'.[11] Elsewhere, as in Poland and Hungary, it was Soviet military support that enabled the Communists to neutralize and immobilize their opponents and set up totalitarian régimes.

If Khrushchev had attributed all these upheavals, which related to a central strategic plan, to Stalin, it would have removed an obstacle to Communist-socialist rapprochement in the West. But he would then have been challenging the entire system, going against the Soviet Union's vested interests and those of the ruling parties in the People's Democracies. And he, his successors, and all the Eastern leaders were to maintain this fiction of the peaceful victory of the Communist parties, won with the aid of the majority of the population and whose gains could not be questioned. Thus V. Novy thought of the Prague coup as the beginning of the Czech path to Communism.

It is precisely at this point that the Khrushchevists, who wished to modify the practice of power while preserving everything that had been handed down to them as a result of the 1948 coups, parted company with the revisionists, who felt that the wrong path had been taken in 1948 when anti-democratic and illegal means had been used to seize power. After the Twentieth Congress the spectres of democracy and national sovereignty stifled in 1948 permanently haunted the élites of the People's Democracies.

4

The Eastern Leaders and De-Stalinization

The immediate impact of the Twentieth Congress and the disclosures of 'Stalin's crimes' varied greatly from country to country in Eastern Europe, depending on national characteristics and the political and economic situation. The initial effect of the Congress was to stimulate further the rapprochement and co-operation between Tito's Yugoslavia and what seemed to be Khrushchev's Soviet Union. In Poland and Hungary, where there had been stirrings since 1955, it widened the split in the upper echelons, and encouraged liberal elements, reformers, revisionists – Gomulkists and Nagyists – who felt justified in the direction Soviet policy had now taken. In countries where the party leadership was not seriously threatened, the leaders aligned themselves formally with the Kremlin, while keeping a tight control over reforms and stifling any opposition.

Thus the process of diversification that began immediately after Stalin's death with the varying interpretations of the 'new course' continued; and the gap between Warsaw, Prague, Budapest and Bucharest widened. In the end, fear of being overwhelmed by the wave of de-Stalinization and the awakening of centrifugal democratic and national forces led the Soviet leadership to shift the emphasis from reform to continuity, from rediscovered patriotism to international solidarity. But this retrogressive movement came too late and was too equivocal to stem the rising tide in Poland and Hungary, and it led to a deterioration in relations between Moscow and Belgrade.

The Moscow–Belgrade Axis and the Dissolution of the Cominform

Belgrade was the only Communist capital to welcome the Twentieth Congress with sincere enthusiasm. Edvard Kardelj gave a very positive assessment of the work of the Congress.'It is making', he said, 'a significant contribution to peace and peaceful coexistence'; it is encouraging 'the establishment of contacts and democratic collaboration on an equal footing between the different progressive and socialist movements'; and finally, 'the ideological trend of the Congress constitutes a magnificent affirmation of democratic socialism'.

In other words, Belgrade regarded the Twentieth Congress as a victory for Khrushchev over Molotov, for Titoism over Stalinism. This favourable impression was further strengthened when the Yugoslav leaders came to know of Khrushchev's secret report rehabilitating Tito that went even further than earlier public pronouncements. From now on the feeling in Tito's entourage was that Khrushchev had crossed his Rubicon, that the Soviet leadership's break with concentration-camp Communism was final. It seemed, therefore, that the stage of formal rapprochement between states was passed, and that there was now a chance of real ideological collaboration that might inject new life into the movement. Tito was determined to give Khrushchev all the help he could to consolidate his position in the socialist camp and to act as an intermediary for him in his attempt to secure a rapprochement with the West. This role of principal ally and supporter of Khrushchev's Russia appealed to Tito even more in that it reinforced his own prestige and influence throughout Eastern Europe.

The Yugoslavs had fresh cause for satisfaction when, on 17 April 1956, *Pravda* and the papers of the other European Communist countries simultaneously published a resolution announcing the dissolution of the Cominform. This body, it will be remembered, had been set up by Stalin in 1947 to centralize the European Communist movement, and to control the parties of the People's Democracies. It was under cover of the Cominform that the Kremlin condemned the Belgrade rebels and reorganized the Soviet bloc on a cold-war basis. After the expulsion of Yugoslavia and the Soviet leadership's assumption of full control over strategic planning, the Cominform became superfluous; it had an entirely nominal existence, and its only act was to issue a multilingual publication called *For a Lasting Peace, for Popular Democracy*. It was only reasonable for it to be abolished after the reconciliation with Tito, the theoretical acknowledgement of the independence of the parties, and at a time when the U.S.S.R. was seeking to de-escalate the cold war and re-establishing its links with the socialist movements. The Yugoslavs had been urging this course for a year. 'The establishment of the Cominform', one of Tito's associates had written, 'has once again made it clear that it is impossible and even harmful in the present international situation . . . to create any centre whose object is to control the working-class organizations in the different countries.'[1] In Yugoslav eyes, Stalin's centralization of the international movement had stifled 'the remarkable impetus world Communism received from the dissolution of the Comintern in 1943'. They pointed out somewhat slyly that in this respect their ideas coincided with those of the Chinese, who as early as 1943 were insisting on their right 'to work out their own political line independently and to pursue it, taking into account the actual situation and the particular conditions of their country'. The Yugoslav Communists had not enjoyed regular relations with Peking, but it seems that they counted on Mao Tse-tung's assistance in persuading the Kremlin to give up any idea of prolonging the existence of the Cominform, and to adopt instead a form of co-operation that amounted basically to an exchange of experience and criticism.

The declaration of 17 April 1956 seemed to be pointing in this direction. 'The Communist and workers' parties', it stated, 'will without any doubt continue to exchange views on general questions concerning the struggle for peace, democracy and socialism, as it suits them and, taking into account the concrete conditions under which they are pursuing their activities . . . , at the same time as they consider problems of collaboration with parties and movements that are leaning towards socialism.' It looked as though the Kremlin was about to discard monolithism and the absolute control it had hitherto exercised over the Communist parties.

When Tito came to Moscow at the beginning of June 1956, therefore, it was triumphantly as an ideological ally. On 20 June he and Khrushchev signed a declaration making official the reconciliation between the two parties and their future co-operation on a basis worked out by the Yugoslavs. The declaration insisted that this co-operation

... be based on completely free agreement, complete equality, friendly criticism and a friendly exchange of views on matters in dispute. The parties hold the view that the paths of socialist development vary according to the country and the conditions that prevail there. They agree that the diversity of forms of development of socialism is a positive factor. Both parties are opposed to any attempt to determine the paths and forms of socialist development of others.

The representatives of the C.P.S.U. and the L.Y.C. regarded their mutual co-operation as an integral part of their relations with the other Communist and workers' parties, as well as with the socialist and other progressive movements in the world.

For the Yugoslavs and for many other anti-Stalinists in the East European countries, the declaration seemed a charter of decentralized internationalism, of that polycentrism that Togliatti had hailed in an interview published in the journal *Nuovi Argomenti* also on 20 June 1956. Togliatti was, in fact, the first Western party chief to visit Belgrade in Khrushchev's footsteps (May 1956); he got on very well with Tito, and even though fluctuations in Soviet policy and his circumspection concerning the Kremlin forced him subsequently to modify his autonomist and polycentrist position, he remained to the end of his life closer to Tito's pluralism than anyone else.

Yugoslavia's Relations with the Other Countries of Eastern Europe

The leaders of the other People's Democracies had serious differences to settle with Tito's Yugoslavia. After the Twentieth Congress, they turned to this task with greater or lesser alacrity. Late in March 1956 Novotny, head of the Czech party, announced to his Central Committee: 'We attach particular importance to the development and consolidation of economic co-operation with Yugoslavia.' On 11 May, Siroky, chairman of the Council, declared at Bratislava that 'all those parts of the Slansky trial that were directed against Yugoslavia and Zionism were inaccurate'. The Bulgarians also felt it incumbent on them to make a gesture: they announced the full rehabilitation of the head of their party, Kostov, who had been executed at the end of 1949; and the resignation of the Prime Minister, Chervenkov, most rabid and also most gifted of the anti-Titoist Stalinists of the East, was timed to coincide with the arrival in Sofia of a Yugoslav parliamentary delegation under Moshe Pijade.

On 21 April the Hungarian government resumed the economic negotiations broken off in the autumn, and showed itself much more flexible. But this approach and Rakosi's conciliatory words could not revive Tito's interest; he was convinced that only a radical change could repair the damage to Hungary of seven years of repression. Apparently he found it easier to forgive Gheorghiu Dej his past errors, and on his way back from Moscow in June 1956 he signed a declaration in Bucharest. Relations between Belgrade and East Berlin remained cold, and with Tirana they were thoroughly bad.

In spite of Suslov's and Pospelov's intervention, Enver Hoxha refused categorically to rehabilitate his old rival, the pro-Yugoslav Koci Xoxe, who had been hanged in 1948; with a cynicism that shocked Belgrade, he turned Xoxe into the Albanian Beria, and blamed him for the introduction of the personality cult and its effects on relations with Yugoslavia. At the local party committee meeting in Tirana in April 1956, elements favouring a rapprochement with the Yugoslavs nearly overthrew Hoxha, but he had taken precautions and frustrated the 'plot'. The leader of the Titoist, or rather Khrushchevist group, Panayot Plakon, fled to Yugoslavia and in 1957 was given political asylum in the U.S.S.R.[2]

In Belgrade there was unrestrained criticism of 'the little Stalins' in the People's Democracies, and support for de-Stalinization was encouraged. Especially in Hungary and Poland, open reference was made to the example of Yugoslavia. Three aspects of the Titoist model were particularly noted by the proponents of 'socialist democracy' in Poland and Hungary; de-collectivization,[3] decentralization, and the struggle against bureaucracy, and finally the institution of workers' councils, which from spring 1956 the left wing of the Polish liberals and certain proletarian sections of the party saw as a vehicle to change the system and to give 'real power' to the workers.[4]

Yugoslav proselytism began to worry even Khrushchev: Tito's influence was pushing the movement in a direction that ran counter to Soviet interests. The Poznan rising, seven days after the signing of the Moscow declaration, marked a turning point in the Kremlin's policy towards Eastern Europe. Hope of a gradual, smooth transition to Khrushchevism gave way to fear that things were getting out of hand. Khrushchev lent a more ready ear to the views of Novotny, Ulbricht and Maurice Thorez. Intransigence in the Kremlin's attitude was reflected in a restatement of its position issued by the Soviet Central Committee in *Pravda* on 30 June, censoring Togliatti for having spoken of the 'degeneration of Soviet society' in connection with the Stalin cult and calling for vigilance in the face of 'new intrigues on the part of imperialist agents' and the strengthening of 'ideological unity and international fraternal solidarity'.

Then in late summer the Soviet Central Committee sent a confidential circular to the other Communist parties affirming in no uncertain terms its own dominant role in the Communist world. 'Enduring collaboration is possible only with parties that adhere strictly to the doctrine of Marxism-Leninism', it reminded them, adding that 'socialism can be achieved only under the banner of internationalism, in close contact with the socialist countries, and not under the banner of nationalism and apart from the socialist countries'.[5] The letter was obviously intended as a warning against the Yugoslavs, who at the time were siding more and more openly with Gomulka in Poland and those most opposed to Rakosi in Hungary. In Belgrade there was no doubt as to its significance, and the shock and disappointment at this step backward by the Kremlin was evident. Even so, Khrushchev apparently wanted to dispel the doubts that had been raised and to secure Tito's agreement to the compromise solutions he was working out, in order to avoid the unrest in Eastern Europe. This is the reason for his sudden trip to Belgrade in September and Tito's subsequent visit to the Crimea, where Khrushchev introduced him to Rakosi's successor, Ernoe Geroe, whose appointment as First Secretary of the Hungarian party was being sharply criticized in Belgrade. But in spite of evidence of goodwill both before and during the October crisis by Tito, who wanted de-Stalinization to proceed in an orderly fashion and not by means of rebellions, the Soviet-Yugoslav agreement could not stand the strain. Stalinists in the U.S.S.R. and the People's Democracies took advantage of the disturbances to blame Yugoslavia for unleashing centrifugal forces. Pluralism was said to be a Trojan horse, enabling nationalist and bourgeois-democratic tendencies to infiltrate the Communist citadel and corrupt the militants and public opinion.

Poland. Ochab Succeeds Bierut

The Polish party leader Boleslaw Bierut, who headed his party's delegation at the Twentieth Congress, fell ill, and died in Moscow. The funeral of this Stalinist personality paradoxically provoked an anti-Soviet demonstration in Warsaw, for his death occurred at a moment when public opinion was in a particularly sensitive state, following the revelations of the Twentieth Congress concerning the extermination of the old party élite. Dimitrov's death in 1949 and Gottwald's immediately after Stalin's funeral were recalled. It was a sign of the times that on this occasion Polish anti-Russian feelings found an outlet in a Communist figure. The Gomulkists were able to take advantage of these sentiments, which were the basis of the national Communism that was to assert itself in the face of pressure from Moscow.

This became apparent during the election of Bierut's successor on 20 March. Khrushchev appeared personally in Warsaw to influence the decisions of the Polish Central Committee, thereby showing that, despite his assurances to the contrary, he was determined the Kremlin should continue to supervise the fraternal parties in matters of importance.

He found the leadership of the Polish party split among several groups: the Stalinist, also named after Natolin, the suburb of Warsaw where they met; the Pulawy group, led by Roman Zambrowski, a former Stalinist who now supported moderate liberalization; and finally the group around the Prime Minister Cyrankiewicz, who favoured a policy of appeasement. The majority seemed to be behind Zambrowski, but Khrushchev opposed this, letting it be known that it would be better for the Polish party not to be led by someone with a name like 'Ambramovich'. Zambrowski was, indeed, of Jewish origin. Khrushchev tried to tip the scales in favour of Zenon Nowak, the leader of the Natolinians, because, from the Soviet point of view, this party seemed more reliable than the others; but the Central Committee found this intervention out of place, and settled finally for Edward Ochab, a veteran Communist considered a good organizer within the party machine. Ochab had voted for Bierut against Gomulka in the 1948 crisis, but he had consistently refrained from accusing the former General Secretary of being an imperialist agent or a spy.

All things considered, Khrushchev was not displeased with the choice: Ochab started implementing a policy of moderate, controlled liberalization. In March 1956 the Soviet party leader could not foresee, any more than others, that Ochab, Gomulka's future deputy, was to prepare the path for the latter's return, at first reluctantly and then increasingly deliberately. While trying to restrain the popular movement, Ochab was to lean towards the liberals; in October he played the part of mediator between the party apparatus torn between its fears of the people and its fears of Russia, and the man of destiny whom liberal propaganda had painted as a national hero. It was to a large extent thanks to Ochab, almost unknown before his appointment, that a last-minute compromise solution to the Polish crisis of 1956 was found, whereas the Hungarian one, with no Ochab on the scene, was to turn into a blood-bath.

Costly Rehabilitations

One of the most delicate aspects of the Kremlin's new political course was the rehabilitation of victims of the Stalinist purges and the dismissal of those guilty. In this regard, the Polish leadership was the promptest and most thorough. Immediately after Ochab's election as party leader, full liberty was restored to Gomulka, his friends Marian Spychalski and Zenon Kliszko, and then to Generals Tatar, Kirchmajer, Moczar, Kuropieska and Komar, who had been sentenced for having allegedly plotted in support of Gomulka. Many former officers of the Army (*Armia Krajowa*), former socialists and peasant leaders were also freed. These measures were crowned by the amnesty of 25 April 1956, which freed about 30,000 political prisoners sentenced for periods of five years or less. An extensive purge was then carried out among those responsible for the arrests and arbitrary trials, which involved the dismissal of the former Ministers of Security and of Justice, as well as the Attorney General. Finally, on 5 May, Jakob Berman, who seemed to personify the old régime, resigned from the Politburo.

Gomulka's popularity was enhanced by the fact that he had been condemned as a nationalist and anti-Soviet, and Ochab tried to make it quite clear that his release should not be taken for complete political rehabilitation. He drew a clear distinction between himself as the representative of the 'centrist', Khrushchevist and pro-Soviet line, and Gomulka, 'whose views had been justifiably resisted', since he had 'interpreted the correct concept of a Polish path to socialism in an alien manner that amounted to a renunciation of socialism in Poland'. Gomulkism, therefore, was still banned, even though Gomulka's arrest in 1951 was recognized as having been unjustified and based on false allegations. There was a tacit understanding that the way back into the party was not completely closed to Gomulka, but he would have to redeem himself by self-criticism. Gomulka, however, was sure that the public would not be satisfied with the half-measures taken by Ochab and Cyrankiewicz, and that his best tactics would be to hold himself in reserve for the crisis he could see coming.

In Hungary, the rehabilitation of one dead man, Rajk, and one living, Imre Nagy, hung in the balance. No one at home or abroad was unaware of the part played by Rakosi in Laszlo Rajk's conviction and his execution in 1949. When investigation of his trial began during the first thaw under Nagy, Rakosi was as obstructive as he could be and did his utmost to slow it down. For the moment, under pressure from Khrushchev, Tito and the survivors of the trial who had been unobtrusively rehabilitated in the meantime, Rakosi had to give way. At a meeting of activists in a provincial town he announced casually that Rajk had been rehabilitated by the Supreme Court. 'Other cases have also been reviewed', he said; 'the innocent have been rehabilitated and the others pardoned.' This applied particularly to a number of social-democratic leaders. Those responsible for these judicial crimes, like Gabor Peter, had been exposed and disarmed. The main thing now, added Rakosi, was to see that enemies were not able to take advantage of the new development; as the rule of law had now been restored, everyone should concentrate on the economic aspect of Marxism.

This off-hand way of resolving questions of crime and punishment, however, did not satisfy the spokesmen of public opinion, the party intellectuals, whose opposition to the régime continued to grow from late 1955. On 30 March 1956 Sandor Lukacsi, a young Communist literary critic, voiced his indignation at seeing Rakosi, who was responsible for the deaths of Rajk and his colleagues, now condemning their murder. He called the party leader 'a Judas whose hands are red with Rajk's blood'. The poet Laszlo Benjamin asked when poems dedicated to Rajk and banned by the censors might appear. A representative of the censorship replied: 'Never!' But the unrest showed no signs of subsiding. Many militants demanded the publication of the documents relating to the investigation into the Rajk trial. Others expressed doubts as to the legality of Imre Nagy's conviction in March 1955.

But even if Rakosi admitted under pressure from the militants that he was implicated (through carelessness) in the violations of the law between 1949 and 1953, he remained inflexible on the subject of Imre Nagy. On 18 May 1956 he declared that both left sectarianism and right deviationism – that is, Nagyism – must be resisted if the spirit of Twentieth Congress was to be followed. A few weeks later, to pacify widespread demand for his retirement, he sacrificed a particularly hated former associate, Mihaly Farkas, the ex-Minister of Defence. Rakosi did everything in his power to remain in office himself, and for a while was able to convince Moscow that he was irreplaceable.[6] But he gradually lost his grip on the party; his threats were no longer convincing and he dared not make use of the machinery of repression for fear of annoying Khrushchev.

On 19 June 1956 at a meeting of the Petöfi Circle, a club of young intellectuals, Rajk's widow (who had herself been imprisoned for six years without trial) asked the militants to help her avenge her husband and have those responsible for the judicial murders expelled from the party and government. Mrs Rajk was also in contact with Imre Nagy, who was in retirement and avoiding all political activity. Like Gomulka, only more passively, he was waiting for the party to summon him. His friends – journalists, writers and economists – were expounding his ideas in the Petöfi Circle, and in a press that was becoming increasingly free. The trial of strength between the rebellious militants and the party leadership was approaching.

The Czech leaders meanwhile were concerned with the memories of Slansky, Clementis, and the others executed in 1952. From the winter of 1955 there were rumours in Prague of an investigation into the trials which had had such a profound effect on the political life of the country. On 11 June 1956 at the national party conference, these rumours were confirmed by Novotny, who then revealed the special board that had been secretly set up within the Central Committee in 1954 to examine 'the legal and juridical circumstances' of the trials. The chairman of this board, Rudolf Barak, the Minister of the Interior, made it clear that a reconsideration was called for only in respect to the charge of Titoism. Otherwise, the 1952 verdict was correct. According to Barak, it was Slansky, Beria's accomplice, who had introduced to the police the sort of methods to which he himself had subsequently fallen victim. Nevertheless, a number who had survived the trials were quietly released: Vilem Novy, formerly editor-in-chief of *Rude Pravo*; Artur London, formerly Deputy

Minister of Foreign Affairs, who was sentenced to life imprisonment; Eugen Loebl, formerly Minister of Foreign Trade; the poet Laco Novomesky, a former member of the Slovak government; and also the Israeli implicated in the Slansky trial, Mordecai Oren, who was, however, deported immediately on his release. 'There were no limits to the methods used in making those who had been convicted on fabricated evidence confess their crimes', London said later to Western journalists. 'I was not drugged, but I suffered physical violence. However, it was not the tortures to which I was subjected that made me confess. After my arrest in January 1951, initially I refused to plead guilty. But I was an innocent caught in such a vast plot that there could be no resistance. The most distressing aspect was to be wrongfully accused by the very people who had been my friends, my superiors, my comrades in the party. Finally I realized that it was preferable to confess so as not to allow our enemies to cast doubts on the infallibility of the party and harm the socialist cause.'

At London's side was his wife, the sister-in-law of the French Communist leader Raymond Guyot, who at the time of the trial had asked in a letter to the President of the Court that a harsh sentence be imposed on her husband. She now asserted that she had written this letter 'in all good faith', because the statements she had been shown had convinced her that London was a traitor. 'I began to have doubts later, especially after the rehabilitation of the Jewish doctors in the U.S.S.R. and the disappearance of Beria.' In November 1954 Mrs London had asked for her husband's rehabilitation. He was released on medical grounds in July 1955, but it was only after the Twentieth Congress that his request for rehabilitation was granted.

London's case was exceptional; as regards the Slovaks, Clementis and his friends in particular, Prime Minister Siroky declared at Bratislava on 11 May 1956 that they had not been sentenced for criminal views or political deviation, but for actions 'threatening the building of socialism'. Only in the second wave of de-Stalinization, following the Twenty-Second Congress of the C.P.S.U. in October 1961, did Novotny, yielding to increasing pressure from Slovak militants, withdraw from his 1956 position and agree to a fuller review of the 1952–4 trials. After the Twentieth Congress

Novotny was still strong enough to obstruct de-Stalinization. He had the advantage over Rakosi, who was pursuing the same policy, of a less compromised past, of incurring less hatred, and, above all, of heading a far more coherent team, solidly united by its fear of the liberalization that threatened to overwhelm it. The Prague leaders were anxious to avoid what they regarded as the mistake made by the Poles and Hungarians, in permitting conflicting opinions within the party. Nascent independence shown at the writers' congress in April 1956 and widespread agitation by the students, who on 20 May 1956 organized a mammoth demonstration calling for a reliable press, free import of foreign books and newspapers, and the trial of those responsible for extorting confessions, were quickly and savagely repressed. Prague's tactics, in fact, were still those of 1953 : one step forward, one step back. The step forward was the declaration of intention with regard to socialist legality, a few dismissals, some wage increases, and the release of prisoners as described above; and the step back was the isolation of agitators and the preventive action taken by the security organs which, unlike those of Hungary and Poland, were significantly neither demoralized nor disorganized. On 24 May 1956 they were urged by the Minister of the Interior to pursue 'a merciless fight against the subversive activity of the enemy, who is extending his spy network over the whole country'.[7] But if the reformist movement initiated by the Twentieth Congress had already subsided by June 1956, the ideas and frustrated hopes survived and were to surface again in 1963, at a time when Poland and Hungary, which had exploded so spectacularly in the summer and autumn of 1956, were passing through a period of disillusionment and depression.

In East Germany, as in Czechoslovakia, the external threat was used by the leaders as an argument against critics who demanded that light be shed on Stalinist crimes. On 29 April 1956 the official organ *Neues Deutschland* explained why the leadership did not think it necessary to follow the example of Poland, Hungary and other People's Democracies. 'In fact, our party's general line has always been correct. There have been no Rajk or Kostov trials here; such errors are not relevant in our case.' Prime Minister Otto Grotewohl was of the same opinion : what

Poland, Czechoslovakia and Bulgaria were doing now in dismissing ministers the G.D.R. had done as long ago as 1953. 'We will not give our enemies the pleasure of turning everything upside down here.' Nevertheless, Franz Dahlem, who had been cleared as a result of investigations into the Slansky trial, was released along with eighty other militants, about seven hundred Social Democrats, and twelve thousand other political prisoners. That was as far as de-Stalinization went.

The Rumanian leaders acted similarly to Ulbricht, claiming that there had been no mistakes, and that there was nothing to correct. The 'purge victims' of 1952, Anna Pauker, Vasile Luca and their companions, were described as 'dogmatists', 'sectarians' or 'opportunists' who were justly sentenced. Gheorghiu Dej fraternized with Tito as though he had always been Yugoslavia's true friend; he also fawned upon Khrushchev and successfully strengthened his hold over the party.

The Bulgarian dictator Chervenkov did not escape so lightly. He was forced to exchange his post as Prime Minister for that of First Deputy Prime Minister. His successor Anton Yugov, who came from Bulgarian Macedonia, was reputed to be a 'more national' Communist. Although forced to make a self-critical statement in 1949 at the time of the Kostov trial, he had continued to progress through the administrative machine and, it was alleged, had long been in charge of subversive operations against Tito. Consequently his appointment was coldly received in Belgrade, even though it was accompanied by the official rehabilitation of Kostov.

On 11 April 1956 at a meeting of Sofia activists, the First Secretary of the party Zhivkov announced that the charges against Kostov, notably the accusation of criminal relations with the Yugoslav leaders, had been false. The survivors of the trial were released, rehabilitated and reinstated in the party. But the new leadership was united in its determination to resist the liberal demands heard faintly, and the press warned militants against 'the mania for criticizing everything'. Like Rumania, Albania and the G.D.R., Bulgaria chose the conservative path.

Substitutes for Democracy

In Poland and Hungary, where the pressure for democratization was greatest, the leaders, with Moscow's permission, contemplated moderating the party's rigid monopoly over the political life of their countries on the Yugoslav pattern. Imre Nagy had already been thinking along these lines in 1954, when he tried to invest the Patriotic Popular Front, a mass Communist but non-party organization, with a degree of autonomy to give it a real existence that would enable it to counterbalance the party machine and serve as a corporate vehicle for public opinion. His plan had been frustrated by Rakosi, who saw in it a threat to party domination. Ochab, in the spring of 1956, was both more cautious and more articulate; an important element in his programme was the revitalization of Parliament. For him, as for Gomulka later on, this did not mean a return to genuine parliamentarianism, which would have involved free elections and the dismantling of the one-party system; the Polish leadership was looking for an intermediate formula that would enable the party to seem to be engaging in a dialogue with highly selective representatives of public opinion without endangering its own monopoly.

The session of the Polish Diet that began on 23 April 1956 gave expression to these concerns. It opened with an appeal from Prime Minister Cyrankiewicz, urging deputies (not all of whom were Communist) to speak freely, to criticize the government if necessary, and to use their own initiative. To the astonishment of Western observers, a clash of opinions actually took place.[8] The discussion concerned a bill legalizing medically approved abortions in cases where the pregnant woman was either in poor health and living in bad conditions, or had been raped. The spokesman for the progressive Catholics (just returned from the Vatican) spoke energetically against this bill, protesting that it contravened not only Christian but also Communist morality. But the bill was passed by a large majority, with five Catholic deputies voting against it. These deputies intervened on other occasions; one asked for a separate Catholic youth organization. Drobner, a former Social Democrat, successfully demanded that all discrimination against non-Communist wartime resistance fighters should cease. Two speakers, the journalist Korczinski and the writer Osmanczyk, of the liberal wing of the party, appealed for more freedom for the press, 'which must reflect public opinion'. The publicity accorded debates in the Diet stimulated the political consciousness of those sections of Polish society that had remained passive and distrustful of the changes promised. But it was the opposition that benefited most from the revival of interest in public affairs.

In Hungary Rakosi, in his report to the Central Committee on 12 March 1956, considered the reactivation of the Patriotic Popular Front discouraged after Nagy's fall.[9] But the rights he was prepared to grant the Front were derisory. On 18 May, when public opinion had been stimulated by the session of the Polish Diet, Rakosi proposed that the Patriotic Front be strengthened through a merger with the Peace Movement, the Union of Democratic Women, and the Hungarian-U.S.S.R. Friendship Society – all of which were controlled by the party, and completely discredited. After Rakosi's forced resignation, Prime Minister Andras Hegedues (who continued in office) on 31 July promised the National Assembly an enlargement of its legislative powers. But this was entirely disregarded.

The Writers, the Students and the Revisionist Trend

In Marxist and other dictatorships, at certain moments in their history, the writers, journalists, artists and students proclaim themselves as 'heralds of springtime', the dynamic forces behind social and political thaws. This is perfectly understandable. In spite of basic differences in structure, direction, political and social programmes, between Communist and essentially reactionary authoritarian régimes, they resemble each other strikingly in one respect: their refusal to allow an overt opposition to form. Student youth is highly organized and subjected to continuous indoctrination, and strict censorship ensures that every manifestation of discontent, all criticism of the system and the leaders, is nipped in the bud, so that pockets of opposition survive only in exile, underground or in prison. But, as soon as the pressure is relieved, censorship slackens, the government shows signs of hesitation and weakness, the writers and young intellectuals take the lead. Being trained to think, criticize and discuss, they are the natural bearers of a social and political message. Of course, writers and artists also work for the state, especially when its prestige is in the ascendant, as long as they can identify themselves with it to some extent and are given some scope for creative, if limited, activity. But when a state matures into rigidity, dogmatism and reaction, and at the same time loses its capacity to inspire fear, the intellectuals become disillusioned and their chains seem intolerable. It is then that the desire to think for themselves, speak freely and to abolish all controls seizes them, and turns them into the spokesmen of long-despised and silenced public opinion.

Stalinism was originally grafted on to a genuine revolutionary movement, so that many left-wing intellectuals, whether Marxist or not, collaborated with it. Initially, in the Eastern countries, it managed to win the ascendancy, and to inspire and mobilize a considerable section of the youth behind a grandiose programme of radical social change. The Communist intellectuals and the youth-movement leaders were given prominent roles in the building of socialism, and from their ranks the imposing propaganda machine was recruited. Even those who had not become state or party officials were obliged to 'help the party educate the people',[10] a task to which many intellectuals turned out of conviction. 'When I rejoined the revolutionary ranks', a Polish Stalinist turned revisionist wrote in 1956, 'I knew what I was doing. We were absolutely convinced not only of the righteousness of the cause, but even more of its splendour ... A new socialist morality, new aesthetics, new customs, a new man, a new world ... Up till now no ideologist had promised so many things.'[11] Of course, the material and moral advantages guaranteed to intellectuals turned propagandists also attracted many opportunists whose insincerity was not immediately apparent. Even among the sincere, according to one of their number, 'arrogance, lust for easily acquired fame and unmerited privileges grew, while concern for ordinary people, who lived more impoverished, more silent ... and truer lives than our own, diminished'.[12]

The desire to treat the common people as beings capable of rational thought came from the top, in the first place from the Soviet leadership when it realized that it had lost touch with its browbeaten, apathetic population, and that the powerful propaganda machine was working in a vacuum. The main object of the de-Stalinization drive initiated by Khrushchev was to establish contact, to encourage the people to express their opinions, and to give them some grounds for hoping that their wishes would be fulfilled. However, it was easier to carry out this programme of gradual, peaceable national revival in the Soviet Union, where the régime had lasted nearly forty years, and men were sufficiently conditioned not to be carried away, than in the countries of Central Europe, where democracy had been strangled only a few years before on orders from outside, and where many prominent writers and artists had resisted government pressure and harassment, and preferred a dignified if precarious retirement to participation in the official cult.

It was above all with these silent comrades that the zealots of Stalinism, after the self-criticism of the leaders and the revelations of Stalin's crimes, felt they had lost face. They had refused to heed the evidence of their senses, had sung the praises of Stalin and fulminated against Tito, Rajk and Slansky. They had betrayed their own consciences, lied, cheated – 'ad maiorem gloriam Dei. But this god had been exposed by his own high priests, and turned out to be only an idol. To appreciate the full extent of the disgust, shame and remorse that overcame Stalinist writers at this time, one has but to read Temps Modernes (Nos. 129–33, 1957), collections of writings published in Poland and Hungary in 1956.

Their moral and intellectual crisis led them to a much more radical and violent challenge than the authorities were prepared to tolerate. The writers were pejoratively described as 'revisionists' or 'modern revisionists', recalling the controversy between Bernstein and Karl Kautsky at the beginning of the century. The term was undoubtedly much abused: from 1957 the Yugoslav leaders were condemned as 'revisionists', and strongly denied the charge; their own revisionist was Djilas. Khrushchev, who regarded himself as the upholder of orthodoxy, was finally stigmatized by the Chinese and Albanians as a revisionist. In 1957

Gomulka made a great effort to tame his rebel intellectuals, but this did not stop the Prague and East Berlin leaders suspecting him of revisionism, and in fact a number of the ideas put forward by the rebellious intellectuals were subsequently absorbed into the system.

Revisionism is exemplified principally in words of literature, poems, essays and newspaper articles, and has never hardened into a body of doctrine. It is a state of mind rather than a system; a heretical tendency that sprang up within the propaganda organization itself – as Protestantism did from among the clergy – and strove to revitalize the Leninist faith by returning to the spiritual sources of Communism. Starting from a critique of Stalinism, the revisionists moved on to challenge Leninism and ended up – like Imre Nagy – either on the way to reformist, social-democratic pluralism or, like certain Polish intellectuals, with a left-wing, idealistic, national, revolutionary socialism.

The main theses advanced by the revisionists can be classified as follows:

Rejection of the dictatorship of the proletariat, which, according to the revisionists, simple refers to monopolistic party dictatorship inevitably leading to bureaucracy. In Poland, Julian Hochfeld resurrected Rosa Luxemburg's criticism of Lenin's authoritarian ideas. The revisionists call for Socialist Democracy as opposed to dictatorship.

Questioning of the historical mission of the proletariat. 'Is the working class fit to lead?' asked the Polish *Po Prostu*. The revisionists emphasize the leading role of the intelligentsia.

Internationalism. Revisionists protest against 'the absence of complete equality' in relations with the Soviet Union. The Polish and Hungarian opposition tends to refer to Togliatti in advocating 'new, full, brotherly relations between equals among equals'. All revisionists are in effect national Communists. They acknowledge neither the exclusiveness nor even the superiority of the Soviet model.

Hostility to censorship. In the intellectual sphere the revisionists categorically reject party control over cultural activity. They have fought for the complete independence of intellectual organizations where Communists and non-Communists work together as colleagues. They place truth above the interests of the party.

In the economic and social sphere, revisionists launched the great campaign against centralized planning and for decentralization that survived the catastrophe of 1956. But the movement's most distinctive contribution is the idea of workers' councils, rediscovered in the middle of 1956 by the Polish workers and intellectuals, who made it the cornerstone of the new democratization. At the same time the revisionists stimulated sociology by popularizing public-opinion polls and condemning the privileges of the 'new class' of inefficient and conceited bureaucrats.

In aesthetics, revisionism means a break with socialist realism, a return to avant-garde traditions, and the restoration of cultural links with Western movements in the arts.

In philosophy, the revisionists rediscovered the moral roots of socialism under the debris of vulgar materialism. The revisionist thinker and spokesman Leszek Kolakowski, formerly professor in the Polish party university, summarized the case : 'The fact that we regard the advent of Communism as historically inevitable does not make us Communists. We are Communists because we are for the oppressed against the oppressor, for the poor against the masters, for the persecuted against the persecutor. Every practical choice is a choice of values, a moral choice.' According to the Polish professor Adam Schaff (an orthodox Marxist later to allow himself to be infected by the heresy, like the Frenchman Garaudy) philosophical revisionism is the product of 'a marriage between Kantian philosophy and existentialism'.

But over and above these not always original ideas and formulas, what distinguished the 1956 revisionist movement (and reappeared among the 'progressive' Czechoslovak intellectuals in 1967–8) was a sort of collective enthusiasm, an impassioned search for truth and justice, a fierce hope of renewal, which spread through the press, clubs and party organizations to intellectual and student circles and began to reach a larger public in the summer of 1956.

It was then that Poland and Hungary parted company from Czechoslovakia, East Germany and Bulgaria, where the intellectual opposition had been stifled in the spring. In Poland and Hungary oppositional bases formed which resisted interference from the party leadership. The most important of these was the writers' union. As early as 23 April, the Polish writers' union expelled the Stalinists Putrament and Kruczkowski from its own leadership, and went so far as to demand a renewal of the party leadership. The greater part of the Hungarian writers' union found itself engaged in a battle with Rakosi from October 1955, when it had protested in a memorandum signed by the most prominent Communist writers and artists against the crude administrative interference in literary affairs.

In Hungary, and even more so in Poland, the Communist opposition writers were in control of the main literary magazines, whose readerships increased considerably in 1956. Thus the Budapest *Irodalmi Ujsag* increased its circulation from 8,000 to 30,000. In Poland copies of *Nowa Kultura*, *Przeglad Kulturalny*, *Zycie Literackie* (Cracow) and *Tworcosc* were in great demand.

The daily and weekly press and the radio gave more and more space and time to publicizing revisionist ideas. A large section of the journalists supported the cause of reform. Between 1954 and 1956 Rakosi had to replace forty-six of the fifty-two staff members of the official party organ, *Szabad Nep*. Miklos Gimes, one of the journalists who was dismissed, was the first to ask publicly for Rajk's full rehabilitation and Rakosi's punishment. In Poland the newspaper *Zycie Warszawy* was highly instrumental in rousing public opinion.

Finally, a number of clubs sprang up, as they had done before the French Revolution. In Hungary the first and most famous of these was the Petöfi Circle, named after a poet of the 1848 revolution. The Circle was founded at the end of 1955 under the aegis of the (Communist) Union of Democratic Youth to serve as a meeting place for young intellectuals. For a while its sessions were closely supervised by the Central Committee, but after the Twentieth Congress the Circle broke free, and its audience began to grow. On 14 June, 1,600 people heard old Gyoergy Lukacs, to a chorus of catcalls and whistles, placing himself in the vanguard of the struggle against sterile dogmatism (without, however, recanting his own orthodox past). On 27 June 6,000 people attended a discussion on the freedom of the press, during which the Communist writers Tibor Dery and Tibor Tardos demanded total abolition of the censorship and Rakosi's resignation. Three days later the two were expelled from the party, the Circle was forbidden to meet, and Rakosi forced a harsh resolution through the Central Committee condemning the 'hotheads'. Eighteen days later he fell from power.

In Poland, the rebellious youth initially gathered round the weekly *Po Prostu*, run by Eligiusz Lasota. The most popular debating centre was the Krzywe Kolo, which had many local branches. In April 1956 a National Centre for Inter-Club Co-Operation was set up. There was much agitation at the headquarters of the Union of Polish Youth, and in late summer the more active members left to found a new Union of Communist Youth; the Catholics also were getting ready to set up their own separate organization. The University of Warsaw (like the University of Budapest) and the technical colleges became centres of ferment which the party leaders were unable to control.

In Hungary, until almost the last minute reformist agitation was limited to intellectual and student circles, but in Poland the revisionist movement had a number of working-class centres as well. Thus the party organization in the Zeran motor works in Warsaw became a very active centre in the spring of 1956. The anti-Stalinists were at first in a minority, but, borne along by the wave of press criticism, they ended by taking over the committee. At the party meeting in Warsaw in April 1956 the Zeran delegates, in the presence of the stupefied members of the Politburo, were already demanding 'rapid democratic changes, greater freedom for the press ... and the establishment of the alliance with the Soviet Union on healthier foundations'.

For the first time, the 'base' was giving evidence of a desire to have a say in policy formation. The idea of reviving the great tradition of workers' councils that flourished in the early days of the Russian revolution occurred independently of the anti-Satalinist Zeran Communists and was immediately taken up and publicized, with references to the Yugoslav workers' councils, by the youth weekly *Po Prostu*. Towards the end of the summer the Zeran workers made contact with the so-called revolutionary students. Then, in September, the first workers' councils were organized in the Zeran and W.F.M. works in Warsaw. Gradually the Warsaw party organization, led by the ex-Stalinist and now revisionist Staszewski, was carried away by the movement.

The Zeran workers, though far more radically inclined than the moderate liberal leaders and the Gomulkists, provided them with additional and invaluable assistance in taking control of and diverting the movement when the explosion came in October. This is one of the keys to Gomulka's success and Nagy's defeat: the latter had no organized base in the party organization or the factories capable of giving him support.[13]

Poznan: An Alarm Signal

On 28 July 1956 Poznan repeated what had happened in Kronstadt, Plzen and East Berlin, and gave a foretaste of what was to happen in Budapest. The short-lived rebellion that broke out in this west Polish town was a portent and at the same time served to separate the two sides to a greater extent: after Poznan the liberals became more liberal, the Stalinists more Stalinist. The power struggle became more acute: some wanted Gomulka to arbitrate in the matter; others wanted to appeal to the Kremlin. In these circumstances, the attitude of the Centrists (moderate Stalinists) around Ochab was of decisive importance.

Since 1955 there had been a certain amount of unrest in the Zispo locomotive, carriage and armament factory in Poznan, employing 15,000 workers. As in the case of the East Berlin workers three years before, this was caused by the increasing of production schedules; as a result, wages, which were already low enough, fell by about 3.5 per cent. Stoppages caused by irregular supply of raw materials also affected earnings, and taxation was oppressive. The factory management rejected all demands. The party organization, though it contained 38 per cent of the workers, showed itself as powerless to help them as the trade-union organization, which had been completely bureaucratized and had long since lost the ability to defend workers' interests.

On 25 June 1956 a delegation made up mostly of members of the party and the factory committee arrived in Warsaw to tell the Ministry and metallurgical trade-union headquarters of the workers' grievances. The Minister, Tokarski, saw the delegates, but announced that he would not be able to satisfy their basic demands. They replied that if their mission failed, the disappointed workers would undoubtedly strike. In that case, said Tokarski, tanks would be sent in. The delegates sent a message to Poznan on the result of the talks, and prepared to catch the train home. On the morning of 28 June, before their arrival, a rumour having circulated that the entire delegation had been arrested in Warsaw, the Zispo workers stopped work to form a procession to hand in a list of their demands at the town hall. They carried placards asking for bread, price reductions and wage increases.

The march started off in an orderly and peaceful manner, but as it got closer to the town centre, thousands of other workers, especially young ones, swelled the ranks, excitement mounted, the crowd's mood changed, and they chanted slogans that became increasingly audacious: 'Long live freedom, bread and justice!' and 'Down with the U.S.S.R.! ... Down with Soviet occupation ... Free Cardinal Wyszynski ... Give us back religion!' The demonstrators sang patriotic, religious and socialist songs. The militia tried in vain to disperse them. One of the groups invaded police headquarters and seized some weapons. Other groups attacked the radio building and the court house, and broke into the prison. A section, led by 'armed provocateurs', made for the security headquarters to free any who had been arrested. As in Budapest four months later, it is difficult to determine who first opened fire, but the atmosphere became increasingly explosive. Soon after midday, army tanks appeared on the scene, followed by units of the internal security forces (K.B.W.) and the civil militia. The rebellion was crushed in the evening, and the following day the troops mopped up the last pockets of resistance. There were 54 dead, 300 wounded, and about 320 arrests.[14]

It is likely that the short-lived Poznan rising was largely instrumental in saving Poland from an explosion similar to that in Hungary in October 1956. In Budapest the Hungarian troops were uncertain as to whether to intervene and fraternize with the crowd; and the subsequent Soviet intervention spread the conflagration far and wide. The fact that the Poznan uprising did not spread was probably due to the prompt and strong intervention of the Polish armed forces. Furthermore, the party leadership drew the correct conclusions from it.

The Prime Minister stressed that 'the blood spilt at Poznan will not stop the party and the government from continuing their efforts to democratize our life, and to realize our aims of national, economic and cultural development. Our chief concern is to raise the standard of living of the working population as quickly as possible.' His objective was clearly to forestall any attempt by the Stalinists to use the disturbances to get back into the saddle.

The inquiry into the Poznan rising carried on in the press enabled the public to appreciate the gravity of the country's condition. The workers were dissatisfied, disheartened and driven back on themselves. They were frequently deprived of hard-won traditional privileges. Their living conditions 'became more and more easily advantageous to hostile elements', while the party organizations, in the words of the secretary of the Poznan committee, 'were unable to oppose this with sufficient vigour, given the fact that the workers' demands were justified in the main'.[15] It also became clear that the supposed activity of foreign agents was imaginary. 'We have not yet found any evidence of the activity of any espionage organization ... The attempts at organization, with isolated individuals forming groups and the groups establishing links with each other, took place during the fighting.' Exactly the same thing was to happen in Hungary : there was explosive material and an explosion took place. There was such a clear separation between the nation and officialdom that one can, without exaggeration, speak of a pre-revolutionary situation. 'Obviously they had had enough', Gomulka said later. 'One can never overstep the line with impunity.'

The Soviets and Khrushchev himself realized the danger, and reacted hesitantly. The West, it was felt, would not hesitate to exploit the unstable situation created by a relaxation of control. The entire Communist press, with the exception of Yugoslavia's, was unanimous in denouncing the machinations of imperialist agents and calling for vigilance. The Stalinists in Warsaw echoed it, criticizing Cyrankiewicz's forbearance with the revisionists.

The conflict between the two wings of the Polish leadership

burst out violently at the Seventh Plenum of the Central Committee in Warsaw between 18 and 20 July 1956. The Kremlin showed its own interest in the meeting by sending President Bulganin and Marshal Zhukov to Warsaw, ostensibly as its representatives on the occasion of the 22 July national celebrations. The Soviet statesmen were kept away from the Plenum, but Bulganin, in a speech at the Palace of Culture and Arts (a gift from the Soviet government), warned against 'the enemy that wishes to drive a wedge between us, so as to be able to pick off each socialist country one by one'.

Bulganin blamed the newspapers for having 'allowed poisonous seeds to be sown', and denounced those who 'on the pretext of democratization are undermining the power of the people'. His speech also contained a warning, apparently directed at both Tito and Gomulka: 'We must not permit a weakening in the international links of the socialist camp through an appeal to national determinism.'

The Russian leadership, fearing that Poland might drift out of the Soviet orbit, leant towards the 'hard-liners', the Natolinians, who were unquestioningly loyal, and kept in constant touch with the Soviet ambassador, Ponomarev. Encouraged by this support, their leader Zenon Nowak laid before the Central Committee a programme that included strengthening ties with the U.S.S.R., active repression of nonconformist intellectuals, demagogic promises to the workers (e.g. a 50-per-cent rise in the standard of living) and, to cap it all, a purge of the party and state machine on a national, or racist, basis. Once again the Natolinians were counting on using the Jews as scapegoats. They did not, however, possess a majority in the Central Committee.

Always opposed to Gomulka, the Natolinians were cynical enough to propose his appointment to the Politburo (possibly because they hoped to win him over to their side, or perhaps simply to embarrass the liberals). Indeed, Cyrankiewicz and his friends still hesitated to call on the man who alone had sufficient prestige and energy to surmount the crisis of authority that was affecting the whole country; they were afraid of annoying the Soviets, who still regarded Gomulka as a national deviationist, a potential Tito.

The Central Committee in the end confined itself to an inconclusive gesture. Gomulka was fully rehabilitated and reinstated in the party (the decision was made public on 4 August 1956), but the exact definition of his status was deferred.

Gomulka himself did nothing to make it easy for those negotiating with him. As a condition of his return to political life, he demanded the resignation of Hilary Minc, whom he regarded as the symbol of the harmful economic policy pursued since 1949. Two months of valuable time were lost while he awaited satisfaction of this demand.

Every decision taken by the Seventh Plenum was partial or temporary. The Politburo was enlarged by the admission of a few moderates : Rapacki, Gierek and Roman Nowak, as full members; Jedrychowski and Stawinski, as provisional members. It was decided to continue with the struggle against bureaucracy. The programme outlined by the Central Committee promised a higher standard of living, the promotion of the artisan class, the encouragement of agriculture and workers' participation in the management of enterprises. But there was absolute silence on the one question regarded as crucial by the public and by Gomulka himself : the need to redefine Poland's relationship with the Soviet Union. Also, in spite of the fact that undoubted progress had been made, the Plenum failed to administer the 'psychological shock' needed to restore the country's confidence in its leaders.

In this respect too, Poland in late July 1956 resembled Hungary after Rakosi's fall and, *mutatis mutandis*, Czechoslovakia at the beginning of 1968 after Novotny's resignation as head of the party. Partial concessions and promises of improvement were no longer enough; it required more radical and positive changes, more sweeping concessions to the national spirit and the democratic principle to stabilize the country now.

5

The Revolutions of October 1956

The Polish October: A Revolution Channelled

Gomulka took power under extraordinarily fluid and ambiguous circumstances. The convict of 1948 was lifted into office on the wave of a quasi-revolutionary popular movement, for which he was the symbol of national independence and democratic revival. At the same time he was supported by the liberals and centrists of the party apparatus who looked to him to organize and direct the revolution, and to save the foundations of the régime. It was Poland's good fortune – if the avoidance of civil war and foreign intervention at the price of renouncing the initial revolutionary objectives can be described as 'fortunate' – that, at the critical moment, the nation was able to organize itself behind a man of character who enjoyed considerable prestige, and that Gomulka and his supporters found the nucleus of some kind of organization in the popular movement, whose support would be crucial in the final confrontation.

The main instigators of the movement pursued ends different from those of Gomulka, who pre-eminently represented the authority of the centre. For them the word 'democracy' carried wider and deeper implications that were revolutionary, and perhaps naïve and Utopian. But the first stage in the realization of their national and liberal aspirations had to be the overthrow of the discredited régime, and the radical elimination of the Polish Stalinists and of all the symbols of the country's subjection. In order to be able to use Gomulka in the future, they were prepared to put themselves at his disposal first, and to help him get rid of his enemies, who were also theirs. But they were foiled; for, once in power, though he immediately took steps to make life more bearable for the majority of Poles, Gomulka bent all his energies towards restoring order, the party's authority, and its monopolistic position; and to gaining the support of the politico-military organization and reassuring the Russians.

Gomulka's Poland was not to turn out the way the intellectuals and excited workers hoped it might on the night of 19 October 1956, when no one slept in Warsaw; nor the way the young people stirred by 'the hope of real socialism' desired. But for several years, at least until economic difficulties and the leader's own weariness overshadowed events, Poland was more open, more in touch with her traditions, much freer intellectually, than the other Communist countries. In the final analysis, Polish development after 1958 is a good illustration of the vulnerability of liberalization not based on firm guarantees.

The memorable night of 19 October witnessed the encounter, or rather clash, of the main protagonists in the drama: the thoroughly roused popular movement; the liberal leaders, seeking a solution to the crisis in an appeal to Gomulka; Gomulka himself; the Polish Stalinists, trying to redeem their failed *coup d'état*; and finally the Soviets, who after some hesitation decided to back a man they never suspected they would be able to exploit so well.

Unrest and the pressure of public opinion had increased steadily after the Seventh Plenum, though the party leadership and government worked desperately to recapture the initiative. On 13 August 1956 general elections were announced for 16 December. The government obtained a new credit of 100 million roubles from the Soviet Union, an increase in the price the Soviets paid for Polish coal (till then a tenth of the world price), and the repatriation of thousands of Poles who had been kept in the U.S.S.R. after the war. Early in September the Diet passed a law taking prison administration out of the hands of the police and giving it to the Ministry of Justice. General W. Komar, a former resistance fighter of Jewish origin and a victim of the Stalinist purges, was appointed head of the internal security forces. His name was a pledge that the de-Stalinization of this organization was being taken seriously.

The trial of the Poznan rebels, which opened on 23 September, took place in the presence of numerous Western journalists and was remarkable for the mildness of the sentences. The unprecedentedly open and frank proceedings gripped the public imagination. But all this only encouraged the champions of radical reform. The revisionists penetrated the sanctuaries of the party press itself, and Nowe Drogi, the theoretical organ of the Central Committee, published in September Kolakowski's article, 'Intellectuals and the Communist Movement', which commended in a scarcely orthodox manner the part to be played by the intelligentsia in the 'reconstruction of Marxism'.

In late August nearly a million Catholics turned up in Czestochowa to worship the Virgin. The demonstration was calm and dignified and showed the Church's continuing strength. At the beginning of September, the University began to stir again. AntiStalinist students, after a lively discussion of the political situation, came to the conclusion that 'things could not go on in the same way'. The party organization in the University of Warsaw was already completely in the hands of the revisionists, who invited Gozdzik, Secretary of the Zeran factory party committee, to their meetings. Workers and students were thrilled at their new-found brotherhood and eagerly discussed everything from the current economic and political situation to 'Communism as such throughout history'. The trade unions also began to move. At a meeting of their Central Committee on 20–21 August, the Stalinist leader Zolkiewski was booed for defending the interests of the State and not those of the workers. On 30 September Po Prostu proposed the establishment of workers' councils as a basis for the real workers' democracy of the future. The influence of the Zeran agitators was already predominant in the Warsaw party committee and growing in the provincial industrial centres. And everyone was demanding Gomulka's return.

Negotiations were taking their time, however. Urged by the liberals to speak out, Gomulka raised the bidding. He insisted on his immediate appointment as First Secretary of the party, to head a new Politburo; Hilary Minc's resignation on 9 October did not prevent him from demanding Marshal Rokossovsky's recall to the Soviet Union from the Ministry of Defence, and thereby he raised the issue of Polish-Russian relations.

At the beginning of September Ochab left for Peking to attend the Chinese Party Congress. There he had discussions with Mao

Tse-tung, Chou En-lai and Mikoyan, who was representing the Soviet party. Chou En-lai seems to have encouraged Ochab to pursue a policy of emancipation, even at the risk of displeasing the Soviets. This advice accorded with Mao's ideas at the time; without disputing the predominance of the U.S.S.R. and the need to strengthen the bloc, he advocated genuine independence for all parties whether in power or not.[1] In any case, shortly after his return to Warsaw Ochab agreed to the Gomulkist solution proposed by the liberals. On 13 October the Politburo met with Gomulka present. The majority agreed on the changes to be made, and to call a Central Committee meeting for 19 October. Thus, eight years after his dismissal from the post of General Secretary of the party, eighteen months after his release, and scarcely two months after his rehabilitation, Gomulka found himself nearing his objective, which was quite simply to pick up the threads of the situation as it was in 1948.

Alarmed by Gomulka's intransigence and fearing that his return to power meant the end to their own political ambitions, a few Natolinian leaders tried to reverse the trend by a *coup d'état*. They first alerted their friends in the Kremlin, who on 17 October called the Polish Politburo to Moscow. Sensing danger, Ochab declined the invitation on the pretext that it was impossible for him to put off the Central Committee meeting that was to take place two days later.

In the meantime the ex-fascist writer Piasecki, leader of the Catholic movement Pax and a friend of the Natolinians, had made threatening sounds in an article published on 7 October: 'If we do not carry on the discussion in a framework of responsibility instead of democratization, we shall bring about a situation in which the State will have to assert itself savagely, under conditions reminiscent of a state of emergency.' The Stalinists counted on Rokossovsky, his deputy, General Witaszewski, and a few other (mostly Russian) army generals. They wanted to present the Central Committee with a *fait accompli* by placing 700 leaders of the other side under arrest on the eve of their meeting. This list of 700 names, however, was obtained by the Zeran committee, which warned those in danger to leave home. A few detachments of the regular army under the command of Stalinist generals were already marching towards the capital. The opposition, however, united around Gomulka, and with the Warsaw party committee, the Zeran workers, and the Po Prostu group as its most active centres, proceeded to a kind of general mobilization. From 17 September the people were warned to avoid all street demonstrations which might result in the use of armed force. When the students of the military academy called a meeting, every means was used to get it cancelled. The Zeran factory sent cars to warn party organizations in the suburbs, the factories and the university faculties. The liberal and Gomulkist leaders made sure of the support of the secret police; they already had that of the internal security forces under Komar. Many army officers clearly sympathized with the opposition, and refused to obey orders issued by the Stalinists. Thus if the latter persisted in their attempt to effect a coup, they would come off the losers, unless the Soviet army intervened on a massive scale. Everything, therefore, depended on Moscow.

On the morning of 19 October, a few hours before the opening of the Eighth Plenum of the Polish Central Committee, a very high-powered Soviet delegation, consisting of Khrushchev, Mikoyan, Molotov, Kaganovich and Marshal Konev (Commander-in-Chief of the Warsaw Pact forces), with eleven generals in full dress, landed at Boernerowo military airport. Their arrival was, to say the least, unexpected. Two days before, Khrushchev had told Ochab of his decision to come to Warsaw, and Ochab had suggested the postponement of his visit until after the Plenum but Khrushchev was hard-pressed, anxious, and in danger of losing control of the party leadership; his Stalinist opponents were renewing their attacks and accusing him of being unequal to the task in hand. The Soviet high command, acting on information from inside Poland, took precautionary steps. There were reports of troop movements and concentrations in East Germany and near the Polish borders in the U.S.S.R., and that Soviet motorized troops stationed in the neighbourhood of Wroclaw had started moving towards Warsaw. It was also rumoured that Marshal Rokossovsky had ordered Polish units under his command to co-operate with the Soviet troops in checking the activities of subversive forces.

Nevertheless, the Polish Central Committee met as planned, and hastily proceeded to make changes in its own membership. Gomulka and three of his associates – Spychalski, Loga-Sowinski and Kliszko – were co-opted on to the Committee, and Gomulka's candidature for the post of First Secretary was announced. The Committee then decided to suspend its activities in order to enter into discussions with the Soviets. Gomulka was a member of the chosen delegation, which also included Ochab, Gierek, Zawadzki, Cyrankiewicz, Rapacki, and also Rokossovsky, whose future was one of the points at issue in the talks.

On receiving information from their ambassador and the Natolinians, the Soviet leaders seemed to have lost their heads at the prospect of a mounting wave of nationalism that might lead to the secession of Poland, a vital link in the East European security system. They did not trust Gomulka, and feared that popular agitation might prove too much for the party and undermine the whole basis of the régime. Khrushchev and Mikoyan shared these fears with the hard-liners Molotov and Kaganovich, and with Konev, who at the time of the Berlin crisis in 1953 had shown his determination to protect the gains of the Second World War. They no doubt hoped that a show of force would be enough; they knew that armed intervention in Poland would create difficulties in their relations with the West, with Yugoslavia and even with China. But they would not have hesitated to take this step if the risk of non-intervention had seemed greater than that of intervention (as in Hungary two weeks later).

Hence the crucial nature of the very hasty talks with the Polish delegation that continued through the night of 19 October. The workers of the Zeran and most of the other Warsaw factories were in a state of mobilization. The streets in the capital's centre were empty, but inside the darkened buildings the population was awake. Throughout the day thousands of letters of support from workers, young people and students had poured into the Central Committee. It was this national solidarity that in the last analysis enabled Gomulka and Ochab to withstand Russian pressure. They were able to counter the Soviet show of force with a demonstration of working-class support and also the support of those pillars of government in Communist countries, the secret police, frontier guards and internal security troops.

A few hours earlier this moving resolution had been passed by the Zeran party organization: 'We strongly affirm that we have committed ourselves to the power of the people as a matter of life or death. We contend with all who believe that our democratization represents a first stage on the way back to bourgeois democracy.' Ochab did not hide the fact that the Polish conception of de-Stalinization differed from the Soviet, which was considered too 'authoritarian and dogmatic', but, like Gomulka, he made it clear that he was determined it should proceed within a Leninist framework, and in no way yield to 'reactionary bourgeois' pressure. As regards the question of national independence, Gomulka, not allowing himself to be intimidated by insults and accusations, laid down the principles on which relations between the two parties were in future to be based, whether the Kremlin liked it or not.

'It is up to our Central Committee and to it alone to determine the membership of our Politburo ... The composition of the leadership of a Communist party cannot, in my opinion, be discussed with a fraternal party.' This statement of principle conformed with the assurances given by Khrushchev at the Twentieth Congress, and in the declaration jointly signed with Belgrade, concerning the independence and equality of the parties and the validity of the principle of non-interference. But in practice, as we have seen, the Soviet leadership always insisted on its right of surveillance and arbitration as supreme guardian of the interests of the socialist camp.

Gomulka did not recognize this right, nor did he give way over Rokossovsky. But he assured the Soviets that he had no intention of threatening the strategic interests of the U.S.S.R. in any way or withdrawing Poland from the Warsaw Pact, and that he was more than ever convinced (and would be himself able to convince others) that Poland's national interest, as well as ideological unity, required the preservation and even strengthening of the alliance with the U.S.S.R. and the other socialist countries on a sounder basis.

Subsequently Gomulka showed that he had meant what he said, and was able to keep his word. For the moment, at least he made the Soviets hesitate, and on the morning of 20 October the Soviet delegation returned to Moscow. A short communiqué stated that the talks would be continued at an early date in the Soviet capital. Gradually Russian troop movements were halted, and the Central Committee returned to its work. Gomulka delivered a speech which was to go down in the annals of the international Communist movement.[2] It was a Polish complement to Khrushchev's secret report, a stern indictment of the satellization and Stalinization of Poland, and a declaration of the legitimacy of different models.

The invariable in socialism is simply the abolition of the exploitation of man by man. The means whereby this end may be achieved can be and are multifarious. The socialist model also can vary: it may be of the kind created in the Soviet Union, it may follow the Yugoslav pattern, or it may be yet different from them.

Gomulka outlined his own plan for Poland, carefully defining the limits of the liberalization he had in mind. It was based on decollectivization (but with the ultimate objective of socialization of the countryside on the basis of free consent); religious freedom (provided that the Church supported popular power); the development of 'socialist democracy'; and economic reforms. 'We shall not permit anyone', he emphasized, 'to take advantage of the process of democratization to the detriment of socialism. Our party places itself at the head of the process of democratization.'

As for relations with the Soviet Union, the past, 'where all has not been as it should have been', had to be buried. Relations between the socialist countries would have to be based on the recognition of the full independence and autonomy of each party; but 'if some people imagine that anti-Soviet feelings can be stirred up in Poland, they are profoundly mistaken. We shall not allow the vital interests of the Polish state and the building of socialism in Poland to be prejudiced'.

The Central Committee approved this principle, and elected a new Politburo, in which Gomulka was at last appointed First Secretary, and his friends were in a majority. It remained to be seen whether Gomulka could impose the required limitations on the popular movement that had swept him to power, and that in the following days, further excited by the Hungarian rising, ecstatically gave vent to its aspirations for freedom. On this the Soviet attitude certainly depended.

Ever since the closing stages of the Plenum, there had been an unprecedented flow of resolutions, proposals, appeals and letters to the Central Committee. The officer cadets of the military academy hailed Gomulka's return, and their meeting was a signal for an avalanche of meetings throughout Poland. On 24 October at a huge meeting on the vast esplanade in front of the Stalin Palace, Gomulka was able to assess the mood of the country. When he declared that Soviet troops would have to stay on in Poland as long as NATO military bases were maintained in West Germany, his words were received in complete silence. Anti-Soviet incidents were reported here and there, notably in Wroclaw and Gliwice (Silesia).

Many Poles regarded the revolution as having just begun, and there were indeed factors that might have led it to follow the same disorderly, violent course that it did in Hungary, where the ill-considered intervention of Soviet forces on the night of 23 October provoked a rebellion. But Gomulka and his team displayed remarkable energy and tactical skill in controlling this explosive situation, convincing the party, the army and the whole population of the absolute necessity not to step over the line, and to make sure that Soviet interests were not threatened. At the same time, they did everything humanly possible to get the Kremlin to accept them as legitimate and indispensable intermediaries. They were aided in this double task by the Chinese and the Yugoslavs, and also by Soviet fears lest the Hungarian conflagration should spread to Poland. Had these two crises merged into one, the consequences would have been disastrous for the bloc. In the light of the Hungarian disturbances, the Soviets realized their good fortune in being able to negotiate a reasonable compromise with an organized opposition in Poland; Gomulka's victory suddenly seemed a lesser evil and the solution of the Polish crisis reached on 20 October a model for that of the Hungarian crisis.

This change was reflected in the Soviet government's declaration on 30 October, giving fresh guidance for inter-Communist relations, which Belgrade and Peking both welcomed eagerly. The document reflected a willingness to tolerate the national and democratic aspirations of the Poles and of the Hungarians, provided 'the legitimate and progressive movement of the workers', dissatisfied 'with irregularities and mistakes in relations between socialist countries', did not overstep the bounds set by Gomulka himself. The Soviet government announced that it was prepared to revise its economic relations with the socialist countries 'on the basis of national sovereignty, mutual interest and equality before the law', and prepared also to reconsider, together with the other Warsaw Pact countries, the question of Soviet troops stationed on their territory. But, for the present, it was vital that 'foreign and internal reactionary forces should not be allowed to shake the foundations of the Popular Democratic régimes', to shatter the unity of the camp, or to question the European *status quo* resulting from the Yalta and Potsdam agreements.

Gomulka, alarmed by events in Budapest and the spectre of a rebellion that was both anti-Soviet and anti-Communist, responded positively. Whatever his personal feelings towards the men in the Kremlin or his opinion as to the expediency of the first Soviet intervention in Hungary, Gomulka's interests coincided with the Soviets': a Hungarian secession must be prevented and Imre Nagy and Kadar, who were still co-operating with each other, must be helped in their efforts to stabilize the situation while making large, limited concessions. To promote a Gomulkist solution, the Polish Central Committee sent two of its members, Starewicz and Naszkowski, to Budapest. On 2 November the Polish Central Committee declared its solidarity with 'the Hungarian workers and with all those who are fighting with them for social democratization' and expressed its confidence that external intervention would not be necessary.

The failure of the attempts at stabilization and the break between Nagy, swept along by the rebellion, and the Soviets, won over by Kadar, were bitter blows to Gomulka. The violent reaction of Polish public opinion to the second Soviet intervention in Hungary renewed the threat of serious disturbances. However, Gomulka was able to use the Hungarian example to strengthen his argument that acceptance of the compromise of 20 October was the only path of salvation for the Polish people. The crushing of the Hungarian rising and the complete inaction of the West showed the folly of insisting on a 'maximalist' solution under the present circumstances. Once the party united behind Gomulka and his moderate policy, Poland would be guaranteed against both a return of Stalinism and foreign intervention.

One might have thought that the Hungarian tragedy, isolating Poland as it did, would make it particularly vulnerable to the combined pressure of the Soviets and the Stalinists in the international Communist movement, who were for a long time to regard Gomulka with suspicion. But in fact it helped Gomulka consolidate his power on the foundations he had already laid. Backed by public opinion, he was able to gain some sovereignty for the Polish leadership, as indicated by the dismissal of Rokossovsky and all the Russian generals in the Polish army, the expulsion from the Central Committee of those individuals who were most compromised, and the initiation of a series of liberal reforms that were to differentiate Poland appreciably from all the other Communist countries apart from Yugoslavia. These measures included the abandonment of collectivization (at the end of 1956 only 1,700 of the 10,600 collective farms remained intact); the enlargement of the sphere of private enterprise; the release of Cardinal Wyszynski and an agreement with the episcopate; the establishment of an economic council to construct a new model for planning; the recognition of workers' councils (whose privileges, however, were then progressively limited); a rise in salaries and wages; the revitalization of local government and of the Diet (without going so far as to allow an organized opposition); more liberal and more lively universities and press, freed from Soviet influence; and greater autonomy in foreign relations, particularly in regard to contacts with the West (negotiations were opened with the United States with a view to obtaining economic aid).

On the other hand, playing on his compatriots' fears of Poland's powerful and apprehensive neighbour, ever ready to intervene if her interests were threatened, Gomulka gained easier acceptance of the *modus vivendi* formalized in Moscow on 18 November which, while confirming the alliance, and the stationing in Poland of Soviet troops (under the control of the Polish government), contained many positive features: the cancellation of Polish debts, amounting to two thousand million roubles, the granting of new credit facilities, and a commitment to supply 1.4 million tons of wheat.

The elections of January 1957 were, in effect, a plebiscite in support of Gomulka. With this popular backing he was to spend the whole year re-establishing and strengthening party control over all institutions, at the risk of displeasing and alienating many of his former ultra-democratic and revisionist supporters. He gave Poland a government that was relatively tolerant, pragmatic (not to say opportunistic) and flexible, but also authoritarian – a government that reflected his political views and temperament.

The Hungarian October: Revolution Crushed but Fruitful

With similar origins and characteristics, the Polish and Hungarian movements came to very different initial conclusions – compromise as opposed to confrontation, appeasement as opposed to catastrophe. But subsequently they converged on a similar kind of de-Stalinized Communism. The sequence of events in the two countries is mutually revealing: for example, might not Gomulka have suffered Nagy's or Kadar's fate if incidents had arisen between the Polish population and the Soviet troops on the night of 19 October, and vice versa? Given similar conditions, might not Nagy have become a Hungarian Gomulka? It seems that Poland was only a hair's breadth away from rebellion and Hungary a hair's breadth from avoiding it. Yet there was nothing arbitrary about the result, as the factors that, on the one hand, operated in the direction of a peaceful outcome and, on the other, detracted from it had been building up for a long time.

Basically the developments in the two countries may be summed up as follows: Poland avoided Soviet repression because, first, the Polish party showed itself capable of acting relatively independently of the Soviet leadership as early as April 1956; secondly, it was in Poland's national interest to preserve the alliance with the U.S.S.R.; and thirdly, the extent to which the

Gomulka group wanted to break away and de-Stalinize was not irreconcilable with basic Kremlin objectives. Developments in Hungary, on the other hand, led to Soviet intervention because, in the first place, after the Twentieth Congress the Hungarian party showed itself incapable of strengthening its popular base by a more independent policy; secondly, it was in Hungary's national interest to acquire international status and institutions similar to those in Austria, Finland or Yugoslavia; and thirdly, the aims of the Hungarian majority constituted a direct assault on the strategic and ideological positions of the Soviet Union.

The Hungarian tragedy can to a large extent be blamed on Matyas Rakosi – the most hated of all Stalin's lieutenants – who, according to his own close associates, was obsessed with the idea of repression.[3] He clung to power too long without having his earlier means of exercising it. The Poznan riots gave him an excuse for taking preventive action against the Hungarian intellectuals. On 30 June 1956 he called a meeting of the Central Committee and pushed through a resolution condemning 'the open opposition to the party and Popular Democracy organized mainly by Imre Nagy's group'. Dery and Tardos were expelled from the party, and the Petöfi Circle was asked to discontinue its meetings. Nor did Rakosi stop there. He tried to mobilize the workers from the large factories against the rebellious intellectuals, who were accused of being 'agents of the bourgeoisie'. The workers, however, wanted more information before signing motions condemning the Petöfi Circle. Rakosi accordingly contemplated arresting the main opposition spokesmen, including Nagy, and banning their newspapers.

However, even if his schemes were reasonable enough in the Hungarian context, they did not accord with the de-Stalinization policy laid down by the Kremlin. On 17 July Mikoyan and Suslov arrived in Budapest. The decision they forced on Rakosi reflected the balance of power in the Soviet leadership and Khrushchev's wish to keep to his side of the bargain with Tito: Rakosi was requested to hand in his resignation.

But a scarcely less discredited Stalinist, Ernoe Geroe, succeeded him as First Secretary, and this half measure merely served to demoralize Rakosi's supporters and even further alienate the opposition. The ineptness of the choice – which also displeased Tito – was only slightly redressed by the appointment to the Politburo of a number of 'centrists': Janos Kadar and Gyoergy Marosan (former victims of Rakosi), as well as Karoly Kiss (a relatively moderate Stalinist). Kadar was appointed Geroe's deputy in the secretariat of the Central Committee, and, perhaps to balance his appointment, Jozsef Revai, the intellectual dictator of the Stalin era, was recalled to the Politburo.

This reconstituted body was too heterogeneous to act effectively. The political resolution it adopted promised more rapid rehabilitations and an expansion of the role of parliament, but it referred also to the continuation of the policy of collectivization and insisted on the priority of heavy industry. This plan conceded far less to public opinion than the resolutions adopted by the Seventh Polish Plenum. Whereas the Polish leaders began to break away from Moscow after Poznan, Geroe and his colleagues owed everything to Mikoyan, and were entirely dependent on the Soviet Union. The fact that Nagy was still being kept in the background only served to enhance his prestige, and liberal and patriotic opinion developed more strongly about his person.

Kadar, like Ochab in Poland, might have built a bridge between the party and Nagy, but he shared the suspicions of Nagy held by the organization, and especially of his entourage of revisionist intellectuals. Kadar probably thought himself better suited than the former Prime Minister to put Khrushchev's ideas into practice.

After his election, Geroe, while admitting that there were 'some good things' about the Petöfi Circle, decried its tendency to set itself up as a 'second political centre' in opposition 'to the only true political centre in the country', the Central Committee. The authority of the Central Committee was, in fact, severely shaken, whereas attempts to create an organized opposition were obstructed by Imre Nagy, whose scruples would not allow him to establish a 'group' as certain of his friends suggested. Nagy's 'legalistic' convictions were expressed in a letter to the Central Committee on 4 October,[4] in which he upheld the 'Leninist principle of democratic centralism' and stressed the need for ideological, political and organizational unity of the party. Nagy hoped to convince the party organization of his loyalty; he said he considered his place to be 'in the party where I have spent nearly forty years, and in whose ranks I have fought to the best of my ability with gun in hand, through my work and by means of the spoken word or the pen, for the cause of the people, the country and socialism'. Gomulka's views were no different, but this did not prevent his making use of contacts in the Warsaw party committee and among police and army chiefs, in anticipation of his return to power. Nagy relied on the party alone, and this was in a state of dissolution.

In the three months between the July changes and 23 October 1956, excitement continued to mount, and confusion grew. The crisis became more acute, but no group was strong enough to take control of matters firmly – as was the case in Poland – either in the leadership or the opposition. Public opinion had its spokesmen, but it had no leader. At the beginning of September the writers' congress rejected the 'gradualist' proposals put forward in the name of the party leadership by Gyula Kallai, a friend of Kadar's. The writers demanded 'complete freedom for literature'. The impunity with which the writers rebelled showed up the impotency of the government, contributed to creating a pre-revolutionary climate and reinforced the illusion, common to intellectuals in all periods, that it is sufficient to formulate popular aspirations for the course of history to be altered.

The Petöfi Circle resumed its discussions, and discussion groups sprang up in all the university towns. The apathy of the authorities in the face of this spiritual awakening, and the concessions made by Geroe, were correctly taken as signs of weakness and confusion.

After an initial refusal, on 6 October the party leadership authorized state funerals for Rajk and three of his friends who had been fully rehabilitated. More than 300,000 people marched through the streets of Budapest: high-school students, office staff, writers, workers, artisans – party members and non-party people. The police feared disturbances like those in Poznan, but there was no incident, not even a shout. Imre Nagy walked at the head of the procession, and it was he who embraced Rajk's widow. The restraint shown in this demonstration was a triumph for the Nagyists, who had promoted it. The opposition was able to mobilize the masses and control them.

Now was the moment for the party leadership to make a spectacular gesture, on the occasion of the reconciliation of party and country. But the Hungarian leaders lacked imagination and were afflicted with a curious blindness. Nothing better demonstrated the extent to which they were out of touch with the nation than the prolonged visit of Geroe and his principal colleagues to the Soviet Union at the end of September and beginning of October. As a former high Comintern official, Geroe persisted in believing that the key to Hungarian affairs lay in the U.S.S.R. He had several meetings with Suslov and Mikoyan in Sochi, after which Khrushchev introduced him to Tito, thinking that the Yugoslav's moral support for the Geroe–Kadar team (even if he viewed it as a preliminary to the replacement of Geroe by Kadar at the head of the Hungarian party) might contribute to the pacification and stabilization of Hungary.[5] As a token of his goodwill, Tito, who was anxious to consolidate the Soviet-Yugoslav agreement, which had been somewhat unsettled by Poznan, finally acceded to Khrushchev's requests, and invited his ex-enemy Geroe on an official visit to Yugoslavia. There is reason to believe that Geroe was influenced by Tito when he had Imre Nagy reinstated in the party, and thus cleared the way for Nagy's return to power.

On 14 October Geroe went to Belgrade, accompanied by Kadar. He returned on 23 October without having gained any political advantage from his trip, as in the meantime Hungary's attention was drawn to events in Poland. Hanging on the news from Warsaw, the Hungarians interpreted Gomulka's victory over the Stalinists and the Soviets as a portent of what they might themselves expect.

'The Hungarian path to socialism' now seemed a possibility, provided the party leadership seized the opportunity and acted swiftly. In spite of the apparent weakness and remoteness of the Central Committee, none of the leaders of the Petöfi Circle considered anything more than reform of the Communist régime. There was nothing revolutionary in the ten-point programme the Circle adopted on 22 October. It envisaged an emergency meeting of the Central Committee with Imre Nagy's participation, the reorganization of the Patriotic Popular Front (which even in 1953 Nagy had wanted to turn into a mediating body between the people and the party), factory autonomy (an echo of the Yugoslav system of self-management), Rakosi's expulsion, a public trial of the police chief Mihaly Farkas, and finally the establishment of 'even closer links with the U.S.S.R. on the basis of the Leninist principle of absolute equality'.

The Petöfi Circle was the Gironde of de-Stalinization to the Jacobinism to be found among the students, whose demands formulated the same day were less restrained. These included the evacuation of Soviet troops, general elections with several parties participating, and a revision of the entire economic system 'in accordance with the conditions prevailing in Hungary'. The students called a big demonstration of solidarity with Poland for 23 October; they plastered their battle-cries over the walls of the capital.

That was how it started. The demonstration was at first banned by the Ministry of the Interior, and the writers, the Petöfi Circle and the students sent several delegations to the Central Committee to get this decision annulled. Hours were spent discussing and quibbling over details until the procession had already virtually got under way. That morning Geroe had returned from Belgrade. He was inclined to be harsh, but other leaders urged him to give in. The Nagyists were afraid of provocation. Nagy himself was not in Budapest, and did not return till about midday. Shortly after one o'clock the ban was lifted.

The demonstration took place in an orderly fashion in front of the statue of Jozef Bem, the Polish general involved in the 1848 Hungarian revolution. But, instead of petering out, it grew. The whole population was on the streets, and workers flooded in from the suburbs. The curbs had failed, and the political vacuum caused by the decline of governmental power was filled by an inarticulate crowd waiting for 'something positive', 'something momentous ... and truly significant'. There were spontaneous bursts of activity: finding Imre Nagy, destroying the Stalin monument, occupying the radio building, hoisting the national flag with the emblem of the People's Republic removed. As yet there was nothing beyond the control of a powerful personality.

But nobody ready to take action came forward; instead the crowd was treated to a speech, Geroe's clumsy broadcast, that emphasized Hungary's debt to the Soviet Union and condemned the demonstration as chauvinistic. As much by what it said as by what it left unsaid, this absurd performance inevitably exacerbated the situation.

During the evening, shots were heard near the radio building. The security police, the A.V.H., were unable to disperse the crowd, the government was unsure of the army, and the Central Committee, hastily convened in circumstances that are not clear, panicked and took two conflicting decisions. On the one hand, Imre Nagy was appointed Prime Minister (leaving the party leadership in Geroe's hands); on the other, an appeal was made to the Soviet garrison to restore order.

The circumstances under which Nagy was recalled prevented him from carrying out the tasks he had been preparing for. He had wanted to be the man of reform, but for this he needed at least the basic elements of power still intact. The appearance of Soviet armoured vehicles in the streets of Budapest emphasized the utter impotence and unpatriotic character of the party and state. From then on, national, democratized Communism became a chimera. Overtaken by events, Nagy did everything humanly possible to repair the damage done by Geroe, to restore conditions to the point where a new start could be made, to harmonize his aims with the people's hopes. But their aspirations soon got out of hand, and manifested themselves in spontaneous outbursts of passion.

Thrown back on himself, cut off from his own people, Nagy did his best to win some ground in which to manoeuvre; he tried to limit, moderate and impede the repression, to get rid of Geroe and his minions, to persuade the Soviets to withdraw, the insurgents to moderate their demands, and both the Soviets and the insurgents to trust him and accept him as a mediator.

It took him several days to discover that he was confronted with a national rebellion against foreign domination and the totalitarian régime, and for democracy. Like Kadar, Geroe and everyone else, he thought at first that the disturbances were caused by a minority of inflamed young people, possibly under

Western orders, and that it should be possible to deal with them quickly.

On the evening of 24 October the Kremlin's emissaries, Mikoyan and Suslov, arrived in the Hungarian capital and went to party headquarters, where Imre Nagy was. They seemed prepared to listen to Nagy; they admitted that the appeal to Soviet troops had been a mistake, and showed themselves willing to make sweeping concessions. Geroe was dismissed, and Kadar took his place. The populace was called on to put out flags. Spokesmen for the writers urged the rebels to lay down their arms and fall in behind Nagy and Kadar, who were beginning negotiations with the object of forming a more representative government. But the rebellion spread to the provinces, street fighting continued, the party disintegrated and the administration was paralysed. The strike that began in Budapest on 24 October became general. Soviet armoured columns and the united security forces did not stamp out the centres of resistance in the capital – Corvin Arcade and Kilian Barracks – perhaps because of reluctance to do so. In nearly all the provincial towns, sometimes after bloody clashes with the police but more often peacefully, power passed into the hands of revolutionary committees and workers' councils, who as a rule accepted Imre Nagy as a potential tool.

The new government announced by Nagy on 27 October was greeted sceptically; it did not inspire confidence as it incorporated too many survivors from the old régime regarded by the public as Rakosists. The higher patriotic feelings rose and the more articulate public opinion became, the more radical the demands grew. The sudden removal of restraint sparked off feverish outbursts of enthusiasm.

For a few days the Hungarians felt miraculously free. The young people's excitement was contagious. The nation unified in pressing for independence, free elections and the withdrawal of the Soviet troops.

Nagy himself became more and more involved. On the one hand, as a loyal Communist, a realistic patriot, he was bound by the compromise with Mikoyan and Suslov which he regarded as basically satisfactory. On the other hand, he was under pressure from the committees with which he was in communication.

Every day he made new concessions, hoping to restore order. He tried to regain control by legalizing the rebellion, ordering the police and the Russians to cease fire, and taking rebel leaders such as Pal Maleter into his confidence. But, having freed himself from the Rakosists in the machine, whose prisoner he had been in the early days of the rebellion, Nagy succumbed to the rebels. In dealing with them he was aided by his prestige and the fact that state interests were on his side, but he had no material strength.

The Prime Minister had to accept the facts: the single-party system and Communism had no popular basis. They were wholly dependent on Soviet power, and now, emboldened by the failure of the first intervention, the people were ignoring that power, and thought they had defeated the Soviet army. For Nagy, since more forceful intervention would be the negation of everything he stood for, the only hope of salvation lay in the reorganization of the political parties. He looked to the leaders of the peasant and Social Democratic Parties, who had some political experience, to help him win the race against the irresponsible extremists who were trying to bring him down, and to drag the country along what was under the circumstances a very hazardous path.

On 30 October Nagy announced the return to 'a system of government based on the democratic co-operation of the coalition parties, as they existed in 1945'. He was convinced, and the leaders of the former democratic coalition assured him, that the multi-party system was not incompatible with the maintenance of the socialist economy. But now the intoxicated rebel spokesmen went still further, demanding the condemnation of the Warsaw Pact, complete independence and neutrality. For several days Nagy held out against them; then he yielded, thereby hastening his own and the rebellion's downfall.

The final stage in the drama remains obscure. It is known that on 29 October Mikoyan and Suslov returned to Budapest, bearing the government's declaration that was published the following day, which appeared to reaffirm the compromise of 25 October. However, the introduction of a multi-party system and the imminent condemnation of the Warsaw Pact placed the Soviet leaders in a novel and extremely awkward situation.[6] Later, in 1959, Khrushchev admitted in Budapest that opinion in the Kremlin was not unanimous on the course to follow: 'Certain comrades were afraid the intervention might be misinterpreted.' Nevertheless, it is hardly surprising that those in favour of intervention carried the day.

The Kremlin had every reason to believe that, if the Hungarian rebellion were not suppressed, the situation would be repeated. Leaders in Prague, East Berlin, Bucharest and Sofia already regarded Gomulka's advent to power and the tolerance shown the Polish revisionists as a threat to the stability of their régimes. A neutral, parliamentarian Hungary, leaning towards the West, would have demonstrated to the peoples of Eastern Europe that the course of history could be reversed. Even the Chinese, who were so hostile to 'great-power chauvinism', agreed on this point. They had sympathized with Nagy as long as they thought he would keep the situation from getting out of hand and would introduce national Communism, but he became counter-revolutionary in their eyes in going over to parliamentary democracy. Mao Tse-tung, while continuing to support Gomulka against the Russians, put pressure on them to suppress the Hungarian rebellion without delay. Together with Czechoslovakia, East Germany, Rumania and Bulgaria, Mao gave the Soviets the international mandate they so badly needed. Soviet military leaders whose pride had been hurt by the set-back in Budapest were pushing in the same direction. Of course Hungary was not of the same strategic importance to the Soviet Union as Poland, but its loss was clearly not acceptable to Soviet strategists. Finally, the split between the Americans and the French and British over the Suez crisis conspicuously reduced the risks of intervening to the Soviets. Russian diplomatic soundings in Western capitals must have shown that in spite of overt sympathy for the Hungarian rebels no power would take military action on their behalf.

At dawn on 4 November, the Soviet troops regrouped around Budapest, and began to move. Red Army tanks opened fire on the barricades erected by the rebels. A few hours before, the authorized agents of the Nagy government, Generals Maleter and Kovacs, who had been invited to Soviet headquarters to continue negotiations begun on 1 November, were placed under arrest.

Exhaustively planned, the Soviet intervention quickly overcame the rebels' resistance. The latter were poorly organized and had few fortified positions and little ammunition. The regular army troops, in their barracks mainly under the command of Stalinist officers, remained passive during the first stage of the rising, only intervening sporadically at the end. In all events, the struggle was an unequal one. It was the workers from a few large factories in Budapest, Csepel and Dunapentele, and the miners of Pecs who put up the longest resistance. They fought as a matter of honour, out of their despair. The terrain did not lend itself to partisan warfare. Hopes of Western aid which some had entertained quickly collapsed.

In deposing the Nagy government, whose legality was unquestionable, and crushing a rebellion whose strength lay not in arms but in the rebirth of national consciousness, the Soviets invoked the Warsaw Treaty which, as the Soviet delegate in the Security Council emphasized, empowered the U.S.S.R. 'to protect Hungary against subversion'. An appeal was, in fact, made to the Soviets by Janos Kadar, who on the morning of 4 November announced his break with Nagy over the radio and the formation of a 'revolutionary workers' and peasants' government'. Kadar did not repudiate 'the mass movement' begun on 23 October, whose 'noble aim was to right the crimes committed by Rakosi and his accomplices against the party and democracy, and to uphold national independence and sovereignty'. But 'the exploitation of this movement by counter-revolutionary elements inadequately resisted by the Imre Nagy government' had endangered 'socialist conquests, the people's state, workers' and peasants' power, and the country's very existence'. Hence the need to set up a new centre of power which, 'on behalf of the working class, the people, the entire country', asked that the Soviet army 'come to our aid, so that the sinister forces of reaction might be crushed and calm and order restored in the country'.

Kadar's sudden change seemed surprising. As recently as 1 November, he had spoken over Radio Budapest announcing the reorganization of the party and extolling the rebellion. However, if one looks closely at this speech – broadcast shortly before his secret visit to the Ukraine where he was to form his counter-government – it provides the key to his volte-face. In fact, Kadar spoke of the dramatic choice facing the country 'between the consolidation of our conquests and a move over to counter-revolution'. As a party man, brought up in the cult, any challenge to its supremacy seemed to him to smack of counter-revolution, and it is true that from 28 October the Hungarian rising was clearly taking an increasingly anti-Communist turn.

After the withdrawal of the Soviet troops a number of extremist rebels began hunting down A.V.H. agents, and sometimes even party militants. In the factories and ministries an anti-Communist purge was under way (which paradoxically continued for several months, even after the revolt had been crushed). But as the rebellion became progressively better organized politically, the democratic parties revived, and the workers' councils, originally created by the rising, consolidated their position, it seemed likely that a sovereign Hungary would provide itself with institutions that were both socialist and democratic, and would resist a return to a Horthyist régime, which appealed only to a minority.

Nagy and his friends were willing to continue functioning in such a context, but for Kadar, Münnich and their supporters it was unacceptable. They condemned the excesses of Rakosi, and were prepared to follow Khrushchev along the path of de-Stalinization 'from above', but they were bound to support the Soviet decision to prevent the overthrow of the one-party system and Hungary's secession, whatever the cost. One may assume that Kadar, like Nagy, dreamed at first of reconciling devotion to the party and loyalty to the U.S.S.R. with patriotism, and even with Hungarian nationalism, of whose strength he was well aware. But when the time came to make a choice, absolute priority was given to the interests of the party over national independence, and this – whatever the immediate or long-term drawbacks – necessitated Soviet intervention.

In view of the outcome, it is as important to understand Kadar's motives as those of the Soviet leaders. The world was stunned by the ferocity of the intervention and the perfidious attempts to justify it, which seemed to demonstrate the permanence of Stalinism. Later, however, it became evident that Stalinist methods of repression had been used, not to restore

Stalinism, but to institute a Khrushchevist régime similar to Gomulka's, although it was unlike his in that it would always bear the taint of having been directly imposed by Russian tanks.

National unity, which had arisen during the October days, survived the military defeat. It found its expression in the general strike and its mouthpiece in the Greater Budapest Central Workers' Council established on 14 November, which for several weeks acted as a second government representing the disarmed but united nation as opposed to Kadar's government, which was clearly embarrassed by having to rely on Soviet tanks alone.

At the head of his so-called 'workers' and peasants' government', which had no links with the working class or peasantry, Kadar keenly wanted to win supporters for his programme, which took in nearly all the points in Nagy's, except for the multi-party system and neutrality. The workers' representatives tried to exploit the weakness of Kadar's position, having to search for a minimum of legitimacy for his rule, to extract concessions from him – including Nagy's return – which would have endorsed the political victory of the militarily defeated rebellion. The representatives of the democratic coalition parties and the writers, whom Kadar tried to win over as well, displayed the same intransigence.

Finally Kadar lost patience, and at the beginning of December he arrested the leader of the central workers' council. Nagy and his companions, who left the Yugoslav embassy where they had taken refuge on 4 November on the understanding that no action would be taken against them, were deported to Rumania. The political police were restored and repressive 'workers' militias' were set up, composed of the hardest Rakosist elements. Thus the Hungarians were given a new lesson in the terror they had freed themselves from in October. Excitement gave way to resignation, romantic nationalism to bitterly disillusioned realism.

Then, once the opposition had been completely crushed and the nation demoralized, Kadar not unskilfully embarked on a gradual, careful course of liberalization. On the ruins of his compatriots' dreams and appealing to their sense of realism, he erected a system that was appreciably less oppressive than the earlier measures of Rakosi and Geroe, or those which Hungary's Czech or Rumanian neighbours had to endure for years to come.[7]

6

A Holy Alliance against Revisionism and National Communism

Hungary

'Disturbances are unfortunate, but we can learn something from them . . . In this sense, a bad thing can be the source of good.'

Thus Mao Tse-tung commented in February 1957 on Hungary, paraphrasing a two-thousand-year-old aphorism of Lao-tse. In his view, the 'good' engendered by the Hungarian revolution was the impulse it gave Communism towards solidarity. The initial reaction of most of the leaders of the Eastern countries was to close their ranks and confirm the unity that had been so rudely shaken in 1956: de-Stalinization, Poznan, Warsaw, and now Budapest.

As in 1928, 1939, and 1948, so now the Communists found themselves isolated, opposed and abused, after an interval of relaxation, of attempts at co-operation with the non-Communist left, and of approaches to the West. The threat of Hungarian disagreement had driven them to violence, and that in turn led to a fresh insistence on ideological orthodoxy.

Conditions now favoured a revival of sectarian attitudes. Given the doctrinal preoccupations of the régimes and the entire movement, the quest for greater unity inevitably involved a search for a unified interpretation of Marxism-Leninism. However, it soon became clear that, even if everyone, from Ulbricht to Mao, including Khrushchev and Tito, was agreed on the need to unite, countries and parties had already grown so far apart that there could be no identity of opinion on the means of achieving this unity. The debate on what was to be learnt from the Hungarian revolution degenerated rapidly into a search for scapegoats, and reactivated the quarrel between Stalinists and anti-Stalinists.

The situation was further exacerbated by the fact that for most of the proponents of internationalism (i.e., total devotion to the U.S.S.R.) the reassertion of orthodoxy was a pretext for the strengthening of police dictatorship, while for others – notably the Chinese – it masked a growing ambition to take the Soviets' place, or at least to gain acceptance for the idea of collective leadership of the camp as an anti-coexistence strategy. Nevertheless, the common front of Russia, East European and Chinese Stalinists that emerged at the end of 1956 was able to drive a wedge between Gomulka and Tito, and to inspire with inquisitorial spirit the resolutions taken by the Moscow international conference in December 1957, which marked a clear retreat from the decisions taken at the Twentieth Congress of the C.P.S.U.

The execution of Imre Nagy in June 1958 was the most spectacular victory gained by this strange 'holy alliance', which was directed not only against 'real' revisionists and Titoists, but also against Khrushchev, and which aimed, at least as far as the Chinese were concerned, to separate the U.S.S.R. from the West once again. But the Stalinist or neo-Stalinist offensive suffered from lack of realism in its objectives. Conditions allowed neither for the restoration of unity under Soviet leadership, of which the Czech, French, East German, Bulgarian, and 'nostalgic' Communist leaders in the Kremlin dreamt, nor for the establishment of the new type of unity envisaged by Mao, according to which the Kremlin would have had to share much of its responsibility for strategic planning with China. Ultimately, the search for unity exacerbated their differences.

National Communism in the Dock

'Those who believed that Czechoslovakia was setting out along the path of vague liberalization and dubious democratization ... must have been very disappointed', declared President Novotny in Bratislava in April 1957. The Czech leaders prided themselves on having understood the Hungarian situation clearly from the outset. When not only Polish but even Chinese newspapers were still showing some sympathy for the Hungarians, the Prague press had already revealed the 'counter-revolutionary' nature of events. In Prague these served as a pretext for strengthening police surveillance, for clamping down on discussion and criticism. The job of bringing the intellectuals into line was entrusted to Kopecky (who had already distinguished himself in the pre-1953 anti-Titoist campaigns), Vladimir Koucky and Jiri Hendrych, who remained in office up to 1968, and were no less dogmatic in their orthodoxy than were Suslov or Ponomarev themselves.

Novotny had joined Ulbricht in pressing Gomulka 'to put an end to reactionary activity in Poland, and to check the spread of mistaken views that are affecting public opinion, and even the ranks of the party'. Even after the ban on Po Prostu, the organ of the Polish revisionists, the ruling Czechoslovak bureaucracy displayed outraged disapproval of Warsaw's moderate policy.

Prague placed itself in the forefront of the struggle to restore a unity between the socialist camp and the international movement that, in its view, should be rigid and unconditional. The Czech leaders were indignant at an article that appeared in Nowe Drogi of 14 December 1956, calling for a frank and friendly discussion on the points at issue among the Communist parties: the interpretation of Stalinism, the evaluation of the Yugoslav experiment, the choice of centralism or polycentrism, the nature of the Hungarian rising and the Soviet intervention. For Prague there could be no such thing as differences between true Communists.

A few days after the Polish article appeared, Novotny and Ulbricht published a joint declaration condemning 'national Communism' as the gravest of heresies; they claimed that 'unshakeable friendship with the U.S.S.R. is the condition for the victory of socialism in every country', gave their warm approval to the Soviet intervention in Hungary, and called for vigilance. On 22 January 1957 the Czech party leaders, together with a French party delegation, signed a similar declaration. The nucleus of an unconditionally pro-Soviet front had been created, as became even clearer when in the same month Soviet, Bulgarian, Czech, Rumanian and Hungarian leaders met in Budapest with the object of strengthening Kadar's position.

Nowhere did Togliatti's and Tito's polycentrist ideas meet with such opposition as among the Czech leaders, who would have liked to see the Comintern rise again from its ashes. Their furious internationalism was not, however, due solely to their devotion to the Soviet Union or their loyalty to Stalin's memory. There was also a certain uneasiness about Khrushchev and the indecision of Kremlin policy. The real strength of Czech Stalinism lay in the mentality of the men in power, who had come up through the ranks, and who wanted clear, firm principles for their government.

In this respect they were the true heirs of the stiff-necked, obscurantist officials of the Habsburg monarchy. Like them, they tended to identify liberalism with anarchism and were suspicious of intellectuals. Khrushchev's report on Stalin and his approaches to Tito had shocked them, and for that reason, though they had pledged themselves to unconditional loyalty, they kept their distance from the Kremlin, and did not hesitate to take action in the field of ideology or internal affairs. In November 1957, for instance, they appointed Novotny President of the Republic after Zapotocky's death, and allowed him to remain as First Secretary of the party. 'It is politically expedient to merge the offices of chief-of-state and party leader', declared Prime Minister Siroky in Parliament. But collective leadership still prevailed in the U.S.S.R.; Khrushchev, the party leader, shared power with Bulganin, the head of the government, up to March 1958. Thus, in a sense, Czechoslovakia showed the Soviet Union the way to follow.

Khrushchev, for his part, appreciated what was to be gained from winning over a team of men that had given proof of their tenacity, loyalty and political ability. On a visit to Prague in July 1957 after the defeat of the Molotov–Malenkov group, he was effusively complimentary about Novotny. No doubt on a personal level he preferred Tito, who was colourful, imaginative and passionately fond of political schemes, though difficult to handle; but from the point of view of the Soviet state, he knew the value of a methodical, dull but reliable man.

Bulgaria

The Sofia government reacted as strongly as Prague had done to events in Hungary, reaffirming their absolute loyalty to Moscow. It was the Bulgarians who first struck the familiar key-note: 'the attitude towards the U.S.S.R. and the Soviet party is the criterion and touchstone of proletarian internationalism'. The revival of internationalist obligations, for which the Kremlin immediately recompensed them with an economic subsidy, went hand-in-hand with the strengthening of control over the country. 'The organs of proletariat dictatorship exist in Bulgaria. They are growing more and more powerful', announced Zhivkov in a speech on 28 November 1956. To give point to his words, the police proceeded with the preventive arrest of several thousand alleged opponents of the régime. Yugov, the chairman of the Council, sternly denounced the young 'hooligans' of the University who, several weeks before the outbreak in Budapest, had demanded a reduction in the number of hours devoted to the teaching of Marxism-Leninism. Intellectuals were called on to submit unconditionally to party discipline. This new insistence on orthodoxy was accompanied by material concessions such as rises in old-age pensions, family allowances, the minimum wage and unemployment benefits.

Albania

For the Albanian leaders the Hungarian tragedy simply confirmed 'the collusion between Tito and the imperialists'. Indeed, the cooling in relations between Moscow and Belgrade immediately after 4 November 1956 was a great relief to Tirana. Having been under pressure from Moscow for several months to come to terms with Yugoslavia and rehabilitate the Titoist Koci Xoxe, Hoxha now, in November 1956, had the satisfaction of being invited to submit articles to *Pravda*. He seized the opportunity to attack those 'who claim to have discovered new forms of socialism and refuse to be guided by Soviet experience', and rashly declared that the insistence of 'certain people' on sovereignty and independence was the produce of 'reactionary, bourgeois ideology'. At the same time, his friend Mehmet Shehu, the chairman of the Council, announced that 'the Albanian government has never suffered from the slightest Soviet interference in the affairs of the country'. (Five years later, after the break with Moscow, Hoxha demanded sovereignty, and accused the Soviets of having put strong pressure on him since spring 1956.)

As in Bulgaria, the Albanian declarations of orthodoxy were followed by repressive measures. The most striking was the trial and execution, announced on 25 November 1956, of three Titoist leaders or supporters of a rapprochement with Yugoslavia: Mrs Liri Gega, a member of the Politburo (who, according to Khrushchev at the Twenty-Third Congress, was pregnant, and was shot despite a Soviet attempt to intercede on her behalf), General Dale Ndreu and Petro Buli. Thus Hoxha, the champion of obedience, savagely asserted his autocracy as a national despot, heir to the all-powerful *pashas* who had ruled the little country in the name of the Sublime Porte.

Rumania

The Rumanian leaders reacted to events in Hungary less uncompromisingly. Gheorghiu Dej was in Yugoslavia at the time of the Budapest rising. Treated with much consideration, he made his peace with Tito and, if it is an exaggeration to speak of his 'conversion' to the latter's ideas, he took back from Belgrade the impression that there was 'a firm basis for the strengthening of fraternal links between the two countries' (*Scanteia*, Bucharest, 9 November 1956). It was probably due to Tito's influence that he tried to handle the feeling in his country aroused by the Hungarian rising, notably among the Hungarian minority in Transylvania, by means of concessions rather than increased repression. (He waited until after Nagy's execution in 1958 to carry out a thoroughgoing purge of the Hungarian intellectuals who had formulated demands in 1956 and 1957.) Immediately after the insurrection, Dej was the first Eastern Communist leader to go to Budapest to offer Janos Kadar moral and material support; Kadar repaid him in 1958 by officially renouncing all territorial claims on Rumania.

One should guard against anticipating the sudden revelation in 1963 of a Gheorghiu Dej fiercely resisting Soviet integrationism. At the end of 1956 Rumania was still occupied by Soviet troops, who were even strengthened after demonstrations of sympathy for the Hungarian rebels in Cluj, Tirgu Mures, Timisoara and even in Bucharest. Nevertheless, there is some justification for believing that the events of late 1956 prompted Dej to reduce his dependence on Moscow by enlarging the popular basis of his power and improving his country's international status. (In the speeches and articles of the most prominent Rumanian leaders of the time there is a striking number of references to China, which Gheorghiu Dej had visited in September 1956 on the occasion of the Chinese Party Congress.) The chairman of the Rumanian Council, Chivu Stoica, in a speech to the National Assembly on 23 March 1957, first made use of the phrase that was to crop up again and again in the speeches of Eastern leaders until 1959: 'The countries of the socialist camp under the leadership of the Soviet Union and People's China.' But on the same occasion Stoica also expressed the desire to develop economic and cultural relations with France and Italy, 'with whom we are linked by traditions of friendship and co-operation, and with the other Latin peoples of Europe and South America, with whom we share a common cultural background'.

This insistence on Rumania's Latin culture was a fresh aspect following years of russification. While attacking national Communism on a theoretical basis and reproaching the Yugoslavs in a friendly but firm manner for seeing a contradiction between internationalism and national sovereignty, the Rumanian leaders took steps to come to terms with the current of nationalist opinion. Without relaxing the police dictatorship, slackening the party's control, or ceasing to pay homage to the wise leadership of the U.S.S.R., Gheorghiu Dej began ingratiating himself with nationalist forces that had been so strictly suppressed in past years. Dismissed professors were restored to their chairs, silenced writers appeared again, and professional officers in the old army were granted pensions. Gradually, imperceptibly, Rumanian Communism nationalized itself at the expense of the Jewish, Hungarian and German minorities.

This change of front, only apparent several years later, was facilitated by the great strides made in industrialization. By the end of 1956 industrial production had increased by 330 per cent over 1938. The standard of living remained appreciably lower than in Czechoslovakia and Hungary, but the government's success in the sphere of industrialization impressed the population and especially the technical intelligentsia, hitherto sceptical and deeply anti-Communist.[1]

Mao versus Tito

The most significant feature at this period was the penetration of the People's Democracies of Eastern Europe by Chinese influence. This was made possible by the internecine struggles taking place in the Kremlin and the eclipse of Soviet authority. The Russian intervention in Hungary caused Soviet might again to be feared and respected, and most leaders were relieved to find that Moscow was not prepared to sacrifice them in times of crisis. But they were not unmindful of the wavering of the Kremlin or of Peking's firmness when the moment of decision came. The moral prestige of the Soviet leadership had declined while that of the Chinese had risen.

Immediately after the crisis, the conflict between Khrushchev and his opponents in the Kremlin became more acute. Not until June 1957 was it resolved, for better or for worse, and in the meantime, with the need for a strong man at the wheel only too apparent, the governments in the People's Democracies remained uncertain as to what direction Soviet policy might take.

It is not surprising that Mao Tse-tung, who since the beginning of 1956 had been following Khrushchev's progress with concern, seized the opportunity to gain recognition for his own theoretical and practical contribution to the common cause. He put himself forward as arbitrator in the inquest on the Hungarian rising, in which the Yugoslav leadership found itself on the opposite side to most of the other Eastern Communist leaders.

The Yugoslavs were in an embarrassing position after the rising. Apparently Tito had been consulted by Khrushchev and Mikoyan at a secret meeting and had been persuaded to give his approval to Soviet intervention. However, in Richard Loewenthal's words, 'it would be unfair to accuse Tito and his associates of treachery towards Hungarian democracy; they are Communists and not democrats, and cannot therefore betray principles they have never held'.[2] It is true that Belgrade had supported Imre Nagy, but in accepting the multi-party system Nagy overstepped the line separating Tito from Djilas, and 'single-party democracy' from parliamentary democracy. The Khrushchevist Kadar was closer to Tito than was Nagy; and in any case his was the lesser of the two evils.

Tito's main concern, after having made a choice that Yugoslav opinion strongly condemned, was to limit the damage and to hold on to the gains he had made in 1955 and 1956 by co-operating with Khrushchev. His intention was to join forces with Gomulka, Khrushchev (under pressure from Molotov and Suslov), and the Italian Communists to prevent the Stalinists from outmanoeuvring them. While assuring Kadar of his support, he attacked the 'inveterate' Stalinists of Prague, Tirana, Paris and other places and called for collaboration with the Polish comrades. In a speech to the National Assembly on 7 December Kardelj even deplored the fact that the Kadar government, which was making 'fruitless attempts to restore the party', had not relied on the workers' councils, which in fact had sprung from the proletariat.

There was a general outcry of indignation at these remarks. The orthodox leaders saw in them fresh proof of Belgrade's 'fractionalism' and 'interventionism'. At this point the Chinese *People's Daily* of 29 December summarized the conclusions drawn from the Hungarian rising by the Politburo of the Chinese party. This significant document impugned Tito, who had opined that the Hungarian rising had begun as a genuine popular movement, and only later had been taken over by the forces of reaction. Peking took the Stalinist view that international imperialism was 'the principal, the crucial' force behind these events. It admitted that Stalin had made mistakes (great-power fanaticism, unwarranted interference in the internal affairs of fraternal countries and parties), but emphasized the Soviet party's ability to rectify these without any need for a 'struggle between the anti-Stalinists and Stalinists'. 'If one must speak of Stalinism, it can be said in the first place that Stalinism is Communism and Marxism-Leninism.' Peking sprang to the defence of those parties denounced by Tito as Stalinist: such attacks 'could only divide the movement'. Kardelj had gone too far in praising the workers' councils, 'which had fallen into counter-revolutionary hands' ... 'One cannot contrast socialist democracy with the dictatorship of the proletariat.' Finally, while emphasizing that Communist parties must keep their independence, and that it is through 'genuine and not just formal consultation that they must achieve unity of opinion and action', Peking declared that the U.S.S.R. 'still remains the centre of the international Communist movement', and that the strengthening of the solidarity of the international proletariat must be based on its pre-eminence.

It may seem surprising that Mao Tse-tung, who from the start had looked like a potential Asian Tito, should have come down so firmly on the side of the Moscow-oriented Stalinists against the Yugoslav champions of independence for the Communist countries. But there was a logic in the Chinese position. Mao rejected the Kremlin's hegemony, but none the less he believed strongly in the importance of maintaining discipline and having a unified strategy for all. In his view, solidarity came first: the socialist countries must form a united bloc in the face of imperialist pressure. The neutral partnership that Tito was seeking seemed absurd to him, and the Yugoslav's influence over Khrushchev pernicious; his cordial relations with the Western powers were cause for suspicion, while his proselytism in the Third World posed a threat. On the other hand, Mao, not without reason, hoped to gain some moral and material advantage from his protection of the Eastern Stalinist governments against interference from the Kremlin. Czechoslovakia and the German Democratic Republic, though not Yugoslavia, could supply him with some of the industrial equipment he needed, and his dislike for Tito grew steadily over the following years. In emphasizing solidarity and drawing attention to the 'common roots' of Leninist doctrine, Mao put forward a platform that was at the same time to serve the socialist camp and the international movement.

Chou En-lai went on a tour of Eastern Europe at the beginning of January 1957. On his arrival in Moscow on 7 January, the Chinese Prime Minister at once entered into discussion with a delegation from the German Democratic Republic under Grotewohl, which he won over to his point of view without difficulty. On 10 January he met Kadar, who was glad to receive the support of the great Far Eastern fraternal party long regarded by the Nagyists as their friend and protector.

Chou then proceeded to Warsaw, where his mission was more difficult. The Soviet-Polish agreement of 18 November 1956 had not resolved all misunderstandings between the Kremlin and Gomulka, who was concentrating on consolidating his power, while under pressure from Moscow, Prague and East Berlin to have done with the revisionists and to align himself publicly with the rest. Gomulka hoped that Mao's envoy might understand, and lend him some support. No sooner had Chou En-lai alighted from the plane than he embarrassed the Polish leader by denouncing 'the imperialist diversions in Hungary' and extolling 'the solidarity of the socialist countries with the U.S.S.R. at their head' – formulas that Gomulka avoided so as not to offend Polish public opinion. On the Soviet Union's leading role the Polish leader remained adamant throughout the five days of the talks; but he finally gave way over Hungary.

The joint communiqué issued on 16 January contained neither a condemnation of Imre Nagy nor a specific approval of Soviet intervention, as Chou would have liked, but it did uphold the Kadar government and its programme, a major concession on Gomulka's part in view of Polish hostility to a political body regarded as anti-national. No doubt in return Gomulka obtained Chou's promise of Chinese support for his resistance to interference from the Kremlin, which still would not concede that Gomulka was the best judge of how to run his own country. The Warsaw talks did not resolve all differences between the two parties; if a 'Peking–Warsaw axis' began to form in the spring of 1957, by summer Mao's hardening attitude to the revisionists had alienated him from Gomulka. Nevertheless, even when the Sino-Soviet conflict was in full swing, when Gomulka's position was closer to Moscow's, Sino-Polish relations remained courteous and considerate, no doubt reflecting a common suspicion of the 'fanaticism' of that great power that lay between them, at whose hands they had both suffered in the past.

Khrushchev's Victory and its Repercussions

The Soviet Union, however, was in a state of turmoil. At the end of June 1957 the crisis that had been brewing in the Kremlin since November 1956 came to a head. Finding himself in a minority in the Presidium, Khrushchev transferred his quarrel with Molotov, Malenkov and Kaganovich to the Central Committee, where his friends and supporters were in a majority. Meeting between 22 and 29 June, the Committee decided in his favour. The First Secretary's victory over his opponents, the so-called 'anti-party group', was immediately represented as that of 'the course approved by the Twentieth Congress'.

Once again Khrushchev and his supporters played on the theme of de-Stalinization in order to increase their popularity at home, and to oil the wheels for Soviet diplomacy. The resolution adopted at the close of the meeting castigated Molotov and his friends for having opposed the internal reforms and the international *détente*. It stigmatized Molotov's hostile attitude to a reconciliation with Yugoslavia and the negotiation of a State treaty with Austria, his refusal to acknowledge 'the possibility of averting war under the present circumstances ... the possibility of different paths to socialism in different countries' ... 'At the root of Comrades Molotov's, Kaganovich's and Malenkov's attitude ... is the fact that they are prisoners of old ideas and methods', that they are 'dogmatic and sectarian'.

This new attack on Stalinism served to bring out the difference between the trend in the Soviet Union as opposed to most of the other Communist countries, including China, where it was rather towards rigidity. It ought logically to have led to a new breach between Moscow and the other bloc capitals; if this did not happen, at least initially, it was because Khrushchev hastened to reassure the Stalinist leaders, notably in Rumania and Bulgaria, who on the pretext of following the Kremlin's lead began purging their enemies and personal rivals. Thus, in Sofia, Todor Zhivkov expelled a 'hard-liner', Chankov, from the Politburo, and took the opportunity of getting rid of another dangerous rival, Terpechev, a notorious Titoist. In Bucharest Gheorghiu Dej acted likewise, expelling Joseph Chisinevschi and Miron Constantinescu from office; the Central Committee resolution published on 2 July 1957 accused them of having opposed the party line, at one and the same time, out of dogmatism and extreme liberalism. They were alleged to have 'attacked the security organs', and 'tried to deflect the discussion on the lessons of the Twentieth Soviet Congress'. What mattered to Gheorghiu Dej, who was closer to Molotov than to Khrushchev, was to strengthen his own position and render the party leadership less vulnerable to Moscow's influence. To carry out this policy he called on one of his old friends, Ion Gheorghe Maurer, to take over the Ministry of Foreign Affairs. A former lawyer, Maurer had secured Dej's release from prison in 1944. Appointed Secretary of State for Justice in 1945, he sank into obscurity during the Stalinist period, to reappear only in 1956. He was known as an able and approachable man, whose firm political convictions had never involved a sectarian puritanism. Over the next few years, he was to help to reshape Rumanian policy with brilliant results.

In Hungary, it was Kadar's centrist group that benefited from the changes in the Kremlin. His Stalinist opponents, such as Jozsef Revai, had counted on Molotov's victory. Their patron's defeat banished their last hopes of restoring Rakosi. However, holding to his strategy of a 'battle on two fronts', Kadar lost no time in making it clear that he had no intention of modifying his attitude towards the 'revisionists', Nagy's supporters. It was significant that, to justify his intransigence towards the Nagyists, Kadar pointed to Mao Tse-tung, who despite his declared taste for 'the hundred flowers' had also just embarked on a harsh purge of revisionists.

In Warsaw, the fall of Molotov, symbol of Soviet hegemony, was received with satisfaction, though Gomulka was inclined to be cautious. One of his friends, the trade unionist Loga-Sowinski, expressed the hope that the events in Moscow 'would improve the chances of democratization, not only in Poland, but also in the other socialist countries'.

This is what Tito seemed to believe as well. He suggested to Khrushchev that they resume the dialogue that had been interrupted at the end of 1956. The two arranged to meet in Bucharest at the beginning of August, but before this Khrushchev went to Prague to reassure the leaders there; he defined the limits of the projected rapprochement with Tito, and publicly criticized Yugoslav presumption in proposing workers' councils – an institution particularly detested by Czech bureaucrats – as a model to be copied. 'We recognize the existence of different paths', he went on. 'But what matters most is the general path.' Thus Khrushchev showed that for him bloc unity under the aegis of the Kremlin, and supported by the most loyal parties, took precedence over everything else. It should not be forgotten that it was with the help of 'hegemonistic' figures such as Suslov and Marshal Zhukov that Khrushchev was able to defeat the opposition. Henceforth, he applied himself to dispelling the suspicions that his sympathy for Tito had aroused in Moscow as much as in the other Eastern capitals. His aim now was to draw Yugoslavia into the camp by his flexible and broad policy, and he wanted the approval of the men in Prague.

Tito, it seems, still entertained illusions about Khrushchev's liberalism and pluralism, and the possibility of influencing the policy of the U.S.S.R. and the People's Democracies through him. To help Khrushchev strengthen his position, he made substantial concessions at their meeting in Bucharest, promising to take part personally in the international conference called for November in Moscow and to recognize the German Democratic Republic.

However, when Tito learned of the draft resolution of the international conference a few weeks after this meeting, he realized that he had been taken in. This document, a joint Sino-Soviet enterprise – a point that Tito scarcely found reassuring – bore the stamp of Mao's dogmatic, aggressive spirit rather than Khrushchev's 'flexibility'. To be sure, in order not to alarm the Yugoslavs, Poles and Italians prematurely, those responsible for the draft had avoided all mention of the 'leading role of the U.S.S.R.' and the re-establishment of the Comintern. The document did, however, stress internationalist discipline to an extent that Tito considered excessive; in Loewenthal's words, 'it was a crude, unsubtle document, in the spirit of the cold war, according to whose logic Yugoslavia would be forced to choose between unqualified adherence to the Warsaw Pact or being denounced as revisionist'. Bitterly disappointed, Tito cancelled his plans to attend the conference in Moscow and instructed his envoys, Kardelj and Rankovic, to make it clear from the start that, unless the joint declaration was considerably modified, Yugoslavia would not sign it.

The 1957 Moscow Conference and the Anti-Yugoslav Campaign

During the fortieth anniversary celebrations of the October Revolution in November 1957 the first international conference of Communist parties since the dissolution of the Comintern met in secret. There were two successive sessions: one, from 14 to 16 November, of the parties in power, which, after detailed discussion, passed the draft declaration, a new charter for the movement, which the Yugoslavs did not sign; the other, a conference of sixty-eight Communist parties out of the seventy-five in the movement, which adopted a peace manifesto prepared by the Soviets and Poles. This the Yugoslavs signed, not wishing to burn all their bridges.[3]

Mao took the lead in the conference. Khrushchev seemed to want to stand aside in favour of Suslov, a strict doctrinarian expert in relations with the fraternal parties, who put up scarcely any resistance to the Chinese drive, which was supported by the most militant East European Stalinists: Ulbricht, Hoxha, Zhivkov and Hendrych. Mao's double objective was to strengthen the centralist side of the declaration so as to preclude any compromise with the Yugoslavs and to turn it into a militant, revolutionary document that would commit the Soviets to an offensive strategy. He showed himself to be an extremely skilful tactician: no one insisted more strongly on the 'leading role' of the U.S.S.R., but in fact it was he who consolidated and manipulated the majority at the conference.

Cut off from the Yugoslavs and only half-heartedly supported by Kadar, Gomulka went on the defensive. Referring to his internal difficulties, and the mood of the population highly sensitive to any apparent threat to the national interests, he tried to blur the outlines of the 'formulas' dealing with proletarian internationalism. But his objections were brushed aside. 'We must have a leader', said Mao Tse-tung, stressing that the Chinese Communist party was not worthy of fulfilling this role. 'China is a large country, but its industry is small. China does not have even a quarter of a Sputnik, whereas the Soviet Union has two. Without the Soviet Union, we should all have been taken over by other countries.'

In the end, the U.S.S.R.'s leading role in the socialist camp was proclaimed. The conference came to the conclusion that the principles of equality, independence, sovereignty and non-intervention which the Poles and Yugoslavs had stressed did not adequately define the relations among the Communist countries and parties; solidarity found its expression in close co-operation and mutual fraternal aid.

The centralist majority led by Mao also had its way over the question of dogmatism and revisionism. There again, Gomulka, who could not be accused of tenderness towards the revisionist intellectuals in his country, put forward a less rigid formula that treated dogmatism and revisionism as two equally dangerous deviations. One might have thought that the Soviets, who had just got rid of the dogmatic Molotov, would support him on this point, but Suslov, together with Mao and Ulbricht among others, took the view that there was no similarity between dogmatism, a permissible deviation, and revisionism, which reflected a bourgeois ideology that 'paralysed revolutionary energy and aimed at the restoration of capitalism'.

It is true that, to save Khrushchev's face, the 'popular front' strategy laid down at the Twentieth Congress was not openly repudiated; but the Moscow conference did mark a return to the 'class versus class' and 'camp versus camp' strategy of 1947-53. It emphasized the 'struggle against the internal enemy' and the defence of the dictatorship of the proletariat. War is not inevitable, it declared, taking up the formula of the Twentieth Congress; however, as Mao loved to point out, 'as long as imperialism exists there is a danger of war'. It was also Mao who caused the proposition that 'if imperialism unleashed a war, it was imperialism that would be destroyed', to be written into the declaration. Mao's utterances on this subject made everyone at the conference uneasy. He asserted that the balance of power had altered considerably in favour of the socialist camp, and that therefore they must not hesitate to take risks in order to expand world Communism. Above all, they must not be intimidated by the nuclear blackmail of the United States (a barb aimed at the Soviets). China had a population of 600 million; even if half this number were to die in a war, 300 million would be left to rebuild a prosperous, happy, socialist China on the ruins of the old. This optimism scared the Eastern European leaders, with the exception of Hoxha. Mao's rashness in defining his 'adventuristic' ideas made it easier for Khrushchev subsequently to counter Chinese influence, and to secure the approval of the governments of the People's Democracies for his more cautious and flexible foreign policy, although not without its share of calculated risks, like the one he took in Cuba in 1962 without consulting them.

Khrushchev's action ensured that Mao's success at the Moscow conference would prove short-lived. He certainly managed to gain acceptance for the principle that the strategy of the bloc and of international Communism must be determined, not as before by the Kremlin on its own, but through bilateral and multilateral consultation. But he was mistaken if he thought he could thereby influence the Soviets' and the bloc's foreign policy.

No doubt in order to avoid any obstacle to their freedom of action, the Soviet leaders brushed aside all plans for the re-establishment of the International, advanced principally by the French and the Czechs. They preferred to control the movement without the encumbrance of a permanent supervisory body. The furthest they would go was to agree to the founding of an international magazine called *Problems of Peace and Socialism*. This multilingual publication, under the editorship of the Soviet Rumyantsev, printed news articles and formal pronouncements on doctrine. It never had much influence, and in 1962 the Chinese withdrew from its editorial board.

The most significant result of the Moscow conference was to provide ammunition for the ideological rearming of the Communist rank and file, which had somewhat lost its sense of direction during the 1956 crisis. It put new life into the Leninist tenet that revolution was inevitable and of the effectiveness of the dictatorship of the proletariat. But at the same time, by encouraging the leading cadres in their schematic way of thinking, it further delayed a more realistic consideration of the problem awaiting solution. The ideologists still took precedence over the pragmatists.

Finally, the theoretical condemnation of revisionism gave the Stalinist leaders a good excuse to stifle criticism and purge nonconformist elements. It led logically to the resumption of the campaign against Yugoslavia.

The Moscow declaration did not specifically identify the Yugoslavs as revisionists, and after the meeting Khrushchev still had hopes of bringing Tito back into the fold. But the Yugoslavs themselves provided the excuse for the new campaign. Angered by what he regarded as Khrushchev's alignment with Mao and the Stalinists and abandonment of the resolutions of the Twentieth Congress, Tito entrusted his party's best thinkers, notably Kardelj and Vlahovic, with the task of drawing up a programme to contain the essence of the Yugoslav way – de-Stalinized Marxism-Leninism – for the Congress of the Yugoslav party in April 1958. The draft was published on 13 March. It contained nothing new: everyone was familiar with the Yugoslav theses on the atrophy of the state, the dangers of bureaucratic centralization, the diversity of paths, workers' management as the basis of socialist democracy, and so on. Nevertheless, despite its circumspection with regard to the U.S.S.R., and the many references to a 'common fund' of doctrine, the draft programme appeared to be a rejoinder to the Moscow declaration, with its insistence on equality, the independence of parties and non-interference in internal affairs, its defence of the Yugoslav party's policy of nonalignment, and its uncompromising condemnation of Stalinism and monolithism.

The Kremlin could not let the challenge go unanswered. On 5 April 1958, Khrushchev informed Tito of his decision not to send a delegation to the Congress and to publish a refutation of the programme. To avert the danger of a break, the Yugoslav leaders then suggested certain alterations, but they were considered inadequate. On 19 April *Komunist* published a harsh critique of the draft programme, for the first time since 1955 accusing Yugoslavia of 'national Communism'. A few days later, at the Congress in Ljubljana, Tito, Kardelj, Rankovic and Koca Popovic defended their ideas, rejecting the attempts to interfere in Yugoslav affairs.

The die was cast. This time the initiative for a witch-hunt came from Peking and not Moscow. On 5 May the *People's Daily* accused Yugoslavia of having abandoned the path of socialism, and recalled that the Cominform resolution of 1948, condemning Yugoslav revisionism, and confirmed by the attitude prevailing in Belgrade, was still in force. This was the signal for a fresh stream of abuse, especially from Sofia, Tirana and Prague. Khrushchev, outflanked by his followers, allowed himself to be drawn into a course of action that was probably more vigorous than he had intended; had he not himself blamed Stalin for bringing ideology into the sphere of intergovernmental relations? The Soviet government yielded to Chinese pressure, and on 27 May 1958 it suspended the 285-million-dollar loan promised to Yugoslavia in 1956. Then, at the beginning of June, Khrushchev visited Sofia, and in a long speech condemned Yugoslav revisionism as a Trojan horse in the socialist community; he also suggested that the Yugoslav leaders were engaged in subversive activities against the Communist countries in return for the American aid they were receiving. Khrushchev was no longer bothering to be consistent. He himself had made it clear, in a message to Eisenhower a few weeks earlier, that the U.S.S.R. would willingly accept long-term loans from the United States, and he had closed his eyes to Poland's receipt of American aid.

In his Sofia speech Khrushchev publicly condemned Yugoslavia's role in the Hungarian uprising. During the 'counter-revolutionary *putsch*' of 1956, he said, the Yugoslav embassy in Budapest 'had become the centre for those who were struggling against the Popular Democratic régime', and then 'the place of refuge for the treacherous, capitulationist Imre Nagy–Losonczi group'. From that moment it looked as though Imre Nagy's fate was sealed, especially as the Hungarian party daily *Nepszabadsag* had argued a few days before that 'revisionism inevitably leads to treason, as is shown by the case of Imre Nagy'.

In 1949 the struggle of the orthodox Muscovites against the nationalist heresy had culminated in the trial of the Hungarian Rajk, who represented Tito. In 1958 it was another Hungarian, Imre Nagy, who was chosen as the scapegoat. Everything indicates that the decision to put him on trial and execute him, in spite of Kadar's pledges to the contrary in 1956, was taken, not in Budapest (as it was not in Kadar's interest to shock public opinion), but at an international level, perhaps at the Warsaw

Pact meeting in Moscow at the end of May. It was only out of consideration for the Yugoslavs that the trial, which was demanded particularly vehemently by the Chinese government (no doubt in order to make things still harder for Khrushchev), had been put off for so long. But, now that relations with Yugoslavia had deteriorated, Khrushchev no longer had the will or the desire to protect the man whom he had himself helped to bring to power.

On 17 June 1958 the Hungarian telegraphic agency announced the execution of Nagy and three of his friends. The Peking press rejoiced; Prague, Sofia and Tirana also expressed satisfaction. Poland bowed its head. Hungary, overwhelmed by the loss of some of her best sons, was stupefied, humiliated, and impotent.[4]

As for Khrushchev, Nagy's execution had given the ultimate proof of his orthodoxy, and of his determination to fight revisionism; he did his utmost to bury this judicial crime by making it seem the end of a particular chapter in history rather than a signal for the intensification of the cold war. He attended the East German Party Congress in July 1958 and delivered a long attack on the Yugoslavs, blaming Tito for trying to make mischief between Moscow and Peking. But at the same time he urged the fraternal parties to keep the anti-Yugoslav campaign within reasonable limits. Probably he was already aware that he was the target of Mao Tse-tung's attacks through Tito. In any case, the campaign against Yugoslavia was inconsistent with the 'popular front' tactics once again being employed against Western socialists and progressives and the neutral, socializing countries of the Third World.

For his part, Tito was well informed about the difficulties that had cropped up in Sino-Soviet relations. He foresaw that Khrushchev would need worldwide support, including Yugoslavia's, in this dispute, and therefore he forgave the Soviet leader the insults he had suffered. From October 1958 contact between Moscow and Belgrade was renewed, and their animosity subsided. In the following years Tito worked hard to strengthen his connection with Moscow; he obtained new Western loans, and went on an Afro-Asian tour to reactivate the club of non-committed nations of which, together with Nehru, Nasser and Sukarno, he was one of the principal founder-members.

All-Out Collectivization, without Poland

The most striking expression of the new aggressive line defined by the Moscow conference in 1957 was the resumption in several Eastern countries of agricultural collectivization. This coincided, for a very good reason, with the 'great leap forward' and the people's commune movement in China. The two movements, in fact, reflected the same spirit of continual agitation, stormy progress and permanent revolution, now centred in Peking and not Moscow. But, quite apart from Chinese influence, the plunge into collectivization resulted from the new, dynamic spirit of the European Communist 'counter-reformation'. With the exception of Gomulka, who remained true to his idea of voluntary collectivization, the other Eastern leaders all thought that the moment had arrived – with the revisionists in disarray and retreating – to reduce the last strongholds of private property, whose continued existence they believed to lead to the resurgence of capitalism. For China, the 'great leap' of 1958 also reflected the desire to distinguish herself from the U.S.S.R., and to overtake that country in pursuit of Communism. In the Eastern countries it was more a question of adhering more closely to the Russian pattern.

Russian and Chinese influences were very apparent in Bulgaria where, after collectivization had been carried out, a 'great leap forward' was undertaken in October 1958, raising industrial production targets of 1957–62 between 60 and 100 per cent. Agricultural production was to double in 1959 and treble in 1960 that of 1958, but these targets were not achieved. The government embarked on a large-scale concentration of collective farms, reducing their number from 3,450 to 680, with an average size of 7,000 hectares. As in Peking, officials were required to undertake a thirty to forty-day stint of manual work, and these measures were accompanied by reforms based on the 'Sovnarkhoz' administrative reform in the Soviet Union by Khrushchev in 1957.

In Hungary more than 60 per cent of the collective farms had been disbanded in 1956; after the rising, these amounted to only 10 per cent of the arable land. As Kadar's main concern had been to neutralize the peasantry, he had shelved collectivization, and gone so far as to abolish compulsory state deliveries. However, by the end of 1958 the government already felt secure enough to resume collectivization. Some leftist elements, headed by the pro-Chinese Dogei, wanted to speed up the movement; the right wing of the party feared economic repercussions and pointed to the caution exercised by the Poles. Kadar took up a middle position; he decided to carry out collectivization through a judicious mixture of persuasion and force. By 1961 the greater part of the land had become collective property.

It was the same in East Germany: by 1960 the proportion of collective land had been raised from 38 to 80 per cent. In Rumania this was achieved by 1962.

The Chinese were proud of the impulse they had given to this new advance in socialization, based on a principle dear to Mao: politics first, production next. But, while West European agricultural production rose by 25 per cent between 1945 and 1960, that of the Eastern countries remained roughly at the pre-war level.

Mao tried to get the People's Democracies to go even further. In June 1960, at the opening of a horticultural exhibition in East Germany, the Peking delegate suggested people's communes, 'the highest form of the agricultural production co-operative', as a model for all Communist countries, but this was politely rejected.

We have already mentioned that Poland remained outside the movement. In 1957, only 1,700 out of over 10,000 collectives registered a year earlier remained; 87 per cent of the arable land was in the hands of private peasants, 12 per cent in state farms, and only 1 per cent in Soviet-type collective farms. Nothing, in fact, was more alien to Gomulka's temperament than the large-scale, sudden upheavals promoted by Peking, but while the Soviets criticized the people's communes as an anti-Marxist experiment, Gomulka regarded them as a phenomenon peculiar to the historical development of China. Neither did he share the view of Khrushchev and the other Communist leaders that agricultural collectivization was essential for the consolidation of the socialist régime. Thus, while joining in the unitarian, anti-revisionist movement of 1957–9, Poland continued to follow its own middle, semi-orthodox, semi-heretical course within the bloc.[5]

7

The Moscow–Peking Conflict and the People's Democracies

The Moscow conference in 1957 reconciled two opposing attitudes: the Soviets' peaceful coexistence and the total, anti-imperialist war of the Chinese. The synthesis, however, did not survive for long. It turned out to be harder to harmonize Soviet and Chinese interests than had been anticipated.

The Chinese did not find Moscow so sympathetic towards their territorial claims in Formosa and India as they had expected; Soviet economic aid seemed inadequate to them; refusal to give them the atomic bomb annoyed them intensely; and they could not tolerate Khrushchev's presumptuous claim to speak for the whole community, or his policy of rapprochement with the United States. In view of the basic conservatism of the Soviet leadership at the time, Mao became more and more convinced that it was he and People's China who represented the revolutionary Marxist-Leninist tradition. Of course, the U.S.S.R. was far more advanced technologically, industrially and militarily, but Peking was now the repository of the revolutionary ideal and theory. Underlying the ideological offensive launched by Mao in April 1960 with the publication of his pamphlet *Long Live Leninism!* is a basic confidence in the power of doctrine. Mao identified himself with Lenin in his struggle against the opportunists of the Second International. Like Lenin he did not allow the fact that he was in a minority to deter him, but counted on winning over the majority by sheer persuasion and by virtue of the truth that had been vouchsafed him.

However, it became clear fairly soon that the determinant of the attitudes of the various East European Communist governments to the Moscow–Peking quarrel was not ideological but the interests of the leaders. Hence the tendency generally to espouse the Soviet cause, while also trying to make use of the quarrel between the giants to enlarge their own sphere of freedom.

Khrushchev's policy of coexistence was more in accordance with the interests of the Eastern countries than the total war advocated by the Chinese. In effect, Soviet policy in Europe was basically defensive, and aimed at the maintenance of the status quo, and consequently the preservation and consolidation of the Communist régimes that had developed from the Second World War.

Chinese policy, on the other hand, was expansive. It meant taking risks that the Eastern governments did not feel were justifiable; in fact, it boiled down to using the U.S.S.R. and her European dependencies as an auxiliary force in the struggle with the United States, which China wanted to assume a more dynamic, aggressive form. Nevertheless, the Eastern leaders' basic agreement with Soviet foreign policy aims was qualified by a certain fear (especially among the East Germans and Poles) of some East–West, Moscow–Washington, Moscow–Bonn, or Moscow–Belgrade deal at their expense. To ensure against such an eventuality, they welcomed any external support, including support from China, which eagerly took up the role of champion of community interests as a whole against the egotistic interests of the U.S.S.R.[1]

Thus, from 1958, and increasingly after 1964, the Kremlin was subject to pressures from East Berlin and Warsaw for a tougher West German policy. These pressures, however, would probably not have had much effect had not China been at the same time harassing, obstructing, and restraining the U.S.S.R.

The Eastern leaders (with the exception of the Albanians, for whom 'coexistence' meant the realization of their worst fears – rapprochement with Yugoslavia) were aware that their relationship with the Soviet Union was basically one of dependence. Gomulka gave clear evidence of this in January 1963 when, at the East German Party Congress, he declared: 'No Communist country could hold out against capitalist pressure without the Soviet Union.' At the 1957 conference Mao Tse-tung had given this as the reason for his support for the U.S.S.R.'s leading role. Since then, however, his views, always fluid in this matter, had changed. Under the present circumstances, he felt that the Soviet Union would offer him an atomic shield in the sole eventuality of unprovoked war with the United States. However, the Chinese Communist régime seemed to him sufficiently well established already to be able to withstand the consequences of isolation. The Eastern countries were much more vulnerable in this respect (although the Rumanians, for example, and then the Czechs gradually realized they were less so than the others).

The need for protection, however, does not imply a willingness to be submissive. With the exception of Novotny and Zhivkov, wholehearted pro-Soviets, no leader of the People's Democracies wished to return to the centralized discipline of the recent past. They were all anxious to preserve the greater or lesser degree of autonomy gained since Stalin's death, due partly to Chinese (and Yugoslav) pressure. And they were all afraid that Moscow might try to reassert her hegemonic control indirectly, through her condemnation of Chinese aberrancy and nationalism; this explains why the East European Communist leaders, again with the exception of Novotny and Zhivkov, while officially supporting Moscow, did not hesitate to obstruct Khrushchev, if cautiously, when he pressed for China's excommunication.

In fact, it was not to the advantage of the Eastern countries for the Soviets to come to terms with Chinese dogmatism, which would have left them free to deal with their recalcitrant European allies, or to reject it entirely, which would have impelled them to seek compensation in the West. The real hope for the East lay in the prolongation of the conflict; if, on the one hand, China's unrelenting theoretical assault 'inhibited' the Soviet Union from evolving in a revisionist direction, on the other, it made her more sensitive to charges of hegemonism, and forced her to pay with new concessions for positive evidence on the disinterest of her internationalism.

Thus the Eastern countries had certain interests in common with China in her struggle with Soviet imperialism, and it would have been surprising if this had not been reflected in some form in their policy. When Mao Tse-tung, in conversation with Japanese socialists in the summer of 1964, allowed himself to condemn Russian annexations in even harsher terms than would have been used in Washington and Paris, on recalling that Bessarabia was torn from Rumania, and that East German territories were given to Poland, an indignant chorus, particularly from East Germany, supported Moscow's protest. Such remarks would only benefit Bonn; but the Rumanians could scarcely conceal their pleasure.[2]

The Eastern countries were as dependent on the U.S.S.R. economically as they were politically, though some were in the process of carefully freeing themselves. Most of their trade was with the Soviet Union; the aid they hoped to receive in the form of loans and investment was incomparably more than China could offer those who chose her fellowship (with the exception of tiny Albania, whose needs were easily satisfied). In any case, the Soviet model, with all her faults, bitterly experienced by the Eastern countries, was more congenial, especially since strenuous efforts were made to improve it, than the Chinese, however fascinating it might have seemed.

Peking's extreme demands tended to repel the Eastern countries back to the Soviet Union. Eastern Europe had played a not inconsiderable (and not unprofitable) part in the industrialization of China. But from 1958 the Chinese began to demand an appreciable increase in aid, without taking account of the pressures on East European governments to satisfy the growing needs of their own peoples. The Russians and the Czechs accused the Chinese of wanting to obstruct the development of the more advanced countries to enable the Asiatic People's Republics to catch up.

However, the most industrialized Eastern countries, notably the G.D.R. and Czechoslovakia, were not overjoyed at the prospect of being forced to sacrifice a satisfactory customer from solidarity with the Soviet Union. Pankow, the seat of government in East Berlin, was particularly sensitive to the gains West German trade might make as a result of a deterioration in Sino-East German relations, and thus favoured a moderate policy towards China. Nor could the bloc countries remain indifferent to the positive effects of China's stubborn struggle against the U.S.S.R.'s colonial methods of exploitation, including the pressure she exerted in order to 'buy cheap and sell dear'. Peking tried to exploit Rumanian displeasure at Khrushchev's concept of the 'international division of labour' and 'specialization', in voicing aloud what the satellites only dared to whisper: she condemned the U.S.S.R.'s 'national egotism', which 'requires that the fraternal countries fulfil her needs unilaterally', and demanded that 'economic co-operation be based on the principles of complete equality and reciprocal advantages'. The Chinese had done all the U.S.S.R.'s allies an immeasurable service.[3] They showed the East European countries the way, providing them, especially the Rumanians, with the theoretical arguments upon which to base their defence of the right to a diversified economy.

On the whole, Peking's challenge to Moscow's political and economic domination, under the right conditions, could have furthered the cause of the emancipation of the Eastern countries more effectively than little Yugoslavia's rebellion against Stalin in 1948 had been able to do. Even the most Stalinist leaders – Ulbricht, Novotny, Zhivkov, Gheorghiu Dej, all of whom in 1956–7 had supported Mao – now recognized the need for a change in methods, for the régime to be adapted to changing political and economic circumstances. Their main concern was that they themselves should be allowed to determine how quickly and in what manner Khrushchevist reform was to be implemented, without interference from the Soviet Union. It was not too hard for them to repudiate Stalin, provided they kept their position and authority, and these Moscow, in the light of the 1956 experience, was willing to concede them. Finally, the people of the Eastern countries reproached Khrushchev not for having unmasked Stalin, but for having stopped half-way. They were, to say the least, not opposed to revisionism; they preferred the prospect of a 'goulash socialism', as propounded by Khrushchev in Budapest in 1964, to that of the permanent revolution (with poverty and terror) implicit in Mao's purist doctrine. There were far fewer 'Chinese' in the Eastern parties than in the more bourgeois parties of France and Italy.[4]

Albanian Stalinism

Alone among the European socialist countries, Albania came down wholly on China's side, after breaking completely with the Soviet Union two years before the Moscow–Peking conflict was made public. More than any of the other satellite leaders, the Albanians feared that they might be sacrificed on the altar of coexistence, and that they might be used for bargaining in a Soviet rapprochement with Yugoslavia and Greece. Since 1955 Enver Hoxha had been subjected to almost continual pressure from Moscow to change his policy, and in April 1956 he was nearly ousted by supporters of Khrushchev. Since that period Hoxha had placed himself under the protection of Mao Tse-tung, who sympathized with his Stalinism and fervent anti-Titoism. When the time of decision came, in 1960, honour as much as personal and perhaps national interest impelled Hoxha to give his entire allegiance to Mao.

His choice was the easier in view of the somewhat primitive social and economic conditions in Albania. The curtailment of Russian, Czech, Bulgarian and other subsidies, which had enabled the country to survive and even develop slowly, was a blow, but the transition to Chinese aid did not present insuperable problems for either side. Albania's territorial security was still guaranteed, paradoxically enough, by the interest of her neighbours – Yugoslavia, Greece and Italy – in maintaining the *status quo* rather than effecting a partition which would bring them face to face with each other. And in his opposition to the Yugoslavs and defiance of the Russians, Hoxha could call on his countrymen's patriotism and their love of a good fight, and thereby increase his own popularity. It was in this way that he managed to introduce Stalinism and Maoism.

But one must not forget that it was ultimately the Russians who forced this choice on the Albanians; Hoxha tried to avoid a break for a long time. He only wanted to get himself into a better bargaining and blackmailing position with Peking's support. The split was precipitated by Khrushchev's humiliating, indeed Stalinistic, methods in trying to obtain an unconditional surrender.

In June 1959, accompanied by Marshal Malinovsky, Khrushchev visited Tirana. There were spectacular demonstrations of friendship. Soviet economic aid was increased, and Khrushchev once more stressed Albania's strategic importance, threatening in a published speech to install rocket bases there, as in Bulgaria, if Greece and Italy admitted United States bases.

Nevertheless, clouds appeared on the horizon as early as autumn 1959. The Kremlin was displeased with the 'Chinese' tone of certain declarations and articles coming from Tirana. In January 1960 Mikoyan paid a secret visit there with the object, according to the Chinese later on, of turning the Albanian party against China. It was probably this visit that caused a ferment in the Albanian leadership. A number of individuals – Liri Belishova, her husband Mazo Como, Rear Admiral Sejko, and the chairman of the Control Commission, Koco Tasko – protested against Hoxha's unilaterally pro-Chinese course, and warned the party against the consequences of a conflict with the U.S.S.R. Hoxha was not unaware that his critics were acting with the Kremlin's approval, if not actually on its instructions. He reacted with his customary speed and ferocity, denouncing the rebels and expelling them from the Central Committee.

It was while this was going on that Khrushchev, heading a Soviet delegation to Bucharest to attend the Rumanian Party Congress, tried to take advantage of the presence of representatives of most of the parties for holding an impromptu secret conference to condemn Chinese 'sapping activities'. On the eve of the meeting he had a newsletter circulated among the delegations which criticized bluntly Mao Tse-tung's theses in Long Live Leninism!, which had been widely distributed throughout Communist countries. Then, at the secret meeting, Khrushchev condemned Mao's nationalism, adventurism and Trotskyism with unprecedented vehemence. The Peking representative, Peng Chen, at this time considered the leader of the 'hard-liners' in the Chinese party, but superseded and denounced as an opportunist and revisionist in May 1966, stood up bravely to Khrushchev and the delegates of the fraternal parties. Only the Albanian delegate, Hysni Kapo, rose in his defence, protesting against the 'putsch-like' tactics of the Soviet leader to get the Chinese position censured by the conference.[5]

The Albanians' open support of the Chinese seemed to Khrushchev the height of insolence. On 13 August he summoned Hoxha to Moscow, but, no doubt with the support of Peking, Hoxha declined the invitation. Shortly afterwards Maurice Thorez visited Tirana to try to influence Hoxha, but was shown out.

The tension between the U.S.S.R and Albania became apparent at the General Assembly of the United Nations in September 1960. Khrushchev appeared in the company of Kadar, Zhivkov, Novotny and Gheorghiu Dej. Hoxha's representative, Mehmet Shehu, was boycotted. This was all the more striking because Khrushchev, meeting Tito for the first time since 1957, embraced him. Nevertheless, Hoxha and Shehu, president of the Albanian council, went to Moscow at the beginning of November to attend the conference of the eighty-one Communist and workers' parties, which, in the absence of Mao, was electrified by the Sino-Soviet dispute. They were invited to come before the meeting opened, the appointment being fixed for 9 November and then postponed for three days. According to Khrushchev, Hoxha and Shehu behaved like 'provocateurs' during this discussion. According to Hoxha, Khrushchev in a fit of fury said to him: 'I find it easier to get on with Macmillan than with you.'

Hoxha took the stand on 16 November. Never before had the Soviet leadership been subjected, in its own house as it were, to such a violent and furious onslaught. Hoxha echoed the most radical Chinese views in criticizing the decisions of the Twentieth Congress, de-Stalinization, and the principles on which Khrushchev's foreign policy was based. But the major sensation came when he spoke of Soviet-Albanian relations. He accused the Russians of seeking revenge for the pro-Chinese attitude of the Albanian representative at the Bucharest conference by refusing to deliver the 10,000 tons of wheat promised to Albania when she was suffering from an unusually severe drought. 'This pressure is intolerable. Soviet rats have food, but Albanians are dying of starvation.' Hoxha also accused the Russians of having interfered crudely in the affairs of the Albanian party, so as to force it to choose, in Khrushchev's words, 'between the 200 million Russians and 650 million Chinese'.

The first speaker after Hoxha, Luigi Longo, the head of the Italian delegation, described the Albanian leader's words as 'not only disloyal but also infantile', and Thorez declared: 'The members of our delegation have listened to [Hoxha's] speech with a feeling of shame. As militant Communists, they have never heard such language, either in their party meetings or in the meetings of the international Communist party ... The path followed by the delegation of the Albanian party is a very dangerous one ...'

The following day Hoxha and Shehu 'made a spectacular exit from the conference, indicating their refusal to consider the collective views of the fraternal parties', according to Khrushchev at the Twenty-Second Congress.

Even though the conference ended – after extensive bargaining – in an ephemeral Sino-Soviet compromise, Soviet-Albanian relations remained thoroughly bad. On 21 December 1960, Tirana, in a new challenge to Khrushchev, ostentatiously celebrated the anniversary of Stalin's birth. Moscow tried to bring Albania to heel by applying greater economic pressure. At the beginning of 1961, Soviet specialists working in Albanian industry were recalled, as they had been from China the previous summer. Economic negotiations between the two countries were suspended, Moscow having decided that the new agreement should be discussed 'at top party and governmental level', in effect calling on Hoxha to make a journey of penance. 'The Soviet government is treating these matters in an incorrect fashion, in a spirit alien to that which should inform relations between socialist countries. We cannot accept', came the Albanian Central Committee's reply.

In February 1961, at the Albanian Party Congress, the Kremlin was represented by P. Pospelov, who castigated dogmatism and sectarianism and appealed for unity. The Congress responded by applauding Stalin's name. The Chinese delegate, alone among the guests, gave his unequivocal approval to Hoxha's 'doctrinal purity'. On 26 April Kosygin, then First Deputy Prime Minister, officially notified the Albanian government of the termination of Soviet aid. 'The Soviet people and the peoples of other socialist countries would not understand if we were to continue to deprive our own country of material resources in order to satisfy the needs of the Albanian leaders, who are jeopardizing the interests of their peoples by ignoring the elementary rules of conduct in their relations with the Soviet Union and her government.' The Albanians protested against 'the extension of ideological differences . . . into economic or political and military spheres'. On the eve of the Twenty-Second Soviet Congress they sent a letter to the Central Committee, to be elected by the Congress, condemning 'the crude, anti-Marxist activity of N. Khrushchev and his group'.

The Albanians took steps to ensure that their charges were brought to the notice of the leaders of the fraternal parties; and the Chinese did not seek to hide the fact that they agreed with Tirana. Khrushchev, therefore, knew that his silence would be taken for a sign of weakness. He also wanted to show the Chinese leaders that, however great his desire to prevent a break, he was no longer prepared to tolerate the damaging propaganda they were still pouring out against his person and policy.

This, no doubt, was why he decided to make an example of the Albanians, and to condemn them, and through them the Chinese, from the rostrum of the Twenty-Second Congress. 17 October 1961 is a date to remember. It was the day when Khrushchev, in denouncing the anti-Soviet attitude of the Albanian leaders, initiated the great split in the Communist movement. Three days later Chou En-lai spelt it out for Khrushchev's benefit. 'Any public and unilateral condemnation of a fraternal party', he declared didactically, 'is an attack on the unity of the socialist camp. One cannot regard the disclosure to the enemy of discussions between fraternal parties as showing a proper Marxist-Leninist attitude.' The same day the Albanian Central Committee, in a declaration published in Tirana, went further, accusing Khrushchev of having 'rudely violated the 1960 Moscow declaration', which provided for fraternal exchanges to settle disputes between the parties. 'We shall not retreat, and we shall not give way before the slanderous attacks, blackmail and pressure of N. Khrushchev or others.'

In his closing speech on 27 October Khrushchev answered Chou, who meanwhile had left Moscow for Peking, after placing a huge wreath on Stalin's tomb. 'We share the anxiety of our

Chinese comrades; we appreciate their concern for the strengthening of unity', declared Khrushchev. 'If the Chinese comrades were prepared to use their influence to normalize relations between the Albanian party and the fraternal parties, it is highly unlikely that we should find anyone better qualified to bring this task to a successful conclusion.' He then launched into a fresh diatribe against the Albanians, who 'keep themselves in power through violence and arbitrary behaviour' and have produced 'an abnormal and unhealthy atmosphere' in the party. 'The day will come when the Albanian Communists, the Albanian people, will have their say. The Albanian leaders will then have to answer for all the harm they have done their country and their people.'

This was the signal for wild disputes to commence, anticipating the verbal battles in the Sino-Soviet dispute two years later. The Albanian ambassador in Moscow had circulated the documents relating to the quarrel, and the Soviet government decided to break off diplomatic relations with Albania. It was thus once more demonstrated that the adoption of the socialist system did not automatically make relations between countries more brotherly. Stalin and Beria had been accused of bringing about the 1949 Soviet-Yugoslav split through despotic methods that had nothing to do with socialism. Now, Khrushchev, the de-Stalinizer, Stalin's and Beria's accuser, was himself instrumental in bringing about a new diplomatic break between two socialist countries, and furthermore after a Congress where he had reactivated the campaign against Stalin and the Stalinists, to silence his enemies at home.[6]

As early as the Bucharest conference the Chinese had taken Khrushchev to task for his 'patriarchal, arbitrary and despotic attitude' in the discussion. In fact, Marxist-Leninist ideology did not make it easy to settle differences; on the contrary, the contradictory interpretations it provoked, and the doctrinal passions it aroused, complicated the task of arriving at a straightforward settlement. The Kremlin's 'papism' – its claims to the spiritual leadership of the world Communist movement – made its 'caesarism', its claim to the leadership of the alliance of socialist countries, more inflexible and more intolerant. The recalcitrant ally was treated first and foremost as a heretic. The Soviet government's theoretical acknowledgement, as in its declaration of 30 October 1956, of the equality and independence of the Communist parties and governments made little difference; there was still a large gap between theory and practice.

Albania, for her part, exchanged her status as a Soviet satellite for dependence on China. For the Chinese the maintenance of dissident Albania was a matter of prestige: they had to show that they were able to support their adherents, and ensure that they did not drift into the enemy camp, as did Yugoslavia.

In February 1961, therefore, they made Tirana a loan of 125 million dollars for the purchase of industrial equipment. Together with the previous loan of 13.75 million dollars, this bridged the gap produced by the cancellation of Soviet and East European agreements.[7] Soviet technologists were replaced by Chinese technicians, and China's share in Albania's trade rose from 4.3 per cent in 1960 to 46.6 per cent in 1964. Poor at the start, the country remained poor, effectively sealed against all Western and even East European influences. But her leaders gained great satisfaction from being linked with the 'great Chinese brother', from being the bridge-head in Europe and the spokesman at the U.N. of that revolutionary spirit whose victory, so they believed, could not be long in coming. It is this waiting for the day of judgement that gives the austere, stagnant, regimented life imposed on the Albanians by their leaders its quasi-religious character. In no other Communist country is the contrast between advanced theory and backward living conditions so striking as in Enver Hoxha's.

Rumania's Disengagement

Albania's dissent was precipitated by the Kremlin's drive for ideological unification, provoked by the Chinese challenge. Rumania's disengagement and gradual emancipation, the development of what might be called her 'national Communism', was based on opposition to the Kremlin's policy of economic integration. Its de-satellization was more remarkable in that the country was an immediate neighbour of the Soviet Union, and for the first fifteen post-war years had seemed the most submissive and the most loyal of her satellites. Coming after the break with Yugoslavia and Albania, Rumania's own 'uncoupling' showed that, in the long term, 'the Balkanization of Communism has prevailed over the Communization of the Balkans', in Pierre Hassner's words.[8]

Undoubtedly ideological and personal factors, which were the basis of Albanian dissent, also played some part in the case of Rumania. Like Enver Hoxha, the Rumanian leaders had been subjected to pressure from Khrushchev with regard to de-Stalinization. Dej's skill in safeguarding his own position, giving verbal approval to the Soviets and then going his own way, has already been mentioned. Thanks to the purges of 1952, and subsequently those of 1957, the chief of the Rumanian party and government succeeded in consolidating his team, and was one of the first satellite statesmen to see the possibility of exploiting the Sino-Soviet conflict to gain a better position for himself and his country, initially in the economic sphere and then, in J. F. Brown's words, 'going from brilliant improvisation to brilliant improvisation', in the spheres of culture and foreign policy.

It was in 1961 that the economic ambitions of Bucharest clashed directly with Soviet ideas on the subject. At the Moscow conference in August, Khrushchev, goaded by the success of the Common Market and worried by the appearance of centrifugal tendencies, proposed turning the Council of Mutual Economic Aid (Comecon), established in 1949, into a real instrument for planning, specialization, and the international division of labour.

Contrary to what was believed in the West, until that time the economies of the Eastern countries had developed on an independent basis, but were tied together – and to the Soviet Union – by more or less long-term commercial agreements. On the Soviet model, each country strove to industrialize, to make itself increasingly self-sufficient, without paying much attention to the profitability of the newly created industries. Thus Rakosi and Geroe had wanted to turn Hungary into a country 'of iron and steel'. Rumanian planning followed the same course, with the difference that the country's mineral resources enabled it to develop very rapidly. In 1958 industrial production had risen by the record figure of 9.5 per cent over 1957 (whereas a rise of only 7.5 per cent had been forecast). The government forecast a rise of 10 per cent for 1959, and that figure also was exceeded: the increase was in the region of 11.1 per cent, and steel production increased by 52 per cent. In June 1960, at the Third Party Congress, Dej, in Khrushchev's presence, announced proudly: 'Our country has taken a gigantic step forward on the path of economic and social development; it has laid the foundations for even more rapid progress.' The experts had just prepared a new and extremely ambitious five-year plan aiming at more than doubling 1959 industrial production by 1965. In addition to the construction of a large steel-works in Galati (producing four million tons per year), the new plan envisaged the development of the chemical and ship-building industries, and the manufacture of such equipment as machine-tools, tractors, oil installations.

However, just as the Rumanians were about to put their plan into action, Khrushchev came to the conclusion that the Communist countries could not compete successfully with the West unless they specialized to some extent, and this could be brought about only through planning above national level. The experts of East Berlin and Prague had suggested such a course as early as 1958, for East Germany and Czechoslovakia had everything to gain by obstructing the development of competitive industries in the more backward countries. Their delegates therefore enthusiastically supported the integrationist proposals put forward by Khrushchev in August 1961 and then at the Comecon summit conference in June 1962. The Bulgarians and Poles were less forthcoming. The Chinese pricked up their ears from afar. From that moment the division between the more or less developed countries in Comecon and the underdeveloped ones could no longer be ignored. Rumania, despite its progress, was still underdeveloped. Her *per capita* industrial production in 1962 was only 36 per cent of East Germany's. In that year the Rumanian national income *per capita* had risen to 45 per cent of Czechoslovakia's and East Germany's.[9] According to her economists, acceptance of the Soviet plans for integration would have kept Rumania in an unfavourable position in relation to the more developed bloc countries, which were accused of selling the Rumanians industrial products and equipment, which were frequently inferior, at higher than the world market prices. At successive meetings of Comecon in November and December 1962 the Rumanian experts successfully resisted Soviet, Czech and East German pressure.

In March 1963 the Central Committee of the Rumanian party, acting on information received from the government's delegate to the Comecon Council, Alexandru Birladeanu, on the latest developments in the debate on integration, unanimously approved the stand taken by its representatives, emphasizing that Rumania intended basing her co-operation with the other socialist countries 'on the principles of national sovereignty and independence, equality of rights, fraternal aid and mutual interest'. These principles were, of course, written into the declaration of the eighty-one Communist parties at the 1960 conference in Moscow, but the Rumanian use of them was nevertheless political dynamite. It expressed their determination to develop a nationally oriented policy within the socialist camp, on the premise that the aim of turning Rumania into a powerful member of the Communist bloc in no way contradicted Marxist internationalism.

At length, at the summit conference of leaders of the Comecon countries in Moscow during July 1963, the Rumanians won their case. Faced by a Rumanian veto, the Soviets and their supporters agreed to shelve the plans for economic integration; the communiqué issued at the close of this meeting stated that bilateral preliminary consultation on long-term economic co-operation constituted the best basis for co-ordination of plans. This was precisely what the Rumanians were arguing.

Gheorghiu Dej had pulled off a brilliant coup. He had prevented Comecon from being transformed into a supranational authority, and thereby had created a precedent for the economic (and later political) restructuring of the whole bloc. If the Chinese destroyed Soviet dominance of the international Communist movement in 1957,[10] the Rumanians six years later signalled the disintegration of Soviet dominance in Eastern Europe.

At another time the Soviets would not have taken this so passively, but at the end of 1962 and the beginning of 1963 Khrushchev had good reason to exercise moderation and avoid any new scandal. The repercussions of the Caribbean crisis had not yet died down; relations with China were at the breaking point; and economic and political reprisals against Albania had had no effect. Under these circumstances, the Soviet Union had limited means at her disposal to bring Rumania under control. The use of military force, as in the case of Hungary in 1956, was out of the question, since the Rumanian challenge did not immediately affect Soviet strategic interests. Greater economic pressure would have led the Rumanians either to follow Albania's example or, much more likely, to throw themselves into the arms of the West, with whom they had gradually been resuming commercial relations since 1959. In fact, the risks the Rumanians were taking were no greater than those being taken at the same time by De Gaulle's France in opposing American supremacy. In both cases, a particular situation was promoted, if not actually produced, by an international *détente* that enabled the two countries to attain a measure of independence without immediately jeopardizing their position.

It was, as we know, the Moscow nuclear agreement signed at the end of July 1963 that led to the disruption of party contacts between Moscow and Peking. Rumania supported Moscow over this agreement, though without great enthusiasm. But, unlike all the other European Communist countries, Rumania abstained from the violent polemics over a pact that Mao regarded as an attempt to obstruct China's achievements of nuclear status. Her neutral position had become evident as early as 1963, when Peking issued the famous twenty-five 'propositions' summarizing China's grievances against Moscow's position in a most unflattering tone. There were obvious allusions in this document to the dispute between Bucharest and Moscow over economic integration, and while all the other Eastern Communist countries ignored it – it was banned in the U.S.S.R. – the Rumanian press published lengthy extracts. And, whereas the Soviet Union and her followers appreciably reduced their trade with China, Rumania's increased after 1962. In March 1963 Bucharest resumed diplomatic relations with Albania; these had been virtually defunct since the Soviet-Albanian split of late 1961.

Thus, in the increasingly bitter Sino-Soviet conflict the Rumanians took up a position much like that of the Vietnamese, anxious to maintain good relations with both contestants. In an article published in *Problems of Peace and Socialism* in November 1963, Prime Minister Maurer, while supporting the Soviet foreign policy aims of peaceful coexistence, condemned open, abusive polemics, from whatever source, and advocated reconciliation through patient, courteous negotiation. When in February 1964 the Soviets were about to disclose the contents of a report by Suslov to the Central Committee on the quarrel with China, which urged an 'emphatic rebuff to the schismatic actions' of the Chinese, the Rumanians intervened, asking the Kremlin to postpone publication of the report, and to await the results of a final attempt at reconciliation that they themselves had offered to make in Peking. Maurer then visited Mao Tse-tung, who received him in a very friendly fashion but remained obstinate. But even this failure did not lead the Rumanians to abandon their conciliatory attitude. They continued to oppose the international conference advocated by the Kremlin to excommunicate China, though most of the other People's Democracies except Yugoslavia had agreed.

Gheorghiu Dej had good reason to fear that the condemnation and isolation of China would mark the first stage in the establishment of a greater degree of discipline and cohesion in the bloc. This fear was shared by Gomulka, Togliatti and other Communist leaders, although not so acutely. Dej's response to Soviet pressure was to get his Central Committee to pass a resolution which, when published in Bucharest on 27 April 1964, was at once regarded as a virtual declaration of independence.

The Rumanian document echoed the Peking 'propositions' of a year earlier. But the calm objectivity of the Bucharest leaders in stating their views prevented the Soviets from denouncing them publicly, particularly as each of their offending remarks was accompanied by protestations of friendship and professions of faith in Marxism-Leninism. Khrushchev's pressure and his attempt to stimulate opposition to Gheorghiu Dej within the party leadership simply resulted in the Rumanian leader's refusing to take part in the 'family reunion' in Moscow to celebrate Khrushchev's seventieth birthday in April. Tito, after a brief encounter with Khrushchev in Leningrad in June 1964, visited

Dej in Timisoara and apparently unsuccessfully tried to reconcile the two men. Nevertheless, the Rumanians were as careful as the Soviets to prevent this personal quarrel from affecting intergovernmental relations. Maurer was warmly received in the U.S.S.R. in July, after his spectacular visit to Paris. Then the Soviets sent Mikoyan to attend the twentieth anniversary celebrations of the liberation of Rumania. He, as it were, set the seal on Rumanian claims by stressing that 'the friendship and co-operation between the peoples and parties of the Soviet Union and the People's Republic of Rumania are based on the inviolable Marxist-Leninist principles of socialist internationalism, mutual respect for national independence and sovereignty, equality of rights, and [most important of all for the Rumanians] non-interference in internal affairs'.

The more independently Dej acted (already in May 1964 he had sent the economist Gaston Marin on a mission to the United States), the more his country approved of him. This encouraged him to extend the movement into the cultural sphere. Historians were urged to rewrite the history of the country's liberation, drawing attention to the role of the resistance and the part played by Rumanian troops in the war against the Nazis. In September 1963 the Rumanian government closed down the Maxim Gorky Institute, the main centre for the diffusion of Russian culture in Rumania. The Russian language ceased to be compulsory in schools, and was given the same status as the other important languages. In 1964, no doubt in response to Soviet pressure on behalf of the maltreated Hungarian minority in Transylvania, Bucharest reopened the question of Bessarabia, and published a forgotten work of Marx condemning tsarist annexationism. She did not wish to be associated in Mao's fulminations against the Soviet Union but simply to state her views in a less inflammatory historical form.

Even with Gheorghiu Dej gone, Rumania will doubtless remain a People's Democracy run by its Communist party. But the party, which has more than doubled in size between 1955 and 1966 as a result of the rise of a new generation, is adopting a patriotic outlook. It no longer regards itself as the 'Rumanian detachment of the Muscovite International', but as a native body, the highly integrated instrument of Rumanian nationalism and Rumanian greatness. In propaganda, in education, in everyday behaviour, the focus is shifting imperceptibly from bloc solidarity to national interest, while attendant philosophy has led to a rejection of the Stalinist practices of the very man who set the whole movement going – Gheorghiu Dej. There was a similar transformation in Yugoslavia, but there ideological fervour to create a new political and economic model in place of the obsolete Stalinist one took precedence, whereas the Rumanians are less interested in theory than in pragmatic action.

Gheorghiu Dej certainly drew his inspiration from Tito, but he ended by being even more flexible. In fact, Rumania's gradual disengagement from her subordinate position, the achievement of Gheorghiu Dej and his main associates, Maurer and Ceausescu, who were to take up where he left off, is a remarkable example of diplomatic plain-speaking and perseverance allied to an astonishing sense of just how far it is possible to go.[11]

8

Liberalization under Khrushchev

Albania's disenchantment and Rumania's gradual disengagement were largely brought about by the Sino-Soviet conflict, and especially the Soviet Union's attempt to strengthen its ideological and economic hold over the recalcitrant People's Democracies. But the two instances remained isolated; the other Eastern countries aligned themselves with the U.S.S.R. in the dispute. This is not to say that their leaders did not try to strengthen or increase their freedom of action with regard to Moscow. But their main attention between 1960 and 1964 was not so much national independence as internal political problems and, above all, problems of re-equipment and economic co-operation.

If these countries broadly speaking adopted the Soviet path of Khrushchev, it was because it was appropriate to their level of development and to their particular difficulties. At the Twenty-Second Party Congress in October 1961, Khrushchev gave de-Stalinization a fresh impetus. As Michel Tatu has clearly shown, Khrushchev's concern for his image as the man responsible for the *détente* in internal and foreign affairs was not devoid of any demagogic ulterior motive, and his renewed attacks on Stalinism and the Stalinists just before and during the Twenty-Second Congress were dictated principally by his determination to consolidate his personal position. The methods he used against Molotov and other adversaries, more dangerous because closer to the source of power, remained the old methods of intrigue and denigration. Nevertheless, with all its contradictions and limitations, the policy laid down by the Twenty-Second Congress confirmed the course inaugurated by the Twentieth Congress in 1956, and provided arguments and ideological weapons to all those who, whether for national or for opportunistic reasons, rejected Stalinism and supported liberalization of the party dictatorship.

The liberalizing effect of Soviet policy was particularly felt in Hungary and Czechoslovakia. In the former, Khrushchev's victory at the Twenty-Second Congress, symbolized by the new Soviet party programme, destroyed the last hopes of Kadar's Stalinist opponents for return to power of the Molotovites. In Czechoslovakia it encouraged the reformist elements in the party. In Poland, where de-Stalinization had reached its peak in 1956, it was more a question of maintaining and consolidating the existing position than of going further. The East German leaders were to continue de-Stalinization while limiting reform to the economic sphere. There was a slight improvement in Bulgaria, though it is impossible to speak of a real political and intellectual thaw.

Janos Kadar and the Liberalization of Hungary

Kadar did not wait long after the Congress to embark on the 'new course' which, in practice if not in theory, has turned Hungary into the most liberalized Communist country apart from Poland. The foundation for the fresh policy had been established as early as the Hungarian Party Congress of November–December 1959, from which Kadar, warmly backed by Khrushchev, had emerged in a remarkably stronger position. More than any other Eastern leader Kadar benefited from Khrushchev's friendship, and demonstrated that it was possible to re-establish party authority after the 1956 upheaval without returning to Stalinism. In January 1960 the Hungarian government was reorganized; Kadar resumed the chairmanship of the Council that he had yielded two years earlier to Ferenc Münnich, thereby concentrating party and State power in his own hands, like his Soviet mentors. Kadar chose as his deputy his old centrist colleague Gyula Kallai (who was to replace him as Prime Minister from 1965 to 1967), and dismissed two men who were likely to get in his way, the notoriously incompetent Gyoergy Marosan, and Imre Dogei, the Minister of Agriculture who had made himself unpopular by overdoing collectivization and had a reputation for being a 'pro-Chinese dogmatist'.

Kadar's aim was to build a bridge between the Communist government and the other people (especially the intelligentsia), who had still not forgiven him for the Soviet armed intervention. From 1961 onwards, a number of factors contributed to creating a climate of *détente*. First was the consolidation of the economy. Thanks to Soviet aid and a substantial reduction in armament spending, it was possible to raise the standard of living appreciably : *per capita* income in 1960 was 20 to 35 per cent higher than in 1956. Secondly, the party recovered its lost legions (who numbered 96,000 members in December 1956, 402,000 in December 1959, and 512,000 in December 1962) and a certain unity, though Stalinists and revisionists cancelled each other out, while the majority of the party consisted of pragmatists, if not opportunists. Thirdly, the intellectuals, who since 1955 had considered themselves the mouthpiece of national and democratic aspirations, had developed a more realistic attitude and were open to compromise. In 1962 one of the country's most respected writers Laszlo Nemeth, published a play, *The Journey*, whose hero, an old nationalistic professor, returns from a visit to the Soviet Union convinced that his country must shed its illusions and come to terms with reality, provided the rulers in turn showed as much good will. Not all the intellectuals were in agreement with this point of view, although an increasing number of people understood the folly, and even the risk for the country, of a totally negative attitude. And finally, the Twenty-Third Soviet Congress gave grounds for hope of the possibility of the kind of peaceful national development that Hungary needed so vitally. Paradoxically, Khrushchev, who had been responsible for the 1956 intervention, began to acquire popularity in Hungary three or four years later.

Under these circumstances, Kadar gave the signal for the commencement of the third Hungarian relaxation (the first was in 1953, and the second in 1956) by declaring in an article in *Pravda*[1] : 'Despotism is not a socialist phenomenon', and launching his slogan, 'He who is not against us is for us'.

His liberalization policy contained three important decisions, which together brought about a change in the political climate :

1. The former *kulaks* and well-to-do peasants were allowed to

join the collective farms. This ended the terrible discrimination against these peasants who were often the most efficient but found themselves social outcasts.

2. An end was put to educational discrimination against children of formerly middle-class parents, and even children of the intelligentsia, very few of whom had been able up till then to acquire any higher education.

3. A growing number of non-Communists were appointed to high State and economic positions.

The last of these three measures met with stubborn resistance from the party apparatus, where there were a large number of workers' cadres whose appointments were made from political motives, and not from considerations of efficiency, and who enjoyed considerable support. Yugoslavia had a long experience of this class struggle, and Czechoslovakia was shortly to become acquainted with it. But Kadar and his team, in spite of ties with old comrades, held their ground. 'The party is determined to arrive at a situation where senior positions in industry, agriculture, the civil service and culture are occupied by the most competent people' (Nepszabadsag, 3 June 1962), But control remained in Communist hands, and those in charge of cadre selection tried to take on people who were both qualified and Red.

Nevertheless, relations between Communists and non-Communists gradually improved in the years 1962–3. The intelligentsia benefited most from the new policy, and Kadar did much to conciliate their nationalistic feelings. Most of the writers sentenced after the rising (Dery, Hay, Zelk, Tardos) had been released as a result of the partial amnesty of April 1960. The amnesty of March 1963 freed the best contemporary Hungarian thinker, the sociologist Istvan Bibo, who was Imre Nagy's Secretary of State. A Central Committee decision in August 1962 finally rehabilitated Rajk and 190 other victims of the Rakosi purges; Rakosi, Geroe, and seventeen others chiefly responsible for Stalinism in Hungary were expelled from the party; and Karoly Kiss, chairman of the party Control Commission, was dismissed from his post for opposing de-Stalinization. The new industrial town, Sztalinvaros, was renamed Dunaujvaros. The government became increasingly open-handed in granting foreign visas, and foundations were laid for the resumption of tourism, which was to develop over subsequent years. Censorship was relaxed; publishing houses were permitted to publish a considerable number of translations of Western works; cinema and theatre productions were renewed, and a number of excellent magazines like *Nagyvilag* and *Uj Jras* brought the best works of contemporary world literature before the public.

The Eighth Congress of the Hungarian party in November 1962, a very unspectacular but useful affair, set the official seal on the new course that was already beginning to bear fruit not only inside but also outside the country. At the beginning of 1963 the Hungarian question vanished from the agenda of the United Nations; in July U Thant visited Budapest; in the autumn Kadar was invited to Belgrade and was reconciled with Tito. In September the Hungarian government signed an agreement with the Vatican which, although it left in abeyance the question of Cardinal Mindszenty, who had been in the U.S. embassy since 4 November 1956, settled the appointment of six new bishops and the question of the clergy's oath of loyalty to the government. Thus gradually the Hungarians, defeated in 1956, were granted 'many freedoms, if not freedom itself', in the words of an émigré writer Paul Ignotus; and a Slovak journalist stirred his compatriots' imagination when he wrote: 'There, freedom bears the name of socialism and Kadar is the most popular man in the country.'[2]

A First Relaxation in Czechoslovakia

The development of the People's Democracies is full of paradoxes. As Raymond Aron says, 'there is no apparent correlation between the degree of liberalization and the degree of independence in the field of international politics'.[3] A liberalized but very dependent Hungary bordered on a Rumania that was becoming more and more independent and yet remained relatively immune to liberalizing influences. A comparison of the histories of Hungary and Czechoslovakia in 1960–64 shows that there is no strict causal relationship between the economic situation and the political and cultural temperature; whereas Kadar's experiment in de-Stalinization was made possible by the consolidation of the economy and the party's recovery of its authority, in Czechoslovakia it was the deterioration of the economic situation in 1961–3 which led to a long-overdue relaxation, and in the same period economic difficulties in Poland led to the increasing authoritarianism of the régime.

Until 1961 de-Stalinization in Prague was a matter of speeches and insignificant gestures. In spite of the appointment of a committee in 1956 to review the Stalinist trials of 1949–52, little was done to rehabilitate the purge victims, and even less to punish those responsible, many of whom were still in positions of authority. Of course, it was not so easy to maintain this conservative line; we have already pointed to the growing dissatisfaction of the intellectuals, who deplored the fact that Czechoslovakia was so slow in following Russia's, Poland's, and even Hungary's example.

But these grievances would probably not have had any repercussions if the economic recession had not added to the number of dissatisfied people, which resulted in disagreements in the upper echelons of the party. The rate of increase in production reached its peak in 1960 (11.7 per cent), slowed down in 1961 (8.9 per cent), dropped even further in 1962 (6.2 per cent), and ceased altogether in 1963. Measures of decentralization taken in 1958 to give the economy a fresh boost had turned out to be inadequate, no doubt in failing to give management sufficient incentive to assess demand.[4] The third five-year plan, launched on 1 January 1961, had to be abandoned in the summer of 1962. An interim plan was implemented for 1963, while the general structure of a seven-year plan was worked out. Throughout 1961–2 the industrial centres suffered from meat, vegetable, fruit, and butter shortages, resulting from the collectivization drive of 1959–60 and bad weather.

This halt in expansion in a highly industrialized country, which up till then had been the Communist world's showplace, took the leaders by surprise and shook the popular belief in the superiority of the socialist system. To the upper echelons of the party an opposition apparently began to crystallize around

Rudolf Barak, Minister of the Interior and vice-chairman of the Council, a brilliant, energetic, ambitious man who was reputed to have Khrushchev's ear and to favour reform. The anti-Stalinist resolutions of the Twenty-Second Congress encouraged this faction to move into the offensive.

However, once again, Novotny under pressure displayed his remarkable capacity for survival. Immediately after the Soviet Congress, he came before the Central Committee as the most ardent exponent of Khrushchev's ideas. Announcing the forthcoming demolition of the Stalin monument in Prague, he cast all the blame for the 'violations of legality' on an ageing and ill-advised Gottwald. He stressed that during the great purges he, Novotny, had had no say in the matter. Then in February 1962 he removed Barak from the Ministry of the Interior, a first stage in the process leading to his ultimate arrest in June 1962 on charges of sabotage and illegal use of state property. Barak was accused of having wanted to seize power, and was sentenced to fifteen years in prison by a military court in August 1962. Thus Novotny got rid of his chief rival, who was more dangerous in that, as chairman of the body charged with reviewing the purges, he had amassed a great deal of damaging evidence concerning the part played by Novotny and his friends. The illegal nature of his trial was only acknowledged after the Plenum of April 1968.

Khrushchev, whom Novotny won over by his energetic support of his plans for integration, made no move to save his protégé. But, though he carried the day in Prague, Novotny could not prevent the current of opinion manifested in the intellectual circles of the Slovak party from spreading; reformism here was compounded not only of liberal but of national aspirations as well. The Slovaks, whether Communist or not, could not forgive the centralizing Czechs for having taken advantage of the 1949 Moscow anti-Tito campaign to destroy the last vestiges of Slovak autonomy, won after the war, as the fruit of the defeated but glorious rising in 1944.

The new 1960 constitution, which conferred the title of Socialist Republic on Czechoslovakia in contrast to the more usual description People's Republic accorded to Communist countries other than the Soviet Union, confirmed Slovakia's subordination to Prague, which was the more bitterly resented by most Communists because it put them in a very difficult position with their compatriots, who, although not separatists, had not given up the idea of an autonomous Slovakia within the framework of a Czech-Slovak state. The only chance they had of regaining their popularity was by getting rid of the anti-national opprobrium that clung to them, and the best way of accomplishing this was to secure the political rehabilitation of the Slovak Communist leaders condemned after 1950 on account of their patriotism. With the party vanguard, the intellectuals, as well, the struggle against Stalinism merged with the struggle for the rehabilitation of the autonomist Communists and thereby of Slovak autonomy as such. The battle to make (or remake) Czechoslovakia into a 'state of two nations equal in law' was based on ideas made current at the Twentieth and Twenty-Second Soviet Congresses.

The long-delayed thaw now set in. At the writers' congress in March 1963 the Slovak Communist novelist Ladislav Mnacko delivered a moving speech in which, criticizing himself for having in his time applauded Clementis's and Novomesky's arrests, he urged his fellow-writers to do everything in their power to improve the tenor of public life by 'telling the truth, the whole truth'. A few days later, an article published by the Bratislava *Pravda* demanded the removal of Prime Minister Siroky and others implicated in the purges. While making some concessions, Novotny did his utmost to put a stop to the agitation. He severely reprimanded *Pravda* for having printed the article, and announced that neither Slansky nor the 'bourgeois nationalists' of Bratislava would be rehabilitated. These threats, however, carried no weight. The party had lost control of the writers' union weeklies, *Literarni Noviny* (Prague) and *Kulturny Zivot* (Bratislava); they published jointly a manifesto in May declaring: 'The writers are the living conscience of the nation', and this amounted to setting themselves up as a rival power to the party. It was an outburst of suppressed fury.

In September 1963 the opposition won an important victory: Novotny dismissed Siroky. The new Prime Minister, the Slovak Josef Lenart, was known as a moderate in favour of 'controlled liberalization'. On 22 August 1963 the High Court had delivered its verdict on the rehabilitation of Slansky, Clementis and seventy others. The rehabilitations were incomplete, as the charges of violation of the law and abuse of power against Slansky were upheld. Finally, three months later, the Czech Central Committee admitted that the charge of 'bourgeois nationalism' levelled in 1950 against leaders of the Slovak party and maintained ever since was totally unjustified. The Slovaks had won, and the cause of Slovak autonomy was redeemed. It is true that the victory was far from complete; if the powers of the Slovak National Council (Parliament) were subsequently somewhat enlarged, the important questions were still decided in Prague. But antagonism was reduced in so far as the central authorities henceforth took rather more notice of Slovak demands.

These concessions to Bratislava enabled Novotny to stabilize the situation for a while, as there was a *modus vivendi* between the party and reformist elements. Concessions to the intelligentsia made it possible to halt the process of radicalization. In a few months Czechoslovakia caught up with Poland and Hungary: the powers of the censorship were restricted, contacts with the West facilitated, and artistic activity gradually freed from the impositions of the ideologists. There followed a renaissance in literature, the theatre, cinema and the fine arts. Historians, sociologists and philosophers were able to deal with subjects formerly prohibited.

At the same time, the serious economic situation caused by a balance-of-payments deficit, a fall in the return on investments to a sixth of what it had been in 1950, accumulation of stocks of unsaleable goods, and exhaustion of labour reserves forced the economically as well as ideologically orthodox Novotnyites to initiate a reorganization of the system of planned management. At the beginning of 1963 the economist R. Selucky's attack on the deficiencies of the plan was still being angrily denied by Novotny. A few months later, similar criticism from Eugen Loebl, a rehabilitated Slansky trial victim, and Ota Sik, the new director of the Academy of Sciences' Institute of Economics, was more favourably received. At the end of 1963 a conference of leading economic experts came to the conclusion that the plan must no longer be regarded as an end in itself, but only as a means; that the economy must be governed by the law of supply and demand; that capitalist managerial methods should be pursued; and that economists should be given the task of working out the scientific basis for the government's economic policy. This was the beginning of the long struggle of the liberals for radical reform of the economic structure of the country, a struggle that became central to Czechoslovak political life because of increasing difficulties in the sphere of foreign trade in 1965.

Novotny's tactics in 1963–4 were to make minor concessions and to adopt a more permissive attitude, so as to keep his own power and that of the administration basically intact. But this short-sighted policy of vacillating half measures led to the gradual disintegration of his authority. The President was wide open to criticism. Little by little, even the sphere of international politics came under fire. The official spokesmen still claimed that close economic co-operation with the Soviet Union and the other Communist countries was of critical importance, but they were already admitting, under pressure from the economists, that Czechoslovakia had often been forced to buy too dear and sell too cheap, and that Stalinization had retarded the country's development by preventing it from following the Czechoslovak course projected in 1945. The Czech party supported every Moscow initiative as enthusiastically as ever (especially condemnation of the Chinese heresy), and Novotny (like Kadar) remained a pillar of Khrushchevism to the end, but the official party organ was already coming out against 'satellitism', and noting 'the growing independence of the U.S.S.R.'s partners'. The days of Czech isolationism were numbered. In September 1963 the Minister of Foreign Affairs, Vaclav David, an out-and-out Novotnyite, made an official visit to London, an unprecedented event since 1947. At the same time, the Iron Curtain between Czechoslovakia and Austria was lifted at Bratislava. When it was seen that this could be done without leading to large-scale defection, other crossing-points were established. In 1964, for the first time, 'Visit Czechoslovakia' posters appeared in Western tourist agencies. Kafka was rehabilitated as a Czech writer, but Czechoslovakia herself was no longer imprisoned in that Kafka-like world that had existed for almost fourteen years.[5]

Stabilization and Stagnation in Poland

The Twenty-Second Congress of the Soviet party did not have so profound an effect in Poland as in Hungary and Czechoslovakia. At the most it stimulated intellectuals to reflect even more critically on the origins and social roots of Stalinism. At the very time when the Hungarians found themselves being granted the 'small liberties' of Khrushchevism and the Czechs were being carried away by moral indignation and visions of reform, the Polish régime was hardening into an authoritarian form. There are several reasons for this: the independence won in 1956 meant that Gomulka no longer felt compelled implicitly to follow the erratic course of Soviet policy and, in any case, Poland at the end of 1961 had already attained that degree of liberalization which Russia, Hungary and Czechoslovakia were now approaching; also, the failure of the Polish government to provide the country with a new, viable economic model ruled out any further attempt at democratization, even if Gomulka had wished it. The way Polish policy developed between 1958 and 1964 demonstrated Gomulka's dictatorial temperament, his distrust of intellectuals and of the bourgeois West, his preference for strong men, his adherence to the basic principles of Leninist Communism. He still rejected the use of terror, the cult and ideological fanaticism, and certainly would not tolerate a return to Stalinist methods, of which he had never approved. But, like Pilsudski before him, he believed in the need to suppress the natural anarchic tendency of his people by means of strong government. Without having a totalitarian turn of mind, this 'rough-hewn, dry, unassuming' man, as Hans Jacob Stehle called him, had an instinct for power; he wanted to serve the State, to submerge his identity in it, to be the embodiment of its interests.

At the end of 1958 Gomulka was given a shock by Khrushchev, who in his presence but apparently without having given him any warning of his intentions, delivered his ultimatum on West Berlin, with all its implications of a renewal of international tension. Subsequently, however, he drew gradually closer to the Soviet leader who, for his part, respected the autonomy of the Polish leadership to the extent of approving decollectivization in Poland when he was urging the other Eastern countries to carry their own collectivization plans through to completion. In this union of doctrines, Gomulka kept his distance and reserved a certain margin of freedom for himself, even in the international field. Thus he did not take part in the anti-Yugoslav crusade in 1958, and in 1961, despite Chinese and Albanian criticism of his agricultural policy and concessions to the Catholic Church, he did not sever relations with Albania, and tried to maintain formal ones with Peking. When Sino-Soviet relations were approaching the breaking point at the beginning of 1963 after the Caribbean crisis, Gomulka intervened, urging the two parties to adopt a more moderate attitude and to stop the open polemics. When his attempts at reconciliation failed, he took Moscow's side; but his alignment was never unconditional. The Polish attitude to the international conference proposed by Moscow was close to the Italian, Rumanian and Yugoslav line: no objection was raised in principle, but the conference was to be carefully prepared; it must have a chance to restore the unity of the movement, and should not call for excommunication. Gomulka was ready to help the Soviets strengthen international solidarity, but he remained on guard against the slightest hint of Soviet domination.

On another level, Gomulka's main concern had been to strengthen his country's security with respect to the German Federal Republic. In 1957 his Foreign Minister, Adam Rapacki, submitted a plan for the denuclearization of Central Europe to the U.N.; this was aimed, if not at solving the German problem, at least at establishing an independent Polish presence in the international field. The Western refusal to take this plan seriously no doubt strengthened Gomulka's conviction that there was no alternative to an alignment with Russia. In 1959, throwing a veil over former disagreements, Gomulka began to draw closer to East Germany and Czechoslovakia, with a view to tripartite political and economic co-operation in raising a stronger barrier against 'German revengefulness', a barrier perhaps less dependent on Russian support.[6]

The rapprochement with the West hinted at after October 1956 came to nothing, except as regards France, which alone, through De Gaulle, recognized the vagueness of the Oder-Neisse frontier. Relations with the United States remained coldly civil. Poland received some American aid (538 million dollars in loan for the purchase of agricultural surplus between 1957 and 1963, and a loan of 8 million dollars for use in the cultural sphere), but Gomulka always made sure that this aid, to which the Russians (despite murmurings from the other People's Democracies) as well as the Chinese shut their eyes, had no political or ideological strings attached.

No doubt Poland's continuing economic difficulties contributed to reducing her diplomatic potential, just as they had obstructed her internal developments. Yet in 1956 she had made an excellent start in reforming the structure of the economy. The proposals for reform put forward by the Economic Council in December 1956 and approved by the government in July 1957 outlined a new model, based on autonomous enterprises controlled by managers, appointed by the State in conjunction with the workers' councils that had sprung up in October, and they involved a redistribution of salaries and a new national price structure. But the reform inspired by Oskar Lange, the discoverer of 'market socialism',[7] required a radical reorganization for which people were not yet ready. Its haphazard, partial implementation simply increased the confusion. In 1959 Gomulka brought back the ex-Natolinians Szyr and Tokarski, uncompromising believers in State control, to take over the management of the economy and restore the basic elements of centralization and discipline. The hybrid system that resulted could neither repair the foreign trade deficit, due in part to a fall in the price of coal, Poland's main export, and in part to the poor quality of the country's export goods, nor solve the problems of production and the standard of living. In the factories, the workers' councils, their spirit broken, were replaced by 'workers' conferences', controlled by the party apparatus, deprived of any real power and ignored by the wage-earners.

At the end of 1962 the government was forced to introduce austerity measures to stop inflation. The investment programme for 1963 was halved; coal, electricity and gas prices were increased. Wages had risen by 38 per cent between 1956 and 1959, though they were still very low, but hopes for a rapid rise in the standard of living faded. Poverty led to speculation, traffic in currency, theft of public property, moonlighting, and a decline in general enthusiasm for work. In 1963, collective farms accounted for 1.1 per cent of total agricultural production; nevertheless, thanks to more intensive cultivation on the part of the peasants, this had increased by 32 per cent since 1961, thereby making it possible to double the export of agricultural products, which accounted for about 60 per cent of the national earnings in hard currencies. The government, in order to increase agricultural productivity, adopted a fairly generous investment policy which, in a somewhat unorthodox fashion, favoured the *kulaks*. In addition, Gomulka gradually established Agricultural Circles throughout the country, to instruct the peasants in voluntary co-operation. Another encouraging measure was the lifting of the prohibitions affecting small tradespeople and artisans. In 1961 there were 1,900 private shops in Poland, and the number of artisans rose from 96,000 in 1956 to 136,000 in 1962.

In internal politics, the set-back to the liberal ex-Stalinists of the Pulawi group, who had played a crucial part in 1956, was confirmed, though it did not imply a return of the Stalinists. In 1959 Jerzy Morawski left the Politburo, and Bienkowski, who was considered too soft, the Ministry of Education. In July 1963 Roman Zambrowski, the head of the group, was forced to resign. That same year two other leaders of the revolt of October 1956, W. Matwin and Roman Werfel, lost their positions as leaders of the Wroclaw committee.

While these men were falling, the 'Partisans', such as General Moczar – who was appointed Minister of the Interior – Strzelecki and Korczynski, had begun their ascent. They were mostly former resistance fighters who had been pushed into the background if not actually imprisoned under Bierut. They were held together by a curious mixture of Communist orthodoxy, authoritarianism, demagogic nationalism tinged with anti-Semitism, distrust of the liberal intellectuals and reverence for the army.

Gomulka made use of the Partisans by giving them posts in the armed forces and security police. He also promoted a few reformed Natolinians such as Szyr, Tokarski, Gede and General Witaszewski, but relied above all on men who were personally devoted to him: Ochab; Gierek, the energetic, ambitious governor of Silesia; the trade unionist Loga-Sowinski; Zenon Kliszko, who was in charge of ideological affairs; the economist Jedrychowski; and Spychalski, who was raised to the rank of marshal. The former socialists Cyrankiewicz and Rapacki, who represented the right wing, were also re-elected to the Politburo in 1959 and 1964, but their stars were fading. In this heterogeneous group, Gomulka, skilfully holding the balance among the factions, always had the last word.

The party, whose membership rose from 1.1 million in 1959 to 1.5 million in 1965, seemed united, but submissive and undynamic, once its initial revisionist impulse had been exhausted. The struggle of ideas yielded to a sceptical pragmatism, and a number of people hankering after Stalinism tried to form a Maoist group. On the eve of the June 1964 Congress their leader, Mijal, circulated a pamphlet denouncing the opportunistic and ineffectual policy pursued since 1956 and the gradual spread of bourgeois ideology and practice. 'Only the capitalist elements are well off', he wrote. 'Under Stalin, people could at least hope that life would be better one day, but they no longer have that hope.' The activities of the 'splitters' were condemned at the Congress, and arrests were made. Mijal succeeded in escaping to Albania, where he announced the formation of a schismatic party. Another reactionary current centred around the young university teachers Kuron and Modzelewski (the son of a former Minister of Foreign Affairs), whose ideology bore the stamp of the old anti-Stalin 'workers' opposition' and of Trotskyism. Arrested for the first time in November 1964 and then released, these two circulated an 'open letter' which, after quite an interesting analysis of Polish development, called on the working class to initiate an 'anti-bureaucratic revolution', in order to re-establish the workers' councils, the real instruments of the emancipation of the proletariat. Arrested again in 1965, Kuron and Modzelewski were sentenced to three years in prison, and this created a certain stir in intellectual circles. The working class, however, remained indifferent to a message that probably did not get through, and students with an interest in politics tended to look towards revisionism and the West.

During these same years, relations between the party leadership and the intellectuals steadily deteriorated. The revisionists got the roughest treatment, as in Gomulka's view they complicated the task of stabilization and co-operation with other Communist countries, who feared the spread of the infection. In 1962 the Krzyiwe Kolo, where free discussion took place, was dissolved; Kolakowski was subjected to persecution; and two magazines were shut down. Adam Schaff tried to bridge the gap by cautiously introducing a few revisionist ideas into the body of orthodox doctrine, but his attempt failed because of the intransigence of one side and the incomprehension of the other. At a Plenum in July 1963, Gomulka berated the intellectuals for their failure to appreciate the party's realistic aims, and General Moczar warned them against the subversive influence of the West.

Sociology, represented by such distinguished men as Ossowski and Szczepanski, and economics, with Lange, Kurowski, Brus and Lipinski, were given a new stimulus; development in the Polish cinema and theatre, the flourishing of abstract art, and the revival of architecture all bore witness to the vitality of the Polish spirit. In cultural exchanges with the West, Poland was in the forefront of the socialist countries, even influencing developments in the U.S.S.R. and other Eastern countries. But writers, scholars and artists were continually coming up against administrative obstructionism. In March 1964 thirty-four of their most distinguished representatives gave notice of their concern in an open letter to Cyrankiewicz. The text of the letter was published in the West, and the official Polish press raised the cry of treason. Sanctions were imposed, and intellectuals who were party members were asked to dissociate themselves from the rebels. Then the affair died down, leaving a lingering feeling of uneasiness behind it.

In the final count, it was Cardinal Wyszynski's church that benefited from the party's ideological disintegration and the stagnation of left-wing thought. Catholicism was clearly the main spiritual force in the country. The rivalry between this body and the government after 1956 had its difficult moments. In 1961 Wyszynski asked for the establishment of a parliamentary committee to look into violations by the State of the *modus vivendi*. His plea fell on deaf ears. But twenty-five Polish bishops, including him, were allowed to attend the Vatican Council. None of the opposing parties had any interest in provoking a crisis. However, the fact that the Church had won the battle for souls (in an inquiry carried out in 1960, 78 per cent of the young people were convinced Catholics, and only 12 per cent Communists) increased the sense of insecurity and isolation in the upper strata and, like the consolidation of the independent peasantry and the sluggish rate of economic growth, strengthened anti-liberal elements within the organization.[8]

Slow, Cautious Bulgaria

Of all the Eastern Communist parties, the Bulgarian was most closely linked with the Soviet Union. It is hardly surprising, therefore, that Bulgaria suffered the greatest upset after the Twenty-Second Congress of the C.P.S.U., with the fall of Chervenkov. It has already been noted that his disgrace in April 1956 was only temporary. Solidly backed by the hard-liners in the Kremlin and his own political and military cadres, for whom he represented the continuity of the dictatorship, Chervenkov quickly regained his hold. As Minister of Culture in 1957, he silenced the intellectuals pressing for some easement. Then, after his re-election to the Politburo in 1958, he imposed his own line on the party's nominal leader, Todor Zhivkov, and the Prime Minister, Yugov.

During the anti-Yugoslav campaign, Chervenkov, together with the Albanian Hoxha, but displaying greater skill, was one of the proponents of aggressive militancy supported by Mao in Eastern Europe. After a visit to China in September 1958, Chervenkov persuaded the whole Bulgarian leadership to commit itself to a Chinese-style 'great leap forward'. Targets were raised, for example to double agricultural production in 1959 and treble it in 1960, by mobilizing the collective peasantry, and to speed up the rate of industrialization, thus saving two years of the current five-year plan. At the same time, it was considered advisable to give the Kremlin certain assurances. In October 1958 Zhivkov, the head of the Bulgarian Communist party, signed a joint communiqué with Ulbricht condemning as heresy the idea of a 'special path' and emphasizing the leading role of the U.S.S.R. In January 1959 Zhivkov introduced a decree on the reorganization of economic management based on Khrushchev's latest reforms.

Before the end of 1959 it became clear that the ambitious targets of the revised plan were scarcely feasible. Despite almost superhuman efforts, agricultural production rose by only 18 per cent. Moscow's warnings against infatuation with Chinese ideas now fell on fertile ground, particularly since, in order to continue its industrialization – a point of honour for the party – Bulgaria needed Russian aid more than ever. Economic dependence on the Soviet Union strengthened the hands of the Khrushchevist group in Sofia. The Kremlin had to be persuaded to forgive Bulgaria her deviations of 1958–9; thus while the Albanian government identified itself with Hoxha, who became a national hero, the Bulgarian leadership offered Khrushchev Chervenkov's head. The Central Committee, meeting from 28 to 29 November 1961, expelled Chervenkov after hearing Zhivkov's report on the Twenty-Second Congress. Zhivkov warmly sang Khrushchev's praises, and supported his decision not to carry out his threat to conclude a separate peace with the G.D.R., refuting the Albanian charge of capitulation. Bulgarian cadres, who were on good terms with Ulbricht's people and were instinctively hostile to any new concession to the West, had indeed reacted in some degree to this accusation.

In fact, a sizeable proportion of militants wanted Chervenkov back, and were afraid that Khrushchev might try to make the party relax its dictatorial hold – something Bulgaria could ill afford. Zhivkov had to take this into account, so that de-Stalinization was limited to theoretical denunciations of dogmatism, the paying-off of old scores, and the renaming of a few factories. In May 1962 Khrushchev came to Sofia to strengthen Zhivkov's authority, to render an account of his quarrel with China, and to calm Bulgarian apprehensions concerning his recent reconciliation with Tito. Zhivkov was understanding and submissive. He immediately responded by appointing as Deputy Minister of Defence General Transky, who, when head of a wartime partisan group operating on the Yugoslav frontier, had established friendly relations with the Yugoslavs.

Nevertheless, this alignment with Moscow did not please everyone. It produced serious disagreements, and the Party Congress that had been fixed for August 1962 had to be postponed till November. The Congress met when the Moscow–Peking conflict over the Cuban crisis was at its height. Supported by Khrushchev and Suslov, Zhivkov secured a referendum in his favour; Yugov, accused of hostility to the policy of *détente*, of entertaining personal ambitions, and of acting in collusion with Chervenkov, was dismissed from his post as Prime Minister and from the Central Committee. In addition, Zhivkov publicly dissociated himself from the Albanians and Chinese, and the delegate from Peking, Wu Hsi-chuan, took strong exception.

After the Congress, Zhivkov had himself appointed Prime Minister as well. His hands were now a little freer, and he could move, like Khrushchev, towards a cautious policy of reform. He further strengthened his position by appealing to a few rehabilitated Kostovists, such as Petko Kunin, a former Minister of Industry, and the agronomist Chernokolev, who had been sternly condemned in 1951. But when certain intellectuals, encouraged by the relaxation in censorship, began to raise their voices, Zhivkov, with Khrushchev's help, brought them to heel. Khrushchev, who was concerned about the intellectual ferment he had stirred up in the Soviet Union, had made his onslaught on modernist tendencies in March 1963, and in April Ilychev came to Sofia to inform the Bulgarian intellectuals that this applied to the whole alliance.[9]

Thus literary expression was as restricted in Bulgaria as in East Germany and Rumania. The novelist and playwright Emil Manov was sternly reprimanded for his play *Abel's Mistake* (1963), in which the eternal struggle against injustice was unfavourably portrayed. In 1964 the new President of the writers' union, Dimitur Dimov, proclaimed the continued validity of socialist realism.

Nevertheless, slowly but surely, Bulgaria was beginning to show signs of progress and emergence from its isolation. Contact with Yugoslavia was resumed, and at the end of June 1964, after difficult negotiations, relations with Athens were regularized. The idea of Balkan solidarity was mooted again, and the Bulgarians managed to get writers from all the Balkan countries, Turks and Albanians included, around the same table. Attempts were made to develop the tourist industry, and the number of tourists rose from 200,000 in 1961 to 250,000 in 1962. Most came from friendly countries, but there was also an increasing number from West Germany, France and England.

In the great 1962–3 debate over Comecon policy, Bulgaria favoured close co-operation with the U.S.S.R. and the other socialist countries. Bulgaria's basic problem was undoubtedly akin to Rumania's: how to transform an agricultural country into an industrial one. But, unlike Rumania, Bulgaria was not rich in raw materials, and with the elimination of Kostov's group in 1949 national Communism had received a blow from which it had never recovered. It was a matter of prestige for the Kremlin to see that Bulgaria was generously rewarded for her loyalty. In 1964 the U.S.S.R. made Sofia a fresh loan of 530 million roubles in aid of the new five-year plan (1966–70) which meant that large-scale schemes could be put into effect. Bulgaria also increased her exchanges with the German Federal Republic, France, Great Britain and Italy. Zhivkov began taking an interest in Professor Liberman's schemes for reform; collective agricultural management was made more flexible, and peasants were encouraged to work their private plots more intensively, 9 per cent of the arable land, producing 27 per cent of the total meat consumed, 50 per cent of the eggs, etc.[10]

The German Democratic Republic in Search of its Right to Exist

In 1960 Walter Ulbricht had predicted that the following year would be decisive for the German Democratic Republic; and so it was. Ulbricht's hopes of persuading the Soviets to conclude a separate peace treaty with the G.D.R. were not realized. The

Kremlin did not want to bring about a *fait accompli* that would seriously complicate relations with the United States. On the other hand, Khrushchev, in agreement with the People's Democracies, gave Ulbricht permission on 13 August to erect a wall to separate East and West Berlin, a radical attempt to eliminate a permanent cause of weakness and instability. Between 1949 and 1961 more than 2,700,000 people had taken advantage of free movement inside Berlin to flee to Western Germany. This continual drain, the loss of people who were hard to replace – skilled workers, technicians, medical staff, agriculturists – made economic planning difficult.

The frontier with the West was now at least as secure here as in the other Eastern countries; and the West had not protested. It was a great shock to Germans on both sides. The division was now an inescapable fact; the dream of reunification was an illusion. Certainly the G.D.R., with no historical, democratic or even revolutionary roots, still did not look like a genuine state. Its existence, fundamentally dependent as it was on the will of a foreign power, contradicted Communist propaganda in favour of the right of self-determination for the peoples of other continents. However, the G.D.R. did exist, and its government had the means of controlling widespread disapproval on the part of its people. Thus 1961 was for East Germany what 1956 was for Hungary : a lesson in political realities, a demonstration of might over right. Ulbricht's government took advantage of popular disappointment to strengthen his authority, as well as to improve the G.D.R.'s international status, especially with the other Eastern countries, which up till then had often left something to be desired.

Under these circumstances the impetus given to de-Stalinization by the Twenty-Second Soviet Congress could scarcely be expected to have any political effect in East Germany. The Central Committee of the S.E.D., meeting on 28 November 1961 in Berlin, quickly made it clear that de-Stalinization, or liberalization, was irrelevant in the G.D.R. where no cult of personality had proved possible, and all associated errors had been corrected in time. After the purges of previous years, Ulbricht's team, consisting of his 'Crown Prince', Erich Honecker, the Secretary in charge of security, Willi Stoph, Hermann Matern, Alfred Neumann, and other loyal hard-liners, was remarkably like-minded. The East German leadership gave its unqualified support to the denunciation of the 'dogmatist' Enver Hoxha, but in East Berlin this term was merely a name for rebellion against Moscow's foreign policy. Neither the cultural licence in the Soviet Union, of whose limits he was in any case aware, nor the concessions made to intellectuals in Poland, Hungary and Czechoslovakia, persuaded Ulbricht to modify his harshness.

In no other Eastern country, apart from Albania, was governmental control on intellectual life so constant and so oppressive as in the country of Karl Marx, who had begun his literary career with an article condemning censorship. The Marxist philosopher Ernst Bloch (b. 1887), a friend and fellow exile of Bertolt Brecht in the United States, where he had lived between 1938 and 1949, was deprived of his chair in 1956 and unable to publish, and found himself forced in 1961 to seek refuge in West Germany, where there was no obstacle to publication of Marxist writings. In 1963 Professor Robert Havemann, the chemist and philosopher, was accused of revisionism, and was dismissed for having called for 'free and open discussion' in the party. The same year several veteran Communist writers, like Stephan Hermlin, were removed from the bureau of the Writers' Association. Anna Seghers and Arnold Zweig got into trouble with the censor. 'We shall not permit false, dangerous and pernicious ideas to be imposed on the people', declared Ulbricht. 'We shall not tolerate action taken under the guise of the struggle against Stalinism, aiming at obstructing the policy of the party and government and destroying our work.'[11]

At the international conference on Kafka in Prague, the East German delegates, who were chosen from among the most sectarian literary critics, fiercely opposed the rehabilitation of the author of The Trial, who, in their view, was irredeemable because of his pessimism and lack of realism. The dictatorship of intolerant ideologists in East Berlin made the control by Novotny and Hendrych of Czechoslovak literary life, at least from the spring of 1963 until summer 1967, seem a model of liberal laissez-aller.

In contrast, from 1962 the economists received preferential treatment, mainly because Ulbricht needed them to achieve his stated aim of overtaking the West German level of production, which he knew would be impossible if outdated methods were retained. In fact, the East German rate of industrial growth, despite restrictions on home consumption, fell from 12.4 per cent in 1959 to 8 per cent in 1960 and 6.2 per cent in 1961. And it was the G.D.R.'s industrial potential, the greatest in the Eastern bloc, that Ulbricht had counted on to win himself a privileged position in the socialist camp. His régime, lacking any other basis, could at least be justified by its economic efficiency; but this would require a reform of the system. After the Sixth Congress of the S.E.D. in January 1963 (during which Khrushchev vainly called on the Chinese for an ideological truce), Ulbricht summoned a number of highly respected economic experts to the Politburo, such as Erich Appel, who was appointed chairman of the planning body; Günther Mittag; Herbert Jarowinski; and Magarete Müller. Soon East Germany became the most important testing ground for 'Libermanism'. The associations of nationalized enterprises (V.V.B.), which in 1961 were producing 65 per cent of all industrial goods, were granted wide discretionary powers over technological research, detailed planning and disposal of goods. The reorganization, without curing all the faults of bureaucracy, produced results by 1964. It tapped unused resources of skill and energy, and contributed to the birth of a spirit of competition, a sort of economic patriotism which impressed foreign visitors and raised the G.D.R.'s prestige.

It was the growing importance of the East German economy that helped Ulbricht to maintain his own government's special interests against the Soviet Union, despite his political, strategic and economic dependence. Within Comecon, the East Germans, together with the Czechs, were the most outspoken champions of integration; no one condemned Rumanian nationalism and autarchism more harshly than Pankow. The East German position here was comparable to that of the West Germans in the Common Market: the G.D.R. had least to fear from the effects of integration. Ulbricht had taken an extreme pro-Soviet stand on the Sino-Soviet conflict since 1960. However, in view of the importance of trade with China (since 1959 the G.D.R. had been China's second largest customer), Ulbricht curbed the polemics, and continued to send specialists to China after the U.S.S.R. had withdrawn its own in retaliation. More cautiously than Gomulka, and for different reasons – including his fear of losing to the Federal Republic China's much coveted orders – Ulbricht struggled to avoid a break, and hoped to prevent the ideological conflict from impairing relations between the states.

Like the Rumanians and Poles, he had a political as well as economic reason for keeping on good terms with Peking: China's past support (if only to prevent rapprochement between the U.S.S.R. and the United States) had been given him for his demands over Berlin and the separate peace treaty. The improvement after the Cuban crisis in relations between Moscow and Washington, as signified by the 1963 nuclear agreement, worried Ulbricht as much as it did the West Germans; he was afraid that he would be the loser. He now needed allies more than ever, and drew closer to Gomulka, at the same time curbing anti-Chinese propaganda. The satisfaction he felt, on both a personal and a governmental level, at being asked to append his signature to the tripartite nuclear treaty, was neutralized by the Anglo-American declarations that recognition of the signature was in no sense to be interpreted as a first step towards the recognition of the German Democratic Republic. Ulbricht expected the Kremlin to react strongly to this, but it remained silent. Peking at once interpreted this silence as indicating 'de facto recognition of the Bonn régime as the sole representative of Germany' (People's Daily, 23 August 1963). The S.E.D. immediately accused the Chinese of trying to sow discord between the Soviet Union and the German Democratic Republic. However, Ulbricht had not been entirely sorry to hear Peking reflecting his own sentiments. It was, no doubt, in order to give the lie to the Chinese allegations that the U.S.S.R., in lieu of a separate peace treaty, decided to sign a treaty of friendship with the G.D.R. in June 1964.

Once again, the Chinese intervened as the self-appointed spokesmen for East Berlin's unvoiced grievances: the treaty, they pointed out, did not expressly recognize the G.D.R.'s existence as a state; it said nothing about the status of West Berlin as a separate entity. A little later, when Adzhubey, Khrushchev's son-in-law, was sounding Bonn on his father-in-law's behalf, making rash statements about Ulbricht's health and the possibility of his replacement, the Chinese press redoubled its attacks, accusing Khrushchev of wanting to 'sell out' East Germany. Suslov and Brezhnev felt it necessary publicly to answer these attacks by renewing the pledge of solidarity with the G.D.R.[12] If Khrushchev really was thinking in terms of modifying his German policy in order to bring about a *détente* with Bonn, Peking's denunciations were a great help to Ulbricht and all those inside the Soviet faction who were doing their utmost to see that these plans came to nothing. Here one encounters the Rumanian element in East German policy; like Gheorghiu Dej, Ulbricht drew some advantages from the Sino-Soviet conflict; he was enabled to apply pressure, if not to engage in a little blackmail, and to gain a certain measure of independence in his relationship.[13]

9

The People's Democracies
after Khrushchev

On 16 October 1964 *Pravda* announced Nikita Khrushchev's resignation 'for reasons of health', and his replacement at the head of the party by Leonid Brezhnev, and at the head of the government by Aleksey Kosygin. A chapter in the history of post-Stalinist Russia had ended.

Gomulka, who was playing host to Kadar at the time, claimed not to have been surprised, as Khrushchev himself had informed him of his wish to retire shortly. It is possible that Brezhnev, who was in East Berlin just prior to the Central Committee meeting, might have informed certain if not all the fraternal parties of Khrushchev's imminent removal. Nevertheless, the S.E.D. communiqué announcing Khrushchev's fall spoke in terms of 'surprise', while the Czechs expressed 'shock and surprise'. No doubt, most of the leaders of the People's Democracies had been aware of the tensions that existed in the Kremlin, which had nearly led to Khrushchev's departure in February 1964. But it does not appear that they expected the change to take place so soon.

Be that as it may, the various heads of State were too closely identified with Khrushchev to regard his replacement with indifference. This was particularly true of Kadar, Novotny and Zhivkov, who were personally indebted to him, and whose authority was threatened by his downfall. Their first concern, under the circumstances, was to minimize the significance of the change, which they said was a purely 'internal affair'. Kadar, Novotny, Ulbricht and Gomulka accomplished this with some grace (more, at any rate, than Khrushchev's successors), praising the virtues of the man 'responsible for the denunciation of the cult of personality ... as well as for determining the historic line of the Communist parties at the Twentieth and Twenty-Second Congresses'.[1] Novotny in particular, like the French Communists, was bent on recording his displeasure at the off-hand manner in which Khrushchev had been removed.

But the primary concern of the Eastern leaders was to make sure that this change at the top would not lead to any significant modification in Soviet policy. Brezhnev and Kosygin hastened to reassure them on this account. They explained that the reason for Khrushchev's removal was not his having strayed from the general line, but rather his extravagance, his disregard for the principle of collective leadership he had solemnly sworn to uphold at the Twenty-Second Congress. With Khrushchev out of the way, therefore, 'Khrushchevism' could proceed. Brezhnev and Kosygin took the trouble to pay Gomulka a personal visit to give him the assurances he needed. The other leaders of the Eastern countries, with the exception of Novotny, who went on sulking for a while, received the same assurances in Moscow at the anniversary celebrations of the Revolution. Little by little the anxiety subsided, and in fact there seems to have been no change in the Kremlin's relations with the East European governments. Two questions do, however, arise: to what extent did Khrushchev's policy towards the People's Democracies contribute to his fall? and what effect had his fall on the subsequent development of these countries?

In view of the secrecy surrounding the Central Committee session of 13–14 October 1964, there can be no positive answer to the first question. Nevertheless, details of the indictment that Suslov read out at the meeting indicate that Khrushchev's 'regrettable attitude' to Gheorghiu Dej, whom, it seems, he 'bullied' at their last meeting, was one of the points made about his behaviour.[2] Soviet policy towards Rumania, which (like the policy towards China) was determined by the whole Soviet leadership, was not questioned, but rather Khrushchev's behaviour, which had led to a breakdown in personal relations. His successors tried to use his departure to resume the dialogue with Dej and normalize relations with Bucharest; and they succeeded, at least temporarily.

It seems that Khrushchev was also blamed, not so much for the mission to sound out Bonn (18 July–2 August 1964) entrusted to his son-in-law Adzhubey, but for the way the mission had been completed.[3] But the fact is that Khrushchev, in advocating a policy of rapprochement with the Federal Republic, was (like Beria in June 1953) storming 'a sacrosanct bastion of Soviet foreign policy'.[4] He clashed with the 'East German lobby', which supported Ulbricht through thick and thin, was totally uncompromising on Germany and disapproved of Khrushchev's proposed visit to Bonn to 'break the ice'. In any event, Ulbricht dropped the hint that Khrushchev's German plans were not unrelated to his removal.[5]

The most important indirect consequence of the change in Soviet leadership seems to have been a fresh decline in the prestige of the Kremlin, which then showed some instability and disunity (as it had done after Stalin's death and at various stages of the succession struggle). Whatever Moscow's account of the matter, the whole affair looked like a palace revolution, and showed up the arbitrary, occult and unsettled character of Soviet power. The Eastern leaders were inclined to keep the Kremlin at arm's length, and to insist that they were not involved in the sudden changes affecting the U.S.S.R. Ulbricht recalled that he himself had never followed Khrushchev's advice on agriculture. Kadar waited till the end of June 1965 before relinquishing the prime ministership to his friend Kallai, so as not to be accused of having imitated the new two-part Soviet model of leadership.

Brezhnev's and Kosygin's new style ('fewer words and more deeds'), their sober and cautious, not to say hesitant, realism encouraged this tendency towards emancipation and concentration on national problems. Of course, Khrushchev, unlike Stalin, had been no god or idol, and this had helped smooth the transition to a new leadership. The age of myths, cults and great demagogic flights of oratory was over; inspired improvisation from the platform was succeeded in Russia by objective, bureaucratic, impersonal conservatism, which also claimed to be scientific.[6]

This change in climate was not unwelcome in countries where the old dogmatic leaders of the Stalinist era were beginning to give way to administrators who, while certainly authoritarian, were pragmatic in their outlook: men like Biszku in Hungary, Verdet in Rumania, Cernik in Czechoslovakia, and Gierek in Poland, all sought their justification, no longer in Moscow's backing, but in their own administrative efficiency. The more flexible, 'anti-imperialist', 'united-front' tactics of Brezhnev and Kosygin enabled the U.S.S.R. to regain some of the lost ground in the Far East, in Vietnam and in North Korea; but neither the Yugoslavs nor the Rumanians returned to the fold. Even Czechoslovakia, for so long the most unquestioningly loyal of the satellites, sought 'new formulas and a new conception' for her relationship with the U.S.S.R.

The emancipation and diversification of the Eastern countries occurred on an economic as well as ideological level. The various party congresses put structural economic reform first on the list of priorities. The radical Yugoslav experiment and the very cautious 'Libermanism' practised by the Soviets served as points of reference, but each government looked first to its own national conditions and interests. In the summer of 1967 even Rumania, where the centrist tradition was stronger than anywhere else, began experimenting with decentralization. This course was actually forced on the Communist leaders by economic circumstances beyond their control. The increasing industrialization of the less developed bloc countries, combined with the inevitable resumption of trade contacts with the capitalist countries, destroyed the closed system which, if it had effectively protected the socialist economies, did not provide them with sufficient incentive to raise their technological standards.[7]

Czechoslovakia, because of her extreme economic dependence on the outside world, had suffered most from the hidden disadvantages of this system. But what was true for Czechoslovakia was broadly true for the other People's Democracies as well. They all began to feel the spur of Communist and capitalist foreign competition; a return to the past seemed impossible (unless economic considerations were sacrificed on the altar of politics, as in the Chinese 'cultural revolution'). It was the exigencies of foreign trade rather than the pressure of internal consumption (which was easier to check) that made reform of the economic system imperative for the Eastern leaders. Centralized planning could no longer resolve the complex problems arising.

The different steps taken by the governments to reorganize the management of the economy are summarized below (Part II, Chapter 17). It is sufficient for the present to notice the difficulties of the Communist leaders in restricting criticism and the desire for renovation to the economic sphere alone, and preventing the relaxation of administrative control over the economy from leading to an erosion of the party's power. Certain technocratic reformers, like the Hungarian economist Istvan Friss, believed that the political stability guaranteed by a strong government, the undisputed authority of the party, provided the most favourable conditions for the success of the new experiment.[8] Nevertheless the view prevailed, first in Yugoslavia, and then in Czechoslovakia, after a hard political battle, that only fairly extensive democratization could produce a climate in which economic reconstruction could be realized.

The years 1966–8 saw political struggle in the People's Democracies. Behind the opposing forces of 'progressives' and 'conservatives' one glimpsed the interests and ambitions of two social entities (not to say classes): the technical and artistic intelligentsia and the party machine (the Establishment, or new Communist class). And in the background was a new, unknown, amorphous, politically unformed working class that could be manipulated.

The starting-point was the same in Yugoslavia, Poland, Czechoslovakia (and even the U.S.S.R.). Political and ideological development lagged behind the economic needs of the moment, causing a crisis in which the intellectuals, particularly Communists, were once again the first to give expression to the real feelings, grievances and aspirations of the country. This was not surprising; the public had no other established means of voicing its demands than through the few professional associations (the writers' or journalists' unions) over which party control had relaxed, and the party cells in the universities, where the critical spirit refused to be stifled. No doubt, writers, journalists and artists in post-Khrushchev Poland, Czechoslovakia and Hungary enjoyed considerable freedom of expression. 'In our country socialism is open to all progressive ideas', wrote W. Sokorski, a supporter of the Polish régime. 'What more do you need? What freedom is being asked for?'[9]

In fact, what was being demanded was the right to criticize the policy of the party and government with impunity, to discuss all the country's vital problems freely – in other words, to function as an opposition. This was of course incompatible with the party's monopoly. If in Yugoslavia and then in Czechoslovakia, thanks to increasing progressive and centrist influences in the upper echelons of the party, the intellectual ferment opened up prospects of liberalization, Poland, the G.D.R. and Bulgaria would develop in a contrary, anti-liberal, repressive direction.

The course taken by these three countries coincided with that of the Soviet Union. In fact, the influence of neo-Stalinists in the Kremlin – especially in positions of authority over intellectual life – grew steadily after Khrushchev's fall. The Sinyavsky-Daniel trial in February 1966 was the signal for a new ideological freeze characterized by close co-operation between the pressure group of ideologists and conservative bureaucrats – Pospelov, Fedoseev, Rumyantsev, Grishin, Mikhailov, Yury Zhukov – and neo-imperialist military circles, the most dynamic representatives of which were Marshals Grechko and Yakubovsky and General Yepishev (appointed head of the political department of the Soviet army at the beginning of 1968). These elements skilfully exploited the fear of top bureaucrats with reformist tendencies among the country's intellectuals, as well as the movements for national emancipation in Rumania and then Czechoslovakia. They launched a general attack on all those who still hoped to carry on the work of the Twentieth and Twenty-Third Congresses, and began the process of rehabilitating Stalin.

So it was that the internal development of the Soviet Union, paralleled in Poland, the G.D.R. and Bulgaria (Kadar's Hungary, inhibited by its memories of 1956, occupying an intermediate position), created the conditions for a new internationalism, which crystallized into a kind of holy alliance of the conservative, authoritarian, anti-liberal Communist régimes, and culminated in political and later military intervention in Czechoslovakia and a campaign of intimidation against Yugoslavia and Rumania.[10]

10

The Second Yugoslav Revolution

Between 1961 and 1967 nearly all the Communist countries began to change, to take the first steps in the process of renewal. The disintegration of the bureaucratic, monopolistic system inherited from Stalin accelerated. One after another, the socialist states began introducing economic reforms, rethinking their political structures and their relations with the Soviet Union. The parties tried to redefine their leading role and the meaning of the dictatorship of the proletariat.

However, in the two countries representing the two opposite poles of the Communist world – Yugoslavia and China – the movement took on such a radical character that it does not seem too far-fetched to speak of a second revolution. It was no coincidence that 'the great proletarian cultural revolution' initiated by Mao or the Maoists in 1965 occurred in the same period as the great Yugoslav reform. Despite all the demographical and historical differences, and their violent doctrinal clash, these two Communist countries shared from the start a revolutionary dynamism, inspiration and imagination that distinguished them from the more apprehensive fraternal countries. Tito's Yugoslavia, like Mao's China, was the product of a civil war; both leaders had come to power on the wave of a genuinely national movement. They were consequently not disposed to play the role of satellites, feeling on the contrary the need to make their own experiments and to establish patterns of development different from those of the Soviet Union.

At this point, of course, their paths separate. Yugoslavia, with her workers' councils and self-management, had been in the vanguard of the reformist Communist movement from the early fifties, had increasingly enlarged the scope of private initiative and had opened herself to Western influences; on the other hand, after 1958 China took the opposite direction: extreme internationalism, adherence to the concept of revolution, implacable hostility to the West, permanent mobilization, and militarization of political and economic structures. In 1955 Yugoslavia drew closer to the Soviet Union, whose post-Stalinist leaders looked to some extent to the Yugoslav experiment in de-Stalinization. China moved further away from the U.S.S.R. and set herself up as the determined opponent, not only of Russian hegemonism, but of all forms of ideological or practical revisionism. Nevertheless, these two contrasting courses led to strikingly analogous crises, in which the dominant role of the party, based respectively on Leninist and Stalinist principles, was challenged. In China, long after Russian opportunism had been denounced, the party apparatus under Liu and Teng Hsiao-ping continued to use organizational methods and criteria of political and economic efficiency drawn from Soviet experience. Thus the disease had taken root; the Stalinism of the Chinese administration contained the seeds of Khrushchevist revisionism and, to that extent, Maoists were justified in calling the strictly orthodox Liu Shao-chi a 'Chinese Khrushchev'.

In Yugoslavia the party's central machine, while in principle accepting the reforms promoted by the liberals – which went beyond Khrushchevism and Liu's concessions made between 1961 and 1965 to the Chinese technical intelligentsia and the peasants – jealousy guarded its totalitarian privileges; it had no intention of surrendering its position as a state within a state. Its dead weight stood in the way of talent and obstructed effective decentralization. In China, too, the party machine obstructed Mao's grand design for the creation of a completely new type of permanent, egalitarian war Communism, without bureaucrats and anti-intellectual.

Finally, in China, as in Yugoslavia, there was one potentially explosive factor: the succession. In 1966 Tito was seventy-four, and Mao Tse-tung seventy-three. Both leaders were showing signs of fatigue, but the prestige of neither was shared by any of their associates. They were, and still are, the symbols and guarantors of the unity of party and state. They stood above the fray; below them there were simply rival individuals and groups competing for their favour while formulating their own political plans. The struggle between individuals, cliques and tendencies had broken out even before the rulers had disappeared from the scene. 'Doesn't this remind you of what happened under Stalin?' Tito asked his associates at the height of the 1966 crisis. 'In my opinion, the resemblance is rather striking.' And indeed the situation in both countries was similar to that in the Kremlin prior to Stalin's death.

In order to safeguard the future of the régime and prevent the factions from getting the upper hand, Stalin had put his trust in Beria, the chief of his secret police. This 'super-efficient, super-competent' organization was at the very heart of Soviet power.[1] Mao Tse-tung's Beria was Lin Piao, who was head of the military commission, and controlled both police and army. Tito's Beria was Rankovic, the creator and chief of the formidable U.D.B.A. Lin Piao had no hesitation in pushing through an egalitarian and anti-bureaucratic revolution in order to bring all the other organizations in the country, including the party, under his own politico-military administration. But Tito, for his part, sacrificed Rankovic. China moved towards a variant of totalitarianism in which the manipulation of individuals and crowds was perfected as never before. Yugoslavia set herself the task of reconciling the leader's enlightened despotism with unprecedented individual and collective freedom. In both cases, forces were unleashed that threatened the unity of the state. The second revolution may have unforeseen consequences for both, and may lead to the development of forms of government whose success or failure, as with the experiment in socialist democracy begun in Czechoslovakia, will serve as an example to all the countries in the world, Communist and non-Communist.

The origins of the second Yugoslav revolution date from early in 1961, when the liberal leaders introduced a whole series of measures to breathe new life into an economy that was flagging, despite successive steps taken to decentralize it since 1950: the discretionary power of the workers' councils in regard to distribution of income was increased; prices were freed; and a new credit system was instituted by which banks gradually took over from the state. In order to give the experiment some chance of success, the Yugoslav government took considerable advantage of Western aid. The United States made a loan of 100 million dollars; the International Monetary Fund, 75 million dollars; a group of Western states, 100 million dollars. In January 1961 the United Nations Development Fund made three more loans totalling 27.7 million dollars; in February there was a loan of 6,100,000 dollars; and the World Bank made a loan of 30 million dollars to facilitate Yugoslavia's gradual integration into the international market through devalutation of the dinar (750 instead of 300 to the dollar).

Several years were needed for the country to adapt itself to this experiment, but Tito retreated at the first sign of difficulty. No doubt the old leader was anxious about the long-term effects of an economic reform, which to succeed must effectively and not just theoretically end the party's control over the economy. Up till then, there had been a precarious balance in Yugoslavia, a paradoxical coexistence of totalitarian structures, and a kind of bureaucratic polycentrism; Western influence and friendship with the U.S.S.R., which, *de facto* if not *de jure*, ensured the survival of the Communist régime. The full reform programme might have destroyed this equilibrium and pushed Yugoslavia into the Western community. Paying more and more attention to the conservative elements around him, Tito therefore applied the brakes sharply. The violently anti-American stand he took at the conference of uncommitted nations that met in Belgrade in September 1961 disappointed the American ambassador George Kennan, and relations with Washington became strained. In November, at Skopje, Tito delivered a speech stressing the League's (the Yugoslav party's) leading role. The course pursued by the Soviet Union after the Twenty-Second Congress, when Khrushchev took up Mao Tse-tung's challenge, reminded Tito of the part he might well play in the international Communist movement as the Kremlin's valuable aide, if not guide. It seemed to him an opportune moment to restore contacts that had been destroyed in the wake of the Hungarian rising. In April 1962 Gromyko came to Belgrade and was warmly welcomed; in September Tito received Brezhnev, the Soviet head-of-state at the time; in December, after the Cuban crisis, Tito went to Moscow and threw his weight behind Khrushchev. 'We are', he said on his return, 'on the side of the anti-dogmatic forces in the international Communist movement.'

This abrupt change of front in foreign policy was accompanied by a left-wing trend in home affairs. At a meeting of the League Executive Committee (Politburo) in March 1962, there was a violent clash between the liberals and the conservatives headed by Rankovic. Tito intervened in favour of the latter. Four years later it became known that these highly confidential Politburo deliberations – where there had been much plain talk – had been taped by Rankovic's men for future use. At the time, however, Tito was unaware of these machinations, and trusted Rankovic implicitly. In June 1962, at Split, he delivered a speech that showed that his attitude towards the intellectuals and liberals was less flexible. In December it was Rankovic and not Kardelj (who was disliked by the Russians) who accompanied Tito to Moscow, while in June 1963, when the top posts came up for redistribution according to the new constitution, Rankovic was elected Vice-President of the Republic, and Kardelj had to make do with the presidency of the Assembly. The Serb Stambolic, a supporter of Rankovic at the time, was appointed head of the federal government. It was clear that Tito wanted Rankovic as his successor.

Because Rankovic was a Serb, this choice was a momentous one. It complicated and exacerbated conflicts by reawakening national hostility between Serbs on the one hand and Croats and Slovenes on the other. It was no accident that the strongest supporters of liberalization, decentralization, and the pro-Western trend were to be found among the Slovenes and Croats, the most Western of the southern Slavs. The liberals launched a counterattack. On the eve of the Eighth Party Congress Rankovic tried to get himself appointed General Secretary of the League, on the pretext of taking some of the strain off Tito's back, but really in order to consolidate his own position. However, Kardelj, seeing the danger, got to the Executive Committee before him. 'I have been authorized to announce', he said apparently, 'that Slovenia will make use of its constitutional right of secession if Tito does not remain at the head of our federation.' Bakaric supported him. There was a split in the Serbian leadership, and Stambolic, Todorovic (Vice-President of the National Assembly), and Milentije Popovic came out in favour of Tito and reform. The Eighth Congress also backed Tito's authority and acclaimed him as never before.

Then the pendulum swung to the right again. Khrushchev's fall showed up the instability of the Kremlin, and weakened the position of the Russophile wing, particularly when it became clear that Yugoslavia could not depend on substantial aid from the U.S.S.R. The economic situation, moreover, had worsened; currency reserves were exhausted; there was galloping inflation; many industrial enterprises were working at only half-capacity; and the number of unemployed had risen.

These were the circumstances under which Kardelj and Bakaric disregarded conservative objections, and relaunched the economic reform of 1961. This time a real start was made on introducing a market economy, rejecting state control and derived – as *The Economist* (London) pointed out with some irony – from the Manchester school. By the terms of the 1965 'great economic reform', the enterprises were to keep 71 (instead of 51) per cent of the net product; the so-called political factories (enterprises established and maintained regardless of their profit-earning capacity) had to adjust or to disappear, the dinar was devalued once again (1,250 to the dollar) to stimulate exports; all price controls were to be lifted till 1968; the function of banks was better defined; the finance for industrialization in the underdeveloped regions was entrusted to a central fund for the poorest regions. Convinced this time that Yugoslavia meant business, the experts of the International Monetary Fund recommended a new one-year loan of 80 million dollars to support the dinar, and released the 60 million dollars of the previous loan which had been retained in view of Yugoslavia's dishonouring of obligations undertaken in 1961. Once again the United States showed its readiness to subsidize the Yugoslav experiment: 1.35 million tons of wheat were supplied, a new long-term credit of 86 million dollars was granted, plus 40 million dollars to finance purchases and equipment; finally, a moratorium was placed on the repayment of 17 million dollars owed to the Export-Import Bank. Italy also announced that it was prepared to grant credit. The experiment began. Its promoters were aware of the risks they were taking: the ultimate closure of about 2,000 factories, a massive laying-off of personnel, an increase in unemployment and a rise in prices. But there was no alternative, they believed, to an extremely hard two- or three-year transitional period. The whole success of the experiment depended on these measures of purification and rationalization being carried out firmly and to the letter.

Conservative elements tried to sabotage the programme, taking advantage of the disorder and confusion it caused. At a Central Committee meeting at the end of February 1966, Rankovic and his supporters – most of the Serbian and Montenegrin members of the Committee – attacked the new economic policy on the grounds that it favoured mainly the Croats and Slovenes. On the eve of the meeting several hundred senior Serbian officials resigned in protest. However, the reformers stood fast and Tito lent them his support. 'There is no room in the League for those who do not carry out its decisions. They must go', he said. But the opposition did not give up. In March the Central Committee met twice more without reaching a firm conclusion. The two sides prepared for a test of strength. The liberals invoked the principle of rotation laid down in the 1963 Constitution, to strengthen their position in the central organization and eliminate Rankovic's supporters (including Lukic, the Minister of the Interior). This operation would certainly have failed if Tito, Kardelj, and Bakaric had not been able to depend on the support of the head of the army, the Croat General Ivan Gosnjak, Minister of Defence; the head of military counter-espionage Kreacic, who was appointed to the Central Committee; and the higher cadres of the secret police in Croatia and Slovenia, most of whom backed the liberal leaders of their republics.

Rankovic, it seems, was waiting for Tito's departure for the Far East, which was due autumn 1966, before setting in motion a plan similar to that which had brought Nkrumah down. Tito apparently learned of this scheme just at the moment when military counter-espionage found out that Rankovic had 'bugged' his offices and private apartments in Belgrade and Zagreb. He decided to strike first.

Tito confronted Rankovic before the Politburo on 16 June. The latter, while protesting his innocence, handed in his resignation.[2] A board of six, representing the six republics, was appointed to investigate. This inquiry, concluded on 22 June, established Rankovic's personal responsibility; he was accused of fractionalism, chauvinism, misuse of police powers and plotting. A meeting of the Central Committee was called for 1 July in Brioni, and special police and military precautions were taken. Slovene army units were hastily moved to Belgrade to prevent a coup. Military garrisons and the regular police forces, generally ill-disposed towards the U.D.B.A., were put on the alert. The Central Committee members arrived in Brioni by military air transport or in armoured trains, and the island guard was strengthened.

This was the most dramatic meeting in the history of the Communist régime in Yugoslavia: it was opened by Tito, who, in a voice choked with emotion, arraigned the man he had trusted implicitly for so many years, now accusing him of having betrayed him by setting up a 'fractional group whose object was to seize power'. Then the chairman of the board of inquiry, the Macedonian Krste Crvenkovski, submitted his report – a document that throws considerable light on contemporary history. It showed, in effect, that in de-Stalinized Yugoslavia, with its workers' councils and ultra-democratic constitution, that on the surface seemed so liberal, Rankovic's secret police had constituted a state above the State, a clandestine government entirely independent of Tito, the Central Committee, and Parliament. 'State security had become the monopoly of a few individuals', said the report. Comrade Marko (Alexander Rankovic) had set himself up as 'the incarnation of the Central Committee'. He had established control over the whole of society, 'right up to the highest levels'. Aided by Svetoslav Stefanovic, chairman of the Federal Executive Committee Commission for Internal Affairs, Rankovic had placed security men in every department, even the Ministry of Foreign Affairs, without consulting the appropriate ministers. 'All of which shows', declared Crvenkovski, 'that certain basic norms of democratic procedure ... norms laid down and developed in our society, have been greatly neglected, have not been respected and have been inadequately developed.'

The police-state nature of the Communist state had never been so eloquently unmasked, not even in the U.S.S.R. after Beria's removal, though the no less important role of military intelligence was left unexplored. It is understandable that Tito, as he admitted in his closing speech on 2 July, had long hesitated to join battle on this issue : 'One could not be sure of the effect it would have on the internal life and development of the country, nor how it would appear to our people or be judged abroad, where our country enjoys the prestige gained for it by its people.'

In fact the preventive July strike, eliminating Rankovic from the succession, had serious dangers for the régime. The first was that of unsettling the secret police, essential to every state, especially to a one-party state where it alone could prevent an opposition from forming. The victors were fully aware of this, and that is why Crvenkovski, who read the report, urged that 'the criticism should not be directed against the department as a whole'; he anticipated the transformation of the security police into 'a modern organization charged with the defence of the socialist system and independence of our country'. According to the report, the blow struck at the secret police in Yugoslavia was similar to the reorganization of the Soviet secret police after Beria: it was the organization's autonomous status that had to be eliminated. Henceforth, the U.D.B.A. was to be subject to the control of the government and the Central Committee. Even more significant, from the point of view of Yugoslav development, is that U.D.B.A. branches in the different republics were made subordinate to the governments and parties of those republics. In this way Greater Serbia lost its most powerful weapon.

This brings us to the second danger: a significant section of Serbian opinion (even among those who detested the U.D.B.A.) regarded Rankovic's elimination as a defeat for Serbia. Rankovic had to be prevented from utilizing this potential support to regain power. Kardelj and Bakaric, therefore, were well advised to tread cautiously. While initiating a thorough purge of the U.D.B.A., the League leadership hoped to give the Serbs some satisfaction. Two Serbian party leaders, Todorovic and Milentije

Popovic, were appointed in Rankovič's place – the former on the League's secretariat, the latter on the Politburo. A third Serb, Koca Popovic, former Minister of Foreign Affairs, was appointed Vice-President of the federation.

Tito also did his utmost to reassure the Soviets that Rankovic's departure was not a signal for a diplomatic turnabout in favour of the West. In late September Brezhnev came to Belgrade, bringing with him a loan of 160 million dollars for the purchase of industrial equipment. He was warmly greeted, but, despite this fresh proof of the Kremlin's goodwill, Tito still refused to take part in a new international conference of Communist parties.

Doubtless to avoid shocking the Russians and turning him into a Serbian martyr, Rankovic was simply expelled from the party and the federal assembly. Thus, although pronounced guilty, he and his principal colleagues were pardoned.

In theory, the way was now clear for implementing the great reform of 1965. But, in fact, not all the obstacles had been eliminated. The disbanding of the secret police had shaken the régime to its core; the time had come for the reorganizaton of the state on new foundations, for stabilization. It was no coincidence that Bakaric, who up to the summer of 1966 had shown himself very indulgent towards the group of revisionist intellectuals in Zagreb gathered around the magazine *Praxis*, chose this particular moment to penalize the magazine's contributors and to suspend its publication, although it reappeared eight months later. A few weeks after this, Mihajlov, a young writer of Russian origin, author of a remarkable work on Soviet intellectual life, was arrested in Zadar for having planned to bring out a 'Djilasist' magazine independent of the League and opposed to it.

Bakaric and Kardelj, like their Serbian political colleagues Popovic and Todorovic, wanted to make it quite clear from the start that their support of decentralization and democratization did not mean that they were adepts of Western-type parliamentary democracy. Though they showed much greater flexibility in their dealings with the intellectuals than Gomulka or Novotny in the same period, the Yugoslav leaders never surrendered control over the dissemination of information.[3]

In July 1966, when the memorable session opened, the Central

Committee appointed a board of forty members to formulate plans for the restructuring of the League. These plans were submitted in the form of 'theses' in April 1967. Before this, however, there was a very extensive and enlightening discussion in the press of the League's proper role in a largely decentralized Yugoslavia. It may be noted at this point that even though Crvenkovski went as far as to suggest that factions be permitted in the party, most of the leaders were anxious to stay within the limits of the Marxist-Leninist tradition.

Tito especially was determined not to jettison the Leninist concept of power, but not simply for internal reasons: he also wanted to keep a place for his party in the great family of Communist parties. This is why, from the beginning of 1967, he sought as many opportunities as possible for the exchange of views with leaders of fraternal parties: having met with Luigi Longo, Ceausescu and Zhivkov, he visited Moscow at the end of January, and on his return met Kadar. It is true he would not alter his position on the issues under discussion: the meeting of the new 'council', the conference of European Communist parties, called for April 1967 in Karlovy Vary (Karlsbad). Like Ceausescu, he did not want to limit his freedom of diplomatic action by committing himself. But this intransigence on his part was not intended to lead to Yugoslavia's isolation, and Tito was clearly not indifferent to the cautious reservations about the Yugoslav party's plans for reform expressed by *Pravda* on 20 February 1967.[4]

The theses on the reorganization of the party published in 1967 showed that even the most liberal members of Tito's circle were in agreement on the need to preserve the system of dictatorship exercised through the single party, while somewhat reducing the party's role and extending the scope of the alliance of socialist forces, the trade unions, and the republican and federal communal assemblies. Substantial progress was made on this last point. In December 1966 there was a ministerial crisis in Slovenia, the like of which had never been experienced under any Communist régime: finding himself in a minority in the Assembly, the chairman of the Council, Janko Smole, resigned. His decision was the more electrifying in that he omitted to give the Central

Committee prior notice of it, whereas according to the rules laid down three months earlier by Kardelj, 'if the government must be answerable to the Assembly, Communists are answerable to party organizations'. It was only after a compromise solution had been worked out with the Central Committee and the Assembly that Smole withdrew his resignation. The deputies of the Federal Assembly, elected in June 1967, also took their new prerogatives seriously, and made considerable use of the right to criticize the government. Nevertheless, the respective roles of federal government, party, assemblies, and the organs of self-government have yet to be precisely defined, and the new federal model, substantially extending the scope of the republican governments and parties at the expense of the central power, has yet to be worked out in detail.[5]

While the debate was raging over party and state reform, Tito's powers seemed greater than ever. Thus when the Middle East crisis came (May–June 1967), he seemed to be acting on his own authority when he espoused the Arab cause with even fewer reservations than the Soviets. No doubt his personal friendship with Nasser made matters easier and the close links with the U.A.R. had long been one of the planks of Tito's foreign policy. If Tito agreed to take part in the two Kremlin-sponsored conferences of socialist countries on the Middle East, held in Moscow and Budapest in June 1967, it was not in order to make common cause with the Soviets, but rather to urge them to give Nasser more positive support and to take stronger political action against Israel. Tito was in no way deterred by the reluctance of certain members of his government and a significant section of the public, who would have preferred a more moderate response, like Rumania's, so that Belgrade might mediate later. In September 1967, after Tito's trip to Cairo, Damascus and Baghdad, Yugoslavia put forward a more flexible plan for a political solution than the Indo-Yugoslav proposals submitted to the special session of the General Assembly in June. But Yugoslavia's position had already been compromised by its unilateralist stand at the height of the crisis.

Tito interpreted the Israeli victory after the military coup in Greece as the beginning of an American offensive to alter the balance of power in the Near East and the Balkans, and therefore as a threat to the security of Yugoslavia. He decided that it was necessary to put a brake on the liberals' activity and to rely more on conservative elements in the army, the great body of veterans of the partisan war (somewhat demoralized by Rankovic's expulsion), and the reorganized political police, whose importance in the struggle against infiltration by foreign intelligence services had been stressed in a series of articles in *Borba*.[6] On 1 August 1967 Tito appointed as his Chief-of-Staff the veteran General Milos Sumonja, a Serb from central Croatia, whence had come the largest guerrilla contingents between 1941 and 1944. It is not surprising that the army's political influence should have increased at the time of Yugoslavia's second revolution (as in China, where the party also was split), even if this increase was not translated, as it was in China, into a direct takeover of the administration. Thus there was simultaneously a tendency towards decentralization, the distribution of power, and the transformation of Yugoslavia into a kind of presidential republic, with the army standing as a symbol of the unity of the state, until the party revived.

On the other hand, there was again a noticeable deterioration in relations between Moscow and Belgrade at the beginning of 1968. The Yugoslavs did not yield to Soviet pressure for their participation in the preparations for the new council; they expressed their concern (notably at the Conference of Progressive Mediterranean Forces which took place at the end of May in Rome) at the presence of Soviet naval forces in the Mediterranean, and finally directly opposed the Kremlin on 'democratization' in Czechoslovakia and the anti-intellectual purge in Poland. Tito's talks with the Soviet leaders on his brief visit to Moscow at the end of April did not narrow the gap between them. Apparently the Yugoslav leader indicated that he would regard any Soviet attempt to put pressure on Czechoslovakia, or to intervene, as a serious mistake, and he would oppose such a move without hesitation.

At the same time, contacts between Belgrade and Bucharest became more frequent, and renewed friendship was demonstrated in Bakaric's visit to Rumania in May and Ceausescu's to Yugoslavia. The Rumanian leaders, without approving of all the 'internal' implications of the Prague liberalization movement, did not fail to appreciate the advantages they might draw from a revitalized Czechoslovakia's adoption of a more independent foreign policy, like their own. As opposed to the 'bloc of the five unshakeables' – the U.S.S.R., Poland, the G.D.R., Hungary and Bulgaria (the last two being 'followers' rather than 'leaders') – Yugoslavia, Rumania and Czechoslovakia were beginning to form a triangular union of their own, recalling the Little Entente of the inter-war period.[7]

The Yugoslav leaders clearly showed more imagination in the field of diplomacy than in that of the national economy, which continued to give cause for anxiety. The drastic anti-inflationary measures of 1966–7 substantially slowed down industrial production (the rate of growth fell from 8 per cent in 1965 to 4 per cent in 1966 and 5.6 per cent in 1967), and led to a rise in unemployment (344,000 at the beginning of 1968). 'The introduction of a market economy', wrote E. Bettiza in the Milan newspaper *Corriere della Sera*, 'had a savagely palaeo-capitalist effect not experienced elsewhere.' Nevertheless, the balance sheet drawn up by the O.E.C.D. experts at the end of 1967 stressed the positive aspects of the development: a better balance between supply and demand; a healthier balance-of-payments situation; an improvement in productivity; and more efficient use of investments.[8] The movement in favour of the importation of Western capital grew steadily stronger. ('It is better to import capital than export labour,' observed Zagreb's *Vjesnik u Srijedu* on 6 December 1967.)

In this confused, almost anarchic, edifice of political, economic and social structures, Tito's presence as the supreme arbitrator seemed more than ever essential. The old head-of-state made full use of his still very great prestige in June 1968, when Belgrade's students rose as did the French *enragés* in May, except that the majority of rebellious students in Yugoslavia did not question the whole basis of society or the régime. Their demands reflected a curious, but understandable, mixture of egalitarian, Maoist, and liberal 'Djilasist' ideas. They wanted social and political practice to reflect more closely the principles professed by their leaders;

the socialist republic to be more social (with an equable division of labour, sanctions against the new rich, the 'Red bourgeoisie', and emergency measures to reduce unemployment, particularly among the young technicians) and also freer and more democratic (democratization of the party, press and radio, freedom of speech and assembly, and the extension of self-government to the institutions of higher education, which had retained their authoritarian structure).

There was the danger in Yugoslavia, as in France, that the student explosion might spread to other sectors – that it might inflame the working class, who had many reasons for dissatisfaction, and rekindle national antagonisms. Tito, however, faced the crisis, and displayed remarkable skill in avoiding it. Instead of attacking the students, he admitted the justice of most of their demands. 'I promise you', he told them in his televised speech of 9 June, 'that I shall give my full attention to solving your problems. You must help me in this task. If I prove incapable of settling this matter, I must no longer remain in my post.' The students responded enthusiastically to this display of enlightened, vigorous and concerned paternalism. Moreover, the first positive result of their movement had come on 5 June, when the Serbian League of Communists decided to impose a graduated tax on high salaries, to raise the minimum wage, to establish self-governing bodies in the universities and to give the students parliamentary representation.

Thus the Yugoslav students emerged as an identifiable political force, and succeeded in reminding the leaders, almost exclusively concerned with administrative and economic problems, of the 'social' vocation of a socialist régime. Nevertheless, the main problem remaining to be solved in Yugoslavia is the creation of institutions strong enough to ensure the unity and development of the federal State, even after the man of destiny has disappeared. In this respect, the invasion of friendly Czechoslovakia in August 1968, against which the government and the League of Communists immediately protested in the most vigorous terms, has acted as a catalyst. The relaunching of the anti-Titoist campaigns by the U.S.S.R., Poland and Bulgaria, Sofia's renewed reference to the Macedonian question, the threat of intervention against the

Balkan dissidents ('unlikely but possible', according to Tito's speech at Pula on 23 September 1968) have served to remind Yugoslavs, of whatever ethnic origin and shade of opinion, of the vital need to remain unified. Once again, the Yugoslav peoples are mobilized and ready to fight in defence of their dearest possession: national independence.[9]

11

The Czechoslovak Tragedy
and its Implications

A Peaceful Revolution

At the beginning of 1968, twenty years after the 'Prague coup'
marked the seizure of power by the Communist party – both a
cause and effect of the cold war that divided Europe into two
separate and hostile blocs – Czechoslovakia surprised and enthral-
led the world with the spectacle of a political, ideological and
social resurgence, a boisterous and yet at the same time level-
headed reawakening whose significance transcended national
boundaries.

Novotny was removed from his post as First Secretary of the
party on 5 January 1968. At first the ensuing events that shook
Czechoslovakia, until then the firmest bastion of the Communist
order in Eastern Europe, seemed a continuation of the process of
de-Stalinization, which had been too long delayed there. The end
of Novotny's personal power had the same 'liberating' effect in
Prague and Bratislava as had the end of Rakosi's in Hungary in
summer 1956, and the eclipse of party authority in the same
period in Poland. As in those two countries twelve years before,
the explosion of democratic aspirations and the irrepressible resurgence of national feeling coincided. But in Czechoslovakia, the
political élite which initiated and directed the process of renewal
benefited from Hungarian and Polish experience in its efforts to
avert both an uncontrolled explosion and a degeneration of the
original impetus. Furthermore, the Czech movement was also
related to the changes that had occurred over recent years in
Rumanian policy, to the search for new socialist paths in Yugo-

slavia, and more remotely to the tendency towards questioning, change and renewal that appeared simultaneously inside and on the fringes of the Communist, socialist and progessive Western parties and movements.

The complexity of the Czechoslovak movement, its connections both with the West and the East, is due as much to the country's situation in the heart of Europe as to its high level of industrial, intellectual and technological development and the evidently indestructible nature of its liberal and democratic traditions. These traditions sharply contrasted with the bureaucratic, totalitarian, and socially and nationally fissiparous character that the Communist leadership, burdened by the Stalin cult, its loyalty to the U.S.S.R., and its dogmatism, had imposed on the socialist régime after seizing power. 'The Czechs and the Slovaks', wrote one of the protagonists of the revival, the historian and theorist Edo Fris, 'are among those peoples that possess a national memory... History is omnipresent in our social consciousness, both as a warning and a stimulus.'[1] But to the Czechs and Slovaks (whether Communists or not) with their historical consciousness, the centralist, monopolistic system established by Gottwald and continued by Novotny did not seem to be the modern expression of their national personality, as during the first Republic and later the 1944 Slovak rising, the 1945 Prague rising and the first three post-war years, but something alien, grafted on.

The renewal, the political awakening that took place at the beginning of 1968, had many and complex causes, but its principal source lay in the deep desire of the Czechs and Slovaks to rediscover their confused and repressed identity, and to restore the continuity between their past and their future. This desire is common to all the peoples of the East, traumatized by the war and Soviet domination; it has led nearly all the Communist parties of Eastern Europe, at different times and in different ways, to reconsider their purpose, and to try to establish themselves as representing the national interests.

What distinguished the Czech development from those in the other People's Democracies was the double operation of democratization and de-Stalinization effected by a large and strong Communist party in a spirit of realism, taking into account the international situation, the precariousness of the country's position as the 'forward bastion of the socialist bloc', and with due regard for the essential interests of the hegemonistic super power.

The aim of Novotny's successors was to succeed where Imre Nagy, carried away by the tidal wave of popular rebellion, and Gomulka, with his stranglehold on the vital forces in his country, had failed: to construct a socialist model that was both pluralist and national, stable and efficient.

The Crisis of 1967–8

The origins of the crisis that culminated in the gradual expulsion of Novotny and his Stalinist colleagues go back to the aftermath of the Twelfth Congress of the Czechoslovak Communist Party in December 1962, when Novotny, yielding to pressure from those encouraged by the new wave of de-Stalinization in the Soviet Union and the Soviet-American *détente*, made a few tactical concessions; the dictatorship changed its style, and became more liberal. Rehabilitation, only partial, but with repercussions for fairly large sections of the party, enabled many survivors of the 1949–54 purges to be heard again. Intellectual and artistic life revived, and a spirit of inquiry sprang to life in Prague, in the writers' union, the party High School, the party History Institute and the Institute of Economics; in Brno, in the magazine *Host do Domu*; and in Bratislava, where the influence of prominent figures who had been rehabilitated (Husak, Novomesky, Loebl and Fris) was increasingly felt.

In 1963–7 Novotny and his principal associates, Dolansky, Hendrych, Kolder, Koucky, did their utmost to stabilize political life at the level of semi-liberalization attained in 1963, while preserving the party's basic prerogatives. But these were devastatingly challenged by experts led by Professor Ota Sik, who called for decentralization and rationalization to combat the stagnation, technical backwardness and decline in the standard of living. The people, and particularly the intelligentsia, were more conscious of this backwardness and decline, in that they now had a basis for comparison with neighbouring capitalist states, thanks to the resumption of tourist, commercial and cultural exchanges with

Austria, West Germany, and the West generally. Blame attached both to the state-controlled system and to the inefficiency of the cadres, most of whom had been selected by the party leadership for their firmness and ideological orthodoxy, not for their competence.

At the beginning of 1967 the government brought in an economic reform, a compromise between reformist aspirations and centralized planning, which from the start was obstructed, if not sabotaged, by conservative cadres. Uneasiness grew, especially since Novotny, at the Central Committee meetings in February and March, tried hard to bring the country back into line ideologically with the Soviet Union, where the neo-Zhdanovist, antirevisionist current was getting the upper hand. Sinyavsky and Daniel were in prison, and Solzhenitsyn was being subjected to increased pressure from the censors. The establishment of a Czech Ministry of Culture, the appointment of a dogmatic bureaucrat, Havlicek, to head the committee on ideology, Hendrych's repeated warnings to film directors, writers and journalists forgetful of the party's primacy in doctrine, were sufficient evidence of the uncertainty of the gains of 1963 and of the dictatorship's incompatibility with free artistic and scientific development.

The Middle Eastern war and the government's unqualified conformity with the U.S.S.R.'s pro-Arab policy further exasperated the intellectuals. The crude anti-Zionist campaign initiated by the government was not only patently unjust and out of all proportion, but its overtones and implications recalled the anti-Semitism of the Slansky trial period, and – viewed against the moderate, neutral stand of the Rumanians – was fresh evidence of the leaders' lack of dignity and independence. For many Czechs there was no doubt about Israel's right of self-defence, even if it involved making the first move, in the face of an increasingly obvious threat of annihilation.

At the writers' congress in Prague on 29 June 1967, a number of speakers criticized the government's policy. Pavel Kohout compared Israel's destiny with Czechoslovakia's after the Munich agreement. The novelist Jan Prochazka, deputy member of the Central Committee and a former confidant of Novotny, read out a letter addressed to the party leadership protesting against the anti-Israel campaign. A few weeks after the congress, the Slovak novelist Mnacko left for Israel and denounced in the Western press the servility and the regressive, anti-Semitic tendencies of the Prague government. For this he was deprived of his citizenship, to be restored in March 1968, when Mnacko returned to his country.

The writers' congress marked a turning-point in the relations between the intellectuals and the government. For the first time writers, with the courage of desperadoes, had led an assault on the leadership. The resolution, agreed after lengthy discussions with the authorities who were represented at the congress by Hendrych, indicated that the liberals had already made considerable progress; it recalled the 'high level of democracy and freedom' enjoyed by Czechoslovakia before the war, when 'the most eminent representatives of Czech and Slovak literature freely decided in favour of socialism'; it stressed that 'the continuity of Czechoslovak literature was broken in 1949 ... the creative process was shackled, put in the service of propaganda; culture and ideology were identified with each other in an intolerable and crudely utilitarian fashion'. Referring to this resolution, a number of writers demanded amendment of the 1957 press law which, according to the playwright Ivan Klima, was far less progressive than the press law abolishing censorship promulgated a hundred years earlier by the emperor Francis Joseph. Kohout revealed the contents of the dramatic letter which Solzhenitsyn had sent to the Union of Soviet Writers in May, and the fiery young novelist Vaculik remorselessly indicted the system, whose greatest crime, in his opinion, was to have turned a nation of citizens into a herd of faceless, terrified subjects. He called for a revision of the 1960 Constitution, so that citizens might be guaranteed against abuses of power.[2]

In other times or places such disrespectful and inflammatory speeches would have led to arrests and severe penalties. Nothing, however, better illustrates the decline in Novotny's authority than the contrast between the violence of the verbal condemnations and the relative mildness of the reprisals taken against the rebels. They were merely subjected to disciplinary measures: the

Central Committee meeting in September expelled Vaculik, Liehm, and Klima from the party, while Prochazka was relieved of his functions as a deputy member of the Central Committee. The organ of the writers' union, *Literarni Noviny*, was placed under the control of the Ministry of Culture. It soon ceased publication, and was replaced by a new weekly that was boycotted by the writers and the public; it reappeared under the name of *Literarni Listy* in February 1968.

But this alone was insufficient. Czechoslovakia's oppressive summer was marked by Mnacko's exile; the trial of the young writer Benes, because of his contacts with émigrés; the mysterious death of Jordan, vice-chairman of an American-Jewish organization; and by incidents on the Austrian frontier deliberately provoked by a police force that seemed completely independent of government control. Novotny still hoped to destroy the writers' opposition by shattering their organization and restricting the activities of the publishing houses which supported them. But when it came to the actual implementation of repressive measures, the party Presidium split. Contrary to hard-liners such as Chudik, chairman of the Slovak Council, and Dolansky, a number of others like Kolder and the economist Cernik urged moderation; Hendrych wavered, and Alexander Dubcek, the Slovak party chief, continued to defend the Slovak liberals and independents whose mouthpiece was the magazine *Kulturny Zivot*. The arguments over repression, over the economic reform, the first effects of which had been inflationary, over a new definition of the role of the party, and over the Slovak demands for independence had accelerated the dissolution of the party leadership's monolithic unity.

The first symptoms of a crisis appeared at the Central Committee session of 30 October 1967. It was now that Dubcek took over the leadership of the opposition, in his questioning of Novotny's methods. The latter ill-advisedly responded by calling him a 'bourgeois nationalist'; this was the last straw.[3] The savage repression, on Novotny's personal orders, of a demonstration of students from the quarters in Strahov who were motivated by material grievances, rapidly politicized, increased the unpopularity of the party chief and head-of-state whose replacement, at least as First Secretary, was being openly advocated. The anti-Novotny group of Professor Goldstuecker, the writers' spokesman, and the rehabilitated veterans Smrkovsky, Kriegel, Svermoda and Josef Pavel met regularly in the party's Institute of History and won support in the party organization, the press, radio, television and the University.[4]

Sensing the danger of a union between the Czech liberal group and the Slovak autonomists led by Dubcek and Husak, Novotny appealed to Brezhnev, who arrived in Prague on 8 December 1967. But all the head of the Soviet party could achieve was to persuade Prime Minister Lenart (a Slovak), David (Minister of Foreign Affairs) and Lomsky (Minister of Defence) to give Novotny their support. Brezhnev denied wanting to interfere in party affairs, but argued that, in the existing international situation – with Bonn engaging in disruptive manoeuvres, and with the need to strengthen the northern flank of the Warsaw Pact and to show solidarity on the eve of the preparatory conference in Budapest – a change of leadership in Czechoslovakia would be playing into the hands of the enemy propagandists. In answer to this it was pointed out that the concentration of power in Novotny's hands was an anachronism, even from the point of view of the international movement. It was Novotny's mistakes that were lowering the party's prestige and reducing its effectiveness.

On 19 December the Central Committee met in a tense atmosphere. The party's Parliament, formerly Novotny's submissive tool, found itself placed in the role of arbitrator, called on to make a decision in the face of a Presidium split equally. The opposition speakers – Ota Sik; Slavik; the Rector of the Charles University, Stary; and Dubcek's deputy in the Slovak party secretariat, Bilak – called for the separation of powers, the reorganization of the police, etc. Faced by a mounting storm of criticism and deserted by several of his supporters, including Hendrych and Koucky, Novotny made a vague self-critical statement, and indicated his readiness to withdraw, if that was the price to be paid for the maintenance of party unity.

On 21 December, the Central Committee adjourned to consider the matter, until 3 January. A twelve-member preparatory committee of representatives from the large regional organizations was charged with the task of helping the Presidium to work out a solution to the crisis. Novotny tried, with the help of Mamula, head of the Central Committee department of the armed forces, to use this period to mobilize the generals, the police and the people's militia, that 'private army of the party' raised in strict adherence to Stalinism; he also tried to get the Soviets to use their influence, and Ambassador Chervonenko intervened on his behalf with many of the leaders. General Sejna, head of the party organization at the Ministry of Defence, planned to lobby the Central Committee with the principal military leaders, and at the same time to move some armoured columns in the direction of Prague.

The situation resembled that which had existed in Poland in October 1956, before Gomulka's election. However, General Dzur, Deputy Minister of Defence, and Prchlik, head of the political administration of the army, both friends of Dubcek and the liberals, proceeded to a counter-mobilization; the plot, of which the organizers, like Rakosi and the Polish 'Natolinians' in 1956, aimed at arresting the main opposition leaders, failed. Meetings were called in Bratislava to demand Novotny's resignation. In the Central Committee, which resumed work on 3 January, the preparatory sub-committee proposed a compromise solution: Novotny was to surrender his position as head of the party, but retain that of President of the Republic. After a last attempt by Novotny's friends to save him, this proposal was accepted. At a nocturnal session on 4 January the Central Committee, presented with the alternative of Lenart, the Novotnyites' candidate, and Cernik, the candidate of the liberals, selected a third man to succeed Novotny as First Secretary – Alexander Dubcek, whose candidature had been held in reserve.

This choice turned out to be a very wise one. A moderate and honest Communist who was anxious to win the support of both the party and the public, Dubcek brought the Prague liberals the votes of the Slovak independents. He had set out his programme in an article in the *Pravda* (Bratislava) for 31 December 1967. 'We are living', he wrote, 'at a turning-point in history, a period of transition to a qualitatively new type of socialist society ...

We must declare war on all preconceptions and on all subjectivism, and defeat the attempt to impose the party's will on society through coercive and despotic methods.' After his election, in a speech broadcast on 1 February 1968, he was even more explicit: 'The party', he said, 'exists for the working people; it must be neither above, nor outside, society, but an integral part of it. Democracy is not simply possession of the right and means of free expression of opinion, but also the government's attention to the opinion so expressed, and the genuine participation of everyone in the process of decision-making.'

It is true that public opinion was not allowed to influence the actual decisions affecting the nation's future during the crisis. The Czech public could find out what was going on in the Plenum only by listening to foreign radio broadcasts. But the logic of the struggle against the Novotnyites, who were a long way from giving up, led the most dynamic elements in the progressive wing of the party – Smrkovsky, Cisar and Sabata, among others – to bring the discussions down into the market place, so as to persuade the people that what was at issue, over and beyond the changes in officials, was a radical reshaping of methods of administration, a liberal, humanistic Communism based on pre-1949 traditions, and rejecting totalitarian methods. The writers, who had chosen Goldstuecker as their president, and the journalists and commentators, now virtually uncensored, enthusiastically joined in the campaign to rouse first the intelligentsia and then larger sections of the public.

The intellectual élite, which the Novotnyites denounced to the workers as neo-bourgeois, had never felt itself so close to snatching the reins of power from the administrative élite. There was a strange excitement in the air; people felt a flow of creative energy; it was very much like what the Hungarian and Polish élite had experienced in 1955-6 and a part of the young French intelligentsia in May 1968, but with the difference that the excitement was limited to the various sections of the intelligentsia, and the political awakening, the clash between old and new, the great confrontation, did not lead to any disturbances or outbursts of violence.

The non-violent character of the Czech revival needs some explanation. It was no doubt largely due to the temperament of the people, who are especially cautious, serious-minded and moderate, and to the democratic tradition, which had suddenly reasserted itself, after twenty years, with great force and yet with moderation. For students of the history of political thought it is a good example of the survival of deeply-rooted national, political, religious and social traditions in the face of oppression.

After twenty years a new generation had grown up in Czechoslovakia, shaped by the system and kept in such ignorance of the past that memories of the anti-Nazi resistance and the Slovak rebellion, most of whose heroes had been sentenced, persecuted and annihilated politically, had been largely forgotten. The works of T. G. Masaryk were on the index, and no one at school or in the Komsomol (Youth Organization) told the young about Jan Masaryk and his tragic end. And yet one of the first collective acts of the Prague students after Novotny's resignation in January was to make a pilgrimage to the graves of the two Masaryks who lie side by side in the little cemetery of Lany, 60 kilometres from Prague.

The salient feature of this dramatic rediscovery of the past was the emphasis on discussion rather than violence. What occurred in Prague and Bratislava was revolution *in camera*. For weeks the streets were empty after the working day was over, everyone was at a meeting, especially party cells and committees. Then came the writers and scholars, trade unionists, and co-operative peasants, students and journalists, economists and victims of the terror, ex-servicemen and Pioneers. The leaders of the former political parties, which in 1948 had become mere satellite bodies (Father Plojhar's Catholic-oriented People's Party, the Czech Socialist Party), all the organizations serving simply a nominal purpose and providing alibis, and the prelates of the various religious faiths, were sitting on committees, electing themselves by getting rid of discredited dignitaries and discussing plans for the future.

Thus the initiation of legislation, which had been so long monopolized by the party, was restored to individuals and groups, all freely giving expression to their grievances and demands without fear of reprisal. In the future, considerable credit will probably be due to Dubcek for allowing freedom of speech full play for a while, postponing the time when some measure of stabilization would have to be introduced, trusting in the people's civic sense and wisdom like an easy-going monarch who had been converted to liberalism. A relevant factor here is that the people, especially the inhabitants of the Czech and Moravian regions, were inclined to the left; contrary to what happened in 1956 in Hungary and Poland, there was no real danger of the situation being exploited by rightist or extreme right-wing elements.

This did not stop Novotny's supporters inside and outside the country from condemning the threat to the 'gains of February 1949' from the encouragement of 'anti-socialist forces', the unmasking of all the defects of the former régime, including the judicial crimes, which were more numerous than had been thought. But these forces were not clearly defined: intellectuals like Ivan Svitak the philosopher, or the playwright Vaclav Havel, who urged the need for an opposition party, were cited, as were the attempts of the former social democrats to reform; the claims of the ex-satellite, and now emancipated, parties to a greater say in government; demands for the dismantling of the workers' militia, or the re-establishment of the pre-war *sokols*; and the broadcasting by press and radio of facts and opinions that might discredit the party and provoke the Russians.

At the Central Committee meeting in late March, a Novotnyite painted a sombre picture of the collapse of party authority: in certain factories, he said, the workers had evicted the director; in other places honest officials had been threatened with dismissal. There were calls for the re-establishment of private enterprises with under fifty employees. There was a spirit of vendetta abroad, judges were committing suicide, and there were other symptoms of tension.[5] In the months following the January Plenum, Novotny and his friends did their best to play on the fear aroused among the new bureaucratic class by the removal of restraints on freedom of speech; such people were frightened of losing their privileges and of having to answer for their illegal acts. They identified themselves with socialism and the pre-Soviet course, and they still had considerable influence among the workers. They believed that the Soviets would not allow revisionism to triumph in Czechoslovakia at a time when every challenge at home was being met with renewed vigour and when the influence of neo-Stalinist elements was becoming more and more noticeable in the Soviet leadership.

Dubcek Caught in Cross-Fire

In fact, from the beginning of the Czech crisis the Soviet leaders, surprised and worried that a country that previously had given no trouble was slipping out of their grasp, had kept up a steady pressure on Dubcek and his team. They intervened first in favour of Novotny; then, seeing that the latter had definitely lost all his authority, threw their weight behind the conservatives who, like Bilak, Dubcek's successor at the head of the Slovak party, then Kolder, Indra, Svestka and others, rallied to Dubcek more or less wholeheartedly, on condition that he maintain the party's position with a minimum of concessions and call to order the press, whose frankness was continually shocking them.[6]

From the Dresden conference of 23 March when Dubcek received his first serious formal warning, the new party leader was constantly being torn between the Soviet Union and the other allies, and the progressive wing of his own party. The Soviets demanded that he slow down the movement, and on no account overstep the bounds that the most liberal of the Communist leaders, Janos Kadar, had, in consultation with the Kremlin, set for liberalization in Hungary. The Czechoslovak progressives on the other hand – Smrkovsky, Cisar, Spacek, besides others – spurred by the support aroused among the militants, in the press and among growing sections of the public, were urging Dubcek to espouse the cause of renewal more resolutely, to eliminate all traces of Novotnyism, and to embark on an original and bold experiment in democratization.

Dubcek, for his part, hoped at first to accomplish his aims, which were, after all, moderate enough, on the basis of the January compromise: he wanted to steer a middle course between the party's left (conservative) wing, supported by the Russians, and its right (radical) wing. His object was to satisfy the Russians without upsetting public opinion. After each meeting with

Brezhnev (in January and February), and with the Five (in March), he did his best to slow things down, and to urge a more realistic attitude and more patience. However, each of his attempts to stabilize the situation, and each impulse from conservative elements in the party made the progressives, who had the advantage of almost total press support, react more and more strongly, so that Dubcek and his centrist friends – Cernik, Kriegel and Mlynar – were gradually carried away. Imperceptibly the drift of this internal development forced Dubcek into a more radical position. He certainly thought he was telling the truth when he explained to the Five at Dresden that the party was in control of the general situation and that there was no reason for serious concern, despite a few negative developments in the country, especially in the press. But the party leadership was in control only in so far as it identified itself with popular aspirations and the overriding desire for change. And the more Dubcek gained the confidence of the country, the more he lost that of the Soviets and their allies. His path is somewhat reminiscent of Imre Nagy's in 1956. Nagy also started off as a paternalistic Communist of the centre, a believer in enlightened dictatorship; events turned him, in spite of himself, into a popular leader, a national leader. Dubcek accomplished the same metamorphosis between March and August 1968.

In January he was still quite prepared to collaborate with a less powerful Novotny. But the latter, still counting on Russian support, would not resign himself to a secondary role, nor accept his defeat as final. He tried to redress the balance by turning the workers against the liberal intellectuals, who were depicted as the gravediggers of socialism intent on creating the conditions for a return to capitalism; but in January, General Sejna, Novotny's protégé, a friend of his son's and one of the backers of the abortive plot of December 1967, fled from the country and this enabled the anti-Novotnyites to launch a powerful counterattack. On 15 March Novotny was forced to append his signature to the dismissal of two of his most active supporters, the Minister of the Interior and the Attorney General. A week later he was forced to resign as President of the Republic. (This prompted the Five to call Dubcek urgently to Dresden on 23 March.) On 28

March the Central Committee unanimously proposed General Ludvik Svoboda, a survivor of T. G. Masaryk's and Benes's generation, as its candidate for the presidency. The National Assembly having confirmed this choice, which was regarded by the public as a turning-point in the life of the country, the Central Committee met again and on 6 April adopted the 'party's action programme', each paragraph of which reflected the contradictory concerns of reactivating public opinion and strengthening the party's authority.[7]

The Czechoslovak Model

The most important feature of the programme was the Communist party's denial, not of its leading role – this was the guarantee of progressive, socialist development – but of the totalitarian power it had enjoyed since 1949.

'The Communist party', it stated, '... does not wish to assert its leading role by bringing pressure to bear on society, but by serving it devotedly with an eye to its free, progressive, socialist development. The party cannot impose its authority; it must earn it continually by its action... The party's aim is not to become a universal administrator of society, to bind and shackle the organizations and the whole life of society by its directives... The party's policy must in no way make non-Communist citizens feel that their rights and their freedom are being infringed by the party.'

The authors of this programme (in which one recognizes the hand of the jurist Zdenek Mlynar, Dubcek's grey eminence) did not go so far as frankly to allow pluralism, real contests for power or an institutionalized opposition. But they did advocate a clear separation of the powers of the party and the government, the latter being in addition responsible to a parliament that should be more representative and more dynamic; and a system of 'counterweights', based primarily on the restoration of the National Front, the remains of the great coalition of 1945–8. The programme provided for the partial freedom of the non-Communist parties in the Front, which were now permitted, if not to oppose, at least 'to express different and contradictory points of view ... but from a socialist viewpoint, through agreement ...' The interested parties – trade unions, the new national organization of co-operative peasants, the youth movement, the unions of writers and artists – were also called on to 'exercise a direct influence over state policy'.

What the programme laid down about the dissemination of news was more radical. 'We must have done with delayed, distorted and incomplete news', it stated, promising to abolish censorship, which was effected by the press law of 25 June 1968, to guarantee the right of foreign travel, to rehabilitate and compensate victims of the arbitrary persecution of former years, and to purge and reorganize the security services, which 'should no longer be directed or used to resolve political problems'. There was also provision for the completion of the decentralization process, the restoration of the economy, the normalization of relations between Church and State, and finally, the framing of a new constitutional law to give the country a federal structure, in conformity with Slovak wishes and based on the complete equality of the Czech and Slovak nations, with a considerable degree of independence for national minorities.

A new and mainly centrist government under Cernik, but containing a few representatives of the progressive wing (called 'Communists of the right' in Czechoslovakia) such as Ota Sik, who became vice-chairman of the Council, and Kadlec, the Minister of Education, was appointed on 8 April to carry out the programme. The appointment to the Ministry of the Interior of General Pavel, a former prisoner who had been tortured by the police, was a guarantee of the active fulfilment of measures for the purging of the security apparatus.

On 18 April the National Assembly, by 148 votes to 68, elected Josef Smrkovsky, the most effective advocate of reform, as its President. Not without humour, he expressed satisfaction at the fact that by voting against him at least 68 deputies in the Assembly had shown that a lot had changed since the days when the vote did not express the real opinion of those who voted. Nevertheless, the vote did show how unreal the Central Committee's unanimity had been a few weeks earlier in approving the new party programme. It began to look as though Dubcek would be making a mistake in trying to govern with a Central Committee and National Assembly most of whose members owed their positions to Novotny and his followers. Immediately after the National Assembly session, another leading progressive, Cisar, expressed the hope that the Central Committee would be replaced throughout, which would only be possible if the anticipated Party Congress were called. He thereby defined in advance the stakes for which the two sides were playing in the intense struggle that took place the following week at the Party's regional conferences.

The Hostility of Poland and the G.D.R.

The adoption of the action programme, despite its moderate character, was a great success for the Czech liberals. It consolidated the gains of the previous months, notably freedom of the press and of expression, and this is why the Polish and East German leaders, as well as the Soviets, watched Czechoslovakia's progress with apprehension bordering on panic. Most of the Eastern leaders did not believe in the possibility of democratizing Communism, and they regarded Dubcek's aim, to give socialism a human face, as absurd and insulting. If a revisionist government established itself successfully in Prague, the game would be up for the neo-Stalinists and neo-Zhdanovists in such countries as East Germany, Poland and Bulgaria, and liberal trends in all the Eastern countries would be given a boost that might prove decisive.

In particular Czechoslovakia's development created a chasm with Poland, which was embarking simultaneously on a diametrically opposed course. Indeed, at the beginning of 1968, the removal of Mickiewicz's play *The Forefathers*, on the pretext that the production gave the anti-tsarist piece an anti-Soviet tone, led to violent student demonstrations.

The Warsaw students and the teachers and writers who joined them, excited by the political spring in Prague, thought their movement might act as the signal for a similar national and democratic reawakening in their country. But the reverse happened. Moczar's group seemed to have been waiting for just such an opportunity to move into attack and secure an advantageous position in the struggle for the succession to Gomulka. The militia's occupation of Warsaw University transformed a relatively calm protest movement into a rebellion that was brutally suppressed. Reviving the language of the 1952 trials, the Partisans at once attributed all the disturbances among students and intellectuals to the action of 'a group of conspirators affiliated to the Zionist Centre ... and which was plotting a *coup d'état*'.[8] They initiated a great purge of the party machine, the press, radio, cinema and the University, the first victims of which were liberal Communists of Jewish origin accused of Zionism.

The charge was sheer nonsense; the 30,000 Jews who had survived from the pre-war community of 3 million (a few tens of thousands having emigrated to Israel or the West between 1945 and 1957) had given sufficient proof of their opposition to Zionism. But anti-Zionism enabled the Partisans to arouse the latent anti-Semitic feelings of the working masses – a working class strengthened by the influx of hundreds of thousands of politically naïve and suggestible peasants. As it grew, the anti-Zionist campaign turned into a purge directed against all liberal and revisionist elements, not sparing even those close to Gomulka.

Surprised by this Partisan offensive, Gomulka tried to temporize and to place himself at the head of the movement so as to be able to check it. In a speech on 19 March 1968, he asked the party to draw a distinction between Zionist Jews, who would have to go; cosmopolitan Jews, who could stay but must be barred from positions of responsibility; and patriotic and Communist Jews, who should be treated the same as loyal Poles. The Partisans, however, while paying lip service to Gomulka's wishes, continued to drive home their advantage and to consolidate their position. Gierek, the leader of the technocrats, apparently supported the movement, which was carrying Poland towards a régime based, apart from anti-Semitism and anti-revisionism, on a flamboyant patriotism (directed against West Germany and secretly against the Soviet Union) and an ideological inflexibility in the party – a régime, therefore, which would be a Red variant of the pre-war Colonels' rule, not unlike that of Greece after the *coup d'état* of April 1967.[9]

The Warsaw riots produced a sharp reaction in Prague and Bratislava, where students and intellectuals publicly demonstrated in sympathy with the victims of repression in Poland, and the press surpassed itself in denouncing the repressive line being taken by the neighbouring countries. The ensuing war of words led to a deterioration, not only in inter-party, but also in diplomatic relations.

There was a similar deterioration in relations between Prague and East Berlin. Ulbricht and his friends saw Czech democratization as nothing but 'fits of hysteria ... over freedom of opinion and of the press, an attitude which amounts to a celebration of pure bourgeois democracy'.[10] The East Germans were the first to pass from suggestive, abstract criticism of Czechoslovak developments to personal attacks on certain of Dubcek's associates, like Smrkovsky and the economist Snejdarek. In May the Czechoslovak public got some idea of what the East German leadership thought of them when *Literarni Listy* published a confidential document produced for the benefit of G.D.R. activists, which included these comments:

The Czechoslovak Communist Party is, in fact, powerless. Loyal Communists have been expelled from top governmental bodies, and their positions have been taken over by secret enemies of the party and the people, deliberate and involuntary servants of imperialism. ... Counter-revolution is getting a grip on Czechoslovakia, and the elements of a return to the bourgeois system have seeped into the party's programme of action. ... On the pretext of granting freedom to the press, freedom has been given to the counter-revolution. This policy has already driven countless honest Communists to suicide. The way is open for anti-Soviet propaganda ... Assurances given by Czechoslovak representatives of their friendship for the U.S.S.R. and the socialist allies are worthless, since these people are no longer in control of internal developments in their country. The situation is equally out of hand on the Czechoslovak frontier, which class enemies and imperialist agents are crossing unimpeded. The development has reached the point at which it ceases to be an internal affair of Czechoslovakia. The present régime's laxity over the infiltration of enemy agents into Warsaw Pact territory threatens the security of all the member countries. The socialist countries cannot maintain a passive attitude to this state of affairs.

Doubtless Soviet officials were less direct than this, at least in public. In May Dubcek and his associates, from General Svoboda to Cisar and from Hajek to Smrkovsky, still did not despair of convincing the Kremlin that the principle of alliance with the U.S.S.R. and the other socialist countries remained sacred for them, and that all they wanted, as regards internal and external policy, was to take more account of Czechoslovakia's particular political, economic and cultural interests; this would enable them to consolidate the régime, which had been discredited under Novotny's management. But it became increasingly clear that Dubcek and Brezhnev were not speaking the same language.

After the May Plenum: The Growing Crisis

At the end of May the Czechoslovak Central Committee met in a tense atmosphere. Conservatives and liberals clashed with unprecedented violence. Dubcek, for his part, had resolved to try to appease the Soviets on the lines of the gentlemen's agreement just reached with Kosygin: the resolution he laid before the Plenum placed a certain restraint on the April programme by stressing that the party's leading role could not be questioned, that no opposition party would be permitted, and that the party would resist the anti-socialist forces of the right. But at the same time the liberals managed to impose their own terms with regard to two important points which, in fact, nullified the concessions to the Soviets. After a moving speech by Husak, who had a personal score to settle with Novotny, the latter was not only expelled from the Central Committee, but his party membership was suspended with that of six of the main organizers of the Stalinist purges – Bacilek, David, Kohler, Rais, Siroky and the public prosecutor Urvalek – 'pending an investigation into their role in the 1948–54 trials'. The second gain for the liberals was that the Fourteenth Extraordinary Congress of the party was called for 9 September.

Under the circumstances, a Congress involved drawing the mass of militants into the debate between the Czechoslovak liberals and the Soviets operating through their intermediaries; it meant calling on the main body of the party, the 1.6 million

Czechoslovak Communists, to act as arbitrators. An election fever swept the country; everyone knew that the fate of the Czechoslovak experiment would depend on the Congress delegates elected by the different echelons of the party, as it was these delegates who would elect the new party leadership and approve its programme. This was precisely why the Novotnyites and neo-conservatives such as Indra, Kolder and Svestka had done their utmost before the May Plenum to prevent an early Congress.

Once the date for it had been fixed, a race for time began. The conservatives made a last desperate attempt to mobilize all the support they could still muster in the party machine, the administration and the workers' militia. It was clear that they were receiving encouragement from abroad. The liberals responded to this Stalinist mobilization by a counter-mobilization, which was launched by an appeal in *Literarni Listy* on 27 June, entitled '2,000 Words' and addressed both to Communists and the mass of the population. It called on them actively to engage in the struggle against 'the old forces', a struggle which would no longer take place only in the upper classes, but in every enterprise and every office within the organizations of the National Front, the municipal committees and elsewhere. The appeal called for the vigilance and militancy of the masses, to eliminate 'all those who have abused their power, who have degraded the collective heritage'. It urged the supporters of renewal to take the initiative, to organize public meetings of criticism as well as demonstrations, resolutions and strikes. It recommended the setting up of committees for the defence of freedom of expression. Finally – and it was this section that caused the Soviets most consternation – for the first time openly pointing out the possibility of foreign intervention, the signatories assured the government 'that we will support it, even if it comes to bearing arms, as long as it fulfils its mandate'.

The '2,000 Words' threw the Czechoslovak conservatives, and even more so the Soviets, into a frenzy. On 11 July *Pravda* saw it as a 'platform for those forces in Czechoslovakia and beyond its frontiers which, under cover of playing with liberalization, democratization, and other things are trying to depreciate the whole of Czechoslovak history since 1948 ... to discredit the Czechoslovak party, to deny its leading role', and followed with more in like tone. The Kremlin told Dubcek to deal severely with the offenders. Dubcek replied that 'the Presidium of the Central Committee was discussing the subject, that this appeal would be sternly condemned, and that energetic steps would be taken'.[11] But while Dubcek and Prime Minister Cernik officially condemned the '2,000 Words' as inopportune and too extreme, they recognized the good intention of its authors and refused to invoke any penalty against them, particularly as public opinion took a very favourable view of the appeal, and saw nothing counter-revolutionary about it. When representatives of the conservatives in the party machine appeared in the factories to rouse the workers against the allegedly anti-socialist intellectuals, they were shown out, often forcefully. Committees for the defence of the freedom of the press sprang up in many large enterprises.

It was in this period – late June and early July – that the reform movement that had started in January extended its scope, so that liberalization was no longer only the concern of the intelligentsia, but of the intelligentsia and a working class that had recovered their unity. No doubt the threat to the liberalization drive posed by increasing Soviet pressure contributed to this change, which led the different sectors of Czechoslovak society – workers, intellectuals, militants and non-Communists, Czechs and Slovaks – to bury their differences and to find a common cause in patriotism and the defence of the sovereignty of the party and the nation. The strength of this new-found solidarity became evident in mid-July after the Five had delivered their ultimatum and the Central Committee, to everyone's surprise, voted unanimously in favour of Dubcek's proposed reply rejecting Warsaw's demands.

It would be wrong to assume that, therefore, the entire Central Committee had been converted to patriotic socialism, as at least a third of its membership was composed of Novotnyites and neo-conservatives, several of whom did not hesitate, a few weeks later, to put themselves at the disposal of the occupying forces. But on 18 July no one dared run the gauntlet of popular scorn by voting against Dubcek. In a sense, the pro-Soviets were intimidated by the overwhelming majority of their compatriots.

This partial unanimity, it must be emphasized, was in no way anti-Communist. The Central Committee's reply to the Warsaw letter was scarcely exaggerating when it stressed 'the growing authority of the party's new democratic policy in the eyes of the great mass of the workers and the absolute majority of the population' as the determining factors in the Czechoslovak situation. Indeed, 'the great majority of citizens from all classes and levels . . . came out in favour of free speech and the abolition of censorship'. The entire population, in fact, supported the Communist party in its attempt to show that it was 'capable of governing politically without the use of bureaucratic and police methods'.[12] A few voices were calling for neutrality, and the public reacted somewhat nervously to the long delay in the withdrawal of Soviet troops that had entered the country for combined exercises in June. But the majority of the 'political class', including the liberals, were realistic enough to appreciate 'that it was impossible to alter the balance of power in Europe without a European conflict'.[13]

The tragedy of Czechoslovakia lay in the fact that, right up to the last moment on 21 August, the leaders, the militants and the public continued to hope that the absence of any deep resentments or bitter hostility towards the Soviet Union, the absence of any tendency to withdraw from the alliance or to alter the socialist foundations of the régime, would induce the Russians to give Dubcek the benefit of the doubt in his efforts to strengthen the régime through reform. The people and their leaders refused to believe that this policy could be regarded by the Soviets and their associates as unacceptable, as constituting 'a danger to the socialist system as a whole'.

Czechoslovakia Occupied

No doubt Dubcek's pleading to be excused attendance at a new Warsaw Pact meeting on 14 July (without the Rumanians, who since March had been excluded from these sessions on Czechoslovakia) was the last straw for the Soviets. What happened in Czechoslovakia was worse, or at least more embarrassing, from the Russian point of view than a Hungarian-type insurrection would have been. It would have been easy, in disturbances and riots, to find a suitable pretext for intervening. But Soviet and East German agents, acting in collaboration with a few Czechoslovaks, completely failed to provoke the population. The press showed great restraint in answering the attacks made by Soviet papers, which no longer even avoided mention of prominent party officials. However, after the Soviet leaders, on receiving the Czechoslovak Central Committee's negative reply, pretended to give way and suggested a bilateral meeting of the two Presidiums in late July in Cierna-nad-Tisou on the Slovak-Ukrainian frontier, *Literarni Listy's* 26 July appeal for support of Dubcek produced an enthusiastic and determined response in the country. All sections of the Czech and Slovak population turned up at the improvised centres for the collection of signatures; it was a spontaneous plebiscite in favour of Dubcek and his programme, and against the return to old practices and interference from abroad. How could the country's leaders, however moderate or realistic, and whatever their misgivings, resist this mighty appeal coming from the very depths of the national soul?

For the Soviets, however, this spontaneous movement was but further evidence of subversion and counter-revolution. In their view, if Czechoslovakia had been allowed to develop freely, the Congress of 9 September would have ended in a triumph for the liberals, and the Czechoslovak party would have turned into a democratic, revisionist, national Communist party which, in the natural course of events and even taking into account the realism of its leaders, would have pursued a Rumanian-type foreign policy. This much was clear from the eagerness with which people were awaiting the visit of those symbols of independence, Marshal Tito and Ceausescu, which had been announced a long while back and delayed till after the Bratislava conference.

If only the Czechoslovak leaders had been prepared at least to give fresh proof of their loyalty to the Warsaw Pact by agreeing to the insistent demands over several months of the Soviet Marshals Grechko and Yakubovsky for the permanent stationing of allied troops along the country's western frontier! But there was no question of their doing so. On the contrary, they persisted in repeating publicly that the Czechoslovak army was strong enough to protect its own frontiers. One of the Czechoslovak military leaders, General Prchlik, went so far as to call, at a press conference, for a revision of the structure of the Warsaw Pact in terms similar to the Rumanians'. To calm the storm of protests that these remarks provoked in the U.S.S.R., the Czechoslovak government dismissed the general on the eve of the Cierna conference. But this gesture did not satisfy Moscow, especially as the Kremlin knew that the Minister of Defence, General Dzur, shared Prchlik's opinions.

From then on, the Soviet leaders, not to prevent a counter-revolution in Czechoslovakia, but to keep effective control of the country from slipping out of their hands, were determined to find a substitute team, a Czech Kadar, or men unquestionably loyal to the U.S.S.R. and having, as Kadar did, the courage – or, perhaps, bravado – to defy public opinion, to call on the Soviets for help in subduing the people and breaking their unity, and to restore Soviet influence through the party's absolute control of the administration and the press. This is probably why the Kremlin took the initiative in organizing the two conferences at Cierna and Bratislava. Their object apparently was to produce a last-minute split in the Czechoslovak leadership, to isolate Dubcek, Smrkovsky and the other liberals who were regarded as 'right-wing opportunists',[14] to impose terms corresponding to the Warsaw ultimatum on the leaders of Prague and Bratislava, and, finally, to set them against the Rumanians and Yugoslavs.

As things turned out, it appears that the decision to intervene had already been taken in principle before Cierna and Bratislava; only the methods and the actual date remained to be fixed.[15] The military aspect of the invasion seems to have been worked out well in advance, and the June–July manoeuvres enabled the Soviet military leaders to put the finishing touches to their plans; this explains the technical perfection of the actual deployment of troops on 21 August, and made the occupation of Czechoslovakia one of the most complete and successful military operations since the war.

Psychologically and politically, however, the operation was a total failure. It was not that the Soviets, wanting to impose a 'Budapest 1956' solution on Czechoslovakia, failed to find men ready to do their bidding. For better or for worse, there was a network of such people.[16] The security chief, Salgovic, was in their pay, and took steps to facilitate the landing of Soviet airborne troops once he knew when the invasion was to take place. They could also count on the head of security in Prague, Bohumil Molnar, and a few other police officials. Moreover it is likely, if not certain, that several members of the party leadership had been told about the invasion plans. The article in *Rude Pravo* on 20 August, the eve of the invasion, by the paper's editor-in-chief Oldrich Svestka, a notorious new-conservative, may be regarded as an attempt to prepare people psychologically for the political change that was about to occur. Svestka spoke of 'serious reason for concern', condemned the campaign which aimed at 'discrediting honest, vigorous officials', and blamed 'certain journalists' for 'creating an atmosphere of moral, social and political disintegration around politicians and civil servants'. The same issue of the paper reproduced a pamphlet distributed in Brno demanding the dissolution of the workers' militia. The general effect of all this – echoing what was appearing at the same time in the press of the Soviet Union and its allies – was as though Czechoslovakia were being threatened with a kind of anti-Communist pogrom. The anonymous appeal for help published in *Pravda* on 21 August, which Svestka failed the next day to get into his paper, was written in the same spirit.

Much is still obscure about the political aspect of the invasion. It seems that Dubcek was not expecting it to happen, despite Kadar's enigmatic warning at a secret meeting on 15 August. With most Czechoslovak politicians and observers, he thought that the Soviets had embarked on a long-term war of nerves, but that they would not dare to use force, in view of the disastrous effects an armed intervention would have on their relations both with the West and with Yugoslavia, Rumania, and a considerable section of the international Communist movement.[17]

Apparently Dubcek was warned of the impending coup on the evening of 20 August by a mysterious telephone call, perhaps from the Czechoslovak embassy in Moscow. At the time he was attending a Presidium meeting in which Piller, Bilak and Indra began to attack his policy. Indra, it seems, accused him of 'practising the cult of personality'. Alerted by the telephone call, Dubcek interrupted the discussion to draft a proclamation to the nation.[18] The proclamation, passed by seven votes to four (those of Svestka, Indra, Kolder and Bilak), called the invasion 'an act contrary to the fundamental principles governing the relations between socialist states' and a 'violation of the principles of international law'. But it asked the people and the armed forces not to resist 'the troops on the march'.

After the meeting, Dubcek went to the Central Committee, where he was joined by Smrkovsky, Spacek and Kriegel, who, like him, had decided not to accept the *fait accompli*. Cernik called an urgent meeting of the government. Meanwhile Prague, like all the other principal centres of the country, was occupied with a minimum of bloodshed. Only the occupation of the Prague radio centre involved a violent skirmish. The Central Committee building was one of the first to be taken over by the Russians. Salgovic's agents arrested Dubcek, Cernik, Smrkovsky and Kriegel, who were handcuffed and forced to remain standing facing the wall for hours on end. They were then transferred to a prison in sub-Carpathian Ukraine.

All that remained to be done was to install a Kadar-type 'revolutionary workers' and peasants' government'. Indra, Secretary of the Central Committee was mentioned in Warsaw since April as Dubcek's successor, and was ready to take over the reins of government. Accompanied by the Commander-in-Chief of the invasion forces, the Soviet General Pavlovsky, and by Chervonenko, the Soviet ambassador in Prague, as well as by Kolder and Svestka, he arrived at the castle where President Svoboda, like Istvan Dobi twelve years before in Hungary, was asked to confirm his appointment.

But here the first obstacle was met. The old man, a hero of the Soviet Union, whom Marshal Konev in his war memoirs had called 'a real hero of the people, one of the bravest men I've ever known, a soldier in the highest sense of the word',[19] was determined to follow in Masaryk's rather than Hacha's footsteps. He insisted that he was the guardian of national sovereignty, asked to see Dubcek and Cernik and showed his visitors out.

The conspirators experienced a similar failure with the Central

Committee. About fifty of its members met on the afternoon of 21 August at the Praha Hotel. Apparently escorted by Soviet officers, who remained in the room, Indra, Kolder, Bilak and Barbirek tried to win their colleagues over to the idea of collaboration. (The radio, which after a few hours off the air resumed its broadcasts by means of a secret transmitter, was to call them 'capitulationists' on account of this action.) But, thoroughly confused by the conflicting issues, their desire to serve the U.S.S.R. and their fear of being spurned by the people, the majority of the Committee hesitated to follow them. The resolution adopted at the close of this meeting reflected their indecision: it appealed for calm, proclaimed its loyalty to the party's action programme, and its opposition to any return to pre-January conditions, and at the same time vaguely recommended that relations should be established with the occupying forces.

The group of pro-Soviet conspirators, acting on this part of the resolution, sent all the regional organizations anonymous instructions to make contact with the local commanders of the Warsaw Pact troops. This order, however, was immediately rejected by its recipients. Thus, the regional committee of Northern Bohemia replied in a broadcast message demanding, first and foremost, the withdrawal of the invasion armies. 'We are a sovereign state possessing sufficient strength to ensure the development of socialism, our security, and to fulfil our obligations to our allies. We support the Central Committee represented by Dubcek, the government represented by Cernik, the Parliament represented by Smrkovsky, the National Front represented by Kriegel, and the President of the Republic, Svoboda.' Similar declarations were made by nearly every party organization, at every level.

Legal Resistance

On 21 August several party organizations took the initiative of summoning the Fourteenth Extraordinary Congress for the next day in Prague (the original date had been 9 September). This Congress, held in the C.K.D. factory, with an attendance of 1,095 of the 1,543 elected delegates under the protection of the workers' militia, was a masterpiece of organization, a resounding victory for the spirit of resistance.

It showed that over a period of eight months the Communist party had transformed itself root and branch, and had ceased to be a passive instrument in the hands of the leaders.[20] The entire party rejected the role of collaborators, and chose instead to become the party of legal resistance. One of the speakers at the underground Congress, Martin Vaculik, former Novotnyite First Secretary of the Prague party committee and now a supporter of Dubcek, condemned the attitude of Bilak, Indra, Piller and the others who, he said, 'accept the occupation as a reality, forgetting that other reality − the clear, unanimous antipathy of the people'.

The Congress, whose resolutions were broadcast over the underground radio network, elected a new Central Committee from which all the actual and prospective 'collaborators' were eliminated; the Central Committee in turn chose a new Presidium of twenty-eight members and a new secretariat with a majority of progressives. Dubcek was confirmed as First Secretary, and Venek Silhan, a young professor of working-class origin, was appointed to deputize for him. The Congress called a general protest strike between 12.00 and 13.00 hours on 23 August, and this took place.

The same spirit of resistance manifested itself simultaneously throughout the various political institutions which for years had been staffed by nominees of the former party leaders, and had been totally unrepresentative, but which, when put to the test and given a unique opportunity to restore their prestige with the population, behaved with as much dignity, courage and resolution as would have freely elected and representative bodies in their position.

Recovering quickly after the initial shock, the goverment, Presidium of the National Assembly, Czech National Council, Slovak National Council, National Front, National Committees, trade unions and professional organizations condemned the intervention over the radio and through the newspapers that reappeared, protested against the violation of Czechoslovak sovereignty in notes and resolutions dispatched to the capitals of the Five, and demanded the withdrawal of the troops and the release of the leaders who had been arrested.

From the Moscow Compromise to Normalization

From the evening of 22 August the Soviets realized that their plan for a political solution to the crisis had failed. Therefore, Svoboda's proposal to go to Moscow with Gustav Husak, General Dzur and Kucera, the Minister of Justice (the representative of Benes's old party in the government), probably came as something of a relief to them. Svoboda was received in Moscow with all the honour due to the president of an allied country. But the Russians made sure of extending the negotiations by summoning, besides the delegation appointed by the government and the Czechoslovak Assembly, Bilak, Piller and Indra, who had just been ejected by the Extraordinary Congress. Nevertheless, any hopes that the Kremlin still held of persuading Svoboda to agree to the appointment of a quisling government were to be disappointed. The President still insisted on the participation of Dubcek, Cernik, Smrkovsky and Kriegel as a condition for any negotiations. In the end, he got his way. Dubcek and his companions were brought to Moscow, and the 'unusual' negotiations began, resulting on 26 August in the signing of the Moscow protocols, the whole text of which was never published.

It was Smrkovsky who, on 29 August, after the delegation had returned to Prague, most frankly described the dilemma in which the Czechoslovak negotiators had found themselves. 'We could have refused all compromise', he said, 'and let things progress towards the establishment of an occupation régime, with all the consequences that held for the sovereignty of the state, political rights, the economy and the loss of human lives that such a development would have entailed. I must say that we did not forget that there comes a point where one may be driven to refuse agreement and to have recourse to arms to evict soldiers from one's territory and safeguard the character of the nation. But in the end, we considered ... that, despite everything that had occurred, there was another possibility which, as statesmen, we were bound to examine. That is why we did our utmost to reach an acceptable compromise.'

In fact, the characters of Dubcek, Svoboda and their fellows, with their political pasts and convictions, made any other choice inconceivable. When he learned of the invasion of the country, Dubcek apparently exclaimed: 'How is it possible? How can they do that to me? I have devoted my whole life to co-operation with the U.S.S.R. This is a personal tragedy!' It was, indeed, a tragedy to be cut out for the role of conciliator and mediator, and to find oneself trying to reconcile two irreconcilables - the U.S.S.R.'s determination to dominate the proceedings, and the nation's desire for independence. The defence of national independence - as was shown by the attitude of Rumanians and Yugoslavs over these tragic months - means acceptance of the risk of armed intervention, of a radical break; for the Czechoslovak leaders, however, this possibility was excluded *a priori*. As a Slovak leader pointed out, Dubcek, in spite of his total failure to get through to the Soviets, never cut the spiritual umbilical cord with the Kremlin. He could not see beyond the confines of the socialist camp. Therefore, after 21 August, when he realized that the Soviets needed him as well, even if only for the time being, Dubcek seems to have set himself the task of trying to salvage something from the January policy, the great dream of a humanist democratic socialism, by identifying himself with the nation which had been loyal to him in so stirring a manner over the last few months.

And yet the Moscow protocols, as far as one can judge, left little room for an independent political programme, however restrained. They, in fact, amounted to a *Diktat*, only slightly tempered by a few concessions with no guarantee whatever. Czechoslovakia became a state under tutelage, and under strict surveillance. It is true the protocols stipulated that military units and 'other bodies' would not interfere in Czechoslovakia's internal affairs, and that the allied armies would be gradually withdrawn 'as soon as the threat to socialism has been eliminated'.

But the illusory nature of these promises became clear in the weeks that followed. If the occupation forces, on the whole, abstained from interference, the Soviet Union maintained a steady pressure on the Czechoslovak leaders through diplomatic channels, through its press, indicating in detail what measures should be introduced to achieve 'normalization'. In addition, the Soviets on 16 October pressed home their advantage and compelled the Czechoslovak government to sign a treaty for the permanent stationing of a certain number of Soviet troops; this treaty had no expiry date, nor was there any reference as to how it might be terminated. Thus, for the withdrawal of the bulk of some 600,000 occupation troops, the Czechoslovaks accepted the Soviet Union's military presence, and the invasion of the country was tardily given a legal basis; Czechoslovakia had become an occupied country for an indefinite period.

Although the Moscow protocols were drawn up in as ambiguous terms as the Cierna and Bratislava declarations, they provided the basis for continual interference. They required the Czechoslovak leaders strongly to oppose counter-revolutionary forces (this meant all those elements that did not rigorously adhere to Moscow's line); to re-impose censorship; to prohibit non-Communist organizations such as the Club 231 and that of the non-party militants; to dismiss those minsters who, like Ota Sik and Jiri Hajek, had made pronouncements that were regarded as unacceptable, or like the Minister of the Interior, Josef Pavel, had resisted the occupants' demands too effectively. The protocols obliged Dubcek to declare the Fourteenth Congress null and void, to defer the calling of another Congress, and to put a stop to the removal of people the Kremlin regarded as 'firmly attached to Marxism-Leninism and proletarian internationalism'. This last provision was further strengthened after new Soviet-Czechoslovak talks at the beginning of October. Dubcek had to undertake to employ people approved of by the Kremlin in party and state organizations.

The main danger threatening Dubcek and his colleagues after the signing of the protocols was that they would lose the trust of the party and the people without gaining that of the Russians, East Germans, Poles and Bulgarians, who still doubted their sincerity and suspected them of playing a double game. They had embarked on a supremely thankless task, and they were bound to lose in the end. All their efforts to show the people that the essentials of the January programme would still be implemented must displease the Russians, while their attempts to comply with the latter's demands would increasingly exasperate their own supporters.

Paradoxically, the political situation in Czechoslovakia at the close of the first stage of 'normalization' (the end of October 1968) in many respects resembled that which had existed before the intervention. On the one hand, the conservative, ex-Novotnyite and wholeheartedly pro-Soviet elements who had been demoralized and paralysed by the unanimity of the August resistance, came out into the open again, this time with obvious Soviet backing (*Pravda*, 4 November). On the other hand, the journalists, writers, artists, scholars, regional and municipal party organizations and workers in the large enterprises, whose political awareness had been greatly sharpened by recent events, made their voices heard, calling on Dubcek to oppose the conservatives resolutely, to call the Party Congress, and to continue with democratization, as they had done earlier in June and July.

This is one of the most novel aspects of the Czechoslovak crisis. The Soviets, in fact, could only think in terms of a Hungarian solution. But, as we have seen, the situation on 21 August was different. In Czechoslovakia, unlike Hungary in 1956, there was no political vacuum; it was the Communist party itself, its organizations, and the institutions controlled and inspired by it, that were at the very heart of the resistance movement and the movement of democratization. It was, therefore, not enough gradually to pressurize Dubcek himself into becoming more and more the spokesman and instrument of foreign domination until he lost his identity and his self-respect; it was not enough to replace him and his friends by other more amenable people, better suited for the part. Kuznetsov, Soviet Deputy Minister of Foreign Affairs and a skilful and subtle diplomat, who was sent to Prague at the beginning of September to work out a satisfactory political formula, had to accept the fact that the main obstacle to 'Kadarization' was the Communist party itself. The machinery of repression had to be set in motion against the party; but this was something the Soviet leadership, for reasons of prestige before the international Communist movement, was loath to do. The Kremlin preferred to let the situation stagnate, to split the leadership, and to sow the seeds of discord and disillusionment.[21]

Hence, a prolonged crisis, with equivocations, waverings, gropings, where the two realities, the foreign presence and the will to survive of the Czechs and Slovaks, more closely united than ever before in their history, coexisted and struggled without either disappearing altogether. The most striking description of this confrontation has been given by the Marxist philosopher Karel Kosik (in an article published in the first number of the writers' weekly, which reappeared in February 1968 under the name of Listy):

In the sphere of politics, the dialectic of master and slave means that the victor forces the vanquished not only to accept his vision of the world, but also to assimulate the formulas whereby he must accept his capitulation. In other words, in the political game the vanquished is the one who lets another's attitude be imposed upon him and who judges his own actions through the eyes of the enemy. The Czech problem is to know whether the nation can survive as a political entity . . . or whether it will turn into a nation of wheat and steel producers, speaking Czech and Slovak, living in a strategically important area, with democracy giving way to fascism, and humanism to barbarism.[22]

Part II:

Structures and Tendencies

12

Contradictions within the Communist System

The Basic Contradiction

The intervention of the forces of the Warsaw Pact countries in Czechoslovakia had as its purpose to force the Czechoslovak government and party leadership to follow a course approved by the Soviet Union and its partners, if not to overthrow them. The pretext on which the attack was launched was that of 'defending socialism in Czechoslovakia'.[1]

This event has certain features in common with the Slansky affair, though the context of the international situation differed considerably in each case. These features arise from similar structures and tendencies, and reflect certain constants in the history of the U.S.S.R. and the People's Democracies.

The cyclical nature of the developments is substantiated in part by the fact that the Slansky trial followed in the wake of the large-scale Cominform offensive instigated by Stalin against Tito's Yugoslavia. Sixteen years later, Yugoslavia again felt herself directly threatened by the invasion of Czechoslovakia, with whom she had ties and ideological affinities. She reckoned that she might be the target for the next blow. The Soviet, East German, Polish and Bulgarian press revived the old charges levelled against the 'Yugoslav way', of anti-socialism, treachery and collusion with imperialist forces, all of which had been supposedly buried for good after 1955. The People's Democracies, which had seemed to be making real, if erratic, progress towards *détente* and normalization, were abruptly flung back twenty years into the past.

Several weeks before the intervention of the Five, a Yugoslav newspaper stated in an article commemorating the twentieth anniversary of the Cominform anti-Yugoslav resolution[2]:

Stalin believed he was fully entitled to meddle in the internal affairs of the other socialist parties and countries in the name of the Soviet Communist party and the U.S.S.R. Moreover, he acted on this belief. He regarded the path to socialism followed by the U.S.S.R. to be the universal path and binding on all. The Stalinist creed was imposed on the other parties. . . Those who first dared to question the justice and cogency of these postulates of Soviet policy were asking to be anathematized. We were the first.

It was Yugoslavia's good fortune to be the first and to have to suffer only excommunication, a blockade and a four-year campaign of denigration. The worst was avoided, thanks to the determination of the Yugoslav leaders, who foiled the N.K.V.D. plot and resisted all attempts at interference. They were also aided by Stalin's fear of bedevilling the international situation through an armed attack, in view of the real or supposed support that Tito might expect from the West.[3] But if Stalin allowed Yugoslavia to make a relatively easy exit from the fellowship camouflaging the U.S.S.R.'s political defeat by the drastic expedient of expelling the offending state, he compensated for the loss by relentlessly tightening his hold on the other Eastern countries – especially Czechoslovakia, with the Slansky trial. Thus what one might in Marxist-Leninist terminology call the 'basic contradiction' in the socialist system was already apparent in this initial period. On the one hand, there was the peculiar Soviet form of hegemonism (simultaneously imperialistic and ideological), and on the other, the tendency of other Communist parties and states to seek to win or recover their internal and external autonomy.

Again, it was the Yugoslavs who showed up the imperialistic nature of Soviet policy. They were not afraid to call a spade a spade. 'The U.S.S.R.', said Tito in a report to his party's Sixth Congress, a few months before Stalin's death, 'initiated its expansionist, imperialistic policy before the last world war, when it concluded the pact with Hitler, sharing spheres of interest with him, and invading foreign territory . . . The same policy was pursued after the war . . . When it is dealing with a socialist country', he added, 'the U.S.S.R. tries to justify its use of imperialistic methods by claiming that it is necessary, in the supposed interest of world revolution, for the small socialist countries or People's Democracies to subordinate their own interests (to the point of sacrificing their independence) to those of the Soviet Union, the leader of the socialist camp. In actual fact, the enslavement of these small nations, as was shown in the case of Poland, and subsequently Rumania, Hungary, Bulgaria and Czechoslovakia, and others, had only one object – and that was not world revolution, but world hegemony – the Soviet Union's domination, as an imperialist power, of the other nations.'[4]

After Stalin's death, and particularly after Khrushchev's journey of penance to Belgrade in 1955, the Yugoslavs softened their criticism of Soviet imperialism, partly for tactical and opportunistic reasons and partly because they had been won over (Tito having believed Khrushchev's declaration on the normalization of relations between socialist countries). However, the Chinese played their former role with even greater polemical fervour. In a letter of 14 June 1963 addressed to the Soviet Central Committee, Peking's leaders accused the U.S.S.R. of 'great-power chauvinism', of 'exploiting the fraternal parties to its own ends, of applying pressure in seeking to impose its will on others'. Mao Tse-tung, in an interview with a group of Japanese sympathizers in July 1964, went even further than Tito in 1952, castigating the Russians for having 'annexed everything they could' at the end of the Second World War.[5]

In August 1968 China and Yugoslavia, despite the ideological gulf that separated them, found themselves on the same side, stigmatizing the occupation of Czechoslovakia as an act of imperialist aggression and a violation of the national right to independence. If the contradiction between hegemony and the drive for independence of the Communist countries was already apparent in the 1948–52 crisis, it became more acute with the Soviet military interventions in Hungary and Czechoslovakia, with the passage from political, ideological and economic pressure to the use of military force. To use Communist terminology once again, this contradiction must inevitably lead to fresh economic and social upheavals.[6]

Individual Paths and Stalinism

The determination of the Soviet leadership to act as police within the sphere of interest appropriated by the U.S.S.R. after the Second World War, of which the European People's Democracies form the major part, is a constant factor. The other constant, manifesting itself now in one country, now in another, is the desire of the political élites (even those created by Stalinism) to build a socialism adapted to the individual traditions, conditions and potentialities of their countries.

Again, it is Czechoslovakia's recent history that best exemplifies this situation. The programme the Czechoslovak Communist party adopted in April 1968, on the initiative of Alexander Dubcek, was issued as a pamphlet, with the significant sub-title 'The Czechoslovak Way to Socialism'. In fact, this programme, the implementation of which was one of the reasons for the Soviet military intervention, harked back to the Czechoslovak party programme immediately after the Second World War. The plan for a 'Czechoslovak path to socialism' advocated then by Gottwald and his associates sprang from the conviction that the particular conditions in Czechoslovakia made a peaceful, parliamentary transition to socialism more feasible. The country had attained a high level of industrial and cultural development, possessed democratic traditions, and a powerful Communist party that had practically a majority and could expect the backing of the U.S.S.R. The plan was conceived for gradual implementation, and safeguarded the essential features of the democratic institutions while rejecting the savage methods of collectivization and measures against small tradesmen and artisans. There were to be religious toleration and artistic freedom, as well as other characteristics of a free society.

Contrary to popular belief, the end of 'the Czechoslovak way' was not marked by the 'Prague coup' of February 1948 – the defeat inflicted by the Communist party supported by the trade unions and workers' militias, that 'private party army', on the non-Communist parties that had banded together to overthrow it. The party leadership, intent on consolidating its power, still had no specific change in view. The impetus, if not the order, for a total change of direction, the application of new methods and concepts, came from Stalin through the Cominform. By subscribing to the Russian excommunication of Yugoslavia on 28 June 1948, the Czechoslovaks, like the other Communist parties that were signatories to the resolution, surrendered their own right to individuality and independence. The condemnation of Yugoslavia amounted to a permanent legitimization of Soviet intervention, an identification of internationalism with strict control by the U.S.S.R. The ideological cover for this transformation (it was, in fact, a transfer of sovereignty) was provided by the famous Stalinist doctrine of 'the inevitable sharpening of the class struggle in the period of the building of socialism'.

The Slansky trial, as Eugen Loebl correctly emphasized in his account published in 1968, was in fact the trial of the Czechoslovak party of 1945–8 and its policy. The key passage in the arraignment reads: 'Slansky's subversive centre had, like the Yugoslav Titoists, developed the so-called theory of Czechoslovakia's individual path to socialism, in order to disguise its real aims. Under cover of this theory – which amounted, in fact, to the restoration of capitalism in the republic – the centre was completing its preparations for a radical reversal of the situation in Czechoslovakia on the Titoist pattern and directed by English and American imperialists.' Loebl, however, has shown convincingly that this individual path condemned at the trial represented Gottwald's political views and the policy of the entire Communist party leadership, confirmed by the Party Congress.[7]

Slansky and his companions were simply scapegoats. In the same way, the 1968 intervention, by destroying Dubcek, who was called a 'right-wing opportunist', was intended to eliminate the whole Czechoslovak party leadership, its policy as defined by the April programme, and its attempt to construct a new model of socialism. The occupation of Czechoslovakia was a Slansky trial conducted by other means, on a larger scale. It was the act of a great power that was not content with maintaining a dominant position over the small nations within its strategic ambit, but was determined to impose on them its own creed and method of government.

This latter-day Stalinism is the result of the attempt to overcome the basic incompatibility between Soviet hegemonism and the autonomism of the satellite states through compulsion and ideological expedients. The methods used to unify and centralize the Soviet Union after the October Revolution were, after 1948, extended to the whole bloc. In this way a theoretical and practical system was evolved, incorporating all the political, economic, social and cultural activities of the countries as a whole, and based on coercive integrationism.

Three factors made this extension of Stalinism to the Eastern countries possible.

The first was the international power structure, which, after the Yalta and Potsdam agreements, exposed the Central and East European states to the direct, unilateral pressure of the Soviet Union. The U.S.S.R. occupied East Germany militarily, and maintained forces in Poland, Hungary and Rumania (where troops were not withdrawn until 1958). Czechoslovakia (up to 1968) and Bulgaria avoided military occupation only because the Kremlin felt it could rely on the completely loyal Communist parties in these two traditionally Russophile countries to safeguard its vital interests.

The second important factor was ideological. It was the conviction of the local Communist leaders, as well as at least a majority of the militants, that there could be no conflict of interest between the different detachments of world Communism and the Soviet state which was their centre and guide. This conviction, inherited from the Stalinist Communist International, was associated with the idea that the first socialist state, with its heroic pioneering history, constituted the only valid model for countries embarking on the path of socialism.

The third factor, and perhaps the most important for successful application of Stalinist practices, was the efficiency of the Soviet Union's secret police. It was through the police that Stalin had been able to establish his absolute personal dictatorship, and his system was characterized by the precedence of the secret-police network over the Soviet party and even the personnel of the machine. When Stalin decided to impose a greater degree of integration on the Eastern countries, it was natural for him to entrust the execution of this policy to that Soviet organization on which the Soviet system itself was based. The secret police undertook to liquidate or neutralize the native Communist leaders (Gomulka and Spychalski in Poland, Kostov in Bulgaria, Rajk and Nagy in Hungary, Clementis, Husak and Loebl in Czechoslovakia, Patrascanu in Rumania) who would have preferred to continue along the gradual, patriotic path pursued between 1945 and 1948.

Cardinal Errors: Subjectivism and Voluntarism

Howeyer, even when taken as far as totalitarianism, police methods, by their very nature, can only superficially overcome and resolve conflicts and tensions in the social organism. They drive them beneath the surface, into the subconscious of the oppressed and repressed peoples. This applies to the basic contradiction we have noted, as well as to the minor ones affecting the economic, political, social and cultural sectors in each country.

These various conflicts in the Communist system have one thing in common: opposition between spontaneous, natural, organic social activities on the one hand and the dominant ideology on the other. Stalinism means the ascendancy of an all-embracing ideology, effected by means of coercion and brainwashing. Even though this ideology, which the Eastern Communist parties took ready-made from the hands of Stalin, was described as 'scientific socialism', it was, and is, astonishingly prejudiced, Utopian and voluntaristic. Supposedly expressing the 'historical interests of the modern proletariat', it has long reflected only 'an unconscious urge to discover its roots and develop its potentialities'[8] – the desire of an extremely powerful police and political organization to transform national societies of great economic, political and cultural diversity into a single, absolutely controlled organism. Behind this ideology there was, of course, a lofty, Faustian, Promethean conception of man as master of his destiny. However, when the idea was implemented in the conditions that prevailed at the time, the result was that a handful of men, who were truly masters, ruled over the mass of men, who were subjugated. After Djilas and the Hungarian Gyula Hay, the Slovak writer Mnacko and the Czech L. Vaculik have shown how contemptuously the leaders treat the mass of men, like so much malleable, expendable raw material, or cannon fodder.[9] The Czech philosopher K. Kosik astutely traces the anthropological theory underlying his country's official ideology back to 'analysts of man as disposable and manipulable', that is back to Machiavelli, Hobbes and, before them, Plato.[10]

Attempts were made to explain the origins of Stalinist terrorism and despotism in terms of Stalin's own authoritarian personality; but when it was realized how futile and un-Marxist such an explanation is, 'production relations', the political and social structure of Russia, and even Russian tsarist traditions were invoked. However, it appears that the Communist scheme for the radical transformation of the world, which was systematically expressed in Stalinism, was rooted in a fundamental ideological misconception of the nature of man and the limits of the malleability of human society, what Pierre Fougeyrollas calls its 'irreducible cultural multiplicity'. This misconception – and the incredible obstinacy displayed in adhering to it – explains the irrationalism, the aberrations, the evils, even the crimes of the system in all their various economic, political, social and cultural manifestations.

After twenty years of experience in Eastern Europe and fifty in the Soviet Union, even certain official theoreticians have learned to recognize the error, to trace its origins further back than Stalin and Lenin, to Marx and Engels. This is especially true in the economic field, where mistakes are most expensive. 'Marx and Engels, and subsequently Lenin in his pre-October writings,' wrote a Soviet economist, 'thought that, with the abolition of private ownership of the means of production, market-oriented production, the idea of value, money and all other related concepts would be eliminated too ... Practice has, however, shown that socialism cannot do without market-oriented production and a type of market, the law of value and other concepts ...'[11]

One of the principal Hungarian party economists, Istvan Friss, has been even more explicit. 'Marx, Engels and Lenin', he wrote, 'have drawn from their analysis of capitalism the conclusion that, after the socialization of production, ... society would be able scientifically to evaluate its needs and the sources of energy necessary to fulfil them – that it would be able also to control the distribution of produce according to needs ... These ideas have not been borne out by reality. Our society is not yet able to measure present and future social needs accurately. Nor can it control the application of human and mechanical labour in accordance with social needs.'[12] Indeed, society, or those who identified themselves with it – the party machine and leadership – has, even with the unprecedented concentration of power at its command, been unable really to eliminate the market economy and replace it by a planned economy. 'The law of value still holds good', said Friss. 'It has continued to operate indirectly' – secretly, as it were – 'by making increasingly intolerable the distortions of production and distribution caused by prices not corresponding to the law of value.' The law, adds Friss, 'is the expression of objective relations which assert themselves in the economy, whether we like it or not. In which case it is better for us not to close our eyes to the effects of the law of value'.

The Eastern Communist leaders, owing their power to Stalin or his heirs, have on political, social and cultural questions adopted an attitude that harks back to the same unrealistic economic model described by Pachkov and Friss. One finds the same ignorant, off-hand contempt for 'objective relations', the same romantic, adventuristic belief in the omnipotence of the force and idea bequeathed to them by men who initially, under exceptional circumstances and driven by a fierce thirst for power, seized the reins of government in Russia. Carried away by their success, the Bolsheviks had thought that their technique of organization, mobilization and repression would break down all attempts at resistance, all the 'laws', forces and structures of the society that had been subdued. Tito in 1945, and subsequently Mao Tse-tung and Fidel Castro, were inspired exponents of the same faith that the lesser luminaries of the Eastern countries displayed in a more absurd form. But in each case, the same mistakes produced the same disappointments.

Thus the political scene corresponds to the economic laws of value, of supply and demand – in short, to the market. This means the competitive coexistence under constitutional guarantee of ideas, tendencies, groups and political parties. Democracy ensures a creative balance between authority and the freedoms, and stimulates the active participation of all citizens in public affairs.[13] The one-party system, with its extreme centralization, has been as unsuccessful in eliminating democratic aspirations as economic planning has been in neutralizing the law of supply and demand. In Part I we saw how political aspirations, patriotism, the taste for freedom and truth, deprived of any means of political expression, nevertheless survived and are still active under the surface. They affected the party itself, so that finally Communist leaders (and not the most insignificant ones at that) came to realize how intolerable was the gulf separating government and governed, word and deed. In the end, an entire Communist party – the Czechoslovak party – was converted, transformed into a socialist, democratic and national organization.

The same goes for the illusion that the abolition of private property, the elimination of the old propertied classes, would finally resolve the social problem. The theoretical elevation of the working class to the rank of ruling class did not put an end to exploitation or subordination of the wage-earner. The leadership's policy of out-and-out levelling did not eliminate differences in status, standard of living, skills, age and sex. The distinct and often contradictory aspirations and interests of the different classes and strata remained active. At the first signs of a *détente*, they sought to express themselves publicly, either through the professional bodies that were regaining their independence, or outside these domesticated structures.

The party also proved incapable of creating administratively a substantially new literature, art, science, or a fresh outlook by decree or by fiat. It was unable to eliminate all traces of the traditional religious, national and liberal cultures from the popular consciousness. 'Socialist culture', wrote a Yugoslav neo-Marxist, 'is nonsense, unless one is talking about what might be called the cultural policy of socialism.'[14] The party's or the party bureaucrats' interference in literary and artistic life, on the pretext of the need to wage a permanent struggle against the influence of bourgeois ideology, created confusion, destroyed values, stifled initiative, and has caused untold damage. What the Czechoslovaks, at their June 1967 Congress, found had happened to their own literature sums up the general cultural effects of Stalinism through the socialist countries.[15]

Diversification

If the history of the People's Democracies between 1945 and 1953 seems to be dominated by a vast movement of integration, standardization, repression and restriction, the history of the years 1953–68 displays a reverse trend. It is concerned with the growing struggle, sometimes in a disguised form, sometimes openly violent, between the forces of conservation and those striving for the recovery of national and social identity and the re-establishment of pluralistic bodies. The Soviet Union, the world's second most powerful military power, still dominates the scene, and is able to impose its will on its Warsaw Pact subordinates. But the People's Democracies are diversifying, gradually rediscovering, at different points and in varying degrees, their individual identities.

Diversification simultaneously affects the relationship of each country to the dominant power, the extent to which freedom of action is regained, and developments in internal structure. Thus, fifteen years after Stalin's death, Yugoslavia stands out as a country which, in spite of the confused state of internal development, has been able to preserve a remarkably large area of independence in a world where nuclear power alone seems to guarantee full sovereignty. Rumania, for its part, has achieved the quasi-independent status of an 'awkward ally', playing a role similar to France in the Atlantic Alliance. A third Balkan country, Albania, defies the Warsaw Pact from the flank, much as Cuba does the United States. The leaders of this country of barely two million inhabitants, under the moral and financial protection of distant China, continually criticize, not only Russian hegemonism (which has failed to subdue them) but also the alleged revisionism of the Soviet leadership. Hungary, after its ill-fated attempt to secede in 1956, has become a satellite again, though treated with some consideration and held up as a model of enlightened paternalism. Poland, Bulgaria and even the German Democratic Republic, strengthened by the wall erected in 1961, adapt their commitments and allegiance to the U.S.S.R.

to agree with their individual interests as member nations. Finally, Czechoslovakia, for nearly twenty years the most subservient of the allies, an outstanding example of voluntary self-discipline, aroused Big Brother's ire, and provoked an intervention. It suddenly displayed its will to transform its internal and foreign policy and, while standing by its obligations and alliances, to take account of Czech and Slovak traditions. The military occupation of the country has not stifled the united patriotism of the Czechs and Slovaks.

Although progress has been interrupted by Soviet intervention, the general movement in Eastern Europe has been towards emancipation and independence. Gradually and imperceptibly, the stress has shifted from what unites to what separates, from internationalist solidarity imposed from outside to the adumbration of a new order founded on the sovereignty of states. To the extent that Soviet ascendancy over the Eastern countries can be termed colonialism, the history of the fifteen years that have elapsed since the death of Stalin looks like a European version of decolonialization.

Does the anti-hegemonistic, national movement necessarily lead to internal liberalization – to the replacement of the party's monopoly by pluralistic structures? The tendency of the movement, its content, and its tempo are determined by the conditions specific to each country, the level of development, the traditions, the strength, vigour and ideological convictions of the national Communist parties. In 1948 Hungary, Poland and Czechoslovakia were simultaneously deprived of their sovereignty as states and of their democratic institutions. It is hardly surprising, therefore, that national and democratic aspirations in these countries should be closely associated, and that a return to pre-June 1948 political pluralism (which does not mean a return to the bourgeois, capitalist system) should have been advocated even by Communist leaders and theorists. Without going so far as to abandon the leading role and political and ideological monopoly of the party, normalization, liberalization and the introduction of pluralistic elements, or 'socialist democracy', have to a certain extent been realized in nearly all the Eastren countries. The exception is Albania, which has kept her Stalinist structures intact.

Nevertheless, the picture is a very complex one. The situation varies not only from country to country, but from year to year. In 1963, Kadar's Hungary was regarded by Czech and Slovak intellectuals as an oasis of free creativity. In 1968, however, Czechoslovakia, to the delight of some and the amazement of others, placed itself in the vanguard of socialist democratization. Poland, astonishingly free and diverse between 1956 and 1959, has stiffened into a kind of 'Red fascist' mould, despite Gomulka's attempts at camouflage. Bulgaria's and the G.D.R.'s régimes, under cover of an inflexible Marxism-Leninism, are coming more and more to resemble 'regular authoritarian governments such as are found in other parts of the world'.[16] The régime in Rumania is attempting, at one and the same time, to develop its technological potential, and to enlarge its popular esteem by appealing to national pride and ambition.

Whether one studies economic organization, the peasant situation, the role of the intelligentsia, the development of cultural life, the increasing contacts with the West, or relations with the Churches, one is struck by the great variety of methods employed and solutions reached. Before drawing an overall picture of the process, we shall try (fully aware of the risks involved) to determine the direction of the movement and the forces behind it. We must determine the origin and nature of the initial impetus behind de-Stalinization and the main forces encouraging de-satellization, modernization and democratization. We shall then turn to discuss the forces of cohesion, and the institutions and organizations that reflect them.

The Impetus for Normalization

The Soviet model of government and of economic control was not easily adaptable to the small and medium-sized countries of Eastern Europe, which had embarked on the path of socialism while already possessing political and social structures far more advanced than Russia's had been at the start.[17] But the impetus for change, as we have seen, did not originate in the Eastern countries; after five years of subjection and manipulation, they were exhausted, and to both leaders and population the system seemed inevitable. Obsessed by Stalin's omnipotence, paralysed by their own convictions, terrorized by their overlords and isolated from the people, the leaders of the People's Democracies were incapable of acting on their own initiative.

Under these circumstances, any impetus for improvement had to come from above – from the sole, independent, decision-making centre: the Kremlin. De-Stalinization (like Stalinization) bore the Russian imprint. It was the post-Stalinist Soviet leaders' own revision of their methods of government and economic management that lay behind the first impulses in the Eastern countries for internal *détente*, collective leadership, limitation of the powers of the secret police, and the introduction of the new course based on Lenin's N.E.P. Accustomed to identifying their interests with those of their client states, the Kremlin leaders were convinced that the organizational reforms envisaged for the U.S.S.R. would be equally valid in the Eastern countries. However, de-Stalinization, which was put into operation without the interested parties being consulted or their agreement secured, simultaneously weakened the authority of the Kremlin, Leninist-Stalinist doctrine and the leaders, who were forced to engage in self-criticism. It provoked immediate crises in Hungary and Poland and a delayed one in Czechoslovakia. It also goaded certain Stalinist leaders (in Albania and Rumania) into loosening their connections with the Kremlin.

The general effect of the reformism identified with Khrushchev's name was to throw the Communist parties of the People's Democracies back on their own national Communist traditions along separate paths. It encouraged them to reduce their dependence on the Soviet leadership.

The problem was quite a different one in the Soviet Union, where Communism and patriotism had merged long ago during Stalin's lifetime, encouraged by him or in spite of him, especially during the war. Communism fitted into the great hierarchical and bureaucratic Russian tradition. Stalin realized the expansionist dreams of the greatest tsars, while Khrushchev's reforms were in the tradition of Catherine II, who gave the ruling nobility back its dignity and confidence. As Jean Laloy has pointed out, 'Soviet chauvinism has been the cement holding the social structure together in the midst of the great upheavals between 1956 and 1964',[18] The East Europeans, with the exception of the Bulgarians and for a while the Czechs, were not similarly compensated for the forced sacrifice of their freedom and well-being. Hence, the first and most durable consequence for them of the change-over from terrorist dictatorship to a more enlightened and tolerant form, from the tensions of the cold war to more relaxed relations with foreign countries, was a revival of national aspirations. The hegemonistic power that had elicited this response was to find it hard to control and repress.

The Impact of Yugoslavia and China

No doubt, the post-Stalinist Soviet leaders never intended to dissolve the hegemonistic structure, or to allow any of the Communist countries of Eastern Europe to regain their full external and internal sovereignty. Their object was to promote their hegemonistic aims through other more flexible and rational means. If they went further than they intended along the path of this 'neo-imperialism' or 'neo-colonialism', it was due to the dual, separate pressures of Yugoslavia and China, each of which, in its own way, pressed for the transformation of the empire into a community of independent socialist states. It was under pressure from Mao in 1954 that the Soviets dismantled the mixed companies, the colonial instruments of exploitation of the Eastern countries.

The reconciliation between the U.S.S.R. and Yugoslavia, a socialist country outside the community, created a precedent, the historical significance of which was not lost on the other Communist countries. The principles recognized by the U.S.S.R. in the Belgrade Declaration of 1955 were relevant to all of them, unless it had been decided to apply a double standard and to reward secession. By acknowledging the diversity of paths to socialism and the right of independence, and by rehabilitating Tito, the Soviet leaders encouraged the rehabilitation of all the national Communists sentenced for their refusal to recognize that the Soviet model of socialism was binding on all (Rajk, Kostov, Gomulka in 1956; Clementis, Husak in 1963; Patrascanu in 1968). The Soviets thus returned theoretically to Lenin's view of diversity: 'All the nations will achieve socialism, but they will not all take the same path to reach it.'

The five Bandung principles (national independence, sovereignty, equality of rights, territorial inviolability and non-interference in internal affairs) had as deep, if not deeper and more lasting, repercussions in the People's Democracies than the principle of pluralism endorsed at Belgrade. These principles were put forward by Chou En-lai and Nehru to govern the relations between different countries and régimes. The Neo-Hegemonists claimed that they were obsolete, and therefore irrelevant when it came to relations between socialist countries. To invoke them in these cases was to base one's actions on 'chauvinistic nationalism'.[19] It is in this sense that we should interpret Khrushchev's declarations at the Twentieth Congress regarding the 'new socialist pattern of international relations' which, according to him, was already current in the socialist community. 'These relations', he said, 'are characterized by complete equality of rights, sincere friendship, brotherly co-operation in the political, economic and cultural fields, and mutual aid in constructing a new life. They are conditioned by the nature of the economic system of the countries of the socialist community, by the unity of their basic interests and their lofty ultimate aim, the building of Communism, and finally by the Marxist-Leninist idea common to the Communist and workers' parties.'

The second part of this statement, of course, reduced the significance of the first. Khrushchev was willing to ease the situation a little, and to allow a certain amount of decentralization; but it was clear from what happened later that same year (1956), at the time of the Polish and Hungarian crises, that the Kremlin still reserved the right to set a limit – if necessary by means of military intervention – to the sovereignty of the socialist countries, to arbitrate internal conflicts of opinion and, finally, to prevent secession. In the case of Hungary, however, the U.S.S.R. found itself, for the first time, forced to turn to China to give what was in fact a military operation dictated by hegemonistic interests an internationalist stamp.

It was under pressure from the Chinese and Yugoslav popular movements jointly that the Kremlin agreed to further concessions in the autumn of 1956.[20] The Soviet government's declaration of 31 October 1956 conceded to the whole bloc of People's Democracies what it had admitted in 1955 only with regard to Yugoslavia: that mistakes had been made, which 'endangered the principle of equality of rights in relations between socialist states'. In particular, it stated that the Soviet government was prepared 'to consider, together with representatives of the governments of the other socialist states, measures whereby economic ties between socialist states may be developed and strengthened, so as to eliminate any possibility of infringement of the principles of national sovereignty, mutual interests and equality of rights.'[21]

This declaration, which the Chinese eagerly hailed as a new chapter for inter-Communist relations, served as the basis for the Polish-Soviet compromise and the establishment of an authoritarian, Communist, but not Rakosist, régime in Hungary. Of course, once the crisis in the autumn of 1956 was past, the Soviets tried to restrict their new concessions, if not to Poland alone, where Gomulka succeeded in consolidating his margin of self-determination, at least to the other People's Democracies. In 1957, after the suppression of the Hungarian rebellion, Khrushchev had no hesitation in calling Kadar's Hungary an 'independent state with its own independent government and an independent policy'.[22] We have already seen how skilfully the Kremlin exploited the Communist leaders' fears of the growing wave of revisionist and pro-Western sentiment in Poland and Hungary to strengthen their hold on all the People's Democracies, this time with China's conditional support. The declaration signed by the representatives of twelve ruling parties (apart from the Yugoslavs) at the end of the 1957 international Communist Conference represented a victory for the U.S.S.R., in that it confirmed the leading role of the Soviet party and called for a struggle against 'the vestiges of bourgeois nationalism and chauvinism'. It announced that 'it is the solidarity and close unity of the socialist countries that constitutes a guarantee of the sovereignty and independence of each'. It is true that it attributed to Lenin the view that basic Communist principles had to be adapted to the particular conditions of each nation, but it denounced the tendency to exaggerate or overestimate these particular characteristics. Once again, Communism was presented as a universal, supranational doctrine and system of which the U.S.S.R. was the proper guardian.

However, its universality was resisted by a growing conflict of interests and opinions. From 1960, the Albanians and Chinese defied the Kremlin, more or less under the same conditions, in the same terms, and with the same fury of disappointed love as had the Yugoslavs in 1948. They were far more critical than Imre Nagy, in whose execution in 1958 for anti-Soviet views they had had a part. After Khrushchev had condemned them at the Twenty-Second Congress in October 1961, the Albanian leaders accused the Soviets of betraying proletarian internationalism, 'trampling on the principles of consultation and equality of rights, by its arrogant and patriarchal methods', and trying 'to impose their opinions on the Albanian party and state through all kinds of economic, political and military pressures, through threats and a blockade.'[23] Thus the Albanians, encouraged and protected by the Chinese, demonstrated the Kremlin's failure to adapt the community's structures to new conditions. The harmonization of Soviet interests, masquerading under the principle of proletarian internationalism, with those of individual nations turned out to be at least as difficult as the harmonization of the interests of the Atlantic Alliance with those of certain of its members.

Unfortunate Consequences of Coexistence: The Development Towards Polycentrism

The post-Stalin pattern of relations between the socialist countries was conditioned by splitting the world into two camps, which took place under Stalin and was both cause and effect of the cold war. However, the increasing *détente* and the reinforcement and consolidation of the West European states shattered the cohesiveness of the monolithic blocs. The slow economic progress of the U.S.S.R., its set-backs in Cuba, the failure over Berlin, the circumstances of Khrushchev's fall, and the split with China – all contributed to the decline of the Kremlin's authority and accelerated the move towards independence.

Rumania and Czechoslovakia exemplify the almost inevitable nature of a development in which integrationist and interventionist pressures give rise to increasingly strong nationalist, anti-hegemonistic counter-pressures. It is true that the dispute between Bucharest and Moscow sprang from economic and not ideological differences. But, under the circumstances, national grievances crystallized around economic considerations. The Rumanian position, as expressed in the April 1964 declaration, clearly drew its inspiration from the Chinese 'propositions' of June 1963. Like Peking before it, but less aggressively, Bucharest proposed 'a qualitatively new system of relations' based on 'the principles of independence and national sovereignty, equality of rights, reciprocal advantages, fraternal mutual aid, non-interference, respect for territorial integrity and the principles of proletarian internationalism'.[24] In order to forestall any doctrinal quarrels, such as those between the Chinese and Albanians on one side and the Soviets on the other, the Rumanian declaration stated that 'no party must label the fraternal party with which it differs anti-Marxist and anti-Leninist'.

Hence the author of this declaration, the once ultra-Stalinist Gheorghiu Dej, came to the same conclusion as the Hungarian Imre Nagy and the most radical Polish revisionists of 1956: that the independent national state is the necessary intermediary in the progress of society. The old internationalist model misused by Stalinist and post-Stalinist Russia has been destroyed. Socialism (supranational or centralized) does not guarantee independence, but on the contrary fully realized independence enables the nation to develop socialism, and may serve as the basis for regional groupings and an international order.

Certainly the Soviet Union, too, is a country where Communism has become naturalized, and where national interests take precedence over ideological solidarity. The national character of Bolshevism was underlined by Stalin in 1931: 'Do you want our socialist homeland to be defeated and to lose its independence? If not, then we must put an end to our backwardness as quickly as possible.' In the same spirit Khrushchev in 1959 observed that 'the Soviet people fulfils its internationalist duties by building Communism at home'. But Stalin and Khrushchev set a fashion. A whole series of ruling Communist parties – the Yugo-slavs, Albanians, Rumanians and, most recently, the Czecho-slovaks – have claimed to be adapting Marxism-Leninism to their own needs and interests.

In the Marxist-Leninist-Stalinist scheme, nationalism is re-garded as a progressive force with a positive part to play only in so far as it aims at the destruction of the colonialist, reactionary empires of the Western powers. Within the Communist bloc, nationalism directed against Soviet hegemony can only be nega-tive. It is defined as 'the main weapon of the international reaction to the unity of the socialist countries'[25]; but doctrine is somewhat uncertain on the point. Little by little, even certain Soviet theorists are having to acknowledge that the 'simplified, optimistic, bureaucratic formulas', formerly used to settle this question are no longer applicable. 'A new situation has arisen,' wrote *Izvestia* (21 September 1966), 'a situation that requires the creative application of Marxist-Leninist principles ... How are the interests of the national state in each socialist country reconciled with the interests of the entire system? How are the different interests of separate states harmonized? How is the surge of national consciousness and national pride, reinforced by the achievements of socialist construction and the acquisition of genuine national independence, to be oriented in the direction of socialist integrationism?'

That is, indeed, the question. The terms in which it is pre-sented are similar to those in which the Austrian Marxist Otto Bauer in conversation with his supranationalist socialist colleague Karl Renner defined the nationality problem of Austria-Hungary fifty years ago. He thought that, after a long period of full-scale oppression, liberation could not be achieved simply by a change at the top. Any new synthesis, according to Bauer, presupposed a 'negative movement', the break-away of nations that would set themselves up as independent states.[26]

Sovereignty, Solidarity and the Right of Intervention

The recovery of national sovereignty became the principal objec-tive of the peoples and Communist states of Eastern Europe; but the Soviet Union, in order to preserve its gains, did its utmost to secure acceptance of its right of protection and intervention. This new concept was first openly formulated in the letter sent to the Czechoslovak Communist party by the representatives of the five 'interdependent' powers – the U.S.S.R., the G.D.R., Hungary, Poland and Bulgaria – meeting in Warsaw, on 14–15 July 1968. 'Our parties are not solely responsible to their own working classes, but also to the international working class, to the international Communist movement ... They cannot abdicate their responsibilities.'[27]

One of the aims, if not the main one, of the Bratislava conference of 3 August 1968 was to force the recalcitrant leaders of the Czechoslovak party and government to acknowledge that 'the defence of socialist gains in each socialist country is the common cause of all the countries of this system'. The implication was that the socialist allies had the right to intervene in cases where they felt the situation in a fraternal country (as in Czechoslovakia on its new course) posed an intolerable threat to their interests.[28] This claim was pressed further in the same declaration: 'The fraternal parties steadfastly, resolutely and with unshakeable solidarity resist all intrigues of imperialism and all anti-Communist forces trying to weaken the leading role of the working class and the Communist parties. They will never allow anyone to drive a wedge between the socialist states.'[29]

After the intervention, the Soviet press did its utmost to show that the occupation of Czechoslovakia, although carried out against the wish of that country's government, was the logical consequence and in fulfilment of common engagements entered into at Bratislava. Soviet theorists performed feats of casuistry to show that the principles of sovereignty, and respect for independence, as well as other matters guaranteed by the Warsaw Pact and confirmed even by the Bratislava declaration, must be interpreted from a 'class' point of view. 'In a class society, no right exists independently of class.' The Five had, it seems, intervened against a Communist party that 'has not taken the interests of the other parties into account and has forsaken its international obligations'.[30]

The Chinese were the first, but not the only ones, to tear away the Marxist-Leninist, internationalist veil under which the Soviets and their partners tried to hide the brutality of an action that world opinion, with a rare show of unanimity, regarded as unprovoked aggression. Chou En-lai's analysis of the situation made sense even to those who reject the frequently distorting simplifications of Maoist thought. 'The ruling Soviet clique', said the Chinese Prime Minister on 23 August 1968 at the Rumanian embassy in Peking (without any objections being raised by his host), 'has behaved exactly like Hitler in his aggression against Czechoslovakia, and like Amercan imperialism in its present aggression against Vietnam . . .' The Soviet leadership, he added, 'long ago degenerated into social-imperialism and social fascism.'[31]

It is true that, in order to crush Czechoslovak socialist democracy and to humiliate the country's leaders, the Soviets employed methods recalling those of Hitler in 1938 and 1939. It was to recall the Munich agreement and its consequences that young Czechs and Slovaks painted swastikas on Soviet tanks halted in their streets. In certain other respects Soviet policy in 1968 was also strikingly reminiscent of the Third Reich's. There were the attempts to drive a wedge between Czechs and Slovaks, threats to disintegrate the country by setting up an independent Slovakia; appeals (unavailing, as it turned out) to a fifth column; the use of Hungarians and Poles, as well as East Germans, in the occupation of a country against which they harbour long-standing resentments; threats to subject Czechoslovakia to military rule, to turn it into a protectorate; and finally, anti-Semitic agitation faintly disguised as 'anti-Zionist', which had already shown what it can do in Poland.[32]

One could carry the analogy even further with respect to the pressure put on Rumania and Yugoslavia, Czechoslovakia's natural allies, immediately after the latter had been occupied, which might be regarded as a repetition of the Nazi Reich's policy of expansion in the Balkans. The parallel cases of the exploitation of the anti-Rumanian feelings of the Hungarians (over Transylvania) and of the anti-Yugoslav feelings of the Bulgarians (over Macedonia)[33] are not mere coincidences; they suggest that Russian imperialism has, to some extent, taken over the role of German imperialism. The fact that the victim has been a country whose inhabitants had for long regarded themselves as the brothers and privileged Slav protégés of the U.S.S.R. shows not only that the internal contradictions of the Soviet empire are getting worse, but also that the influence of militarist and 'national socialist' forces (or social-imperialist, as the Chinese call them) is prevalent in the Kremlin.

It is impossible to explain the military intervention in Czechoslovakia convincingly in terms of real state interests: the real danger of losing Czechoslovakia and seeing the gains of the Second World War wiped out. The true danger in Dubcek's Czechoslovakia was the more or less long-term challenge to the privileges of the police and anti-liberal bureaucratic régimes of the U.S.S.R., Poland and East Germany. The Czechoslovak intervention was clearly a panic move, an arbitrary and violent impulse on the part of the Soviet bureaucratic governing class, increasingly influenced in the sixties by the East German bureau-technocrats.[34]

A Reactionary Power

In 1888 Friedrich Engels expressed the opinion that the destruction of the Austro-Hungarian monarchy 'would be a disaster for European civilization if it occurred before the triumph of the Russian revolution'.[35] Thirty years later, the disintegration of the monarchy actually occurred, closely following the Russian revolution and collapse of the tsarist empire. The peoples of Central and Eastern Europe began to build an independent life for themselves on the ruins of the monarchy. But the precariousness of their new-found independence became apparent from the thirties, when Hitler's Germany made good its claim that Danubian and Balkan Europe was to be regarded as its natural area of expansion.

However, the Soviet Union's participation in the great anti-Nazi struggle made most Europeans forget that, after the turmoil of the revolution and the civil war, greater Russian imperialism had returned in a Marxist-Leninist guise, and that on the eve of the Second World War it had shown itself only too willing to divide up Danubian and Balkan Europe with German imperialism. Later on, after Stalin's devastating interventions between 1948 and 1953, Khrushchevism – despite the Hungarian episode, which could be regarded as a historical accident – awakened hopes for a liberalization of the Soviet system. This, in its turn, would enable de-satellization to take place, that is, the peaceful progress of the bloc countries towards international status and social and political régimes reflecting native interests and traditions.

The Czechoslovak tragedy shattered these hopes. This time, the Soviet Union has used force not against a people that wanted to rid itself of its current Communist régime and repudiate the Russian alliance, like the Hungarians in 1956, but against a Communist party and government whose declared aim was to overhaul the political and economic structures and improve the functioning of the alliance. Thus the Czechoslovak episode has shown that Soviet hegemonism constitutes as great an obstacle and threat to the development of countries in the Soviets' sphere of domination as nineteenth-century tsarist expansionism and interventionism and twentieth-century Nazi imperialism had done. Perhaps the French Communist writer Claude Roy has drawn the moral most sharply: 'It should be realized that the Soviet state, as it has developed, is neither socialist, nor popular, nor democratic, nor revolutionary; that it gives off a pervasive stench, as Bertolt Brecht wrote; and that a co-opted oligarchical government, the private property of a privileged bureaucracy, identifying its caste interests with the national interest and the good of the people, is nothing but a crude caricature of the socialist design; that the celebrated Soviet model held up before the so-called People's Democracies is the exact equivalent of the famous Procrustean bed of mythology – on which they are invited to lie down, helped by their executioners disguised as advisers. That socialist grass does not grow again on the ground over which the *Arturo Ui* Marxists called Brezhnev or Grechko pass.'[36] After the nations of the People's Democracies, who have suffered it for twenty years, the Western Communists and progressives have also begun to realize that the system exported by the Soviet Union to the countries of Central and Eastern Europe has merely usurped the name of socialism.

13

The National Revival

'A spectre is haunting the world: the spectre of nationalism', wrote Pierre Hassner in an excellent study, 'Nationalisme et relations internationales'.[1] This observation applies as much to the Eastern countries as to the Third World, and even more so than to the West. From Budapest to Tirana, from Bucharest to Prague, the disintegration of the internationalist myth, the contagious revival of nationalist feelings have raised complex issues. They concern not only the hegemonistic power, which since 1966 has grown increasingly nervous and inflexible, but also the parties, governments and populations of the People's Democracies. These issues are on several levels: they influence the behaviour and ideology of the Communist leaders, who are having to redefine their attitude to the bourgeois national legacy; relations between the nations making up the multi-national states; and finally, the position of minorities in these countries.

The Communist States, the Nationalist Bourgeois
Legacy and the Federal Idea

The national revival in the Eastern countries has, in the first place, taken the form of a return to national traditions, history and origins. However, this return, which is a natural enough reaction to the standardization and russification imposed between 1948 and 1953, has resulted not only in a revitalization of national values but also a revival of former rivalries, and a search for ways and means of overcoming them.

The present-day Communist states of Central and Eastern Europe are the successors of the bourgeois and nationalist states, which owed their origin or growth to the Wilsonian principle of self-determination written into the Versailles and Trianon treaties of 1919–20. It should be remembered that Hungary was the principle victim of this settlement. Two thirds of its traditional domains were divided among Czechoslovakia, Rumania and Yugoslavia, all three of which were presented with large Hungarian minorities. Throughout the whole inter-war period, Hungarian national feeling, fanned by a chauvinist education, gathered around the demand for a revision of the 'unjust treaties'. The Hungarian Communists could scarcely escape the pressure of a practically unanimous public opinion. After the Second World War Rakosi and Geroe hoped to obtain some frontier adjustments, like those made at the expense of Slovakia and Rumania in 1940, through Hitler's agency. These hopes seemed justified, particularly as the Russians and the Communist International had always opposed the territorial arrangement of the 1919–20 treaties. In 1945, however, after having annexed Bessarabia and sub-Carpathian Ukraine, Stalin announced that he was satisfied with the existing frontiers. The Western powers were no more inclined than Stalin to yield to Hungarian pressure.

Thus, this time under the aegis of the U.S.S.R., Eastern Europe with only a few adjustments settled back into its pre-1938 mould. The Hungarian Communists had to accept their situation; they were unable to prevent the expulsion from Slovakia of tens of thousands of their compatriots, who were made collectively responsible for the exactions of Hungarian troops during the war, and equally unable to protect their harassed compatriots in Transylvania.

The first to raise the banner of national independence against Austria in the nineteenth century, the Hungarians were the ones to suffer most from Danubian nationalism.[2] In 1849 Kossuth's struggle for an independent and liberal Hungary had been crushed by the joint forces of the Austrian emperor and the tsar, with the help of the Czechs, Slovaks, Rumanians and Croats. The latter saw him simply as the representative of the 'master race' which oppressed them socially and nationally. In 1919 with the help of the *entente* Czechs and Rumanians frustrated the

Communist Bela Kun, who with Lenin's approval attempted to save his country from being disintegrated by turning it into a Soviet federal republic. We have already noted the Hungarians' defeat in 1945, when they were once more expelled from Transylvania and southern Slovakia. Their most recent defeat was in 1956. The rising for independence led by the national Communist Imre Nagy was crushed by the Red Army with the approbation of the neighbouring governments, which feared not only the contagion of liberal ideas but the renewal of Magyar (territorial) revisionism.

So many traumatic reversals have made Hungarian national consciousness profoundly pessimistic. This pessimism finds expression in contemporary literature (as in Gyula Illyes's work), and is also reflected in a population decline which is a source of much concern to the authorities and the intellectual élite.[3] They also explain Kadar's embarrassment and that of his colleagues in the face of the national revival among the neighbouring peoples which, particularly in the case of the Slovaks and Rumanians, has often taken an anti-Hungarian turn. Indeed, unlike the leaders of the other People's Democracies, the Hungarians, with memories of 1956, are scarcely in a position to exploit the nationalist sentiments of their people to increase their own popularity. Hungarian nationalism is too clearly identified with antiSovietism and with claims on the territory of neighbouring states. This is why the Hungarian representatives have adopted an 'internationalist', extreme pro-Soviet position in the debate within the socialist camp and the international Communist movement over the Chinese, Albanian, Rumanian and Czechoslovak 'nationalist heresies'. They have opposed their 'nationalist' neighbours as resolutely as Horthy's Hungary opposed Benes's Czechoslovakia, Titulescu's Rumania and King Alexander's Yugoslavia.[4]

No doubt, in combating the nationalism and chauvinism of the other Eastern governments, Kadar was merely paying off the debt to the tutelary power incurred in 1956. But even historians and writers regarded as genuinely representative of nationalist sentiment feel that Hungary's salvation must lie in transcending the arrogant and xenophobic nationalism of the past, though this should not be confused with submission to a hegemonistic power. This was what the Hungarian delegates tried to convey to their colleagues from the other Eastern countries at historians' conferences between 1964 and 1968. They suggested that 'each nation should critically examine its own chauvinism' and that 'not only the reactionary bourgeois legacy from the war should be eliminated ... but also the nationalistic narrow-mindedness of the bourgeois, democratic legacy'. But most of the ideologists and historians of the other People's Democracies took a different path. Whether Marxist or not, they accepted nearly the whole of the national past as far back as 1848–9, when the first confrontation between the rival nationalisms of Central and Eastern Europe took place.

Thus, the Slovaks and Rumanians called the Hungarian revolution of 1848 a 'revolution tainted with chauvinism'. The Slovaks, in particular, contrasted Kossuth, the champion and symbol of liberal nationalism for the Hungarians, with the founder of Slovak nationalism, Ludovit Stur, the 150th anniversary of whose birth was enthusiastically celebrated in Slovakia. Disappointed by Kossuth, who would not acknowledge the political identity of the Slovaks, Stur had joined with the Viennese court in opposing the Hungarian revolution. The Hungarians refer to Marx and Engels, who supported Kossuth's struggle and sternly denounced the 'Slav brutes' for making common cause with reactionary Austria. But Slav and Rumanian historians have pointed out with some justification that Marx and Engels were badly informed concerning the aristocratic and domineering character of even the most liberal Hungarians. The debate, which was carried on in the press, not only did not allow these old quarrels to be forgotten, but reopened 'wounds that had never healed' and fanned the 'quasi-mythological hatred' of the Slovaks for their former masters.[5]

The controversy soon extended to issues other than those immediately relevant to the 1848 revolution, namely the Austro-Hungarian monarchy. The Hungarian historians asked whether, in the light of the history of the past fifty years, 'the elimination of unifying factors', as represented by the Austro-Hungarian monarchy, might not be regarded as a mistake. Instead of setting up independent bourgeois states divided among themselves, would it not have been better, from the point of view of the security and independence of the peoples, to replace the empire by a federation? As shown in the preceding chapter, this was no hypothetical question for the peoples of Eastern Europe. Hungarian historians pointed out that the idea of federation had been promoted not only by Austrian and Hungarian liberals and social democrats like Otto Bauer and Oszkar Jaszi; Lenin himself, in a (forgotten) letter to the Workers' Council of Vienna in November 1918, had expressed the hope that 'the various nationalities of the monarchy would succeed in putting aside their differences and in working together towards the creation of a Danubian socialist federation'.

This historical allusion of the Hungarians met, apparently, with some understanding from the Soviets. Thus Professor Turok Popov put forward the hypothesis that, while the federalist solution enabled the Bolsheviks to prevent the 'fragmentation' of the tsarist empire, the partition of Austria-Hungary raised more problems than it solved. However, as far as the Soviet Union was concerned, it is quite clear that Lenin's name and the principle of federalism were being invoked simply as a means of combating the neo-nationalism that threatened Russian hegemony. For the Hungarians, on the other hand, the cautious attempt to revive the idea of federalism reflects a profound desire to find a solution that will enable them to set Hungarian patriotism a worthy and realistic objective without awakening the suspicions and hostility of their neighbours.

In any case, the idea has obtained such a hold over the Hungarian intellectual élite that even the leaders have been forced to give it their support, however qualified, and to publicize the concept of Danubian co-operation once again. The occasion for this was provided by the easing of relations between Budapest and Vienna following the 1964 visit of Kreisky, the Austrian Minister of Foreign Affairs, to Hungary. Shortly after this visit, in a speech at the Congress of Young Communists, Kadar stressed 'the common destiny of the nations of the Danube basin, which must unite or perish together'. In 1965 the Hungarian Minister of Foreign Affairs, Janos Peter, went to Vienna and proposed a

summit conference of representatives of the Danubian countries
to seek an improvement in relations between them. Two years
later Chancellor Klaus was given an exceptionally warm welcome in Budapest, and the Hungarian press expressed full and
absolute approval of his declaration which suggested that co-
operation in the Danube basin was 'an essential prerequisite for
European co-operation, especially in the economic field'.[6]

An unofficial spokesman, Tibor Pethoe, took up Klaus's idea,
asserting that 'the way to a European security system lay in
regional co-operation'. He proposed that, for a start, there should
be a greater degree of co-operation between the countries of the
Danube valley: Austria, Czechoslovakia, Hungary and Yugoslavia. This could be achieved by strengthening the framework
provided by the Danube Commission, which Austria joined in
1960. This body not only considers technical, navigational problems, but has also worked on some large-scale schemes such as
the Rhine-Main-Danube and Oder-Danube canals.

The Hungarians' object was clear enough: to escape from
their isolation, and to appease public opinion that was growing
impatient at the government's lack of purpose. [7] 'In our country',
ran an article in a Debrecen magazine, 'any reference to co-
operation along the Danube has been taboo for over ten years
because of dogmatic preconceptions and the allegedly anti-Soviet
implications of the idea ... The time has come to take up this
legacy.' [8] The publication of a historical study of federal schemes
of the past was a political event, as was the publication of the
long-banned memoirs of Count Mihaly Karolyi. As a result, the
new generation learned of the life-long efforts of this passionate,
twice-exiled statesman to bring together the peoples of the
Danube basin.[9]

The persistence of a climate of suspicion in Eastern Europe is
clearly shown by the negative response of all but Austria to
Hungarian appeals. Kadar's visit to Novotny in October 1967
demonstrated that relations between their two countries were
now untroubled, but the idea of co-operation was not raised. The
strengthening of the 'northern flank' of the Warsaw Pact by
means of closer co-operation with Poland and East Germany was
then still a priority for the Czechs. Only an old Slovak historian,

Daniel Rapant (a non-Communist who had been removed from his professorship in 1949), came out in favour of the establishment of a 'federal, neutralized, Danubian empire' to compensate for, and counterbalance, a unified Germany, which should, moreover, also be neutralized.[10]

To the great majority of official historians and ideologists of the Eastern countries up to 1968, the establishment of independent states on the ruins of the monarchy seemed an absolute and undoubted necessity, whereas the federalization of Danubian Europe seemed rather a 'visionary projection'. The shock of Soviet interference and intervention in Czechoslovakia in the spring and summer of 1968, however, greatly increased the attraction of federalist ideas in that country. Publicists such as Budin, chief editor of *Reporter*, and historians such as Karel Bartosek advocated the extension of the 'process of federalization', begun simultaneously in Czechoslovakia and Yugoslavia, in the direction of Balkan-Danubian integration.

It does not take a prophet to predict a great future for this idea, in spite of the apparent victory of Soviet hegemony in 1968. In Eastern as well as Western Europe, the prerequisite for the establishment of independence, or minimal dependence on the super-powers, is co-operation and regional co-ordination. Tito and Dimitrov realized this as early as 1947. But after the savage repression of their federal initiative, the Kremlin, applying the old principle of 'divide and rule', made sure the People's Democracies remained separated from each other. 'On the one hand', wrote V. Kotyk, 'relations between the People's Democracies and the U.S.S.R. were improved; on the other, a kind of isolationism, a provincialization developed in the People's Democracies, which had very little contact with each other.'[11]

In 1948 the Soviets had forced all the Communist countries to boycott Yugoslavia. In 1956 Czechs, Slovaks and Rumanians approved the Soviet intervention in Hungary. The East Germans and Czechs expressed their opposition to Poland's affirmation of nationality. After 1958 the Bulgarians and Albanians were especially enthusiastic about the new campaign against Yugoslav revisionism. In 1963 Rumania's nationalistic policy was openly criticized by the East Germans and Bulgarians, and more discreetly by the Czechs and Hungarians. Finally, in 1968 the G.D.R., Poland, Hungary and Bulgaria took part in the military intervention against Czechoslovakia, in spite (or because) of the sympathy felt for the Czechoslovak liberal experiment among large sections of their populations.

But if numerous divisive factors still operate, encouraged by Soviet hegemonism, there are also contrary indications. Apart even from the cautious Danubian initiatives we have mentioned, contact has been resumed among the Eastern countries; rapprochements are taking place like the Rumanian revival of Balkan co-operation, and the spectacular, if rapidly stifled, reconciliation between Rumania and Yugoslavia in summer 1968.

It is true that the Balkan Pact, signed in August 1954 by Yugoslavia, Turkey and Greece, never came to anything. It was a temporary expedient for Yugoslavia, which was isolated as a result of the Soviet blockade and wanted to make sure of a connection with NATO. But immediately after the Soviet-Yugoslav reconciliation, the military aspects of the Pact were played down and, at the beginning of 1959, according to a Belgrade spokesman, the Balkan Pact in effect ceased to exist.

Meanwhile, the initiative passed to the Rumanians. The appeal of their Minister of Foreign Affairs, G. Stoïca, for a Balkan rapprochement in 1957 was, like the Rapacki plan, an integral part of the Soviet peace offensive and for that reason ineffectual, even if one can detect in it the first traces of Rumania's desire for an independent role. The same goes for the revival in 1959 of the Stoïca plan for the denuclearization of the Balkans. The Bulgarian Zhivkov acted as spokesman for it at the United Nations in 1960.

However, since then the situation has changed as much in the East, with Rumania's emancipation in the field of foreign affairs, as in the West with the decline in Atlantic Pact discipline. In the words of an influential member of the Yugoslav leadership, J. Djerdja, 'national and political emancipation creates favourable conditions for the establishment of better relations between states with different systems'.[12] With the Yugoslavs concentrating on their internal problems, the Rumanians, in the full flood of national revival, played the most active part. After Ceausescu came to power in 1965, contacts between Bucharest and Sofia increased, with Ceausescu trying to convince Zhivkov that the different approaches of the two countries to relations with the U.S.S.R. should not stand in the way of their mutual co-operation. At the same time, relations between Sofia and Belgrade and Bucharest and Belgrade also improved, and both the Bulgarians and the Rumanians removed the obstacles that had so long vitiated their relations with Turkey and Greece. In these circumstances Ceausescu's suggestions about the creation of a 'peace zone' in the Balkans assumed an entirely new character. 'History', he said in Sofia in August 1966, 'has shown that the Balkan peoples, who have so often been the pawns of the imperialist powers in their policy of domination and conquest, have a mutual interest in co-operating.' Did not this represent a revival of the old 'Balkans for the Balkan peoples' idea propounded by Titulescu, Nicola Iorga and those bourgeois statesmen and thinkers who are respectfully referred to more and more often in the Rumanian press?

Side by side with these diplomatic efforts, the Rumanians, Bulgarians and Yugoslavs joined forces to reactivate the Committee for Mutual Co-Operation and Understanding Between the Balkan Peoples created after the war, the only regional body with which the Albanians had not broken off relations. In June 1964 a meeting of writers in Sofia resolved to establish a League of Balkan Writers and to publish a journal. In December 1965 there was a meeting of Balkan journalists in Bucharest. Since then, meetings of all kinds, medical, scientific, athletic, youth and student festivals, have increased, and an International Association for the Study of Balkan Civilizations has been created.[13] In 1967 the first signs of an unbending between the Albanians and Yugoslavs were already noticeable. The danger of Soviet intervention in the Balkans after the occupation of Czechoslovakia encouraged the governments of these two countries to draw closer together in 1968, in spite of deep-seated ideological differences.

However, Bulgaria's re-alignment with Soviet policy, which was apparent towards the end of 1967, together with the Greek *coup d'état* shortly preceding it, showed how weak were the links of Balkan solidarity. At the beginning of 1968, on the occasion of the ninetieth anniversary of the Treaty of San Stefano (which gave Greater Bulgaria the whole of Macedonia), the Bulgarian press reactivated the campaign against Yugoslovia. The Yugoslavs responded vigorously. Finally, Soviet pressure on Czechoslovakia created a situation in which the inter-war alignment of forces began to reassert itself. On the one hand, there was an embryo 'little *entente*' of Czechoslovakia, Rumania and Yugoslavia groping for some support in the West; on the other were the former satellites of the Reich, now under the aegis of the Soviet Union. The Hungarians and Bulgarians joined the neo-Prussians of East Germany and Poland under the 'Red colonels' to combat 'that spectre of nationalism' in the shape of liberalism and revisionism, which is more than a haunting memory. It constitutes, in fact, a real motive force, no doubt the most important influence on the development of the Eastern countries.[14]

Nationalization of the Communist Parties and Rejection of the Comintern

The basic tendency of the Eastern Communist parties during the period under review was to take up the 'bourgeois-nationalist' heritage, to concern themselves with national interests, and turn themselves into genuinely national parties. This led the Communists to rewrite party history, blaming Stalin, the Comintern and former sectarian leaders for the political actions that had set the Communist parties at variance with national opinion in the past and had often made them appear mere agents of Soviet policy.

Thus, at a conference of Polish, Czechoslovak and Yugoslav party historians in Belgrade during November 1966, the participants condemned the policy imposed on their parties by the Stalinist Comintern in the first years of the Second World War that forbade them to join battle with the Fascist aggressors.[15] The Rumanian leaders went even further, completely disowning their party's early policy. In contradiction to Rumanian nationalism and under the leadership of militants of Hungarian or Bulgarian origin (Elek Köblös, 1924–32; and Boris Stéfanov, 1932–40), it fought for the systematic application of the principle of self-determination, opposing the dictate of Versailles that severed

Bessarabia from Russia and subjected Transylvania to Bucharest's domination.

Ceausescu, in a resounding speech on 7 May 1966, on the occasion of the forty-fifth anniversary of the Rumanian Communist Party, solemnly repudiated the resolutions of the Third, Fourth and Fifth Comintern Congresses, which had 'wrongly judged Rumania a typically multi-national state, based on the annexation of certain foreign territories', The Rumanian leaders felt that obedience to the 'erroneous' directives of the Comintern (the first of which date back to Lenin's time) 'had isolated the party from the mass of the proletariat, peasantry and progressive intellectuals ... preventing it from promoting the real national interests of the Rumanian people.'[16] This retrospectively self-critical attitude was further displayed in the new manual of party history and in the Central Committee resolution of 26 April 1968 which rehabilitated nineteen leaders put to death in Russia during the Stalinist purges, as well as the national Communist Patrascanu, executed by Gheorghiu Dej in 1954. Ceausescu was evidently determined to convince the public of the genuineness of his conversion to the nationalist path. The function of this review of the Soviet Union's crimes against the Rumanian party in the past was 'to justify the present growing dissociation from Moscow'.[17]

The tendency towards retrospective dissociation also appears among the Poles. They, too, hold the Comintern responsible for the 'false orientation' of their party's policy at the start, when it 'interpreted the emergence of national states in Eastern Europe as a bourgeois attempt to erect national barriers so as to hold back the international socialist revolution.'[18] Indeed, basing themselves on Leninist principles and in conformity with the International's instructions, the Polish Communists had fiercely opposed Pilsudski's nationalism and demanded the restoration of Upper Silesia, Pomerania, and even Danzig to Germany, and of the Polish Ukraine to the Soviet Ukraine, an attitude now condemned as 'sectarian'. The Warsaw government, which does its best to channel Polish nationalism solely against Germany, prides itself 'on having restored to Poland the frontiers it possessed at the foundation of the state'.[19]

All this self-criticism, though its motivation was largely opportunistic, undoubtedly had a solid basis. The policy of the young Communist parties of the Eastern countries reflected a schematic, improvised internationalism based on the conviction that the proletarian revolution would automatically eliminate all sources of national conflict and rivalry. This failure to appreciate the strength of national feelings and resentments was certainly instrumental in turning the Polish and Rumanian parties into small, unassimilated sects. But it would be quite untrue to claim that the impetus which, after 1918, carried Communists, socialists and democrats beyond the simultaneously constructive and divisive nationalist faiths was entirely schematic and based on error. The Eastern Communists' obsession with the coercive methods of the Bolsheviks, their hostility towards Social Democrats and moderate democrats, have isolated them from the nation at least as effectively as their profession of internationalist faith.

There are signs that the critical re-evaluation of their past by Communists, the 'return to grass roots', will lead to their rediscovering the genuine internationalist, democratic, federalist traditions of their respective countries. Thus, in Czechoslovakia, the apprentice Communist party (taking its lead from the Comintern) began with a rigid negation of the Czechoslovak state, 'the product of imperialist quarrels and the unfair Versailles Treaty', and proceeded to a no less hasty Czechoslovak centralism. The doctrines of Bohimil Smeral, one of the party's founders, were rehabilitated on the eve of the political spring. From 1921 Smeral had agitated for the federalization of this multi-national state, giving Slovakia and sub-Carpathian Ukraine a large measure of autonomy.[20] The fact is that the centralist ideology adopted by the party at Gottwald's instigation was a permanent source of weakness for the Slovak Communists; it had enabled the Ludaks (Hlinka's national clerical party) virtually to monopolize the leadership of the Slovak national and autonomist movement between the wars.

From Centrism to Federalism

The shock of de-Stalinization brought to a head, not only the contradiction between Soviet hegemonism and national interests, but also between Czechoslovakism and Yugoslavism, both by-products of Sovietism.

The Prague leaders after 1948, as we know, had taken advantage of the Cominform's centralizing, integrationist line to nullify the independence won by the Slovaks after the rising of 1944. In 1949–50, the leadership of the Slovak Communist party was purged of autonomist elements branded as bourgeois nationalists. For the vast majority of Slovaks, whether Communist or not, this purge was a flagrant injustice, a violation of the 1945 Kosice programme under which the new Czechoslovak state was not to represent a return to pre-Munich days, but rather to become a state of two nations with equal rights, Czechs and Slovaks.

It is true that Slovakia subsequently benefited greatly from the industrialization carried out by Prague. It was transformed from a relatively underdeveloped, largely agricultural region into a mixed industrial and agricultural one, with steel works and modern refineries (notably around Kosice) as well as the basis of a powerful engineering industry.

But in the eyes of the Slovaks this growth did not compensate for what they regarded as the loss of their national identity. Thus long-suppressed resentment against Prague exploded at the first signs of relaxation shown by the central government in 1963. The Slovaks unanimously demanded the rehabilitation of Clementis, Husak, Novomesky and Smidke, the restoration of independence and the dismissal of those Slovak leaders (Bacilek, Siroky and others) who had collaborated with Prague in suppressing the autonomist movement. Novotny's dilatoriness, his grudging concessions, exasperated the Slovaks. 'Today the Slovak national consciousness is hypersensitive and has been provoked', wrote a Bratislava journalist.[21] 'We often encounter symptoms of distrust and anti-Czech prejudices, where they were not to be found before.'

The Slovak intelligentsia enthusiastically took up the search for the roots of its national identity – which was quite distinct from that of the Czechs, whom Bratislava accused of 'chauvinistic paternalism' and a 'jeering contempt' for the Slovak individuality. A first positive step was taken in 1964, when the party leadership formally acknowledged 'the individuality of Slovakia, its right to self-determination and to free national development in every sphere'. But the problem was not so easily solved. The most forceful spokesman for the autonomists within the Slovak party, Husak, called for 'the establishment of state institutions to safeguard the smallest and weakest against oppression, wrong practices, a unilateral interpretation of equality, and against the hegemonistic, discriminatory attempts of the stronger, dominant nation'.[22] The Slovaks were no longer satisfied with 'the vice-chairmanships, with a third share in the administrative appointments'. They wanted to be 'absolutely equal partners'.[23]

Slovak demands extended also to the economic field. They pointed out that their agricultural potential, for lack of adequate investment, was far from being fully utilized. Furthermore, the planners in Prague had not taken into account Slovakia's 'favourable strategic position', closer to Soviet sources of raw materials and still with quite a large reserve of labour.[24]

It was after Novotny's fall that the federalization movement triumphed over all opposition. The appointment of Alexander Dubcek, a moderate Slovak supporter of federalization, as head of the party was in itself a guarantee of its success. The Central Committee Plenum meeting in April 1968 decided unanimously to amend the 1960 Constitution and organize the country on a symmetrical rather than the asymmetrical basis adopted in 1945, which gave Slovakia a dubious autonomy within the framework of a unitary and essentially centralist state. According to a resolution adopted by the Slovak Central Committee in late May 1968, this 'placed no real obstacle in the way of a subsequent limitation of the powers of the Slovak national bodies'.

The Federal Assembly was to be composed of two chambers – a chamber of the people and a chamber of the two nations – or, alternatively, a single chamber divided into two parts, one for the deputies elected in the Czech republic, the other for those elected in Slovakia. The country was to have three governments, Czech, Slovak and federal, with the national prime ministers acting as deputy prime ministers of the federal government. The logical sequel to these changes was a separate Czech Communist party for Bohemia and Moravia, corresponding to the Slovak Communist party which, after January 1968, was virtually autonomous. (Until lately the Communists of the Czech lands belonged to the Czechoslovak party.)

This reform, if it is to have more than a purely theoretical significance, must involve a radical transformation of institutions, a really clean break with the Soviet Union's centralist model disguised as federalism. It is understandable that the framing of the future constitution, which was entrusted to committees representing both parties equally and was closely followed by the press, should have caused a certain tension between Prague and Bratislava during the spring of 1968. Czech liberals reproached the Slovaks for being obsessed with the national problem, and for stressing federalization rather than democratization to such an extent that a large proportion of the former Stalinist leaders were able to hang on to power by identifying themselves with the autonomism of the ultra-conservative Vasil Bilak, who succeeded Dubcek as head of the Slovak party. Slovak spokesmen, notably Vladimir Minac and Laco Novomesky, a friend of Husak's, responded bitterly, recalling that in 1963 de-Stalinization had been initiated by them in Bratislava.[25]

Arguments over the relationship between federalization and democratization, further complicated by a resurgence of anti-Semitism, led to a split in the Slovak élite as early as April. Breaking with the progressives of *Kulturny Zivot*, Novomesky and his political friends started a more outspokenly nationalist, and on the whole anti-liberal, weekly, whose articles were obligingly quoted by Moscow's *Pravda*.[26] Throughout the summer of 1968 the Kremlin did its utmost to exploit the anti-Czech and anti-liberal feelings of the Slovak autonomists. For the benefit of Bratislava, the five Warsaw Pact countries stressed in their letter to the Czechoslovak leadership that they were not criticizing 'the settlement of the problem of Czech-Slovak relations on the healthy basis of brotherly co-operation within the framework of the Czechoslovak Socialist Republic'. Nevertheless, at the time of the Soviet intervention concern for the sovereignty of the state seemed to take precedence with most Slovaks over particularist grievances and reservations about the new course. The Slovak Party Congress, meeting at the end of August in Russian-occupied Bratislava, expelled the 'collaborator' Bilak from the party leadership, electing Gustav Husak in his place. Subsequently, it is true, the latter gave the impression of being more pro-Soviet, assuming an apparently more realistic attitude to the Moscow 'protocols' than Dubcek. But, however convinced that he was better suited than Dubcek to lead the country as a whole under the difficult conditions of occupation, he had to take the opinion of his compatriots into account. And the great majority of Slovaks rejected the idea of a Slovakia independent of Prague but becoming – like Tiso's 'independent' Slovakia of 1940 – a protectorate of the Soviet Union. On 18 September Cestmir Cisar, who in spite of strong Russian criticism was kept on as chairman of the Czech National Council, declared : 'The four weeks that have elapsed [since the occupation of the country] have produced abundant evidence of the unanimous desire of the Czechs and Slovaks to work together within a common Czechoslovak state.' Far from impeding the federalization movement, the intervention of the Five seemed paradoxically to accelerate it, while at the same time revealing the fundamental solidarity on which it must be based.

In Yugoslavia too, centralist tendencies revived national conflicts. After the war the Communists had given the country a federal structure, but they contradicted it by the highly centralized organization of party, police, army and the main sectors of the economy. The concentration of power in Belgrade – capital both of the Yugoslav federation and the Republic of Serbia – apparently enabled Serbia to play a dominant part in running the country, despite substantial representation of the other nationalities in the government. For Tito, Yugoslavism (pre-eminently Serbian) displaced federalism, which he tended to regard as a transitional stage leading to the merging of nationalities, the creation of an economically, politically and culturally unified Yugoslav nation. As late as 1963 Tito was still defending the idea of an integrated Yugoslav culture, but this was so much wishful thinking.[27] For years the leaders of the League of Communists in

Ljubljana and Zagreb had been subjected to increasing pressure from intellectuals and executives, who accused them of not defending the special interests of Croatia and Slovenia forcefully enough against Belgrade's centrism, which they saw as a new, barely modified version of King Alexander's Yugoslavism.

The resurgence of nationalism first appeared in the economic field. On the one hand, Slovenes and Croats complained that they had been handicapped and obstructed in their development by planning and distribution of investments over which their representatives had no influence. On the other, Bosnians, Macedonians and Montenegrins accused the Croats and Slovenes of 'exploiting' them.[28]

This problem was further complicated by the fact that, at the outset of the Communist experiment, the new Yugoslavia was composed of two republics (Croatia and Slovenia) that were industrially and technically fairly advanced, and four that were distinctly underdeveloped (Serbia, Bosnia-Hercegovina, Macedonia and Montenegro).[29]

The country's leaders tried gradually to eliminate these inequalities by making the relatively advanced republics grant considerable subsidies for the industrialization of the underdeveloped regions. The gap between advanced and backward republics may have been reduced, but Croat and Slovene economists consider that because of bad planning this progress has cost their own countries too much.[30] Far too many factories were built in Montenegro, Macedonia and Serbia which were not economically viable, whereas Slovene and Croat industrial centres were allowed to stagnate. The Slovenes and Croats felt that they were being exploited on behalf of their less-developed sister nations, whose frequently incompetent leaders had wasted a large part of the funds put at their disposal.[31]

This was the main reason for the prominence of the Croat and Slovene leaders, Bakaric and Kardelj, in the struggle for economic reform and decentralization, which would enable the advanced republics to control the use of their national income once they had made their contribution to the federal budget and the central financing fund. The economic decentralization they desired, however, could hardly be realized without political decentralization;

and a large section of the Serbian party and public opinion (represented by Rankovic) regarded Croat-Slovene plans as a threat to the position of Serbia, already weakened by the post-war federal organization. As we have seen, in 1966 the struggle for and against reform was on the verge of degenerating into civil war. It was a major victory for Tito, as also for Kardelj and Bakaric, to have been able to ward off Rankovic by winning over the most enlightened representatives of Serbian public opinion.

Bakaric and Kardelj are aware that an anti-Serbian Yugoslavia would be as impractical as pre-war anti-Croat Yugoslavia. Their aim is to lay more solid foundations for national unity through decentralization, or in Bakaric's words, 'to federalize the federation'. To achieve this end, the Croat and Slovene 'liberals' felt it necessary to open an offensive on two fronts: against centralizing Yugoslavism (also called 'unitarism') and against separatist tendencies. Hence the violent reaction of the leadership of the Croat party to the writers and intellectuals who, in a memorandum published in March 1967, called for the complete separation of the Croat and Serbian written languages. There was widespread indignation in Serbia, and the authors were penalized. Bakaric would not allow the intellectuals (among whom were many of his old friends, such as the novelist Krleza) to take action over his head, independently of the party and government and ignoring the tempo he wanted to set.

A few months later, when discussions were taking place on the reorganization of the League of Communists and the convening of the republican Party Congresses in 1968 (before the federal Congress of the League), it became clear that the Croat and Slovene leaders, the main inspirers of the movement, wanted to extend the republics' powers considerably, without, however, undermining the federal foundations. According to their plans, the republics would have their own secretariats of national defence, and would come to exercise an increasing influence over foreign policy.

The main problem still to be resolved, of course, concerns the reconciliation of the very different economic interests of advanced and underdeveloped republics. However, the Soviet intervention in Czechoslovakia and the subsequent political and military pressure on Yugoslavia was a timely reminder for the nationalists of the need for overall solidarity in the face of hegemonistic foreign powers. In early September 1968 'committees of defence', comprising state, party, and parliamentary leaders, were set up in Serbia, Macedonia and Montenegro, and on the Hungarian, Rumanian and Bulgarian frontiers. As in the heroic days of the guerrilla war, Slovenes, Macedonians, Croats and Serbs united under the banner of a rejuvenated Tito, prepared, if needs be, to take up arms in defence of the right of their common country to follow 'a separate path to socialism'.[32]

The Fate of the National Minorities

One of the evils of the Stalinist system in the People's Democracies was the despotic attitude of the bureaucracies of ethnically dominant groups towards the numerous minorities within the framework of national and multi-national states, the various constitutions of which stipulated equality of rights of all the nationalities. It is, therefore, not surprising that the revival of nationalism should have provoked a more or less general movement among the minorities, who also asked for a certain degree of administrative, cultural, and even economic autonomy. Tensions, grievances and conflicts supposedly resolved manifested themselves again.

The process was not uniform, however. In Rumania, and to a certain extent in Bulgaria, where the nationalization of Communism reinforced the unitary, centralist character of the national state, there was at least initially some deterioration in the position of minorities. In Yugoslavia and Czechoslovakia, on the other hand, where the resurgence of national feeling has led to decentralization and federalization, the minorities seem destined to benefit considerably from the new development.

The approximately 1.5 million Hungarians in Rumania – most of whom live in Transylvania, a Hungarian province up to 1918 – were subjected from 1958 to increasing pressure from the central authorities, determined to strengthen the Rumanian hold over the region.[33] The Hungarian autonomous region, established in 1952 as a framework for Hungarian cultural autonomy (79 per cent Hungarian, 20·5 per cent Rumanian), was reorganized in 1960 so that several almost wholly Hungarian districts were placed under Rumanian administration. Rumanian districts were also incorporated, and the name was changed to 'the Autonomous Mures-Magyar Province'. As a result of this new arrangement, the region lost its basically Hungarian character.[34] In 1959 the merger of the old Hungarian university of Cluj with the Rumanian university and the closure of the famous college of Nagyenyed caused a certain commotion. In 1962 a few leading Hungarian intellectuals from Transylvania managed to transmit a memorandum on the subject to the West; they complained bitterly of the systematic destruction of their nation as a separate entity.[35]

The Rumanian government justified its actions in terms of economic and administrative convenience and the need for industrialization. It is true that as individuals the Hungarians have been in no way discriminated against; on the contrary, they were rather well represented in the Civil Service and in economic life, and about 250,000 of them had settled in Bucharest. Theoretically Hungarian cultural activity was subjected to no greater administrative restraints than Rumanian, and a certain 'linguistic liberalism' characterized the primary and secondary education system (although great efforts were made to see that the Rumanian language gained ground).

But as an ethnic group attached to its language, traditions, culture and links with Hungary, the Hungarian minority complained of being ridiculed and cut off from the mother country. Its complaints did not go unheard in Hungary, where the public reproached Kadar for not trying to get Bucharest to abandon its assimilation policy. In an attempt to reduce the tension, Ceausescu in frequent visits to the autonomous region between 1965 and 1968 stressed 'the equality of rights and opportunity for all citizens of whatever nationality', and urged the inhabitants of Transylvania to eliminate all traces of their former differences.

The administrative reorganization decided on at the end of 1967, setting up two 'counties' (Hargita and Mures) which together contained a large Hungarian majority, acceded to some of the demands of this minority.[36] Hungarians have been brought increasingly into the administration, and energetic steps have been taken to develop the region industrially. The Ceausescu–Maurer government's more sympathetic policy, as well as its refusal to take part in the invasion of Czechoslovakia, commended it to the Hungarians of Transylvania, who joined their Rumanian compatriots in condemning the invasion and pledged their loyalty and support to the national government in the face of the Soviet pressure of late summer 1968.[37]

Hungarians form the largest minority group in Czechoslovakia also (in 1961 there were 540,000 Hungarians, as against 67,000 Poles, 55,000 Ukrainians and 140,000 Germans). Most of them live in southern Slovakia, and they often had to depend on the central authorities in Prague to protect them against the 'chauvinism' of the local Slovak authorities, who were both anti-Czech and anti-Hungarian. The 1960 Constitution guaranteed the rights of the Hungarian minority, which at the time possessed a score of newspapers, publishing houses, many schools and a cultural organization (Csemadok) that was fairly active even though strictly conformist. A subsequent administrative reorganization in Slovakia put the Hungarians at a disadvantage, since knowledge of Czech or Slovak became a prerequisite for responsible and remunerative jobs.

From 1963 the growth of Slovak nationalism and the development of the autonomist trend revived former misgivings and resentments. Determined to achieve equality with the Czechs, the Slovaks, even the liberals, often treated the Hungarians in an overbearing and contemptuous fashion. However, the latter, who were very attached to their culture and their past and less isolated from Hungary than the Hungarians in Rumania, strongly resisted Slovakization. In a resolution published in Bratislava in March 1968, Csemadok, claiming to represent the entire Hungarian minority, demanded economic, political and cultural equality for the 600,000 Hungarians in the country. It asked specifically for representation at all levels of political life and for educational reform, an increase in the number of schools, and the establishment of a Hungarian university.[38]

These demands met with stern opposition in Slovak political and intellectual circles, where 'the age-old oppression of the ancestors of the present-day Slovaks by the Hungarian masters of

Slovakia' was recalled. But gradually the Slovak leaders came to see that they could hardly refuse the Hungarians what they themselves were demanding of the Czechs in the name of justice and the rights of man. The committees working on the federalization project took into account the legitimate interests, not only of the Hungarian, but also the German, Ukrainian, Polish and gypsy minorities.

The ethnic map of Yugoslavia, with some fifteen peoples and nationalities, is even more of a mosaic than that of Czechoslovakia. But it is in this country that, from the onset of the Communist régime, minority rights, at least formally, have been best respected. The 500,000 Hungarians of the autonomous region of Vojvodina enjoy flourishing cultural institutions, quality magazines, radio programmes, and many schools. The region has benefited from decentralization. Hungarians evidently coexist there peacefully with their Serbian and Slovene compatriots and communicate freely with the mother country.

The 1,100,000 Albanians form the largest minority in Yugoslavia. About 67 per cent of them live in the autonomous region of Kosovo-Metohija (Kosmet), which, like Vojvodina, is part of the republic of Serbia. The formal autonomy they enjoyed was restricted because of the tension between Albania and Yugoslavia and Tirana's anti-Yugoslav propaganda campaign, and Rankovic's police devoted itself to stifling any nascent Albanian nationalist movement. Belgrade's suspicions also explain the relative neglect of a region whose natural resources (70 per cent of the country's lead and zinc deposits and 50 per cent of its lignite) have only been partially exploited. However, the resolutions passed by the Brioni Plenum of June 1966 have encouraged the minority's spokesmen to ask for 'substantive acknowledgement' of their rights in Yugoslavia. The new generation of the Albanian intelligentsia has set itself the task of developing its national individuality within the framework of a decentralized Yugoslavia and in partnership with the Serbian, Turkish and Montenegrin inhabitants of the region. It would like to 'act as a bridge' between Yugoslavia and Albania, as the Albanian representative on the Presidium of the League of Communists, Fadil Hoxha, indicated in his statements of 5 and 18 October 1967, which made a deep impression. The minority's leading journal proposed to Tirana that it put aside ideological differences, recognize Yugoslavia's interest in the defence of Albanian independence and integrity, and establish close links between the cultural institutions of Pristina (capital of Kosovo-Metohija) and Tirana for the greater good of their common language and culture. Tirana was not indifferent to these appeals from the Albanians of Yugoslavia, who represent a third of the entire Albanian population.[39]

If the question of the Albanian minority has long bedevilled relations between Yugoslavia and Albania, the Macedonian question, too, is still a source of dispute between Yugoslavia and Bulgaria (and also Yugoslavia and Greece). After the Balkan wars of 1912 and 1913, Macedonia, the age-old battleground of Greeks, Byzantines, Bulgars, Serbs and Turks, was divided between Serbia (Vardar Macedonia), Bulgaria (Pirunic Macedonia) and Greece (Aegean Macedonia). Although the Bulgarians and Greeks go as far as to deny the existence of a Macedonian nation, it was officially recognized in Yugoslavia after the Second World War. The 1,045,000 Macedonians in Yugoslavia (1961) are one of the six peoples in the federation with their own republic. Moreover, in 1947 Macedonian nationalists under the protection of Belgrade came close to realizing their most cherished dream: the establishment, within the framework of the Balkan federation planned by Tito and Dimitrov, of a Macedonian state formed by the union of Yugoslav, Bulgarian and, at a later stage, Greek Macedonians. The real purpose of the Greek civil war (1946–9) was to establish the Balkan federation and the unified Macedonian state. However, Stalin's opposition to the federal project, the expulsion of Yugoslavia from the Comintern, and the failure of the Greek rebellion (which the Greek Macedonians supported in large numbers) put an end to these hopes.[40]

Macedonia, under the aegis of Yugoslavia, has made substantial economic and cultural progress. There are 164 secondary schools, and the University of Skopje has 12,000 students. In February 1967 an Academy of Sciences also was set up in Skopje. The Macedonian Church has gained a degree of autonomy under the Patriarch of Belgrade and, supported by the political leaders of the Republic, is trying to win complete independence. Thus Macedonian nationalism now possesses a powerful base from which it can influence its two neighbours. Its leaders in Yugoslavia aim at persuading Sofia and Athens to recognize Macedonian nationality and at winning cultural independence for their brothers in Bulgaria and Greece. These requests, however, have been categorically refused, and this has led to endless disputes and tense relations. On the visit of a delegation of writers from Yugoslavian Macedonia to Sofia in November 1966, the president of the Bulgarian writers' union refused to sign the communiqué, which was in both Bulgarian and Macedonian, on the pretext that there was no such thing as a separate Macedonian language – it was the same as Bulgarian – and proposed that the communiqué be issued in Bulgarian and Serbo-Croat. The Macedonian writers walked out, slamming the door behind them.

The dispute flared up again when Tito and Zhivkov were trying to come to terms : the Yugoslav press pointed out that the Bulgarian census of 1967 indicated only 8,000 Macedonians, whereas the 1958 census had given the number as 178,000. *Borba* (9 February 1967) asked what had happened to the others. The Macedonians also took the Bulgarian authorities to task for obstructing the translation of works from the Macedonian throughout the People's Democracies. Skopje and Belgrade reacted strongly in 1968 to the noisy celebration in Bulgaria of the treaty of San Stefano, which had for several months placed the present Yugoslavian Macedonia under Bulgaria. The situation was exacerbated by the publication of a historical work in the U.S.S.R. supporting Bulgaria in this matter, just as the tsarist régime had done in the past.[41]

At the time of the Czechoslovak crisis in the summer of 1968, Skopje's leaders condemned the participation of the Bulgarian army in the occupation of Czechoslovakia even more vehemently than did Belgrade. They saw in this 'a very edifying illustration of the aims of the anti-Yugoslav and anti-Macedonian campaign being conducted at present in Bulgaria'.[42]

The Bulgarians also had some trouble with the Turkish minority (750,000, or 10 per cent of the population), which refused to be assimilated. In 1951, 154,000 Turks of Dobroudja were repatriated in Turkey, but after that Ankara, unable to absorb these immigrants, shut its gates. The majority of Turks in Bulgaria, however, were immune to the propaganda aimed at persuading them to accept Bulgaria as their country and to renounce their Turkish nationality. Their resistance was partly for economic and religious reasons: the Turkish peasants are especially opposed to collectivization and attached to the Muslim religion, and they were irritated by the press campaigns against Islam and Turkey.

The Jews of Eastern Europe and Anti-Semitism

Compared to the problems of the large national minorities – Hungarians, Turks, Macedonians or Albanians – the problem of the Jews, who do not exceed 250,000 in the Eastern countries ought not to have been of more than marginal importance.[43] It is even misleading to refer to a Jewish problem in the same sense as the Hungarian or Macedonian problem. The majority of the Jewish survivors of the Nazi massacres remained in the country of their birth when they might have emigrated. They did not regard themselves as of separate nationality, and wanted to be assimilated as completely as possible. 'They are Jews', said a Czechoslovak writer 'only by descent, by virtue of the fact that their ancestors practised the Jewish religion; apart from that they feel ... Czech, Ukrainian, or Slovak and are, for the most part, atheists.'[44] There is less a Jewish problem than a problem of anti-Semitism, either as a survival of the religious, popular anti-Semitism of the past or as a useful tool in the hands of police and fascist elements in Communist parties. Thus, the attitudes of the régimes to this problem can be taken as an index of the degree of liberalization attained by them.[45]

The People's Democracies have on the whole been more tolerant than the Soviet Union of those Jews wishing to adhere to the religion or cultural traditions of their ancestors. In Poland, the government subsidized the Cultural and Social Association of Jews, which in 1967 still counted 7,500 subscribing members (nearly a third of the Jewish community), and published a newspaper (*Volkstimme*, with a circulation of 6,000), and books in

Yiddish. Until 1968 there was a Yiddish theatre in Poland (as in Rumania) which also toured abroad. The religious Jewish community in Poland numbered 7,000. In Rumania there were 72 religious communities, with 300 synagogues and some 40 schools. The religious Jews of Hungary have 34 synagogues, a seminary, an excellent library, a museum, and a hospital, as well as other amenities. Unlike the Soviet Jews, the Jewish communities in these countries have been allowed to keep in touch with the World Jewish Congress.[46]

Nevertheless, all these communities are losing their younger members, and their numbers are declining. Anti-Semitism, which received a fresh stimulus from the revival of nationalism after 1953, is directed less against orthodox Jews, a dying race, than against assimilated Jews, for several reasons. In most of these countries, even before the Nazi contamination, militant nationalism was closely linked with anti-Semitism. Again, the traditional economic and social sources of popular anti-Semitism are far from having disappeared during the last twenty years; many inequalities still persist and, even if commercial and industrial competition has disappeared, the new competition for relatively privileged positions is no less keen in the economic sector, the party machine, the diplomatic service, the press and the university. This is at the root of the revival of anti-Semitism.

Another factor is the important part played by intellectuals and workers of Jewish origin in the propagation of Marxism and the establishment of Communist parties in the Eastern countries. Thus, after the war, the party leaderships and governments – especially in Poland, Hungary, Rumania, and even in Czechoslovakia – contained a relatively high proportion of Jews. This fact enabled the reactionary opponents of the new régimes to describe them, in Nazi terms, as 'Judaeo-Bolshevik'.

It was no doubt the party's dictatorial, anti-national and anti-democratic policy that made Communism so unpopular. But certain autochthonous leaders, envious of the advancement of some of their Jewish colleagues, were greatly tempted to buy themselves an easy popularity by blaming the Jews for the faults of totalitarianism. We have seen how the Kremlin forced leaders like Gottwald, Gheorghiu Dej, Ulbricht and even the Jewish Rakosi to make use of anti-Semitism, disguised as anti-Zionism or anti-cosmopolitanism, as a weapon in the struggle for power. It was also a means of giving their governments – which were, in fact, totally submissive to the Soviets – a more 'national' complexion. The intensification of the internal power struggle caused by de-Stalinization, the search for scapegoats for the mistakes of the past and the revival of nationalist feelings acted as a further stimulus to anti-Semitism. Thus, in Poland, around the time of the Twentieth Congress, the question of Jewish representation in the upper echelons became one of the main topics discussed in the party.[47] The Natolinian group, supported by Khrushchev, made ready use of the Jewish bogy in its efforts to discredit the revisionists and Gomulkists, among whom were to be found a certain number of disillusioned, formerly Stalinist Jews. Later, the Partisans, led by General Moczar and R. Strzelecki, made use of the same arguments against the liberals.

In vain, the Polish philosopher Adam Schaff, who had been the moving spirit behind the anti-revisionist campaign, called for 'an educational campaign' to combat 'anti-Semitism, that typical form of racism', in 1965. To eliminate this danger, he said, 'it is essential to call things by their proper names'. Most of his critics considered that Schaff's concern was exaggerated, and that it was simply a question of sporadic, isolated outbursts of discontent, a 'marginal phenomenon'.[48] One of the philosopher's colleagues, Professor Chaluszinski, went so far as to wonder whether Schaff's internationalist humanism, his opposition to every kind of nationalism, was not due to his Jewish origins and affinities.

The Arab-Israeli war of June 1967 pushed the Jewish problem into the forefront of Czechoslovak and Polish political life. In Czechoslovakia the violent campaign against Israel set in motion by the government incensed liberal intellectual circles, who explained the 'particular fervour' displayed in the condemnation of Israel as the survival of the spirit of the Slansky trial, not all of those responsible for which had been dismissed.[49] After these protests, the authorities in Prague made numerous attempts to show that the condemnation of Israeli aggression had nothing to do with anti-Semitism. However, the mysterious death of the vice-chairman of the Joint Committee, Jordan, whose body was recovered from the river Vltava, increased the feeling of uneasiness.

In Warsaw, pro-Israeli manifestations of public opinion greatly antagonized Gomulka, who, recalling that he had never opposed the departure of Polish Jews for Israel, sternly rebuked 'Zionist circles' and insisted that 'each citizen of Poland must have one country alone, Poland'.[50] Shortly afterwards, a purge of Jews took place in the upper levels of the air force, in other branches of the administration and in the press. 'From one day to the next', wrote K. A. Jelenski, 'every Polish Jew automatically became a Zionist by sole virtue of the fact that, like all other men of good will throughout the world, he refused to recognize Israel as the aggressor.'[51] In Jelenski's opinion, Gomulka was impelled to take such an extreme stand from fear that pro-Israeli sympathy would give rise to anti-Soviet demonstrations. The motives of the Partisans who, at the beginning of 1968, took advantage of the patriotic student demonstrations to stir up a spirit of organized anti-Semitic persecution, were less altruistic. On the pretext of conducting an anti-Zionist struggle, their objective was to gain control of the party and state machine by utterly eliminating revisionist or liberal influence (the dismissal of the country's best economists, Professors Bauman and Brus, is to be noticed). Journalists sympathetic to the Partisans, such as Wladyslaw Machajek, editor-in-chief of *Zycie Literackie* of Cracow, attacked the purge victims in terms reminiscent of the *Stürmer* of days gone by: 'Two-faced men with two countries, those who deride national values...'[52]

It is true that Gomulka, alarmed by negative foreign reaction and the many individual human tragedies recorded at home as a result of the anti-Semitic frenzy of the Partisans, tried to curb the movement. But the harm had been done. The Partisans had a grip on Poland, and its anti-Semitic reputation was reinforced. Hundreds of the most able Jews, disillusioned and ruined, left. General Moczar, for his part, remained true to his convictions when, expressing in August 1968 his satisfaction at the 'blow struck by the Five against the counter-revolution' in Czechoslovakia, he attributed the crisis to an 'imperialist, revisionist and

Zionist plot' against socialism and national independence ... Indeed, if Bebel could define anti-Semitism as 'the socialism of the poor in spirit', the example of Poland clearly shows that anti-Semitism today is the 'nationalism of the police'. It is a substitute for genuine patriotism and democracy put forward by the most reactionary Communist elements, those most enslaved by the hegemonistic outlook.

14

The Lure of the West

The most striking development in the Eastern countries since Stalin's death is perhaps their rediscovery of historical national characters, but no less important is the renewal of contacts with the West. The iron curtain that lay between East and West in Stalin's time has been partially lifted. A period of rapprochement, of exchanges and incipient co-operation has succeeded isolationism, suspicion and cold war. Gradually the emphasis has been shifted from divisive to unifying factors.

The Soviet Union has itself embarked on a policy of *détente*, and can hardly prevent the People's Democracies from following its own example, in turn normalizing their relations with the Western powers. But relations with the West cannot be allowed to interfere with the priority of inter-Communist solidarity. Thus *Pravda*, on 4 February 1966, warned the People's Democracies against the danger of succumbing to Western allurements. 'The Socialist countries must more than ever remain unified and vigilant in order to resist ideological deviations.' (This warning was obviously directed at Rumania, but not only at that country.)

An Element of Ambiguity

The attitude of the governments of the Eastern countries towards the renewal of contact with the West firstly reflected ideological hostility, fear of infiltration, subversion and the reinforcement of liberal influence. The fear was particularly great in respect to the United States. The almost frenzied welcome the Poles gave Vice-President Nixon and then Robert Kennedy was a fair indication of the attraction of the American super-power as a counterbalance to Soviet influence. Even in the United States, the obvious danger that the satellites, in their enthusiasm, might run so fast and so far towards the West that the Kremlin would become alarmed was recognized.[1] Those responsible for American policy had learned the lesson of 1956. They no longer wished to raise false hopes, and were intent on constructing a bridge spanning Eastern Europe and continuing in a straight line to Moscow without upsetting the *status quo*.

The Kremlin, however, seemed not to be totally convinced that the Americans had been converted to this view. When President Johnson, in January 1965, expressed his satisfaction at seeing 'the nations of the East gradually recovering their identity', his statement produced a snarling retort from *Izvestia*. The Soviets suspected the Americans of disguising their unchanging determination to alienate the satellites from the U.S.S.R. by adopting new formulas for 'bridge building' and 'peaceful development'. In 1968 they attributed 'the offensive of the counter-revolutionary forces' in Czechoslovakia to the action of 'imperialist intelligence services'.

Quite apart from ideological differences, rulers as well as subjects of the Eastern countries continue to have other reasons for distrusting the West and to avoid too close contact with it. In Czechoslovakia, Munich has entered into the political consciousness of even the most liberal. The Poles, for their part, remember the failure of the allies to carry out the obligations incurred towards their country before the Second World War. The Teheran, Yalta and Potsdam agreements have not been forgotten. The Hungarians in 1956 and the Czechoslovaks in 1968 were able to assesss just how far Western solidarity with them went. The failure to solve the German problem, the refusal of the Western powers (apart from France) to recognize the Oder-Neisse frontier, and Bonn's delay in simply rescinding the Munich agreement remain obstacles in the path of a more positive political rapprochement.

And yet, despite all these objective or subjective, real or alleged impediments, the peoples of the East – especially their intellectual and technological élites – are drawing closer to the West.[2] This trend, which the governments are trying hard to curb, can be explained in the first place by the fact that for most of the Eastern nations, an emotional attachment to the West is a part of their national heritage. For centuries London and Rome were the sources of political and cultural inspiration for the élites. The split with the West occasioned by Stalinism was regarded as running counter to a natural tendency.

In addition, the years of experience of Stalinism made even some leaders realize that exclusive political, economic and cultural reliance on the U.S.S.R. had been a grievous mistake. It is now felt that the establishment at least of some stability in relations with the West and the East is essential to national interests. This desire for more balance in international relations manifested itself first among the Yugoslavs (the policy of equidistance). It was the moving force behind Gomulka's foreign policy before his decline (the Rapacki Plan), behind Rumania's, and finally – with unfortunate consequences – Czechoslovakia's. 'Czechoslovakia's foreign policy', wrote an expert as early as 1965, 'must take into account the country's geographical position in the heart of Europe, at the meeting point of the two systems, as well as Czechoslovakia's traditional relations with the other European states and the fact that Czechoslovak culture is part and parcel of the great current of European culture.'[3]

Economic Needs

Economic considerations undoubtedly played the most important part in the rapprochement with the West. One of the basic dogmas of Stalinism had been the belief in the superiority of the socialist economic system in industrial and technical development. It was assumed that capitalism, threatened by a general crisis and on the verge of bankruptcy, was completely decadent. This belief has exploded. 'Capitalism has not remained at the same stage of development as when Lenin analysed the situation', wrote a Czechoslovak economist. 'It has continued to evolve. It is our knowledge that is dated.'[4] It was impossible to ignore the facts; even the most progressive Communist countries, like Czechoslovakia, were backward compared with the advanced Western countries. This was true not only of the key industries (chemical, engineering and electronic) but also of industrial organization and planning. 'Frankly, I do not see how socialist managerial and planning experts can afford not to make themselves familiar with the managerial methods employed in the large European and American enterprises', wrote one of the champions of reform in Czechoslovakia.[5]

Rapprochement and its Limits

It is understandable, therefore, that the governments, under pressure from their own economic experts, should have seized the opportunity offered by the U.S.S.R.'s policy of *détente* and approaches from the West, to enter into closer contact with the West. There were undeniable advantages to be drawn from a rapprochement that economic consideration made imperative, in spite of the risks involved. The governments might hope to acquire a certain international status, and hence greater prestige for themselves at home.

Thus, from 1964 the normalization of relations proceeded at a faster pace, as much on a diplomatic level as in the economic and cultural spheres. There was even an improvement of relations with the United States. In November 1965, Washington decided to upgrade its diplomatic missions in Hungary, Rumania and Bulgaria to the rank of embassies, on a reciprocal basis. However, the United States was too involved in the Vietnam war and problems in Latin America, Asia and Africa to be very active in Eastern Europe. As far as the governments of the Eastern countries were concerned, a rapprochement with Western Europe was a less perilous enterprise.

Of all the Western countries, General de Gaulle's France was looked on with greatest favour. This was due, in the first place, to the French government's determination to combine a policy of rapprochement to the ex-satellites with a Franco-Soviet rapprochement. France made no political or ideological conditions for the resumption of relations. Furthermore, its campaign to reduce North American influence in Europe, its stand on the Vietnam war and Middle Eastern conflict, and its differences with Bonn reassured Moscow and the other Eastern capitals. France strenuously opposed German nuclear armament. The Rumanians in particular cited the Gaullist idea of a Europe of mother-countries, to justify their independent line.

Nevertheless, the limits to this rapprochement were emphasized by De Gaulle's visit to Poland in September 1967, the foundations for which had been painstakingly laid by years of diplomacy. De Gaulle, as it were, put Franco-Polish friendship to a 'plebiscite', but he did not shake Polish conviction that the maintenance and strengthening of the G.D.R. were vital to Polish security. He was unable to reassure Gomulka of Bonn's intentions (however moderate these might now seem), or of any prospect of the reunification of Germany. As regards De Gaulle's proposal for the abandoning of the military blocs, the Polish leaders emphasized the value of the Soviet alliance for them and the other countries of the Warsaw Pact, 'the keystone of Polish policy'. The visit to Zabrze (formerly Hindenburg), situated in former German territory, and De Gaulle's speech describing it as 'the most Silesian of Silesian towns, the most Polish of Polish towns', was as gratifying to Warsaw as it was infuriating to the West German press, public and government. But the hope De Gaulle expressed that 'Poland would not allow itself to be absorbed by some vast foreign apparatus', his appeals to Poland's spirit of independence, were censored by the press; they conflicted with Gomulka's attempt to turn Polish nationalism exclusively against Germany. In fact, the Polish, Hungarian and Bulgarian leaders – like the politicians of the NATO countries – prefer conservative bi-polarism to De Gaulle's revisionistic multicentrism. The former, they believe, 'offers a better chance of effectively controlling international relations and preventing conflicts from breaking out'.[6] The Gaullist message evoked a positive response only in Yugoslavia and Rumania, where, to quote G. Maurer, 'the ideals of national independence have not been rendered obsolete, but have, under the present circumstances, taken on a deeper and broader meaning'.[7]

Cultural Reunification

If Polish misgivings and the precautions taken by the five Warsaw Pact countries against Czechoslovakia's tentative rapprochement with the West showed up the obstacles in the path of a political agreement, the cultural reunification of the two halves of Europe has made considerable progress. Abstract art, new fiction – Ionesco's plays, the works of Beckett, Sartre, Adamov, Albee, Dürrenmatt and Peter Weiss – have reached Poland, Hungary and Czechoslovakia. A Czechoslovak art critic was not exaggerating when he said that 'the Prague theatre repertoire is sometimes far more representative of what is going on in the theatrical world generally than the Parisian one'.[8] New Polish, Czech, Yugoslav and Hungarian films have been well received in Western capitals. In Prague as in Warsaw, in Belgrade as in Budapest, existentialism, personalism, and various schools of structuralism have been assimilated. Experimental forms of art are practised, even 'happenings' and pop art. Sociological investigations, which had long been banned, have made public opinion conscious of itself as a force to be recognized by the rulers. The discovery of Anglo-American 'Kremlinology' has stimulated historical research and self-critical investigations into the recent past. Even Marxist anthropology and sociology have become revitalized through contact with French and Italian 'open Marxism' in the thought of such men as Gramsci, Henri Lefebvre, Roger Garaudy, Lucien Goldmann, Edgar Morin, Pierre Fougeyrollas, Kostas Axélos and C. Wright Mills.

Communication between the two sectors of Europe is growing, with exchange of official delegations of all kinds. Round-table conferences and international discussions, fairs and exhibitions are becoming increasingly frequent. The tendency towards unification has extended into the fields of fashion, leisure, dance and gadgetry, but its most spectacular expression is in the revival of tourism.

The Dynamic Role of Tourism

In this sphere economic considerations were of course the dominant factor. The Eastern governments went all out to procure the necessary foreign currency to buy patents and equipment.

Yugoslavia led the way, the first to face the dangers of a change-over from the habitual isolationism of dictatorships to an open-door policy for more wealthy and liberal régimes. The Yugoslav experiment proved a success: from 1960 the tourist industry expanded, making the country, because of its relatively low prices, one of the most popular in Europe, with Spain and Italy. In 1963, 1,700,000 tourists visited Yugoslavia; in 1965, 2,600,000, 560,000 of whom were from the German Federal Republic; in 1966, 12 million, bringing the country 230 million dollars, which almost covered its trade deficit. Yugoslavia's example was quickly followed by Hungary, Rumania, Bulgaria, Czechoslovakia and Poland.[9]

The rebirth or birth of a tourist industry benefited even those who did not have the means of travel to the West. In Stalin's time, it was scarcely easier for a Czech to spend his holidays in Hungary or Yugoslavia than to get a passport to visit France; the Communist countries were isolated from one another. Possession of a passport was not a right but a privilege, and it was extremely difficult to obtain a visa. All this is changing. 'The craze for foreign travel has swept our country like a summer storm', wrote a Czech journalist.[10]

But the most notable effect of the increase in foreign contacts, especially with Western Europe, has been to enable the people of Eastern Europe to put their own position and development into better perspective. It may be that prolonged stays in the West have enabled some to acquaint themselves not only with the splendours, but also with the defects, contradictions, inequalities and dilemmas of Western civilization.[11] In the main, however, the East Europeans have been impressed by the achievements of progress, the prosperity, vigour and freedom. The Czechs in particular were painfully shocked by the discovery that they had been left far behind by countries whose productivity and standard of living before or even after the war had been on a level with theirs. The leaders were hard-pressed to give a convincing explanation of this backwardness. This was due, they said, not only to the bad methods of centralized management, but also to the need to help the less advanced socialist countries and the national liberation movements, as well as to essential military expenditure. The man in the street, to judge by press reports, made no attempt to hide his scepticism.

The people of the Eastern countries are inclined to blame their backwardness on Soviet exploitation and economic control based on the Soviet model. Thus tourist and other contacts with the West have precipitated the decline in Soviet influence to an extent that worries the leaders as much as the revival of nationalist feelings.[12]

Between Fear and Attraction

In the language of Communism, Western orientation, or belief in the overall superiority of the West, is called 'cosmopolitanism'. An inquiry in Hungary among young people between the ages of seventeen and eighteen showed that the majority were both 'nationalistic and cosmopolitan'.[13] Similar results were obtained in Poland, Novotny's Czechoslovakia and even Bulgaria. 'Uncritical admiration of the bourgeois West' is naturally regarded by the Communist leaders as a very serious threat to their régimes: 'The myth of the superiority of Western culture is on a par with nationalist distrust and rejection of everything done in the East, and contempt for the achievements of the U.S.S.R. and the other socialist countries.'[14]

Conservative elements in the Communist parties usually attribute the expansion of Western influence to the subversive action of the imperialists. Hence the constantly reiterated warnings against conversations with 'over-inquisitive' foreigners, the appeals to national pride, police pressure to limit the number of passports issued and contacts with tourists. Some leaders believe that socialist society is not yet firmly enough established to dispense with administrative protection against the corrosive influence of the West.[15] The others, however, hope that a combination of discreet but firm surveillance and improved propaganda will be adequate, without the need to return to the isolationism of the past.[16]

One of the most frequently heard slogans in the Eastern countries between 1965 and 1967 was 'no ideological coexistence with capitalism'. But the effectiveness of the anti-capitalist campaigns launched in respect to Vietnam, the Middle Eastern conflict and the Czechoslovak crisis is limited. Economically and technically, the Communist governments themselves are following in the wake of capitalism, copying its organizational methods and innovations, and taking the same values. Ever since the Eastern countries have concerned themselves only with profit, profitability, productivity and the application of the most advanced capitalist methods, and the 'consumer fever' has set in, the Communist system has begun to lose its individuality.[17] One of the main consequences of the rapprochement with the West has been to destroy popular assumptions of the supposed differences between the socialist Utopia – Khrushchev's 'goulash Communism' – and the capitalist one. Both systems seem to be converging on the same ideal of productivity and prosperity.

The Communist régimes are increasingly trying to justify authoritarian rule in terms of its ability to create prosperity and to secure national independence. In choosing such a course they are having increasingly to fall back on the support of the population, and especially of the technological intelligentsia. The latter's pro-Western bias is now openly expressed, and refuses to be limited to the field of technology. The result is that Western influence is steadily gaining ground, acting in favour of the differentiation of régimes, just as centrifugal and native, pluralistic forces, for their part, act in favour of the expansion of Western influence.[18]

As regards a cultural reintegration with the West, the People's Democracies have already drifted appreciably away from the U.S.S.R., where the party curbs and obstructs its development. In this respect, Eastern Europe, in spite of Soviet delaying tactics, is becoming that bridge between the two systems that the best of its sons, such as Mihaly Karolyi and Jan Masaryk, saw as its destiny after the war.

15

Forces of Cohesion and Community Institutions

Centrifugalism – the revival of patriotism and solidarity with the West – could not alter the basic facts of the situation in the People's Democracies. The Communist parties and the countries they controlled in Eastern Europe had commitments to the Communist ideology, the movement and the U.S.S.R., and they were brutally reminded of this fact by the Hungarian and Polish risings of 1956 and the Czechoslovak tragedy of 1968. These commitments were institutionally embodied in the international Communist movement, the Warsaw Pact and Comecon.

The Eastern Countries and the International Communist Movement

At the two great international conferences held in Moscow in 1957 and 1960, all the ruling Communist parties in the People's Democracies (with the exception of Yugoslavia) upheld the Soviet Communist party's claim to the leading role. In October 1961 these same parties approved the Soviet condemnation of the Albanian deviation and hence, indirectly, the Chinese heresy. But their support was not entire. In fact, the attitude of the Eastern leaders to the international movement in the aftermath of the Hungarian rising was determined by two factors: their need for Soviet protection, and their interest in securing as much autonomy as possible within the context of this necessary solidarity. Only the Soviet Union could afford the Communist régimes the necessary material, political and military protection, Yugoslavia and Albania being exceptions that simply proved the rule. On the other hand, the tendency to increase their independence of Moscow, at least in domestic affairs, was encouraged and, to a certain extent, safeguarded after 1956 by People's China, which did everything in its power to obstruct the re-establishment of Soviet hegemony, such as had existed before 1956, over the movement as a whole.

This explains the good relations that existed between the Eastern countries and China up to 1958, when Sino-Soviet relations deteriorated and the moment of choice came. After that date the Eastern leaders sided with Moscow with greater or less alacrity, though they continued to hope that a complete break with Peking could be avoided. Gomulka's policy, pursued with consummate skill over a period of several years, consisted in trying to restrain Khrushchev from taking steps to secure a condemnation of Mao Tse-tung's policy by the great majority of the parties. Outside the Communist camp the Polish leader was supported by the Italians. After 1963, when the Polish resistance began to slacken, the torch was taken up by the Rumanians, who while stressing their loyalty to the cause of unity adopted a neutral position on the Moscow–Peking conflict.

Following the failure of their approaches to Peking after Khrushchev's fall, the Soviets, supported by the Czechs, Bulgarians and French, called a preliminary consultative conference in Moscow on 1 March 1965. Its object was to prepare the way for a new grand council of all the parties that would 'excommunicate' the Chinese rebels. The Rumanians (like six other parties out of the twenty-five that were invited) absented themselves. Furthermore, the conference's official statement to the press, published on 10 March, indicated a retreat from the Soviet-centrist position. Moscow had to be satisfied with the acceptance in principle of a new international conference, but without any definite date for it being fixed. The communiqué stressed respect for the equality and independence of the parties, made no mention of the Soviet party's privileged role and contained no condemnation of 'dogmatism'.

Nevertheless, the Soviets, showing a certain flexibility, used this moderate position, into which they had been forced by the

Italians, Poles, Cubans and British, as a point of departure for a new tactical approach. While apparently abandoning all attempts at excommunication, they aimed at unifying the anti-imperialist front. The object of these tactics – which Togliatti had already recommended in his Yalta memoir of September 1964 – was to win back the neutralist parties that refused to be associated with a condemnation of China even though they disapproved of Mao's intransigence, but did not want to break with the U.S.S.R. and Eastern parties.

These new tactics turned out to be quite effective. They enabled the Soviets to drive a wedge between the Chinese and Japanese Communists, and between Peking and Pyongyang. They also received the support of Gomulka, who tried at the beginning of 1966 to get the Chinese and Albanian leaders to take part in a meeting whose only object was to be the co-ordination of aid to Vietnam, in view of the intensification of American bombing. The Albanians and then the Chinese rejected the offer. They saw no possibility of association with 'the revisionist accomplices of imperialism'. The U.S.S.R. was able to exploit this refusal, which wounded Gomulka deeply, irritated the Italians, and hence improved the prospects for a grand council. Once again this was proposed by Brezhnev in November 1965 at the Bulgarian Party Congress. Votes were taken here, at the Hungarian Party Congress in December 1966 and at the French Party Congress in January 1967. Despite certain reservations and different degrees of enthusiasm expressed, the supporters of the proposal for a council were in a majority. At the S.E.D. Congress in April 1967, Brezhnev announced that seventy parties were in favour.

Meanwhile, a conference of East and West European Communist parties met in Karlovy Vary from 24 to 27 April. The official purpose of this meeting – in the preparation of which the Polish and French Communist leaders had played a major part – was to lay down a common policy on European security, on the basis of the Warsaw Pact declaration of July 1966. The real purpose, however, was to put on a show of unity with the new Soviet leaders; but the absence of the Rumanians and Yugoslavs made it a show of disunity. Urgent approaches by the Russians, Czechs, French and Italians to Bucharest and Belgrade produced no results : the Rumanians and Yugoslavs felt that the question of European security was more the concern of the governments than that of the Communist movement. Tito and Ceausescu, acting together, refused to take part in an anti-Bonn offensive and a demonstration that the Soviets saw as a first step towards the all-party conference.

Ceausescu was determined to keep a free hand, and was infuriated by the Kremlin's attempt to put pressure on him. Shortly after the conference he also referred, without going into details, to various 'attempts at infiltration'. In an article in *Scanteia* on 7 May 1967, he amplified the April 1964 declaration of independence formulated by his predecessor. 'The unity of the Communist and workers' movement', he declared, 'must be based on recognition of the existence . . . of the great diversity of conditions and circumstances under which Communist parties operate, of the different aims and priorities, varying from country to country and party to party . . . Only the Communist party of each country can fully appreciate the actual conditions in which it must carry on its struggle. This is why it is its inalienable right to establish its own political line and revolutionary tactics and strategy.' One of the leaders of the Yugoslav party, the Macedonian Crvenkovski, expressed the same idea: 'Each Communist movement must primarily consider its own working class, its own people.'[1]

Thus Rumanians and Yugoslavs responded to Brezhnev's appeal for unity and solidarity at Karlovy Vary by reaffirming the right of self-determination and their preference for 'bilateralism'. Thereafter, the dispute with Peking was eclipsed by the growing disagreement between 'solidarists' and 'autonomists'. At the time, Czechoslovakia, through its spokesman Koucky, joined Janos Kadar and Todor Zhivkov in politely but firmly condemning the 'neutralist' and 'nationalist' standpoints of the Rumanians and Yugoslavs.[2] Conversations held in Moscow in November, on the occasion of the October Revolution's fiftieth anniversary celebrations – which Tito and Ceausescu also attended – were not successful in reconciling these differences. Not that this prevented Brezhnev from declaring in his jubilee speech that the time was now ripe for a new international conference; this had, in fact, become an obsessive matter of prestige for the Soviet leaders. Having failed to persuade the great majority of the parties to join them in explicitly condemning the Chinese and other deviationists – in 1967 these included the Rumanians and Cubans – the Kremlin seemed resigned to the idea of a meeting that seven of the fourteen ruling parties (the Chinese, Albanian, Vietnamese, North Korean, Rumanian, Cuban and Yugoslav) would not attend.

Soviet policy proceeded in this direction even when, in January 1968, paternalistic internationalism lost one of its last pillars in the person of Novotny. The Czechoslovak political spring cast a shadow over the preparatory meetings for the international conference held in Budapest during February and April 1968. (The first of these meetings was also remarkable for a spectacular walk-out on the part of the Rumanians in protest against the Arab Communist leader Bakdash's criticism of their Middle Eastern policy.) Prague's delegates, Koucky and later Lenart, took up a position close to that of the autonomists. The Soviets, making a pretence of support for the Italian-style internationalism that seemed their last hope of preserving anything of their leading role, managed to get the date for the council to be held in Moscow fixed for 25 November.

No doubt Suslov, the main architect of the international conference, did not foresee the crisis of the coming summer which led the Soviet Union to articulate and then apply a concept of political action diametrically opposed to polycentrism. This was the 'theory of legitimate intervention' which a number of Communist parties, headed by the Italians, Rumanians and Yugoslavs, felt obliged either to censure or to deplore.[3]

While joining the Yugoslavs, Rumanians and Italians in denouncing this fresh proof of Soviet imperialism, the Chinese and Albanians regarded the whole affair as an 'intra-revisionist' struggle, a confrontation between the 'revisionist clique' of Moscow and the 'ultra-revisionist clique' of Prague, whom they accused of having 'shamefully capitulated'. This shows the extent to which Peking's rulers are restricted by their own outlook and prevented from drawing any real advantage from Soviet blunders in Eastern Europe and elsewhere.[4] In fact, the Soviet intervention and the propaganda campaign that sought to justify it demonstrated, not the Kremlin's 'revisionism', but the survival of Stalinist structures in the Soviet Union. These continued to obstruct the *aggiornamento* of the international Communist movement that the Italians particularly wished. The Soviet leaders, for the most part, remained deaf to the argument of Dubcek and his colleagues, that in creating socialism with a human face, in repairing the terrible damage done by the 'Prague coup' of 1968 and its aftermath, they might be able to contribute to the development and consolidation of the Communist world.[5]

In so far as Dubcek's reformism required some loosening of the links with the Soviet Union, the Kremlin and its followers regarded it as potentially counter-revolutionary, no less dangerous than the Hungarian rising of 1956. The Five did not shrink from imposing their own will on Prague, pretending to have the mandate of the 'international working class'.[6]

At one blow, all the patient efforts of Suslov, Ponomarev, Longo and Waldeck-Rochet to make the movement more flexible and lay the foundations for its renewal were nullified. It was claimed in Prague that Suslov – no doubt in an attempt to preserve what had been achieved – showed himself very moderate in Cierna and Bratislava, and that he opposed the intervention. After the Sino-Albanian and Cuban breaks, the Czechoslovak intervention raised the prospect of a new split in the movement, this time between the orthodox bloc and the West European parties evolving towards democratization.

It is true that each side did its utmost to limit the damage. At the meeting of the preparatory committee held in Budapest on 30 September, the Soviets insisted that the timetable set for the international conference of 25 November should be kept. Only a minimum of time was allowed for discussion of the Czechoslovak crisis, but the Italians, French and others took the opportunity of urging the Soviets to revise their attitude towards Czechoslovakia. The International became, in fact, a source of embarrassment for the Russians, instead of a demonstration of their world-wide influence. The new council threatened to turn into a tribunal where the Soviets, for the first time, would appear as the defendants and not the prosecutors. The Kremlin consequently agreed to postpone the international conference for a short while, the final decision being left to a meeting of the preparatory committee fixed for 17 November in Budapest.[7]

'The split in the unity of the Communist movement is, unfortunately, a historical fact that can no longer be ignored', wrote a Hungarian party spokesman at the end of 1967.[8] He did not realize how right he was. Something that had withstood the shocks of the great Moscow trials, the Russian-German pact, the Rajk and Slansky trials and the crushing of the workers' uprisings at Plzen, Berlin, Poznan and Budapest had given way on 21 August 1968. The occupation of Czechoslovakia seems to have destroyed finally the belief in Leninist-Stalinist internationalism. The damage is so great that no patching up seems possible any longer. Those who are trying to salvage the essentials of the internationalist legacy are being forced willy-nilly into making radical doctrinal revisions, into rethinking the concepts of revolution, socialism and democracy. They have no alternative but to break entirely with the superstructures of Soviet hegemonism and dogmatism. This dogmatism, in various equally inflexible and anti-humanistic forms, refuses to acknowledge the inequitable conditions for development that exist, or to recognize the traditions and real forces for change in the world of today.

The Warsaw Pact: Alliance or Instrument of Domination?

When the Soviet government asked the representatives of the European People's Democracies to sign the Treaty of Friendship, Co-operation and Mutual Aid (the Warsaw Pact) in Warsaw, on 14 May 1955, they perhaps anticipated that this document might one day serve as a pretext for military intervention against a recalcitrant member. In the author's view, however, the initial object of the Pact was primarily to give authority for the existing situation, to give a legal structure to the U.S.S.R.'s *de facto* control over the armed forces and territories of the Eastern countries, replacing the 'bilateralist' formula employed by Stalin to the same effect, and finally to absorb the East German army into the unified command. As has been pointed out above, there was no clause in the treaty authorizing armed intervention against one of the signatories.

The structure presupposed in the Pact was evidently modelled on that of NATO, its direct opposite number, although the fourth article of the treaty, with its clause on mutual defence, did not include the terms defining the agreement in the event of attack.[9] Provision was made for a unified command, a consultative political committee and four other subsidiary bodies centred in Moscow.[10] The Commander-in-Chief was a Soviet general with a staff representing the general staffs of the member states and their Defence Ministers. The first Commander-in-Chief of the Pact was Marshal Konev who, in 1960, was replaced by Marshal Grechko and, in July 1967, by Marshal Yakubovsky.

A little over a year after its formulation, the Polish and Hungarian risings put the Pact to its first test. The Hungarian attempt to leave the fellowship and assume a neutral status, like Austria, was crushed by a Soviet intervention approved by all the members.

But the Soviets found themselves obliged to compromise with the new Polish leadership, which wanted to secure greater independence for its own national army. Marshal Rokossovsky and thirty-two senior officers of dual Russian-Polish nationality were sent home. A friend of Gomulka's, Marian Spychalski, who had been sentenced for deviationism under Stalin, was appointed Minister of Defence, and the Polish uniform, Polish insignia and the national flag were restored. On 18 November 1956, the U.S.S.R., in accordance with the pledges made in its declaration of 30 October, signed an agreement with Poland on bases for Soviet troops. Similar agreements were made subsequently with Hungary, Rumania, and East Germany.[11]

In 1967 the strength of the armed forces of the Eastern countries was about 1,200,000 men. Since 1961, these armies had been supplied with new equipment, such as T54 and T62 tanks, anti-tank weapons, MIG21 fighters, fighter-bombers and tactical rockets. (Tanks carrying atomic weapons remained, of course, under Soviet control.) The best equipped and trained armies were those of Czechoslovakia, Poland and Bulgaria. (The East German army is well organized, but its loyalty – like that of the Hungarian army, disbanded in 1956 and subsequently reorganized – is still not taken for granted.)[12]

Since the end of 1962, the Warsaw Pact partners have suffered from the effects of the decline in Soviet prestige brought about by a whole series of factors: the set-back in Cuba, the Moscow–Peking dispute, comparative inactivity in the Vietnam conflict and the technological superiority of the United States.[13] Rumania's emancipation drive, reflected first in economic activity, and then in foreign affairs, alerted the Soviets to the danger. Thus along with their attempt to narrow the intercontinental ballistic missile gap with the United States, they set themselves the task of consolidating the socialist camp. In September 1965, during a speech in Prague, Brezhnev for the first time advocated that the Warsaw Pact be 'improved'. Clearly he had in mind a strengthening of camp discipline over foreign policy, so as to preclude independent diplomatic action. This was precisely why the Rumanians immediately insisted on the right of independence even more for their country than for their party. The Bucharest line on this question was determined by Ceausescu in a speech on 7 May 1966, in which he condemned the 'anachronism' of military blocs and military bases maintained abroad. His statement was clearly inspired by the French position as defined by De Gaulle.

For Ceausescu, military blocs were 'incompatible with independence and national sovereignty, and with normal relations between states'. He therefore proposed the concurrent dissolution of the two hostile Western and Eastern blocs. This had been provided for in the Warsaw Pact, and had been originally justified in terms of a counter to NATO and thus would have no further purpose if the latter ceased to exist. Theoretically, the Soviets also were agreeable to this, and the Rumanians refrained from advocating unilateral action. However, they took advantage of France's withdrawal from the military organization of the Atlantic Pact to indicate their own policy in the light of an already imminent disintegration of the blocs. In the spring of 1966 Bucharest responded to the Soviet plan for strengthening the Warsaw Pact and establishing a kind of permanent directorate by putting forward counter-proposals. According to their disclosures in Moscow, these called for an end to the obligation of member states to maintain Soviet troops stationed in countries other than their own, periodical changes in the supreme command of the bloc's armed forces, and a share in the control of nuclear weapons. Evidently, the aim of the Rumanians was less to secure acceptance of their proposals (whose very existence they promptly forgot) than to neutralize Soviet designs and obstruct any further strengthening of the Pact. And in this they were successful.

The Warsaw Pact consultative committee that met in Bucharest in July 1966 in effect reaffirmed the *status quo*, without making any new decision about the reorganization of the Pact. It is true that its proposals on the question of European security satisfied Ulbricht, as they recognized the G.D.R. and the inviolability of the frontiers as an 'essential component' of European security; but they did not insist on this as a condition for a rapprochement between the member countries and West Germany.[14]

This was another victory for the Rumanians, who wanted a free hand to proceed with normalization of their relations with West Germany. Thus Bucharest, which three years before had obstructed economic integration in Comecon, succeeded in obstructing political integration within the Warsaw Pact. The crisis brought about by Rumania's rebellious attitude subsequently grew more acute as a result of disagreement over the German question, the Middle East conflict, and finally the intervention in Czechoslovakia.

The German Question

The decline in bloc discipline went further when Rumania, disregarding Soviet, Polish and East German objections, responded positively to advances made by the new Federal German government in October 1966. On 31 January 1967 she re-established normal diplomatic relations with Bonn. Ulbricht at once expressed his regret that Rumania should have enabled the Bonn government to put itself forward as the sole representative of Germany.[15] The Bucharest press rejoined coldly that Rumania recognized the existence of two German states, but refused to make this a condition for normalization of diplomatic relations in the interest of peace. Rumania rejected the policy of 'all or nothing'.[16]

The Kremlin refrained from making an issue of the Rumanians' assault on Pact solidarity, and left it to the East Germans and the Poles, who were even more disturbed by Rumania's action. Ulbricht in particular wanted at all costs to prevent Rumania's example setting a precedent. He knew that West German penetration of the Danube basin would ultimately isolate the G.D.R., destroy its economic influence, and perhaps lead to its unification with West Germany. For Gomulka, consolidation of the G.D.R. was a foreign-policy imperative; his main objective was to prevent German reunification.

It was this common Polish-East German front that, with Russian support, prevailed at the conference of bloc Foreign Ministers in Warsaw between 8 and 10 February 1967 in the absence of the Rumanian Minister, who was prevented from attending by a trip to Denmark. The Hungarians, Czechs and Bulgarians, yielding to pressure, agreed to comply with the Ulbricht doctrine that *détente* with the Federal Republic must lead to Bonn's recognition of the G.D.R., the inviolability of frontiers and the renunciation of nuclear weapons. At the same time, the Poles and East Germans took the initiative of replacing the expiring bilateral treaties concluded under Stalin by new ones intended to strengthen cooperation and foreign-policy co-ordination in the framework of the Warsaw Pact (which at the time of the first of the treaties in 1946–8 had not yet existed). Poland and Czechoslovakia signed their new treaty on 1 March 1967.

There followed the Polish-East German and Czechoslovak-East German treaties (March), the Polish-Bulgarian (April) the Hungarian-East German (May) and the Bulgarian-East German treaties (September 1967). In addition, each of these countries concluded a new treaty with the Soviet Union which was, on each occasion, accompanied by a demonstration of friendship and unity.[17]

Only Rumania did not take part in this movement, and the Rumanian party was the only bloc party not represented at the conference of East and West European Communist parties held in Karlovy Vary. Bonn's diplomatic offensive in East Europe was temporarily halted by joint Soviet, East German and Polish action. But the agreement between Prague and Bonn in August

1967 on the exchange of commercial representatives with greater discretionary powers and the re-establishment of Yugoslav-West German relations once again showed to what an extent a rapprochement between Federal Germany and the largely complementary countries of East Europe, especially Czechoslovakia, was dictated by the interests of both sides.

It is understandable that Novotny's fall and the accession of a new leadership with a 'more active European policy' should have given rise to growing concern in East Germany, despite the repeated assurances of Dubcek and his colleagues of their loyalty to the Pact. There was, in fact, no doubt that Czechoslovak liberal opinion was inducing the leaders to adopt a more independent policy, especially on the German problem. From the early months of spring 1968, economic, financial, cultural, scientific and tourist contacts between Czechoslovakia and the Federal German Republic were substantially increased. Under the guidance of Professor Snejdarek, Director of the Czechoslovak Institute of International Politics and Economics, who made several visits to West Germany, preparatory work was begun with a view to re-establishing diplomatic relations.[18]

At the same time, relations between Czechoslovakia on the one hand and the G.D.R. and Poland on the other deteriorated rapidly at the ideological level. The internal liberalization of Czechoslovakia was more a threat to Ulbricht's and Gomulka's absolutist power structures, and to the East German and Polish 'states', than the prospective re-establishment of diplomatic relations between Bonn and Prague. They did their utmost to neutralize this threat of contagion. Thus, Ulbricht's and Gomulka's part in the decision to apply political and military pressure against Czechoslovakia was perhaps even more decisive than that of the Soviet military leaders. It was they who apparently first derived the 'right of intervention' from the 'right of legitimate self-defence'. As embodied in the occupation of Czechoslovakia, this doctrine transformed the Warsaw Pact into an instrument of aggression and domination of the ruling oligarchies over the peoples of the member states.[19] Military and political considerations were merely a pretext; Ulbricht's and Gomulka's purpose in increasingly pressing for the participation of Warsaw Pact forces in the defence of Czechoslovakia's western frontiers was to intimidate and check liberal forces in the country. The Czechoslovak leadership's refusal, communicated by Dubcek to Ulbricht on 13 August, seems to have been the immediate cause of the military intervention. On 5 October 1968 the Kremlin forced Dubcek to agree to the 'provisional stationing' of Soviet troops. Thus, the path not only to a Prague–Bonn rapprochement, but also to the normal development of Czechoslovakia towards democratization, was blocked.

The Middle East Crisis

In the summer of 1967, even before the Czechoslovak crisis, bloc discipline began to crack over the Middle East conflict. From the very outset the Soviet Union took up cudgels for Nasser, casting all blame for the conflict on Israel and her 'champions', the United States and Great Britain. With the exception of Rumania, all the bloc countries, including Yugoslavia, immediately joined the Kremlin's side. After a hastily summoned 'summit' conference in Moscow on 9 June, they also followed the Soviet Union in breaking off diplomatic relations with Israel. The Rumanian leaders, who took part in this meeting, issued a declaration on their return indicating 'active neutrality'. Without naming Israel as the aggressor, Bucharest called for the withdrawal of Israel's forces and advocated that the dispute be settled through negotiations between the belligerent parties. This corresponded to Israel's own wish, and by and large to the position of the United States. On 17 June Ceausescu issued a new appeal for negotiations. Turning to Cairo, he contended that 'democratic development and Arab national unity cannot be served by hatred and dissension', and he called on Israel to 'give up her claims to the conquered territories' in the interests of maintaining a proper balance.

This action helped to gain for Rumania the presidency of the General Assembly of the United Nations at the end of February 1967, an affirmation of the country's increasing prestige. Rumanian policy, in fact, was dictated neither by any particular sympathy for Israel, nor by philo-Semitism (the Rumanian Jews have, after all, complained in recent years of discrimination). It simply expressed the determination to consider national interest alone whenever the country's security was not directly at stake. Thus Rumania also had signed an agreement with Israel for technical and economic co-operation in April 1967, while continuing to maintain good relations with the U.A.R. and Syria.

When on 11 July the Eastern leaders, including Tito, met for a second time in Budapest to express their 'firm support' for the Arab cause, the Rumanians did not send representatives. Their neutrality led to a temporary cooling in Rumanian-Yugoslav relations. But Tito, in fact, before, during and after the crisis, showed himself more resolutely pro-Arab and pro-Nasser than the Soviet leaders themselves. He unhesitatingly supported Nasser's adventuristic demand that the UNO forces withdraw from the Gulf of Aqaba. During hostilities, the Belgrade press criticized Soviet weakness. Upon learning of Nasser's resignation in Moscow, Tito telephoned him, as a personal friend, and urged him to stay on. By springing to Nasser's support he was defending his entire policy of non-alignment based on the Belgrade–Cairo–New Delhi axis. Furthermore, it seems that the Middle East conflict, coming after the Greek military coup, convinced Tito of the existence of an 'American offensive plan' aimed at upsetting the balance of power in the Near East and Balkans. He was also afraid that Nasser's fall might open the way for the growth of Maoist and Castroist influence – already considerable in Algeria and Syria – in the Near East and Africa. Thus, his intimates explained, it was not to cast in his lot with the Soviets that he went to Moscow and Budapest, but to rouse the Kremlin from its apathy; its weakness and indecision frightened him.

However, all these points were insufficient to reassure the liberals, who could not understand Yugoslavia's solidarity with the diehard Arab advocates of a holy war, and feared that Tito's participation in the Warsaw bloc summit meeting might be a first step towards wholesale alignment with the bloc. In the League Central Committee, voices were raised against this policy, and in favour of Israel's right to exist, which Tito had questioned. The Yugoslav government, therefore, under pressure of public opinion and alarmed by the growing Soviet presence in the Mediterranean,[20] subsequently modified its position, joining India and Ethiopia in advocating a political solution to the conflict. Yugoslav-Rumanian relations improved again in 1968, when the two governments took an identical stand on the Czechoslovak question.

The pro-Arab sympathies of the other Eastern countries and the severance of diplomatic relations with Israel led to serious manifestations of discontent, especially in Poland and Czechoslovakia. The existence of such a movement, and the fact that the governments from now on felt obliged to explain their actions, and to defend themselves against accusations of servility or partisan politics, was quite new. Rumania's example was even more disturbing than Yugoslavia's somewhat eccentric one had been. The Soviets' difficulties with this awkward ally – who even raised objections to the plan for a nuclear non-proliferation treaty – reflected the new situation created by the growing economic potential and ambitions of the Eastern states. The Kremlin could master this situation only by throwing its vast military potential into the balance.

Czechoslovakia, the Warsaw Pact and the 'Moscow Protocols'

The summit conference on 6 March 1968 in Sofia was the first time that the 'Czechoslovak problem' – the change of régime in Prague – was raised at a Warsaw Pact plenary meeting. The developments in Czechoslovakia were of concern to its partners in several ways. First was the part played by the Czechoslovak army in the crisis leading to Novotny's fall. The army leaders, the Minister of Defence, Lomsky, and the Chief-of-Staff, Rytir, who were known as out-and-out supporters of the U.S.S.R., had tried to save Novotny at that critical hour by making 'an advance on Prague' with armoured units. Dubcek, with the help of several generals in the political administration of the army, succeeded in forestalling the plot, as a result of which several pro-Soviet generals were replaced. Subsequently one of those implicated, General Sejna, secretary of the Communist cell in the Ministry of Defence, fled to the United States. Marshal Yakubovsky, Commander-in-Chief of the Warsaw Pact forces, was able to judge during the course of a brief trip of investigation to Prague the extent to which disaffection had been increased by this defection.

The Czechoslovakia crisis occurred at a time when the Soviets, in conjunction with the East Germans and Poles, were preparing to strengthen the bloc's defensive capacity in the face of the alleged 'growth of neo-Nazism in the Federal Republic'. Yakubovsky himself, together with Marshal Grechko, was one of the Soviet 'hawks'. For eight years commander of the Soviet army group stationed in East Germany, he had acquired a deep familiarity with the German question, and he took a prominent part in re-strengthening the Soviet infantry, which had been somewhat neg-lected under Khrushchev. At a military conference in Dresden in November 1967, he had taken the view that consolidation of the G.D.R. was the primary objective of the U.S.S.R. and Warsaw Pact. After his appointment as Pact Commander-in-Chief in July 1967, Yakubovsky had made himself the advocate of Pact re-inforcement. On his visits to capitals within the bloc, he tried to convince the governments of member states of the need to in-crease their contributions to the common fund inasmuch as they depended on the U.S.S.R. to raise their military competence to the Soviet level. The G.D.R. was the first to respond positively, increasing its military budget from 360 million marks (5 per cent of the total budget) in 1967 to 580 million marks (8·7 per cent of the total budget) in 1968.

At the Sofia meeting, the Czechoslovaks kept discreetly in the background, and left Ceausescu to make a more open stand. After criticizing the non-proliferation treaty that the Russians and Americans were so eager to conclude, the Rumanian leader, with Czechoslovakia in mind, apparently censured the Russians for not abstaining from interference in the internal affairs of mem-ber states.

Thus it is not surprising that, when the Soviets – under pressure from Ulbricht, who had been virtually reduced to a state of panic by Novotny's total collapse – called a new summit meeting in Dresden on 23 March, the Rumanians were not invited. The Dresden conference was the first of a series with the object either of persuading Dubcek to drop his democratization programme and allow Warsaw Pact troops to be stationed on Czechoslovak soil as a proof of his solidarity and loyalty, or of bringing about his fall.

As Michel Tatu pointed out, Czechoslovakia was given 'special' treatment at Dresden. No one dreamed of calling Gomulka to account for the repressive anti-liberal measures he had just taken, whereas the head of the Czechoslovak party had to submit to a full-scale interrogation on the liberal measures introduced after January. 'In the absence of any other judicial machinery, the Pact and its organization were resorted to when the situation looked as though it might get out of hand.'[21] Various means were used to bring Dubcek to heel. Novotnyite elements were encouraged to resist the new course. Economic pressure was brought to bear, with the Kremlin dragging out negotiations over the Czechoslovak request for a loan of 100 million dollars. Ideological pressure was initiated by *Pravda* on 12 April with a denunciation of anti-socialist forces within the Czechoslovak Central Committee itself, followed by an attack on one of Dubcek's most loyal associates, Cestmir Cisar, who was in charge of cultural affairs. Finally came military pressure: the large-scale manoeuvres held at the end of March in East Germany and Hungary were the first of a series of joint manoeuvres that continued almost until August, and culminated in the invasion of Czechoslovakia.

But before it came to this, there was an escalating campaign of intimidation and blackmail. On 5 May, Dubcek, Cernik and other leaders again stood trial in Moscow. They refused to yield on essentials but, as a pledge of their goodwill, agreed to joint manoeuvres in their country in June, and to the strengthening of the Pact.

On 8 May the 'group of Five' came into being; a summit was held without Czechoslovaks and Rumanians. It was, no doubt, at this private gathering that plans were discussed for a military intervention in the event of all other measures failing to take effect. Kosygin, who was said to favour moderation, visited Czechoslovakia from 17 to 25 May. Talks resulted in a gentlemen's agreement, whereby Dubcek undertook to restrain the press and delay the economic and political negotiations with Bonn.

The Czechoslovak Central Committee, meeting again from 29 May to 1 June, did, indeed, abrogate certain decisions in an effort to pacify the Five. But, at the same time, it resolved to call the Fourteenth Party Congress for 9 September. It was clear that the election of delegates was bound to confirm the ascendancy of the liberal and patriotic Communists, determined to resist external pressures. If the Soviets and their allies were to keep their grip on Czechoslovakia, they would have to act before 9 September. From then on, pressure was increased and provocations were stepped up. The troops were not withdrawn after the conclusion of manoeuvres, despite promises that had been made; the alarm expressed at Vaculik's '2,000 Words' was out of all proportion; *Pravda* (11 July) made a barely disguised appeal to 'honest Czechoslovak Communists to resist counter-revolutionary agitation'; alleged American or West German arms caches were discovered; and Dubcek was summoned to a new summit conference that was to decide on the urgent measures to be taken to help him.

This time Dubcek declined. Recalling how Tito refused in 1948 to attend the Cominform meeting in Bucharest, he proposed instead that bilateral talks should be held to 'clear up the misunderstandings'. The Five, however, met in Warsaw on 14 and 15 July and drew up an ultimatum in the form of a letter to the Czechoslovak Central Committee. The substance of this letter was that, whether the Czechoslovaks admitted it or not, the country was in the grip of counter-revolutionary agitation, its frontiers were no longer safe, and the security of the bloc was at stake. Consequently, either the Czechoslovak leadership was in a position to neutralize these hostile forces, in which case it should at once introduce the emergency measures summarized in five points in the letter, or it was not strong enough. In the latter case, its members, as honest Communists, ought to follow the example set by Kadar in 1956 and call on the socialist countries for help.

On 19 July the Czechoslovak Central Committee unanimously approved its Presidium's courteous but firm reply to this ultimatum: 'We see no justification for describing the present situation in our country as counter-revolutionary.'

On 20 July Marshal Grechko was urgently recalled to Moscow from Algeria. The same day Moscow's *Red Star* announced that 'the Soviet army would know how to protect the interests of the peoples building socialism'. The machinery was set in motion. One final attempt was made to shatter the unity and spirit of resistance of the Czechoslovak leadership before resorting to force. The Kremlin clearly wanted some legal cover for the intervention (a request in due form) such as Kadar had given in November 1956. But the sole result of the meeting between the Soviet and Czechoslovak Presidiums in Cierna between 29 July and 1 August, apart from a tacit agreement to call a halt to the recriminations, was that the Czechs agreed to a new six-nation conference (the Five plus Czechoslovakia) in Bratislava on 3 August.

This conference may have encouraged those Czechoslovaks who believed the Soviets would climb down in the face of a display of national unanimity which surprised and delighted even themselves. On the other hand, the object may have been to drive a wedge between them and Ceausescu and Tito, whose visits to Bratislava and Prague were eagerly awaited; or to force the Czechoslovak leaders to sign a document containing passages that might be interpreted as an acceptance of the 'right of intervention' which had been formulated clearly enough in the 15 July letter of the Five, as well as an abandonment of liberalization.

In view of the use made of the Bratislava agreement by the Soviets and their allies after the invasion, this last interpretation seems the most likely. The agreement provided for the 'common defence' of socialist gains and the 'strengthening of political and military co-operation in the Warsaw Treaty Organization'. It insisted on 'the need to resist anti-socialist forces' and on 'the use of the communications media for the education of the masses in the spirit of socialism and proletarian internationalism'. In the absence of a more adequate justification for intervention, the Five accused 'the leading organs of the Czechoslovak Socialist Republic' of having violated and sabotaged 'the agreement reached at Cierna and Bratislava on the defence of socialism in Czechoslovakia, on the struggle against anti-socialist forces, and on the way imperialist intrigues should be countered'.[22] They went so far as to allege that at Cierna Dubcek, 'with his clearly rightist opportunistic views', had found himself in a minority, the majority taking a 'principled line'. No doubt the authors of this monumentally cynical and untruthful piece in *Pravda* were certain that the occupation, once undertaken, would enable ambassador Chervonenko to find a large minority, if not a majority, in the Czechoslovak Presidium and Central Committee willing to impose a 'Kadar-type solution'.

Three days later, when President Svoboda's refusal to appoint a government of collaborators and the practically unanimous resistance of the party, Civil Service and population had frustrated this plan, the Kremlin resigned itself to dealing with Dubcek and his associates. They were brought from the prison where they were awaiting execution. The unprecedented 'conversations' that took place resulted in the fifteen-point 'Moscow protocols'. The only advantages Svoboda, Dubcek and their comrades had was the knowledge of the unanimous backing of a whole people. For the time being also, they were indispensable to the Soviets, who were reluctant to resort to direct military rule of an allied socialist country. The Soviets, out of shame and as part of a deliberate policy, insisted that the terms of this document be kept secret. According to reliable sources, however, it was an edict only slightly softened by a few Soviet concessions that were more verbal and apparent than real. Dubcek and his colleagues may have believed, when they put their signatures to this document, that there was some hope of preserving the basic essentials: the unity of the people, and the prospects of democratization. In fact, the protocols implicitly legitimized the intervention; Article 5 stipulated that the allied troops would be withdrawn by stages 'as soon as the threat to socialism was eliminated'. The existence of a threat was thus acknowledged, though even the most moderate Czechoslovak leaders, such as Mlynar, continued to deny it publicly even after the agreement had been signed. The same Article specified that units of the Five 'present on the territory of Czechoslovakia' (the word 'occupation' was studiously avoided) and the 'other organs' (a reference to the Soviet secret police or embassy sections) 'would not interfere in the internal affairs of the country'. But no sooner was the agreement signed than the press of the five occupying countries began to screen the activities of the Czechoslovak leadership in detail, laying down in a menacing tone what the Czechs should and should not do in order to achieve normalization as the Kremlin understood it.

In addition, certain undertakings were forced on the Czechoslovak leaders which, despite the calculated ambiguity of their wording, could be used as weapons by their inquisitorial persecutors. Thus, they promised to annul the Fourteenth Congress, which had met clandestinely in their absence (Article 2); to call a Plenum to consolidate party and governmental authority in all spheres of national life; and to dismiss all those whose activities did not conform with the strengthening of the leading role of the party; the implementation of the decisions of the January and May Plenums; the consolidation of socialism in the country; as well as other matters prescribed in Article 3.

The word 'must' kept making its appearance in the Moscow protocols. Anti-socialist and anti-Soviet activities *must* cease in the press, radio and television. The various clubs and anti-socialist organizations *must* be prohibited, nor *must* the anti-Marxist, social democratic party be allowed to operate. Party and state bodies *must* regulate the press, radio and television on the basis of new, concrete measures. Some interim measures *must* be taken, including proceedings against certain individuals (Article 4). Furthermore, the Czechoslovak leaders undertook (Article 7) not to dismiss or take any punitive action against 'those party officials who have fought for the consolidation of socialist positions against anti-Communist forces and for friendly relations with the socialist countries' (in plain English, 'collaborators'), nor to make changes in personnel (Article 12) in the state and party organization.

It is true that Dubcek subsequently tried to interpret Article 3 as an implicit recognition by the Russians of the possibility of continuing with the January–May policy. He compensated for the loss of certain personalities particularly disliked in Moscow, such as Ota Sik, Josef Pavel, Frantisek Kriegel and Cisar, by getting rid of notorious conservatives, such as Bilak, Pavlovsky (a former Minister of Trade), Salgovic (Deputy Minister of the Interior), Karel Hoffmann (a former Minister of Telecommunications), and O. Svestka (a former chief editor of *Rude Pravo*), all of whom had placed themselves at the disposal of the invader on 21 August. Censorship was introduced but the press was not purged; silence was imposed but not brain-washing; the clubs were prohibited, but no arrests were made.

In short, the invader was like the leader of a nation that had been taken into protective custody and who, while yielding to force, was trying to preserve his internal freedom and his self-respect. However, Dubcek was made to understand, first by the increasingly acrimonious press of the Five, and later at a new meeting in Moscow on 2 and 3 October, that the Kremlin would not let him procrastinate indefinitely. In publishing the most exacting clauses in the Moscow agreement, the communiqué issued on 3 October seemed bound to force Dubcek to carry out the Kremlin's will and hence to lose the support of his people. But the Czechoslovak leaders led by Dubcek continued to fight every inch of the way to preserve at all costs their fundamental, essential identity with the people, in spite of the inevitable deterioration in the situation. The Soviets were enraged, and fulminated continuously in their press against the 'totally false' way in which the Czechs interpreted national unity, 'which is, in fact, nationalist, anti-socialist, counter-revolutionary' (Tass commentary, 28 September 1968).

The historical significance of the Czechoslovak affair lay in showing the peoples and governments of the Eastern countries how at variance is the Warsaw Pact, as implemented by the Soviets, with the ideas of national sovereignty and non-intervention in internal affairs guaranteed by that same Pact. All the theoretical concessions to pluralism made since the Twentieth Congress were wiped out at a single stroke. The Soviet Foreign Minister Gromyko, in his defence of the intervention before the United Nations on 3 October, described the action as a 'self-defensive measure' to counter 'imperialist intrigues'. This was, in fact, saying that the Warsaw Pact was an instrument of self-defence for the Soviet Union, which, setting itself above international law and the charter of the United Nations, reserved the absolute right to define what it regarded as a real or potential attack on the 'vital interests of socialism', and 'the inviolability of the frontiers of the socialist community'.

This position was a supremely arbitrary one, and threatened all the U.S.S.R.'s neighbours, especially the socialist countries. The reaction to it, apart from Albania's withdrawal from the Warsaw Pact, the subject of a resolution by the National Assembly in Tirana on 12 September 1968, was open mobilization in Yugoslavia and more cautious mobilization in Rumania. In Czechoslovakia, a pamphlet published on 24 August by a group of young resistance writers seemed to come closest to expressing the general opinion : 'An occupant is not an ally. There is no place in the Warsaw Pact for the Czech and Slovak nations.' The feeling for natural rights as an important factor in the life of the nation should not be underestimated. Henceforward, it is bound, in the case of Czechoslovakia, as for so long in Hungary, Poland and Rumania, to operate against the unilateral institutional links with the Soviet Union. In the long run, the U.S.S.R. will have lost, and the cause of neutrality gained.

The Council for Mutual Economic Aid (Comecon). Compulsory Integration

If the Warsaw Pact was initially conceived in reaction to NATO, the Council for Mutual Economic Aid (Comecon) was set up in 1949 as a counter-blast to the Marshall Plan and the E.E.C., from which the Eastern countries on orders from Moscow were forced to abstain. The purpose of this institution, which included the U.S.S.R. and the European People's Democracies with the exception of Yugoslavia, was to organize economic, technical and scientific co-operation among the member countries.[23] In fact, Comecon under Stalin was a mere cover for economic operations based on bilateral agreements and more a matter of exploitation than of mutual aid. The colonialist nature of these procedures was strongly condemned, first by the Yugoslavs,[24] and then by the Chinese.[25]

It was, moreover, a special type of colonialism. Concerned above all with the reconstruction of its war-disrupted economy, the Soviet Union drained away the raw materials it required. It forced Poland to supply it with coal (13 million tons per year from 1947 to 1950, then 18 million tons per year) at 1.25 dollars a ton, a tenth of the world price. It seized uranium deposits in Czechoslovakia, East Germany and Hungary. By means of mixed companies, it controlled the main economic activities of the Eastern countries. And increasingly from 1950, it urged the People's Democracies to embark on a course of compulsory industrialization, which served two purposes. In the first place, the Soviet Union became the privileged supplier of raw materials to these countries at consistently inflated prices (this practice survived Stalinism, as even in 1966–7 the U.S.S.R. was selling petrol at a higher price to Czechoslovakia than to capitalist countries such as Italy). In the second place, it bought these countries' industrial products at very favourable prices.[26]

But the Soviet Union did its satellites an even greater injury in forcing them to adopt her own system of planned, self-sufficient industrialization, based on her unbalanced development of heavy industry and engineering, without taking local conditions into account. The national economies were thus thrown into a chronic state of imbalance. Frenetic collectivization led to the stagnation of agricultural production; light industry was neglected; wages and salaries were kept at a very low level. Bottlenecks occurred as early as 1951–2, with shortages of industrial raw materials, inadequate power supplies and food shortages. At the same time, stocks of defective and unsaleable articles accumulated in the factory warehouses.

After Stalin's death, his successor realized the need for change. Comecon was revived. In 1955 the bloc experts began to examine the question of the co-ordination of long-term plans. The work was interrupted by the events of 1956, but these, in their turn, made the Soviets more conciliatory. The Soviet government's declaration of 30 October 1956 acknowledged that 'mistakes had been made' in the sphere of economic relations. Shortly thereafter, at Gomulka's request, the U.S.S.R. partially compensated Poland for losses suffered over coal deliveries by cancelling Polish 'debts' amounting to 525 million dollars. Commercial agreements were amended, and the Soviet Union made fairly substantial loans to Hungary (1,200 million roubles), East Germany (420 million roubles), Rumania (270 million roubles) and Bulgaria (200 million roubles).[27]

In May 1958 the party and government leaders decided to re-vitalize Comecon. There was much talk of specialization, which was the main preoccupation of the council in Warsaw in December 1961. The 'basic principles of the international and socialist division of labour' adopted at that time reflected the need to reconcile specialization, championed especially by the Czechs and East Germans, with the clear desire of the less developed bloc countries, in particular Rumania, to concentrate on the creation of as diversified a home economy as possible. In practice, it was very difficult to harmonize these two aims. The Chinese, who kept a close eye on Comecon without being directly involved, were not the only ones to point out that Soviet plans for the division of labour favoured the U.S.S.R. particularly, and also the industrial countries in the bloc. The less developed countries, on the other hand, were in danger of finding themselves reduced to the status of suppliers of raw materials and markets for Russian, Czech, and East German manufactured goods. This was the view of the Rumanian economists. In June 1962, at another meeting of party and government leaders in Moscow, Khrushchev, who was becoming impatient with the slow progress of integration, which contrasted badly with the spectacular advances being made in the Common Market, proposed the establishment of a supranational planning authority and a community-wide investment plan to cover the exploitation of sources of raw materials. But if he was successful in strengthening Comecon by setting up an executive committee consisting of its vice-chairmen from the member states, he was not able to get its statutes altered; the organization was hampered by the fact that decisions were binding only on those countries that voted for them.

Instead of strengthening bloc cohesion through economic unification, the talks held in 1962–3 threw into relief the clash of interests between rich and poor socialist countries, integrationists and nationalists. The Rumanians, as spokesmen for the poorer states, stated that if specialization was to be an instrument for balanced economic progress among the different countries, the various national economies must first attain a more or less equal level of development. Unlike the Common Market countries, the Comecon countries did not fulfil this condition. To illustrate this, the Rumanian experts submitted the following approximate index of industrial production per head of population for 1960, taking the G.D.R. as the point of reference.[28]

G.D.R.	100	Rumania	36
Hungary	55	Poland	60
Czechoslovakia	110	Bulgaria	33

Under these unequal conditions, said the Rumanians, a division of labour based on the existing situation must be disadvantageous to the less developed countries. They therefore urged their partners, in the name of the Leninist principle of equality, to concentrate on bringing all the socialist economies up to standard. This was asking the more advanced countries to make considerable sacrifices, abandoning the manufacture of certain products, which they would then have to import from Bulgaria or Rumania at a higher cost to themselves. However, the Rumanians were exceptionally well placed to put over their point of view and assert their independence. They were self-supporting agriculturally, while petroleum and certain agricultural products earned them a considerable amount of foreign currency. They had no hesitation in purchasing from co-operative Western sources the industrial equipment their partners would not supply. Thus from 1963, Rumanian imports from the socialist countries, although still considerable, were showing a downward trend, whereas imports from the West, especially West Germany, were increasing.[29]

Indeed, the integration proposed by the Soviets met with opposition even from those countries like Czechoslovakia that supported it in principle. All countries cling to their independence, do not willingly give up traditional lines of production, and look on foreign products with a jaundiced eye, frequently dissatisfied with their quality; also business management dreads delays in delivery.[30]

On the other hand, it soon became clear that progress in the division of labour and an increase in commercial intercourse required a more flexible economic structure and a new price system. The existing one, whereby prices were fixed by officials and exchange rates were no less arbitrary, made it almost impossible to calculate comparative costs. The bilateral agreements were concluded in roubles calculated with reference to a mean of world prices rising by degrees over several years. But the rouble was neither convertible, nor transferable within the area. In January 1964, to remedy this situation to some extent, Comecon established an International Economic Bank, with a capital of 333 million roubles subscribed by the member states. Since then, international payments resulting from reciprocal deliveries of goods and other transactions have been carried out through the Bank, which keeps its accounts in transferable roubles. In 1966 prices were re-adjusted on the basis of 1960–64 world prices.

In spite of numerous obstacles, the efforts of Comecon have borne some fruit. Trade between the member states has grown by 500 per cent between 1950 and 1964, and represents 60 to 70 per cent of the bloc's total foreign trade. The engineering and chemical industries benefited to some extent from measures of specialization relating in the former case to 20 per cent of production and in the latter to some 2,000 products. Thus Czechoslovakia increased its export of machine-tools, lorries and buses, East Germany sold more railway carriages, tractors, motorcycles and similar goods. Comecon's standing Transport Committee was responsible for an especially successful operation: the construction of a common depot for goods vans (93,000 in 1964). Joint projects were undertaken. In 1964, phosphorus mines and factories were constructed in the U.S.S.R. with the aid of five Comecon countries. A fuel and power production complex was built in Poland, with the assistance of East Germany, Czechoslovakia and the U.S.S.R. Rumania was helped by the G.D.R., Poland and Czechoslovakia to build its cellulose production combine in Braila.

The two most spectacular achievements of Comecon are the 4,500-kilometre 'Friendship' pipeline to pump Rumanian oil to Poland, the G.D.R., Czechoslovakia and Hungary, and the international high-tension electric grid. Scientific and technical collaboration kept up with this, and between 1950 and 1962 some 38,000 files were circulated. A joint centre for nuclear research was set up at Dubna, near Moscow. Finally, since 1963 many co-operative agreements have been concluded among the countries of the area. Among the international economic associations are

Intermetal, established in 1964, then Interchem, Osmos (the organization of building machinery), as well as an association of bodies dealing with the export of hospital and medical equipment.[31]

A start was also made on organizing the common labour market necessitated by the disparity between the G.D.R., with a shortage of manpower, and Poland (and, to a lesser extent, Bulgaria and Hungary) with a surplus. Doctrinal difficulties have long prevented this matter from being frankly discussed at governmental level; full employment is proclaimed as a real and permanent advantage of the socialist system, a symbol of its superiority over capitalism.[32] Yugoslavia, where rationalization measures resulted in massive dismissals of personnel, was the first socialist country to overcome this self-consciousness, and to bring itelf to export part of its expendable labour force. In 1965 about 200,000 to 250,000 Yugoslav workers were allowed to seek employment in the West, particularly in Austria, West Germany and France. In 1967 their number rose to over 300,000. In 1966, workers employed in the West were bringing Yugoslavia 35 million dollars. Belgrade declared its willingness to lend its workers to East Germany and Czechoslovakia, provided a way were found of transferring part of their earnings back to Yugoslavia. This proposal met with a favourable reception in Czechoslovakia; in 1965 she called on the services of a Yugoslav enterprise to construct a modern glass-works, and *Rude Pravo* (28 September 1965) declared in favour of the organization of labour transfers. The Marxist-Leninist code was further modified to admit of the possibility of labour shortages or surpluses even in socialist countries. During 1965, 7,300 Polish workers (6,300 of them from the frontier regions) were 'lent' to Czechoslovakia, and another 600 went to East Germany for the construction of the German section of the 'Friendship' pipeline. A certain number of Bulgarian forest workers were transferred to the U.S.S.R. In 1967 Hungary and the G.D.R. agreed to the provisional transfer of about 30,000 young Hungarian workers.[33] But the governments of the Comecon countries are still a long way from facing this problem in the way that Belgrade's leaders are doing.[34]

With supranational planning effectively blocked by the Rumanians, the international distribution of labour resources is being promoted on the basis of long-term bilateral agreements, by means of which U.S.S.R. has substantially increased the dependence of all the People's Democracies except Rumania.[35] Thus, according to the terms of the Bulgarian plan of 1966–7, the Soviet Union's share in Bulgaria's foreign trade was to be increased from 57.5 to 60 per cent. Bulgaria buys more than 90 per cent of its petrol from the U.S.S.R., and in 1964 it received a new long-term investment loan of 300 million roubles. The Soviets hope thereby to give the lie to Sino-Rumanian and Yugoslav allegations, and to prove that it does, in fact, support the diversified industrialization of the less developed countries that have faith in its good intentions.

Czechoslovakia, the G.D.R. and Poland also depend almost entirely on the U.S.S.R. for petroleum.[36] To make sure that these supplies continued, Prague agreed in 1966 to grant a 550-million-dollar loan to the U.S.S.R., repayable in petroleum, to be used in the development of new oil fields in the Soviet Union. The Soviet Union remains Czechoslovakia's main cereals supplier, and takes 50 per cent of the Czechoslovak engineering industry's exports. Its share of Czechoslovak foreign trade amounted to 37.5 per cent in 1965 (that of the socialist countries as a whole was 73 per cent). The G.D.R., too, has tended to increase its trade with the U.S.S.R. and Czechoslovakia at the expense of trade, however profitable, with Federal Germany.[37] It solved its fuel problem with the petroleum agreement concluded at the beginning of 1967, guaranteeing it increasing supplies spread out over twenty years. The U.S.S.R. also had its eye on the future when it made an unpublicized agreement in July 1965 that associated it with the construction of nuclear power stations in the G.D.R. Thus 'these two countries have entered on a virtually irreversible course of work undertaken in common', thereby rendering the prospects for the reunification of Germany even more doubtful.[38]

Hungary, too, conducted a third of its foreign business in 1966 with the U.S.S.R., compared with 0.1 per cent before the war. In 1962 she had, moreover, concluded an agreement with the Soviets on the exploitation of bauxite, the only industrial raw material of which the country had abundant resources: with its 80 million tons of reserves, Hungary ranks second or third in Europe, fourth or fifth in the world. The Hungarian government undertook to deliver gradually increasing quantities of alumina, rising to 330,000 tons between 1967 and 1980, to the U.S.S.R. to process into aluminium and return, with Hungary covering the difference in cost by additional deliveries of machines. The Chinese press's view of this transaction – 'plain robbery' – was shared by many experts who felt it would have been more profitable for Hungary herself to produce aluminium sheets from the alumina, with the help of cheap electricity from Yugoslavia.[39]

Objections were raised on two accounts, not only by experts but also by the public, to the growing dependence of the People's Democracies on the U.S.S.R. First, increasing ties with the Soviet Union threatened to invalidate all efforts to achieve political and cultural emancipation. Secondly, the ties seriously obstructed modernization, as in many sectors (for example in electronics) the governments could purchase necessary equipment only in the West. In Czechoslovakia, where after 1966 the 'desire for modernization' was particularly strong, the prevailing opinion in economic circles was that the relative ease with which the country had for so long been selling its industrial products in the protected markets of the bloc, especially the Soviet Union, had slowed down the rate of technical progress. Czech industry, as a result, was becoming increasingly less competitive, not only in the West, but even within the bloc. The Rumanians, Bulgarians, Poles, and often even the Russians preferred selling their agricultural products to the West in exchange for more up-to-date and less expensive industrial products, rather than to Czechoslovakia.[40]

The growing attraction of Western products (especially from Federal Germany and Italy) was reflected in the fact that between 1955 and 1965 the Comecon countries' imports from the highly advanced capitalist countries increased by 247 per cent, and their exports to these countries by 169 per cent, whereas their total exports grew by only 143 per cent, and inter-Comecon trade showed, if anything, a downward trend.[41] However, increase in trade with the Western countries, even aside from political obstacles, is impeded by the restrictive practices of the Common Market, which prevents the export of agricultural surplus; by the falling demand for raw materials like coal (which particularly affects Poland); and by the fact that most of the industrial products of the Eastern countries cannot compete in quality. In 1965 the total value of machinery exported by Comecon to the capitalist countries was 350 million dollars, whereas Federal Germany alone exported 613 million dollars' worth.

Again it was the Yugoslavs who blazed the trail for their neighbours, seeking out possibilities of direct co-operation between Western firms and socialist enterprises by means of the purchase of licences and techniques (contracts were signed by Fiat and Renault with several socialist countries); joint production without amalgamation (the contract between Nihex of Hungary and the English firm, W. E. & F. Dobson, Nottingham, for the production of milling equipment); and the establishment of joint enterprises, such as the Yugoslav firm Rumag with the West German firm Innermann; or the Bulgarian enterprise Balcancar and Japan's Tokyo Trading. One after another, the Eastern governments have asked for long-term investments to speed up modernization.

The Soviet leaders watched this trend with growing concern. On the one hand, they had no hesitation in exploiting the dependence of their partners through economic pressure. Thus, Ceausescu complained in December 1967 of the 'non-fulfilment of the long-term economic agreements, which was obstructing planning'. The following spring the Soviets threatened to suspend wheat deliveries, in order to bring Prague's rebellious leaders to their senses. Throughout the summer of 1968, they put pressure on the Czechoslovaks to turn down Western – especially German – loans offered without any political strings. At the same time, they delayed granting the Czechoslovak government a loan of 400 or 500 million roubles in convertible currency, and advised them against the 'revisionist' economic plans of Ota Sik.

It is not without reason that Soviet-Czechoslovak economic relations have been called 'economic shackles'.[42] One of Moscow's main complaints against Sik and against Cernik's government was that they wanted 'to place economic relations with the U.S.S.R. on a purely commercial basis', whereas the Soviet Union's chief concern was to enable its protégés 'to depend as little as possible on the capitalist countries'.[43] The occupation of Czechoslovakia allowed the Soviet Union to strengthen its economic control over the country and showed up the coercive, restrictive, anti-progressive nature of Soviet integrationism. Rather than subject the machinery of Comecon to a thorough overhaul, the Soviets preferred to keep the Czechoslovak economy in a chronically anaemic state.[44]

16

Development of Internal Political Structures

In 1953, all the People's Democracies possessed political structures usually termed 'Stalinist', after the man who supervised their formation and operation. The system has four characteristics:

1. *Supremacy of the single (or dominant) party over the state.* This means that 'all the important decisions of the party are given legislative expression by the chief organs of the state'.[1] The party organization, in the name of the proletariat, controls all the institutions of the state, and the state controls society, especially the means of communication and education, as well as the professional bodies.

2. *Personalization of power.* Each People's Democracy had a 'little Stalin' at its head. Surrounded by a few grey eminences, his *camarilla* – or 'cabinet', as it was called in Prague – this individual kept the most important, and often even the most minor, decisions for himself. This is what critics of the system called 'bureaucratic centralism' and regarded as a distortion of Lenin's 'democratic centralism'. Personalization went hand in hand with the monolithism imposed on the party, whose members were expected to approve and carry out unquestioningly the decisions taken in their name.

3. The predominance of the police over all other sections of the party and state organizations (the political panoply of the party properly so called, with its hierarchy of secretaries; the administrative machinery, including the government, Parliament and local government; the military and economic organizations; and popular societies). Control of the police apparatus and the closely

linked judicial apparatus gave the leader the last word; he was in a position to 'liquidate' all his rivals, or allies who had become awkward, without having to trouble himself over legalities.

4. To these general characteristics of totalitarian Stalinist régimes may be added a further one peculiar to the People's Democracies: local government is infiltrated by members of the ultra-secret, political police organization, whose job is to enforce 'the centre's' – in other words, the Soviet party's and government leadership's – control over party and State.

The Constant Factor: Soviet Control

The Soviet intervention in Czechoslovakia during 1968, preceded by a period of increased repression in the Soviet, Polish and East German régimes, might lead one to suppose that the structures inherited from Stalin have remained basically unaltered, and that the Soviet Union is not prepared to allow any real progress towards normalization to take place in the Eastern countries. However, as we have seen, this is not the case, and the situation requires rather closer analysis.

In fact, the political climate in the People's Democracies has altered appreciably since 1953, although the content, tempo and prospects of the changes vary from country to country. Thus Hungary under Kadar has turned into an enlightened dictatorship. Poland, on the other hand, has regressed towards a type of neo-Stalinist social fascism. The dictatorship has lost none of its bite in the German Democratic Republic, but it has become more technically-minded, more Prussian. Bulgaria's severe régime has been somewhat modified; Rumania's has Rumanized itself and Albania's has come under Chinese influence. Yugoslavia, where the situation sometimes borders on anarchy, is engaged in the search for a novel solution to the political, national and economic problems that beset it.

It is no longer possible to classify all the Eastern countries under the single heading of totalitarian states, or to use Djilas's description of the Communist system as implying permanent civil war between the party (or its sociological substratum, the new class) and the rest of the population.

However, one should beware of taking the various substitutes for democratization for the real thing. Since 1956 the Communist leaders, with Tito at their head, have displayed great ingenuity in this respect. In the case of the Yugoslav régime itself, measures of decentralization, democratization and self-management have delighted Western political observers as much as they have alarmed the Stalinists. However, it came as something of a shock when, in July 1966, at the time of Rankovic's fall, public opinion woke up to the fact that, all the while democratization was proceeding, the political police network controlled, to quote Bakaric, the Croatian party chief, 'every aspect of social life, from the appointment of company directors to the very composition of the government'. At the same time, it became clear that, despite the freedom of expression enjoyed in Yugoslavia, journalists who were aware of this crucial fact had taken great pains not to reveal their knowledge. No one had dared to criticize Rankovic and his secret police before they were officially condemned. 'Previously', wrote Professor Mihajlov 'we were unanimously in favour of Rankovic. Now we are unanimously against him.'[2] Mihajlov's own arrest and conviction proved his point.

The Czechoslovak régime after 1963 was almost as liberal as Kadar's Hungary. Nevertheless, the Communist writer L. Vaculik was justified in breaking his enforced silence at the June 1967 writers' congress to denounce the permanence of personal power and basic insecurity of all citizens. 'One wonders', he said, 'if even the members of the government are guaranteed the civil rights necessary for any form of political activity.' Indeed, despite the solemn declarations of the re-establishment of socialist legality, 'institutional guarantees for ordinary citizens' were far from secure.[3] With the exception of Czechoslovakia during its liberal interlude and the partial exception of Yugoslavia, the party leadership has kept its monopoly over political decision-making throughout the European Communist countries. It enjoys legislative, executive and judicial powers without having to submit to any effective popular control. The basic features of the Stalinist structures described above have survived.[4]

The durability of the Soviet machinery of control was demonstrated by the Soviet-Czechoslovak crisis of 1968. Evidently, one of the main reasons for the use of force against Czechoslovakia was the conviction that the leaders of the new Czechoslovakia, like those of Yugoslavia, Albania and Rumania, would finish by eliminating all the diehard pro-Soviets and agents of the Soviet Union from the party leadership. This was felt even more keenly than the openly expressed concern at seeing 'the situation slipping out of the control of the Czechoslovak Communist party' (which was more firmly in the saddle and more popular than it had ever been), and the more realistic fear of corruption. According to the Czechoslovaks, the military action was precipitated by information received in Moscow relating to the Fourteenth Party Congress which was due to meet at the beginning of September 1968. It was known that, on the initiative of the Prague party committee (the most progressive local organization in the Czechoslovak party after Brno), the majority of the delegates to the Congress were planning to get rid of seventy-three (out of almost two hundred) members of the existing Central Committee, including the men Moscow regarded as safe. All the evidence suggests that for the U.S.S.R. the survival of these people, through whom the Soviet Union is able to exert its influence, was more important than the popularity of the Czechoslovak Communist party.

Many facts point to this interpretation. The protocols that the Soviets forced the Czechoslovak leaders to accept on 26 August 1968 prohibited them from removing 'those party officials who have fought for the consolidation of socialist positions against anti-Communist forces and for friendly relations with the socialist countries' and required them to get rid of all those whose actions did not meet this specification. In particular the protocols referred to the Minister of the Interior, whose work and activities should be investigated (Article 12). Finally, having recalled Dubcek, Cernik and Husak on 3 October the Soviets directed the Czechoslovak leaders to staff party and state organizations with people devoted to Marxism-Leninism and proletarian internationalism.

The significance of these various demands becomes clear when they are set against events in Prague on 21 August, the first day of the intervention. At that time, the pro-Soviet organization, reconstituted thanks to Ambassador Chervonenko's efforts after Novotny's fall had left it leaderless, emerged from the shadows to take over after the arrest of the Dubcek–Cernik–Smrkovsky group. This political police apparatus consisted of a party secretary, Indra, who was fully prepared to play his allotted Kadar-like part; the security (secret police) chief, Salgovic, assisted by Bohumil Molnar, the Prague state security chief; and two deputies, Josef Ripl and Alois Kozuch.[5] The group also included Hoffmann, the Minister of Communications, who tried to prevent the broadcasting of the party Presidium's protest against the invasion; Svestka, former chief editor of *Rude Pravo*; and Sulek, the suspended director of the C.T.K. agency, who tried to broadcast the appeal for help fabricated by the Soviets. There was also Vokac, a former Minister of Transport, who returned to his post to disrupt communications between different interests and thereby facilitate the progress of the invasion forces. One could also add a few politicians like Kolder, Bilak, Barbirek (members of the Presidium), and Novy and Jakes (members of the Central Committee), who emerged as outright collaborators.[6]

Czechoslovakia's great fraternal ally thus had forces working on its behalf in the police, the press, radio and transport. Their failure was due, first, to Svoboda's courage – he refused to accept the *fait accompli* – and secondly to the resistance of the journalists and officials who refused to obey the orders of the collaborationists. But the most important factor was the drastic action taken by the Minister of the Interior Josef Pavel, who had been convicted and had suffered torture under Novotny. He evaded arrest and, supported by the great majority of officials in the Ministry of the Interior and Public Security, weighed into the attack, thwarting the conspirators' plans. So successful was he that security agents acting on his orders protected radio and television newsmen as well as writers in danger of arrest, helped to distribute the underground newspapers and disrupted the invader's progress.[7]

The fate of the Czechoslovak reformers has shown the limits of free action permitted by the Soviet leadership to the Eastern countries. In Czechoslovakia, a renewed Communist party leadership won over to the ideals of democracy and nationalism thought it would be able to consolidate its power by surrendering its role of 'universal administrator of society',[8] by suppressing bugging devices and engaging in a real dialogue with the people. Neither the one-party régime, collectivism, nor the alliance were questioned; only censorship, the police system and the subjection of the nation, which apparently was the basic point, which explained the Soviet reaction in terms of frustrated partisan ideology and imperialistic egotism. Indeed, Moscow could not fail to see that it was the concern of Dubcek and his colleagues for the national interest and defence of Czechoslovak party and state sovereignty that enabled them to gain popular support for the leading role of the party. (It had been the same story in Yugoslavia, Albania, Rumania and, one might add, China and Vietnam.)

Dubcek hoped that consolidation of the party's influence and popularity, together with a categorical refusal to allow any organized opposition, with pledges of loyalty to the Warsaw Pact, would be enough to allay Soviet doubts. But it was precisely the nationalization and popularization of the party, the extraordinary unity of party and people in July and August 1968 in resisting the Russians, and finally the total loss of direct control over the Czechoslovak party and state that turned out to be the real stumbling block, the final straw for the Kremlin. One of the main objects of the military intervention was to reconstruct the machinery of direct control, dismantled (perhaps unwittingly) by Dubcek.[9]

Changing Factors

1. *The tendency to become less repressive.* Despite repression and intervention, the parties have changed and are changing in their methods, their conception of their leading and guiding role, and their relations with the different strata in society, which in turn have changed and are no longer passive. The police character of the régimes – except in periods of acute crisis, when it becomes apparent that there is nothing that cannot be changed – is also tending to become less severe.

In Stalin's time, not only the population and the militants, but even the leaders were often terrorized by the Moscow-controlled police, who imposed themselves upon the party machine. Beria's fall marked the beginning of the emancipation at least of the Communist leaders. Gradually, under the banner of collective leadership (initially imposed by Moscow), they tried to regain control over the secret police. The elimination of Rankovic in Yugoslavia, the review of the Slansky and other trials, followed by the rehabilitation and indemnification of tens of thousands of victims of Gottwald and Novotny in Czechoslovakia, were the most spectacular episodes in this clearing of the political atmosphere in the People's Democracies. Life stopped, or was about to stop, being nightmarish, Kafkaesque and terrifying. Furthermore, in one country after another, the leadership passed into the hands of former victims of repression – Kadar, Gomulka, Spychalski, Smrkovsky and others – and feelings of guilt turned many former inquisitors into staunch advocates of lawfulness. Progress, in the sense of an internal *détente*, occurred even in Rumania and Bulgaria in 1967.

But if police pressure has generally slackened or become less obtrusive, if the police have been placed under the control of 'politicians', the security services – like the K.G.B., which ostentatiously celebrated it fiftieth anniversary in December 1967 – still tend to set themselves up as the guardians, not only of security, but of ideological orthodoxy. The police are nearly always the natural allies of the most conservative forces. Like that of the military, their influence increases each time the upper echelons of the party are split by conflicting tendencies and cliques. One has only to consider developments in Czechoslovakia in 1967, or in Poland between 1966 and 1968.

2. *The decline of monolithism.* The decline of monolithism and personal power has been no less considerable. The Soviet Union itself initiated this process in 1953. After the cult of personality and the excesses associated with it had been condemned, an attempt was made to consolidate the leader's authority, which was really a new name for the same thing. Certain leaders, such as Ulbricht, Hoxha, Gheorghiu Dej, and Novotny up to 1968, were successful; others were not. However, after Stalin's death, and particularly after the Twentieth Congress, dogmatic Stalinists, Khrushchevite reformists and more radical progressives were

to be found up to the highest levels in each Communist party, and their differences were frequently aired in public.

The economic and intellectual élite became increasingly articulate, and found expression through the Communist cells in their professional organizations. Orthodox officials in charge of cultural activities, such as Adam Schaff in Poland or Hendrych and Koucky in Czechoslovakia, succumbed to the ideas they were supposed to be combating. It became obvious that men and beliefs were not as unchangeable as had been supposed. After Djilas and Imre Nagy, there were Czech and Slovak officials making the leap from Stalinism to humanistic and democratic socialism. After Novotny's departure, *Rude Pravo*, the organ of the Czechoslovak Communist Party, published with the approval of the new leadership a letter from seventy-five veteran militants calling for the restoration 'of an atmosphere of trust' in the party, 'which would enable each Communist to express his opinion freely'.[10]

The disintegration of personal power and the collapse of the belief in the infallibility of the supreme rulers (including the Kremlin) are reflected in the Central Committees, which tend to become, if not the centre of power, at least the arena in which internal power struggles are fought out and resolved. Thus, in 1956 the Polish Central Committee arbitrated in the dispute between Natolinians and liberals. In Czechoslovakia, it was the Central Committee, composed mainly of Novotny's nominees, that in January 1968 rebelled against the chief and gradually brought him down. It was fascinating to see an organization that was supposed to be no more than a rubber stamp suddenly fill out and become alive. 'The final session of the Central Committee', wrote Smrkovsky, one of the people behind this change, 'was entirely unlike any of the previous ones. The Committee members became fully and spontaneously conscious of their responsibilities.'[11]

This renewal, this rediscovery of identity, spread from the top down through the lower ranks. Even in Kadar's pacified Hungary, a party theorist admitted that the Stalinist model of party unity, prohibiting all discussion and requiring absolute obedience, had become an anachronism. Without accepting the 'revisionist model', which turns the party into a 'debating society', this writer hoped that the party would become both a forum for the free exchange of opinion and an instrument for the disciplined execution of decisions.[12] The director of the Institute of Sociology attached to the Hungarian Central Committee took this a stage further. He declared that there was no harm in the coexistence of different concepts in the party, provided the latter retained its guiding role. Party members should have the opportunity of discussing 'various alternatives', which implies that 'some opposition' might exist.[13]

The Yugoslavs and Czechoslovaks went furthest in transforming the Communist party into an internally democratic organization. The draft for new party rules published in Czechoslovakia on 10 August 1968 heralded a break with 'bureaucratic centrism'. (Strangely enough this draft was presented to the Central Committeee by Indra, who a few days later showed his willingness to form a collaborationist government under Soviet protection.) The new rules gave the minority the right to state its point of view, to have it included in the minutes of meetings, and, furthermore, to go on upholding its opinions. While preserving Lenin's 1921 prohibition of organized factions, the new party rules allowed the minority to express its point of view in the party press. They introduced a secret ballot at all levels, and made positions of responsibility subject to a limited tenure.[14]

Democratization entered the fabric of the Czechoslovak party before it was given force of law by a new Congress. The elections in June 1968 of delegates to the Fourteenth Congress amounted to a real party plebiscite in favour of the most progressive propositions and a total rejection of the anti-democratic officials. An opinion poll among the 40,000 Czech and Slovak Communist militants taken in August showed that nearly half were in favour of granting non-Communist parties a role in government, and that 53 per cent wanted the State to abandon direct management of the economy.[15] Finally, when the Soviet intervention came, the regional and municipal committees of the Czechoslovak party displayed a great deal of initiative in organizing passive resistance, and a more radical temper than the centre, which was inhibited by the Moscow protocols. Numerous local committees protested against the Soviet-enforced dismissal of Ota Sik, Pavel, Cisar and other leaders.

The democratic and nationalistic fervour of the party was a strong card in Dubcek's hands. It was no longer simply a matter of replacing a few leaders or subduing the top echelons; the entire party, from top to bottom, would have had to be remodelled.

3. *A workers' party or a party of managers?* Even in countries whose leaders had rejected democracy, the social composition of the parties had been substantially altered by the influx of new generations of officials and graduates, whose motivation was pragmatic (not to say opportunistic) rather than ideological. At the upper levels, the party was becoming more technocratic and the technological intelligentsia was bringing its rationalism, scepticism, its criteria of efficiency and its 'consumerism' to bear on the problems of administration.

The Communist parties of the Stalin era were staffed by men of the 'new class', composed mainly of workers' cadres and veterans of the pre-war party (see Chapter 18 below). Now they were giving way to the 'new new class' of specialists, managers and scientists.[16] The revisionist idea, that 'modern socialism can be established only by the intellectuals, as it is a scientific matter', penetrated to the topmost party levels.[17]

The technological intelligentsia's capture of the parties is one of the main features of the politico-social development of the People's Democracies, despite the survival of proletarianism. The Hungarian party organ has published some statistics showing that 46 per cent of the members of district party committees in the city of Budapest have diplomas.[18] In 1965, 39·2 per cent of the members of the Yugoslav League of Communists were officials, managers and office workers, as against 14.9 per cent in 1947. The proportion of workers had risen from 30·3 per cent in 1947 to 35 per cent in 1965, and that of farmers had declined from 46·9 per cent to 7·4 per cent. 'The social groups that hold and exercise revolutionary power, that fulfil administrative functions, that organize and control labour, are far more highly represented in the League than the others.'[19]

These social changes go hand in hand with ideological ones. 'Economism', the tendency to subordinate politics to economic considerations of efficiency and prosperity, is propagated in all the parties, including the Soviet. And whether one likes it or not, it implies the transference of some decision-making power to the experts, managers and technocrats, who are not necessarily Marxists.

4. *The nationalization of the parties.* Another aspect of this disguised ideological revisionism is the penetration of Marxism by nationalism. The Communist parties, dominated by Moscow, had for a long time resisted this trend as a bourgeois phenomenon. It was condemned as a dangerous heresy in 1948, 1956, 1957 and 1960 in connection with Tito's Yugoslavia, Mao's China and Hoxha's Albania. Nevertheless, under cover of 'internationalist patriotism', all the parties tried to root themselves in national traditions. We have already seen how vigorously the Rumanians applied the concept of Communism's national mission. The appeal to pride and to the spirit of national resistance enabled the Rumanian leaders in the early sixties and the Czechoslovaks in 1968 to rearm the party morally and put it in touch with the people.

We have described the rage provoked in Moscow by the conversion of Dubcek and the entire Czechoslovak party to patriotism, and the summons to resume the 'class positions' that they had deserted. The Soviet leaders seemed to have forgotten the similar accusations of national egotism levelled at them by the Chinese a few years earlier, in connection with the programme adopted on Khrushchev's initiative in October 1961. This was still in force, and was a declaration of intent to transform the Soviet party from a working-class faction to include the whole people. One of the 'crimes' of the Czechoslovak leaders was to put the same programme into practice.

The Revitalization of Citizen Participation

Another Czech 'crime' lay in the measures taken to make 'the state a truly constitutional one',[20] to unshackle the government,

National Front, legislative assembly, judiciary, trade unions and press, and – while preserving the party's leading role and prohibiting any organized opposition – to transform them into representative institutions, through which the citizens might express themselves, exercise control and participate in government.

There are two points to be noted here. First, everything the Czechoslovaks proposed in their plan for socialist democracy adopted in January and set forth in detail in April and May 1968 already existed theoretically, in broad outline, in the other Communist countries. The Czechoslovaks, especially the very moderate Mlynar, who had played a dominant part in elaborating the Czechoslovak path to socialism,[21] simply systematized and put into practice in a direct and effective manner what the leaders of the other Communist countries (with the exception of the Yugoslavs) only spoke about.

Secondly, the Czechoslovak experiment was a clear demonstration of the fact that under favourable circumstances renewal and change can spread through the entire State organism, as well as through social organizations such as Parliament, the trade unions and youth organizations, where the prohibition of pluralism is clearly anomalous. Even after they have been reduced to the status of satellite bodies, these organizations, and individuals in them, remain capable of asserting their independence and putting up an effective opposition – a potential which may be reactivated under certain conditions, when there is a crisis in authority. Thus in Czechoslovakia Lenart, who was regarded as Novotny's lackey, turned on his superior, bitterly accusing him of having prevented him from exercising his functions as head of the government.

An even more striking example is provided by the Czechoslovak National Assembly after January 1968. It had been elected in June 1967 on the basis of the electoral law of 3 November 1966, which was generally recognized as defective.[22] The election was a mere formality, yet it produced the deputies who, in late March 1968, forced Novotny to resign the presidency and elected in his place one who had suffered under him, a man who aimed to follow in the footsteps of T. G. Masaryk. A few days after this, these deputies by a vote of 188 to 65 elected Smrkovsky, one of the promoters of the new model, as President of the National Assembly.

In June they voted for the abolition of censorship, and passed the law on rehabilitation. They laboured honestly in the various parliamentary committees on the draft of a new electoral law which would allow greater freedom of choice, considerably increase the role of the non-Communist parties and introduce a secret ballot. When the invasion came, the great majority of them behaved as though they were indeed the real representatives of the people.[23]

Finally, this inherent capacity of purely formal, ornamental social and governmental institutions to revive applies to the state itself as such. Raymond Aron, in his masterly work *Paix et Guerre entre les Nations*,[24] was right in stressing that Stalin, by formally investing the satellite states with sovereignty, had left the door open for their de-satellization. Hence the transformation, over a period of twenty years, of so many internationalist party leaders loyal to Moscow (Tito, Hoxha, Imre Nagy, Gheorghiu Dej, Dubcek) into statesmen, each one embodying in his own fashion the will to independence of his particular country. As long as there is a framework, it can be reanimated. One should not, therefore, be entirely contemptuous of the formal concessions of autocrats to the spirit of democracy.

The Single-Party or the Multi-Party System?

Every Communist régime has been forced to make concessions, since the Stalinist system leads to apathy and the veiled hostility of the people. East Europeans generally refer to the members of the ruling circle as 'they'. 'We' are the others, the common run of men. The division between subject and ruler is no less clear-cut in the 'Eastern People's Monocracies' (Burdeau) than it was under the old absolutist monarchic régimes. The former, however, lack historical legitimacy. The aim of the reformers has been, and still is, to re-establish contact and strengthen revolutionary legitimacy by means of greater representation and increased participation of the people in government. Dubcek was trying to give expression to this aim when, a few weeks before his election as party leader, and before events had radicalized him, he wrote, 'The party must exist neither outside nor above society, but must be an integral part of it.'[25]

But how could the party be integrated into society if its monopolistic position (at least at the upper levels) were to be preserved? According to many Eastern and Western political theorists, it is like trying to square the circle; there is no middle course between dictatorship and representative democracy. If the Communist party wants democracy, it has to surrender its privileges and submit to the people's decision. This was the conclusion certain Hungarian political thinkers of 1956 drew from their experience during the period of the cult of personality. According to the most representative of them, Istvan Bibo, a plurality of parties was the only effective guarantee of democracy.[26] The Hungarian and Polish revisionists were aiming to extend political democracy through the creation of workers' councils. This development would have enabled them to go beyond 'pure parliamentarianism'.

Their model of socialist democracy was rejected by all the ruling Communist parties, including the Yugoslavs. But after 1965 it again took possession of people's imaginations. A Yugoslav theorist, Vracar, considered the possibility of a two-party or multi-party system within the context of a strong, consolidated socialism. 'If the two- or multi-party system has not endangered the existence of capitalism, but, on the contrary, has strengthened it', he asked, 'why should the same not hold good for socialism?'[27] A year later, Vracar took this idea further, proposing that the one-party dictatorships change over to a two-party system. The aim of both parties would be to build socialism, but they would differ in their structure and their views on particular matters. 'The majority party, the governmental party, would, therefore, have to face an organized opposition. And the two rival parties would accept the fact that they could not perpetuate themselves in power.'[28] Nevertheless, the majority of Yugoslav Communist officials, headed by Tito, like the most liberal of the Czechoslovak Communists, such as Spacek, Smrkovsky or Cisar, turned down the idea of a multi-party system,[29] contrary to the views of some parties in Western Europe.

It should be remembered that non-Communist parties with skeleton staffs have survived formally in several countries. Four non-Communist parties in Czechoslovakia together with the Communists made up the National Front: the People's Party (Catholic) of the former Father Plojhar; the Socialist Party of Benes; the Party of National Revival (a former Democratic party); and the Party of Liberation – the last two in Slovakia only. In Poland there were two other parties, the Peasant Party and the Democratic Party, as well as a small group of Catholic deputies (the Znak) who displayed an extraordinary independence of mind, frequently engaging in astonishingly frank criticism in the Diet after 1956. In Bulgaria there is the Agrarian Union, whose chairman Traïkov was elected head of state in 1964. In East Germany there are four non-Communist parties : Liberal-Democratic, National-Democratic, Christian-Democrat and Peasant.

None of these parties enjoys any real independence. The Czechoslovak reformers, however, had the idea – and immediately put it into practice – of allowing the non-Communist parties to come to life again within the framework of the National Front, to resume their separate identities, to canvass for members, and to 'fulfil democratic functions'. Those of Bohemia, the People's Party and the Czech Socialist Party, turned this new freedom to account. They rid themselves of their collaborationist leaders, and of Alois Neumann; the circulation of their newspapers increased, and they played a very active role after April 1968. They soon were almost playing the part of 'Her Majesty's Opposition', becoming the vehicle for certain independent lines of thought, being particularly concerned with the interests of the technological intelligentsia and 'the little people' before the authorities. This was a very promising development, in spite of the limits placed upon it. The Czech Socialist Party in particular was responsible for reviving the cult of Masaryk, and this was strongly condemned in *Pravda* on 22 August.

The Czechoslovak leaders took an even greater risk in authorizing, or rather in not proscribing, the activities of several new organizations, such as the Club of Committed Non-Party People, of which the philosopher Svitak was the moving spirit, and Club 231, an organization of former prisoners, which occasionally subjected the Soviet system and Soviet interference to very harsh criticism. *Pravda* regarded the existence of these organizations, the quickly stifled attempt of the former Social Democrats to reconstruct their party, and of the Sokols to reactivate their movement, as scandalous and intolerable. But in fact they constituted no threat to public order and party authority in Czechoslovakia.

Elections and Parliaments

Elsewhere the leaders were much more cautious about giving people a feeling of real responsibility again. Nevertheless, they did try to 'reactivate' the parliaments a little, and to raise their prestige – no easy task, as long as elections continued to be conducted, as in Novotny's Czechoslovakia, with a single National Front list (in Hungary, Popular front; in Yugoslavia, Socialist Alliance) prescribed by the Communist party.[30] The governments, however, introduced a few changes into the electoral system intended to make the parliaments more representative. Thus in Yugoslavia, at the elections of April 1967 the electorate was given a choice between two candidates in nearly all districts, and in some places the seats were sharply contested. In Lazarevac (Serbia), for instance, General Jovanovic, who was a friend of Rankovic, appealed to Serbian national feelings, and gained a huge majority despite opposition and pressure from the party authorities.[31]

Under the new Yugoslav system, the candidates are no longer simply nominated by the Socialist Alliance. They are selected beforehand at 'nomination meetings', thus giving the public a voice in the proceedings. In Hungary, the March 1967 elections were organized, on the basis of the new electoral law, more modestly as an experiment. There was a choice between two candidates in seven electoral districts.

Gomulka's Poland, in 1957, was the first socialist country to give evidence of real parliamentary activity, but his authoritarianism soon stifled the democratic spirit. During the Diet session of 1967, a disillusioned Znak deputy remarked: 'We are only a small group, and have no influence over the government. We know also that important decisions are not made in the Diet, but in another building, a thousand metres away' (i.e., the party Central Committee headquarters). In Yugoslavia, on the other hand, the deputies began taking their job seriously, adopting a critical attitude that often embarrassed the government, especially after 1965. In December 1966, the head of the Slovene government, Janko Smole, felt obliged to resign upon finding himself in a minority in parliament.

In Czechoslovakia, Josef Smrkovsky, when elected President of the Assembly, urged the deputies to act as the real representative body of the nation. 'The government', he explained, 'is responsible to the National Assembly. If it takes exception to governmental and ministerial action, there is no reason why it should not pass a vote of "no confidence". If the Constitution is not clear on this point, it should be amended.'[32] Such an amendment, in fact, had been introduced in the 1960 Czechoslovak Constitution (like all other Communist constitutions) in describing the National Assembly as the supreme organ to state power while at the same time entrusting the 'leading state role' to the Communist party. What had to be done, therefore, was to define the respective rights and powers of the Central Committee and Parliament.[33]

The Rumanian Model

While the Communist leaders in Yugoslavia, Czechoslovakia and, more cautiously, in Hungary began increasingly to differentiate the powers of party, State and social organizations, the Rumanians dealt with the problem in an apparently quite different manner. On Ceausescu's initiative, the Rumanian Central Committee introduced an organizational reform on 6 December 1967 that reaffirmed the orthodox doctrine of party supremacy and merged the functions of party and governmental leaders. The fact that one individual (Ceausescu) combined the functions of head of state and party was nothing new. Plurality of offices had existed in the U.S.S.R. under Stalin and after him under Khrushchev (1958–64). It had existed, too, in Czechoslovakia up to January 1968, and still survives in the G.D.R. under Ulbricht, in Bulgaria, where Zhivkov is head of the party and the government, and in Yugoslavia, where Tito is head of the party and state. But in Poland since 1956, in Hungary since 1958, in the U.S.S.R. since 1964, and in Czechoslovakia since January 1968, the offices of head of the party and head of state have been separated, with the party preserving its superior position.

The peculiarity of the Rumanian system lies in the fact that this plurality of offices is repeated at all levels of the hierarchy. The members of the Central Committee Presidium supervising the work of the most important ministries (Foreign Affairs, Defence, Police, Planning) have been asked to assume direct responsibility for their particular sectors; and the same pattern has been followed at every level. One person fills the roles of head of the local council and chairman and secretary of the local party committee, as well as mayor.

This reorganization, on the one hand, gave the party direct control over the Civil Service, eliminating the conflict resulting from the existence of two separate and parallel organizations. On the other hand, its long-term effect was to admit new, qualified administrative cadres, long subordinated to the party puppets, to positions of authority. The party apparatus preserved its customary control in the fields of communications, culture and cadre training. The party leadership ran the state, but the party, as a mass organization, was the state's auxiliary. The trade unions and youth organizations were similarly integrated with the state.

This strengthening of the nationalizing and authoritarian nature of the régime no doubt reflects the determination of Ceausescu's group to create an absolutely unified and disciplined party and administration in the face of pressure and infiltration from outside. Thus it was hoped to neutralize the political consequences of economic decentralization and increase in contacts with the West, which are likely to arouse an appetite for freedom among the intellectuals and managers.

Erosion of Party Authority and Alternative to Democratization: Social Fascism

The greatest threat to Communist parties that are unable to meet the challenge of democracy and patriotism is the erosion of their prestige and authority. The parties are expended as administrators responsible for all the mistakes of government, all the unkept promises and all the disappointed hopes. This erosion was the main concern of the anti-Novotny Czechoslovak writers like Mnacko and Vaculik. It was also the concern of a Polish writer, W. Machajek, who was an ardent supporter of Moczar's group. The nation, he wrote, is tired and angry at the slow progress, particularly in view of the rapid development in other People's Democracies, not to mention the capitalist countries. 'There is a hunger for a clear definition of aims and straightforward leadership, a need for justice, humanity and inspiring examples that the party does not satisfy.' The source of unrest was, in Machajek's view, 'the feeling that it is impossible to improve living conditions in a state that is building socialism'.[34] He concluded that the party must 'take a deep breath' and place itself in the vanguard of the struggle against corruption, injustices in housing, and the increasingly inegalitarian wage structure.

Machajek's ideas are reminiscent of those on which the organizers of the cultural revolution in China based their attempts to mobilize the mass of young people against both the privileged and the liberals. The whole operation was undertaken in the name of egalitarianism and moral regeneration. In fact the response to Maoism was greater in Poland, where reformism and revisionism made no progress against the party organization, and where economic reform met with general scepticism, than in any other People's Democracy. Before escaping to Albania, where he organized a Communist party in exile, the ex-Stalinist K. Mijal had set up an underground group, who demanded that 'the party be purged of class enemies, revisionists, nationalists, *arrivistes*, dignitaries cut off from the masses, and Jews'.

Developments in Poland and the Soviet Union since 1966 have shown that the significance of this neo-Stalinist current should not be underestimated in those People's Democracies where the Communist old guard, veterans of the Spanish Civil War and of the resistance, the régimes' front line of defence, still hold considerable sway in the police and the army. In Poland General Moczar – the Polish Lin Piao – had been able to create an effective politico-military and police apparatus under cover of the Union of

Fighters for Freedom and Democracy (ZBOWiD). The Partisans, advocates of a 'hard and pure' dictatorship, receive considerable support from technocrats and journalists. They hold themselves in readiness to take over from the present exhausted, disillusioned leadership.

The danger of a relapse existed to the time when the Soviets helped Tito to restore national unity, even in Yugoslavia, in so far as the drawn-out struggle between liberals and conservatives, the disintegration of the police, and Tito's advancing years have created a dangerous political vacuum. Furthermore, the radical economic reforms put into practice in 1965 have been the cause of serious misgivings.

In this atmosphere of uncertainty, with a feverish search for new systems going on, the wartime resistance fighters still form a coherent group, the nucleus of party and state. Their representatives, Generals Ivan Gosnjak, Kosta Nadj and Ivan Rukavina, control the army through its party organizations, with their 75,000 members. Soldiers also participate in the activities of local party organizations in towns where they are stationed. In a Yugoslavia where the federal republics are continually extending their powers at the expense of the centre, the army is the only powerful centralized institution left. It has taken advantage of the alarm caused by the coup in Greece and the Middle East conflict to enhance its position. Its generals, both young and old, often deliver themselves of stern judgements on the chaotic state of the country and the aberrations of politicians.[35] The army provides the basis for an authoritarian type of refurbished puritanical Communism.

Thus, an army seizure of control of the party and country seems a real alternative to democratization, in the event of the latter not being thoroughly effected. This is why the Yugoslav experiment is as absorbing as the great Czechoslovak one. In 1968, Czechoslovakia became the pilot country of modernized Social Democracy, just as China in 1966 had become the pilot country of militarized, fanatical and Utopian socialism. Yugoslavia remains the arena in which the two potential types of European Communism confront each other under civilized conditions, comparatively free from Soviet interference. The U.S.S.R.

still controls the fate of the other People's Democracies, as became clear when she invaded Czechoslovakia on 21 August 1968. But what this fate is to be depends also, to a large extent, on how the leaders of these countries solve the problems of economic development.

17

Reforms in Planning and Economic Management

Initial Improvements

'The rationale of the planned economy can be judged only in terms of the sum of its aims,' according to Peter Kende, to whom we are indebted for the most searching analysis that has yet appeared of the 'logic' behind the centralized economy.[1] The technique of economic planning in the People's Democracies after 1948 was based on the Soviet model, with its centralized decision making; priority of heavy industry; contempt for material incentives, and recourse to ethical and political motives; adherence to the theory of the value of work; a rigid production cost structure; free capital, among other considerations. The basic principle of the system was 'to increase production as much as possible, while guaranteeing an adequate minimum for individual consumption'. The 'law' was enunciated by Stalin: 'harmonious and balanced development' in the productive sector.

Initially, the machinery seemed to function very efficiently. Between 1949 and 1953, the industrial production of the six Comecon countries rose by 114 per cent, and in certain countries, like Hungary, where the ambitions of the planners knew no limits, the results had been even more spectacular. Heavy industrial production increased fivefold; the engineering industry was seven times more productive in 1953 than in 1938. Belief in the value of centralization seemed justified. The original targets of the five-year plans were thus raised substantially in 1951 (though this was also not unrelated to the threat to world peace inherent in the Korean situation).

But after 1952 some disturbing symptoms appeared: shortages of provisions, raw materials, labour and capital. The Kremlin, as well as Prague, Budapest and Berlin, must have realized that the five-year plans had been ill-conceived, 'lacking in any scientific analysis, and failing to take profitability into account', according to Imre Nagy. During this period, in fact, no one, even among the most virulent opponents of the Stalinist economists, questioned the system as such. Criticism was directed only at the methods whereby estimates were arrived at and the errors made. Malenkov and Nagy revived Bukharinist ideas that had gone underground in Stalin's lifetime. They were 'gradualists', opposed to 'consistently great leaps forward', inclined to give common sense, moderation, balance and human needs their due. They were advocates of an industrialization tempered by political and social considerations. Thus, Nagy's doctrine, which with the Kremlin's approval was placed before his party's Central Committee (and which more or less applied to most of the other People's Democracies), criticized the course followed between 1949 and 1953 on two grounds: first the tempo of industrialization was out of all proportion to the country's resources; and, secondly, the rapid expansion that had taken place in 1949–50 had been due to the existence of a labour surplus, an under-utilized production capacity. This surplus, however, had been soon exhausted. In 1953 raw-material and fuel supplies were no longer adequate for the needs of a heavy and engineering industry that had grown disproportionately. The gaps between heavy and light industry, and between industry and stagnating agriculture, were too great. In fact, the country's agricultural production might have paid for the equipment and raw materials essential for industrialization, but the planners underestimated the importance of agriculture, and starved it of investments, demoralizing the peasantry by rapid collectivization and taxation that bankrupted private farmers. Wages and salaries rose far less rapidly than the prices of essential goods. All these factors contributed to a fall in the standard of living, estimated at 20 per cent in Hungary in 1953 as compared with 1948. This decline conflicted with the planners' promises, provoked considerable discontent, and hampered productivity, since the planners had given no thought to raising the level of technology. The plans had been based on the concept of independent development, without considering the question of co-operation on an international level. Parallel industries were developed in the various socialist countries, so that inter-Comecon trade grew increasingly difficult to effect, and the trade balance showed a deficit.

The post-Stalinist 'new course' set itself the task of correcting the most glaring mistakes, eliminating the symptoms rather than the organic faults of extreme centralization. The steps taken during 1953–4 in the G.D.R., Hungary, Czechoslovakia and Poland were designed merely to raise the standard of living and slow the tempo of industrialization. Investment in agriculture and light industry was a little increased, and collectivization stopped; individual peasants were less heavily taxed; and the artisan and small trading classes reappeared to some extent.

After Malenkov's fall – which also brought down Nagy in March 1955, before his reform could take effect – the old practices, with a few minor modifications, were soon revived; and the 1956 rebellions were the price that had to be paid for this. However, before and after the Poznan, Budapest and Warsaw uprisings and in connection with the de-Stalinization movement, the first thoroughgoing appraisal of the system was made, notably in Hungary and Poland.[2] This already called for a fundamental revision of the system of planning and management. It revived the concepts of profit, price based on costs and supply and demand; and it urged, furthermore, that enterprises be sustantially freed from obstructive bureaucratic regulations.

The Hungarian reformist economists were censured as revisionists (sometimes by the very people who were, like István Friss, to adopt their ideas in 1964), and were soon silenced. The reformers were more successful in Poland, where the economic council set up by Gomulka developed a new socialist economic model. Taking its cue from the Yugoslav experiment, it envisaged a considerable measure of financial independence for enterprises, the reconciliation of enterprise autonomy with control exercised by workers' councils, and economic relations between state enterprises and the distribution network.

The main mistake of this bold programme was that its target

was too ambitious, at a time when conditions for changing the system were not ripe in Poland or anywhere else.[3] Some of the measures advocated by Lange and his friends were introduced, and the experiment conducted in some forty-five liberalized pilot enterprises in 1957 was not unsuccessful. However, such was the inertia of the planning machinery and the bureaucracy that at the first sign of relaxation central control was once more imposed. Gomulka, who was profoundly anti-liberal and suspicious of innovators, reappointed the practitioners of orthodox state control, and disbanded the workers' councils. The decentralization reforms in Czechoslovakia in 1957-8 were also short-lived. The logic of the system was part and parcel of the mental equipment of the administration, and made short work of these alien concepts. Greater independence in any particular sphere was invariably cancelled out by some control or other, less direct but none the less real. Moreover, once they had recovered from the scare of 1956 the leaders of all the People's Democracies were affected by the wind of optimism and voluntarism blowing from the East. The counterpart to the Chinese 'great leap' was the new wave of collectivization which, except in Poland and Yugoslavia, virtually eliminated private farming in 1962.[4]

The system, thus rounded out, reinforced and to a certain extent improved, continued to govern the economy of the Eastern countries, despite its increasingly obvious drawbacks – the disregard for primary costs, the fixing of relatively low production targets by enterprise directors (to ensure that they were exceeded and the bonuses drawn), general lack of enthusiasm and initiative, frustration on the part of badly paid technicians and workers, an aversion to developing new products and to changing methods, and stagnant agriculture.

Deceleration of Growth

It needed the 1962 recession for the Soviet leaders and those in the more advanced People's Democracies to lend a more attentive ear to the criticisms and suggestions of the economists, who were determined this time to get to the root of the problem. It was, in fact, the decline in the growth rate of industrial production, contrary to all predictions, that seems to have provided the necessary shock and to have played the decisive part in the development of Eastern economic thought and practice. The average annual growth rate of industrial production of the six Comecon members, including the U.S.S.R., which was 13.3 per cent between 1951-5, fell to 10.4 (1956-60), then to 9 (1961-2). In 1963 the overall production of the six increased by only 7.5 per cent. In the five Eastern countries the fall was even more noticeable. The industrial growth rate dropped from 11 per cent in 1960 to 5 per cent in 1963. In Czechoslovakia, overall production in 1963 fell by 0.6 per cent from the previous year. In 1963 plan forecasts were not fulfilled in East Germany, Czechoslovakia or Hungary; in none of these countries did productivity attain the level set by the plan. Only in Rumania, Bulgaria and Albania – the three least advanced countries – did rapid industrial expansion continue, and it was largely because these countries still possessed a plentiful labour reserve and because investments had been substantially increased in 1960 and 1962 (by as much as 46 per cent in Rumania).

The 1962 report in the U.S.S.R. on the progress of the plan for the first time omitted any estimate of the growth of the national income. This omission is readily linked with the permission granted Professor Liberman to publish his celebrated proposals in the Soviet press. Though these were considerably less radical than the reform plans put forward in Poland and Hungary in 1956-7, they aroused huge interest in all the Eastern countries. The fact that they had been formulated in the Mecca of planning greatly strengthened the position of economists denounced as 'revisionists' in the satellite countries: Liberman supplied them with weapons against the defenders of orthodoxy.

Up to this time, and despite the transitory crises of 1953 and 1956, the leaders of the satellite countries were firmly convinced (this providing in large measure their *raison d'être*) that the planned economy was a guarantee of continual growth, or at any rate of substantially more rapid growth than was possible under capitalism, because of its ability to put aside a considerable part of the national income and to give priority to the development of production resources.[5]

In 1962, however, the Communist leaders, headed by Khrushchev, realized that the progress of capitalist Western Europe was more rapid than theirs. The disparity became even more marked during the following years. Between 1955 and 1964, the gross national income of Eastern Europe increased by 48 per cent, against 57 per cent in Western Europe. Between 1951 and 1964, the percentage annual growth of the gross national income was 4.9 in Eastern Europe and 5.4 in the West (due in particular to the rapid growth in Federal Germany – 6.8 per cent).

The East showed up less unfavourably in the growth of its total industrial production : taking industrial production in 1955 as the point of reference, industrial production in Eastern Europe reached 185 in 1964, as against 170 in Western Europe; but this was due in particular to the spectacular advances made in Rumania (244) and Bulgaria (250), whereas Czechoslovakia, which formerly had been leading, stagnated between 1960 and 1964.

In agricultural production the picture is particularly gloomy: in Western Europe in 1963 it was 50 per cent higher than before the war; in Eastern Europe it barely exceeded the 1934–8 level. Only Bulgaria, Rumania and Poland increased their production, the latter largely because of the contribution of the western territories. As regards consumption per head of population, neither Czechoslovakia, Hungary, East Germany, nor Poland reached the pre-war level in 1964. They were all surpassed by Austria, which lagged behind three of these four countries before the Second World War. Between 1950 and 1964, *per capita* consumption increased by 20 per cent in Czechoslovakia, 47 per cent in Hungary, 39 per cent in Poland, and 34 per cent in East Germany, whereas it increased by 100 per cent in Austria, 88 per cent in Italy, and 110 per cent in West Germany. Of course these figures need some adjustment in so far as they do not take into account the considerable increase in the East of social benefits, educational facilities and the low cost of leisure activities. But notwithstanding all this, the gap between Eastern and Western standards of living seems to have widened.[6]

Of course the task facing the socialist countries is not so mountainous as that facing the underdeveloped countries. Industrialization has made a beginning in every East European socialist state, as can be seen from the appendixes. They have all, even the least advanced, reached a level of development equivalent to that of the moderately industrialized countries. In 1964, average *per capita* output in the six Comecon countries (excluding Albania and Yugoslavia) was 880 dollars per year, as against 1,420 dollars in nine of the countries of Western Europe. However, the Communist leaders had aspired to catch up with and overtake the capitalist countries in a short time; but the gap between them seemed to be increasing rather than diminishing.

The economists were not the only ones to notice this. As has been pointed out above, the increase in commercial and tourist communication with the West has led to a feeling of backwardness and inferiority among large sections of the population, and has sharpened appetites, the desire for modernization and the spirit of criticism. Half-measures have been shown to be inadequate, particularly as it is no longer simply a question of raising industrial production at all costs, but also of making investments less costly, and industries more competitive.

Population Growth and the Problems of Labour

In several of the Eastern countries the planners' task is complicated by the existence of a superabundant or badly utilized labour force.

As a whole, the European People's Democracies do not have to face the critical and perhaps insoluble problem that confronts the underdeveloped countries of Asia, Africa and Latin America, in the increasing imbalance between a population explosion and a desperately slow rate of development. The approximate annual population growth in post-war Eastern Europe was similar to that in Western Europe. However, the employment situation varied greatly from country to country. Czechoslovakia and the G.D.R. (the latter because of massive emigration before 1961) were confronted with a shortage of skilled manpower, like the advanced Western countries. Bulgaria and Rumania were in the early stages, when rapidly expanding industry, not yet concerned with profitability, can easily absorb the thousands of peasants seeking employment, although in 1963 unemployment was becoming apparent in Bulgaria.

The same situation had prevailed in Yugoslavia: between 1953 and 1965, annual growth in employment was 19 per cent. There too, the numbers of industrial workers were swollen by hundreds of thousands of peasants leaving the countryside. But the transition in 1962 from 'quantitative productivism' to rationalization exposed the illusory nature of this full employment. Since then Yugoslavia has suffered from growing unemployment, due to the continuing exodus from the fields: between 1962 and 1964, the natural annual population growth was 60,000, against an increase in labour resources of 156,000. The government has tried to overcome this problem by authorizing, and even organizing, emigration, and by directing surplus labour into the unexploited subsidiary sectors: tourism, community services, and crafts and private commerce. However, the halt in emigration, due to symptoms of recession in Western Europe, and the slackening in economic expansion in 1967, have demonstrated the inadequacy of these remedies, and have given rise to serious disaffection.

Poland's position is apparently less, but in fact more, difficult. It has shown the greatest annual growth rate of population (16.8 per cent) after Albania (28.9 per cent). The Polish population explosion was delayed until the 1950s, when there were 750,000 births per year and 250,000 deaths. In 1955, 794,000 babies were born in Poland; these will be aged eighteeen in 1973. During the period of the 1966–70 five-year plan, 3,300,000 Poles reached the age of eighteen and 1,500,000 retirement age. The absorption of some half-million young people per year into economic life is a serious problem, aggravated by the continuing exodus to the towns (549,000 in 1959–60), and the fact that since November 1963 the government has been urging enterprises to reorganize themselves by shedding their surplus manpower. Measures aimed at reducing the birth rate, such as abortion (legalized in 1956, and further facilitated in 1960) and contraception publicity, meet with fierce opposition from the ecclesiastical authorities. 'This land can feed not 30, but 50, 60 and even 80 million Poles', declared Cardinal Wyszynski. Catholic doctrine, under the circumstances, has shown itself more uncompromising than Marxist orthodoxy. Besides, as the Polish writer A. Jozefowicz has perhaps correctly pointed out, 'There is no socialist law of population. It is simply a fabrication of Karl Marx's commentators.'[7]

The Warsaw government is doing its utmost to minimize the problem. Thus in 1966 the official number of unemployed was only 58,422, but a more realistic estimate would be five times this figure, and it might rise considerably (perhaps 600,000 to 750,000 in 1970) unless the authorities abandon the rationalization plans and consequently the projected increase in the average real wage. In any case, it is the threat of unemployment that largely explains the leaders' reluctance to carry out a programme of consistent reform. Logically this should be extended to agriculture, where the present working population of 7,200,000 should be reduced to 4,500,000.

Hungary is faced with the opposite problem. The decline in the birth rate after abortion had been legalized in 1955 was so marked that the public, for patriotic reasons, reacted strongly.[8] Surveys revealed that, apart from the widespread use of contraceptive methods, the ease of divorce, the decline in the standard of living, housing difficulties, female employment and some pessimism regarding the nation's future have all contributed to this decline. In late 1966 the Budapest government introduced a series of measures (increase in family allowances and tax exemptions) aimed at arresting the fall in population, and similar steps were taken in Rumania and Czechoslovakia for the same reasons. At the same time these governments did their utmost to stop the exodus depriving agriculture of a large part of its young workers.[9]

An Agonizing Reappraisal

For the reasons we have noticed, the problem of economic growth was different in Rumania, Poland and Czechoslovakia. In a way, the difficulties Czechoslovakia had to resolve in order to continue expanding were not unlike those of England in 1965–7. Throughout the period that had just ended, Czechoslovak industry readily disposed of its products in the markets of the socialist countries (as England did in those of the Commonwealth). Its partners supplied it with practically all the raw material and foodstuffs it needed, and the quality and technical level of Czechoslovak products were adequate.

But the Czechoslovaks had to pay a high price for the advantages they enjoyed between 1945 and 1962. The system guaranteed them as many outlets as they wanted, but put them under no pressure either to modernize agriculture, or even to improve their industrial equipment. Now the situation has changed fundamentally. On the one hand, the development of certain industries in the U.S.S.R., Rumania and Bulgaria has reduced their demand for the products of the Czechoslovak machine industry. Czechoslovakia's partners are now in a position to purchase the same products, often of a better quality and at lower prices, in the West, and now are able to provide less and less of the raw material and agricultural produce needed by Czechoslovakia. Finally, a partial trade shift to the West has been hampered by the technological backwardness and excessive manufacturing costs of Czechoslovak industry.

At the Twelfth Party Congress in December 1962, Novotny had to admit that the current plan was incapable of dealing with the multitude of complex problems that had to be solved. Once again, the planners had produced a programme that the lack of the necessary equipment and means of construction rendered impossible. 'Thousands of millions of crowns that we were depending on to raise our production growth rate are tied up.'[10] Thus Novotny in 1962 echoed Rakosi's criticism of himself in 1953. After a great deal of discussion, much critical examination, and many tribulations, the Czechoslovak, Hungarian and other leaders had to bow to the facts: the recurrent defects were not the fault of the planners. 'It is the existing planning and control system – the machinery itself – that is reducing the economy's efficiency and holding up progress.'[11] The realization was growing that the Stalinist planning system, designed for a country that was backward but extremely rich in natural resources, worked only under given conditions. Positive results were obtained as long as quantitative factors alone operated (though industrialization created imbalance hard to correct later on), but the system became an obstacle at the next stage: 'qualitative growth', technological improvement, and participation on an international scale.

Few economists made this 'agonizing reappraisal' as courageously and lucidly as the former Rakosist, the Hungarian Istvan Friss. 'The activities of all the economic bodies in a country cannot be controlled by a single central agency', he admitted in the article quoted above. 'Economic decisions can be taken only on the basis of detailed local and professional knowledge.' This amounted to a categorical condemnation of economic totalitarianism. According to Friss, the mistake of the 'centralizers' consisted in wanting to apply Marxist principles of social control to insufficiently advanced economies. Extreme centralization, devoid of the essential statistical and financial control, led inevitably, despite the best efforts of the planners, to an irrational economy, characterized by lack of foresight, wastage, shortage of goods readily made, an abundance of unnecessary products, and high investment costs. The result of this was that 'a comparison between the economic and technical development of our country and that of the highly advanced capitalist countries is extremely unfavourable to us'. 'And this conclusion', adds Friss, 'is not only of theoretical interest, but has great political significance, in view of the competition between the two systems.'

The principal Polish, Czechoslovak and East German economists, and a little later the Bulgarians and Rumanians, came to similar conclusions. The need for decentralization, for a return to a more 'economical economy'–a market economy, in short–impressed itself on everyone; and this lay behind the reforms introduced by one Eastern government after another after 1963, some of them rapidly and boldly, others hesitantly and cautiously. Ulbricht started the campaign with his 'instructions regarding the new system of economic planning and the control of the national economy'.[12] He was followed by the Poles,[13] Czechs,[14] Bulgarians,[15] Hungarians,[16] and finally the Rumanians.[17]

The Main Lines of Reform

The overriding idea behind all the reforms is to liberate the national enterprises from the old type of centralized administrative control, and to give them greater freedom and responsibility. The aim is to expose these new economic units to the more exacting conditions of competition on a national (and increasingly international) scale, to influence in this way the relation between supply and demand, and to eradicate inflationary tendencies. Planning should concern itself with major decisions and the main areas of investment.[18]

The systematic replacement of administrative control by economic influences assumes various forms, depending on the particular character of the national economy, the radicalism of the leaders' economic thinking and the conditions under which the reforms are implemented. Between 1965 and 1967 the Yugoslavs, with their twelve years' start, introduced the most far-reaching measures. Next were the Hungarians and then, some way behind, the Czechoslovaks and Bulgarians. The East Germans, Poles and Rumanians have been more cautious.

Certain common tendencies stand out:

1. The number of compulsory planning index figures, intended to regulate economic activity closely, is being reduced, and replaced by a smaller number of index figures which no longer judge production in terms of quantity, but of quality. Profit is becoming the main criterion of management.

2. Enterprises, singly and in groups, are granted a larger share of the net profit (71 per cent in Yugoslavia and 40 per cent in Hungary, as against 6–8 per cent previously). This sum can be ploughed back, used to finance new techniques, and to create a bonus fund for staff.

3. Control over investments belongs, in varying degrees, to the concerns themselves. They can obtain supplementary credit from the banks to make up for the abolition of subsidies (this implying a reorganization of the banking system). Thus, in Hungary, self-financing has to cover 40 per cent of investments; and in Czechoslovakia, 24 per cent, 60 per cent being guaranteed by bank loan and the remainder being provided by the state.

4. The wages policy has been revised. The reformers are determined to combat the long-established tradition of levelling which (especially in Czechoslovakia, the most egalitarian of all) favours skilled and non-skilled manual workers at the expense of managers, technicians and research workers. Differentiation is to take place within the companies, the state simply fixing a mini-

mum wage (which is 80 per cent of the 1966 wage in Czechoslovakia). Participation in bonuses, distributed in relation to profits, is to be to the advantage of managerial staffs; in Hungary, bonuses can account for up to 80 per cent of a manager's salary, 50 per cent of that of the intermediate technical staff and 15 per cent of that of the workers. Where management is inefficient, executives face a reduction in their salary of 25 per cent, and intermediate staff one of 15 per cent.

5. Mobility of labour has increased; and unnecessary work, even non-profitable enterprises, will be eliminated.

6. Prices have been revised. It has been recognized that the maximization of profit cannot lead to a rational use of resources unless profit is calculated on the basis of real prices, that is prices determined by a free and competitive market. But no Communist country could survive if prices were introduced wholesale, adjusted to the world market. Three price categories have been established in Czechoslovakia and Hungary. Prices of raw materials and of approximately half the consumer goods are still fixed by the state; other consumer goods are allowed fluid prices within prescribed limits; and the prices of luxury goods and of new machines are to be uncontrolled.

7. State enterprises manufacturing the same articles are being urged to engage in competition, to encourage them to try to improve the quality of their products and to reduce their prices. Sale of imported goods should have the same effect. This scheme is meeting with particularly serious obstacles from the measures of concentration taken over recent years to promote mass production. In the G.D.R., 1,500 firms were grouped into 85 vertical and horizontal trusts before the horizontal enterprises were placed under the control of the ministries. In Bulgaria 40 economic associations, employing 650,000 workers, accounted for 35 per cent of industrial production in 1965. In Rumania reorganization into industrial consortia was agreed upon in December 1967. Trusts clearly tend to monopolize production and to restrict the autonomy of enterprises, and their freedom to operate as sellers and buyers on the market.

8. On the whole, the reformers tend to preserve the state's (or party's) prerogatives to represent 'the universal interests of

society', to fix the tempo, to decide on the main lines of national and regional development, to determine the differentiation between individual salaries, the rate of price increases, and so on. The state can intervene at any moment to influence the working of the reforms. The economy is, as it were, in a state of supervised freedom. The problem is how to define the limits of effective intervention and supervision to avoid paralysing initiative when it needs to be stimulated.

First in Yugoslavia, then in Czechoslovakia, the reforms led inevitably to serious disturbances, if only because of the initial distortion of the economic structures. Before it can enjoy the advantages of the new system, the public will have to show restraint and make sacrifices, forget about any immediate rise in the standard of living, and accept price increases necessitated by the removal of subsidies. In Hungary during 1967, the price of dairy products rose by 13 to 19 per cent, meat by 30 to 50 per cent, and the cost of transport by 100 per cent. In Czechoslovakia, manufacturers have taken advantage of the greater freedom to raise their prices sharply, in order to increase their financial resources. Thus, instead of the 19-per-cent rise forecast, wholesale prices of industrial products rose by 29 per cent in 1967. To prevent these rises from affecting retail prices, the government has been forced to increase subsidies from 6,000 to about 12,000 million crowns, thereby raising the inflationary pressure.

There are very few business executives with the necessary business experience and knowledge to make use of the new facilities granted them; Loebl has calculated that in Czechoslovakia such people represent 20 per cent of the total. The party committees and trade unions, ill-adjusted to these new tasks, often obstruct progress; each new difficulty encountered is used by the orthodox to show how absurd the innovations are; at each stage the reformers have to overcome at every level opposition challenging the progress already achieved. The political crises that came to a head in Yugoslavia in June 1966 and in Czechoslovakia in December 1967 reflected the deep split the economic reform caused in the leadership of the Communist parties.

The Yugoslav Experiment

It was in the logic of the anti-conservative struggle that the Yugoslav liberals, who had triumphed in the July 1966 trial of strength, should become more radical. For them, it was no longer a question of simply reconciling the market economy with centralized planning, but of determining to what extent a central plan could still be tolerated in an economic system based as far as possible on the free operation of the law of supply and demand. What the Yugoslavs have undertaken is a radical transformation aimed at making the structural adjustments necessary both to the growth of the economy and to its integration into the world market. Their object has been to create 'a modern, highly productive, stable and rational market economy'.[19]

The results of the first two years of reform enable certain conclusions to be drawn regarding the prospects of this experiment. Industrial prices, which rose sharply at first, by 24 per cent in July 1965, then by a further 10 per cent, subsequently settled down. On the other hand, as has already been noted, there were extensive staff dismissals, and numerous factories were closed down. The dynamism of the economy and especially of industrial production has been substantially reduced: the 16-per-cent growth rate in 1964 fell to 4 per cent in 1966 and to under 2 per cent in the first half of 1967. Employment figures have only slightly risen – 1 per cent in 1965, 2.5 per cent in 1966 – while emigration has practically ceased. Exports rose 30 per cent after the 1965 devaluation, but this gain was reduced to 12 per cent in 1966 and 1 per cent in the first half of 1967. The government's tax policy has not been effective in influencing the distribution of income.

It is to the credit of the Yugoslav authorities that they have persevered, and have not retracted when confronted by these inevitable results. What the experiment demonstrated at once, as in the other Communist countries, was the shortage of experienced managers and, in particular, a lack of capital resources. There are very few concerns capable of financing themselves and of bringing themselves up to a competitive technical and organizational level. The success of the economic reform depends, therefore, largely on external aid. This explains Yugoslavia's attempts to establish co-operative relations with the Common Market, Comecon and EFTA. The Yugoslavs are trying hard to interest foreign participation in Yugoslav enterprises. Foreign partners are encouraged to invest capital, to operate under the latest patents, and to dispose of part of their production in the local market.

Yugoslavia, still in the midst of reform, has been convulsed by the changes introduced and is exhibiting all kinds of symptoms of unrest and disturbance. It seems surprising that these economic upheavals should have had so little effect on the political and social order (although they are not unconnected with the large student demonstrations of June 1968); the reason probably lies in the positive effects of decentralization and political liberalization that preceded and accompanied the reforms. At industrial level, the workers and employees are not merely passive subjects in the experiment; through their councils, they share responsibility for the success or failure of the project. Discussion of all aspects of the reform, advantages, disadvantages and prospects, takes place in the elected local, republican and federal assemblies. Considerable satisfaction is drawn from the fact that Yugoslavia once again is leading the way; though there is confusion, disorder and dilettantism, there is also vitality and hope. Nevertheless, it is understandable that the economists of countries with more complex structures, and possessing less hardened populations, should hesitate before deviating so far from the beaten path of state control; the Czech, Hungarian, Polish, East German and Rumanian governments keep a much firmer grip on the economic situation.

The Rehabilitation of Agriculture

In no sector of the economies of the Eastern countries has the failure of centralized planning been more evident than in agriculture; nor have doctrinal and political considerations impeded other reforms more.

From 1953 the Eastern governments were forced to acknowledge their mistake in treating agriculture and the food industry as minor sectors. Headed by Khrushchev and Nagy, they admitted that stagnation of agricultural production impeded general expansion and lessened the chances of improving standards; and finally, they admitted, in Gomulka's words, that 'you cannot build agrarian socialism without and against the peasants'.

However, the solutions adopted up to 1963 to rectify the mistakes of Stalinism and rescue agriculture were only partially successful and uncertain in their effect. The reasons for this were many and complex, and varied from country to country. There is, however, a common denominator: the Communist leaders' fear of a revival of the peasantry as an independent, comparatively prosperous class, capable of challenging the political structures of the régimes.

This is apparent even in Yugoslavia and Poland, which in 1951 and 1956 respectively, for reasons of expediency, chose the path of 'decollectivization' of farming. In the short term, Tito's and Gomulka's pragmatism has turned out to be more effective than the orthodoxy of the Hungarian, Czech, East German, Bulgarian and Rumanian leaders, who have collectivized virtually all the arable land. In Yugoslavia the return to private farming (87 per cent of the arable land) has brought about a rise in production despite the imposition of a maximum holding of ten hectares. Between 1953 and 1960 there was an annual increase of 8 per cent.[20] Nevertheless, the taxation and price policies and the inadequacy of means of modernization and commercialization have inhibited progress. A new start was made in 1966 when the government authorized the private peasants to purchase small tractors and other agricultural machinery, an example followed by the Hungarians. It would be an exaggeration to talk of a 'restoration of capitalism', as the Chinese and Cubans have done; nonetheless, the principle of complete socialization of the means of production has been breached.

Poland has not advanced as far along this path as Yugoslavia. There the only means of production owned by the peasant is the labour of his family, his tools and his horse. But the fact that he has been confirmed in the ownership of his small estate has given him back his taste for work.[21] Agricultural production between 1956 and 1965 rose by about 30 per cent. Between 1961 and 1965 the net income of the peasants rose by 12 per cent, whereas the average income rise was only about 6 per cent. Productivity, however, remains at a very low level, and Poland has had to import about 3 million tons of cereals per year to meet the needs of its export livestock industry.

The Polish leaders have tried to stimulate modernization by encouraging the peasants to engage in more flexible forms of co-operation, the main instruments of which are the 'agricultural circles'. These circles, which in 1965 included 30 per cent of the farms, are able to buy machinery, chemical fertilizers, and other requisites through the Agricultural Development Fund. The farmers are urged to enter into contracts with the changing industries, and this increases their dependence on the national-ized sector, although a part of the harvest can be sold on the free market.

The 1966–70 plan aims at attaining self-sufficiency in fodder. New steps have been taken to stimulate production: better prices, increased supply of fertilizer and machinery, and above all the redistribution of land to consolidate property by terminating excessive parcelling-out. In October 1967 Gomulka reiterated his agricultural policy. Its long-term aim is socialization, but there is no suggestion of accelerating the transfer of peasant lands to the state farms and the co-operatives. 'Very large-scale farming', wrote the doctrinal organ of the party, 'can, of course, reduce production costs and increase productivity. But it does not always ensure the best use of land ... Under Polish conditions, character-ized by a deficiency of means of modernization and difficulties arising from full employment, very large-scale farming is not demonstrably superior to small-scale farming. Hence, private peasant farming ... is today essential to the development of agri-culture in Poland.'[22]

For the 1966–70 five-year plan, 18 per cent of investments are earmarked for agriculture; this figure is increased to 26 per cent if investments going into industries serving agriculture are in-cluded. Barring a succession of bad harvests, cereal production could rise to 17 or 17.5 million tons, which would be enough to make imports unnecessary, and to creat a solid basis for live-stock farming.

In the countries where collectivization had been carried out the governments are doing their utmost to reconcile the peasants to communal labour and to transform collective and state farms into profitable enterprises enjoying a certain degree of autonomy.

An essential condition for the consolidation of collective farms is an increase in peasant income derived from collective work. Peasant earnings, in comparison with workers' wages, are indeed very low: in Hungary in 1964, 29.2 per cent of the collectivized peasants earned less than 5,000 florins per year, whereas the average wage of the industrial worker was about 12,000 florins; and in Czechoslovakia in 1966 the average income of the *kolkhoz* worker was a third lower than that of the industrial worker, resulting in a massive exodus of young peasants into the industrial centres – the average age of the peasantry is now between forty and fifty. Many co-operatives are forced to hire workers: in 1964 Hungarian collective farms had 721,000 members, and employed 121,000 paid seasonal workers.

As in the other collectivized countries, most Hungarian peasants devote their best efforts to the intensive farming of the tiny allotments of land the use of which they possess in their own right. These allotments represent 9.6 per cent of the agricultural land, yet they accommodate 90 per cent of the poultry, 66 per cent of the pigs, half the dairy produce and 30 per cent of the fruit and vegetables. In Bulgaria in 1960 the peasant allotments, representing 8.7 per cent of total arable land, accounted for 20 per cent of agricultural production, 35 per cent of the cattle, 33 per cent of the pigs and 50 per cent of the poultry.

Since 1963 most of the Communist leaders have abandoned their hard line on allotments. Peasants are granted credit facilities to purchase such requisites as livestock and fodder on their own account. In February 1963 the Bulgarian government issued a decree making individual ownership permanent and hereditary. Still, the governments' main efforts are directed at strengthening the collective farms in accordance with the reform of planning and industrial management. In Hungary, Czechoslovakia, Bulgaria and elsewhere there has been a common tendency between 1966 and 1968 to increase the autonomy of the co-operative enterprises, to raise production prices, and to reduce state monopoly.

The Hungarians have gone furthest in changing the internal structure of the co-operatives.[23] The methods employed by the Red Star co-operative at Nadudvar, a large village in the Great Plain (with its 10,000 acres of arable land farmed by 905 families), have produced excellent results and aroused the interest of economists throughout the Communist countries, including the U.S.S.R. The management of this co-operative has guaranteed the peasants a fixed proportion of the harvest (approximately 20 per cent), whether it be good or bad. In addition, it has guaranteed a share in the profit on a *pro rata* basis of days worked. Work is organized on a family basis, each family looking after three to five hectares after the land has been ploughed and sown by the co-operative. Since 1963 half the Hungarian collectives have employed this system. In 1964 it was extended to livestock farming.

The massive exodus of the most able-bodied peasants from the countryside – especially in the most advanced countries of the bloc – is another factor encouraging agricultural modernization and liberalization. In order to retain and attract skilled labour and to stimulate peasant production, material and also moral incentives are needed, a raising of both the peasant's social and economic status.[24] This course is now being pursued, and agriculture has been moved up in the scale of priorities. Artificial fertilizers, irrigation (in Rumania and Bulgaria), and mechanization are on the agenda.[25] Agronomists are familiarizing themselves with Western research, which has been ignored too long. Co-operatives and state farms are now being urged to specialize and to finance themselves. Prices paid for produce are becoming more realistic.

Social privileges, hitherto reserved for the workers, are beginning to be extended to the peasantry (e.g. the new statutes on Rumanian co-operatives brought into force in January 1966, and the resolutions of the Congress of Czechoslovak Co-operative Farmers held in Prague on 1–3 February 1968). The collective farm workers are encouraged to elect their chairmen from among their most able members, frequently former *kulaks*, and there is a distinct tendency to make the co-operative unions more representative and active organizationally. Only time will show whether these methods can restore the confidence of the Eastern peasants in their rulers and in the future of co-operation as such.[26]

Restoration of Private Enterprise

The policy of the Communist governments with regard to the artisan class and private business has changed in the same way as their attitude to peasant allotments. Immediate economic interest and the need to improve the supplies of commodities operates in favour of small-scale business and private enterprise. And, as in agriculture, doctrinal and psychological considerations are impeding this development. Hence the erratic course continues, tending generally to the restoration of a dynamic 'private sector' within limits not yet accurately defined.

It was Imre Nagy who undertook the thankless task of pioneering in this domain, as in private farming. In his speech of 3 July 1953, he was the first publicly to acknowledge the harmful effects of the policy whereby 'the state had extended its economic hold over those sectors where private initiative and private enterprise may still play an important part and contribute to the greater good of the population'. The new course introduced by Nagy, which permitted the re-opening of many workshops and retail businesses, had a considerable effect on Poland, Rumania and Bulgaria.

But this first relaxation was too short-lived to bear fruit. The doctrinal opposition to even the most inoffensive forms of free enterprise gained the upper hand after 1955. A year later, de-Stalinization produced a fresh upsurge in Poland and Hungary that was to be cut off as rapidly and for the same reasons as the first. Under a crushing burden of taxation, unable to procure the necessary raw materials legally, and harassed by the local authorities, a large number of artisans – 11,000 in Poland during 1960 – surrendered their licences. Czechoslovakia proudly announced in 1961 that small tradespeople and artisans had been almost entirely socialized. Of the nearly 380,000 pre-war artisans, only 3,700 survived in 1962.

But a growing number of leaders thereafter came over to the

side of the economists, who, reviving Imre Nagy's theses (without referring directly to them), held that 'large-scale production is no panacea. In many sectors limited production seems more useful to the people it serves.'[27] It was absurd that it should take weeks to repair a household utensil or a pair of shoes in a major producer of machine-tools and ultra-modern precision instruments like Czechoslovakia. The champions of economic reform were especially sensitive to consumer grievances as regards the shortcomings of the service sector and of distribution. The example of the highly advanced capitalist countries shows that industrialization does not inevitably lead to the elimination of small enterprises; they survive, thanks to their ability to adapt more flexibly to the varying requirements of the consumers. In the socialist countries, full-scale authoritarian nationalization created gaps that the black market and the surreptitious and illicit labour of artisans, frequently with stolen materials, have filled only very inadequately, and it seemed better to legalize the essential contribution of the workers' efforts. The need to improve the sector serving the tourist industry by all possible means has reinforced this trend.

In Yugoslavia, where dogma has been subjected to the most far-ranging revision and where the needs of tourism are most pressing, there were over 3,000 private restaurants in 1963, and in 1965 a further thousand. In 1965–6, 10,000 new licences were granted to artisans, and the number of private carriers grew from 9,000 to 17,000. In Slovenia, in 1964 a special enactment authorized the opening of snack-bars, restaurants, boarding houses and small private hotels managed by the members of one family. In 1967 private restaurant keepers throughout Yugoslavia were authorized to employ up to three, and artisan enterprises up to five, workers. In 1968 private artisan councils were set up in the regional, republican, and federal economic chambers.

Most of the other Communist countries followed the same path, if less resolutely. From 1963, the Hungarian government granted new artisan enterprises tax exemptions for a year, and also guaranteed them supplies of raw materials. The artisans were given most encouragement in the rural districts, which had fewer amenities. In 1965 Hungary already had 35,000 village artisans again, almost 4,000 more than 1964. There were 34,000 in the towns, 17,000 of them in Budapest. A decree issued on 10 June 1968 authorized traders and artisans to operate in seventy sectors.

The Polish government also issued decrees in 1964–5 aimed at enlarging and strengthening the artisan class. In 1965 social security benefits were extended to artisans. The numbers of those employed in the private sector increased from 158,000 in 1961 to 188,000 in 1966. Their number should have reached 315,000 by 1970. The private sector includes some thousand restaurants and bars, 5,000 retail shops, a fifth of the petrol stations and 147,000 artisan workshops.

In Bulgaria and Rumania, where there has been full-scale collectivization, the expansion of the tourist industry has made the governments less inflexible. In the former country, 3,600 people applied for licences in 1965, stimulated by the credit facilities offered by the authorities. Between 1965–6 the number of private artisans grew from 10,000 to 26,000. In Rumania the number of artisans increased from 35,000 in 1963 to 41,000 in 1965.

It was in Czechoslovakia that doctrinal opposition to the restoration of the private sector was the most stubborn. Nevertheless, economic realism had its way there too, even in Novotny's time. In a decree published in April 1964, the government authorized the issue of licences for certain secondary services – laundering, boot-polishing, small-scale dressmaking and alterations. In August of the same year the régime took a further step, and authorized carpentry shops, hairdressers, tailors, and decorators in localities where these services were not provided by state or co-operative enterprises. In 1968 the pace quickened. It was estimated that in May of that year 20,000 new licences to engage in private business would be granted.

In spite of their obvious value, these measures, aimed at reviving the private sector, are meeting with a remarkably strong opposition throughout the socialist countries. It seems that no other aspect of the economic reforms provokes such passionate opposition. The opposition comes, in the first instance, from conservative Communist party members and especially from the local authorities, for whom the re-emergence of contractors and private businessmen is an historical anomaly, a return to the past, and a challenge to their privileged social position.

Indeed, within a short time, certain resourceful contractors were able to make occasional very large profits. This enabled them to achieve the same standard of living as the régime's high officials. In this connection, the Hungarian party magazine indignantly cited the not unusual case of an artisan who changed his old Opel for a new one each year.[28] The anti-liberal puppets, jealous of their privileges, are trying to rouse ordinary people against these *nouveaux riches,* who, because of their recent emergence, glaringly epitomize the inequalities socialism had promised to eliminate.[29]

Of course, only a limited number of small artisans and shopkeepers reach a high income level. In Yugoslavia, where the process has gone furthest, the number of workers such as carriers, artisans and boarding-house keepers capable of earning ten or twenty million dinars a year was estimated at 20,000 at the most in 1967. The fact is that, given the huge demand for services, any individual with a modest sum at his disposal and with some business sense can make much more by working for himself than by working as a labourer, employee or engineer in any national enterprise. It is clear, however, that it is only the hope of gain that induces individuals to take the risks and accept the responsibilities of a private business.

It is no accident that Maoist groups, whose existence has been reported in Poland and Yugoslavia – and which are composed not only of former Stalinists won over by the Chinese doctrine, but also attract idealistic students – keep harping on the private sector, accusing the 'revisionist' leaders of undermining the socialist order and encouraging the revival of a new capitalist class. The left-wing opposition's exploitation of 'anti-new-bourgeoisie' grievances constitutes a not inconsiderable potential danger for the Communist leaders engaged in the work of reform. Since 1967 this has been the subject of a lively discussion in Yugoslav party organizations and the press. In reply to the objections raised by the enemies of the private sector, the liberals have appealed to consumer interests. The state lacks the necessary funds, because of the great disparity between administrative costs and the profitability of very small businesses, they declared. It is simply not equipped to conduct these operations. Whether one likes it or not, the only answer is private enterprise. Besides, in the absence of adequate offers of employment from industry, they added, it is preferable for Yugoslavs to work for private individuals in the country than to sign on with foreign capitalists. If there are abuses, the remedy does not lie in a return to a rigid anti-consumer policy, but in the even more rapid development of a private sector. An increase in the number of workshops, services and hotels, will even out supply and demand, and eliminate speculation.[30]

The government – or rather governments – of Yugoslavia seem determined to persevere along a liberal path. Their spokesmen estimate that artisan establishments and private businesses, which in 1967 were employing 117,000 people, could fairly rapidly absorb 200,000 more workers. In this case 'the population would benefit from quicker and cheaper service', without endangering the socialist framework of the economy. This involves a gamble on the future, intimately bound up with the decisions taken by the Yugoslav leadership in respect to the more significant sectors of economic and political life. These seem to envisage an original model compounded of a mixture of socialists, centrist and capitalist elements.[31]

The Soviet Bridle

After Novotny's fall, the new party leaders in Czechoslovakia seemed inclined to embark on the same course, even if with considerable caution. The liberals blamed the former leader for having, among other things, done his utmost to sabotage the economic reform and to stir up the workers against it by depicting it as a bourgeois affair. Ota Sik, the father of the economic reform, was appointed vice-chairman of the Council and the new party programme adopted in April confirmed the leadership's intention to raise the country from the stage of industrialization to that of the 'scientific and technical revolution'. This aim was clearly formulated by the progressive economists R. Selucky and E. Loebl.

With missionary zeal, Sik and his friends toured the industrial centres to convince the workers that they had everything to gain from liberalization of the economy. The influence of the orthodox was in decline. The spirit of innovation that Liberman, Kosygin and other Soviet reformers were trying to infuse into their officials was about to triumph in Czechoslovakia. Then came the occupation.

In their ultimatum of 15 July, the Five denied wanting to prevent the leaders of new Czechoslovakia from 'rectifying the mistakes that had been committed'. Nor, they insisted, did they wish to intervene 'in the planning and management of the Czechoslovak economy, or in the decisions aimed at improving the structure of the economy and promoting socialist democracy'.

Nevertheless, *Pravda*, in its editorial defending the occupation of 22 August, was already adopting a different tone. In curiously 'Chinese' terms it accused the 'revisionist elements' of the Czechoslovak party of exploiting the economic debate, with the clear aim of bringing the country's economy back to the capitalist path, of wanting 'to replace planning principles by spontaneous market relations, giving over a huge sector to private capital'. A savage press campaign was mounted against Ota Sik, whose dismissal was one of the conditions the Kremlin imposed on a captive Dubcek.

On 16 September thirteen of the leading Czechoslovak economists took up Sik's defence in a letter published by the official organ *Rude Pravo*. They stressed, in the first place, that the new economic model was based on socialist principles and had nothing to do with capitalism; secondly that it had been approved by the government, the party and the public; and thirdly that it constituted 'the most effective means for the development of the socialist economy in Czechoslovakia'.

To the Czechs it seemed that the Soviet press's attacks on Sik, a disciple of Liberman, were aimed also (perhaps mainly) at the Soviet reformers. In this respect, the Czechoslovak drama might be regarded as a projection of a confrontation based on the U.S.S.R., Czechoslovakia being the scapegoat of the Soviet opponents of reform.[52] But whatever the reasons for the objections officially raised after August 1968 by the Soviets to the economic reform in Czechoslovakia, the important point is that they have slowed down if not stopped the implementation of the reform. This is as much by virtue of the serious upheaval and considerable economic damage caused by the invasion and occupation, certain dismissals ordered by the invaders, and the obstacles to obtaining Western loans. All this shows to what extent the freedom of action of the leaders of the European Communist countries is limited, even in the strictly economic field, by their political dependence on the Kremlin.

18

The Development of Social Structures

The economic reforms introduced since 1965 have challenged the old Stalinist social structures in more than one respect. These resulted from a revolution from above that convulsed East European society. Supported by a highly mobilized working class (exemplified by the role of the workers' militias, the 'private army' of the Czechoslovak party, in February 1948), as well as by a party-controlled state organization after the Soviet model, the Communist high commands had effected a radical social transformation.

The main aspects were:

1. The nationalization of industrial enterprises and banks (the expropriation of the big landed estates having been completed in the first, relatively mild phase of People's Democracy), and the elimination of the class of high officials and upper administrative and economic personnel belonging to the former ruling classes. The upper layer of the old society was removed, and its supporters arrested, interned or flung to the bottom of the ladder. The battle against private property and for egalitarianism took the form of an almost total proscription of the small tradesman and artisan class. The process was completed in the early sixties (except in Yugoslavia and Poland) by the collectivization of small peasant property.

2. Assumption of leading positions in the civil service, the economy, professional bodies, by party cadres, veteran Communists, mainly with a working-class background but also from the intelligentsia and lesser bourgeoisie.

3. Mobilization of society as a whole, with a view to industrialization based on the priority of heavy industry. The key idea here was to replace material incentives (personal profit) by moral and ideological incentives by such means as propaganda and appeals to revolutionary zeal, discipline and socialist competition, and fear.

4. Social industrialization reflected in a substantial growth of the technical intelligentsia, the bureaucracy and the working class.

When, after Stalin's death, this revolution from above paused for the first time, new social configurations, or rather undefined and curious mixtures of old and new, were revealed. The so-called socialist societies suddenly discovered that they knew nothing about each other, and that they were not fully self-critical.

The Revival of Sociology

At this point sociology rose from its ashes. Stalinist intolerance of sociological research was no accident. According to Stalinist doctrine, the party, as Jan Szczepanski, one of the advocates of Polish sociology, stressed, was the sole motive force of society, and the party leadership alone could initiate change. This leadership, however, 'was not interested in research into the state of society, as everything worthwhile that took place in society was a reflection of its will. All other phenomena and situations not reflecting the leaders' will were undesirable, and should simply be eliminated.'[1]

The modification of totalitarianism and subsequent emergence of a public opinion after 1953 had the effect of reviving interest in the humanities that had flourished in the past, especially in Poland, Rumania and Czechoslovakia. Public interest in censuses ran high. As Szczepanski says, it was a question of satisfying a real hunger for information on the goings-on in society. This was proof, if such was needed, of the significance of the social and political function of sociology as an instrument of education, reflection and self-correction for societies lacking self-knowledge. At the same time, the vanguard of the rising class – the intelligentsia – has criticized the political élite in sociological terms, putting itself forward as a counter-, or replacement, élite. In Poland and Hungary it has done so cautiously, in Yugoslavia and Czechoslovakia more openly.

Initially, social thought took the most brilliant form in Poland. As early as 1955, a few empirical research centres were opened, and Poland was represented by a particularly outstanding delegation at the World Sociological Congress in Amsterdam in 1956, at which several socialist countries, including the U.S.S.R., were represented. One of the most distinguished contributions was made by Stanislas Ossowski, author of a book that was to become a classic.[2] This was the first scientific attempt to apply the Marxist critical method to Marxist societies. After 1960 some forty research institutes were already functioning in Poland, and Szczepanski's appointment in 1966 as chairman of the International Sociological Association was a confirmation of Poland's new status in a field where objective research so often comes up against the distrust and secretiveness of vested interests.[3]

Hungarian sociology could also claim definite progress. The credit for this belonged mainly to Mrs Aladar Mod, who, in 1963, conducted a highly interesting and sophisticated investigation into social differentiation in the new Hungary, and to Andras Hegedues, who since 1963 has directed a research group under the Academy of Sciences.[4] His case is particularly instructive. Formerly Prime Minister under Rakosi, who together with him was responsible for the appeal for Soviet intervention in 1956, he made use of his exile from politics to meditate on the events in which he had played a part. He turned into a scientist fully aware of the realities of contemporary life, and broke completely with his earlier dogmatism.

Among the champions of sociological thought in Yugoslavia, apart from the pioneer Milovan Djilas, was Mita Hadjivassilev, the author of a remarkable study, 'The Contradictions of Socialism',[5] Svetozar Stojanovic[6] and L. Markovic,[7] who brought Burnham's theories of the 'managerial revolution' up to date and sketched a phenomenology of 'state socialism'. After 1963 the revival of sociology reached Czechoslovakia, where a sociology society of excellent repute was re-established in 1964 and an institute of public opinion research was set up in 1966 under the

Academy of Sciences. Rumania, after the Fourth Party Congress in 1965, revived the tradition that had placed Rumanian scholars like Professor Gusti among the most original pre-war sociologists.[8]

A Glance at Socialist Societies

The conclusions to be drawn from the Polish and Hungarian studies seem generally applicable to the whole bloc.

Szczepanski himself had certain reservations about the continued relevance of the traditional division of society into four strata (working class, peasantry, intelligentsia and bourgeoisie); and indeed this division does not take account of the specific criteria of differentiation, particularly for political power, in socialist societies. Moreover, there is considerable disagreement over these criteria. Thus, according to the Polish sociologist Wiatr, the division ought to be based on differences in the development of the division of labour, in qualification, education, and income. For the Czechoslovak Jodl, social differentiation in the socialist countries is based above all on two criteria: participation in power, and material conditions of life.

All the experts are more or less in agreement over the following definitions of classes and strata :

The intelligentsia. In the East European sense of the word, the intelligentsia is far from homogeneous; it is more a collection of professional categories, including machine bureaucrats (about whom there is significantly little information), technocrats, engineers (30 per cent of the total), intellectuals proper (artists, scholars, teachers, journalists, writers), and the huge stratum of petty officials and employees, often of a very low cultural level and with very low incomes. Unlike the statisticians, popular usage continues to apply the term to the class of 'graduates' as distinguished, not from the bureaucracy in general, but from the unqualified petty officials (the 'new class' discussed below).

The petty bourgeoisie, in 1931 numbering 3.5 million and amounting to 11 per cent of the population in Poland. A significant proportion of this class of artisans and small businessmen was Jewish, and disappeared in the Nazi holocaust. After the war there were still 400,000 small businesses; their number fell to

150,000 in 1955, and then rose again to 188,000 in 1961. It is an unstable class which leads a precarious existence, but certain of its members are able to take advantage of the gaps in the planned economy to make large profits. A small shop in Shmielna Street in Warsaw brings in more than a ministerial position, wrote Szczepanski.

The peasantry. The size of this class in Poland fell from 60 per cent of the population in 1931 to 38.2 per cent in 1960. In Poland, the greatest part is of small landowners, the remainder divided between *kolkhozniks* (135,000 in 1961) and peasant-workers (820,000 in 1960), the majority of whom draw most of their income from industrial work. There are, in addition, peasants working in offices (100,000 to 150,000) and also agricultural workers (280,000 on the state farms and 14,000 on private farms). It is significant that Polish sociologists place these before the working class. In this country where small peasant property has been preserved, the peasants on the whole enjoy a higher social status than the proletariat. In those Communist countries where property has been collectivized, the peasants are usually relegated to the bottom of the social scale.

The urban working class. The numbers of this class in Poland also tripled between 1931 (2.8 million, 830,000 employed in heavy industry) and 1964 (7.6 million, 2.6 million being industrial workers). Most of the recruits to the working class have come from the country, but a not inconsiderable proportion comprises women, whose large-scale integration into social and economic life is one of the most striking developments.[9]

This picture of the class structure needs to be expanded and somewhat modified in the light of the Hungarian census of 1965. Between 1949 and 1965, the proportion of manual workers in Hungary grew from 30 per cent to 48 per cent of the working population. Skilled workers represented 17 per cent, specialized workers 17 per cent, labourers 14 per cent. About 55 per cent of the new working class came from the countryside. In 1949 the lesser artisan and business bourgeoisie and the small agricultural landowners represented 55 per cent of the working population; in 1965 this had fallen to no more than 2 per cent (as a result of nationalization and collectivization). In 1949 the 'intellectual workers' (intelligentsia) represented 10 per cent of the working population; in 1965, 18 per cent. There were three types in this category: 'individuals in leading positions' and 'creative intellectuals', constituting 5 per cent of the working population; mid-level experts (engineers, technicians, etc.), 6 per cent; white-collar workers, 17 per cent.

The peasants, now 'agricultural workers' (in *kolkhozes* and *sovkhozes*), represented only 34 per cent of the working population.

The 'New Class' and the Classless Society

The numerical growth of the technological intelligentsia, the bureaucracy and the working class is a characteristic of all industrial societies. All these societies experience the migration of peasants into the towns and the large-scale assimilation of female labour into industry. In the socialist countries, however, the rise of a class of new men to replace the old propertied and ruling classes is a unique and all-important social phenomenon.

It was Milovan Djilas who coined the phrase 'the new class' in his book. He paid dearly for presuming to tackle this problem. The campaign against his ideas has led the theoreticians of all the Communist countries to perform feats of semantic acrobatics. The men who hold the monopoly of power categorically refuse to regard themselves or to be regarded as a class apart from the rest of society. It is as though the new leaders, springing from a party in which conspiracy has been the rule, still wish to preserve a certain element of secrecy. They like to merge either with the working class from which many of them have come, or with the intelligentsia. The most they will tolerate is for sociologists to refer to them as 'leading personnel' or 'persons in leading positions'. Their dislike of any accurate classification extends to less specific terms, such as 'élite' or 'power élite'. The Polish philosopher Adam Schaff was strongly criticized for having admitted the existence, if not of a 'new class', which he considered 'theoretically absurd', at least of a 'ruling élite enjoying a privileged social position'.[10]

According to one of Schaff's critics, the party and state administration could not be regarded as a privileged élite financially, as 'from this point of view, the technocratic élite, journalists, scientists, artists and finally those in the private sector, were much better off'. Furthermore, the political privileges that the apparatus enjoyed under Stalin have been reduced by a very considerable extent since 1953.[11] In Czechoslovakia, F. J. Kolar, the very orthodox editor of *Zivot Strany*, launched a campaign at the end of 1967 against the sociologists who had 'imported the idea of an élite from the West'. In Yugoslavia, Bakaric, head of the Croat party, acknowledged in 1966 that Rankovic and his group had turned themselves into a sort of 'new class' by amassing excessive powers. However, a year later, this same leader condemned the mistake of describing the political bureaucracy after Rankovic's fall as a new class. The bureaucracy, he argued, does not possess the means of production; it is purely functional, and represents the necessary authority of the state. Instead of resisting it, all that is necessary is to place it under the direct control of the producers.

The official ideologists of various shades of opinion are right in claiming that the social category referred to by Djilas (and before him by Burnham)[12] is not a social class in the sense that the former bourgeoisie was. Its members exercise managerial functions, and enjoy financial advantages without being legally property owners; their prerogatives are not hereditary. As Djilas has stressed, 'the new class played no part in economic and social life prior to its rise to power. It is a special type of organization, with its own distinct discipline based on the identical political and philosophical views of its members'. Sociologically speaking, this hierarchical organization – the party, or rather its officials – takes on the appearance of a class that controls without being controlled, after it has insinuated itself into the leading positions in society. It is the political class, the embodiment of government, the dispenser of state patronage. It can be identified only in terms of the dictatorship of the proletariat, as its title to power is based on this concept. The aim of this dictatorship is to establish the new socialist citadel founded, in the words of a Hungarian sociologist, on 'the fundamental equality of men'.[13] However, this would-be egalitarian dictatorship, this creator of a classless society, has given birth to a system where there are still rich and poor, influential and deprived, and where the degree of participation in power is the main criterion of social differentiation.

Here lies the basic contradiction of socialist society. It postulates the leading role of the proletariat, and yet the social condition of the mass of the workers has not substantially altered. The worker is still badly paid (from which it can be deduced that he is exploited); he is still told what to do, and often by elements 'alien to his class'.[14] The Communist leaders are doing their utmost both ideologically and socially to overcome this contradiction, and to demonstrate the egalitarian, proletarian character of their régimes.

Ideologically, Stalinism, with its myths, its cult of the party leader, its voluntarism, its faith in centralized organization, its dogmatism, intolerant of any critical analysis, serves to safeguard and justify the role of the ruling class. Stalin accepted differentiation, the social privilege of a ruling class, but he made the existence of this class very precarious with his purges and demands for absolute loyalty. After him, under Khrushchev and his successors, the new class has tried to normalize its own position by improving his relations with the other social classes and groups and by reducing the powers of the police.

In the field of social action, the ruling class is endeavouring to show the identity of its interests with those of the working class and its adherence to egalitarian principles through the following series of measures that have had a profound effect, both for good and evil, on the social life of the People's Democracies:

The systematic persecution, especially initially, of the remnants of the former ruling classes. The new class (the party) puts itself forward as the providential protector of the workers against the return of the capitalists, landowners and *kulaks*.

The promotion of workers. A considerable proportion of the new class has been recruited from among proletarian party members. An even greater number of workers and peasants – or at least of their children – have been able to penetrate the ranks of the intelligentsia.[15] In Bulgaria more than half the directors of enterprises in 1966 were former workers who had had no secondary education. In Czechoslovakia in 1962, 52.7 per cent of party members are working-class by origin, but only 36 per cent were actual workers. These 'workers' cadres' – high, middle or low in rank – constitute the strongest social basis of the Communist régimes, although a certain number of them still seem to be under the influence of the former intelligentsia and amenable to liberal ideas.

Levelling of incomes. Generally speaking, there is less differentiation of incomes in the People's Democracies than in the Soviet Union. The income level of the technical intelligentsia and middle-level bureaucracy has fallen, while workers' wages have risen.[16] As a general rule, there is greater differentiation within the social categories than between them. Thus, in Hungary, if we take the lowest income level as 100 points, the income of agricultural workers is 106, that of skilled workers 133, office workers and lower officials 145, middle-rank specialists 155, and high officials and intellectuals 187. However, 10 per cent of households have incomes of under 1,000 florins, and 6 per cent over 5,000–6,000 florins, which is equivalent to a bourgeois standard of living. Among those enjoying a high income are 40 per cent of the 'leaders', 15 per cent of skilled workmen and 6 per cent of collective farm workers. These figures show that differentiation does exist, but that it is moderate, and there is almost parity between the majority of manual and non-manual workers.

It is in Czechoslovakia – where the party was most strongly rooted in a working class that was more advanced than in any of the other socialist countries – that the levelling of incomes was taken furthest, at the expense of the intelligentsia. Egalitarianism had a firm hold in Czechoslovakia even before 1948. After that date the tendency to levelling grew stronger. 'There is no other country', wrote the economist R. Selucky,[17] 'where the bus driver and the district judge, the upholsterer and the medical consultant, the turner and the university professor would have the same salary.' Thus, in Czechoslovakia, as opposed to the other Communist countries, the majority of young people were not attracted by university education, and young doctors, engineers and teachers felt belittled and underrated. The word 'intellectual' took on a pejorative meaning, whereas the social status and prestige of the skilled workman had risen remarkably. This largely explains the longevity of Novotny's régime; a large section of the proletariat regarded the party leader as its protector.

Social mobility. In the other socialist countries, where the technological intelligentsia has retained its social status (though less because of its income than because of its inherited prestige), it was the equality of opportunity for promotion and not equality of circumstances that was put forward as the most significant gain of socialism. The new class showed its proletarian character by giving the sons of workers and peasants priority of access to secondary and higher education. In Hungary, up to 1963, children of former bourgeois and even intellectual families were admitted to institutions of higher education only under exceptional circumstances. In Poland, social class is still taken into consideration in the results of university entrance examinations, where the children of workers and peasants receive supplementary marks. In these countries where, according to a Polish newspaper, 'university degrees appear to be replacing the old titles of nobility', the proletariat has been given advantages.[18] However, these privileges, acquired in the period of the 'great leap forward' of industrialization, when the need for qualified staff was acute, are tending to diminish in the period of stabilization. The good positions are occupied, and an increasing number of skilled people are having to accept jobs not commensurate with their qualifications. Intellectuals do their utmost to hand on their own positions to their children, who have the advantage of a superior intellectual environment, and are in addition helped by their parents. In Poland during 1963–4, 45.8 per cent of secondary school pupils came from the intelligentsia; the figures are 47 per cent in 1964–5, and 50 per cent in 1965–6. In Hungary too, 'the children of people with a higher education and higher cultural level have a greater chance of acquiring secondary education than children from the other classes'.[19]

The development of social security and the guaranteed right to work are strong arguments in favour of the socialist régimes, counter-balancing the unfortunate impression created by the privileges of the new class, its *embourgeoisement.* But here again, subsequent developments have raised doubts as to the reality of these gains. After 1965 the Yugoslav economists and sociologists, and then their Hungarian, Czechoslovak and Polish colleagues, began to point out the artificial, illusory and dangerous character of full employment that ignored profitability.[20] Economic interest has demanded a review of current ideas regarding security of employment, which, like wage-levelling, had, in so far as it was achieved, bred a spirit of conservatism, passivity and indifference among workers and executives to technical and organizational improvements, and had encouraged irresponsibility.

The requirements of economic progress have clashed with the production relations established during the great period of bureaucratic socialism. But the class that has taken the lead in the struggle for the development of the productive forces and the establishment of the socio-political reforms necessitated by this development is neither 'the new class' of organizers and political managers nor the resigned and routine-bound working class, but the technological intelligentsia and the scientific and literary élite.

The New Class at Grips with the Technocrats

To paraphrase the celebrated thesis of the Communist Manifesto, socialist society, erected on the ruins of bourgeois society, has not abolished class antagonisms; it has only 'substituted new classes for the old ones, new conditions of oppression, new forms of struggle'. In fact, the history of the People's Democracies after Stalin's death is the history of these new conflicts. The main struggle is between the ruling class and managers, technicians, engineers, scientists, economists and others whom it has tried to use and to dominate at the same time. 'It is impossible to carry out party tasks correctly without the help of scholars. But scholars are dangerous people', exclaimed Kadar in a speech to an assembly of scientific research workers in June 1966. This was the root of the problem.

As soon as the harmful effects of Stalinist state control became obvious, certain progressive spirits among the Communist leaders realized the need to bring about a reconciliation between the party and the intelligentsia. 'When the unwarranted purges were being carried out, honest intellectuals were often treated in a way unworthy of a People's Democracy, and deprived of the opportunity of putting their knowledge at their country's service', declared Imre Nagy upon coming to power in July 1953. 'The government', he added, 'will take vigorous steps to put an end to these unacceptable practices, and to remedy the injustices. The intellectuals have a right to the respect of the whole of society ... and they must occupy positions worthy of them and commensurate with their ability, whether they be teachers or engineers, doctors, jurists or agronomists ... Respect for education and learning should be reflected in a vast range of opportunities for the work and in material advantages.' Here is a clear exposition of the programme of the reformist Communists, who over the coming years were to militate in favour of an alliance, a sharing of responsibilities, between the 'new class' and the intelligentsia. Nagy's tragic fate showed the difficulty of carrying out this programme. The greater part of the new class retained its distrust of intellectuals. And this distrust was not altogether unjustified. The 1955–6 crises in Poland and Hungary, and those in Yugoslavia and Czechoslovakia betweeen 1965 and 1968 showed that a large section of the intellectuals, especially the young, could not be fobbed off with a few promotions. Their real aim was to replace the politico-ideological bureaucracy by a technocracy or meritocracy.

If Stalinism is the expression in Marxist terms of the authoritarian paternalism of the nascent 'new class', then revisionism, which was particularly active in 1955–7 and 1963–8, primarily reflects the desire of the new generation of the creative intelligentsia to shake off the tyrannical tutelage of the new class, to take over the leadership of party and state, and to remould the socialist system in accordance with its own interests and ideas.

The main argument of all the revisionists, from the Petöfi Circle in Hungary to the Praxis group in Yugoslavia, and the Polish periodical Po Prostu to the Czechoslovak Literarni Noviny, is that neither the working class, nor its vanguard (the party), nor the vanguard's vanguard (the 'new class'), is equipped to manage a modern industrial society efficiently. One could fill a large volume with criticisms of the inadequacies of those who occupy leading administrative and economic positions in the

People's Democracies and stand in the way of properly qualified people.[21]

The intelligentsia's first assault on the new class in Hungary and Poland was broken by the resistance of the administrators. One of the principal objects of the anti-revisionist campaigns of 1957–9 and 1966–8 was to restore the myth of the leading role of the proletariat and the party. This myth is still maintained, and the right to rule has not been abnegated.[22] But, in fact, with the economic reforms, the new class is beginning to fall back on positions that have been prepared in advance. The prevailing tendency is to share a greater degree of economic responsibility with the experts, to give managers more scope, and to seek to satisfy the material demands of the technological intelligentsia.[23] The governments are on the point of granting the aristocracy of skill an honourable place, and even of admitting the rebirth, within certain ill-defined limits, of an aristocracy of wealth. It is the political privileges – the power of decision making – that the new class is determined not to yield to its rivals under any circumstances. But, emboldened by the concessions they have already obtained, a section of the technocrats are not content with an impressive secondary role. They are carrying the battle into the political field, setting themselves up as the spokesmen of national and liberal aspirations. One of the representatives of this movement in Czechoslovakia, the historian Milan Huebl – whom Novotny had dismissed in 1963 from the post of Rector of the party university for his nonconformist views – stressed in 1966 that 'the new model of socialism cannot be limited to the economic field'. It involves 'an improvement in human relations, the development of the personality, a greater degree of personal freedom'.[24] In 1968 the greater part of the Czechoslovak political élite was converted to this view.

The new class, besides, is divided, much as is the Church in certain countries between senior clergy more amenable to modernization and sociological thinking, and traditionalist and reactionary parochial clergy. In Yugoslavia, Hungary and especially Czechoslovakia, the liberal wing of the upper echelons of the new class has drifted further and further away from the unpopular, inflexible section of the rank and file, especially the 'worker cadres', the veteran Communists who are in any case nearing the end of their careers. This trend was reflected in an interesting article in the Hungarian newspaper *Nepszabadsag* of 28 January 1968, which admitted the existence of 'selfish interest groups' in industry and the economic administration, which struggle to preserve their privileges by taking unfair advantage of their authority, stifling all criticism, and persecuting their opponents. They should not be regarded as constituting a ruling class, wrote the newspaper. On the contrary, the party and state leadership are getting ready to destroy these groups with the help of the working class. The new economic arrangements, which put the emphasis on material incentives, will dispose of them more effectively than the appeals to civic and socialist conscience in the past. Indeed, heads of enterprises will henceforth have a personal and real interest in obtaining the workers' greater co-operation by getting rid of their despotic colleagues, and creating a democratic atmosphere in the factories. Furthermore, their own material interests will encourage workers to come forward and denounce abuses of power publicly.

The introduction of economic reforms is giving the top echelons of the new class the opportunity to prove their political and social value. One cannot see how the liberal economists and managers could hope to push through unpopular measures such as staff dismissals or penalties for negligence without the support of the party apparatus. The latter, furthermore, possesses effective means of controlling managers, protecting workers, and mediating in their disputes with heads of enterprises. This new mediating role of the party was apparent in Yugoslavia, where the growth of the system of self-management was used by the so-called liberal leaders to counter-balance the influence of the technocrats.

Rehabilitation of the Trade Unions and the Right to Strike

If the technological intelligentsia is the immediate beneficiary of the change-over to a market economy and of the increasing income differentiation, the working class in the Eastern countries stands to gain equally in the long run. In order to curb the intelligentsia and also to prevent uncontrolled elements (anarchists, trade unionists or even Maoists) from exploiting the workers' discontent, the leaders are being forced to revise their attitude to workers' organizations and in particular to trade unions.

Under the Stalinist régimes the latter had functioned simply as transmission belts for governmental and party decisions. Factory committees, with very few exceptions, were docile instruments in the hands of the leadership. They organized competition between enterprises in the matter of plan fulfilment and the raising of productivity. At the very best, they were 'social welfare offices'.[25]

The workers' dislike for these totally dependent bureaucratic organizations, which had done little to protect their interests, was clearly apparent in Poland and Hungary in 1956 and in Czechoslovakia between 1966 and 1968.[26] Thus, from 1965 there was a cautious upgrading of trade unions in the most advanced People's Democracies. In Hungary a joint resolution of the Council of Ministers and the Union of Trade Unions in June 1966 emphasized that the trade-union movement, as the 'true representative of organized labour, may take an independent line in all spheres of economic, social and cultural life'. According to the same resolution, the unions would have the right to publicize their position in cases of conflict that were not resolved through negotiation. Trade-union party relations were subject to new rules. According to the magazine *Partelet* (Budapest) of July 1966, 'the party continues to guide the trade unions ideologically and politically, but it no longer interferes directly, organizationally, in their activities'. Permanent trade-union machinery of consultation was set up in the enterprises. Factory committees were to have a say with regard to work conditions, wages, bonuses and profit sharing. They were even to be consulted over the appointment of directors.[27] A few months later, the chairman of the Hungarian trade unions urged the factory committees to demand the dismissal of directors who were 'insensitive' over the matter of wages.

The new Hungarian labour code, introduced on 1 January 1968, instituted a very modern – almost democratic – procedure for settling labour conflicts. While codifying the increased disciplinary and organizational rights of management, it made collective agreements binding, and gave the trade unions a suspensive veto over certain decisions of heads of enterprise.

The Yugoslav trade unions, contrary to frequent assertions, were until recently still submissive to the party, but they have also taken steps to improve their reputation with the wage earners.[28] In Czechoslovakia the highly bureaucratic trade unions were also affected by the 1968 spirit of renewal, though somewhat later than the other political and social organizations. But on 22 March they expelled Stalinist devotees such as their chairman Pastyrik from the leadership. On 19 June, 1,200 trade-union officials meeting in Prague applauded Dubcek when he declared: 'The aim of the trade unions, which in the past has wavered between defending the interests of the workers, on the one hand, and those of the enterprise on the other, must once again be the defence of the interests of union members.' The tendency to regard trade unions as cogs in the machinery of state and auxiliaries of the leadership survives only in Rumania and, of course, Albania.

However, even in the most advanced Eastern countries, trade unionism occupies a position not unlike in Spain, where the failure of the official trade unions to protect workers' interests has given rise to uncontrolled strike movements. In Yugoslavia there were 1,365 work stoppages between 1958 and 1966 to protest against low wages. There were also violent strikes in Czechoslovakia, Poland and Hungary. The authorities still refuse to accept the strike as legitimate; in their eyes, to do so would be an admission of failure on the part of the socialist state and the party. Thus, the head of the Czechoslovak metal-workers' union, K. Polacek, in an interview for the West German metal-workers' magazine, stressed that the rights of trade unions and the legal limitations on the powers of management provided an adequate basis for the settlement of disputes.[29] However, voices are increasingly being heard, especially in Yugoslavia and Czechoslovakia, calling for the legalization of strikes as 'necessary complements of market mechanisms'.[30] Indeed, the restoration of the right to strike as a last resort is a logical development of the new socio-economic orientation, which tries to balance divergent interests rather than to resolve them through authoritarian means.

P366 - Not Comm. press.

Workers' Councils

Long before the workers were allowed to use the trade unions to defend their interests, the Yugoslav Communist authorities had invited them to take part in the management of their factories, so as to have the experience of being masters. The basic law of 27 June 1950 setting up workers' councils was a daring challenge to 'state capitalism' and the 'bureaucratic centrism' of the U.S.S.R. and the other Cominform countries. Rebellious Yugoslavia, excommunicated by the Communist world, was showing the most exemplary loyalty to the Marxist-Leninist Utopian principle of the 'withering away of the state' as a 'coercive mechanism' (Tito).

Unlike the workers' councils that were to spring up in Hungary and Poland in 1956, the Yugoslav councils were established by the government itself, the product of a dynamic and imaginative paternalism. Elected by the collectives of manual and office workers, and electing managerial committees in their turn, the workers' councils were supported by the trade unions and manipulated by the party. Notwithstanding these initial defects, the Yugoslav leaders had created the framework of an institution into which active working-class forces in alliance with technical staff would be able to inject real life, should the occasion arise. Thanks to the councils, which were given the right to call for the dismissal of directors who were too autocratic, the atmosphere of work changed.[81] After 1957, when the first national congress of workers' councils was held in Belgrade, the councils – 70 per cent of whose members had come from the ranks of skilled workers and engineers – played the leading part in the struggle for decentralization. Workers and technicians often sided with heads of enterprises to demand greater autonomy for individual factories, as much in the use of investments as in the settling of wages and the distribution of profits. Certain workers' councils, it seems, also campaigned for greater wage differentiation. This showed the influence of the technicians, whose skill was acknowledged by the workers. However, the general tendency was to differentiate only slightly between the wages of skilled and unskilled workers; this resulted in the emigration of a large number of skilled workers as well as technicians.[32]

It is hard to form an overall picture of just how effective the Yugoslav system of self-management is, in view of the differences that exist between individual republics, towns, and even enterprises. There are conservative and ultra-progressive trade unions, as well as active and practically defunct ones, expansive and defensive ones. There are councils that see only their immediate interests and others that display a remarkable sense of social responsibility and economic understanding. From the outset, the workers' councils wavered between their managerial responsibilities and solidarity with the working masses; increasingly it was the latter that prevailed. In February 1964 the government had to bring in a law protecting directors against the 'unfair decisions' of certain councils. After 1965 many managers complained that the councils were obstructing technological progress and the necessary measures of rationalization; although conceived as instruments of education and participation in management, the councils often became a source of friction within enterprises and between the enterprises and the central or local authorities. Khrushchev pointed this out maliciously during the course of a discussion with the members of a council in Slovenia. The reply was that 'friction leads to progress'. In actual fact, if the workers' councils have frequently added to the confusion and complications that characterize economic development in Yugoslavia, they have also enlivened social life. They are now an independent force that the managers, on the one hand, and the party, on the other, try to win over to their respective sides.[33]

Unlike the Yugoslav workers' councils, those that sprang up in Poland and Hungary in the autumn of 1956 claimed to be the direct revolutionary organs of workers' power, destined to replace the party committees and the discredited trade unions. In Poland it was the workers of the Zeran automobile factory who, in September 1956, took the initiative in establishing workers' councils as instruments of socialist self-management. This proposition, which was warmly approved by the liberal intellectuals who dominated the press at the time, proved to be attractive. After initially rejecting the new institution as a 'servile imitation of the Yugoslav model', the party leadership finally adopted it. Many Gomulkists regarded it as an inherent part of the Polish path to socialism, and Gomulka, when he came to power, welcomed the councils, which responded to the aspirations of the working class to a greater share in the management of enterprises. A law passed by the Diet in November 1956 recognized the right of the workers' councils to administer the enterprises, while at the same time limiting their activities to two spheres: output improvement and the distribution of bonuses.

However, the workers' councils, which sprang up throughout the country (there were more than 4,600 at the end of 1957), went beyond these limits. In many cases, they replaced government-appointed directors by their own, and, ejecting party organizations and factory committees, tended to set themselves up as the sole organs genuinely representative of the factory workers.

In May 1957, at the Ninth Plenum, Gomulka, who was anxious to restore party and state authority, condemned these claims. And, backed by the 'revisionists' of the *Po Prostu* group, the movement's champions proposed to replace the existing economic administrative apparatus by a pyramid of workers' councils.[34] This trend towards the establishment of a 'second government' – a government of Soviets! – particularly disturbed the leaders, in view of the fact that the technological intelligentsia, which was more or less openly hostile to the party, now dominated most of the factory workers' councils. Therefore, as soon as the central organization recovered from the shock of 1956, Gomulka took steps to neutralize the danger. In May 1958 he set up a new institution, the 'self-management conference', composed of members of the workers' councils and the factory trade-union and party committees. The decisions taken by this body were binding on its constituent organizations, and the former prerogatives of the workers' councils were transferred to it – assuring the control of the party. The workers' councils themselves were merely responsible for carrying out the decisions taken by the conference in the interval between sessions. Inevitably, the spontaneity of the movement was stifled by the new arrangement; self-management was no longer a reality, and the workers lost interest in the puppet organization that neither gave them any real say in management, nor any longer reflected their aspirations.[35]

The Hungarian workers' councils also sprang from the insurrectional fervour of autumn 1956. The influence of the Yugoslav experiment was even more obvious here than in the case of the Polish workers' councils. During the summer and autumn of 1956, several economists, trade unionists and journalists visited Yugoslavia to see how the workers' councils functioned, and they published articles on their observations. The Yugoslav experiment was also discussed in detail in the Petőfi Circle. In a resolution passed on the eve of the rebellion, the Circle and the Youth Union, where the revisionist influence was dominant, jointly urged the government to promote 'the establishment of a socialist democracy ... by introducing factory autonomy and workers' democracy'. On 23 October the Hungarian writers' union announced: 'The factories must be run by the workers and specialists.'

The first workers' council was set up in the Budapest electric light bulb factory on 24 October, when the street fighting was raging. By the following day several provincial factories had followed suit. Like the municipal and provincial revolutionary committees to which their delegates belonged and where they often played the leading part, the workers' councils plunged into the revolutionary movement. Their resolutions and proclamations, their appeals to the government and public stressed national patriotic and political demands. They insisted on the withdrawal of Soviet troops, the dismissal of the former leaders, the reorganization of the police, and a restoration of normal parliamentary life. Economic and social demands – wage rises, trade-union reform – played only a secondary role.

There was nothing anarchic or anarchistic about the Hungarian councils. They kept the extremist elements at arm's length and expressed their confidence in Imre Nagy, while demanding that he form a government that satisfied national aspirations. In the general confusion, the councils seemed like havens of order and reason. This is what encouraged Imre Nagy to try to take over the movement on his own account and for the party and government. On his initiative, the party Central Committee issued a declaration on 26 October approving the election of workers' councils in all the factories. The council of trade unions published a similar appeal. After this the movement spread. However, the former managerial staff, the director, party secretary and trade-union officials tried – in vain – to get their own candidates elected at the meetings organized in the factories. The declaration, according to which the councils were to be established by the workers, was taken seriously by the latter. Besides, as in Poland, the engineers and other technicians were prominent among the elected council members, and one of the main concerns of the workers was to secure the resignation of the old, discredited cadres.

During the actual ten days of the rebellion the Hungarian workers' councils were in the process of setting themselves up and making their lists of demands; and many of their members were taking part in the fighting. Paradoxically, the Hungarian councils reached their peak after the rebellion had been crushed. Once the revolutionary committees had disappeared, they constituted the only organized national force, a kind of second government. Janos Kadar was at the time very weak, and relied on a few improvised police detachments, apart from the Soviet troops.[36] Following Nagy's example in trying to acquire a popular basis of support, Kadar attempted to strike up a dialogue with the workers' councils, and especially the central workers' council of Greater Budapest, in order to win them over to his side. But it soon became apparent that the councils regarded themselves as embodying the spirit of national resistance and were remaining faithful to the revolutionary aims. Losing patience, Kadar declared that he was ready to co-operate with reasonable workers' councils and in the meantime arrested the leaders of the central council. The movement towards a general strike was broken. Subsequently, Kadar used the same methods as Gomulka to infiltrate, intimidate, dishearten and finally dissolve the councils.[37]

In the new Czechoslovakia of 1968 the initiative for the organization of workers' councils came from the liberal economist Ota

Sik.[38] 'The workers', he said, 'must have the right to control the activity of the heads of enterprises, and also the right to dismiss them.' In July self-management was introduced on an experimental basis in the Skoda factories, and according to one of its sponsors, Rudolf Slansky's son, a C.K.D. engineer, 'the manual and office workers and technicians took such a passionate interest in the proceedings that it was clear their political consciousness had not been destroyed'. In the eyes of many intellectuals, such as the fiery historian Bartosek, self-management represented not only the meeting point of the intelligentsia's and working class's aspirations, but also 'a solid answer to the criticism made against us [the progressive Marxists] by the bureaucrats of certain socialist countries, who claim to be more revolutionary than us.'[39] Apparently the movement for the establishment of workers' councils has not come to an end with the occupation of the country.

From Bureaucratic Socialism to Scientific, Pluralistic, Techno-Democratic Socialism

Compared with the de-Stalinizers of 1956, the reformists of the post-1962 era – especially in the vanguard in Czechoslovakia – seem more realistic. The initiative has passed from the ideologists to the economists (and the ideologists themselves support this trend). The champions of economic reform have been gradually forced to recognize that the introduction of the new economic model must be accompanied by changes in social, juridical and constitutional structures. The aims and methods of socialism must be reconsidered.

However, one of the main social problems the People's Democracies face after the introduction of the market economy is the increasingly obvious contradiction between the egalitarian principles of classical socialism and the increasing inequality of opportunity that favours the intelligentsia and further depresses the proletariat. As we have seen, during the period of bureaucratic socialism, discrimination, based in effect on political influence, was kept within bounds both by the levelling of the intelligentsia and working class and by social mobility.

The economic reforms, however, entail greater discrimination, based increasingly on yield and professional skill. This has come just at a moment when mobility is on the decline and the upper echelons are tending to become entrenched. The technological intelligentsia will not let its children sink to the level of manual workers. Workers' and peasants' children, handicapped by their environment, have much less chance of rising socially, even if limited only by the number of positions available.[40] A possible answer lies in upgrading manual labour through improving the living and working conditions of the workers, whose children would have correspondingly less stimulus to better themselves. But, as a Hungarian sociologist has pointed out, 'such an improvement can be achieved only by putting the new economic model into effect, the very thing that is responsible for increasing existing differences.'[41]

The difficulty confronting the government is to maintain public order and stability in a period of economic reform, which could well be one of class and political struggles. Stability can be guaranteed only by a strong government biased in favour of the Communist leaders, if their authority had not already been seriously undermined by mistakes committed in the past. This is not to say the rulers' ability to rule is being questioned only by the technological intelligentsia; the working class, too, shaking off its lethargy, seems to be considering means of action and is responding to the calls of industrial democracy and co-operation. The student youth is growing impatient and the peasantry, as usual, is biding its time.

Theoretically, of course, there is another path the dictatorships of the proletariat could follow. This is the cultural revolution on which China embarked. Its main features are the rejection of 'economism', or the consumer ideal of industrial societies, and the attempt to substitute ideological, revolutionary and moral incentives for material ones. Having arrived at the stage where Stalinist differentiation was in danger of being reinforced by differentiation based on the division of labour, Mao's China opted for a system in which equality of opportunity was the absolute and sole criterion. Not only are the technological intelligentsia's aspirations to leadership and to a higher standard of living savagely repressed, but even the new class of political officials has to forgo material advantages. Mao, determined to modernize and industrialize, is taking egalitarianism to absurd lengths. His cultural revolution postulates a permanent struggle of each and all against individual selfishness. The enemy is self-interest, with which no compromise is possible. Each man must become a hero of self-abnegation, devoted body and soul to Mao's person and thought.

For historical, geographical, socio-economic and cultural reasons that need not be enlarged upon here, the Chinese path is not workable in the European People's Democracies. These countries, with the exception of Albania and the most backward parts of Yugoslavia, do not belong to those 'rural areas' whose revolutionary potential and mission has been extolled by Lin Piao, but to the urbanized world. Even the bureaucratic, despotic, isolationist socialism of Stalin's period did not eliminate individualistic tendencies or destroy the affinities with the advanced industrial societies.

From Lenin through Stalin and Khrushchev, the leaders and theoreticians of the Communist countries never stopped putting socialism forward as a system competing with the capitalist countries as much in technological development as in the improvement of the standard of living. Furthermore, the Soviet model adopted at the beginning by the European Communist leaders has entailed the acceptance of the traditional framework of the national state. Except in the case of Yugoslavia in its heroic period (1944–8), the satellite leaders have tried to consolidate their power rather than to endanger it by exporting revolution. The Maoist or Castroite idea of international solidarity has always been, and is becoming increasingly, alien to them. The logic of their internal development is leading the People's Democracies (despite Utopian, quasi-Maoist outbreaks, like the Yugoslav student demonstrations in June 1968) to replace the obsolete model of autocratic, Russian-centred socialism by a model or models better suited to their traditional national structures.

The events of 1956 and 1968 have revealed a profound alienation between the social forces and political structures of Stalinism. Whether within the existing structures (party cells in the youth organizations and associations of students, writers, journalists, historians and economists), or in creating new structures (committees of intellectuals, workers' councils), the social classes, broken up, infiltrated and perverted by the political bureaucracy, have displayed a tendency here and there to self-emancipation. It is true that from Hungary and Poland in 1956 to Czechoslovakia in 1968, patriotic aspirations were a common denominator, a factor for integration transcending differences of interest and opinion. It is also true that it was the intelligentsia that everywhere came forward as the representative and natural leader of national society, opposing dependent bureaucracies and foreign imperialism. But it has become clear that there was an 'antagonistic contradiction', in the Marxist sense of the term, only between this anti-national bureaucracy and the rest of the population. There is nothing irreconcilable between the interests of the other classes. Socially as well as politically, the movement promoted by revisionist Marxists tends towards a régime that is socialist, democratic, national and anti-imperialist.

19

Cultural Development: The Breakdown of Ideology

It is on 'the cultural front', as it is currently and significantly called, that the rulers of Eastern Europe have suffered their worst defeat. This is, no doubt, due to the vastness of the attempted transformation of culture, the totality of man's intellectual and spiritual activities, into an instrument of Marxist-Leninist propaganda. The essence of Marxist-Leninist ideology, the 'Leninist faith', lay initially, as Richard Loewenthal has said, in the determination to replace by revolutionary means the alienated, dispossessed, repressed man of former feudal and capitalist societies by a new type of man, integrated in and nourished by society. This man would be of such elevated moral stature that he would no longer even need God. [1]

From disappointing results, we would be inclined to regard this ideal as absurd and unattainable, although we may not entirely sympathize with the pessimism of the Slovene writer and former Communist partisan who writes: 'It must be admitted that Communism as a secularized and positive version of the scriptures, as faith in the power of the intellect and of human goodness, as a concept that holds forth the immediate promise of an earthly paradise, has completely failed. It is now clear that the Communists do not sacrifice themselves for their fellow beings, but work for themselves, for their own interests. This is especially true of the leaders ... The wartime unity of the partisans has broken down. There is no more solidarity. In the promised land, man is on his own.'[2]

Man's terrible loneliness in collectivist society – atomized society – is the leitmotive of the literature and poetry of the socialist countries. It is this that prompted L. Vaculik, another former Communist, to make the following despairing observation: 'In any case, socialism is finished ... What we thought had been accomplished must be redone.'[3] The harmful effects of party control over literary life were detailed by the Czechoslovak writers at the June 1967 Congress that rang the knell of personal power.

The continuity of Czechoslovak literature was broken in 1949, despite its democratic traditions and its richness ... The creative process was obstructed and reduced to a purely propagandist role, and ideology and culture were identified with one another ... with tragic consequences for creativity, labour, and individual human existence ...

The repudiation of certain periods of our national history and of some outstanding personalities has had a harmful effect, especially on the education of the younger generation ... All this sprang from a moral primitivism ...

Our culture and our educational system have been forced to ignore the sources of European culture in antiquity, through the Renaissance and Christianity.[4]

This is a reliable comment on the most striking features of the post-1949 cultural policy of the Communist régimes: a break in continuity, domestication and standardization, a rejection of national traditions (together with a servile imitation of Soviet models), and finally isolation from the West.[5] Nevertheless, culture is not something that can be manipulated at will. One of the most momentous errors of the 'vulgar Marxism' practised by Lenin's followers has been the belief that everything can be reduced to economics, that economic facts (imperfectly understood at that) can be isolated from their socio-cultural context. Spiritual, aesthetic, intellectual and moral values have been degradingly classified as 'reflections', 'superstructures', secondary entities. The practical effect of this heresy has been what Louis Aragon has called the 'Biafra of the spirit'. It is a 'path of violence, of incarceration, torture and destruction of what has been and what has not yet been accomplished'.[6]

The *Soviet Encyclopaedia* defines culture as the 'totality of society's achievements in the fields of science, art and education ... as well as the ability to use them in mastering the forces of nature, in production, and in resolving problems of social development.' The rarefied, narrow, alienating view of culture as expressed in this vision is striking. It is as though it had escaped the notice of the champions of Marxist-Leninist *Kulturpolitik* that, far from being a mere rag-bag of acquisitions and an instrument for the attainment of certain ends, culture is the work of man, poetry in the widest sense of the word, creation. It is, as Malraux has said, a legacy that has been gained (and, one could add, developed). The culture of a nation is its living writers, poets, scholars, artists, thinkers, educationalists, who continue the creative work of their forefathers while drawing nourishment from and contributing to the culture of the other nations in the same civilization. National culture also includes the public, which becomes more literate through contact with these writers, scholars, artists and others.

The attempt to define the cultural needs of the population and to lay down the means of satisfying them from a single centre was as absurd as the idea of controlling all production and distribution of material goods. Nevertheless, this was, and to a certain extent remains, the aim of the ruling party. In 1952 one of the Hungarian leaders under Rakosi, Jozsef Revai, Minister of Culture, a man not without aesthetic sensibility, had expressed the Marxist-Leninist-Zhdanovist view of culture in its most extreme form. 'The writer', he declared at a meeting of literary men, 'struggles to defend his right to handle any theme he likes. However, we do not recognize this right at all. We cannot subscribe to an aesthetic principle whereby the writer's taste and judgement are the main criteria of the purpose and methods of literature ... It is not the people or the state that must adjust to the taste and judgement of the writer, but the writer who must, through his work and teaching, identify himself with the interests of socialism and with socialist construction.'[7]

It is clear that in Revai's opinion it was the party's job to decide what these interests were. However, certain Communist leaders soon realized the disastrous effect of such claims. 'At present', wrote Imre Nagy in autumn 1955, 'it is the party leadership that determines absolutely what must conform to the party spirit in literature and the arts. But this method precludes the search for reality and truth, the exchange of ideas and, above all, criticism. Literature, music, and the arts have become a distorting mirror, in which the people cannot recognize the great and complex problems waiting for an honest solution.'[8]

The result of totalitarianism has been to turn most workers in the field of culture, whether Communist or not, into passive or active rebels, defending cultural values against a party that has continually violated them.

The liberal Communist leaders have tried to resolve this permanent conflict by improving conditions and restoring a certain amount of freedom of expression. The Yugoslav Vlahovic, in particular, proclaimed:[9] 'We have finally rejected the idea that the state determines cultural policy, and that it is the Maecenas and supreme arbiter of culture.' But he admitted that the leadership of the League had been slow and inconsistent in its efforts to find 'a concrete and more progressive alternative' to the idea of planned cultural producton under party control.

What makes it so hard to solve the problem of the relations between the Communist government and culturally enlightened men is not just the determination of the bureaucracy to create an apologetic culture, its inclination to tolerate only those manifestations of culture that serve its purpose; there is also the refusal of many writers, artists and scholars, among others, to restrict themselves to cultural activity alone and to abstain from criticizing and questioning the system.

Indeed, one of the distinguishing features of the culture of the Eastern countries, as compared to that of the liberal countries of the West, is the extent to which it is politically conscious. In trying to defend themselves against the continual encroachment of politics on their domain, writers, artists and scholars of the socialist countries have tended to challenge not only the anti-culture of totalitarian policy, but also its general principles. As against the 'politics first' approach of the totalitarian leaders, the men of culture have upheld the priority of values as a genuine, inalienable expression of national identity. 'If the aim of the socialist régime is to destroy man's sense of alienation, to reintegrate him, and to secure his freedom to develop his own personality,' ran the aforementioned resolution of the Fourth

Congress of Czechoslovak writers, 'then it is not possible to regard culture as something secondary or subsidiary ... The basic purpose of socialist culture is not to assemble a kind of holy writ, but to be continually asking and never finally answering the question as to man's aim and the means whereby he may become ever freer.' And the resolution adds: 'There could be no more damning condemnation of a political régime than a cultural void.'

Opposition Culture versus Cultural Policy

The increasingly acrimonious dispute over culture encouraged the Hungarian and Polish writers, journalists, artists and scholars in 1956, and the Czechoslovaks in 1963 and 1968, to act as 'the conscience of the nation'. They became the spokesmen of all classes of society against governmental abuse of power. This is hardly surprising. 'If one of our organs fails, another one will take over its function as far as possible', wrote the Hungarian poet Gyula Illyés.[10] As Heine pointed out, the repressed political and social passions of romantic Germany sought an outlet in philosophy and the arts. This displacement of cultural activities is even more apparent in the countries of Central and Eastern Europe. 'Hungarian, Polish and Balkan literature', remarked Illyés, 'has in effect, from the outset, been a literature of opposition.' The poets have always symbolized their peoples' will to survive. In their struggle against totalitarianism, artists and scholars, including a large section of the youth, especially of the student youth, have almost inevitably revived the old traditions of resistance to foreign and internal opposition.

After 1949, writers, artists and teachers of the Eastern countries were in fact faced with a situation very like that which confronted their forefathers in the eighteenth and nineteenth centuries in respect to the reactionary censorship and presumptuous police surveillance of the absolutist régimes. The analogy is striking; the Habsburg monarchy, for administrative rather than philosophical reasons, had tried to Germanize the culture of its hereditary domains, such as Hungary and Bohemia, while shielding them from the influence of the progressive cultures of France and England. The situation created by the Russo-Centrist Communist régimes, with their tendency to uncritical adulation of everything coming from Moscow, was a familiar one. It was no accident that the Hungarian intellectuals of 1956 named their club after the liberal, revolutionary poet Petöfi, who died in 1849 fighting against the tsar's army. The Czechoslovak writers at their 1967 Congress compared the press law introduced at the beginning of the year with Francis Joseph's law passed a hundred years earlier, when the Empire was being liberalized. They found the latter considerably more progressive, more liberal than Novotny's and deplored the 'new obscurantism' into which they had been plunged. The Polish student demonstration outside Warsaw's National Theatre at the end of January 1968 against the banning of Mickiewicz's classical play *The Forefathers* (written after the suppression of the 1831 rising) might have taken place a hundred years earlier on the same square to the same shouts of 'Independence! Down with the censorship! Freedom of expression! No censoring of Mickiewicz!'[11]

The Stalinist myths of the party's infallibility, the superiority of the socialist system, the imminent creation of a new man, were exploded. The Eastern Communist régimes, no longer invested with the aura of revolutionary internationalism, and having lost their initial dynamism and aggressive sense of purpose, compared unfavourably with the liberal régimes of Western Europe. In the eyes of their own élites, they seemed repressive, reactionary bureaucracies, and at the same time mere instruments in the hands of a foreign nation. The Soviet Union, which served as a model for the Eastern leaders, had from the outset imported and developed the tsarist tradition of the absolutist, expansionist state, with its double role of maintaining order and introducing modernization. It was quite unable to conceive of social change except as part of a deliberate programme carried out by the administration.[12]

The Nation, a Basic Socio-Cultural Entity

The feeling of having fallen behind, if not in respect to the prewar régimes (Czechoslovakia was the only country to have enjoyed a democratic régime before 1939), at least in respect to the vistas that had been opened up after the Second World War, underlies the entire cultural life of the Eastern countries in the period under consideration. They were conscious of having been held back and abused as sovereign nations. Socially and as individuals, the Eastern peoples had been frustrated and impoverished. Totalitarian Communism reactivated the old resistance to absolutism, 'monarchic arbitrariness'.[13] In this context the idea of a 'nation', the affirmation of national identity and traditions, seemed to the men of culture the only real basis for a new departure. This return to their origins, which is regarded as the main spiritual prerequisite for a revival, a leap forward, characterizes the culture of the Eastern countries, as it does that of the nascent or renascent cultures of the colonial peoples of the Third World.

Echoing the Western Marxist revisionists, the philosophers and ideologists of the Eastern countries have, in the sixties, revived the concept of 'alienation', as encountered in the writings of the young Marx. J.-M. Domenach was no doubt right to criticize the vagueness of this notion, which should perhaps be replaced by less ambiguous terms, such as dispossession, oppression, frustration or expropriation.[14] However, in the Eastern countries, the idea of alienation has acquired a concrete meaning: it implies being forced to become other than what one is, the introduction of a false conscience. This obligation to lie was imposed under cover of proletarian internationalism. If there is one expression that is utterly discredited in the minds of the people of Eastern Europe, it is 'proletarian internationalism'. And if they are certain of one thing, it is of the need for roots in the national culture. They are convinced that 'to surpass himself, modern man must return to his origins' (Edgar Morin). Patriotism and nationalism constitute such an elemental force in the sphere of culture that the Communist leaders themselves have had to yield to it, while trying to control and use it for their own ends.[15]

Integration into European and World Culture

Of course, this cultural and political nationalism, that took such moving and often heroic forms in Poland and Hungary in 1956,

Slovakia between 1963 and 1968, and the Czech lands in 1968, and which on occasion took on an ontological aspect,[16] contained certain negative and retrogressive elements too, reflecting chauvinistic and xenophobic attitudes. It has always been only too easy for demagogues to exploit national feelings. The Communist régimes, who considered that they had solved the national problem by overthrowing the bourgeoisie and persecuted all the truest patriots (Novomesky and Husak in Czechoslovakia, Istvan Bibo in Hungary), made no attempt to rationalize and illuminate nationalism by concentrating on its constructive side. It was fear of the 'shadow' side of nationalism, its exploitability, antipersonalism and retrogressiveness that led Adam Schaff in 1965 to express a certain nostalgia for the lost internationalist paradise and to defend the ideal of universal man against nationalist provincialism and intolerance.[17] 'There is no such thing as cosmopolitan culture', came the rejoinder from Professor Chalasinski, who tried to explain Schaff's search for a supra-nationalist ideal in terms of the latter's rootlessness (i.e. Jewish origins). The memory of the Stalinist, Zhdanovist 'anti-cosmopolitan' campaigns against every kind of modernism – the slogan 'struggle against cosmopolitanism' served also as cover for anti-Semitic purges – was still too alive among Polish intellectuals for them to fail to appreciate the significance of what this 'anti-national nationalist' was saying. The intellectuals of the Eastern countries know that if there is no completely national cosmopolitan culture, there are, in the East as well as the West, many creative spirits, exiles, stateless people, people belonging to minorities, migrants, misfits, refugees, descendants of Erasmus or Kafka. Are they to be refused entry to the republic of letters, arts and sciences? Over and above the national cultures, there is a European and world culture, to which the élites or 'counter-élites' of the Eastern countries fervently want to belong.

As regards the economy and political or social life, the reintegration of the Eastern countries into the European and world context is in its early stages, as we have seen. But culturally 'the point of no return' was reached by most of these countries between 1953 and 1968. The artificial barriers raised between the so-called socialist and bourgeois cultures have crumbled. All that the Communist régimes can do is to impede and delay, to obstruct intercourse between East and West. Under the pretext of the fight against bourgeois influence they are struggling against the basic solidarity of men of culture everywhere. Besides, Czechs, Slovaks, Hungarians, Poles and Rumanians are conscious of sharing this feeling of solidarity with the élite of the Soviet Union, with men like Sinyavsky, Daniel, Ginzburg, whose trials have made a deep impression in the Eastern countries.

The Cultural Contribution of the Eastern Countries

The process of reintegration with the West is inseparably bound up with the revival of cultural pluralism rising anew from the ashes of Marxist-Leninist monopolism. The men of culture are picking up the threads they were forced to drop after 1948. Thus, besides revolutionary Marxism, which seeks to renew itself through contact with the Italian and French 'open Marxists', there are the older tendencies and movements which have gained prestige as a result of Communist persecution. These include the 'populists', who trace their origins to the Russian 'Narodniks' (so called after their paper, *Narodnaya Volya*) and stand for a form of 'democracy that takes national circumstances into account',[18] the 'modernists' of various shades, and the Christians and mystics within and on the periphery of the Churches.

What contribution are these resurgent cultures making to world civilization? Their dramatic, cinematographic, poetic, epic and philosophic products are beginning to reach the Western market. Their political content, the side that is concerned with the struggle for human rights, their breathless affirmation of principles that do not seem to require proof in the West, sometimes appear anachronistic or provincial, especially when the techniques used suffer from comparison with what is being done in the West. To escape the vigilant eye of the censor, these works are often camouflaged, allegorical, allusive and elliptical; and the language is not always easy to interpret.

Yet apart from all this there is such feeling, passion, such a fear of spiritual extinction, that the best creative artists of the East appear as the real heirs to the great Russian and East European cultural tradition. In comparison with their works, those of their Western colleagues in the sixties often seem pale, frivolous, anaemic, absurd and concerned principally with formal experimentation. 'It looks as though a rare type of cultural renaissance has occurred in the shadow of Stalinist repression and Marxist dogma', wrote Maurice Clavel in connection with some new Hungarian and Czechoslovak films.[19]

The fact is that the twenty years of totalitarianism that followed the upheavals, the devastations, threats of war and the Nazi genocides have had a traumatic effect on the Eastern peoples. This is especially true of those concerned with culture, who were subjected to particularly strong pressure aimed at forcing them to act as spokesmen and eulogizers of the party, when all their instincts were to fulfil their natural and traditional functions as spokesmen of their people. For them, it was not a question of being engaged or not engaged. They were engaged, whether they liked it or not. Many fell silent, but when they broke this silence, itself a form of engagement, their understanding had been deepened and enriched. It is these people who inspire most respect. Others employed subterfuge through half-truths, forcing themselves to adjust to the inevitable in order to preserve the essential. Still others allowed themselves to be persuaded to lie for a cause that they wanted to believe was sacred.

But all were injured, all suffered pangs of conscience, torments of the flesh and the soul. For all of them, words like 'air', 'light', 'bread', 'truth', 'country' took on a new, pregnant meaning, full of pathos.

Marxist totalitarianism was an assault on the whole of man's being, challenging human nature in its entirety. Its very existence had been, in effect, denied by the most obtuse Marxists. This is why men of culture, and Easterners in general, suffered a tragic, unexampled crisis of identity and human alienation. In the Nazi extermination camps it was simply a question of degrading and exterminating, whereas in the Stalinist world the destruction was purely incidental, the object being reconstruction and mechanization, brain-washing. This experience, as expressed in literature, art and philosophy, contains lessons relevant to the West, where culture fluctuates between an abstract, formalistic, depersonalized hermeticism, and pop art, which tends to submerge cultural creativity in non-culture or pre-culture and aims at immediate and easy accessibility. The best writers, artists and philosophers of the Eastern countries oppose both forms of contemporary cultural nihilism and anti-humanism. They are the proponents of a culture that believes in itself, in man, and that has something to say.

The Communist governments have not succeeded in establishing or promoting that superior socialist culture, which men like Lunacharsky, Gyoergy Lukacs, Bertolt Brecht, and so many other revolutionary militants after Marx had dreamed about. On the contrary, they have stifled, distorted or debased the creative élan, the hopes for a full life and for renewal raised by the Russian Revolution. Whatever has been and is being achieved in the East in the field of culture is in spite of the repressive action of the party's 'ideological committees'; it has been undertaken in opposition to and not on behalf of the official ideology. Ideology has in effect, lost the battle for the domestication and instrumentalization of culture. After Imre Nagy, Dubcek, as head of the Czechoslovak party, drew the logical conclusions from this defeat; upon coming to power, he solemnly promised to 'eliminate everything that obstructs and stifles artistic and scientific creation'.[20]

A Glance at Education

It would be wrong to conclude from what has been said that the Communist régimes' activity in the field of culture has been purely negative and destructive. There is a positive side that should not be ignored. By making the centralized state the sole agent of history, the régimes inherited not only dynastic absolutism's bureaucratic structures, its abstract rationalism and propensity for controlling or supervising everything, but also its dynamism, its drive for efficiency and progress, and its taste for grand administrative enterprises. Throughout the hereditary lands, the reigns of the enlightened Habsburg monarchs Maria Theresa and Joseph II were notable for the construction of countless public buildings. These include barracks, hospitals, prisons, prefectures and law courts, but also and especially primary schools and 'gymnasia', universities, theatres and museums, architectural edifices that still give towns like Vienna, Prague, Bratislava, Budapest, Ljubljana, Zagreb and Cracow their particular atmosphere. Joseph II's aim was for the state to take over from the Church the upbringing and training of citizens, especially efficient and loyal public servants.

The Communist régimes followed in this tradition of state management. They gave a new impetus to the campaign for literacy and – a Social Democratic legacy, this – the democratization of the educational system. The expansion of education was necessitated by large-scale programmes of industrialization which needed a greater volume of professionally qualified staff for their efficient implementation. The considerable effort made to adapt school personnel and programmes to meet the needs of economic life is to the credit of the Communists – as are achievements in the field of social security. Without furnishing a detailed account of what has been accomplished in each country, we give in Table 1 figures to illustrate the advances made in higher education in Poland.

Table 1

ACADEMIC YEAR:	1937–8	1947–8	1957–8	1965–6
High Schools	42	56	76	76
Faculties	118	162	331	350
Chairs	782	1,348	2,360	2,735
Students	49,534	94,785	162,680	251,864
Graduates	6,114	4,147	19,424	25,218
Professors and Docents	907	2,044	2,954	3,669
Assistant Masters and Assistants	2,107	5,223	12,888	15,050
Lecturers and Assistant Lecturers	157	391	1,525	1,960

At the end of 1964, 328,000 of the people employed in Poland's nationalized economy, including 100,000 women, had had a higher education. Besides normal education, advanced, evening and correspondence courses organized by the workers played a prominent part in social advancement in Poland as in the other Eastern countries. In 1965–6, out of about 250,000 students, 100,000 were taking evening or correspondence courses. It should also be remembered that education is entirely free in the higher schools. In the academic year 1966–7, 70,000 students received grants. Seven years of general education (and since 1966 eight years), an extensive network of secondary schools (340,000 students in 1962–3 as against 114,000 in 1937–8) and free education and scholarships brought higher education within the reach of many working-class and peasant children. In 1965–6, 27.3 per cent of those receiving normal education were of working-class origin, 16.7 per cent of peasant origin, and 50.7 per cent came from the intelligentsia. Polish scientific publishing houses, run by the Ministry of Higher Education, issued 1,280 titles in 1965 and published 82 scientific journals.[21]

The figures for Hungary are no less impressive. The number of students in higher education increased from 11,000 in 1937–8 to 67,000 in 1962–3 (including evening and correspondence course students). In Rumania student numbers increased fivefold between 1938 and 1966, when there were 46 institutions of higher education, with 101 faculties, as against 33 in 1938: and 13,000 teachers, as against 2,200 in 1938. In Serbia in 1967 there were 645 secondary schools, as against 60 or so before the war. In Serbia again, progress in other branches of education is exemplified by the following figures: 28 intermediate agricultural colleges, as against 2 before the war; 28 medical colleges, as against 1; 70 technical colleges, as against 4; 31 teachers' training colleges, as against 10. Over the twenty post-war years, 3,000 schools have been opened in Serbia and the number of school children and students has tripled.[22]

Thus the Eastern countries fully participated in the academic explosion that has characterized the post-war development of all the industrialized countries, or countries that are being industrialized. The technological and cultural level has risen everywhere. But, as in the field of economics, this educational advance has had certain disadvantages, leading to growing dissatisfaction among teachers, parents and students to such an extent that the intellectual movement initiated by them has turned against the Communist régimes. The following are the most important of these negative aspects:

Hastiness and defective planning. An article in a Czechoslovak newspaper published at a time when liberalization was only in its early stages observed:

In many schools, with the term already well under way, it has been impossible to establish syllabuses in accordance with the education plan. The students of many schools have been urged to take part in apple-picking or to join work brigades. There have been delays in the distribution of school books and requisites, which this year are free for the first time. School life is often disrupted by the many social engagements of teachers. Many of the latter complain that they spend more time in organizational activities than in teaching.[23]

As in the economic field, the planners' projections have often turned out not to be feasible. Thus in Bulgaria the 1962 plan forecast an extremely rapid rate of growth which would raise the number of university students to 220,000 in 1980. After 1963 the government realized that this plan was unrealistic and it was substantially modified.

Russification and the mechanical imitation of the Soviet educational model. The tendency to integrate with the Soviet cultural system has been reflected simultaneously in the privileged place given to the teaching of the Russian language and literature at the expense of Western languages and the wholesale application of Soviet educational methods.[24] In Czechoslovakia, immediately after the Prague coup, a 'school-type discipline' was introduced into the universities, which were deprived of all independence. Everywhere the higher educational institutions had to cut all their traditional links with Western institutions and model themselves entirely on the Soviet universities. Certain areas of research, like cybernetics, automation, genetics and the social sciences, which were ill-regarded in the U.S.S.R., were neglected.[25]

In 1958 Khrushchev, concerned about the increasing gulf between intellectual and manual work that socialism had promised to eliminate, introduced his celebrated educational reform. Education was 'polytechnicized', and every candidate for higher education had to spend a two-year compulsory period working in production. This reform, which conflicted with the whole tenor of social development in the U.S.S.R., and which provoked widespread opposition among teachers and parents of Soviet students, was even less appropriate for the traditions and needs of the People's Democracies. It was nevertheless introduced in the Eastern countries, Bulgaria and Rumania carrying it out literally after 1959 and East Germany and Czechoslovakia applying it with some discretion. Hungary and Poland, on the other hand, managed to modify it to a considerable extent. Though based on theoretically uniform principles, the syllabuses, methods of poly-technical education, and co-ordination of schools and industry varied to a certain extent. In Poland, an eight-year period of compulsory schooling was introduced in 1961, whereas in East Germany and Hungary ten years was already the rule, and in Czechoslovakia from 1960 the period was nine years.[26]

From autumn 1963, when Bucharest's Maxim Gorky Institute was closed down, the Rumanian government began 'de-russifying' Rumanian education and culture as zealously as they had russified it between 1948 and 1958. Russian ceased to be a compulsory language at university and education was gradually westernized.[27]

The ideological content of education. The large place occupied by the teaching of Marxism-Leninism at all levels of education, and the poor quality of this teaching, provoked the greatest number of protests among teachers as well as students in the Eastern countries. In Novotny's Czechoslovakia, pre-military physical training, plus Russian and Marxism-Leninism, took up 30 per cent of the curriculum, whereas, according to the teachers, 'the stimulation of interest in the sciences ought to be the kernel of Communist education'.[28] Throughout the Communist countries a major student demand was the reduction, if not the elimi-nation, of the teaching of Marxism-Leninism, which was nothing more than 'a superficial apology for current policy'.[29]

In Poland the government, yielding to the pressure of public opinion, agreed in 1956 to do away completely with the teaching of the 'rudiments of Marxism-Leninism' (which was, in fact, limited to the study of Stalin's works, especially his *History of the Communist Party of the Soviet Union*). But the organization could not resign itself to abandoning the party altogether, particularly as the gound abandoned was rapidly taken over by the Church. Consequently there was a new drive in 1959 – a year of ideological hardening – 'to teach economics and philosophy in a Marxist spirit'. However, the lack of qualified instructors prevented the scheme from getting off the ground. In 1965 there was a new departure, with the attempt to make Marxism-Leninism a more attractive subject, introducing the study and discussion of problems of contemporary politics, sociology and economics. But once again the régimes were forced to choose between stimulating the students' interest and arousing their critical spirit, at the risk of enabling opposition groups to form, and insisting on indoctrination, which inevitably led to apathy.

Whatever tactics were employed, they were insufficient to halt the decline in the influence of Marxist-Leninist dogma. Only heretical revisionist Marxists like Kolakowski in Poland, or the philosophers associated with *Praxis* (Zagreb) and *Delo* (Belgrade), succeeded in stemming the tide, but with consequences that were not to the governments' liking. The fact that even the Rumanian leaders, who were firmly attached to Marxist principles, ended by dropping Marxism-Leninism from its place of importance in the university curriculum takes on a symbolic significance. Throughout the Communist countries in the sixties, the emphasis has been on patriotic education and professional training.

The Students and the Younger Generation

Periodically the leaders of the Eastern countries complain of the indifference of students, and young people generally, to ideological and political matters. According to them, the young are excited only by 'jazz and decadent dancing'.[30] Yet compared with their colleagues in the West, the students of the Eastern countries seem, or at least seemed prior to 1967, to be rather politically conscious. Since 1956 the Hungarian, Polish, Czechoslovak and Yugoslav students have been playing an opposition role in the political and social life of their countries similar to that of the Spanish, Turkish or South American students in their unstable dictatorships. They have deliberately placed themselves in the vanguard of the movement for progress, liberalization and national independence. In Hungary in 1956, in Poland in 1956 and 1968, and in Czechoslovakia in 1963 and 1967–8, active student elements formed a natural link with the liberal writers, journalists, teachers and artists. There is a tendency for them to define the intelligentsia's political and social demands in more radical, more extreme terms than their elders. Educated in and disillusioned by Marxism, responsive to socialist ideals but indignant at the gap between fact and theory, the students, even though largely of working-class origin, have since 1956 become a source of trouble for the régimes and of hope for the peoples.

If one takes only the post-1956 period, a number of incidents spring to mind. In Warsaw in October 1957 the students demonstrated against the ban on the revisionist weekly *Po Prostu*. There were scuffles with the police and purges. In April 1964 the students supported the thirty-four writers who signed the letter of protest against the government's cultural policy. Penalties were inflicted, and meetings were banned. The next year the expulsion of two young teachers, Modzelewski (son of a former Communist Minister of Foreign Affairs) and Kuron, from the University, and their subsequent arrest, led to disturbances. The philosopher Kolakowski, while not sharing the leftist, anarcho-Trotskyist ideas of the two men, testified in their favour in the name of freedom of opinion. After sentence had been passed, there were new protest meetings, and new interventions by the authorities. On 21 October 1966, the tenth anniversary of the 'little revolution', Kolakowski addressed a crowd of excited students, condemning the restrictions on freedom of organization and criticism, the absence of parliamentary life, and governmental inefficiency. He called for the removal from the penal code of those articles under which Kuron and Modzelewski had been tried and sentenced.

The next day the philosopher was expelled from the party. Kliszko, Gomulka's right-hand man, came to the University to defend the penalties that had been imposed, and accused Kolakowski of having been in contact with notorious foreign anti-Communists. Fourteen of the fifteen teachers in the department supported their colleague. The students for their part met the representative of the leadership with scepticism. In February 1968 there were fresh disturbances at the University over the ban on Mickiewicz's patriotic play. The victory of the liberals in Czechoslovakia acted as a catalyst. On 8, 9 and 11 March student demonstrations reached an unprecedented size, overflowing into the streets. Taking advantage of the presence among the students of the children of several Jewish former dignitaries and high officials, the authorities blamed the disturbance on the action of 'Zionist' elements. They mobilized the workers' militia controlled by the Partisan group, and used the occasion to carry out a new anti-Jewish purge.

Paradoxically, the forces of order in Warsaw came down on the students who marched to cries of 'Independence! Democracy! Gestapo!' on the very day when the Minister of the Interior in Prague was apologizing to the students who had suffered from police brutality during their large demonstration on 31 October 1967.

The Czechoslovak students did, in fact, make a great contribution to the victory of the liberals. It was towards the end of 1965 that they reappeared on the political scene. At the national conference of students in Prague in December 1965, under the aegis of the Union of Youth Movements, a militant, Jiri Mueller, carried a resolution calling for the 'federation' of the youth organizations – that is, the establishment of separate organizations for working-class youth, peasant youth and student youth – within its framework. The students also demanded that their organization be granted an independent political status, including the right to oppose the party, and representation in the National Assembly.[31] The party leadership categorically refused these demands and expelled Mueller from the University's youth union; and he was immediately called up for national service. But the emancipation movement was not destroyed so easily. In autumn 1967 the students of the philosophical faculty protested against the penalties inflicted on the anti-Novotnyite writers. On 31 October several thousand students of the student hostel district of Strahov organized a 'march on Prague' to present the authorities with their demands. The procession was broken up by the police, who lost their self-control; eleven students were wounded, two of them seriously. Public opinion reacted violently, and the dispute among the leaders over who was responsible for the police brutality precipitated the political crisis.

After the January 1968 Plenum, the students' spokesmen again raised the question of the establishment of an independent student organization. They accused the Central Committee of the Youth Union of being 'the most conservative institution in the country'.[32] On 28 February the committee of the Prague philosophy department youth union resigned and made way for a university students' council. The Czechoslovak Dutschke (or Cohn-Bendit), Jiri Mueller, was rehabilitated and reinstated. Reparations and apologies were made to the students wounded on 31 October. On 26 May, in the presence of Cisar and delegates of the non-Communist parties, student representatives of the fifty-three faculties of Bohemia-Moravia adopted the programme of 'the union of students in higher education'. One of the points in the programme dealt with student participation in the management of their schools.

Over the following months, the students remained in the forefront of the struggle. They supported the '2,000 Words' and took part in the organization of the campaign in support of Dubcek launched by *Literarni Listy*. After the Bratislava conference they demonstrated in Jan Hus Square to cries of 'We want the truth', 'We want a Masaryk policy', 'Free elections', 'Long live Israel'.

The leaders, anxious not to offend the Russians, were thankful that the majority of the students were away on holiday. Had they been present in large numbers in the major towns when the invasion occurred, it would have made it considerably more difficult to avoid bloodshed.

The Young and the Struggle for the Future

The outcome of events in Czechoslovakia explains why the Communist authorities in other Communist countries are so strongly opposed to the autonomy of student organizations. Party control is more easily maintained over youth unions when members come from all social classes, and where, as a result, the activist students are submerged in the mass of young workers, peasants and clerks, who are easier to handle. Even so the apparatuses of the unions are being put under increasing pressure by the young, who are no longer prepared to be 'subjects of indoctrination', but are demanding 'equal partnership'.[33]

In Yugoslavia the youth federation put forward its own demand for independence in November 1966. 'Instead of being an organization *for* the young', announced its president, 'we want to be an organization *of* the young.'[34] In the press debate that followed, several young people argued that institutions should take into account 'natural conflict [sic] between old and young, between the older and younger generations – a conflict that is an inherent feature of the social process'.[35]

The 'conflict between the generations', which is simply the conflict between the young and the Communist establishment, has become one of the great subjects of controversy throughout the Eastern countries. The young sulk over the party and the party scolds the young for indifference, ingratitude and nihilism. In Yugoslavia, where, in 1958, 23.6 per cent of the militants were under twenty-five, the young accounted for only 13.6 per cent in 1964. In Czechoslovakia, only 16 per cent of the party members were under thirty in 1966.

In the latter country numerous surveys among the young revealed that 'the enthusiasm of the fifties that made hundreds of thousands of young people engage in voluntary, unpaid work to help in the building of socialism no longer exists ...' 'Life has not educated the young people as our engineers of the soul hoped it would ... And this failure is due above all to the disparity between words and deeds, between what the young had been told about life and what they encountered in practice.'[36] Inflated and increasingly formalistic propaganda that is being contradicted by the gradual uncovering of Stalinist errors has given the rising generation a kind of 'built-in allergy to political indoctrination'.[37] The 'old' pretended to regard this scepticism of the young as a total lack of idealism, a 'bourgeois consumerist infection'[38]; in actual fact, it was an expression of frustration, of disillusionment with their elders who had let 'their spirits be broken', and 'discredited great ideas'.[39] The younger generation detests the supercilious, authoritarian paternalism of the rulers and, not without reason, accuses them of hypocrisy, moral and political schizophrenia and, above all – this particular charge is constantly recurring – incompetence.

Young graduates and technicians are also critical of the 'gerontocracy' of the aged cadres who despite their lack of qualifications occupy all the best positions because of the confidence they enjoy in the upper echelons.[40] Young graduates, together with students, make up the shock troops of the technological intelligentsia, demanding the rotation of cadres, the appointment of 'experts democratically chosen' to managerial positions.[41]

The youth of the Eastern countries shares with Western youth a certain disillusioned positivism and distrust of slogans and obsolete ideologies.[42] Tired of unkept promises – all the propaganda about 'the unlimited possibilities of socialism' – the young demanded action, proof; they believed only in science and technology.[43] 'The young do not always know where truth is', wrote the Czechoslovak poet Miroslav Holub, 'but they know where the lie is.'[44] It is this rejection of the social and political lie, the rejection not of ideals as such, but of false ideals, not of heroism, but of false heroism, that is driving the young to seek satisfaction in their private lives, or in setting up groups, more or less secret clubs in which they can escape the control of their elders. The young, after their own fashion, are searching for truth, beauty and justice.[45]

This also accounts for the prestige, so frequently lamented by the authorities, of nearly all the long-banned products of Western literature, art and fashion among the young of the socialist countries. Within a few years, jazz, jiving, rock and roll, beatnik styles, abstract and pop art have broken through the official barriers to the extent that even the leader of ultra-puritanical Bulgaria, Zhivkov, felt it necessary in December 1967 to preach 'tolerance towards the experimentalism, the crazes of the young, which should not be combated by sectarian methods'.

'Cosmopolitanism', the boundless admiration of the young for everything Western, from Faulkner to the Volkswagen, is on a par with their patriotic, even nationalistic, hypersensitivity, which merges into their rebellion against the Soviet model.[46] In order to establish some kind of control over the rising generation, to reconcile it with the régime, the Bulgarian, Polish and East German leaders appeal increasingly for 'the patriotic and military-patriotic [sic] education of the young'.[47]

The army and para-military organizations are trying to fill the gap left by school and family, to make the young more politically responsible in the sense of identifying the party with the country. This is what the Novotnyite leaders of Czechoslovakia, where the ideological morale of the young reached its lowest ebb, had been trying to do before their defeat. At the Party Congress in 1966, the secretary, Koucky, pointed out that the army was the best recruitment ground for the party; 75 per cent of the officers were, at the time, party members and many young soldiers had been persuaded to apply for membership.[48] However, in 1968, it became clear that the great majority of these recruits to the Novotnyite party supported the cause of renewal.

It was in Bulgaria and Rumania that the national Communist (not to say chauvinistic) indoctrination of the young was carried out with greatest vigour. In Bulgaria, the Congress of the League of Communist Youth in January 1968 was given the theme of 'the great nineteenth-century romantic period of the Bulgarian national renaissance'. Members of the youth organizations received uniforms. However, it was also decided to teach them a 'socialist patriotism, the main feature of which was a strong love for the U.S.S.R. and its Leninist party'.[49] The socialist patriotism propagated by the Rumanian party, on the other hand, is certainly not cordial towards the Soviet Union. The emphasis is placed on the 'traditions of the struggle for independence and national and social freedoms': the enemy being, of course, primarily Russia. But the objective and technique are the same. In December 1967 the Plenum of the Central Committee, on Ceausescu's initiative, decided on the 'modernization' of the Union of Communist Youth, which counted 2,300,000 members. While insisting on patriotic education, the new directives took into account the 'individual' aspirations of the young, 'their enthusiasm for culture, their artistic inclinations, their love of sport, their taste for open-air leisure activities and entertainment'.

The Communist Régimes, the Churches and Religious Belief

In the great struggle for the souls of future generations, the main rival of the ideologists of the Communist countries – apart from the unfavourable influence of the Western way of life and pluralistic culture – is the Christian faith.

If it be in the nature of faith, as Paul Tillich says, that man is entirely bound up with what concerns him absolutely, unconditionally, then one can also talk of a Marxist-Leninist faith.[50] The original Communist *praxis* rests on an act of faith in human potentialities. Of course, this faith claims to be anti-religious, originating in a radical critique of religion, that 'opium of the people'. Atheistic militancy, the aggressive denial of God's existence, lies at the heart of Marxism. The ideal of the new man, whose 'relations with his fellows and with nature are transparent and rational',[51] presupposes the rejection of everything transcendental. At the same time, the most significant and dynamic expressions of Marxist revolutionism – Stalinism and Maoism later on – seem to indicate the impossibility of making a clean break with religion without replacing it by some form of religiosity or idolatry. It seems to be impossible to eliminate God without introducing under a different name and in a disguised form what God represents, that is, the Absolute.

After Berdyaev, Pasternak exposed the religious core of Communism very well. In his view, it was a Judaeo-Christian movement, a modern, materialistic, pseudo-scientific version of the messianism of the past, a grandiose attempt to integrate the Absolute in history, to transform the transcendental into a socio-political immanency, and finally to defeat the demons of egotism and possessiveness by means of a thorough-going economic, social and political revolution. It was these perverted Judaeo-Christian passions that were responsible for the Communists' eagerness to destroy the old order, to lay the economic foundations for a new order where equality, fraternity and justice would reign. The Communist régimes, as Raymond Aron has said, are above all 'ideocracies'. And what is ideocracy other than a secularized derivative of theocracy, just as ideology is a secularized derivative of theology?

This is not the place to embark on a full-scale psychoanalysis of Communism. For this the reader should turn to Jules Monnerot, Ignazio Silone and Arthur Koestler. Suffice it to say that, in the end, it is the refusal of Marxist-Leninist ideologists to acknowledge the roots of their beliefs and the real nature of their faith that largely explains the ambiguous and contradictory character of the relations between the Communist régimes and the Churches and religion. According to Marx, religion is nothing but a mystical cloud that enshrouds social life, as long as it is not transformed through social revolution into 'the work of freely associating men, fully conscious of and in control of their own actions'. It follows that Communism should concentrate on achieving a more rapid transformation of the conditions of work and socio-political relations, of which religion is only a reflection, and wait calmly for this reflection of disappearing conditions to vanish from men's minds.

However, Communist activists were, and are, impelled by a faith which like any religious faith is much more than a mere reflection. It is, quite apart from its transcendental sgnificance, a basic component of the structure of social life, and its disciples wish to spread it among their compatriots, and especially the youth, as rapidly as possible. Totalitarian Communist propaganda, controlling the means of information, education and influence, tends naturally enough to become exclusive, to turn Marxism-Leninism into a monopolistic state ideology (religion), and for that reason clashes with the traditional propaganda of the Churches. This is why the Churches that were tolerated initially and allowed to function constitutionally are now persecuted and their field of action is being systematically restricted.

It has been claimed that the ruthless struggle of the Communist régimes against the Churches during the Stalinist period was justified in that the Churches, and in particular the Catholic Church, represented political forces traditionally linked with the nationalistic right, the former privileged classes and anti-Communist political parties, some of which were associated with Christianity. According to this theory, the *Kulturkampf* between Church and State would have broken out even had the Eastern régimes remained democratic instead of going over wholesale to

Stalinism. This may be so; but in that case it seems likely that the conflict would have been more restrained (as under France's Third Republic), and legality would have been respected. On the other hand, it is conceivable that the Stalinist régimes would have persecuted the Churches, even if the episcopate, the clergy and the believers of the Eastern countries had been more to the left. After all, during the terror, the non-Communist left – especially the Social Democrats – suffered as cruelly as the extreme right. The principal aim of Stalinism in this field was to eliminate the Churches' spiritual autonomy, their ability to pass on a great tradition, their international status and, at the same time, close identification with the national communities. All these things were incompatible with the spiritual and cultural monopoly that the ruling parties demanded.

On the death of Stalin, most of the leaders of the Catholic Church were in prison. The Primate of Croatia, Archbishop Stepinac, had been sentenced in 1946 to sixteen years' hard labour for his alleged collaboration with Ustashi, a Croatian ultra-nationalist group controlled by A. Pavelic. The Primate of Hungary, Cardinal Jozsef Mindszenty, was sentenced in 1949 to hard labour for life after a distressing trial. His successor as the senior of the Hungarian episcopate, Jozsef Groesz, was sentenced to fifteen years in 1951. The Primate of Czechoslovakia, Archbishop Beran, was deposed in 1959, and was kept under house arrest. The Catholic Bishop of Alba Julia in Transylvania, Aron Marton, and the Bishop of Iasi, Anton Durcovici, were thrown into prison in 1950, and the Catholic Archbishop Cisar of Bucharest followed them in 1951. In Poland several bishops were arrested in 1951–2, in contravention of the 1950 agreement between the State and the Church, and in the autumn of 1953 the Primate, Mgr Wyszynski, was placed under house arrest in a convent. The head of the Albanian episcopate, Archbishop Prennhushi, died in prison in 1952. Thousands of priests and refractory monks had been imprisoned or interned throughout the Eastern countries. On the whole, the Orthodox Church, the chief denomination in Yugoslavia, Bulgaria and Rumania, which was traditionally more susceptible to the influence of the Patriarch of Moscow, was better treated.

As for the Calvinists and Lutherans, the Communist leaders had tried to exploit their minority resentment of the Catholics and place weak men at the head of their synods. Thus two bishops, Albert Bereczky and Janos Peter, who collaborated wholeheartedly with the Communist leadership, were made heads of the Hungarian Calvinist Church. The Protestant community got rid of them in October 1956. Janos Peter became Minister of Foreign Affairs in Kadar's government.

After intimidation came infiltration. The Communist governments tried to establish organizations of 'progressive' Catholic priests (the movement of the Czechoslovak Father Plojhar, the Catholic section of the Peace Movement in Hungary and the famous Pax in Poland), by means of which they hoped to destroy Church unity, separate the Church from the Vatican, and exert an influence over the faithful. The most successful of these movements was Pax, led by the former fascist Boleslaw Piasecki, a highly skilled organizer and polemicist. Piasecki's propaganda combined Catholic traditionalism with a predilection for Stalinist authoritarianism and complete devotion to Russia. Powerfully backed by the government and enjoying a virtual monopoly over Catholic publications, Pax was able to attract up to five thousand 'patriot-priests', among whom a certain number were sincere Catholics who hoped to avoid a break between the Communist State and the Church.

Between 1945 and 1952, all the People's Democracies had broken off diplomatic relations with the Vatican, expelled the papal nuncios, and condemned the existing concordats. The Catholic press was reduced to a minimum. Only in Poland did religious education remain theoretically compulsory, but even there the authorities found a thousand and one excuses to flout the law. Catholic schools ceased to exist, with the sole exception again of Poland, where, in accordance with the 1950 agreement, 600 infant schools, 300 primary schools, 400 secondary schools, and the Catholic University of Lublin continued to function.

The extent of the damage to the Churches, especially the Catholic Church, in the Eastern countries can be gauged from the example of Czechoslovakia. Before the attempt to regularize the situation in April 1968, the position of the Church was objectively examined. At that time, only four of the twelve Roman Catholic dioceses (six in Bohemia-Moravia, six in Slovakia, and one Byzantine-Slav diocese) were headed by bishops. The Byzantine-Slav (Greek Orthodox) diocese had been annexed by the Russian Orthodox Church in 1950, on Moscow's request, and despite the protest of the faithful. Eight bishops had been sentenced to terms of imprisonment (four of them died in prison) on the most various pretexts. Others had been deprived of their sees by administrative means. (One of these, Archbishop Beran of Prague, who was freed in 1963, was forced into exile at the beginning of 1965.)

In addition, 1,500 priests were prevented from practising as ministers. Though not legally abolished, the religious communities were in effect eliminated: in a single night all the monks were deported and interned. At the same time, 2,000 nuns were ejected and forced to work under conditions of strict surveillance in state factories or farms. All the seminaries were closed (two re-opened in 1963). An anti-religious campaign of unparalleled severity was launched in the same year (1950) by the ultra-Stalinist Minister of Culture, Kopecky (who died in 1961), following the 'exposure' of the alleged 'spurious miracle' of Cihost, where the crucifix over the tabernacle bowed each time the priest Toufar invoked the name of God. When arrested, the priest admitted having caused this miracle by operating a concealed system of pulleys. An examination of the court record of his trial revealed that the priest had confessed under torture, and that the mechanism that had been discovered had been fitted by the police.[52]

Also in 1950 the government set up two theological faculties, one for Bohemia-Moravia and the other for Slovakia, but reserved the right to select the professors and senior lecturers. Religious teaching was restricted to the primary schools, and frequently obstructed. There were three authorized Catholic periodicals, but these were run by members of the only permitted Catholic body, Plojhar's clerical Peace Movement, controlled by the Communist party.[53] The number of churches in use declined from 10,473 in 1948 to 3,200 in 1965, and the number of priests from 7,040 to 4,700.

Those of the Communist leaders who took the trouble to reflect realized as early as 1953 that the persecution of the Church and the anti-religious campaigns were merely a further cause of discontent. It had not produced the desired result in a real reduction of the Church's influence and that of religion generally. What, indeed, emerged from the few inquiries carried out on this subject in the sixties,[54] and from the many articles published in the Eastern press, was that, if the process of de-christianization made some progress in these countries, this progress was, on the whole, slower than in certain capitalist countries where the Churches were subject to no persecution.

'Strange as it may seem, it is likely that we atheists are doing more to preserve the religious spirit than the secular bourgeois states, not to mention those that use religion openly and cynically for their political ends,' wrote the Kadarist Lajos Mesterhazi (*Nepszabadsag*, 25 July 1963). A liberal Czechoslovak Marxist sociologist came to the same conclusion. 'If we continue with our bureaucratic methods,' he wrote, 'we will have more believers in the next century than we have now.'[55]

To illustrate this, we give the results of a few surveys. In 1965, in northern Moravia, 30 per cent of the population under twenty were atheists, 30 per cent believers, and 40 per cent undecided. But 58 per cent of the people questioned stated that they were members of a Church (44 per cent Roman Catholics, 9 per cent Protestants, 4 per cent members of the Czech Church and 1 per cent belonging to other denominations). The proportion of atheists was highest among qualified people, and practising believers were numerous among women, elderly people, peasants and small-town inhabitants.[56] In 1966, out of 250,000 people questioned in the industrial region of Ostrava (northern Moravia), 30 per cent were believers, 30 per cent atheists, and 40 per cent undecided.[57] In Poland, a radio survey produced the following results: 78.3 per cent of the 2,746 young people between the ages of fifteen and twenty-four questioned said they were Catholics, and 4.3 per cent atheists.[58] In the same year, according to an inquiry carried out in the workmen's garden cities, 48 per cent were practising believers, 28.5 per cent believers who did not attend Mass regularly, and 9.5 per cent atheists.

The general impression of observers who have visited Eastern Europe – especially the basically Catholic countries like Slovakia, Poland, Hungary, Croatia and Slovenia – is that the number of practising believers is at least as great as before the persecution and that persecution has made the Churches more popular.[59] Communism has not won the battle against religious belief, and this failure largely accounts for the fact that, after 1962, most of the Communist régimes responded to approaches from Popes John XXIII and Paul VI, and tried to normalize relations with the Vatican by putting 'competitive coexistence' with religion on a new basis.

Here, too, the pioneering roles of the Hungarians Imre Nagy and Gyoergy Lukacs, the former in politics and the latter in the field of ideology, should be remembered. In his programme speech to Parliament in Budapest on 4 July 1953 Nagy declared: 'We must be more patient in religious matters. Administrative methods such as have been used in the past are inappropriate here. The government is adopting the principle of toleration, the methods of which are persuasion and elucidation; it condemns the use of administrative methods or other means of coercion, and will not tolerate them.' In June 1955 the Hungarian government suspended Cardinal Mindszenty's sentence. He was neither pardoned nor rehabilitated, but kept under house arrest and allowed to receive the senior bishop, Mgr Czapik. In May 1956 Mgr Groesz was freed. The Cardinal might have been treated likewise had he not insisted on full rehabilitation and reinstatement in his see at Esztergom. However, in October 1956, Imre Nagy's new government did rehabilitate him. In these stirring days, he returned to the capital and behaved very tactlessly. On 4 November, the day the Soviet army occupied Budapest, he sought refuge in the United States Embassy, where he remains today, despite the efforts of the Vatican and the Hungarian government to settle the matter.

Gyoergy Lukacs, for his part, was the first official Marxist thinker to discover (ten years before Gilbert Mury, Roger Garaudy, and well before Lombardo Radice) what, for the Marxists, had up till then been the *terra incognita* of modern Catholic and Protestant theology and, in particular, the research undertaken by Christian theologians in Marxist anthropology. Rejecting persecution and isolationism as signs of an inferiority complex and defeatism, lack of faith in the creativity and intellectual competitiveness of Marxism, Lukacs courageously came out in favour of an open and honest discussion.[60]

In Poland, the *détente* between Church and State began later. October 1956 saw Wyszynski back in Warsaw after his August pilgrimage to Czestochowa, when over a million Poles from all parts of the country made a spectacular demonstration of their attachment to the Church. When Gomulka came to power, he negotiated an agreement with the Cardinal, who showed himself sensitive to the critical situation in Poland. It was largely due to the Church's help and moderating influence that Gomulka was able to get the situation under control. In 1959, after the death of Mgr Stepinac, who for a number of years had been under house arrest, the Yugoslav government also began to regularize relations with the Church and the Vatican. Marshal Tito made an unprecedented gesture when he authorized an official funeral for the Cardinal.

All these steps have opened a new era in the relations between most of the Eastern Communist states and the Churches, especially the Catholic Church. Stalinist rigidity has persisted, in fact, only in three countries. The first is Albania, where after the 1966 Party Congress, under the impulse of the Chinese cultural revolution, militant atheism was carried to its extreme. All the churches and mosques (2,169 in all) were closed and turned into cultural centres. In October 1967 Albania celebrated the fiftieth anniversary of the October Revolution and proudly proclaimed itself 'the first atheist state in the world'.

In 1967 Bulgaria, where the Patriarch Kiril and Archimandrite Gorazd had acted as zealous propagandists for the régime, announced that 'the great majority of the people have already freed themselves from the shackles of religion and religious morality'.[61]

In East Germany, Ulbricht and his right-hand man in religious matters, Seigewasser, have been able to depend, in their efforts to assimilate the Lutheran Church and separate it from Federal Germany's Evangelical Church, on the compliance of Moritz Mitzenheim, Bishop of Thuringen. Not that this prevented

'Christian work circles' that were believed to be completely submissive from asking Ulbricht in August–September 1968 to withdraw troops from Czechoslovakia; nor Lutheran pastors from sending a message of sympathy to the churches of Czechoslovakia from the pulpit on two Sundays running.[62]

It was Yugoslavia that went furthest towards acceptance. In June 1966 it signed an agreement with the Vatican on the exchange of representatives. This was the first time a Communist state had concluded an agreement with the Holy See. The seeds sown by John XXIII, described in Belgrade as 'the greatest Pope of all time', have taken root and borne fruit after his death.[63] In January 1968 Tito was one of the first heads of state in the world to support the Pope's proposal for a world peace day, and the 1966 agreement was confirmed on the occasion of the visit of the head of the Yugoslav government, Mika Spiljak, to Paul VI. Despite the cordial relations existing at the top, some difficulties remain. Communist authorities, especially in Croatia and Slovenia, worry endlessly about the encroachments of the leaders of the Church – Cardinal Szeper, Primate of Yugoslavia, and Mgr J. Pogacznik, Archbishop of Ljubljana – into politics. 'The difficulty', Pogacznik has said in his own defence, 'is that the atheists persist in treating the Church as a political and social organization. They cannot understand its essentially supernatural character.'[64] In fact, referring to the general lines laid down by the last Council, the Croatian and Slovene bishops called for State neutrality in matters of education, and asked to be given radio and television time. They restored the Catholic youth associations, and organized pilgrimages. The Croatian and Slovene Churches, taking advantage of the appeal of novelty, and imitating the modernism of the Italian and Austrian Churches, have swiftly recovered their lost ground. The failing Communist youth organizations, bureaucratized and disillusioned, have not as yet discovered the means of counter-attacking, nor have they found any way of co-operating smoothly with the religious organizations.

In the Communist countries in the process of liberalizing and reorganizing themselves, though an opposition is still prohibited, the Churches, and particularly the best organized and strongest of them, the Catholic Church, are tending once again, by the very nature of things, to become a political force. This force concentrates within itself, besides the unsatisfied spiritual hunger, all anti-governmental currents. The case of Poland after 1956 clearly demonstrates the endless causes for conflict inherent in this situation. In a letter to *Le Monde* (24 April 1968), Cardinal Wyszynski protested against Western commentaries attributing political motives to his pastoral work. This was in connection with the campaign he launched in February 1968 against the dangers to the Church and its believers of atheist propaganda, incitement to hatred, demoralization and alcoholism. The Cardinal denied that he wanted to become a leader of a political opposition. And, indeed, Wyszynski's incessant demands, becoming increasingly uncompromising after 1957, rarely exceeded the bounds of what the Catholic Church and the Churches in general legally enjoy in the non-Communist, pluralistic countries.

However, in Poland, with its minority dictatorship, this type of demand often takes on a subversive character. The Church appears as the rival to the party, aspiring to the succession, and the true embodiment of the national spirit. Cardinal Wyszynski, who seems to have grown more intransigent in his long struggle with the government, has progressed from liberalism to an almost Spanish integrism, and has missed no opportunity (e.g. General de Gaulle's visit to Poland or the thousandth anniversary of the foundation of the State) to stress the basic Catholicity of the Polish nation and state, as well as his own guardian role.

Nevertheless, numerically speaking the Polish Church appears to be in a flourishing state. In 1956 Poland had 6,558 parishes as against 5,224 before the war, 13,000 churches as against 7,527, 17,700 priests (two thirds more than before the war) and 28,500 monks and nuns. It possessed many seminaries, a Catholic university and a theological academy in Warsaw.[65]

The Communists accuse the Cardinal of wanting to call the separation of Church and State in question, and himself to replace the State's representatives (as in December 1965, when, in the name of the Polish episcopate, he had sent a letter of conciliation and pardon to the German bishops). Wyszynski, on his part, accuses the government of not honouring the concessions it made in 1956 and of trying to create a nation of atheists (sermon of 3 December 1967). Indeed, in January 1961, religious education once again had been banned in the schools,[66] and processions were prohibited. In December 1966 four seminaries were closed. The State insisted that education dispensed by the free schools be controlled by its officers. The construction of a church in the new town of Nowa Huta was delayed. In addition, Wyszynski blamed the government for encouraging the Pax organization and Piasecki's activities, the latter having sacrificed the Church's interests to his own political ones.

In 1967–8 we find an embittered Gomulka, harassed by the Partisans, disappointed with his people, crossing swords with a hero-Cardinal who might just have stepped out of a Montherlant play, and in whom the fanaticism of the great prelates of the Counter-Reformation lives again. Both men operate from positions of strength – all the government's attempts to drive a wedge between the intransigent Wyszynski and the more moderate bishops having failed – and both are aware of the limits of their strength.

This curious conflict is one of the most striking aspects of contemporary Poland. It springs from the imposition of an anomalous political and social régime on countries where the Church, despite its medieval characteristics, appears to many agnostics, who nevertheless cherish freedom and justice, as a haven, a refuge from the intolerant totalitarianism of the State. Yet in 1968, at the time of the anti-intellectual, anti-Semitic unrest stirred up by the Partisans, the Church disappointed liberal opinion. Wyszynski did not bring his influence to bear in condemning the anti-intellectual and anti-Semitic repression; he did nothing to defend the liberal Catholic Znak group, which remained loyal to him while trying to co-operate as far as possible with the party and government.[67]

In Hungary, where the Catholics represent 60 per cent of the population, the coexistence of State and Church has been more successful, no doubt because of the greater open-mindedness of the authorities on the one hand and of the bishops on the other. After a year of negotiations, and leaving the question of Cardinal Mindszenty open, the Hungarian government signed a concordat with the Vatican in 1964, dropping its plan to impose 'peace priests' on the Church as bishops. The Holy See, for its part, agreed that the bishops appointed after consultation with the government should swear an oath of allegiance to the constitution of the Republic. However, the activities of the diocesan committees are still closely supervised by the State Office for Ecclesiastical Affairs, and the state still controls the Protestant Churches.[68]

In Rumania there was a *détente* between the State and the Catholic Church at the end of 1967, following a visit of Cardinal König, Archbishop of Austria, who had previously played a part in bringing about a rapprochement between Budapest and the Vatican. Bishop Aron Marton was allowed to move freely about his diocese of Alba Julia, and the Patriarch Justin, head of the Rumanian Orthodox Church, loyal to his government but imbued with the ecumenical spirit, came out publicly in favour of lifting 'certain restrictions' on the Catholic Church. In January 1968 the rapprochement between Bucharest and the Holy See was strengthened by the visit of Prime Minister Maurer and Foreign Minister Manescu to the Pope.

Finally, in Czechoslovakia, Novotny's fall opened the way to making amends for the mistakes committed. The new government, as an immediate token of goodwill, appointed Mrs Kadlecova, a liberal Marxist expert on religious matters, to head the Religious Department of the Ministry of Culture. The 'silent Church' was allowed to speak again. The Catholic Clergy for Peace movement, a crypto-Communist organization, was dissolved and replaced by a new organization, the Movement for Conciliar Renewal. Mgr Tomasek, Apostolic Administrator of the Archbishopric of Prague (in the absence of the exiled Mgr Beran), a man known for his moderation and honesty, took over direction of the organization personally.

According to Mgr Tomasek, the negotiations between the government and the four active bishops begun in April revealed a mutual desire for settling the painful and complicated dispute.[69] The diocese of Tresov (Byzantine-Slav) was restored, to the great joy of the faithful who had remained secret adherents for eighteen years. The banished bishops were reinstated; the officials who had supervised the activities of the bishops, even censoring their correspondence and attending all their meetings, were dismissed. Catholic periodicals once again came under the control of the Church.[70] Preparations were made for negotiations with the Vatican on the appointment of bishops to replace deceased prelates and for a resumption of diplomatic relations.

Czech and Slovak believers celebrated Easter 1968 in an atmosphere of renewed hope. However, the Soviet intervention slowed down progress in this field as in others. Yielding to Soviet pressure, the Czechoslovak government has banned the Movement of Conciliar Renewal as well as the 231 Club (of victims of persecution) and the Club of Committed Non-Party People.[71]

The Collapse of Socialist Realism and the Literary and Artistic Revival

The September 1956 Hungarian Writers' Congress, the June 1967 Czechoslovak Writers' Congress and the late February 1968 Extraordinary Congress of Polish Writers are all milestones in the pioneering struggle of literary men and their allies in the world of art and science for the liberalization of the Communist régimes. In this battle Communist writers and artists were in the front line. They realized fairly soon that they could not wage a successful struggle for freedom of expression without demanding the same freedom for those creative artists who did not share their ideas, and furthermore that freedom of expression was an integral part of freedom as such. Censorship, party control of literary life, was simply an expression – the most striking one – of the totalitarian attempt to deprive society, all the social groups and classes, of independence.

In turning their association into bodies 'as free and diversified as possible', 'living unions, run in a democratic way',[72] the writers created the first models of socialist pluralism, the first centres of independent thought and activity.[73] Political and social reform began everywhere with reform in the field of culture, with the writers' gaining of independence. Students, young people and intellectuals, hungry for truth and sincerity, soon recognized their real spiritual leaders among these writers.

This is not the place to list all the authors who came to the fore during the period under consideration; it will be enough simply to trace the main lines of development. This has varied from country to country, and everywhere has followed an erratic course.

Between 1956 and 1959, literature and the arts enjoyed an exceptional freedom in Poland that was the envy of all creative artists throughout the socialist countries. Then the climate worsened, and the rift between the government and the men of culture steadily widened; finally, in February and March 1968, there was a serious clash between the majority of writers and the party bureaucracy.

Between 1962 and 1965 Hungary seemed an oasis of toleration and a model, if not of absolute freedom, at least of freedom that was not too closely controlled (this distinction was drawn by the Hungarian exiled writer Paul Ignotus). Then, here too, the authorities began putting on the pressure. After 1963 it was Czechoslovak literary and artistic life that enjoyed a period of revival. In 1967, 'frontier incidents' between the commissars and the authors blew up into a sharp struggle that ended with the victory of the writers and the abolition of censorship, an 'unbelievable and crazy' development in the eyes of the bureaucracies of the fraternal countries.[74]

In the U.S.S.R., East Germany, Poland and Bulgaria, the state did not relax its grip on intellectual life. Once again, it was the East German leadership that distinguished itself by its Prussian rigidity. Party ideologists were continually reminding writers and artists of their 'responsibilities to the first German worker's and peasant's state', their duty to concentrate on 'describing the possibilities for socialist solutions'.[75] Despite their distinction and their irreproachable militant past, the best East German writers – Stefan Heym, the singer Wolf Bierman, the poet Stefan Hermlin, and the novelists Anna Seghers and Christa Wolf – were periodically called to order by official critics for their slightest deviations from the official aesthetics.

The situation was similar in ultra-orthodox Bulgaria, where Zhivkov took a paternal interest in literature and the arts, an interest that was sometimes repressive, sometimes permissive, modelled on that of his patron Khrushchev. No sooner did the latter launch an attack on the modernists, abstract artists and pessimists than Zhivkov, too, called a meeting of the writers and artists of his country on 14 April 1963 to advise them 'not to stray from socialist realism'. Writers who, like Boris Delchev, had the audacity to suggest that the Central Committee was perhaps not competent to censor literature, were reprimanded. Literature continued to be regarded as one of the most significant ideological weapons, an instrument of patriotic education. The Committee for Art and Culture that was set up in 1967 re-opened an offensive on the cultural front.[76] However, the literary and artistic stagnation produced by this bigoted state control forced Zhivkov to loosen the reins a little. The official critics, the guardians of ideology, were urged to show greater indulgence towards writers and artists, and to refrain from treating them like 'mentally retarded children'.[77]

In Rumania, too, a certain relaxation in control was noticeable after 1965. 'We ask our men of letters and our artists to place their talent at the service of socialist construction, but they are at liberty to determine how they should write, paint and compose', announced Ceausescu in June 1966. Avant-garde poets like the 'Rumanian Mallarmé', Ion Barbu, and the spiritualistic Lucien Blaga have been rehabilitated; the cultural past and Western contributions to civilization are regarded in a more sympathetic light; the magazines *Secolul* and *Amfiteatru* are more receptive to modernist ideas.

The débâcle of socialist realism, initiated in 1952 by the great Croatian novelist and playwright Miroslav Krleza, is spreading. Its orthodox supporters are contenting themselves with a rearguard action, periodically issuing warnings – as on 1 February 1968 at the meeting of the heads of the Warsaw Pact writers' unions in Sofia – against 'imperialism's ideological diversion, its attempt to sow discord among the intellectuals, and especially among the writers'. The Communist leaders, anxious about this cultural development, are aware of the artificial and sterile nature of the aesthetic dogma in whose name they have tried to get the highly-paid creative artists to accept an arbitrary optimism, a simple glorification of the ruling apparatus, a vision of the external world based on its precepts, a literature and art devoted wholly to edification. Of course the Soviets, especially after 1965, have continued to use their influence against liberalization, and the Sinyavsky–Daniel, Ginzburg, and Litvinov–Daniel trials have encouraged those who believe in repression. On the other hand, the champions of pluralism and of cultural autonomy find support among the 'open Marxists' of the West, who, like Roger Garaudy and Louis Aragon, are extending the idea of socialist realism so that it embraces 'everything human', every style, everything of literary and artistic value that is not directly counter-revolutionary.

A renaissance is in the offing. The threads that were dropped in 1948 are being taken up again. Well-meaning and opportunistic mediocrities, who as mouthpieces of the state philosophy had held the limelight, are giving way to those with real talent. In Hungary writers, poets and dramatists who were long kept in the background, are coming into their own: for example Lajos Kassak, Milan Fuest (who died in 1967), Janos Pilinszky (a Catholic), Sandor Weoeres (an esoteric writer), Laszlo Nemeth (a populist), Tibor Dery (a revisionist Communist), and Miklos Meszoely (a surrealist). In Poland real writers and poets are praised, people like Aleksander Wat (who died in 1967), Zbigniew Herbert, Roman Brandstäter, the grand old lady of classical realism Maria Dombrowska, Slonimski, Andrzejewski and Mrozek. In Rumania, Marin Preda, the author of a great peasant epic, has been enthusiastically received by the public.

There is a new diversity for which it is hard to find a common denominator. However, the dominant feature of the literary life of the Eastern countries is the 'remembrance of things past', the search for the image of a reality that has been suppressed, an unconquered past. Solzhenitsyn's masterpiece, *One Day in the Life of Ivan Denisovich*, was the first and most outstanding expression of this search. The literature of the Eastern countries in the sixties is above all a literature of reconstruction and elucidation of the war years, the occupation, the liberation, the purges, the internments, collectivization and terroristic expropriation, the useless sacrifices and the suppressed anger and sorrow. The works of the Slovak Mnacko (*Deferred Reports; The Taste for*

Power; *Death's Name in Engelchen*); of the Hungarians Jozsef Lengyel (*From Beginning to End*) and Gyula Oszko (*The Seventeenth Sunday*); of the Bulgarian poet Nicola Lankov; of the Rumanians Ion Lancranjan (*Solar Eclipse*) and Marin Preda (*Mirometii, I-II*); of the Poles Andrzejewski (*The Twilight of a World*) and the playwright Slawomir Mrozek; of the Yugoslavs Cosic and Bulatovic; and a whole series of neo-realist or fantasy films (Wajda's *Ashes and Diamonds*, Jancso's *The Cold Days*, Nemec's *The Feast and the Guests*) are the most characteristic manifestations of this.

Writers and film-makers are the exponents of a kind of collective psychoanalysis. Those who are Communists are concerned with ridding themselves of their guilt complex,[78] while the non-Communists, through irony and sarcasm, are taking their revenge for twenty years of silence and humiliation. The young, who are neither accomplices nor victims, express their amazement at the aberrations of their elders, and are calling them to account. A Slovak writer has rightly compared the literary and artistic movement of the sixties with the romantic movement after the French Revolution and the Napoleonic wars.[79] As in the great period of romanticism, creative artists are faced with the immense task of rendering an account of the upheavals in the social order, the innumerable individual and collective tragedies, of exploring and defining a new, unreal, confused, contradictory reality. One has the impression in reading the best works and seeing the most striking films of the Eastern countries that their creators are being driven by an irresistible force making them act as witnesses in a vast, unique trial, the trial of socialism betrayed, of faith scoffed at, of conscience violated. It is as though this trial were the means appointed for surmounting a past where evil, lying and cruelty in a variety of unexpected guises had overwhelmed man. The literature and art of the socialist countries can be summed up in the exclamation : 'Let all be light.'[80]

The Great Battle against Censorship

Printed, spoken and filmed journalism, with its double purpose of providing news of what is happening inside and outside the country, and acting as a medium for the expression of individual and collective opinions, is both a political and cultural activity.[81] Like the writers, journalists in the Communist countries enjoy a privileged socio-economic status.[82] However, what initially drives so many writers, the best of them, into opposition, is the ethical concern to a certain extent inherent in the profession; the same goes for the journalists. The Stalinist system, by reducing them to party propagandists, prevented them from acting as spokesmen of public opinion, from speaking their minds, and from telling the truth as they saw it. It stopped them from doing their job, and turned them into cyphers. This is why one finds so many journalists in the post-1953 period struggling with the writers against censorship in Hungary, Poland and then Czechoslovakia.

Indeed, a few years of totalitarian rule between 1948 and 1953 turned a living, imaginative, varied and interesting press, which had no cause to envy its Western equivalent, into a press that was as dull, uniform, tedious, badly written as that of the Soviets and their dependents in the West. Each People's Democracy had its *Pravda*, *Izvestia*, *Komsomolskaya Pravda*, *Trud*, and a magazine like Moscow's *Komunist*, all following the same pattern, and publishing endless statements by official personages of the country and of the socialist camp. The only items of any interest, apart from articles on sports and chess, were the editorials and leading articles written in a coded language, from which initiates and Kremlinologists, after careful deciphering, could get some idea of the aims of the leaders, the conflicts that divided them, and the purges that were in prospect.

As in the other spheres of cultural life, the contrast between quantity and quality was striking. The leaders took pride in the substantial increase in the number of publications and their readership, in radio programmes and in the development of other media. In Czechoslovakia every family had a radio in 1960, and one in two had a television set. Circulation of daily newspapers reached four million (one million in Slovakia). But press and radio standards were very low, their main function being propaganda; everyone realized that the public had no faith in what was offered by way of political news, but increasingly turned to foreign sources : Radio Free Europe, the Voice of America, the

B.B.C., West German and Austrian stations, whose broadcasts, as a result of the policy of coexistence, were jammed to an ever-decreasing extent. It is this foreign competition that has finally forced the leaders to try to make their press more attractive and informative. An example was set by the Soviet Adzhubey, Khrushchev's son-in-law, who tried to modernize the layout of *Izvestia* and make its contents more varied. But the main obstacle to an improvement was, and remains, the deeply rooted desire of the Communist leaders to operate annd deliberate in the greatest secrecy possible, to disclose nothing of their quarrels, and to present a façade of unity and infallibility at home and abroad, even if the facts belied it. To give only a few examples: the proceedings of the famous meeting of the Hungarian Central Committee in June 1953 which led to Rakosi's first defeat were never made public. It is true that in October 1956 the Polish press was allowed to publish the proceedings of the Central Committee session which brought Gomulka to power, but this was not to prove a precedent. Likewise in Czechoslovakia, the Central Committee discussions in January 1968 were kept secret despite the strong current of liberalization.

It is understandable that one of the liberal Communist demands should be concerned with the publicizing of the deliberations of those bodies concerned with the most important decisions. In this respect, the great conflict between Czechoslovak journalists and officials over the 1967 press law takes on a particular significance. This had introduced preventive censorship, responsibility for which was vested in a government agency called the Central Publications Administration. This body, on which the journalists were not represented, had the right to prevent the publication of any information that might prejudice the country's defence, security or economy, and also 'other interests of society'. It was this last point, the vagueness of which opened the gate to arbitrary interference, on which the journalists concentrated their attack. They insisted, as has already been noted, that the 1967 law was far more reactionary than Francis Joseph's law of 1867. Hendrych, the chairman of the party's ideological committee, indignant at such a comparison, upbraided the journalists 'for mixing up freedom and anarchy, democracy and liberalism, socialism and bourgeois concessionism'.[83] However, after the January 1968 Plenum progress was made towards revision of the law.[84] After the end of February the newspapers, radio and television took practically no notice of the recommendations of the censor and the authorities. They had become free.

This victory turned out to be short-lived, but in the history of the Communist countries it marks a turning-point, a sunrise that will be remembered in spite of the eclipse that followed. On 13 June 1968, the Czechoslovak government actually abolished censorship, disbanded the Central Office of Publications, and decided that senior editors of newspapers, magazines, and radio programmes would be fully responsible in law for the news published or broadcast.

Dubcek kept the promise he had made in January. In so doing, he showed considerable courage, as, according to *Pravda* on 22 August, great pressure had been brought to bear on him since the Dresden conference in March by the Soviets and their allies to put the political and literary press in order. But the action programme that emerged from the discussions of the March–April Central Committee Plenum confirmed the promises of freedom, and the Czechoslovak press, radio and television made extensive use of this freedom even before it became law.

Summoned to appear in Moscow on 4 May and confronted with a bulky file of incriminating evidence compiled with the help of Chervonenko and Udaltsov, Dubcek and Cernik, it seems, admitted (in a secret protocol which, however, was leaked by *Pravda*) that 'the negative aspects raised in the press were not of purely internal significance, but concerned the fraternal countries, especially the U.S.S.R. and Poland.' Furthermore, at the Central Committee Plenum at the end of May, in order to appease the Soviets, Dubcek urged the press to behave responsibly, and not to make the government's job more difficult. However, according to *Pravda*, the steps taken 'had remained dead letters'. The press, in fact, did help Dubcek and the progressive wing of the party by assisting them to mobilize public opinion, to give the militants a voice, and to resist the neo-Stalinists. It played the major part in the transformation of the Czechoslovak Communist party, and in making Dubcek, Svoboda, Cernik and

Smrkovsky popular leaders. As the Soviets fully realized, press, radio and television were largely instrumental in the crushing defeat suffered by conservative candidates in the elections of delegates to the Extraordinary Congress in June and July. It was the press which, by publishing Vaculik's '2,000 Words' and then organizing the campaign in support of Dubcek, literally created national unity.

It is understandable, therefore, that in wanting to disarm Dubcek and stifle the sovereignty of the Czechoslovak state and party, the Five should, in the first instance, have attacked the press, radio and television, which according to the ultimatum of 15 July, had 'fallen into the hands of anti-socialist and revisionist forces'. The ultimatum demanded that the Czechoslovak party re-impose control over all the means of mass information, and this was repeated at Cierna and Bratislava. According to *Pravda*, the Czechoslovak representatives 'gave assurances that they would take specific steps', but 'they did nothing'. Hence the need for intervention, leading to the Moscow order of 26 August.

What an admission of defeat on the part of leaders claiming to head an international revolutionary movement, that, in order to preserve the legacy of Marx and Lenin, and to help man to free himself from slavery, they had to send 60,000 men into a socialist country to force its government to muzzle a press in whose freedom this government saw no danger for itself! This demonstration of its fundamental hostility to freedom must undoubtedly have harmed the Soviet régime in the long run, and have nullified the effects of its victory over the weekly *Literarni Listy*, whose disappearance has been one of the main results of the invasion.

The Czechoslovak leaders are still trying to reconcile the course they are obliged to follow with the possibility, theoretically admitted by the Soviets, of 'not returning to the situation existing before January 1968'. Press and information offices have been set up in the Czech lands and in Slovakia, but it is still hoped that their activities will be limited to supervision only. What is envisaged is a kind of self-censorship, a censorship in the hands of the editorial delegates. But the Soviet guardians are watchful. They increase their demands daily, condemning the slightest deviation. They have secured the dismissal of the heads of radio and television, Zdenek Hejzlar and Jiri Pelikan, and they have not forgotten the great deeds of the clandestine radio stations and newspapers which, during the week of 21–8 August, frustrated every attempt to break the nation's spirit.

'The re-establishment of censorship', announced the Prague delegate, A. Polednak, over Czechoslovak television on 27 September 1968, 'is a very sad duty ... unavoidable but temporary.' Czechoslovak journalists and writers are being forced to relearn the language of silence and symbolism. Some of them – Goldstuecker, Mnacko, Budin (those most under fire) – have chosen exile. Those who remain are aware that they are running the risk of suppression, against which, so they believe, only 'public and recognized international guarantees' could give them any protection.[85] But who is in a position to give them such guarantees? What can public opinion, what can Italian and French Communists and progressives do to protect the Solzhenitsyns, Sinyavskys, Modzelewskis, Kolakowskis, Mihajlovs and Istvan Bibos against their inquisitors?

From the dissolution of the Hungarian writers' union and the banning by Gomulka of *Po Prostu* in 1957 to the re-establishment of censorship in Czechoslovakia, the history of the press in the Eastern countries on the way to liberalization has been one in which journalists and writers, who have made themselves the voice of public opinion, have had to bear the brunt of government disapproval.

It is no exaggeration to say that the position of the press is a barometer, an index of the political and socio-cultural situation as a whole. At the present moment, control of the press and all media is as rigid in East Germany, Bulgaria and the Soviet Union as it was under Stalin. A more lively presentation has had only a superficial effect. The Polish press after 1957 first retreated into a boring provincialism, and then returned to the most aggressive and stupid Zhdanovism. The way in which the Warsaw papers described and commented on the student demonstrations of March 1968, attributing them to a 'German-Zionist plot', the way they handled the Czechoslovak affair in August and September, provide innumerable quotations for future anthologists wishing to illustrate how the limits of decency were exceeded, and where the art of lying received its most cynical expression. It also demonstrated the weakness, the reversibility of progress unaccompanied by institutional guarantees.

The Hungarian press reflects the mediocre, apprehensive, shameful paternalism of the country's leaders who, nevertheless, have given the nonconformists some leeway by permitting a few avant-garde magazines with a limited circulation to exist. They have admitted that 'Marxism may do without a monopoly in the fields of ideology and culture.'[86]

It is to the credit of Yugoslavia, and more especially of Czechoslovakia, that they have become subjects of research for a new model of liberal socialism, where organizations and professional groups, if not groups of individuals freely associating – trade unions, youth bodies, writers' unions, parties – are 'allowed to publish newspapers and periodicals and influence public opinion free from external interference'.[87]

Ideas once born cannot be destroyed by tanks. The élite among the East European peoples will not forget the stirring part played by the press, radio and television in awakening the national conscience, in the national and democratic integration of the Hungarians and Poles in 1956, the Slovaks in 1953, and the Czechs and Slovaks in 1967–8. The scholars and intellectuals have made history. The seed sown by them will bear fruit.[88]

Prospects

We shall end with a number of observations, in place of a formal conclusion, for how can one conclude a story that is in the process of unfolding, where any comment may be contradicted tomorrow?

In the autumn of 1952, I cautiously suggested that the dictatorship of the proletariat, the revolution from above in the Soviet manner, did not seem to have provided an adequate and lasting solution to the problems of security, sovereignty, economic modernization and cultural development facing the East European peoples and governments after the war. The second period of revolutionary development, with which we have been concerned here, has confirmed me in this opinion, although it cannot be denied that there have been a few rather ephemeral improvements.

The people and governments of the Eastern countries propose, but it is always the Soviet leaders who dispose, as has been shown by events in Hungary and Czechoslovakia. The People's Democracies are, as it were, caught in the Soviet net. Djilas and Chou En-lai, elaborating on the theses of the unorthodox Trotsky, are no doubt right in claiming that the Soviet Union is no longer a revolutionary state – this role has been taken over by China – but something far more powerful and menacing: a conquering world power, an empire.

After an initial period of tentative and contradictory decolonialization under Khrushchev, the Soviet leaders since 1965 seem to have opted for a kind of cynical, aggressive neocolonialism or neo-hegemonism, as indicated by the Czechoslovak invasion. This has shown that, as far as liberalization is concerned, the post-1956 Hungarian model, which entails absolute loyalty to the Kremlin and is necessarily preceded by a disciplining of the intellectuals, is the most Moscow will tolerate. According to the new doctrine as expressed in the 1968 documents, amounting basically to a reassertion of the Stalinist, Zhdanovist and Cominform creed of 1948, the Communist leaders in power (and also those not in power) are responsible, not to their own party and people (that is of secondary importance), but to the International – the Soviet leadership posing as the latter's agent.[1]

The U.S.S.R. has shown that it will not shrink from the use of force in pursuing its aggressive policy against recalcitrant nations, however moderate they might be. It is now clear that the peaceful transition from Stalinism to a socialism that is democratic and national, a peaceful transformation directed from above, which was the aim of the Czechoslovak leaders between January and August 1968, is not possible, so long as power in the Soviet Union remains in the hands of a neo-Stalinist, neo-colonialist group.

Party dictatorship after the Soviet model is not for the peoples of the Eastern countries. What they all want is socialist democracy – independence leading to a free association of federated states.[2] But it will be impossible to experiment with such a solution before there has been a considerable political shift in the Soviet Union itself.

In so far as these countries have become part of the world Communist system, the Communist political élite in the People's Democracies has been stricken by the great crisis in international Communism brought about by de-Stalinization. In unmasking the idol to reveal the cruelty and madness of the father figure, Khrushchev released unknown forces, feelings, doubts, grievances, aspirations hidden till then. After the great purges of 1935–8 and 1948–52, it was thought that Bukharinism, Trotskyism, nationalism, the unorthodox Communist doctrines, had been wiped out, but in 1953 it became clear that they had only been pushed under the surface: ideologists who had long been on the Index, and politicians who had been cast into secret dungeons, were rehabilitated and returned to active life. It seems that Khrushchev would have liked to rehabilitate even Bukharin, but that he was prevented from doing so by his colleagues. The Hungarian Imre Nagy was a convinced Bukharinist, and the Italian Communists have started treating Bukharin and Trotsky as Church Fathers. In the spring of 1968, theoreticians of the Czechoslovak party discovered Isaac Deutscher's *Stalin*[3] and preparations were made for the publication of a duly annotated edition of Trotsky's *The Revolution Betrayed* in an official series.

In fact, Khrushchev, with his frequently improvised and irresponsible speeches and his joint declarations with Nehru, Tito and Nasser, introduced the idea of relativity, the leaven of pluralism, into Communist ideology. He dealt a mortal blow to the dogma of Moscow's infallibility. The first commandment of the Stalinized International, which took respect for the Kremlin as the touchstone of internationalist and revolutionary purity, is crumbling. The Chinese and Albanians have left the holy Muscovite church; others have remained in it, in order to contest the U.S.S.R.'s hegemony from within. Togliatti's alliance with Tito has encouraged the Rumanians and contributed to the climate of opinion favouring the decentralization of power, to which Togliatti gave the name of 'polycentrism'. The Czechoslovak party will doubtless not have been the last to seize on the principle that each Communist party is the best judge of its own strategy and tactics, and that the trust of its own people is much more precious to a government than the trust of a foreign government.

However, throughout the entire period we have covered, the Kremlin has persisted in its attempts to get its caesaro-papist claims, its undisputed authority in the defence of Marxism-Leninism (as interpreted by itself) recognized. But each assertion of this authority, aimed at strengthening bloc cohesion, has increased the tensions and disturbances and produced new schisms. In vain *Pravda* and *Izvestia*, followed by *Neues Deutschland* and *Trybuna Ludu*, have accused Ceausescu, Cisar, Dubcek, of heresy, either directly or by implication. The tendency for the revision of Marxism-Leninism, for the de-mythologization of Moscow's authority, is making progress in all the Communist parties.

The resurgence of Soviet aggression and repression can doubtless be explained by the fear inspired, not only by American imperialism or German revanchism, but by the crisis in the system, the sharpening of what we have called the basic, antagonistic contradiction, as well as the secondary contradictions, in their system of domination. For a section of the Soviet leadership, obsessed by the thought of anti-Communist pogroms to which a consistent reformation of Dubcek's type might lead, the sole means of maintaining an empire and a dictatorship lies in the use of force, in police control and in censorship. Their reactions at the time of the Czechoslovak crisis were terrifyingly blind, irrational and obsessional. A clear-sighted observer has pointed out how the Soviet bureaucracy at all levels showed signs of an infantile mentality at the time of the Czechoslovak invasion and after.[4] Dubcek's conflict with Brezhnev was not simply a repetition of John Hus's with the Emperor three centuries before. It was also that of a human, straightforward, civilized man with a raging barbarian bureaucrat.

Are we, therefore, moving inexorably into a new period of repressive obscurantism, a period of explosions, catastrophes, with the Soviet leaders rushing headlong into another world war? Must we echo the cry of the great, insane Hungarian poet Voeroesmarthy, bewailing the suppression of his people's rebellion in 1849: 'There is no hope, no hope!'? No; the wavering of the Soviet leaders, even in the first eight months of 1968, before they embarked on a course of military repression, shows that in the U.S.S.R. too, and in the opmost echelons, there exist forces for moderation, toleration and peaceful development.

What visitor to Czechoslovakia in April 1967 would have thought that a year later a group of Communist leaders would raise the banner of patriotic and democratic renewal? Who in Prague at the time had heard of Dubcek, Smrkovsky, Spacek, Sabata, Simon? The intellectual élite was dispirited, isolated, reduced to impotence and defeatist; the working class was passive; Novotnyism triumphed. Yet what happened eight months later was no miracle (though it looked like one): it was an explosion of forces that had been suppressed in the subconscious of the Czech and Slovak nations. It was the result of objective economic and socio-cultural developments, whose premises, *mutatis mutandis*, exist equally in the Soviet Union.

Socialism, usurped, distorted, devalued by Stalinism, disgraced by Gottwald's and Novotny's crimes, nevertheless showed its vitality in Czechoslovakia, its capacity for regeneration. Why, therefore, should one exclude the possibility of a 'step forward' in the Soviet Union towards a democratic reform of socialism?[5] Why exclude the possibility of a return to the fount, the neglected thought of the prophet Lenin of 1923-4, who saw and foresaw the tragic consequences of the bureaucratization of the party and the régime he had conjured up?[6] It is conceivable that the Czechoslovak leaders and intellectuals, in taking up the work begun by the Hungarian followers of Nagy and the Polish revisionists, might have helped in accelerating the slow awakening of conscience in the Soviet Union.

One may hope – certainly the people of the Eastern countries hope – that the next Dubcek will appear in the nerve centre of the system : Moscow.

Epilogue I (1971): After Prague and Postscript on Poland*

'Normalization' in Czechoslovakia

The process of normalization, followed by consolidation, which has taken place in Czechoslovakia under the vigilant eye of the occupying power deserves careful study, since it reveals the mechanism by which the Soviet leaders assert their control and domination over countries within their sphere of influence. To recover the authority which almost slipped from their grasp in 1968, to re-establish absolute power the Soviet experts and their Czech and Slovak collaborators have shown themselves to be formidable and skilled technicians.[1]

Thus the 'salami tactics' so called by the former Hungarian Stalinist leader Matyas Rakosi) that were used successfully in 1947–8 against the elements of Popular Front coalitions that would not accept Communist hegemony were now employed against the leaders of the Czechoslovak Communist party and against that party itself. Despite the failure of the attempt by Indra, Bilak and Kolder on 21 August 1968, the Kremlin stuck to its purpose of installing a group of leaders who, if they did not all see eye to eye on every question, were at any rate a hundred per cent pro-Soviet. The cardinal importance that the Kremlin attached to the composition of the Presidium of the Central Committee – the supreme party organ and virtual government of a Communist country – was shown in Dubcek's plea to the Central Committee at the end of September 1969, in which he revealed that during his four hours' tête-à-tête with Brezhnev at Cierna in July 1968 the latter had laid particular stress on his demand for 'personnel changes, especially in the Presidium'.

To secure a team who would carry out Soviet wishes, it was necessary first of all to break down the alliance between the four

*Translated by Paul Stevenson.

principal figures of the 'Prague spring' – Dubcek, Cernik, Svoboda and Smrkovsky – who, in the hour of trial, had sworn to keep faith with one another. Time and patience achieved this end: the first step, in November 1968, was to oust Smrkovsky, Moscow's chief enemy among the four. Later, wedges were driven between Dubcek on the one hand and Cernik and Svoboda on the other. In April 1969, when the population's delirious joy at an ice-hockey victory over the Russians degenerated into rioting, Marshal Grechko's threat of a fresh Soviet military intervention brought about Dubcek's removal and his replacement by Husak as head of the party.[2]

Dubcek's dignity and weakness. By turning back on Dubcek, Cernik secured only a few months' respite: in January 1970 he had to relinquish the premiership to Lubomir Strougal. Further reshuffling purged the Presidium of all elements that were suspected of right-wing or opportunistic views. Dubcek was expelled from it in September 1969; in January 1970 he was made to resign from the Central Committee and, at Husak's suggestion, was sent as ambassador to Turkey. In March he was suspended from party membership by the commission of inquiry set up to ascertain the leaders' responsibility for the 'deviations' of 1968. Later he was recalled from Ankara and expelled from the party on 26 June. Alone of the original four, Svoboda remained in power, helping thereby to demolish his patriotic image in which he had taken pride in 1968. His fate illustrates the grim prophecy of the philosopher Karel Kosik: 'The master-slave dialectic operates in politics in such a way that the conqueror not only forces his adversary to accept his viewpoint, but to embrace the very formulas in which his surrender is expressed.'

As for Dubcek, he lost the gamble to which he committed himself after signing the Moscow *Diktat* and which was based on the same false premises as his tactics in the summer of 1968. namely the hope that the Russians would allow him time to prove the efficiency of his political system and its harmlessness from their point of view. As he said on 11 October 1968 in a long speech which one cannot re-read without compassion: 'It is our desire to continue political work in such a way as to maintain the positive principles of our present policy, including the union of the party with the people and the workers' share in carrying out the party's policy.' After the Munich-type agreements signed at Moscow which legalized the presence if not the entry of Soviet troops, such declarations were a Utopian attempt to square the circle. Under the Moscow agreements the first obligation of the Czechoslovak leaders was to combat anti-socialist forces – by which term, as was quite clear, the Russians and the orthodox Czechoslovak Communists meant to designate the élite of the party and country and all elements which sought to uphold national sovereignty, the participation of citizens in government and the abolition of totalitarian centrism. This being so, everything Dubcek felt obliged to do to appease the Russians aroused protests from his own followers, and everything he did to soothe public opinion incited the Russians to step up their pressure and encourage his adversaries.

Later, in June 1970, Husak boasted of the 'strong and consistent policy' by which he had put an end to the 'anarchy and disintegration' that prevailed under his predecessor. He forgot to say, however, that the anarchy, instability and repeated crises from August 1968 to April 1969 were due first and foremost to the Kremlin's incessant pressure, the centralization and censorship measures taken at its behest, and the unremitting encouragement of Dubcek's enemies and those who sought revenge against him.[3]

Husak's policy was undoubtedly 'consistent', but it was based on a choice that was not open to Dubcek. No doubt the advocate of 'socialism with a human face' lacked the exceptional qualities he would have needed in order to cope with highly complicated situations. Although a thoroughly decent man, he was certainly not a great statesman. Goodwill, of which he had plenty, was not a sufficient cure for an internal crisis aggravated by an external one. But it must not be forgotten that the root cause of Dubcek's weakness lay in the role that he had chosen and was determined to play: that of a conciliator between the party and people, a mediator between his country and the tutelary power. He was the victim of a double allegiance which prevented him from taking up a clear, unequivocal position, either by challenging the Russians and accepting the consequences or by sacrificing his own ideas and popularity in order to carry out their will in a 'strong and consistent' manner. True, he held out against the Kremlin, for example when he refused to attend the Warsaw meeting in July 1968, but he had not provided himself with the means of effective resistance. Instead he was profuse in gestures and pledges of loyalty towards Moscow, which were to cost him dear. From the record of his talks with Waldeck-Rochet on 19–20 July 1968, it appears that Dubcek and Cernik themselves invited the Russians to hold the summer manoeuvres in Czechoslovakia – thus preparing the way for the invasion – in order, as Dubcek explained, 'to show the world that we are an integral part of the Warsaw Pact'.[4]

Dubcek refused to believe that the Russians would intervene by force, and he would not listen to the generals who urged him to take precautions. When the Russians did move in, Michel Tatu argued that a more skilful politician could have turned to his own advantage the new situation of 'political guerrilla warfare' that spontaneously swept the country during the first week of the occupation. At that stage it was Brezhnev, not Dubcek, who needed a political solution, and the latter might have made terms.[5] But Dubcek, bound hand and foot by an ideology whose touchstone was devotion to the U.S.S.R., saw no alternative to 'forming a part of the socialist world', and this made him helpless in dealing with men who had no such internationalist scruples. All that he could and did do was to fight a rearguard action that was doomed to failure. Thus he was made use of, disarmed, cut off from his real friends and prevented from replying to his slanderers, until finally, after his recall from Ankara, he stood at the mercy of new leaders some of whom were his bitter personal enemies. Convinced that he had acted rightly, he stubbornly refused to perform the self-criticism on which his accusers insisted.

Husak and Kadar. Dubcek's team having been split up by 'salami tactics', the 'Kadar system' was put into operation in order to secure a purged leadership agreeable to Moscow. The Kremlin had a choice of executants for this policy, from the veterans Indra, Strougal and Bilak to the political newcomer

Husak. But Indra was discredited in public eyes by the fiasco of 21 August 1968; Strougal was in disfavour for his opportunism in joining the anti-Soviet resistance (as Cernik's deputy, when the latter was under restraint, he had signed government protests against the invasion); and Bilak did not seem qualified for more than a secondary role. Husak's advantage over his rivals was that his moral position resembled Kadar's in 1956: as a former victim of Stalinism who had never given way under torture, he enjoyed a reputation for integrity. His leadership of the party seemed to afford a guarantee against the worst excesses of the past, with its mass arrests and arbitrary rule.

It should be emphasized that in Czechoslovakia in 1969, as in Hungary in 1956, the Russians did not set out purely and simply to re-establish the discredited former régime. In Hungary they did not restore Rakosi, and in Czechoslovakia they had no thought of recalling Novotny and his chief henchmen – although, for lack of other material, they used a number of vengeful extremists from the 'leftist front' who presented a threat to Husak in 1970. By and large, in both countries the Kremlin favoured pragmatic men of the centre who, while they certainly had no love for revisionism, showed flexibility and discretion and did not cultivate repression for its own sake. In this spirit, Soviet official statements endorsed the 'policy of January 1968' which Husak promised to continue, while depreciating its 'excesses'. What exactly the policy consisted of was far from clear, since all that had happened in January 1968 was Novotny's departure and the vague promise of a new style of government, while Novotny himself was differently judged at different times: in 1968 he was chiefly blamed for personal despotism and breaches of legality, whereas now it was alleged that during his last years of power he had shown 'excessive liberalism' towards 'rightist' elements, intellectuals and writers. Equally absurd charges had been levelled against Rakosi after the suppression of the Hungarian rising.

Be that as it may, Husak set about his task in the same way as Kadar: a stern policy first in order to restore the party's authority, which meant dictatorship by Kremlin-approved leaders, followed by a policy of conciliation when the dictatorship had dug itself in and the population had been cured of the nationalist virus and any ambition to influence the course of politics. The parallel with Kadar's actions in Hungary – 'an object-lesson in strong, ideological leadership' – was explicity drawn by Jiri Hajek, an ex-disciple of Novotny's converted to Husakism, in a series of articles published during Kadar's visit to Prague in December 1969 and entitled 'What our Hungarian comrades have to teach us'. Kadar himself encouraged Husak to endure present obloquy in order that he might become popular in the future: as he declared at Prague, 'Many people hated us for taking measures for which they are now grateful.' Husak, indeed, did not await the completion of 'normalization' before borrowing Kadar's conciliatory slogan, which earned him so much popularity: 'He who is not against us is with us.' Husak's words, addressed to the Central Committee in January 1970, were: 'In our eyes, anyone who does not work against the party is a potential ally and not an enemy.' Similarly in a speech of 28 August 1970 Husak expressed the hope that 'after the present period of crisis is over' the country might return to 'the normal forms of socialist democracy'. This theme was taken up a few days later by the Budapest *Magyar Nemzet*, which attacked the extremists in Czechoslovakia who 'wished to drag the country back into the errors of dogmatism'. The success or failure of Husak's experiment will largely depend on the outcome of his battle against the extreme left, which took advantage of the downfall of the 'progressives' to corner several important jobs in the party apparatus, the press and radio.[6]

The great purge. One essential difference between Husak's situation in 1969 and Kadar's in 1956 is that whereas in Hungary the Communist party and the whole state apparatus were disintegrated by the revolt, so that the Russians and their agents were opposed for a time only by such forces as the workers' councils and hastily-formed revolutionary committees, in Czechoslovakia it was the party itself, the largest in Central Europe, and its dependent political and social institutions, which constituted the focus of resistance and was supported by almost the whole of public opinion. The Fourteenth Extraordinary Congress showed that the bulk of party members, ignoring the hidebound 'appara-

tus', had turned themselves into a democratic and national socialist party, whose regional and local organs showed an almost
revolutionary vitality during and after the six 'glorious days' of
21–6 August.[7] The militants' spirit and their demand for a share
in public affairs was not broken once and for all by the occupation.
In September–October 1968 the Central Committee received more
than 70,000 resolutions and letters from party organizations in
industry and the public service, calling for continued democratization, the eviction of 'collaborators' and Quislings, the summoning of a constituent party congress, and so on.

Thus it was clear that in order to neutralize opposition the
party would have to be destroyed and rebuilt, not from the foundations, which were contaminated, but from the top downwards.
As Brezhnev had urged even before the invasion, the party of the
masses must be replaced by a party of the élite – a living, active,
demanding organization by an obedient one. This meant the
severest purge that the Czechoslovak Communist party has ever
undergone, and one from which it may well not recover.

After purging the Presidium and the Central Committee – the
latter being only too eager to make amends for its resolutions and
loyalty to Dubcek in 1968 – the next step was to reform the
party apparatus and the provincial, district and municipal committees. The hardest hit was the committee for the city of Prague,
bastion of Dubcekism which was now accused of being a 'second
party headquarters' and a hotbed of resistance to Soviet pressure.
As with the Presidium, the purge took place in stages. On 3 June
1969 the principal officers of the Prague committee were made to
resign collectively and its first secretary, Bohumil Simon, was
replaced by an ex-Novotnyite, Oldrich Matejka. On 24 September
all the 'progressives', including Simon and the historian Milan
Huebl, were expelled from the committee. Finally, on 16 December Matejka was replaced by Antonin Kapek, a former general
manager of the C.K.D. engineering works, who had been among
the members of the Presidium accused of collaboration in 1968
but was subsequently whitewashed. He now showed his mettle
by completing the purge. By the end of 1969, 147 members of the
municipal committee and district councils in Prague had lost their
jobs. A similar purge was carried out by stages in the provincial

committees such as that of Northern Moravia, under its new secretary Miroslav Mamula who had been one of Novotny's most trusted aides. Seventy-five former teachers at the Central Committee's School of Advanced Political Studies were dismissed from their posts and expelled from the party.

Next came the turn of the rank and file. A purge began early in 1970 by means of the issue of fresh membership cards; before this, many had left the party of their own accord in protest at the expulsion of Dubcek, Kriegel, Smrkovsky, Spacek and Slavik. From April 1969 onwards, according to an estimate which Dubcek quoted to the Central Committee in September, barely 16 per cent of party members attended meetings. By 1970 some 600,000 had left the party, including 200,000 in Slovakia, leaving something like a million to be scrutinized. On 2 April 1970 Indra declared : 'It will not hurt the party to lose two or three hundred thousand members.' In point of fact it lost many more, with particular detriment to its working-class character : by March 1970 only 24 per cent of members were workers, as compared with 38 per cent in 1968.[8] In the Skoda works at Prague the appointment of Kapek as First Secretary was followed by the resignation of 323 out of 350 workers from membership of the party organization.

But the purge wrought most havoc among the party intelligentsia, a fact which must have given the régime some concern. In Hungary before the rising, most of the intelligentsia were not Communists. In Czechoslovakia party members comprised 70–80 per cent of the manager class, 85–90 per cent of high State officials, 70 per cent of 'cultural workers' (writers, artists, journalists etc.), 55 per cent of secondary school teachers, 60 per cent of university teachers, 40–45 per cent of scientists, 30–40 per cent of technicians and 25–30 per cent of doctors. The great majority of these Communist intellectuals had compromised themselves by showing sympathy with Dubcek's ideas or condemning the occupation. In many cases (over 20,000 in Bohemia and Moravia up to August 1968), those who were expelled from the party also lost their jobs. Philosophers, scholars, journalists and writers of worldwide reputation were dismissed and were often unable to find other work, even of a manual kind. The Prague weekly *Tribuna* for 18 June 1970, from which the above figures are taken, suggested that the purged Communists would have to be replaced by 'bourgeois' specialists. Thus, as in Hungary after 1956, the re-Bolshevization of the party meant to a large extent the de-Communization of intellectual life and the whole machinery of State.

The purge of the administration went *pari passu* with that of the party, the success of both operations involving a reorganization and strengthening of the machinery of repression. In March 1970 Strougal was able to tell the Federal Assembly (itself considerably purged and reduced to its former role of a rubber stamp) that 'the security forces are once more a guarantee of safety on the home front'. The security organization had been shaken up by Josef Pavel when Minister of the Interior – a post to which Dubcek appointed him on the recommendation of Husak, his former comrade in captivity – and about 150 of its agents were then dismissed; it was now hastily reconstituted, with the dismissal of about 30 per cent of the police force who disapproved of the new régime. They were not easy to replace. Kaska, the new Minister of the Interior, admitted to the Assembly that 'recruitment was hampered by the unpopularity of the police', but he announced that some 500 officers had been sent to the U.S.S.R. for practical and ideological retraining. A large force was necessary not only for detecting and foiling any opposition moves but, first and foremost, to inquire into people's past activities, especially those of the vast number who in 1968 had operated secret radios, printed and distributed pamphlets, given information to foreigners or in any way displayed hostility to the occupation. A questionnaire addressed to the teaching profession by Hrbek, the Minister of Education, caused a stir both within and outside the country; similar inquisitions followed in other professions such as the army, where every officer was questioned on his activities and those of his friends and relations in 1968–9.[9] As in 1949–52, Czechoslovakia is once more the scene of a Kafkaesque 'trial', a grotesque and enormous arraignment of the whole nation.

Were the interrogations intended to lead to a spate of actual trials? Husak, on 12 February and 25 June 1970, and Strougal on 29 May, declared that 'the party would not so debase itself as to fabricate trials' like that of Slansky, and Husak added: 'We shall only use administrative methods when there is a clear violation of the law.' But from September 1969 onwards the Federal Assembly passed amendments to the laws which 'turned the exception into the rule and conferred full powers, sometimes of an excessive character, on numerous institutions and persons'.[10] Meanwhile the press and radio continued to refer to the 'Prague spring' in terms of foreign plots: on 21 April 1970 the Bratislava *Pravda* accused Smrkovsky, Slavik, Pavel and General Prchlik of treason. Kriegel and Goldstuecker were denounced as accomplices of Zionism, and V. Cerny, the eminent Romance scholar, as a 'spirit of counter-revolution'. Some of the charges levelled against Dubcek were so serious that expulsion from the party seemed the mildest foreseeable penalty. The demand that 'counter-revolutionary and anti-socialist forces should be brought to trial' was voiced by an extremist member of parliament, Mrs Zdena Dohnalova, and in the Central Committee by General Rytir, a former Chief of Staff. However, up to the spring of 1971, the only noted follower of Dubcek to be brought to trial was General Prchlik, who, in March 1971, was condemned by a military tribunal to three years of prison.

From April 1969 the judicial system was also reorganized: judges and magistrates, the public prosecutors and the Supreme Court were purged and the rehabilitation commissions set up in 1968 were dissolved. (However, the new Procurator-General, Jan Fejes, was a moderate 'Husakist'.) The new Minister of Justice, Jan Nemec, expressed the view that at least a third of the rehabilitation pleas put forward in 1968 were inadmissible, as the persons concerned had deserved their sentences. The newly rehabilitated were once more suspect. The weekly *Tvorba*, in its review of the film made in France from Artur London's *On Trial*, did not hesitate to accuse London, Loebl, Smrkovsky and the other survivors of the great purge of complicity in the judicial murder of Slansky, against whom they had given evidence – not a word was said of the methods by which that evidence was extorted. In the same way Rakosi in 1956 blamed Rajk, whom he had had executed seven years earlier, for having deceived the party by confessing himself guilty.

Censorship and self-censorship. The re-establishment of press and radio censorship was no less important in the eyes of the 'normalizers' than the regeneration of the party apparatus, the army and the security service. The weekly *Politika* was suppressed on 2 April 1969; the party's own organ, *Rude Pravo*, was rebuked for stepping out of line. *Listy*, the writers' organ, and *Reporter*, the weekly published by the Journalists' Union, were subjected to preliminary censorship.

After Dubcek's eviction the regimentation of the press became speedier and more thorough. The resignation of *Rude Pravo*'s chief editor, Jiri Sekera, was the first of a long series of resignations and dismissals ending, on 21 November 1969, with that of J. Suk, the director of the C.T.K. agency. *Literarny Zivot*, the organ of liberal Slovak writers which took the place of *Kulturny Zivot*, was suppressed in April 1969. *Listy* and *Reporter* closed down a few weeks later, as did the progressive Brno review *Host do Domu* in the spring of 1970.

In an article published in the Moscow *Pravda*, *Rude Pravo*'s new editor, M. Moc, wrote: 'The party's interests have obliged us to part company with journalists who have shown themselves to be the ideologists and inspirers of the anti-party opposition ... The press has once more become a weapon in the hands of the Communist party, fighting for the success of its policy.' Indeed the press and radio, deprived of the services of practically all talented journalists, display the same monotonous uniformity as in the 1950s – nor is the tone of aggression and denunciation wanting, in articles that usually bear no signature. On 16 July 1969 *Rude Pravo* declared for the first time that Soviet troops came to Czechoslovakia in August 1968 'to defend freedom and socialism' – a triumph for the normalizers' policy. The new, approved weeklies *Tribuna* and *Tvorba* vied each with other in denouncing all the main figures of the 'Prague spring'; while all the other papers, as well as the radio and television under extremist control, insulted public opinion daily by uttering the wildest charges against men who had enjoyed its favour and could no longer defend themselves. Thus *Rude Pravo* on 12 March 1970 accused Dubcek's Minister of the Interior, Josef Pavel, of having carried anti-Sovietism so far as to have his agents spy on Soviet troops during the 1970 manoeuvres; while on 23 July Prague Radio announced that the former directors of the mining and uranium industry had had the audacity to suggest to the government that it should terminate the *de facto* Soviet monopoly on the exploitation of uranium ore, which the Czechs were obliged to deliver at prices below those on the world market. A book could be filled with quotations slandering Dubcek, Smrkovsky and the writers Jan Prochazka, Vaclav Havel, Antonin Liehm, Cerny, Pelikan and others. Again in imitation of 1952, and also of the Polish press in 1968, official propaganda sought to discredit the liberal movement by stressing the Jewish origin of some of its leaders, such as Kriegel and Goldstuecker. A security chief, Bohumil Molnar, declared that 'the 1968 movement had close links with Zionism'. The revival of anti-Semitism was expressed most clearly by the Bratislava *Pravda*, which on 5 August 1970 noted with satisfaction that the Plenum of April 1969 at which Dubcek was overthrown had marked the end of the period of 'Judaization' of the mass media and the efforts of 'a clique of Jewish intellectuals to manufacture a Jewish problem that does not exist in Czechoslovakia, the Soviet Union or any other socialist country'. Much publicity was given to a book by Frantisek Kolar, *Zionism and Anti-Semitism*, which was put out by the party's official publishing house and attacked the best-known Jewish intellectuals in terms worthy of *Der Stürmer*.

In May 1970 the President of the Federal Assembly spoke with satisfaction of the progress achieved in the sphere of information, declaring that 'the authorities have less and less cause to intervene'. Indeed there was no need of prior censorship: the editors themselves did all that was necessary, aided by self-censorship on the part of writers. The only blemish on this success was a slump in the sale of newspapers.

To judge from an article in *Tvorba* of 20 August, the authorities themselves were slightly embarrassed by an extremist broadcast which accused the writers as a body of 'receiving inflated fees for their counter-revolutionary works'. On this charge the party weekly commented that 'one of the greatest blessings one can have is a stupid enemy. Must we go on providing our opponents with this unmerited advantage?' Continuing, *Tvorba* emphasized that 'misinformed and inept comments' only reinforced 'the cohesion in the ranks of ideological adversaries, and sympathy for them in the public mind'.

Literature and the arts underwent the same treatment as the press. As M. Claude Roy wrote in Le Monde of 10 June 1970 after a visit to Prague and Bratislava: 'Czechoslovak culture, which its leaders have upheld against every oppression, from the Counter-Reformation to the domination of Austria, from Comenius to Masaryk, from the Nazi protectorate to the great Stalinist freeze – that culture which the resolution of a people has kept afloat in spite of every tempest – is now at the mercy of a handful of intolerant fanatics.' Apart from some Slovak writers belonging to the review Nove Slovo who are personal friends of Husak's, not a single author or artist of any repute has lent his moral authority to the régime. On 22 May 1969 the members of the Cultural Front who held their last meeting at the Cinema Club in Prague registered a solemn protest against the 'return to the era of the monologue'.[11] Since then they have been silent.

The Czech cultural associations, having refused to give in, have been suspended or dissolved. So, in January 1970, was the Slovak Union of Artists and Film Actors. At the end of 1969 the Czech Writers' Union was deprived of the funds which, even under Novotny, had given it a certain independence; in future, publishing contracts were not to be entered into through its agency. The film studios, so active until 1968, were at a standstill. In May 1970 the Komorni Theatre had to take Molière's Le Misanthrope out of its repertoire because of 'irresponsible reactions' by audiences who discovered a topical relevance in the hero's scorn of compromises. On 1 April 1971, Otomar Krejca, one of the greatest directors of the Czech theatre, was relieved of his post at the Za Branou theatre. The gulf between the Cultural Front and the new rulers is so deep that it will certainly be a long time before it is bridged and a modus vivendi achieved on the lines of that reached by Kadar with the world of letters, art and science.

Social organizations. The purge of the party, the National Front and the various State bodies – including the army, where hundreds of high-ranking officers were dismissed – was followed by that of all social organizations which had regained a measure of independence in 1968 and were on the way to becoming centres of representation, initiative and participation.

This applies particularly to the trade unions, which, like the party organs, were in the forefront of resistance in August 1968. The debates and resolutions of the national trade union congress held on 4–7 March 1969 showed – in spite of the self-restraint of its organizers, who were anxious not to embarrass Dubcek – that a majority of the working class were still faithful to the cause of democratization. The representatives of the major unions demanded a share in the framing of economic policy, the legalization of workers' councils and respect for national sovereignty. The congress was, as it were, the swan-song of the Prague spring: no sooner had it disbanded than the party leaders set about the destruction of proletarian democracy in all its forms.

At the beginning of 1969 the trade unions were still addressing thousands of petitions to the Central Committee urging that Smrkovsky should remain at the head of the Federal Assembly. A few months later they threatened to call a strike if any harm was done to the writers and students. By 1970, however, the unions were either gagged or side-tracked. In February the Dubcekist Karel Polacek was replaced in the top trade-union post by the highly orthodox Jan Piller. The unions were purged no less thoroughly than the party organizations. According to the Prague Prace for 18 August 1970, 30 per cent of senior members of the Czech unions and 17 per cent of those in the whole country had been dismissed from their posts or expelled, or had resigned. The biggest turnover (50 per cent) was in the leadership of the most powerful union, the metal-workers', which had played a key role in 1968–9. Even such radical purges, however, do not seem to have been altogether effective, especially at the lower levels. A glimpse of the real state of feeling in the purged works committees was given in July 1970, when the Central Council severely rebuked the committee of the metallurgists' union at Mlada Boleslav for defending workers at the plant who had beaten up a party of commissioners appointed to look into the conduct of some of their workmates in 1968. After this the national leaders, from Husak downwards, began visiting the most important factories to explain the party line to the workers, who gave them a frosty reception. In March 1971, the political leaders showed their complete disregard for the working class by naming as successor to Piller, who was dismissed for having been too 'soft' in the purges, Karel Hoffman – a man who had been one of the first to collaborate with the occupation forces and who, furthermore, had no trade-union experience.

The students' union was dissolved in June 1969, after which it took the authorities a year to succeed in launching an embryonic 'Parliament of Bohemian and Moravian students' affiliated to the Union of Socialist Youth. In a petition to the Central Committee the sons of Otto Sling, one of Slansky's fellow-victims, observed that 'it is pointless to talk of the party losing the confidence of youth : it has lost it already'.

However, the chief aim of the realists in power was to be feared and respected, and to nip in the bud any attempt at resistance. After the brutal repression of demonstrators on the first anniversary of the occupation, the government had nothing to fear from street crowds. During the Lenin centenary celebrations in April 1970 some flagstaffs were broken and some posters torn down, but these were isolated incidents. Early in the year the press reported the arrest of some young students and workers belonging to a 'Czech socialist revolutionary party', who were denounced as neo-Trotskyist for distributing pamphlets demanding an 'anti-bureaucratic revolution' (*Rude Pravo*, 13 January 1970). Soon afterwards it became known that groups advocating 'socialism with a human face' had been formed in Prague and the other chief towns, and one of their manifestoes reached the West (*Le Monde*, 1–2 February 1970). There is a strong tradition of underground resistance in Czechoslovakia, and the government imposed by the occupation is almost as much hated as was the Nazi protectorate : this may be judged by, among other things, the nervousness shown by the authorities and the heavy precautions taken for the second anniversary of the occupation. But in the short term the resistance is hampered by the lack of international support, the weariness and despondency of the population and a thoroughly efficient police power.[12]

Economic reconstruction. The Czechs and Slovaks cannot expect any foreign help in shaking off the Soviet yoke, since the Western powers in practice recognize the Soviet zone of influence which includes them and the other members of the Warsaw Pact. The Czechoslovak police, reorganized by the K.G.B. and backed by the Red Army, is capable of crushing any attempt at opposition.[13] As a result, the popular mood is one of resignation, as shown by the calm which prevailed on the second anniversary of the occupation.

Nevertheless there is bound to be sooner or later, as in Hungary, a measure of consolidation and a rebirth of energy which will afford the Czechs both material and psychological compensations, by improving the standard of living, giving them an interest in work and private recreation and alleviating the pressure of propaganda. Normalization will stand or fall in the long run by its effect on the national economy. Aided by the population's traditional good sense and docility, the government has put a stop to galloping inflation by freezing prices and wages, while improving conditions on the home market by releasing, at the end of 1969, some 20 to 25 million dollars for the purchase of good-quality Western consumer items.

On the whole, by 1970 the country had reverted to the economic climate and the almost entirely centralized structure of 1967. This means, among other things, that the problems of stagnation, maldistribution of labour, low productivity, obsolescent equipment and lack of incentives, which combined to bring about the upheaval of 1968, are bound to recur once the country has traversed the reconstruction period during which the main objective must be 'to restore State authority, economic management and labour discipline'.[14] Although the official line is once again to extol central planning and to decry the views of the exiled economist Ota Sik, who is made a scapegoat for all the troubles of 1968, the experts now in control – who include some eminent associates of Sik, such as K. Kouba and L. Veltrusky – have not forgotten that 'we live in a time when a majority of people in the socialist countries are seeking by all means to make their economy more flexible and productive and to prepare the way for the scientific and technical revolution'. Thus the economic reform will probably continue, no doubt on the lines adopted in Hungary, which combine prudence in theory with boldness in practice. 'One of the basic objectives of the State plan is to make room for initiative, to give firms an interest in innovation and in more rational methods of production and management': so ran a declaration signed by eighteen noted economists who had survived the catastrophe of 1968-9 and whose views were endorsed by hundreds of other experts.[15] It was also stressed that Czechoslovakia's closer integration with Comecon would not rule out profitable exchanges with the West.

Thus, while huge economic difficulties lie ahead and are aggravated by the political and social climate, the future in this sphere seems less gloomy than the others. Another aspect which may offer some promise is that of federalization, which came into force on 1 January 1969. Although for the present its effects have been largely neutralized by renewed centralization and the stifling of internal democracy, we may suppose that in the longer term it will be of some benefit to the Slovaks, and that as a result some of them will become more loyal supporters of the Federal government than the Czechs themselves. It is the latter who have suffered most from the occupation and the purge, to the extent that, after the invasion and the collapse of all their hopes of rebirth, Karel Kosik was led to wonder 'whether we can survive as a political nation'.

Eastern Europe since 1968

In the two years that have elapsed since the invasion of Czechoslovakia it has been possible to see that the Russians' action was, in their own eyes, a measure of conservation rather than – as was feared at the outset in Bucharest, Belgrade, Tirana and even Peking – the sign of a turning-point in Soviet foreign policy and a return to the snarling isolationism of the cold war period.

Certainly all the peoples and governments of the Communist bloc recognized the intervention as a serious warning against any attempt to meddle with the political, social and ideological *status quo*. But there were no grave repercussions on relations between the U.S.S.R. and the other bloc countries, unless we regard as such

the Sino-Soviet tension of 1969, which has since been alleviated
by negotiations at Peking and the establishment of a frontier truce.

The intervention brought about some disturbance in relations
between the Communist parties of the five powers and certain of
their fellow-Communists in the West; but this proved to be
neither deep nor lasting. The patient and well-directed efforts of
the Soviet leaders to disarm criticism bore fruit in the conference
of Communist parties which met at Moscow on 5 June 1969, and
which represented a considerable though not a complete success
for the Kremlin's endeavour to reassert its authority. The delegates of seventy-eight parties who attended made little difficulty
about shelving their differences on 'points of detail' – such as the
Sino-Soviet conflict and Czechoslovakia – and proclaiming their
resolution to strive together for unity. Considerable freedom was
allowed to objectors – the Australian delegate's speech condemning the invasion was actually reported in summary form by
Pravda – but this was largely offset by the opportunity given to
Brezhnev and the majority group to state the orthodox, unitary
view and therefore present it as the general consensus. Assuming the right to speak for all the Communist parties present and
absent, Brezhnev declared that 'the parties rightly consider that
the interests of unity demand an intensification of the struggle
against revisionism and opportunism, whether of the right or of
the left'. The 'rightist' Dubcek was thus embraced in the same
condemnation as the 'leftist' Mao. The conference listened without a qualm to Gomulka uttering such phrases as: 'The Soviet
Union is the mainstay of socialism ... whoever opposes it is
playing into the imperialists' hands.' The keynote was struck by
Ulbricht and the others who spoke of legitimate reaction to 'an
imperialist plot which came near to wrenching Czechoslovakia
away from the socialist camp' – a view corroborated by Husak as
head of the Czechoslovak delegation. In short, the conference
perhaps exceeded Moscow's hopes in the encouragement it gave
to the anti-reformist spirit which has prevailed in the Soviet
Union since Khrushchev's fall. The Brezhnev doctrine of 'double
responsibility' was not endorsed on all sides, but it was not contested either. The Rumanians signed the resolution, though with
reservations. Subsequently the Italian Communist party toned

down its expressions of disapproval, while other parties like the Austrian and French 'normalized' their position by expelling those who disagreed with it (Ernst Fischer, Roger Garaudy). The Spanish party alone protested loudly when Dubcek was stripped of his party membership.

The Soviet-Czechoslovak and Soviet-Rumanian treaties. Treaties of friendship and mutual aid were signed by the Soviet Union on 6 May 1970 with Czechoslovakia and on 7 July, after long bargaining, with Rumania. They provide respectively an index of the success and limitations – temporary though these may be – of Moscow's efforts to grasp the Eastern countries more closely to itself.

In a speech to the Foreign Affairs Committee of the Supreme Soviet on 25 May 1970, Gromyko referred to the Czechoslovak treaty as the embodiment in terms of international law of the 'new type of relations between socialist States founded on Marxist-Leninist teaching and the unshakeable principles of proletarian internationalism'. The treaty in fact confers on the leader of the bloc a right of inspection and intervention in both internal and external affairs. The Preamble and Articles 5 and 9 codify the principle laid down in the Bratislava declaration according to which the defence of socialist achievements is 'a joint international duty of the socialist countries'. Both the Soviet and Czech leaders, it is true, have maintained since the signature of the treaty that this does not mean any limitation of the sovereignty of the Soviet Union's allies; as Strougal told the Federal Assembly on 28 May, 'the so-called theory of limited sovereignty is an invention of the imperialists to excite nationalist passion'. In reality, he went on to say, 'the maintenance and defence of socialist achievements against diversion and counter-revolution do not and cannot signify a limitation of the sovereignty of a socialist State; on the contrary, they are the expression of that sovereignty'. Nevertheless, even though the leaders of defeated Czechoslovakia have subscribed to the thesis that the intervention was an act of brotherly aid, it remains an unescapable fact that the Soviet Union used brute force to settle its disagreement with the Czechoslovak government, party leaders and people.

This being so, we may wonder why the Russians did not similarly use force against the other member of the Warsaw Pact
with whom they were at odds, namely Rumania, which, while
protesting its loyalty to the Soviet Union, has held out against
economic, political and military integration. Many reasons may
be suggested: Rumania is a 'vulnerable land, militarily indefen-
sible, economically weak';[16] it was devastated by floods in 1970
and is of minor strategic interest to the U.S.S.R.; the Russians
may feel that they would only have to step up the pressure to
overcome Rumanian resistance. Unlike the Czechs, on the other
hand, the Rumanians would doubtless not have surrendered
without a fight, and even if it had been a walkover this would
have meant international complications. The United States' warning, despite its lack of practical credibility, was also a danger-
signal. Finally, while the Rumanian leaders were nationalistic
they could not be accused of unorthodoxy: the party's supremacy is as well looked after by the Securitate as by the K.G.B. or
the Polish U.B.

No doubt all these factors contributed to the Kremlin's decision
to grant the Rumanians special treatment – or a respite – in
terms of the 1970 treaty. Whereas the treaty with Czechoslovakia covered the whole field of relations – politics, ideology
and defence – the Soviet-Rumanian treaty is a more modest affair
which observers at once saw as an 'inter-State treaty with the
minimum of reference to party ideology'.[17] Instead of speaking of
the 'joint international duty to defend socialist achievements', it
merely emphasizes 'the international solidarity of socialist governments'. The Preamble does not, like that of the Czechoslovak
treaty, relate economic co-operation to 'the division of labour and
socialist economic integration within the framework of
Comecon', nor does Article 2 on the same subject oblige the
Rumanians, like the Czechs, to work towards integration. Article
3 of the Czechoslovak treaty declares that the parties will 'encourage wider collaboration and direct relations between the
respective organs of State power and workers' organizations, so
as to promote mutual understanding and closer relations between
the two nations' – a formula which opens the door to direct
control and intervention by the tutelary power at all levels. In

the Rumanian treaty there is only a reference to 'efforts to develop friendship and solidarity among socialist governments'. Article 5 of the Czechoslovak treaty, which also reflects the Brezhnev doctrine, is missing in the other. Nevertheless, Article 7 of the Rumanian treaty includes the phrase: 'If either contracting party is subjected to an armed attack by any State or group of States, the other party shall at once grant it every assistance, including the military aid necessary to repel an armed attack.'

Did the absence of a limiting reference to Europe mean that the area of application of the Warsaw Pact was being extended, for example to China or the Middle East?[18] As far as Rumania is concerned, this was indirectly denied by the warm reception of the Minister of Defence, General Ion Ionita, in Peking shortly after the treaty was signed: this visit would not have gone off so cordially if he had not reassured the Chinese on this point. In his speech on 31 July Ionita declared that as a member of the Warsaw Pact Rumania was prepared to fulfil her obligations 'in the event of imperialist aggression in Europe' – thus confirming what *Scanteia* had said on 14 May 1970, when the negotiations were in full swing, that 'the aim of the treaty, and its only aim, is to provide defence against an imperialist attack in Europe'.[19]

It is true that Ceausescu, when he presented the treaty to the Central Committee on 8–9 July 1970, described it as 'intended to further the principles of a new type of relationship' among socialist countries. But the facts seem to show that there are two new types of relationship between the U.S.S.R. and its neighbours: the Czechoslovak, based on strict control by the dominant partner, and the other, which gives its ally a certain measure of autonomy in party and government affairs. The contrast between the implications of the two treaties is symbolized by the fact that while Brezhnev triumphantly attended the signature ceremony at Prague, he refrained from going to Bucharest on the pretext of indisposition.

The more permissive type of relationship also seems to prevail between the Soviet Union and Yugoslavia, which reacted almost as strongly to the invasion of Czechoslovakia as to that of Hungary in 1956. When Ribicic, the Yugoslav Prime Minister, visited Moscow at the end of June 1970, the 'serious discussions' which took place resulted in a communiqué stating that 'the existence of different views on some problems should not hinder the development of normal friendly relations'. In other words, the situation was back to the Belgrade declaration of 1955. The Russians, who have been following closely Belgrade's development of links with Bucharest and its rapprochement with China and Albania, are no doubt counting on the effects of time, the weakening of NATO's southern flank and the aggravation of national conflicts within Yugoslavia. Since their advance into the Mediterranean area the Russians have shown increased strategic interest in Yugoslavia's Adriatic coast. The decentralization of the country's government gives them opportunities, of which they take full advantage, to enter into direct touch with official bodies and firms and also to encourage the revival of Panslavism in the Serbian Orthodox Church which, having experienced disappointment in the West, is turning back towards Moscow. Yugoslavia has years of peril ahead of her, and, as the editor of an important Belgrade newspaper put it to this writer, she has to cope simultaneously with 'the heritage of Stalinism and the birth-pangs of capitalism'. Economic reform is gravely hampered by the growth in the defence budget, the demands of the underdeveloped republics, egalitarian pressure from students who play into the conservatives' hands without knowing it, and finally the West's slowness to take advantage of the unprecedented facilities for the investment of foreign capital.

Internal developments in Hungary and Poland were not much affected by the Czechoslovak crisis. The Hungarian leaders, whose minds were on economic reform, found it useful in consolidating their authority: the Hungarian people and especially the intelligentsia, witnessing the fate of the Czech experiment in combining Masaryk with Lenin, have come to appreciate more highly the state of probation which they themselves enjoy and which is the envy of their neighbours. In Poland the anti-revisionist, anti-intellectual and anti-Semitic frenzy of 1968-9 has died down and there is a renewed effort (the third since 1956) to rationalize the economy. On 4 July 1970 the *Monitor Polski* published a decree modifying wage policy by introducing greater incentives. The technocratic element, supported by E. Gierek, has become stronger within the government: Stanislaw Kociolek, aged thirty-seven, was appointed vice-president of the Council of State, and Mieczyslaw Jagielski (aged forty-six) vice-premier, while Stanislaw Majewski is head of the Planning Office. Thus a new chapter has opened in the struggle between the reformers, whose slogans this time are those of efficiency only, and the old guard entrenched in the party apparatus and the trade unions.[20] However, the remarkable efforts of Tito – the new Francis Joseph of the Balkans – to settle the problem of his succession and to bequeath to his country new federal structures based on the consent of the Yugoslav nations, have a chance of success which should not be underestimated.

The Communist bloc, Federal Germany and European security. One of the Soviet Union's objectives in Czechoslovakia was certainly to make it clear, both in the Eastern and in the Western camp, that the road to a *détente* lay through Moscow. Gomulka's pro-Soviet attitude to the occupation enabled him to consolidate his rule, which had been profoundly shaken by the events of March 1968. But the events of December 1970 have shown that he failed to profit from the time he gained.

Before the crisis came to a head the Soviet leaders appeared convinced that in the field of economic relations with the West and especially West Germany, it was necessary both for themselves and for their satellites to move out of the barter phase into that of co-operation and, in fact, Western aid, enabling them to modernize their equipment and develop their resources. The urge in this direction was too basic and powerful to be ignored.[21] Chinese hostility was no doubt another reason for the Russians to come closer to Western Europe. But the stepping-up of exchanges, contracts and two-way travel involves a risk of contamination which must be controlled by political means, above all the recognition and endorsement by the West of the *status quo* whereby the Soviet Union dominates Eastern Europe through subservient Communist parties.

This was the objective which lay behind the renewed call for a European security conference, issued at the first Warsaw Pact meeting after the invasion of Czechoslovakia (Budapest, March

1969), and also the initiative for negotiations with Federal Germany by the U.S.S.R., Poland and East Germany, of which the first concrete effect was the Soviet-West German treaty signed at Moscow on 12 August 1970.

In most Communist countries this treaty was greeted by the press, no doubt with good reason, as 'a success for the forces of peace in Europe and the world', a success for the Soviet Union. Certainly Brandt, the German Chancellor, had done no more than recognize a state of affairs – the partition of Germany, the existence of a second German State and the frontier between that State and Poland – which he could not alter in any case and which his Western allies more or less expressly recognized as unchangeable. The Soviet success was a question of prestige, a moral and legal triumph; but this was just what the Soviet Union needed to reaffirm its status as conqueror and its ability to dictate to the formidable enemy of yesterday which, despite its extraordinary recovery, is today a power of the second rank. From this point of view the treaty – although it put an end to the bogy of a hostile, revanchist, militarist Germany against which the Soviet Union had to protect its allies – serves to consolidate the Soviet hold on Eastern Europe and to buttress the Brezhnev doctrine. Such at least is the implication of a great deal of Eastern bloc propaganda.[22]

The Soviet-German reconciliation removed the chief obstacle to a European security conference which, according to the Soviet thesis, was to perform the function of the peace treaty, envisaged at Potsdam, for the final delimitation of frontiers, and at the same time lay the foundations for a genuine *détente*.[23] All the countries of Western Europe, together with the United States and Canada, were in this way invited to endorse West Germany's recognition of the territorial and political *status quo*. In theory the system of two opposing blocs would then be replaced by a collective security organization on the lines of the League of Nations. But the real objective, as was clear enough from Soviet commentaries, was to eliminate U.S. influence, prevent West Germany being absorbed into the Atlantic community, weaken Europe's economic integration and check the trend towards political unification. The long-term background to Soviet policy in Europe was indicated by *Pravda* on 29 July 1970, which painted a glowing picture of a 'greater Europe' in which the Western countries, turning their backs on Atlantic co-operation and U.S. exploitation, would merge with Eastern Europe (i.e. the Soviet empire, whose solidity is not to be called in question) to form a political and economic entity more powerful than the U.S.

This is clearly more a matter of wishful thinking than a serious prospect. But although Soviet policy is fundamentally defensive, this does not exclude but on the contrary stimulates a certain dynamism which urges Moscow not only to consolidate its gains but, slowly and surely, to extend its influence in order to attain parity with the U.S. This is shown too by Soviet policy in the Middle and Far East, the collective security plan for Asia and the considerable strengthening of Soviet naval power.[24] In the European sphere, this tendency to ideological and political expansion found expression, immediately after the Soviet-German treaty, in the concerted campaign by Moscow-oriented Communist parties, led by the French, for the lifting of the ban imposed in 1956 on the West German Communist party (K.P.D.) – an unusual interference in Bonn's internal affairs. On 25 August 1970 *Pravda* spoke up for the independence of Spain as well as the rest of Europe *vis-à-vis* the U.S. 'The slightest move towards democracy in Spain is seen by the Americans as a threat to their bases' – thus wrote the organ of the C.P.S.U., forgetting the summary treatment of democracy in Czechoslovakia. 'Voices are being raised in Europe for an independent and constructive policy within the European framework.'

The European security system as conceived in Moscow is one in which the East European countries would be the well-drilled auxiliaries of a great imperial enterprise which they would have no hand in controlling but from which they might derive certain incidental benefits, as Poland and the G.D.R. may do from the Soviet-German treaty. But not all the Communist leaders are content with this. As soon as attempts were made in 1966 to formulate a common policy concerning Germany, each of the countries in question put forward demands corresponding broadly to its own national interests, its geographical position in relation to

Germany, its economic needs and the solidity of its régime. The Rumanians took up an extreme position by their decision to negotiate separately; but even those leaders who accepted the need for a common front held out firmly for their respective interests. This was especially true of the G.D.R., the most vulnerable of the satellites, which had no desire to be sacrificed on the altar of 'normalization'. The hindrances which Ulbricht sought to place on contacts with the Federal Republic were resented by the Poles, Hungarians and Bulgarians. In these countries as in Czechoslovakia, public opinion tended to regard closer cooperation with West Germany as a counterweight not only to Soviet absolutism but also to the quasi-imperialistic claims of the G.D.R.

In the same way, differences based on national interest are visible in the satellites' approach to European security. The Rumanians, like the Yugoslavs, hope that the conference will enable them to increase their freedom of action and obtain stronger moral guarantees of their security in the form of a joint reassertion of the principles of coexistence and the non-use of force. All the satellite governments seem interested in improving their international status by closer bilateral relations with non-Communist governments.[25]

To sum up, one may say that the Soviet hold on the People's Democracies has been strengthened since the invasion of Czechoslovakia, but that it is still apt to slip at times. The trend towards diversification and greater independence has been slowed up but not arrested. The same is true of tendencies towards decentralization, pluralism, and the broadening of control by discussion and participation. This is shown by developments not only in Hungary,[26] but also in Russia itself, where, despite the rigours of censorship and the clumsy reactions of the security service, more and more voices are heard – such as those of the academician Sakharov, the mathematician Turchin and the historian Medvedev – in support of the view that 'only a democratization of public life can create conditions making possible the solution of economic problems', the gravity and urgency of which were admitted by Brezhnev to the Central Committee in December 1969.[27]

While one should not underestimate the chances of a return to 'Stalinist authoritarianism', there is some ground for hope that – as Chancellor Brandt seems courageously to have assumed – the development of economic, scientific and technical co-operation with the West will accelerate the evolution which has already begun in all the Communist countries, including the U.S.S.R., and will strengthen aspirations to greater freedom and a climate in which the spirit of creation and innovation is able to flourish. This, of course, would sharpen the contradiction between, on the one hand, a rigid system of hegemony based on conservatism and police power and, on the other, political and social trends within the Soviet empire.[28]

Postscript on Poland: The End of the Gomulka Era

The dramatic events which shook Poland in December 1970 illustrate once again the cyclic character of history in the People's Democracies: the same plot repeating itself with, at most, a few changes in the cast and scenery. Thus the workers' riots at Gdansk, Gdynia, Szczecin, Slupsk and Elblag were, in a sense, a repeat performance of the Poznan riots of June 1956. The circumstances in which Gomulka – a sick man, worn out and disillusioned – was ousted by Edward Gierek, the 'organization man' *par excellence*, recalled in many ways those of Gomulka's takeover in 1956, which had aroused hopes of a 'new model' socialism, more humane and popular, and more in accordance with national feeling. At that time Gomulka inaugurated a 'dialogue' with the Polish people, denounced the clique that had preceded him, and welcomed the workers' councils. Today, in very similar language, Gierek has embarked on a 'dialogue' of his own, condemned his predecessor's autocratic methods and reactivated the workers' councils which Gomulka allowed to fall into eclipse.

But, while history may repeat itself in this way, at each new crisis the contradictions analysed in the present work arise in an acuter and more threatening form. Meanwhile the official ideology, more and more discredited, degenerates into a form of demagogy that in the long run is powerless to withstand the force of events as represented by the disaffection of the masses, pressure from the thinking element of the population, the requirements of *raison d'état* and the working of economic laws.

The immediate cause of the disturbances and strikes that had to be repressed with bloodshed by the K.B.W. (the internal security corps, forming part of the army) under Generals Moczar and Korczynski – the Soviet troops were prudently confined to barracks – lay in the government's decision, just before Christmas, to put up the price of everyday consumer goods. It is curious that Gomulka and his advisers did not foresee the aggravating effects of this measure, itself the outcome of Poland's long-standing economic imbalance and social discontents – paradoxical as these may seem in a country which ranks statistically as the tenth industrial power in the world, directly after East Germany and Italy.

On two occasions, in 1956 and in 1964–5, the Polish leaders tried to remedy the chronic defects of the economy – its declining growth rate, 300,000 out of work, stagnation in agriculture, low productivity, uncompetitive exports – by reforms involving decentralization and increased incentives. On both occasions the reforms were defeated by diehardism in the economic apparatus, the incompetence of cadres and the apathy of the working class.

A fresh attempt at reform was to have come into effect on 1 January 1971. It was, to say the least, ill prepared, and it involved, to begin with, a further onslaught on the workers' standard of living. This touched off a more violent reaction than that of Poznan in 1956, as enraged workers hung militiamen on lamp-posts, lynched them or flung them into the sea.

It was noticed that the angry crowds of Gdansk, Gdynia and Szczecin directed their attack first and foremost against the premises of party organizations – thus illustrating the sharp distrust of authority which accompanied the economic crisis. Since the party keeps all the economic controls in its own hands, it incurs the blame for all the difficulties that arise. Gomulka's first reaction on hearing of the disturbances was to lay the blame on 'hooligans', the tools of counter-revolutionary elements. He sent his right-hand man Kliszko to the spot, together with Kociolek and General Korczynski, and, apparently overriding the objections of the military leaders, ordered the army to help the militia restore peace. On the evening of 15 December, before the country at large had heard of the riots, the coast towns were occupied and isolated by armoured troops and a curfew was imposed. Many were killed and wounded in this operation.

Two days later, when the government believed the riots were under control, and the party press was applauding the use of force against 'irresponsible rowdies', the most tragic incident of the revolt took place. On the morning of 17 December troops opened fire on the workers of the 'Paris Commune' shipyard at Gdynia. The workers had downed tools on the previous day but, responding to an appeal by Kociolek, appeared in a body next morning before the shipyard gates, only to find them barred by troops. Excitement rose and a round of shots was fired, causing 27 deaths according to the official version; in a leaflet distributed by the workers next day the figure was given as ten times higher. Kociolek later offered the excuse that there had been a misunderstanding. The military, he declared, had learnt that certain elements intended to wreck the yards, and had therefore decided on the Wednesday evening to keep them closed and to inform the workers accordingly; however, the news had failed to reach a large number of workers who lived in the outer suburbs. Whatever the truth of the matter, a great deal of workers' blood was shed.[29]

Fresh riots also broke out on the 17th at Sopot, and especially at Szczecin, where they were extremely violent. Demonstrators from the harbour and the naval dockyard across the Oder set fire to the villa of the party's First Secretary and to the main post office, threw Molotov cocktails at militia cars and looted shops. The main square, the city's pride since its restoration after the war, was crammed with people when the armoured units appeared, charging through the crowd and mowing down young workers and others in its front ranks. The official count was 14 dead and 117 injured, but local inhabitants informed an American reporter that 147 were killed (Le Monde, 2 January 1971). Here too a curfew was imposed. In protest at the army's action, the workers of the Warski yards and the repair dockyard decided to hold a sit-in and also issued a call for a general strike, which many of their comrades obeyed. A Yugoslav journalist declared with some exaggeration that Szczecin had all of a sudden become 'a true workers' republic in which all powers were exercised by the strike committee'.[30] From other reports and a study of the local press it would appear that the 'workers' power' was confined to the shipyards and factories, where improvised militias took care of security and protected the valuable equipment from damage. Meanwhile talks took place between the freely elected representatives of the ten thousand or so shipyard workers and party representatives of the Voivodship and the municipality. These talks were concluded on Saturday the 20th, and next day the armoured units withdrew from the city. The workers went back to their jobs on the 22nd in response to an appeal by Gierek and on being promised that there would be no reprisals against their leaders and that they would receive pay for the strike period.

On the 17th and 18th there were sympathetic demonstrations in other cities, including Katowice, Poznan and Warsaw. The government was in danger of losing control, and this – as Gierek indicated at Wroclaw on 19 March 1971 – would have meant intervention by the Soviet troops stationed in Poland. The Russians showed no desire to be called on to keep the peace, and apparently urged the Polish leaders to try to achieve a political solution.

It became clear that Gomulka's gamble had failed. The army leaders, vexed at their role of repressors of the working class, refused to obey his orders. At this point Gierek went into action. In March 1968, when Moczar was on the point of seizing power, Gierek had saved Gomulka by rallying to him at the last moment, no doubt with the agreement of his Soviet contacts. This time the Kremlin seems to have left Gomulka to his fate, and Gierek was the only man who appeared capable of retrieving the situation. Compared with Moczar, who played an ambiguous part in the repression, Gierek had the advantage of being a capable administrator, with a reputation for good sense, who had built up a team of competent advisers; at the same time he had an impeccable record as an anti-liberal and had backed to the full the Soviet action in the Czechoslovak crisis.

On 18 and 19 December, Gomulka having refused to summon the Politburo, Gierek organized secret consultations with the army leaders, the police and party functionaries. They agreed that Gomulka must go, and it appears in fact that on the 18th he was summarily removed to hospital. Gierek secured the support of Moczar, his principal rival, by granting him and his followers a large though not decisive share in the party and government leadership. The circumstances in which Gomulka was brought to resign were, it seems, particularly distressing. The *fait accompli* was approved by the Seventh Plenum of the Central Committee, which met at Natolin on Sunday the 20th.[31]

All Gomulka's close associates fell with him : Kliszko, Spychalski, Jaszczuk, Strzelecki. Cyrankiewicz had to give up the premiership and accept instead the figurehead post of chief of state. Loga-Sowinski, whose prestige had suffered badly, retained only till the next Plenum (February 1971) his place in the Politburo and at the head of the trade unions, which had once more shown themselves totally incapable of acting as a link between the government and the working class.

The key posts in the administration were taken over by new men, comparatively young: this, as K. A. Jelenski remarks, represents the latest stage of a 'historical progression' in Poland. The levers of command which had been held successively by the nobility and gentry, the nationalist intelligentsia and professional revolutionaries of the Bierut and Gomulka type, now passed to 'apparatchiks' and technicians presenting the bureaucratic, organizational 'new class' which has also come to the fore in East Germany and Hungary. The virulent pragmatism of this class does not stop short of exploiting nationalist and xenophobic sentiments, and it is prompt to defend the dictatorship against any breath of liberalization. The new team in Poland, it may be noted, also reflects a 'geo-sociological' shift from east to west, with men of industrial Silesia replacing natives of eastern Poland who have ruled the country in the past, from Pilsudski to Gomulka.

One of the first steps of the new leadership was to revoke the price increases of 12 December and to announce that there would be a 'frank dialogue' with the workers. The Polish working class had in fact won a remarkable and unprecedented victory: never before in a Communist country had the workers succeeded in overthrowing the government and bringing about the repeal of measures which their rulers had imposed.

Unlike the Polish and Hungarian revolts in 1956, or the events in Czechoslovakia in 1968, the 'Polish December' and its sequel were not preceded or accompanied by nationalist or anti-Soviet pressure, nor were they inspired or led by reformist intellectuals. The latter, as we saw, had been humiliated, repressed and reduced to silence in 1968. The Polish workers faced the party and police alone. Their revolt was of an economic and social character, and it confirmed the rule that whenever a crisis of confidence breaks out in a Communist country the workers tend spontaneously to create new representative bodies – councils, committees or new workers' commissions – which are completely independent of the Communist party and its puppet trade unions.

At the same time, it should be stressed that the workers' claims once again transcended the economic sphere and affected the political structure of the régime. Thus, on 18 December, the strikers at the Warski shipyard at Szczecin demanded not only a general rise in wages and the cancellation of the prices increases, but also the freeing of arrested persons, the liberation of the unions from party control, the separation of powers between the party and state administration, and the dismissal of the party secretary for the Voivodship, who was blamed for the repression. In addition they demanded that their complaints be published by the press, radio and television. Although the workers were not inspired or led by revisionist intellectuals, by following the course that their interests dictated in the given circumstances they found themselves in tune with the main lines of the revisionist programme for the democratization of the socialist state.

That programme, as it was understood by Imre Nagy or Dubcek, is not one that Gierek and his team aspire to carry out. Their aim is a more modest one: to restore confidence to the working class and the technical intelligentsia by adopting a new style of administration – the 'Kadar style' in Polish terms – and by giving the population some satisfaction in the material and psychological fields – the latter by the restoration of the Royal

Castle in Warsaw, the former by means of higher wages, better prices for farm products and better food supplies, all with the help of emergency Soviet aid.

In the dialogue which has been initiated between the government and all sections of the population, the Church enjoys a special position. It is as if Poland were about to become the first 'People's Republic' in which the Communists, while retaining a monopoly of political power, set out to assure themselves of the Church's co-operation by offering it wide freedom of spiritual activity. (It should, however, be remembered that in 1956–7 Cardinal Wyszynski also gave Gomulka significant help in averting the risk of anarchy.)

In this way the Gierek régime foreshadows a kind of technocratic 'Warsaw spring', marked by the rejuvenation of cadres and an improved technique in human relations and decision-taking. At the time of writing it is hardly possible to estimate the duration and success of this new 'N.E.P.', whose promises arouse much scepticism in Poland, or the staying power of a team that is no more than a coalition of personalities who differ widely in their ambitions and political temperament. Can a system that has worked well in Silesia be transferred to Poland as a whole? Do not Moczar's men control too many posts in the organization, and will they not insist on the new team following up the 'purge' of March 1968? In any case Poland is a sick country, and its ills seem too profound to be cured by an injection of new blood, by Soviet aid and some rationalization of methods. The fact that the 'establishment' intends to turn over a new leaf is not to be despised; but once the honeymoon and the 'dialogue' are over, the new team will be faced with the same problems of political, social and economic development that defeated Gomulka, with all the prestige he enjoyed in the bright days of 1956. From this point of view Gierek's position is very like that of Husak, his opposite number in Czechoslovakia.

On the other hand the 'Polish December' spells a warning to the bloc leaders, of a different kind from the lessons taught them by Budapest in 1956 or Prague in 1968. From these two crises the leaders deduced, first and foremost, that it was essential to nip in the bud any suggestion of intellectual opposition within the party or outside it : the main potential danger to the régimes was, it seemed, the revisionist intelligentsia. But December 1970 in Poland showed that in some circumstances – particularly when the party leadership is worn out or divided, as often happens – the working class itself can become a danger to the dictatorship. This is why, after the events in Poland, the Soviet, Bulgarian, Rumanian, Hungarian and East German leaders were eager to express their concern for the workers, both in words and in actions : higher wages, lower prices, improved housing measures, a shake-up of the trade-union leadership. In the Soviet Union, the five-year plan was revised at the last moment so as to grant bigger credits to light industry.

The organ of the Hungarian Communist Party gave the most overt expression to the new emphasis on social aspects resulting from events in Poland. Condemning Gomulka's 'arbitrariness' and 'lack of realism', which had led to the 'mounting up of tensions of all kinds and to a grave social upheaval', *Nepszabad-sag* laid stress on the value of the lessons which might be drawn from a proper analysis of the experiments and set-backs of a fellow-member of the bloc.[32] But has this analysis in fact been deep enough, and can it ever be? None of the bloc countries has as yet offered so plausible an explanation of the dramatic events in Poland as an Italian Communist observer who, pointing out the essential affinity between the Czechoslovak crisis of 1968 and the Polish one of 1970, remarked that 'what was at stake in both of them was a particular concept of power and way of exercising it which we may call Stalinistic'.[33]

The Polish December was in fact one more instance, and doubtless not the last, of the crisis of bureaucratic socialism. As the unhappy and resounding failure of Gomulka, the erstwhile reformer, has shown, this form of socialism has become, irrespective of the intentions of those who practise it and the degree of their subservience to Moscow, an obstacle to the balanced development of collectivistic society. While therefore Brezhnev was extremely cautious in his references to the Polish events in his report to the Twenty-Fourth Soviet Party Congress, we can guess how deep a shadow they must have cast on the deliberations of the supreme Communist body.

Paris, 1971

Epilogue II: The People's Democracies in 1971-2*

The history of the People's Democracies in the years 1971–2 seems to confirm our interpretation of the broad tendencies governing their development. On the one hand there are the efforts of the Soviet Union to maintain control by means of closer political, military and economic integration; and, on the other, the aspirations of the people, in some degree taken up by the governments, to recover their independence and sovereign functions. Similarly we can see within each country, first, the official Communist organization systematically working to retain the upper hand and, second, nationally rooted economic, social and cultural forces whose development, to the extent to which they are tolerated, leads towards pluralism and towards a stronger constitutional basis for the régime.

On the international level the principal event of recent years has been the reconciliation of the Soviet Union and the German Federal Republic. This was sealed on 12 August 1970 by the signing of the U.S.S.R.–G.F.R. treaty, which was subsequently ratified by the Bundestag, in somewhat dramatic circumstances, on 17 May 1972. These diplomatic developments, which constituted a notable success for the Soviet Union, are part of a total political strategy by which the Kremlin means to bring about a general and permanent recognition of the European *status quo* resulting from the war. The Soviet leaders consider that such a recognition would be a confirmation of the doctrine of 'limited sovereignty', which has come to be considered as the expression of a specifically socialist international law governed by the principle of socialist internationalism, and distinguished from general international law based on the principle of the sovereign equality of states.[1] One of the primary diplomatic objectives of the

*Translated by Peter Byrne.

U.S.S.R. was to bring about the Conference on European Security and Co-operation, where it wished to be seen both as the major European power putting forward its conception of a 'greater Europe' as an alternative to the 'little Europe' of the Ten, and also as the guardian of East European order based on the principles noted above. By receiving President Nixon in May 1972, despite his defiant decision to blockade Haiphong, Brezhnev showed that his priorities lay in Europe and in Soviet-American co-operation.

The attitude of the People's Democracies to Moscow's 'grand strategy' is not unconditionally favourable. Generally their governments and people approve any moves that lessen tension and bring East and West closer together. Indeed an easing of tension between the two blocs seems to be an indispensable condition for social and economic advance. But the *way* the U.S.S.R. works for *détente*, appropriating for itself the prime political and economic benefits, sometimes disquiets both responsible leaders and public opinion (to the extent that it is allowed to be expressed). To take but one example, the Polish government showed signs of strong disappointment and displeasure when the signing and ratification of the Polish-West German treaty was made to depend upon the concluding of the U.S.S.R.–G.F.R. treaty.

Gomulka, by taking part in the occupation of Czechoslovakia in 1968, contributed in no small way to the change of direction in Brandt's *Ostpolitik*. Finding the road to the East closed by client governments, the Federal Republic of necessity negotiated first of all with their master. But Gierek in 1972 is a different figure from Gomulka in 1968; and, although Poland's economic weakness makes it more than ever dependent on Soviet aid, Warsaw's diplomacy strives (if only to satisfy public feeling at home) to show an independent profile. The Poles have not forgotten Rapallo and 1939, and they instinctively fear lest German-Russian co-operation work to the detriment of Poland's interests. This fear has increased since, with Ulbricht's departure, Honecker and his team of ultra-orthodox ideologists have brought the G.D.R. more completely in line with Moscow. Poland now feels caught between Russia and the two Germanies, both of which have a special relationship with the Russians. However, by visiting

Poland – after Russia – Nixon flattered the Poles' proverbial pride, and they also hope to gain something from the competition between the two German states. Furthermore, the ratification of the treaty with the G.F.R., seen in Poland as the recognition of the permanent character of the eastern frontier, consolidated the international position of the country, for which the Polish Party was quick to take all the credit.

For their part, the leaders of the G.D.R., that 'socialist state of the German nation', are clearly seeking to win compensation for the concessions they had to make to ease the reconciliation of Bonn and Moscow. They are intensifying their campaign for recognition of their *Abgrenzung* policy and of their existence as a state. Such an approach will, they hope, lead, with time and the growth of a carefully fostered sense of nation- and statehood, to a conferring of the legitimacy of which they feel the want more cruelly than any of the other Communist leaders of the Eastern bloc. The East Berlin leaders seem especially concerned because the Federal German Republic is better liked than the G.D.R. by most of the People's Democracies – Poland, Hungary, Rumania, even Czechoslovakia. This scarcely veiled preference can be explained not merely by the attraction of West Germany's economic power and technology, but also by the interest the West Germans show in the intellectual life – literary, artistic and scientific – of the East European countries. While the 'Red Prussians' readily adopt the role of supercilious censors, quick to intervene against any sign of independent thinking, the West Germans demonstrate a disarming sympathy, and everything suggests that the re-establishment of normal relations with Bonn – notwithstanding the priority the G.F.R. gives to its friendly relations with Moscow – will open the way to specially favoured cultural and, above all, economic exchanges between the Federal Republic and almost all the East European countries. In the long term any such evolution could undermine Soviet hegemony in the area.

This is all the more likely since the reconciliation with Federal Germany, as well as the increased Soviet-American co-operation, has dispelled the fears of policies based on revenge, of a 'rebirth of German militarism' as the vanguard of Atlantic imperialism, which since 1945 have been the chief binding force of the Soviet bloc and the main justification of the Warsaw Treaty. As H. Birecki,[2] a former Polish ambassador, has explained, the U.S.S.R. is seeking to supply a new cohesion and to justify its continued hegemony by speeding up economic and military integration. One of Brezhnev's most prominent collaborators, Konstantin Katushev,[3] has warned the socialist states against any loosening of the political, economic or ideological ties between them. The general laws of socialism are immutable, he said, and national characteristics must be subordinated to them. In accordance with this doctrine, the procedures of the Warsaw Treaty have been strengthened, and the new programme adopted by Comecon in 1971 attempts to perfect the machinery for co-ordinating plans and to outline a charter to regulate bilateral or multilateral co-operation. Steps were even taken to co-ordinate the ideological activities and cultural policies of Communist parties and governments.

In some sectors progress has been made. However, on the whole, integration seems to be dragging its feet, and one has the impression that the appeal (both economic and cultural) of the West is, throughout the area, on the point of overtaking that of the East. Comecon takes pains to encourage joint ventures with mixed investment financed by member countries, but it has been compelled to postpone the actual co-ordination of long-term plans and to forgo the creation of any supranational organization. Soviet pressure to make the East European countries contribute heavily to the exploitation of its raw materials met with opposition even from the Hungarian government, which, although occasionally expressing mild objections, had hitherto been respectfully submissive.

But it is Rumania especially that continues vigorously and flexibly to resist pressure to bring about integration. This resistance is all the more remarkable when we consider conditions in and around her, which, as in the case of Yugoslavia, have deteriorated strikingly between 1969 and 1972. This deterioration is due to increased Russian presence in the eastern Mediterranean, the uncertain future of Cyprus and Malta, the doubts about what will follow Titoism and, last but not least, the unfavourable economic situation in Rumania itself. Yet Ceausescu imperturbably pursues his objective of 'independence within interdependence'. While addressing the Twenty-Fourth Congress of the Soviet Communist Party, he spoke fearlessly against 'any interference in the internal affairs of other parties' and in favour of 'relationships of a new type between socialist countries'. He further provoked the anger of the Kremlin by his trip to China (1–9 June 1971) and his contribution to Sino-American reconciliation. Throughout the summer of 1971 Rumania was subjected to pressure of all kinds from the U.S.S.R. and its satellites, particularly from Hungary (which called attention to the problem of the Hungarian minority in Transylvania) and Bulgaria. Even military intervention seemed possible. The views of the other countries of the bloc can be gathered from a report presented by Vasil Bilak to the Czechoslovak Central Committee in October 1971.[6] Bilak stated that 'the essential cause' of differences between the other Warsaw Pact countries and Rumania was the latter's 'inclination to further national interests contrary to the international obligations resulting from membership in the socialist community.' Ceausescu was accused of 'seeking to profit unilaterally from the advantages of co-operation', while at the same time not considering himself bound by 'collective commitments'. Bilak reproached him with favouring expressions of nationalism in the cultural field, with failing to reply, when he was in China, to Chinese attacks on the U.S.S.R., the Pact and Comecon, etc.

Ceausescu, however, stood up to these pressures, and his only concession to his accusers (if indeed it turns out to have been a concession) was to strengthen party control of intellectual life and to advocate the elimination of Western bourgeois influences. But at the same time, in the autumn of 1971, he replaced General Serb and a number of other high-ranking officers who, it appears, favoured a pro-Soviet line. This purge culminated in February 1972 with the dismissal of V. Patilinet, the party secretary for defence and security. Then, by putting forward Rumania's candidacy for a special relationship with the Common Market, welcoming Mrs Golda Meir to Bucharest, and making a vigorous contribution to the Helsinki preparatory talks, the Rumanian leader again showed his determination to secure for his country a unique place on the international scene.

The 'nationalism' of Ceausescu might in some ways be considered a tactic to divert attention from his government's slow progress in the economic, social and even political and cultural fields. In the same way, Janos Kadar's policy in Hungary could be called a 'consumer' diversion. The Hungarian government hemmed in by the beneficiaries of the treaty of Trianon and post-Second World War treaties, and under close Soviet supervision since 1956, is in no position to initiate a foreign policy of the kind that would satisfy the people's desire for independence and change. Therefore, to retain some of the functions of a sovereign state, the government fell back on economic and cultural activities. This produced the most substantial economic reform in Eastern Europe, making Hungary the most prosperous country of the bloc – and the most liberal, so far as personal and intellectual freedom is concerned. This privileged position is, of course, precarious. Soviet pressure was doubtless behind the security measures taken by the government of Jenoe Fock in December 1972 on the eve of Brezhnev's visit to Budapest. Because Kadar is given credit for ending in 1961 the repression that followed the insurrection and for introducing a more liberal policy, there is concern about what will happen to the country when he goes. Hungary, like the other Communist countries, is suffering the effects of the institutional instability inherent in one-party régimes given to identifying power with specific individuals. However, for the present, carefully watched by the Kremlin, Hungary serves as the East's show-case for the West. Kadar's methods may be disapproved of in Berlin, Sofia and perhaps (but for different reasons) Bucharest, but certainly Gierek in Poland and probably Gustav Husak in Czechoslovakia seem to want to adopt them.

Moreover, Hungary was the first socialist country whose leaders, even before the shock produced by the Baltic riots, called for a social policy which would lessen the new inequalities, help the most deprived groups of workers, and restore some representative function to the trade unions. The Hungarian model – which the Hungarian theoreticians desperately try to explain as simply a harmless variant of the Soviet form of government – emphasizes fuller use of abilities and skill, and gives experts and 'technocrats' a larger role. Some of Kadar's success in the economic field results from his willingness to employ specialists of Jewish origin to develop the tourist industry and domestic and foreign commerce. This is in contrast to the Polish and Czech leaders, who, as a sop to the most retrograde sectors of public opinion, or in order to establish 'nationalist' alibis or eliminate capable rivals, have removed Jews from all responsible positions under cover of the anti-Zionist campaign.

In the case of Czechoslovakia the process of normalization – which amounts to restoring the Party monolith to power and hamstringing the opposition – was illustrated at the Twenty-Fourth Party Congress (May 1971) and the general elections (November of the same year). The Congress rewarded Husak by consolidating his position, though without completely ending the undercover battle being waged against him by Vasil Bilak and the other exponents of the hard line. These men, whose influence is especially strong in the police organization, are said to have been behind the various waves of arrests (November 1971 and January–February 1972) amongst supporters of Dubcek such as the student leader Jiri Mueller, the historians Milan Huebl and Karel Kaplan, and Slansky's son. These arrests, which it was thought would be followed by trials, caused concern among Western Communists, notably in the French party, which succeeded in making Husak repeat his promise not to proceed against anyone on account of his political opinions or attitude in 1968. Nonetheless trials were held; and contrary to expectations Husak took no action till the spring of 1973 to conciliate the intelligentsia or national opinion. In such circumstances there was a ridiculous side to the election results – with over 99 per cent of the 99.45 per cent of voters choosing National Front candidates.

Albania and Bulgaria have both remained confined within their own particular orthodoxies. In the international sphere the Albanian leaders have to their credit the championing of China's entry to the United Nations. But the Sino-American reconciliation, though not openly criticized, has given rise in Tirana to some concern over Peking's aims. But the Albanians themselves have shown realism by establishing normal relations with the Colonels' Greece and extending their contacts with Yugoslavia.

As for Bulgaria, it continues to prove itself the most faithful ally of the U.S.S.R. After Brezhnev's visit to Belgrade and Sofia the controversy with Yugoslavia over Macedonia was dropped. In domestic politics the important event was the promulgation in May 1971 of a new constitution which legalized the role of the Communist party as the guiding force of state and society. The Bulgarians have thus created a precedent which might be followed by other Communist parties. Their action goes against the opinion which hitherto prevailed among East European jurists to the effect that 'any attempt to define in concrete terms how the guiding role of the party should be fulfilled would inevitably limit the supremacy of the party rather than show it in a more precise and detailed light.'[5] Indeed to give a legal basis to the guiding role of the party means to make it into a quasi-institution of state, whereas traditionally the party has been considered to be above the state.

*

In Yugoslavia discussion of constitutional revision has also been at the centre of political activity. According to the amendments to the constitution adopted on 30 June 1971, the six federal republics were to become sovereign states. But how could the sovereignty of the federation be reconciled with that of the republics? Would Yugoslavia become a federation of states or a federal state? The Croatian Communist leaders, with vast public support, determined to use the debate to get rid of the last vestiges of the centralization which guaranteed the Serbs a predominant position in the state. Their demands concerned not only a better distribution of the foreign currency earned by tourism in Croatia or sent home by its 600,000 workers abroad, but also the placing of Croats in positions of command in the army stationed in Croatia, in the police, administration, banks, etc.

It seems that none of the Croatian government or Croatian Communist party leaders – Tripalo, Pirker, Bjelic (a Serb from Croatia), Mrs Dabcevic-Kucar, Haramija, etc. – intended to press the offensive to the point of separatism. By espousing Croatian nationalism (which erupted vigorously during the summer and autumn, with its focal-point in the Matica Hrvatska cultural association, together with the union of students and the writers' union) they apparently hoped to reshape the foundations of the federation and to strengthen the authority of the Croatian party. Meanwhile the army, the traditional guardian of the country's unity, was urging Tito to step in before it was too late.[6] The student strike that broke out on 23 November in support of economic claims against Belgrade supplied the spark that exploded the powder keg. At a meeting of the presidium of the League of Communists at Karadjordjevo (1–2 December 1971) Tito, backed up by the representatives of the other republics, repudiated the Croatian leaders and called upon the party organizations to remove them if they did not offer to resign.

The highest and middle ranks of the Croatian party, the university, the press and various sectors of the administration were decimated in a vast purge. Hundreds of arrests were made, mainly among the students and the leaders of Matica Hrvatska. The force unleashed by Tito, both political and through the police, discouraged all resistance.

The fact that, in order to bring the Croats to heel, Tito had relied upon the central organization and on the Serbs of Croatia might have created the impression in Zagreb that this was a new victory for the 'greater Serbia' movement that once before, in pre-war days, had put its stamp on Yugoslavia. Tito was seen as a new King Alexander stubbornly crushing by force the Croatian nationalist ambitions.

Any such interpretation has, however, been proved wrong by the events of autumn 1972. These indicated that for Tito, and for his Croatian collaborators, such as Bakaric, the 'normalization' of Croatia was only the prelude to a firm taking in hand of all the republics in the federation.

Everything suggests that Tito had suddenly seen the seriousness of the disorders caused by uncontrolled activity, by 'primitive capitalism', as the London *Economist* called it; and it seems that he realized that the situation, worsened by growing inequalities and selective strikes, could lead to the breaking up of the state when he, its founder, departed. After the decentralizing measures of recent years, the central government retained little or no authority. Croatian nationalism was only the most obvious symptom of the crisis. Particular interests made themselves felt on all sides. The Communist League, conceived as a linking mechanism between the central authorities and those in the republics, had gradually transformed itself, as Tito remarked, into an 'unstable coalition of republican and regional organizations', engendering discussion rather than decision or action. For the aged Tito, a man of energy formed in the Leninist school, who, for all his open-mindedness and flexibility, remains attached to his youthful ideals, this state of affairs too closely resembled the anarchy he so abhors.

When, after much hesitation, Tito finally decided to take firm action to restore central authority and the guiding role of the party, he found that his most powerful opposition came from the heartland of the system, in Serbia at Belgrade. Indeed the leaders of the Serbian party, Nikezic, Mrs Latinka Perovic and Todorovic, were, and have remained, opponents of centralism. They disapproved, it seems, of the authoritarian way in which the Croatian affair was settled, and openly expressed their fears that the reappearance of strong methods might put in jeopardy everything gained by economic reform and modernization. They had made the secretariat of the Serbian party a stronghold of liberalism, buttressed by an intense financial concentration (the Belgrade banks represent 65 per cent of the country's capital) and enjoying the support of the managerial class, the intelligentsia, and the whole of the press.

To overcome this opposition, so much more powerful than the resistance of the Croats, Tito threw into the scales all his prestige, persuasive powers, and skill in political manoeuvre. On 2 October he sent a circular letter – a kind of encyclical – to all the party organizations, announcing his restoration programme. Energetic measures were to be taken to stabilize the economy, to strengthen central planning, and to combat the 'new rich', the '180 millionaires' whose ostentatious wealth had given rise to so much protest during recent years.

Some days later the Serbian central committee was convened. The session went on for four days behind closed doors and was the occasion of a violent confrontation. The incredible happened: Tito found himself, for the first time, in a minority within the supreme Serbian council. But he did not lose heart. Backed up by Dolanc and his personal advisers, the Miskovic brothers, chiefs of security, he called for help to his old comrades, Kardelj and Bakaric, as well as to the new – centralist – leaders of Croatia. His emissaries stirred up local organizations in opposition to Belgrade. After three secret sessions, Nikezic and Mrs Perovic yielded to the pressure and offered to resign. The gravity of the crisis was underlined by the fact that, throwing in their lot with the resigning leaders, Mirko Tepavac, the foreign minister, and Koca Popovic, that extremely popular old friend of Tito, also handed in their resignations.

The fallen leaders were rebuked not only for their liberalism and their want of energy in fighting corruption, but also for their tendency 'to consider the Serbian section of the League as a quasi-autonomous organization.' Likewise, when the purge was extended to Slovenia the president of the council, Stane Kavcic, and his friends were forced to resign, accused of having envisaged transforming Slovenia into an 'autonomous country, dependent on central Europe, a kind of appendage of Austria, Italy and Germany.' It was also because of 'nationalist' tendencies that one of the most prominent Macedonian leaders, Slavko Miloslavlevski, was replaced.

During the early months of 1973 the purges were again intensified within the party and the Socialist Alliance, among the press, the university (particularly in the philosophy and social science departments) and the magistracy. They took on the aspect of a 'witch-hunt', led by the survivors of the old guard of the Rankovic era against the younger generation of liberal or 'technocrat' Communists who took over in 1965. The draft of the new constitution, originally meant to make the system more democratic, was revised with the opposite result. The increased severity of the penal code, the strengthening of police powers, the new press law promulgated in Serbia, which once again places journalists in direct dependence on the bureaucracy, the re-establishment of compulsory courses in Marxism (of a narrowly orthodox stamp), official statements re-emphasizing that 'communism', not 'self-government', is the primary aim: all these seem to go beyond the reimposing of central authority. Rather they show a determination to undertake systematic action for a 'return to the roots', an anti-reform which would bring the

Yugoslav system closer to the classical model of socialism current in the other Communist countries.

This raises the question whether the move to the left, this conservative, anti-liberal offensive, will imply a change in Yugoslav foreign policy. It is a fact that on several occasions Tito has expressed irritation with the Western press, which according to him wrote quite improperly of 'crisis', 'purges' and 'a minor Cultural Revolution' in Yugoslavia, and did so because it was disappointed in its hopes of 'seeing the country drift gradually towards the West.' While the replaced liberal leaders were known to have Western sympathies, the 'centralists' – whose declarations were given vigorous approval by the press in the Soviet bloc countries – tended to lay the blame for all Yugoslavia's difficulties on corrosive influences from the West.

Thus, the 'strong man' of the new team, Dolanc, emphasized the alleged support that the Croatian separatists were supposed to have received from the West. He also rebuked the former Slovene leaders for having 'steered too close to the West'. Belgrade dug up the ancient quarrel with Austria over the Slovene minority in Carinthia (a note was sent to the Austrian government on 10 November 1972); the Croatian deputies accused the Italian authorities of having encouraged 'resurgent irredentism among the Italians in Yugoslav Istria'. For the first time a military exercise (the most extensive since 1945) had as its theme the attempted landing of an enemy on the coastal archipelago of Dalmatia. Watched by a distinguished guest, the Polish minister of defence, the enemy who was to be repulsed approached from the west.

Yugoslavia also concluded an important economic agreement with the U.S.S.R. and Hungary, involving credits amounting respectively to 1,300 and 200 millions of dollars. In an interview published in *Vjesnik* (Zagreb) on 5 February 1973, Tito hinted that the U.S.S.R. might rise from third to first place in Yugoslavia's foreign exchange. At the same time he repudiated those Yugoslav leaders who – following the 'line' established since 1958 – interpreted non-alignment to mean a position equidistant from the two superpowers. 'The Soviet Union is a socialist country at war with no one ... What happened in Czechoslovakia is over and done with.' Shortly afterwards, Tito accepted Husak's invitation to Prague, where on an earlier visit, in August 1968, he had given his full support to Dubcek. Finally, while reaffirming his desire to remain outside the Sino-Soviet conflict and to increase his contacts with Peking, Tito insisted that Yugoslavia's relationship with the Soviet Union was much more fully developed, and also extended to relations between the two Communist parties. This was not the first time, of course, that the Marshal, for domestic reasons, had stressed the distance between himself and the West, whose attraction – in Serbia quite as much as in Croatia and Slovenia – works towards a liberalization which alarms him. Throughout all his calculated shifts of position, he has always managed to keep his balance. It is hardly likely that before leaving the scene Tito would wish to sacrifice the independence of Yugoslavia. But he wants to leave behind him a *Communist* Yugoslavia; and his new course, with its anti-liberal measures, could in the long run favour the growth of Soviet influence, especially if economic relations with the West were impeded.

The situation, however, remains too unsettled – at the time of writing – to yield any clear perspective. Especially in Serbia, Tito is far from having won the day. The advances made during the last ten years in independent thinking and in day-to-day living, the growth of democracy in ordinary life, seem to be irreversible. Will a change of course – however strongly it is applied – be enough to transform mental habits, reinvigorate anaemic ideology, and put new life into the Party? Will administrative action of a repressive sort succeed in rendering omnipresent nationalism innocuous? Is it certain that Yugoslavia can be governed only by force, and that it can regain its stability without the whole-hearted agreement of the Serbian, Slovene and Croatian élites?

Questioned on the problem of his successor in a B.B.C. interview (16 October 1972), Tito replied with surprising optimism: 'Nothing will change when I go. Everything will go on just as it is now.' But the fact is that *now* everything is turbulent, full of fears and question-marks. Are we witnessing a passing crisis or the death throes of the Yugoslav experiment? Will Tito himself consent to, or even, without the Russians having to lift a finger, undertake, the destruction of everything that was original and attractive in Titoism? Will the Yugoslav régime abandon its great aim of being a laboratory of modern socialism and work its own transformation into a Balkan-type 'national Communism' of the Rumanian or Albanian variety? Or a Communist version of the royal dictatorship of 1929? What is beyond doubt is that the defeat of the Yugoslav liberals was a psychological shock for public opinion in the neighbouring countries comparable to that of 1968, and that conservative leaders in the U.S.S.R. and the People's Democracies see it as confirming the correctness of their view that any democratic and decentralizing alternative to socialism is impracticable.

Paris, April 1973

Notes

Introduction: Stalinism at its Apogee and in Decline

1 English translation published by the Foreign Language Publishing House, Moscow, 1952.

2 cf. *Current Soviet Policies: the Documentary Record of the Nineteenth Party Congress and the Reorganization after Stalin's Death,* New York, 1953.

3 cf. Peskova and Veber, 'Notes on the History of the Cult of Personality in Czechoslovakia', *Acta Universitatis Carolinae,* Prague, 1966.

4 cf. 'Document interne du P.C. tchécoslovaque sur les crimes de la période stalinienne', *Le Monde,* 29–30 May 1966.

5 For Hungary, these events are described by S. Nogradi in *A New Chapter of History Begins,* Budapest, 1966, which also contains an interesting portrait of Matyas Rakosi.

6 Lange, Oskar, 'Towards Socialist Democracy', in *Trybuna Ludu,* 5 December 1956.

7 cf. Elias, Z., and Netik, Jaromir, 'Czechoslovakia', in *Communism in Europe,* II, M.I.T. Press, Cambridge, Mass., 1966.

8 As quoted by Rudolf Barak, then Minister of the Interior and chairman of the Central Committee sub-committee charged with re-examining the files on the Slansky trial in 1956. See *Rude Pravo,* 13 June 1956. Barak himself was arrested in 1961 and sentenced the following year for 'abuse of power and theft'.

9 In his book on the trial (*Die Revolution rehabilitiert ihre Kinder,* Europa, Vienna, 1968) Loebl describes how he was beaten by Svab during an interrogation.

10 *Mlada Fronta,* 31 March 1968.

11 *Smena,* Bratislava, 28 April 1968.

12 cf., besides Loebl, op. cit., the testimony of Artur London, another survivor of the trial and a former Deputy Minister of Foreign Affairs, *L'aveu,* Gallimard, Paris, 1968.

13 *Svobodni Slovo,* 24 May 1968.

14 *Pour une paix durable, pour la démocratie populaire*, 25 November 1952. It should be noted that after June 1956 Novotny, the head of the Czechoslovak party, asserted that all the confessions made by Slansky and his associates implicating the Yugoslavs were totally untrue. But twelve more years elapsed before the entirely false and fictitious character of the confessions, the evidence and the charges was officially acknowledged.

15 According to Ben Gurion, Slansky had been the only Czechoslovak leader bitterly opposed to Prague's delivery of arms to Israel. See the interview reported in *Yediot Aharonot*, Tel Aviv, 30 April 1968.

16 cf. Fejtö, F., 'Le procès de Prague', *Esprit*, March/April 1953; Barton, P., *Prague à l'heure de Moscou, analyse d'une démocratie populaire*, Paris, 1954; Fejtö, F., *Les juifs et l'antisémitisme dans les pays communistes*, Plon, Paris, 1960; Burks, R. V., *The Dynamics of Communism in Eastern Europe*, Princeton University Press, Princeton, N.J., 1961, Ch. 8.

17 Fejtö, F., *Histoire des démocraties populaires: l'ère de Staline*, Seuil, Paris, 1952, pp. 273–8; Ionescu, G., *Communism in Rumania 1944–1962*, London, 1964; Fischer-Galati, S., *The New Rumania*, M.I.T. Press, Cambridge, Mass., 1967.

18 cf. Burgin, J., 'The Contagion', *Przeglad Kulturalny*, 13 February 1957.

19 cf. Stern, Carola, *Ulbricht: A Political Biography*, trans. A. Farbstein, Pall Mall, London, and Praeger, New York, 1965; and *Porträt einer bolschewistischen Partei*, Kiessenheuer und Witsch, Cologne, 1957, Ch. 4.

20 It seems that in June 1963 Beria nearly succeeded in totally eliminating Rakosi and his Jewish clique from the leadership of the Hungarian party. A resolution to this effect was about to be carried by the Hungarian Central Committee (unanimously, as always) when Khrushchev informed Rakosi over the telephone of the 'liquidation' of Beria, and ordered him to rescind the resolution. Rakosi remained at the head of the party, and Malenkov's protégé, Nagy, became chairman of the Council.

21 Hamsik, D., *Literarni Listy*, 29 March 1968.

22 The New Economic Policy (N.E.P.), instituted in the Soviet Union in 1921, under which a wide range of private economic activity was legalized.

PART I: THE EVENTS

1 *The New Course*

1 cf. Leonhard, Wolfgang, *N. S. Krouchtchev: Ascension et chute d'un homme d'État soviétique*, Rencontre, Paris, 1965, p. 49. After 1955 Khrushchev in a sense took over 'Malenkovism', but then a new current was becoming manifest, especially in Poland and Hungary: revisionism. On the main political currents in the People's Democracies, see also the article by Ryszard Turski and Eligiusz Lasota, 'The Polish October', *Po Prostu*, 28 October 1956.

2 As early as 6 June 1953, Molotov proposed to Tito that the two countries exchange ambassadors, and Tito agreed on 15 June. At the same time the U.S.S.R. regularized relations with Turkey and Israel, and gave China, exhausted by the Korean war which she was largely financing, the go-ahead to re-open negotiations for an armistice, finally signed after prolonged bargaining at Panmunjom on 27 July 1953.

3 Despite official and unofficial explanations, the Beria affair is still shrouded in mystery. There was apparently a close association between Beria and Malenkov, at least during the first few months after Stalin's death; it seems probable that the coup against Beria was directed also, and perhaps primarily, against Malenkov. In any case, the one who stood to profit most from Beria's removal was Khrushchev, who, in September 1953, was appointed First Secretary of the Central Committee – that is head of the party machine.

4 cf. Seniga, Giulio, *Togliatti e Stalin*, Sugar Editore, Milan, 1961.

5 Kraus, Wolfgang H., 'Crisis and Revolt in a Satellite', Noordwijk Conference paper, 1965 (unpublished).

6 cf. correspondence in *Bund*, Berne, 22 April 1953.

7 See Spittman, Ilse, in *Süddeutsche Zeitung*, Munich, 10 March 1963.

8 Stern, C., *Ulbricht*, op. cit.

9 On Kronstadt, see Gletcher, G., 'Against the Stream: Resistance to Totalitarianism within the Soviet Empire, 1917–1966', in *Ten Years After* (ed. T. Aczel), MacGibbon & Kee, London, 1966.

10 cf. Jaenicke, M., *Der Dritte Weg*, Cologne, 1964.

11 cf. 'The New Course and the Party's Tasks', *Neues Deutschland*, 28 July 1953.

12 cf. Imre Nagy's political memoirs, written in 1955–6 and published as *On Communism: in defence of the New Course*, Thames & Hudson, London, 1957.

13 Nagy's accounts of the talks have never been contradicted, and we have every reason to believe in their authenticity. Regrettably Nagy mentions nothing said by Beria who had played an important part in the decisions taken 'by common consent'.

14 cf. Fejtö, F., *La Tragédie hongroise*, Horay, Paris, 1956, p. 211.

15 According to evidence collected in Prague, Gottwald had been only a shadow of his former self since the Slansky trial. The death sentences of so many of his old friends had broken his spirit, destroyed him as a human being, and turned him into a drunkard.

16 cf. Kaplan, K., 'From Monetary Reform to the Tenth Czechoslovak Party Congress', *Sbornik Historicky*, October 1962.

17 'Czech Currency Riots', *The Times*, London, 9 July 1953.

18 A gigantic memorial to the Generalissimo was erected in Prague in May 1955, to be removed only in 1962.

19 Regarding the similarities between the French and Czechoslovak parties, see Fejtö, F., *The French Communist Party and the Crisis of International Communism*, M.I.T. Press, Cambridge, Mass., 1967, p. 86.

20 *Rude Pravo*, 24 February 1954.

21 cf. Fejtö, F., *Histoire des démocraties populaires*, op. cit., pp. 260–68.

22 *Nowe Drogi*, December 1954.

23 *Nowa Kultura*, 13 and 20 June 1954.

24 cf. Gozdzik (party secretary in the Zeran factory) in *Pologne-Hongrie*, 1956, p. 22.

2 Relations between the U.S.S.R. and the Socialist Countries

1 cf. Fejtö, F., *Chine-U.R.S.S. La fin d'une hégémonie*, Plon, Paris, 1964, Ch. 5.

2 Djilas, Milovan, *Lénine et les rapports entre États socialistes*, Livre Yougoslave, Paris, 1949.

3 These words were reported by Severyn Bialer, whose account was confirmed later by the Czech historian V. Kotyk in *Cesko-slovensky Casopis Historicky*, No. 3, 1965.

4 Popovic, M., *Des rapports économiques entre États socialistes*, Livre Yougoslave, Paris, 1949.

5 Nagy, Imre, *On Communism*, op. cit., p. 83.

6 Seniga, G., *Togliatti e Stalin*, op. cit., p. 49.

7 Quoted in 'Is Yugoslavia a Socialist Country?', an editorial which appeared in *Red Flag* and *People's Daily*, 26 September 1963.

8 In *The Struggle of the Albanian Workers' Party Against Right-Wing Opportunists between 1945 and 1955*, 1967, S. Mahdi states that the Albanian leadership was not informed of the Soviet plan to 're-examine' the Cominform resolutions condemning Titoism, to dispense with the Cominform, and to come to terms with Yugoslavia, until three days before Khrushchev's departure for Yugoslavia on 26 May 1955. Hoxha replied on 25 May in a letter calling for a meeting of the Cominform to decide on the course to be followed. But no notice was taken of his proposal. cf. *Studime Historike*, No. 3, 1967.

9 cf. the League statutes in *Questions actuelles du socialisme*, 15 December 1952.

10 On the Yugoslav experiment, see Moch, Jules, *La Yougoslavie, terre d'expérience*, Paris, 1953; Bobrowski, C., *La Yougoslavie socialiste du plan quinquennal de 1947 au bilan de 1955*, Paris, 1956; 'La démocratie socialiste en Yougoslavie', *Notes et études documentaires*, *Documentation française*, January 1963; 'Le fédéralisme yougoslave', *idem*, 16 June 1961; 'L'évolution des institutions yougoslaves d'après les constitutions de 1946–1953 et 1963', *idem*, 5 March, 1964; 'L'économie yougoslave', *idem*, 5 March 1965; 'L'évolution du communisme yougoslave', *idem*, 9 June 1966.

11 Thames & Hudson, London, 1957.

12 *On Communism: in defence of the New Course*, op. cit., p. 82.

13 cf. Fejtö, F., *Histoire des démocraties populaires*, op. cit., p. 288.

14 Formal agreements on the stationing of Soviet troops were concluded in 1956, after the Hungarian and Polish risings. Rumania, on the other hand, secured the withdrawal of Soviet troops in 1958.

15 Article in *Red Star*, Moscow, 14 May 1965. In January 1968, in the great struggle against Novotny, Lomsky was one of the latter's strongest supporters and so compromised his position.

For a fuller treatment of the Pact see Part II, Chapter 15, of this book.

3 *The Twentieth Congress of the C.P.S.U.*

1 cf. Rossi, A., *Autopsie du stalinisme*, containing the full text of the secret report, Horay, Paris, 1957.

2 cf. *People's Daily* and *Red Flag* editorial on Stalin, 12 September 1963.

3 No. 14, 1955.

4 cf. Gruliow, Leo, ed., *Current Soviet Policies*, No. 2, Columbia University Press, New York, 1957.

5 Opat, J., in *Prespevky k Dejinam Kec*, No. 1, 1965.

6 cf. Daniszewski, T., *Droga Walki K.P.P.*, Warsaw, 1949. The Polish Communists during the war had revived the movement as the Polish Workers' Party, with the Kremlin's permission. This name was changed in 1948, after the merger with the Social Democrats, into the Polish United Workers' Party.

7 cf. Varga, Eugene, in *Pravda*, 21 February 1956; 'Portrait de Béla Kun', *Est et Ouest*, 16–31 October 1957; Honti, Françoise, 'La fin de Béla Kun', *Le Monde*, 14 May 1949; Szélpál, Arpad, *Les 133 jours de Béla Kun*, Paris, 1955.

8 cf. Ceausescu's statement, 7 May 1966, and Voicu, S., in *Lupta de Clasa*, No. 6, 1966.

9 cf. *Z Pola Walki*, No. 1, Poland, 1966, p. 21.

10 cf. Hervé, P., *La révolution et ses fétiches*, Paris, 1956.

11 *Red Flag* and *People's Daily* editorial, 30 March 1964, and Lacina, V., 'The Conference on the Fifteenth Anniversary of the February Revolution', *Ceskoslovensky Casopis Historicky*, No. 3, 1963, which draws attention to the role of the army chief Svoboda in the negotiations with Benes.

4 The Eastern Leaders and De-Stalinization

1 Vlahovic, V., *Komunist*, Belgrade, 25 August 1955.

2 cf. Hoxha's speech, 7 November 1966, in *Notes et études documentaires, Documentation française*, No. 3139.

3 See for example Zochowski, T., 'For the Restoration of Agriculture', Po Prostu, 30 September 1956.

4 Gozdzik, L., and Waclawek, J., 'Thus Was the Vanguard Formed', *Trybuna Ludu*, 12 November 1956, and Hajnicz, A., in *Nowa Kultura*, 1 July 1956.

5 *Manchester Guardian*, 1 October 1956.

6 On 5 April Bulganin sent Rakosi a telegram congratulating this 'tested veteran of the revolutionary movement' on the measures he had taken to strengthen the system of People's Democracy.

7 On the situation in Czechoslovakia immediately after the Twentieth Congress, see Freeman, John, in *New Statesman and Nation*, 21 July 1956, and Ferney, B., in *France-Observateur*, 27 July 1956.

8 See Crossman, R.H.S., in *New Statesman and Nation*, 5 May 1956.

9 cf. *Magyar Nemzet*, 15 March 1956.

10 Revai, Jozsef, in *Tarsadalmi Szemle*, Nos. 8 and 9, Budapest, 1952.

11 Braun, Andrzej, in *Nowa Kultura*, 18 March 1956.

12 Woroszylski, V., 'Matériaux pour une biographie', *Temps Modernes*, February–March 1957.
13 Labedz, Leopold, ed., *Revisionism: Essays on the History of Marxist Ideas*, Allen & Unwin, London, 1962; Jordan, Z. A., 'The Philosophical Background of Revisionism in Poland', *East Europe*, June–July 1962.
14 See *Avanti*, Rome, 8 July 1956.
15 See Woroszylski, Victor, in *Nowa Kultura*, 29 July 1956.

5 The Revolutions of October 1956

1 cf. especially Ben, P., *Le Monde*, 20 October 1956. Ben's daily articles from Warsaw, and Sydney Gurson's in the *New York Times* over the same period, are the best sources for understanding the course and context of events in Poland.
2 *Notes et études documentaires*, *Documentation française*, 16 November 1956.
3 Nodradi, E., *Memoirs*, Budapest, 1966.
4 See *Szabad Nep*, 14 October 1956.
5 cf. Fejtö, F., *Budapest 1956*, Julliard, Paris, 1966, p. 129.
6 The Soviet position on the question of parties had been made clear in *Pravda*, 6 July 1956: there was no social basis for other parties in the U.S.S.R. The People's Democracies, on the other hand, might permit the participation of other parties in the government, provided they submitted to the leadership of the Communist party.
7 On the Hungarian rebellion, see also Meray, Tibor, *Ce jour-là, 23 October 1956*, Budapest, Laffont, Paris, 1966; Marie, J.-J.; Nagy, B.; and Broué, P., *1956, Pologne, Hongrie*, E.D.I., Paris, 1966; Zinner, Paul E., *Revolution in Hungary*, Columbia University Press, New York, 1962; Vali, Ferenc A., *Rift and Revolt in Hungary*, Harvard University Press, Cambridge, Mass., 1961; Kecskeméti, Paul, *The Unexpected Revolution*, Stanford University Press, Palo Alto, Calif., 1961.

6 A Holy Alliance against Revisionism and National Communism

1 cf. the analysis of policy in 1956–7 and the birth of 'Gheorghiu-Dejism' in Fischer-Galati, S., *The New Rumania*, op. cit., Ch. 3.
2 Loewenthal, Richard, *Khrouchtchev et la désagrégation du bloc communiste*, Calmann-Lévy, Paris, 1964, p. 110.
3 The minutes of the debate at this first meeting have not been published; but see Ebert, Friedrich, in *Neues Deutschland*, 30 November 1957.

4 Ten years after Nagy's execution the Czechoslovak writers' weekly was the only one to do justice to this man, who 'by his criticism of absolute dictatorship and his humanitarian conception of socialism was the advocate of democratic and national socialism', and who 'based his attitude on an understanding of the fact that a totalitarian régime is always dedicated to copying foreign models'. According to *Literarni Listy*, 13 June 1968, 'Nagy's defeat was due to the fact that he had little understanding of the international realities. The world situation at that time, basically because of the Suez crisis, was extremely unfavourable to his policy'. cf. also Schreiber, T., *Le Monde*, 18 June 1968.

5 For the whole period see Loewenthal R., op. cit., Brzezinski, Z., *Soviet Bloc*, rev. edn, Pall Mall, London, and Praeger, New York, 1963; Brown, J. F., *The New Eastern Europe: The Khrushchev Era and After*, Pall Mall, London, 1966; Griffiths, W. E., ed., *Communism in Europe*, I, II, M.I.T. Press, Cambridge, Mass., 1964–6.

7 The Moscow–Peking Conflict and the People's Democracies

1 See the Chinese 'Propositions' of 14 June 1963 in 'Documents sur les relations sino-soviétiques', *Documentation française*, No. 3037.

2 Mao remarked to the Japanese: 'The territories occupied by the U.S.S.R. are many. In accordance with the Yalta Agreement, the Soviet Union, on the pretext of guaranteeing Mongolia's independence, placed that country under her domination ... The Soviets seized part of Rumania, and they cut off a part of East Germany, and drove its inhabitants to the West. After cutting off a part of Poland, they incorporated it in Russia, and compensated Poland with a part of East Germany. Finland was subjected to the same treatment ...' *Asahi Evening News*, Tokyo, 13 July 1964, quoted in *Pravda*, 16 September 1964. See also *Einheit*, East Berlin, 1964, Nos. 9–10, and Doolin, D. J., *Territorial Claims in the Sino-Soviet Conflict*, Stamford, 1965.

3 See 'Propositions', op. cit.

4 Griffith, W. E., ed., *European Communism*, 1965, M.I.T. Press, Cambridge, Mass., 1966; 'La Polémique soviéto-albanaise', 'Documents fondamentaux sur le communisme international, 1961–62', *Documentation française*, No. 3139; Rakowski, M. F., in *Politika*, Warsaw, 28 September 1963; Mlynar, Z., in *Kulturni Tvorba*, Prague, 10 September 1964.

5 Kapo requested that the matter be discussed further at the all-party conference that was to take place in November in Moscow.

Other parties must have inclined to moderation as well, because in the end Khrushchev abandoned his scheme and was satisfied with the publication of a vague communiqué which left the question open.

6 Tatu, Michel, *Le Pouvoir en U.R.S.S.*, Grasset, Paris, 1967, pp. 127–240.

7 By the end of 1966 Albania's total indebtedness to China was approximately 200 million dollars. cf. Prybyla, Jan S., 'Under China's Economic Tutelage', *East Europe*, January 1967.

8 *Change and Security in Europe*, Institute of Strategic Studies, London, 1968, Pt I.

9 cf. Rachmu, I., article in *Probleme Economice*, Bucharest, July 1963.

10 Fejtö, F., *Chine-U.R.S.S.*, op. cit.

11 Brown, J. F., *The New Eastern Europe: the Khrushchev Era and After*, op. cit.; Fejtö, F., *Chine-U.R.S.S.*, op. cit.; Fischer-Galati, S., *The New Rumania*, op. cit.; Floyd, David, *Rumania: Russia's Dissident Ally*, Pall Mall, London, 1965; Griffith, W. E., 'Eastern Europe and World Communism' in Fischer-Galati, S., ed., *Eastern Europe in the Sixties*, New York, 1963; Griffith, W. E., *The Sino-Soviet Rift*, Allen & Unwin, London, 1964; Ionescu, G., *Communism in Rumania, 1944–1962*, O.U.P., London, 1964; Logoreci, A., 'Albania: The Anabaptists of European Communism', in *Problems of Communism*, May–June 1967; Montias, John M., 'Background and Origins of the Rumanian Dispute and Comecon', *Soviet Studies*, October 1964; Montias, John M., *Economic Development in Communist Rumania*, M.I.T. Press, Cambridge, Mass., 1967.

8 Liberalization under Khrushchev

1 26 December 1961.

2 *Kulturny Zivot*, No. 16, 1961. On the development of Hungary, see Fejtö, F., 'Hungarian Communism', in *European Communism*, I, op. cit.; Schreiber, Thomas, and Dethoor, Nicole, 'L'évolution politique et économique de la Hongrie, 1956–1966', in *Notes et études documentaires*, Documentation française, 8 November 1966; Brown, J. F., *The New Eastern Europe*, op. cit.

3 *Preuves*, March 1966.

4 See the *Economist*, 19 August 1967.

5 The most thorough study of the development of Czechoslovakia in this period is: Elias, Z., and Nelik, J., 'Czechoslovakia' in *European Communism*, II. There is also much valuable material in

the special issue of *Survey*, London, April 1966, on Czechoslovakia.

6 cf. Wladislaw Tykocinski's interview, 'Poland's Plan for the Northern Tier', *East Europe*, November 1966, and *Neue Zürcher Zeitung*, 29 March 1963.

7 cf. Lange, Oskar, *Some Problems Relative to the Polish Road to Socialism*, Belgrade, 1957.

8 See Stehle, Hans Jakob, *Nachbar Polen*, 1963; and his contribution, 'Polish Communism', in *European Communism*, I; Jelenski, K. A., 'La Pologne à l'heure du polycentrisme', *Preuves*, January 1964; Tatu, Michel, 'La Pologne va aux urnes', a series of articles in *Le Monde*, 25–7 May 1965; Gamarnikow, M., 'Poland's Economic Recession', *East Europe*, March 1963; Strobel, G. W., 'Probleme und Reformmassnahmen in der polnischen Wirtschaft', *Osteuropa*, April 1964; 'Les Policiers à l'assaut du pouvoir en Pologne', *Est-Ouest*, April 1965. The best summary of Gomulka's views on the role of the intellectuals is contained in his speech to the Thirteenth Plenum, in *Ostprobleme*, 5 October 1963 (a number devoted to Poland). On international policy, Rapacki, A., 'What has become of the Polish Plan for a De-Nuclearized Zone', *International Affairs*, London, January 1963; 'La Pologne et l'Europe orientale face au différend Sino-Soviétique', *Notes et études documentaires*, *Documentation française*, 20 November 1965.

9 Editorial in *Rabotnichesko Delo*, 24 April 1963.

10 Meier, Viktor, 'The Political Struggle', *East Europe*, October 1961; and 'Bulgariens Weg im Ostblock', in *Neue Zürcher Zeitung*, October 1963; Gabensky, I., 'L'industrialisation de la Bulgarie', *Faits et Opinions*, *Documentation française*, 13 July 1963.

11 *Neues Deutschland*, 4 March 1963.

12 'The relation of socialist friendship and solidarity linking the U.S.S.R. and the G.D.R. cannot be bought or sold, not for all the gold in the world.' *Pravda*, 6 October 1964.

13 Stern, Carola, 'East Germany', in *European Communism*, II, and *Porträt einer bolschewistischen Partei*, 1957; 'The Refugees of East Germany', *East-West*, 1–15 May 1962; 'Directives for the New System of Planning', *Neues Deutschland*, 17 July 1963; Vogel, D., 'Ulbricht sucht Generaldirektor', *Frankfurter Allgemeine Zeitung*, 7 March 1964; Jaenicke, Martin, 'Eastern Germany Today', *Problems of Communism*, No. 4, 1963; Stolpe, Wolfgang, F., *The Structure of the East German Economy*, Harvard University Press, Cambridge, Mass., 1960; Spittmann, Ilse, 'The G.D.R.', *Problems of Communism*, July–August 1967.

9 The People's Democracies after Khrushchev

1 Resolution of the Hungarian Central Committee, 25 October 1964.
2 Agence France-Presse dispatch, 30 October 1964.
3 See H. Schewe's report in *Die Welt*, 21 October 1964.
4 Tatu, M., *Le Pouvoir en U.R.S.S.*, op cit., p. 423.
5 Speech in *Neues Deutschland*, 6 December 1964.
6 Brzezinski, Z., 'Victory of the Clarks', *The New Republic*, 14 November 1964; Boffa, G., 'The U.S.S.R. after Khrushchev', *Rinascita*, 23 January 1965; Féron, B., *L'U.R.S.S. sans idole*, Paris, 1966; Romensky, S., *L'U.R.S.S. a cinquante ans, les révisionnistes conservateurs*, Seuil, Paris, 1967.
7 'Despite the rises in productivity recorded, the technological gap between ourselves and the more advanced countries, whether capitalist or not, has on the whole widened.' Friss, I., *Kozgazdasagi Szemle*, Budapest, June 1967. As regards Czechoslovakia, see A. Staub's apposite analysis, 'Market Perspectives', *Hospodarske Noviny*, 18 June 1967.
8 Friss, I., 'The Laws and Management of the Socialist Economy', *Tarsadalmi Szemle*, June 1967.
9 *Miesiecznik Literacki*, March 1967.
10 On internal developments in the U.S.S.R. after Khrushchev's fall, see Tatu, M., *Le Pouvoir en U.R.S.S.*, op. cit., Bourgois, Christian, *L'Affaire Siniavski-Daniel*, Paris, 1967; *Survey*, January and April 1968.

10 The Second Yugoslav Revolution

1 Arendt, Hannah, *The Origins of Totalitarianism*, 2nd edn., Allen & Unwin, London, 1958.
2 Rankovic denied having opposed the League's policy and having had any ambition other than of being an 'executive'. *Borba*, 3 July 1966. cf. 'Liberalization or Disintegration?' *Review*, No. 6, London, 1967.
3 Given a five-month suspended sentence in 1965 for his *Moscow Summer 1964*, Mihajlov was sentenced on 23 September 1966 to one year's imprisonment for his articles 'Why we remain Silent' and 'Djilas and Yugoslavia today', published in *The New Leader*, New York, as well as for his attempt to create an opposition group.
4 Without mentioning Yugoslavia by name, *Pravda* wrote that 'any restriction on the role of the party, any limitation of its function to the sphere of ideology alone, would be totally unacceptable and detrimental to the cause of socialism'.

5 See Part II, Chapter 13, of this book.

6 31 October; 1, 2 November 1967.

7 'Nach den Gesprächen Titos im Kreml', *Neue Zürcher Zeitung*, 4 May 1968.

8 cf. the analysis of this report in *Neue Zürcher Zeitung*, 22 December 1967. See Stankovic, S., 'L'économie yougoslave et ses problèmes', *Est-Ouest*, 16–31 May 1968, on the struggle against the party organization for the radical application of the economic reform.

9 Meier, V., 'Yugoslav Communism' in *Communism in Europe*, I, op. cit.; Ionescu, G., *L'avenir politique de l'Europe orientale*, Éditions Futuribles, Paris, 1967; 'L'évolution du communisme yougoslave de 1950 à 1965', *Notes et études documentaires*, *Documentation française*, No. 3298; 'Constitution de la R.S.F. de Yougoslavie', ibid., No. 3055; 'Les nouveaux statuts des communes yougoslaves d'après les constitutions de 1946, 1953 et 1963', ibid., No. 3168; 'The Yugoslav Experience' *Economist*, 16 July 1966; *Les Documents du IVème Plénum*, Paris, 1966; 'Theses on the Development and Reorganization of the League of Communists of Yugoslavia', *Review of International Politics*, Belgrade, No. 411, Suppl.; Stankovic, S., 'Yugoslavia's Critical Year', *East Europe*, August 1967; Mihajlov, M., 'Djilas and Yugoslavia Today', *The New Leader*, New York, 4 July 1966; and 'The Defence That Could Not Be Used', *The New Leader*, 8 May 1967; Reismüller, I. G., 'Titos Macht ist noch gewachsen', *Frankfurter Allgemeine Zeitung*, 6 September 1967; 'Vingt ans de dépérissement du P.C. Yougoslave', *Est-Ouest*, 1–15 March 1968; 'Let's Blame the Federal Chaps', *Economist*, 4 May 1968; 'Titos aussenpolitische Kurskorrektur', *Neue Zürcher Zeitung*, 24 October 1968.

11 The Czechoslovak Tragedy and its Implications

1 Fris, Edo, 'Eine historische Chance', *Das Tagebuch*, Austria, January–February 1968. Fris was editor-in-chief of *Pravda* (Bratislava) up to 1952.

2 For the text of Vaculik's speech see *Die Weltwoche*, Zurich, 21 July 1967, and *Esprit*, April 1968.

3 cf. Tatu, M., in *Le Monde*, 14–15 January 1968, and Razumovsky, A., in *Frankfurter Allgemeine Zeitung*, 19 January 1968, based on first-hand evidence.

4 See the 'Letter of Seven Old Communists', in *Mlady Svet*, 22 March 1968, and in *Est-Ouest*, 16 May 1968.

5 See *Rude Pravo*, 7 April 1968.

6 See Part II, Chapter 15, of this book.

7 'The action programme of the Czechoslovak Communist Party', Prague, April 1968.

8 See Kakol, K., in *Prawo i Zycie*, 24 March 1968.

9 Jelenski, K. A., 'La Pologne: une Grèce du monde communiste', *Preuves*, June–July 1968.

10 See Honecker, Erich, in *Pravda*, Moscow, 24 June 1968.

11 *Pravda*, 22 August 1968.

12 'Réponse du Comité central tchécoslovaque à la "Lettre de Varsovic"', *Articles et documents, Documentation française,* Special number, 16–23 August 1968.

13 *Literarni Listy*, 23 May 1968.

14 *Pravda*, 22 August 1968.

15 According to *The Times*, 6 August, the invasion was envisaged by the Soviets and East Germans in mid-July. The first phase of the plan was to have commenced on 19 July with *Pravda's* revelation of the discovery of an important cache of Western arms in in Bohemia. However, moderate elements in the Soviet leadership succeeded at the last minute in persuading the interventionists to give up their project and accept the Cierna conference.

16 See Part II, Chapter 16, of this book.

17 See Fejtö, F., 'Prague, Pourquoi?', *Preuves*, October 1968.

18 Salvan, Georges-Albert, 'Nouvelles précisions sur la crise soviéto-tchécoslovaque', 20 August 1968.

19 Konev, I. S., *L'Invasion du IIIème Reich: memoires de guerre 1945,* Plon, Paris, 1968.

20 This transformation is discussed in Chapter 16.

21 cf. Tatu, M., in *Le Monde*, 9 November 1968.

22 cf. among the abundant French literature on the Czechoslovak developments, Mnacko, Ladislav, *La septième nuit*, Flammarion, Paris, 1968; Vichniac, Isabelle, *L'ordre règne à Prague*, Fayard, Paris, 1968; Tigrid, Pavel, *Le Printemps de Prague*, Seuil, Paris, 1968; Salomon, M., *Prague: la révolution étranglée, Janvier-Août 1968*, Laffont, Paris, 1968.

PART II: STRUCTURES AND TENDENCIES

12 *Contradictions within the Communist System*

1 'The Defence of Socialism, a Supreme International Duty', *Pravda* editorial, 22 August 1968.

2 *Borba*, Belgrade, 28 June 1968.

3 Fontaine, André, *Histoire de la guerre froide*, II, Ch. XVII.

4 The text can be found in *Notes et études documentaires*, Documentation française, 3 March 1953.

5 cf. Fejtö, F., *Chine-U.R.S.S.*, op. cit., II, Chs. XX and XXI.

6 Khrushchev, in his report to the Twentieth Congress, after a somewhat sketchy analysis of the antagonisms of the capitalist world predicted that 'capitalism must inevitably lead to fresh economic and social upheavals'.

7 Loebl, E., and Pokorny, D., *Die Revolution rehabilitiert ihre Kinder*, Europa, Vienna, 1968.

8 cf. Pallas, Jan, 'Idéologie et société socialiste', *Esprit*, February 1968.

9 cf. Djilas, M., *The New Class*, Praeger, New York, 1957.

10 Kosik, K., *The Dialectic of the Concrete*, Prague, 1963, quoted by Pallas, J., in *Esprit*, February 1968.

11 Pachkov, A., *Komunist*, No. 9, Moscow, 1966.

12 *Tarsadalmi Szemle*, February 1968.

13 Calvez, J., *Introduction à la vie politique*, Paris, 1967; de Jouvenel, B., *De la politique pure*, Paris, 1963.

14 Lansic, *Praxis*, No. 4, Zagreb 1965.

15 cf. Chapter 19 of this book.

16 Meier, V., 'A l'Est : une Europe des patries?', *Preuves*, June–July 1968; see also Bettiza, E., 'Les Technocrates de Pankow', loc. cit.

17 For an excellent assessment of the effect of the adoption of the Soviet model on the Czechoslovak economy, see Kaplan, K., 'Economic Democracy Between 1945 and 1948', *Ceskoslovensky Casopis Historicky*, No. 6, 1966.

18 Laloy, J., 'L'évolution internationale du communisme', *Cahiers Reconstruction*, April 1967.

19 Imre Nagy, when accused of this, retorted that 'as long as nations and national states exist – and there is still a long history ahead of them – the ideas inherent in the five principles will remain the key factors in the development of the socialist system'. cf. Nagy, I., *On Communism: in defence of the New Course*, op. cit., Nagy and his friends invoked the Bandung principles and the Belgrade declaration to justify their demands for the transformation of Hungarian-Soviet relations.

20 In a paper at the Noordwijk Conference on World Politics in 1965, Professor György of Boston University characterized the movements in Poland and Hungary during 1956 as anti-Communist (opposed to the totalitarian régime) rather than anti-Soviet.

In fact, both the Hungarians and Poles took prominent Communists, regarded as patriots, as their leaders. The main demand of the two movements was independence.

21 Fejtö, F., *Budapest 1956*, op. cit., p. 206. The declaration dealt mainly with economic relations, but promised also to 'reconsider' the question of Soviet occupation forces.

22 Interview with Turner Catledge in the *New York Times*, 10 April 1957.

23 *Zeri i Populit*, 25 March 1962.

24 cf. Part I, Chapter 3, of this book.

25 Programme of the Soviet Communist party adopted by the Twenty-Second Congress, October 1961.

26 cf. Bourdet, Yvon, ed., *Otto Bauer et la Révolution*, E.D.I., Paris, 1968.

27 *Le Monde*, 19 July 1968.

28 This interpretation of the Bratislava declaration is put forward in the article by Dadiants, M., in *Le Monde*, 20 September 1968.

29 For the complete text of this declaration, see *Le Monde*, 6 August 1968.

30 This thesis was put forward with great assurance by Kovalev, M., in *Pravda*, 26 September 1968. It should be remembered that the Warsaw Pact, signed in 1955, contains several articles prohibiting any foreign interference in the internal affairs of member states. One should remember, too, that the Czechoslovak leaders signed the 'solidarity' passages in the Bratislava declaration only because the declaration pledged all signatories equally to do everything in their power to strengthen the co-operation of their countries on the basis of the principles of equality of rights, respect for national sovereignty and independence, territorial integrity and mutual fraternal aid. Dubcek and his colleagues probably did not anticipate the strange shape this 'mutual fraternal aid' was to assume seventeen days after the signing of the declaration.

31 *Peking Information*, No. 34, 26 August 1968. Commenting on this declaration, the *People's Daily* of 23 August observed : 'Social-imperialist refers to socialism's disguised imperialism'.

32 It is significant that General Moczar, secretary of the Polish party and leader of the Partisans, attributed the 'situation created in Czechoslovakia' to the 'treacherous appeals of the imperialists, revisionists and Zionists to humanize and democratize social and economic relations in the socialist countries'. These appeals, according to this typically Marxist-fascist theoretician, were in fact 'aimed against socialism'. (Agence France-Presse, dispatch

from Warsaw, 15 September 1968.) A leading Czechoslovak revealed at this time that the Soviets, in order to justify their intervention, intended staging an anti-Zionist trial where the accused would be Frantisek Kriegel, the only Jewish member of the Presidium of the Czechoslovak Central Committee, and Professor Edward Goldstuecker, president of the writers' union, who was also of Jewish origin and who had been sentenced to life imprisonment at the time of the Slansky trial. cf. 'Un nouveau chapitre de la tragédie tchécoslovaque: l'exode des intellectuels', published anonymously in *Le Monde*, 12 September 1968.

33 Philippe Ben got the impression in Rumania that, because of the uncertainty as to the Kremlin's intentions, people he spoke to felt they had been 'plunged thirty years into the past, a time when the future of the whole continent depended on a decision taken in the eagle's nest, on a Bavarian mountain peak' ('La Roumanie devant l'orage', *Le Monde*, 28 September 1968).

34 On Ulbricht's role in the Czechoslovak intervention, see Fejtö, F., in *La Nef*, October 1968, and Martinet, Gilles, 'La nouvelle lutte des classes', *Le Nouvel Observateur*, 26 August 1968: 'If the Russian bureaucracy took the initiative (armed intervention) ... it was to suppress a movement that might spread to all the other socialist countries, *including the Soviet Union*.'

35 Quoted in Jaszi, O., *The Dissolution of the Habsburg Monarchy*, University of Chicago Press, Chicago, 1929.

36 Roy Claude. 'Arturo Ui occupe Prague', *Le Monde*, 10 September, 1968.

13 The National Revival

1 *Revue française de la science politique*, June 1965.

2 In *Dynamics of Communism in Eastern Europe*, Princeton University Press, Princeton, N.J., 1961, R. Burks compares the Hungarian position with that of the Jewish minorities. They are the two 'rejected peoples', the two butts and scapegoats of Eastern Europe.

3 Fejtö, F., 'Hungarian Communism', in *European Communism*, I, op. cit., p. 183.

4 On this relatively little known period in the history of the Eastern countries, see Woolf, S. J., ed., *European Fascism*, Weidenfeld & Nicolson, London, 1968. John Eros's essay on Horthy's Hungary in that volume is the first objective analysis of pre-war Hungarian policy.

5 See Husak, G., 'A Revolutionary Generation', *Kulturny Zivot*, 8 October 1965, and V. Minac's articles in Nos. 42 and 44, 1965; E. Andrics in *Valosàg*, April 1966.

6 Austria's role as bridge-builder between her Communist neighbours and the West has been brilliantly dealt with by Otto de Habsbourg in an article in the *Revue générale belge*, June 1967.

7 cf. 'An Alternative Policy for Hungary', *Radio Free Europe Research*, 29 March 1966.

8 Peter, L., Tiszataj, March 1966.

9 cf. Merei, M., *Federal Schemes in South-Eastern Europe and the Austro-Hungarian Monarchy*, Budapest, 1965. Mihaly Karolyi's *Memoirs* were published in London in 1956 (Jonathan Cape), and a censored edition appeared in Budapest in 1966 due to the efforts of his wife.

    Born in 1875 into one of the greatest Hungarian families, Karolyi became President of the Hungarian Republic in 1918. Overthrown by Bela Kun, he went into exile. As chairman of the Anti-Fascist Committee formed in London in 1943, he tried to win over English public opinion and the exiled Czechoslovak politicians to the idea of a Danubian federation. Hungarian Minister in Paris from 1947 to 1949, he resigned in protest against the Rajk trial and the bolshevization of his country. He died in Venice in 1955 and his ashes were sent home in 1962.

10 Rapant, D., 'On Dualism', *Slovenske Pohlady*, November 1967.

11 Kotyk, V., 'Several Aspects of the History of Relations between the Socialist Countries', *Ceskoslovensky Casopis Historicky*, No. 4, 1967.

12 *Revue internationale de Belgrade*, 30 September 1965.

13 cf. C. Popisteanu's article in *Contemporanul*, 3 September 1965, and Brown, J. F., 'The New Initiatives in the Balkans', *Radio Free Europe Research*, 20 September 1966.

14 cf. Koevago, L., 'The Events of 1918 in the Works of Czech, Rumanian and Yugoslav Historians', *Valosag*, October 1966; Mod, Aladar, 'The Significance of the National Question', *Uj Jras*, March 1966; Horvath, Zoltan, 'On the Habsburg Monarchy', *New Hungarian Quarterly*, November 1964; *Annals of the Rumanian Party Historical Institute*, Vol. 10, 1964. On the causes underlying the collapse of Austria-Hungary, see Kolnai, Aurel, 'Das unvollendete Völkereich', *Rheinische Merkur*, 29 September 1967. See also the papers of the 1965 Noordwijk Conference by W. E. Griffith, Kurt London, Remy C. Kwant and Andrew György.

15 See the report in Z Pola Walki, No. 2, 1967. The Comintern's policy changed only on the eve of the Nazi attack on the Soviet Union. The French party, it should be noted, never gave as frank an account of its behaviour in this matter as the East European Communists.

16 cf. Goldberger, N., in Annals of the Institute of Historical Studies, Bucharest, Nos. 2–3, 1966.

17 Lazic, B., 'Les communistes roumains dénoncent leur passé du temps de Staline et de Gheorghiu Dej', Est-Ouest, 16–31 May 1968.

18 J. Kowalski at a conference of Polish historians in March 1966. cf. Z Pola Walki, No. 3, 1966, and Tych, F., in La Révolution d'Octobre et le mouvement ouvrier européen, E.D.I., Paris, 1968.

19 Declaration by Professor Jablonski on the occasion of the thousandth anniversary of the creation of the Polish state, Le Monde, 19 July 1966.

20 Mlynarik, J., 'Dr B. Smeral and the Slovak National Question at the Outset of the Communist Movement', Ceskoslovensky Casopis Historicky, October 1967.

21 Pavlik, O., 'The Cult of Personality and Morals', Kulturny Zivot, 17 August 1963.

22 Kulturny Zivot, 8 October 1965.

23 Novomesky, L., in Kulturny Zivot, 23 June 1967.

24 cf. Velas, S., 'To Escape the Vicious Circle', Smena, Bratislava, 6 July 1966.

25 cf. Minac's address to the Congress of Slovak Writers, published in Uj Szo, Bratislava, 22 April 1968.

26 cf. Michel Tatu's excellent analysis in Le Monde, 7 May 1968.

27 According to the 1961 census, the constituent elements of the nations of Yugoslavia (excluding the national minorities) are as follows: Serbs, 7,806,213; Croats, 4,293,860; Slovenes, 1,589,192; Macedonians, 1,045,530; Montenegrins, 513,833. Only 317,125 people gave their nationality as 'Yugoslav', and 972,954 as 'Muslim'. In the previous census (1953) there had been 998,698 'Yugoslavs', of whom 891,800 were in Bosnia-Hercegovina. The reason was that at the time the Muslims (most of whom live in Bosnia-Hercegovina), not wishing to be taken either for Serbs or Croats and not being allowed to call themselves Muslims, had given 'Yugoslav' as their nationality. But as soon as they were permitted to describe themselves according to their religion, most of them did so, discarding the term 'Yugoslav'. Thus, statistics show that the unitary concept of a 'Yugoslav nation' is an abstraction that has not gained popular currency.

28 Jankovic, P., 'Une Passion nationale en Yougoslavie', *Le Monde*, 3 May 1968.

29 Serbia comprises two autonomous regions: Vojvodina, with a large Hungarian minority, and Kosovo-Metohija, with an Albanian majority. The former is comparatively advanced.

30 The following table shows that in 1965, when the great reform was initiated, the inequalities were still considerable:

Republics and autonomous regions	Percentage of total population	Percentage of national product	Income per head (average 100)
Yugoslavia	100	100	100
Bosnia-Hercegovina	18	12.1	67.7
Montenegro	2	1.6	63.6
Croatia	23	27.5	121.8
Macedonia	7	4.7	66.8
Slovenia	8	16.7	191.4
Serbia	42	37.4	92.3
Vojvodina	9	10.9	110.9
Kosovo and Metohija	5	1.7	30.9

According to a spokesman of the Albanian minority the relative position of developed and underdeveloped regions in 1964 was the same as in 1947. cf. *Perparimi*, June 1967.

31 In 1958 Slovenia, with 8.6 per cent of the Yugoslav population, was providing 37.2 per cent of the federal budget, corresponding to 45.6 per cent of the Slovene national income.

32 Dispatch from G. A. Salvan, the Agence France-Presse correspondent in Belgrade, 3 September 1968.

33 For a detailed account, see Michel Tatu's excellent study, 'En Transylvanie, carrefour des nationalités', *Le Monde*, 11–14 November 1967.

34 The Hungarian population of the region was reduced from 564,000 to 473,000, whereas the Rumanian population was increased from 147,000 to 266,000.

35 *Observer*, London, 14 April 1963.

36 In Hargita county, 280 of out of total of 330 schools are Hungarian.

37 See P. Ben's report, 'La Roumanie devant l'orage', *Le Monde*, 1 October 1968.

38 cf. *Uj Szo*, Bratislava, 15 March 1968.

39 See Hairedin Hoxha's article in *Perparimi*, Pristina, June 1967; 'Kosovo-Metohija: A Nationality Case Study', *Radio Free Europe Research*, 30 October 1967.

40 Burks, R., *The Dynamics of Communism in Eastern Europe*, op. cit., Ch. V.

41 *The Liberation of Bulgaria from the Turkish Yoke*, produced under the joint auspices of the Moscow Institute of Slavic Studies and the Sofia Institute of History, Nauka, Moscow, 1968. See also the *Rabotnichesko Delo* editorial of 21 December 1967 on the treaty of San Stefano and the counter-attacks of *Nova Makedonija*, Skopje, 30 December 1967 and *Politika*, Belgrade, 14 January 1968. There seems in fact to be a certain ambivalence about this matter in the U.S.S.R. where – as *Vjesnik u Srijedu* of Zagreb stressed on 10 January 1968 – a Russo-Macedonian dictionary (as distinct from the Russo-Bulgarian dictionary) was recently published.

42 cf. the report to the Central Committee of the Macedonian Communist party by B. Stankovski, *Nova Makedonija*, 17 September 1968.

43 In 1967, the number of Jews was estimated at 110,000; there were 75,000 to 80,000 in Hungary (90 per cent of whom were in Budapest); 25,000 in Poland; 15,000 to 18,000 in Czechoslovakia; 6,000 in Yugoslavia; 7,000 in Bulgaria. See the statement by Nahum Goldmann, chairman of the World Jewish Congress, reported by Agence France-Presse, 12 April 1967.

44 Kolar, E., 'Zionism and Anti-Semitism', *Rude Pravo*, 18 July 1967.

45 See Fejtö, F., *Les Juifs et l'antisémitisme dans les pays communistes*, Plon, Paris, 1960.

46 cf. statement of N. Goldmann, cited above; and Nos. 1–21 of the bulletin *The Jews in Eastern Europe*, Jewish Contemporary Library, London.

47 In 1956, at a party meeting in Lodz, a piece of paper with the following question was handed to Ochab: 'Why are the best positions in the party, government and civil service occupied by Jews?' See Jelenski, K. A., 'Antisémitisme et déstalinisation en Pologne', *Évidence*, August–September 1956.

48 Schaff, Adam, *Le Marxisme et l'individu*, Gallimard, Paris, 1967. See the report on the debate in *Nowe Drogi*, December 1965.

49 See L. Mnacko's statement on the occasion of his protest flight to Israel in *Frankfurter Allgemeine Zeitung*, 11 August 1967.

50 *Trybuna Ludu*, 19 June 1967.

51 'La Pologne: une Grèce du monde communiste', *Preuves*, June–July 1968.

52 As Antonin Slonimski pointed out at a meeting of the Warsaw section of the Polish writers' union, the only difference from Nazism was that the latter had blamed all misfortunes on a Judaeo-Communist conspiracy, whereas the Partisans spoke of a Judaeo-anti-Communist conspiracy. This is the latest version of the tale of the elders of Zion, whose sources have been so learnedly traced by Léon Poliakov in his *Histoire de l'antisémitisme*, Calmann-Lévy, Paris, 1955–68, 3 v.

14 The Lure of the West

1 *New York Herald Tribune*, 25 May 1964. These same fears were expressed by Paul-Henri Spaak after the occupation of Czechoslovakia: 'Not only should the member states of NATO refrain from embarking on any course calculated to weaken the Warsaw Pact, but they should firmly declare their support for the present set-up ... The policy of *détente* can be carried out only through the two existing blocs.' *Le Monde*, 2 October 1968. It goes without saying that this conservative view does not conform to the aspirations of the East Europeans.

2 cf. Klaus Mehnert's very well documented account, 'Westerly Wind over Eastern Europe', presented at the Noordwijk Conference, November 1965.

3 Sedivy, J., 'Our foreign Policy', *Voda A Zivot*, September 1965.

4 Rab, V., 'Scientific Work and the Party', *Zivot Strany*, July 1964.

5 Selucky, R., 'Us and the World', *Literarny Noviny*, 5 September 1964.

6 An article by the pro-government Catholic S. Stomma, 'Geopolitics or Glassboro', *Tygodnik Powszechny*, 23 July 1967, justified this preference simply for reasons of State. See also Jean Lacouture's report, 'Ces Polonais qui se méfient', *Le Nouvel Observateur*, 11–17 September 1967, which quotes an unofficial Polish source: 'Poland for the first time in its history has acquired a degree of security and equilibrium based on Russia protecting us against Germany, and America protecting us against Russia ... We, therefore, have no alternative but to uphold the *status quo*.'

7 See the proceedings of the Rumanian Grand Assembly, 24–6 July 1967, *Agerpres*; Fejtö, F., 'La portée d'un message', *Réforme*, 16 September 1967.

8 Liehm, A. J., in *Le Monde*, 21 January 1965.

9 The following tourist figures illustrate this development:

Hungary: 1963, 584,000 tourists; 1965, 1,320,000 (300,000 from the West), 20 million dollars.

Bulgaria: 1961, 200,000 tourists (10,000 from the West); 1966, 1,500,000 (580,000 from the West), 53 million dollars.

Rumania: 1965, 260,000; 1966, 800,000, the majority from the West.

Czechoslovakia: 1965, 3,715,000, 30 per cent from the West, especially W. Germany. 1967, 4,000,000.

Poland: 1964, 819,000 (86,000 from the West); 1965, 1,167,000 (190,000 from the West); 1967, 1,300,000 (300,000 from the West).

There is not much precise information on the reverse flow, which is considerably less because of the authorities' caution and the shortage of foreign currency. Thus, only 1,132 Hungarians, nearly all officials, visited the West in 1953. In 1958 there were 21,000; in 1960, 33,000; in 1963, 120,000.

10 *Predvoj*, 17 June 1965.

11 Szabo, L., *Magyarorszag*, 1 February 1964.

12 Public preference (especially among the skilled workers) for Western products and methods is often unfavourable to the Russians. See Rab, V., 'Scientific Work and the Party', *Zivot Strany*, July 1964.

13 Perjes, G., 'Confusion about National Pride', *Latohatar*, July–August 1967.

14 Starewicz's statement to the Polish Central Committee, *Trybuna Ludu*, 12 July 1963.

15 cf. Darvas, I., *Partelet*, Budapest, April 1966; Giberti, E., *Vychodo-Slovenski Novini*, Bratislava, 7 September 1966.

16 cf. Szirmai, I., in *Tarsadalmi Szemle*, Budapest, November 1965: 'To close the frontiers again would only make the West seem more attractive.'

17 E. Loebl, the great Slovak economist, gives a typical expression of this view: 'Economic efficiency, like surgery, is not a matter of Communism or capitalism, but of science, of executive skill.' Quoted by Salomon, M., in *Prague, la Révolution étranglée*, op. cit.

18 It is this penetration of Western influence that Polish hard-liners have cynically called the 'internal violation of Czechoslovak sovereignty', cf. the Agence France-Presse report of 20 September 1968, on a discussion on Polish television in which two members of the Central Committee, S. Stefanski and S. Trepczynski, took part.

15 *Forces of Cohesion and Community Institutions*

1 *Revue de la politique internationale*, Belgrade, 20 April 1967.

2 *Problems of Peace and Socialism*, August 1967; *Pravda*, 17 and 30 September 1967.

3 cf. with regard to this theory, the *Unità* editorial of 3 September.

4 On 30 September Chou En-lai, in condemning the concentration of Soviet forces in Bulgaria, came forward as the protector of Balkan sovereignty in general, disregarding the ideological dispute with the 'Yugoslav revisionists'.

5 Reply of the Presidium of the Czechoslovak Central Committee to the letter of the Five, Prague, 18 July 1968.

6 Letter of the Warsaw Five to the Central Committee of the Czechoslovak Communist party, 15 July 1968.

7 cf. Tatu, Michel, *Le Monde*, 3 October 1968.

8 Puja, F., 'On the International Conference', *Partelet*, December 1967.

9 cf. 'Le Pacte de Varsovie et l'inventaire des forces de l'Est', *Est-Ouest*, 1–15 July 1967.

10 A standing committee charged with drafting foreign policy recommendations and a joint secretariat composed of representatives of the member states were set up in January 1956.

11 Before the Czechoslovak intervention, estimates relating to Soviet troops stationed in Eastern Europe were as follows: 20 divisions in East Germany, half of which were armoured; 4 divisions in Hungary; 2 divisions in Poland. Soviet troops were withdrawn from Rumania in 1958. In September 1968 it was estimated in Washington that there were 51 Soviet divisions in Eastern Europe, 17 of which were in Czechoslovakia and 10 in Poland.

12 The following table of Warsaw Pact forces, plus those of Yugoslavia, is based on figures compiled by the Institute for Strategic Studies, London, and published in *The Military Balance 1970–1971*.

> *Bulgaria*: Regular forces: 149,000 (Army: 130,000; Air Force: 12,000; Navy: 7,000); Paramilitary forces; 17,000; Militia: 150,000.
>
> *G.D.R.*: Regular forces: 129,000 (Army: 92,000; Air Force: 21,000; Navy: 16,000); Paramilitary forces: 52,500 frontier guards, 21,000 security troops; Betriebskampfgruppen (armed workers' organizations): 350,000.
>
> *Hungary*: Regular forces: 101,500 (Army: 90,000; Air Force: 10,000; Navy: 1,500); Paramilitary forces: 35,000 (frontier guards and security troops); Militia: 125,000.

Poland: Regular forces: 242,000 (Army: 195,000; Air Force: 25,000; Navy: 22,000); Paramilitary forces: 45,000 (frontier guards and security troops).

Rumania: Regular forces: 181,000 (Army: 165,000; Air Force: 8,000; Navy: 8,000); Paramilitary forces: 50,000; Militia: 75,000.

Czechoslovakia: Regular forces: 168,000 (Army: 150,000; Air Force: 18,000; Navy:—); Paramilitary forces: 35,000 (including 15,000 frontier guards); Militia: 90,000 (numbers to be increased to 250,000).

Yugoslavia: Regular forces: 238,000 (Army: 200,000; Air Force: 20,000; Navy: 18,000); Paramilitary forces: 19,000 frontier guards. The Territorial Defence Forces are planned to reach a strength of 3 million men and women.

13 Griffith, W. E., *The United States and the Soviet Union in Europe*, M.I.T. Press, Cambridge, Mass., October 1967.

14 Although Ulbricht tried to see that the declaration issued by the conference was interpreted this way. cf. his statement in an A.D.N. dispatch from East Berlin, 9 July 1966.

15 *Neues Deutschland*, 3 February 1967.

16 *Scanteia*, 3 February 1967.

17 The 1965 Soviet-Polish treaty served as a model for the new treaties. It stressed the bilateral and multilateral (ideological) character of the alliance. However, Articles 1 and 2 place the emphasis on 'equality, respect for sovereignty and non-interference' and on 'the mutual advantage' of co-operation. The Hungarian-Soviet treaty, signed in September 1967, stresses the 'internationalist' character of the alliance. Both parties undertook 'to strengthen the unity and cohesion of the socialist countries' and to 'take steps to consolidate the might and power of the world socialist system'.

It is possible that one of the objects in consolidating the network of treaties, as Manlio Brosio suggested at a NATO council meeting (cf. *Le Monde*, 21 November 1967), was to establish a bilateral second line of defence in the event of the dissolution of the Warsaw Pact alliance itself.

18 cf. the violent attack on Snejdarek in *Neues Deutschland*, 12 May 1968.

19 For Ulbricht's role, see Winter, Bernard, 'L'Allemagne de l'Est et la Tchécoslovaquie', Agence France-Presse, 5 September 1968.

20 An assessment of these forces is in *Il Secolo*, Rome, 20 June 1968.

21 Tatu, Michel, 'La conférence de Dresde', *Le Monde*, 26 March 1968.

22 cf. 'The Defence of Socialism and the Supreme Internationalist Duty', *Pravda*, 22 August 1968.

23 In 1961, Albania withdrew from Comecon. Outer Mongolia joined in 1962, and in 1964 Comecon agreed to Yugoslavia's request to be represented on a number of its standing committees.

24 See Popovic, M., *Des rapports entre États socialistes*, Paris, 1949.

25 cf. especially the article in *People's Daily*, 8 May 1968, quoted by the New China News Agency the following day.

26 According to the *People's Daily* article quoted above, which does not specify its source, trade with the Soviet Union from 1955 to 1961 had cost the 'fraternal countries' 1,400 million dollars.

27 After the 1956 rising, Hungary received loans from the Communist countries totalling 300 million dollars, to be repaid during the course of the sixties.

28 Rachmut, I., in *Probleme Economice*, July 1963. It should be noted that, over the following years, the situation changed in that the G.D.R., which was more dynamic, took over the lead from Czechoslovakia, and Rumania improved her position. On 15 January 1966 the Czechoslovak journal *Hospodarske Noviny* published the following *per capita* table of industrial production, based on the Polish figures:

(1) G.D.R.: 201; (2) Czechoslovakia: 177; (3) U.S.S.R.: 120; (4) Hungary and Rumania: 107; (5) Poland: 100; (6) Bulgaria: 73.

29 The West's share in Rumania's foreign trade was over 34 per cent in 1966, as against 22.3 per cent in 1960. The Soviet Union's share fell from 47 per cent in 1959 to 34 per cent in 1966, while that of the Comecon countries as a whole fell from 66.4 per cent to 54.1 per cent.

30 cf. Sekera, J., *Nova Mysl*, 5 May 1963.

31 On this new form of co-operation see Trend, H., 'International Economic Associations of East Europe', *Radio Free Europe Research*, 20 September 1967.

32 *Shorter Dictionary of Economics*, Prague, 1963.

33 The existence of this agreement was revealed in *Polityka*, Poland, 26 August 1967.

34 cf. Milicevic, O., 'Exchange of Labour Force between Socialist Countries', *Borba*, Belgrade, 19 November 1967.

35 On this point, see the Comecon resolutions during the session of 12–14 December 1967, held in Budapest, attended by Yugoslav delegates.

36 The Czechoslovaks admit that they buy Soviet oil at a higher price than it is sold in Italy. They claim, however, that it would cost them even more in the Middle East, and that the U.S.S.R. compensates them by buying Czechoslovak machinery and consumer goods at higher than world market prices (which is debatable). cf. Sedwy, Z., *Kulturni Tvorba*, 2 November 1967.

37 It was, apparently, in protest against this tendency, which he regarded as harmful, that Erich Appel, the head of planning in the G.D.R., committed suicide in 1965. The Soviet share in East German foreign trade is calculated to rise from 43 per cent in 1966 to 46 per cent in 1971; and that of Comecon, as a whole, to 71 per cent in 1971 (1 per cent more than in 1966).

38 *Le Monde*, 26–7 November 1967.

39 For the Chinese view, see *People's Daily*, 15 November 1967. The embarrassed explanation of the vice-chairman of the Council is reproduced in Apro, A., 'On Hungarian-Soviet Co-Operation'. *Tarsadalmi Szemle*, November 1967.

40 The Soviets, after having purchased twenty-five sugar refineries from Czechoslovakia, ended up buying more up-to-date ones from England, France and West Germany.

41 According to *Zycie Warszawy*, 19 February 1967, the growth of inter-bloc trade was 85 per cent between 1950 and 1955, 71 per cent from 1955 to 1960, 55 per cent from 1960 to 1965, and the probable growth for 1966 to 1970 is between 40 and 50 per cent. *Tanyug* (dispatch from Warsaw, 5 September 1968) speaks of stagnation. According to the U.N. report published in January 1968, the rate of growth of East European purchases from, and sales to, Western Europe was about 15 per cent in 1966.

42 *Le Monde*, 14 September 1968.

43 *Pravda* editorial, 22 August 1968.

44 The following are some of the most significant general works among the vast number devoted to Comecon and the development of the bloc's foreign trade: Wszelaki, J., 'New Patterns of Trade', *Eastern Europe in the Sixties*, Praeger, New York, 1963; Agoston, I., *Le Marché commun communiste*, Droz, Geneva, 1964; 'La Coopération économique au sein du bloc des pays de l'Est', *Bulletin de la Société des banques suisses*, No. 1, 1966, and *East Europe*; 'A Special Survey', *Economist*, 19 August 1967; 'New Forms of Economic Co-operation (Industrial Co-operation between East and West)', *Rynki Zagraniczne*, Warsaw, 11 November 1967.

16 Development of Internal Political Structures

1 Vracar, S., in Gledista, Belgrade, Nos. 8–9, 1967.

2 Mihajlov, M., 'The Defence I Did Not Use', The New Leader, New York, September 1967.

3 Huebl, Milan, in Kulturny Zivot, 5 January 1968.

4 cf. Ionescu, G., L'avenir politique de l'Europe orientale, Futuribles, Paris, 1967, which gives a detailed analysis of the political structures of the Eastern countries and their trends and tendencies.

5 cf. Agence France-Presse dispatch from Prague, 24 August 1968, announcing the dismissal of these individuals at the hands of Pavel, the Minister of the Interior.

6 cf. Michel Tatu's brilliant analysis in Le Monde, 7 September 1968.

7 Interview with Pavel on the free Prague radio, 25 August 1968.

8 Speech by Dubcek, 27 May 1968.

9 In certain respects, Dubcek reminds one of the good soldier Schweik face to face with a vast military and administrative apparatus. The Poles are perhaps not entirely wrong in describing him as being 'naïve to the point of credulity' (cf. Trybuna Ludu, 13 September 1968). Innocence and integrity always contain a good dose of naïveté.

10 30 January 1968.

11 Pravda, Bratislava, 7 February 1968.

12 Santa, I., Tarsadalmi Szemle, Budapest, June 1967.

13 Lakos, S., Nepszabadsag, 4 June 1968.

14 See Michel Tatu's analysis of these truly revolutionary rules in Le Monde, 11–12 August 1968. Pravda, in its inquisitorial article of 22 August, attributed the democratic tenor of the new rules to the action of 'right-wing forces'. One should remember, however, that – apart from the fact that it was Indra who presented the new rules to the Committee – as early as 13 February 1968, in the columns of Rude Pravo, the moderate theorist Mlynar was urging that minority rights in the party as well as in Parliament and elsewhere should be guaranteed. The Soviets never attacked him.

15 Rude Pravo, 15 August 1968.

16 See Kolar, F. J., 'Democracy or Elite', Kulturny Tvorba, 19 October 1967.

17 The Slovak economist E. Loebl is one of the most brilliant advocates of this notion. See Salomon, M., Prague, la révolution étranglée, op. cit.

18 Nepszabadsag, 2 December 1967.

19 *Revue de la politique internationale*, Belgrade, 5 February 1968.

20 Smrkovsky, after being elected President of the National Assembly, 14 April 1968.

21 See his article, 'Our Political System and the Separation of Power' *Rude Pravo*, 13 February 1968.

22 'I would go into the polling station,' wrote Mrs Dohnolova, a contributor to *Kulturny Noviny*, on 25 February 1968, 'get my electoral card, then report to the committee that made a note of my attendance. Was I to enter the booth hidden away in a corner? No, since there were too many eyes watching. Was I to strike out any names? No, since we were all of one mind and, besides, the result would be 98 per cent for, anyway. Everything had been arranged beforehand ... As long as elections are not free and secret, as long as I cannot choose freely between candidates, the act of voting must be a mere formality.' This periodical was put out by the Ministry of Information and Culture that had replaced *Literarni Noviny* when it was banned by Novotny in autumn 1967.

23 The critical part played by the press, radio and television in rousing public opinion should be noticed, however.

24 Eng. trans. *Peace and War*, Weidenfeld, London, 1967.

25 'A Year of Action', *Pravda*, Bratislava, 31 December 1967.

26 See his memorandum in *Esprit*, November 1957, written after the Soviet intervention. cf. also Kiralykuti, Andras, 'Contestations démocratiques et révolutionnaires (1953–1956), l'octobre hongrois', *Esprit*, February 1958. It should be noted that more than twelve years after the rising, Bibo is still condemned to silence.

27 In *Pregled*, Sarajevo, March 1966.

28 Vracar, S., 'Party Monopoly and Political Power', *Glodista*, Belgrade, August–September 1967.

29 See *La Marche de la France au socialisme*, Éditions Sociales, Paris, 1966; and Cisar's statements reported in *L'Humanité*, 30 April 1968.

30 In January 1968 a secretary of the League of Yugoslav Communists proposed, as an alternative to the multi-party system, the transformation of the Socialist Alliance into a real arena of confrontation between the Communists and the 'large masses of the population'. Imre Nagy, in 1954, had already had the idea of turning the Patriotic Popular Front into a living organization where there could be a real 'dialogue'. But as soon as his idea began to take shape, the party apparatus under Rakosi stepped in to put a stop to this experiment, on the pretext that an autonomous front must inevitably develop into a kind of 'second party'.

However, a front without independence could have no attraction, and its collapse contributed to the 'depoliticization' of the people. Until that time, this has been the fate of all the alternatives to democracy advanced by Communists.

31 In December 1967 he was forced to resign after a protracted and savage campaign in which he was taken to task for having been supported by reactionary forces.

32 In a speech over Prague radio, 2 February 1968.

33 Mlynar envisaged a real separation of power between government and party. These two were to be 'independent political bodies'.

Czechoslovak and Yugoslav reformers and Hungarian theorists wanted to give actual independence also to such bodies as the trade unions, youth and student organizations, and writers' unions. See, in addition to the following chapter, Bihari, O., 'On Representative Democracy', *Tarsadalmi Szemle*, August–September 1965; Lakatos, M., 'Some Problems of Socialist Democracy', *Pravny Obzor*, Bratislava, March 1966.

34 *Zycie Literackie*, Cracow, 18 February 1966.

35 cf. the series of articles by Bettiza, E., 'The Drama of the Yugoslav Reform', in *Corriere della Sera*, Milan, December 1967, and Antic, Z., 'Army Influence in Yugoslavia Growing', *Radio Free Europe Research*, 5 February 1968.

17 Reforms in Planning and Economic Management

1 Kende, P., *Logique de l'économie centralisée*, Sedes, Paris, 1964.

2 On Hungary, see the article by Peter, G., in *Nepszabadsag*, 12 July 1957; and on Poland, Lipinski, E., 'Oskar Lange and Michal Kalecki', in *Nowe Drogi*, December 1956.

3 Gamarnikov, M., 'The Growth of Economic Revisionism, II', *East Europe*, May 1964.

4 On the advance of collectivization, cf. 'The U.S.S.R. and East European Agricultural Situation', *U.S. Department of Agriculture*, March 1966, p. 2.

5 Novotny, in an interview with *The Times*, London, 13 July 1963, stated that in Czechoslovakia investment accounted for at least 34 per cent of the national income.

6 On these comparative assessments, see M. Ernst's survey in *The World Outside*, Washington, 1966; and Vernant, Jacques, 'Europe(s)', *Notre République*, 7 January 1967.

7 Jozefowicz, A., in *Zycie Gospod.*, 17 November 1957.

8 The Hungarian birth rate of 13.1 per cent in 1964 was the lowest

in Europe. Birth rates elsewhere were: Poland 19%; Czechoslovakia 16.9%; Bulgaria 16.4%; Rumania 15.7%.

9 Srb, V., Kucera, M., and Vysusclova, D., 'Une enquête sur la prévention des naissances et le plan familial en Tchécoslovaquie', *Population*, Paris, January–March 1964; Guthart, A., 'Situation de l'emploi dans les pays d'Europe orientale et en U.R.S.S.', *Le Courrier des pays de l'Est*, Paris, 2 February 1966; Miklasz, C., 'La population polonaise, doctrines, politique et conflits religieux', *Population*, April–May 1960; Kuszinski, L., 'The Demographic Problem of Contemporary Poland', *Poland*, Warsaw, February 1966; Ortutay, Z., 'The Birth Rate and the Family', *Tarsadalmi Szemle*, Budapest, October 1966; Lorince, G., 'An Impending Population Explosion in the Balkans?' *New Statesman*, London, 3 February 1967; Gamarnikow, M., 'Perspectives à court et à long terme de l'économie polonaise', *Analyses et Prévisions*, 1967.

10 *Rude Pravo*, 5 December 1962.

11 Friss, I., 'The Laws and Management of the Socialist Economy', *Koezgazdasagi Szemle*, July 1967.

12 *Neues Deutschland*, 17 July 1963.

13 Decree of the Council of Ministers, 29 July 1964, elaborated by Jedrychowski in July 1965.

14 Reorganization plan passed by the Central Committee in January 1965 and put into effect on 1 January 1967.

15 Central Committee theses published in December 1965, and elaborated by Zhivkov at the Party Congress in November 1966, the 'new course' to be effective from January 1968.

16 The new economic system developed in 1966–7, introduced on 1 January 1968.

17 Central Committee decision, 7 December 1967.

18. cf. the excellent report by the French Commercial Councillor in Prague, M. Rivaille, in 'Problèmes économiques', *Documentation française*, 13 June 1968; and G. Ardant's comparative study of Czechoslovak and Hungarian reforms in *Le Monde*, 8 October 1968.

19 Gligorov, K., Deputy Prime Minister, 'Two Years of Economic Reform', *Revue de la politique internationale*, Belgrade, 20 October 1967.

20 Of the 7,000 co-operatives in 1951, only 500 have survived. The wealthiest are in Vojvodina.

21 Of the 10,000 collective farms in 1955, 1,803 were preserved after the events of 1956. In 1966, 1,268 remained, covering an area of 160,000 hectares, the total area of arable land being 20 million.

Twelve per cent of Polish land is cultivated by state farms.

22 *Nowe Drogi*, 1 January 1967.

23 Much light was shed on the basic problem of socialist agriculture by the Hungarian journal *Valosag* in May 1966. The peasants work just enough for the *kolkhoz* to keep the State from withdrawing its financial support. Generally speaking, the co-operatives – where the land is poorly cultivated, the buildings badly maintained, the machinery badly exploited and livestock declining – are growing poorer, while the peasants themselves, thanks to their allotments, are becoming prosperous, building houses, buying cars and other luxury goods.

24 cf. 'Reflections on Rural Emigration', in *Alfold* (Hungary), April 1966.

25 In Rumania in 1948 there was one tractor per 1,957 hectares of arable land, in 1966, one tractor per 108 hectares. (The corresponding figures for other East European countries are 29 hectares for Czechoslovakia, 30 for the G.D.R., 59 for Hungary, and 70 for the U.S.S.R.)

26 Among the few general accounts and numerous specialized works on the subject are: Dumont, R., *Sovkhozes, kolkhozes, ou le problématique communisme*, Seuil, Paris, 1964; Gamarnikow, M., 'Reform in Agriculture', *East Europe*, November 1966, and 'Perspectives à court et à long terme de l'économie polonaise', *Analyses et Prévisions*, op, cit.; Kowalka, J., 'Socio-Economic Structure in the Comecon Countries', *Hospodarske Noviny*, 2 December 1966; Màrkus, I., 'What's New in the Countryside?' *Uj Jras*, October 1965; Giosan, N., 'Co-Ordinates of Agricultural Development in Romania', *Agerpres Bulletin*, 1 December 1967; 'The New Czechoslovak Agricultural Model', *Radio Free Europe*, 16 April 1966; 'The New Draft Model of Bulgarian Collective Farms', *idem*, 3 March 1967; 'The Best Methods of Income Distribution and Bonus Payment in the Farmers' Cooperatives in Hungary', *idem*, 18 August 1964; 'A new Era in Hungarian Agriculture', *idem*, 15 March 1968; 'The Seventh Collective Farm Congress in Czechoslovakia', *idem*, 29 February 1968.

27 *Rude Pravo*, 18 May 1966.

28 *Nepszabadsag*, 5 December 1965.

29 On the opposition of the Soviet lower ranks to the development of consumerism, see the excellent study by Romensky, S., *L'U.R.S.S. à 50 Ans*, Seuil, Paris, 1967.

30 See the summary of this discussion by the French commercial councillor in Belgrade, in *Problèmes économiques, Documentation française*, 30 November 1967.

31 Brown, J. F., *Eastern Europe*, op. cit.; Gamarnikov, M., 'The New Role of Private Enterprise', *East Europe*, August 1967; Ariic, Z., 'Yugoslav Marxists Justify Private Initiative in the Economy', *Radio Free Europe*, June 1967.

32 cf. 'Towards the Next Russian Revolution', *Economist*, London, 14 September 1968.

18 The Development of Social Structures

1 Szczepanski, Jan, 'La sociologie marxiste empirique', in *L'Homme et la Société*, No 1, Paris, 1966.

2 English trans. by Sheila Patterson. *The Class Structures in Social Consciousness*, Routledge, London, 1963.

3 See Szczepanski, op. cit.; and another paper of his, 'The Social Structure of Socialist Society', *Kultura*, 22 December 1964.

4 See his 'The Structural Model of Socialist Society and Social Stratification', *Valosag*, May 1964; and Mod, Aladar, *Social Stratification in Hungary*, 1966; with a review by S. Ferge, in *Valosag*, October 1966.

5 In *Current Problems of Socialism*, January–February 1967.

6 The author of 'The Myth of State Socialism', *Praxis*, April 1967.

7 Who wrote 'State Socialism, Classes and Policy', *Borba*, 4 January 1968.

8 Among the many works on the revival of sociology in the Eastern countries see especially Labedz, L., 'Sociology and Social Change' in *Survey*, London, July 1967. On the problems raised by the application of Marxist methods, see Papaioannou, K., *L'Idéologie froide*, Pauvert, Paris, 1967.

9 cf. Nicole Bernheim's excellent essay, 'Suédoises et Polonaises, deux exemples d'intégration socialiste', *Le Monde*, 29 and 30 December 1967, which stresses the fact that in the first six months of 1967, 65 per cent of the market demand for labour in Poland was met by women.

10 Schaff, Adam, *Marxism and the Individual*, Warsaw, 1955.

11 Sokorski, W., in *Kultura*, Warsaw, 10 October 1965.

12 *The Managerial Revolution*, New York, 1941.

13 Ferge, S., *Social Stratification in Hungary*, op. cit.

14 The fact of exploitation has been recognized even by such official ideologists as the Yugoslav Vlahovic (in *Vjesnik*, Zagreb, 31 December 1967), and the Chinese have discussed it at length in their anti-Soviet polemical documents: see 'Khrushchev's Pseudo-Communism and the Historical Lesson it Holds for the World', *Peking Information*, 20 July 1964.

15 See the 1965 Hungarian statistics: 39 per cent of the privileged caste, numbering approximately 500,000 and including high officials and creative intellectuals, were proletarian by origin, and 26 per cent sprang from the peasantry; 46 per cent of the middle-rank intelligentsia (technicians, specialists, office workers) came from the working class and 27 per cent from the peasantry.

16 Thus, in Poland 33.1 per cent of the workers earn over 2,000 zlotys per month and 52 per cent of intellectual workers less than 2,000. cf. Labedz, L., op. cit., p. 37.

17 In Host do Domu, Brno, September 1965.

18 An inquiry carried out in Poland in 1966 showed that the university professors, doctors, teachers, engineers and lawyers occupy the first five places in the 'hierarchy of prestige'. Ministers come seventh, before agronomists and journalists. This demonstrates the difference – which, in my opinion, prevails throughout the People's Democracies, with the exception of Czechoslovakia – between the hierarchy of the 'real country' and of the 'official country'.

19 Szazadok, January–February 1967.

20 'The number of people employed is far larger than can be justified economically', declared Aladar Mod at an Academy of Sciences conference, reported in Szazadok, January–February 1967.

21 On Czechoslovakia, see Loebl, Eugen, in Planovane Hospodarstoi, No. 10, 1965. In Poland, L. Kolakowski, addressing students, said: 'The ruling group is ineffectual, and not answerable to the people.' In Yugoslavia, Branko Horvat, director of the Belgrade Institute of Economic Research, declared in June 1967: 'Many people who occupy top positions in the economy are incapable of adapting themselves to market economy and decentralization.' On 16 August 1968, the Belgrade authorities seized the magazine Delo, accusing its contributors of having 'denied that the working class was capable of running the country and having demanded its replacement by the humanistic intelligentsia.'

22 See Istvan Szirmai's restatement of this in Tarsadalmi Szemle, November 1965; the June 1966 theses of the Czechoslovak party; Ceausescu's speech of 7 December 1967.

23 Szirmai, Kadar ideologist, in his gloomy refutation of the argument that the intelligentsia has a mission to lead, also condemned the sectarians who oppose the workers' (in fact, the intellectuals' and technicians') desire for a comfortable standard of living.

24 Literarni Noviny, 22 October 1966. After Novotny's removal in January 1968, this same scholar hastened to affirm that 'changes

in personnel were not enough'. He called for constitutional guarantees of civil rights.

25 *Przeglad Kulturalny*, 17 May 1962.

26 cf. L. Vaculik's article on this question in *Literarni Listy*, 4 April 1968.

27 *Nepszabadsag*, 19 June 1966.

28 In 1967 the trade-union chairman, Vukmanovic Tempo, a guerrilla veteran, protested against official claims that 'wages had risen more rapidly than productivity'. The trade-union congress of June 1968, with Tito's approval, launched a wholesale offensive against the 'red bureaucracy' and in favour of a bolder social policy.

29 *Der Gewertschafter*, September 1967. In March 1968 Polacek was elected chairman of the Council of Trade Unions.

30 *Vjesnik u Srijedu*, Zagreb, 8 June 1966; *Nin*, Belgrade, 29 October 1967.

31 In 1956, 110 directors were dismissed at the request of the councils.

32 Connock, M., 'L'autogestion a déçu les travailleurs yougoslaves', *Le Figaro*, 22 June 1968.

33 Among the many books on the subject of the Yugoslav workers' councils are: Meister, A., *Socialisme et Autogestion*, Seuil, Paris, 1965; Kolaja, J., *Workers' Councils*, Tavistock, London, 1965; Sturmtahl, A., *Workers' Councils*, Harvard University Press, Cambridge, Mass., 1964; Ionescu, G., *L'avenir politique de l'Europe orientale*, op. cit.

34 *Po Prostu*, 6 January 1957.

35 Sturmtahl, A., op. cit., 1956 *Pologne-Hongrie*, E.D.I., Paris, 1966.

36 The situation was different from that in Czechoslovakia in August 1968. There, the party leadership and party organizations, the government and the Presidium of the Assembly assumed command of the passive resistance movement.

37 cf. Fejtö, F., *Budapest 1956*, op. cit.; and 1956 *Pologne-Hongrie*, op. cit.

38 cf. his lecture to the Prague Economic Society, Agence France-Presse dispatch, 21 May 1968.

39 cf. Michel Tatu's essay on self-management in Czechoslovakia, in *Le Monde*, 21 June 1968.

40 See the results of an inquiry conducted in Hungarian secondary schools in 1967, *Nepszabadsag*, 23 January 1968.

41 Ferge, S., in *Valosag*, October 1966.

19 Cultural Development: The Breakdown of Ideology

1 The party's aim is 'to create ... a new structure of values and

new incentives where man would become master, not only of his material conditions, but also of social conditions.' Suchodolski, Bogdan, 'On Socialist Civilization', in *Nowe Drogi*, No. 11, Warsaw, 1967.

2 Rozane, Marjan, in *Most*, Nos. 9–10, Trieste, 1966. The writer was given a six-month suspended sentence in October 1967 for publishing this disillusioned comment in this Trieste Slovene-language magazine.

3 *Literarni Noviny*, 17 June 1967.

4 Resolution of the Fourth Czechoslovak Writers' Congress, *Literarni Noviny*, 8 July 1967.

5 The exception is, perhaps, Cuba, whose leaders are men of culture and guerrilla fighters, rather than bureaucrats, and have made it a point of honour to tolerate and even cultivate the avant-garde. cf. the opening address of President Dorticos at the Havana Cultural Congress, *Cuba*, February 1968.

6 Aragon, Louis, preface to the French translation of Milan Kundera's novel, *La Plaisanterie*, Gallimard, Paris, 1968.

7 *Tarsadalmi Szemle*, 15 September 1952.

8 *On Communism: in defence of the New Course*, op. cit.

9 'Theses on the Cultural Policy of the Self-Governing Society', *Borba*, 12 February 1968. Maecenas was the patron of Horace and Virgil.

10 *Preuves*, June 1967.

11 *Le Monde*, 2 February 1968.

12 cf. Rigby, T. H., 'Security and Modernization', *Survey*, July 1967; Kecskeméti, K., 'Les grandes lignes de l'histoire de l'Europe centrale', *Esprit*, February 1968; Borsody, S., *The Triumph of Tyranny*, Cape, London, 1960; Bibo, I., 'The Misery of the Small States of Eastern Europe', *Vàlasz*, 1946 (in Hungarian).

13 cf. Calvez, J., *Introduction to Political Life*.

14 cf. his article in *Esprit*, December 1965, and May 1966.

15 Thus, even the ultra-orthodox head of the Bulgarian party, Zhivkov – after so many years of struggle against bourgeois nationalism – condemned the teachers' 'insensitivity' to the country's liberal traditions. 'I know no other country that permits such belittlement and depreciation of its national past' (*Rabotnichesko Delo*, 10 January 1968).

16 See Fejtö, F., *Budapest 1956*, op. cit., p 12.

17 cf. his book, *Marxism and the Individual*, op. cit. See also Chapter 13 of the present work.

18 cf. Kecskeméti, op. cit.

19 *Le Nouvel Observateur*, 21 February 1968.

20 *Rude Pravo*, 22 February 1968.

21 cf. Ratuszniak, Z., 'The Organization of Higher Education', *Polish Prospects*, Warsaw, December 1966; Schreiber, T., 'L'Enseignement en Pologne', *Notes et études documentaires, Documentation française*, 6 May 1964.

22 Vucenov, N., 'Schooling and Education', *Revue de la politique internationale*, Belgrade, 28 December 1967.

23 *Rude Pravo*, 19 March.

24 In Czechoslovakia, the 1953 syllabus called for 104 hours of Russian in the fourth year and 85 hours in the fifth, as against 66 hours of national history.

25 *Vysoka Skola*, Prague, May 1964; *Scanteia Tineretulni*, 21 July 1967.

26 cf. Fejtö, F., 'Réforme scolaire et stratification sociale en U.R.S.S.', in *L'U.R.S.S.*, I, Sirey, Paris, 1962; Pundeff, M., 'Les réformes de l'enseignement en Europe orientale', *Documentation française*, 28 November 1963.

27 Floyd, D., *Rumania: Russia's Dissident Ally*, Pall Mall, London, and Praeger, New York, 1965.

28 *Vysoka Skola*, Prague, March 1964.

29 *Nova Mysl*, Prague, September 1964.

30 The words of the Bulgarian Minister of Public Education, *Uchitelsko Delo*, 7 July 1963.

31 cf. *Student*, Prague, 27 January 1966.

32 *Student*, 21 January 1968.

33 *Pravda*, Bratislava, 2 August 1967.

34 *Borba*, 9 March 1967.

35 *Nin*, Belgrade, February 1967.

36 *Kulturny Zivot*, 23 April 1965.

37 *Literarni Noviny*, 16 January 1965.

38 cf. Hajny, J., 'A Generation without Ideals', *Rude Pravo*, 23 July 1965.

39 Radio Prague inquiry, May 1966.

40 See *Smena* (official organ of the Slovak youth bodies), 15 January 1966.

41 See the preceding chapter.

42 'Is there enough room for adventure and heroism in our lives?' To this question put by the Ostrava Pedagogical Institute's research workers to 183 young people, 16 answered 'yes' and 68 gave a categorical 'no' (*Literarni Noviny*, 16 January 1965).

43 Conversation on Brno radio, February 1967.

44 *Literarni Noviny*, 16 January 1965.

45 cf. Bendova, D., 'What my Generation Feels and Thinks', *Kulturny Zivot*, 23 April 1963, and *Zycie Literackie*, Cracow, 4 December 1966.

46 cf. V. Farago's article in *Latohatar*, Budapest, July–August 1967, which based on an inquiry carried out ten years after the disastrous rising, maintained that most Hungarian schoolchildren between the ages of eleven and fourteen are 'instinctively patriotic', whereas students between seventeen and eighteen are both 'nationalistic and cosmopolitan'.

47 Bulgarian Central Committee decision of July 1967. See also *Polityka*, Warsaw, 12 January 1968.

48 These remarks of Koucky's may be set against the observations of a contributor to the magazine *Smena* (28 December 1965) showing, on the basis of several inquiries, that military service had lost all its attraction to youth, that the majority of young people did not understand the Vietnam war and did not condemn the United States, and finally that military-political subjects were not popular.

49 *Rabotnichesko Delo*, 9 July 1967.

50 *Wesen und Wahrheit des Glaubens*, Evangelisches Verlagwerk, Stuttgart, 1961.

51 Marx, *Capital*, I.

52 *Lidova Demokracie*, 25 May 1968.

53 cf. the information supplied by Mgr Tomasek to the correspondent of *La Croix*, the French daily (2 May 1968), and to the author.

54 The most interesting was the one on the attitude of young people to the religious question carried out by the Czech Academician Mrs Kadlecova (one of the 1967 organizers of the Marianske Lazne Catholic-Marxist discussion) with the Hungarian Institute of Sociology. cf. *Herder Correspondenz*, Freiburg, June 1967.

55 *Osvelova Prace*, No. 26, 1965.

56 *Sociologicky Casopis*, No. 2, 1965.

57 C. T. K., 4 December 1966.

58 *Polityka*, 18 February 1960.

59 Schreiber, Thomas, 'L'Église de Hongrie est devenue plus populaire', *Le Monde*, 6 July 1963.

60 *Tarsadalmi Szemle*, Budapest, August 1956.

61 An inquiry conducted by the Sociological Institute of the Academy of Sciences stated that 64.4 per cent of Bulgarians were avowed atheists (*Politicheska Prosveta*, No. 11, 1967). However, the press is becoming increasingly concerned at the proselytism

of the Adventist, Methodist, and Pentecostalist Churches. In this respect, the situation resembles that in the Soviet Union, where the sects also profit from the official Church's passiveness in the face of persecution.

62 See J. P. Picaper's report in *Le Monde*, 9 October 1968.

63 'Une page tournée', *Le Monde*, 26 June 1966.

64 Agence France-Presse dispatch, Belgrade, 14 March 1968.

65 *Nowe Drogi*, April 1966.

66 In 1956 over 90 per cent of parents had declared themselves in favour of the reintroduction of religious education in schools, and the government yielded to them.

67 See Jelenski, K. A., 'La Pologne: une Gréce du monde communiste', *Preuves*, June–July 1968.

68 See the memorandum on the state of the Protestant Churches in Hungary by an anonymous group of pastors, sent to the West and printed in *Irodalmi Ujsag*, Paris, 15 November 1965, and the article in *Frankfurter Allgemeine Zeitung*, 29 December 1966.

69 Interview published by Agence France-Presse, 26 May 1958.

70 *La Croix*, 2 May 1968.

71 cf. Tatu, Michel, *Le Monde*, 5 October 1968. On the first post-Stalinist period in the development of Church–State relations, see 'The Battle for Belief', in *East Europe*, October 1960, and Schreiber, Thomas, *Le Christianisme en Europe orientale*, Spes, Paris, 1961. It should be remembered that the occupation of Czechoslovakia caused commotion not only in the World Trade Union Federation centred in Prague, whose president, Louis Saillant, condemned the action of the Five, but also in the Christian Peace Conference, a movement organized by the Czechoslovak Protestant Hromadka. This movement, financed by the Czechoslovak government, which for so long had been taking advantage of the good faith and love of peace of many clerics and theologians throughout the world, disintegrated after August. At a meeting of the movement's committee in Paris at the beginning of October, a certain number of those present from the West condemned the intervention of the five Warsaw Pact countries, following a discussion in which Hromadka and the other Czechoslovak participants 'abstained from taking part'.

72 Sotola, S., in *Kulturny Zivot*, 20 June 1967.

73 After the September 1956 Congress of the Union of Hungarian Writers, I called this union an 'independent republic of writers'. Indeed, throwing off the party's tutelage the union turned itself

into a sort of a free enclave within a repressed society. (*Lettres Nouvelles*, November 1956.)

74 cf. *National Zeitung*, East Berlin, 12 September 1968.

75 A. Abusch at the Writers' Union Conference of November 1966.

76 *Narodna Kultura*, 27 Jaunary 1968.

77 Editorial, *Literaturen Front*, 18 January 1968.

78 One of the 'central tasks' of literature, according to Gyoergy Lukacs, is to depict the 'tragic conflict' stemming from the transformation of so many genuine revolutionaries into dogmatic bureaucrats. (Interview with *Nepszabadsag*, 24 December 1967.)

79 Chorvat, M., 'The Revolt of Youth', *Kulturny Zivot*, 29 April 1966.

80 cf. Weiss, T., 'The Guilt Complex in Communist Literature', *East Europe*, May 1966; Urban, R., 'Die Bewaltigung der Vergangenheit in der Tchekoslowakei', *Osteuropa*, May–June 1967. On the Hungarian writers' struggle see Aczel, T., and Méray, T., 'La révolte de l'Esprit', N.R.F., Paris; 'Écrivians hongrois d'aujourd'hui', *Lettres Nouvelles*, special issue September–October 1964; Gara, L., ed., *Anthologie de la poésie hongroise*, Seuil, Paris, 1962; Jelenski, K., ed., *Anthologie de la poésie polonaise*, Seuil, Paris, 1965; Phillippe, P., *Tchécoslovaquie*, Seuil, Paris, 1967; 'L'autre Europe', *Esprit*, February 1968; in addition to the very rich and important literature of Polish, Czech, Hungarian and other émigrés.

81 See above, Chapter 16.

82 In Warsaw, where the average wage in 1968 was 2,200 zlotys per month, 45 writers and artists earned over 10,000 zlotys per month, the salary of a Deputy Prime Minister. Some of them earn up to 40,000 zlotys. In all the Communist countries writers enjoy very high royalties, and often receive special awards. On the moral corruption resulting from this in the Soviet Union, see Frioux, B., in *Le Monde*, 11 October 1968.

83 At the September 1967 Plenum. cf. also the defence of the official line by the former Minister of Justice, Stefan Rais, in *Kulturny Tvorba*, 29 October 1967.

84 cf. the statements by the director of Czechoslovak television, Jiri Pelican, in *Le Monde*, 6 March 1968.

85 cf. 'Un nouveau chapitre de la tragédie tchécoslovaque: l'exode des intellectuels', *Le Monde*, 12 September 1968.

86 Statement of Gyoergy Aczel, Central Committee secretary in charge of cultural affairs, reported in *Nepszabadsag*, 27 April 1968.

87 Lakatos, M., 'The Citizens are looking for their Place', *Kulturny Noviny*, Prague, 24 February 1968.

88 The standard work on the press of the Communist countries (including those of Eastern Europe) is Buzek, Antony, *How the Communist Press Works*, Pall Mall, London, and Praegar, New York, 1964. See also Fejtö, F., 'The Press in the Satellite Countries', *The World Today*, June 1953; 'La presse et la radiodiffusion en Europe orientale', *Documentation française*, Nos. 2735 and 2738, December 1960; 'Aspects de la presse dans les pays satellites', *Libre Belgique*, 22 February 1964; 'Les problèmes de l'information en Pologne', *Articles et Documents, Documentation française*, 5 July 1956; Troscianko, W., 'Polish Journalists and the Censor', *East Europe*, November 1965; Mihajlov, M., 'Perchè non parliamo', *Tempo Presente*, September–October 1965; Osol, B., 'La formation de l'opinion publique dans un pays socialiste', *Questions actuelles du socialisme*, No. 79, 1965; Mond, Georges, 'La presse de l'Europe orientale et centrale', *Revue de l'Université d'Ottawa*, January–March 1965; Stankovic, S., 'The Jugoslav Press to become even freer', *Radio Free Europe Research*, 15 February 1967; 'The Congress of Slovak Journalists', *Kulturny Zivot*, 1 June 1963; Suda, Z., 'Le contrôle politique de la presse en Tchécoslovaquie', *Est-Quest*, 16–30 April 1967; Tigrid, Pavel, *Le Printemps de Prague*, Seuil, Paris, 1968; Salomon, Michel, *Prague, la révolution étranglée*, op. cit.; Molnar, Miklos, *Victoire d'une défaite*, Budapest 1956, Fayard, Paris, 1968; Nagy, Laszlo, *Démocraties populaires*, Arthaud, Paris, 1968; de Jouvenel, B., 'Le système répressif', *Le Monde*, 6–7 October 1968.

Prospects

1 See the exposition of the Soviet doctrine by the Yugoslav Minister of Foreign Affairs before the United Nations, in *Le Monde*, 16 October 1968.

2 On the feasibility of this, see Nagy, Laszlo, *Démocraties populaires*, op. cit.

3 *Stalin: a political biography*, O.U.P., London, 1961.

4 cf. Frioux, B., 'Le procès Litvinov-Daniel', *Le Monde*, 11 October 1968. Unfortunately, one may ask whether the Americans are more adult in dealing with the problems of Vietnam or South America. But crimes of the one do not excuse those of the other.

5 cf. Hochman, Jiri, in *Reporter*, Prague, 8 October 1968

6 cf. Lewin, Moshe, *Le Dernier Combat de Lénine*, Éditions de Minuit, Paris, 1967.

Epilogue I (1971): After Prague and Postcript on Poland

1 See Sartre, J.-P., 'Le socialisme qui venait du froid' : Introduction to Liehm, A., Trois générations, Paris, 1970.

2 On the visit to Prague by Grechko and Semenov on 31 March 1969, see Tigrid, Pavel, La chute irréversible de Dubcek, Calmann-Lévy, Paris, 1970. Grechko presented the Czechoslovak leaders with an ultimatum calling on them to choose between three alternatives: they must either restore order by their own means or accept the Warsaw Pact countries' help in putting down counter-revolution, or, if they refused to do so, those countries would intervene to any extent they thought necessary.

3 The same is true of the anarchical and almost revolutionary trends of the months before August 1968. The Venezuelan Communist leader, Teodoro Petkoff, in his book Cechoslovaquia: el socialismo como problema, Caracas, 1969, rightly pointed out that 'the lack of understanding shown by the present Soviet leaders was the chief factor of instability in Czechoslovakia'.

4 The record was published in Politique Aujourd'hui for May 1970.

5 cf. Michel Tatu's preface to the collection of speeches published as Alexandre Dubcek. Du printemps à l'hiver de Prague, Fayard, Paris, 1970.

6 The differences between the situation in Hungary after the rising and that in Czechoslovakia after the occupation are brought out in a valuable collective study, 'Procès à Prague', in Esprit, June 1970.

7 cf. Pelikan, Jiri, ed., Le Congrès clandestin. Protocole secret et documents du XIVe Congrès extraordinaire du P.C. tchécoslovaque, Seuil, Paris, 1970.

8 cf. 'Le parti communiste tchécoslovaque normalisé. Lettre de Prague', in Politique Aujourd'hui, June 1970.

9 cf. Aragon's outraged protest in Lettres françaises for 8 October 1969 against 'a socialist country turning systematic delation into a national duty'. For the text of the questionnaire to officers, see Le Monde, 4 July 1970.

10 'L'arbitraire légalisé', report by Agence France-Presse, Prague, 19 December 1969.

11 Das Tagebuch, Vienna, July–August 1969.

12 On resistance activities see the excellent report by Philippe Saint-Gilles in Le Nouvel Observateur, 17 August 1970.

13 For the K.G.B.'s activities in Czechoslovakia see the disclosures of Sasha Demidov, a former Czech counter-espionage agent, in Der Spiegel, No. 30, 1970.

14 Svic, O., 'Reconstruction of the national economy', in *Tvorba*, 12 November 1969.

15 cf. 'Nouvelles de Tchécoslovaquie', bulletin issued by the Czechoslovak Embassy in Paris, 3 February 1970.

16 Stuart, A., 'Ceausescu's Land', *Survey*, Summer 1970.

17 Raffaelli, Jean, 'Le traité soviéto-roumain', Agence France-Presse, 8 July 1970.

18 *Der Spiegel* (No. 33, 1970) published what seemed to be well-founded information on the dispatch to Egypt of auxiliary military personnel from Hungary, the G.D.R., Poland, Czechoslovakia and Bulgaria, and also the training of such units in Kazakhstan for desert warfare.

19 On 25 August the New China News Agency, in commenting on the 26th anniversary of Rumania's liberation, praised the Rumanian leaders for 'opposing any interference with their policy'.

20 cf. Gamarnikow, M., 'Die Reformversuche in Polen', *Neue Zürcher Zeitung*, 9 and 11 April 1970, and J.G.G., 'Polen vor neuen Reformprojekten', ibid., 16 August 1970.

21 cf. Levi, Mario, and Schütze, Walter, 'Les relations économiques de la République Fédérale dans les pays de l'Est', in *Politique Étrangère*, No. 4, 1970.

22 Thus the Prague *Mlada Fronta* for 19 August 1970 drew a parallel between the events of August 1968 and the realism which led to West Germany's signing the treaty: 'August 21 [1968] was a turning-point in international affairs, as Soviet strength obliged Western politicians to think more realistically and take more account of facts.'

23 With regard to this part of the Moscow agreements, the Russians would no doubt endorse the statement in the Warsaw *Zycie Warszawy* of 22 August 1970: 'Present-day reality no longer corresponds to the power relations of 1945.' In the vocabulary of the Communist bloc 'reality', when it is to the bloc's advantage, is always presented as irreversible, and its recognition as the essential condition of a *détente*.

24 This policy, as Michel Tatu points out in an article, 'La flotte soviétique dans l'Océan indien: Canonnières progressistes contre canonnières impérialistes', *Le Monde*, 14 August 1970, is a dangerous one, since 'seeking influence for its own sake . . . soon becomes a matter of protecting the advantages thus gained, which are looked on as vital to security, not to mention the "prestige of the flag"'.

25 On the different approaches of the respective countries, see

Klaiber, Wolfgang, 'Security Priorities in Eastern Europe', *Problems of Communism*, May–June 1970.

26 cf. the Agence France-Presse dispatch from Budapest (25 August 1970) analysing the theses presented to the Tenth Congress of the Hungarian Socialist Workers' Party, which emphasize *inter alia* that 'social progress involves an improved social role for the intelligentsia', and that 'artisans and small traders should be given a place in society corresponding to their importance'. It is noteworthy that in 1970, 50 per cent of maintenance and repair services in Hungary were performed by private artisans, the number of workshops being 83,000, or 5,600 more than in 1969 (*Magyar Hirek*, 8 August 1970).

27 cf. the manifesto of these three scholars, couched in highly 'Dubcekian' terms, in *Le Monde*, 11 and 12–13 April 1970.

28 For an interesting discussion of how the West can best take advantage of these cross-currents and the crisis they portend, see Brzezinski, Z., for 'Lenin's Centenary, The Soviet Past and Future', *Encounter*, March 1970, and Hassner, Pierre, 'L'Europe des années 70; Stabilité et Conflits', *Revue de Défense Nationale*, May 1970.

29 cf. the relatively sober and objective account of the disturbances published on 9–10 January by the Gdansk newspaper *Glos Wybrzeza* (Voice of the Coast) and broadcast by Radio Free Europe on the 10th. From 15 December onwards, thanks to its monitoring of Gdansk and Szczecin radios, R.F.E. was the first and most objective source of information in the West regarding the events in Poland. The text of the Gdynia workers' leaflet accusing Moczar and Cyrankiewicz of responsibility for the massacre was published in *The Times* on 27 January. Kociolek's appeal to the Gdansk activists was published in *Glos Wybrzeza* of 9–10 January.

30 Bajalski, R., in the *Politika*, Belgrade, 31 December 1970.

31 For the circumstances of Gomulka's fall see Bethell, N., 'The Downfall of M. Gomulka', in *The Times*, 3 February 1971; 'Wie Gomulka gestürzt wurde', in the *Neue Zürcher Zeitung*, 21 January 1971; an article in the Warsaw *Perspektywy* for 13 February 1971; and Hansen, Per, in *Aktuelt*, Copenhagen, 26 February 1971. This states that Gomulka was relieved of his functions and placed under police guard on 19 December, but not sent to hospital till the 24th.

32 Varnai, F., 'From experiments to lessons', 28 February 1971.

33 Bertone, F., 'Due preoccupazioni della linea polacca', *Rinascita*, 12 March 1971.

Epilogue II: The People's Democracies in 1971–2

1 See Mencer, G., 'Certains problèmes politiques et légaux internationaux', in *Casopis pro Mezinarodni Pravo*, No. 3, August 1971.

2 In a lecture at the Centre d'Études de Politique Étrangère, Paris, 8 June 1972.

3 *Komunist*, 14 April 1972.

4 This report reached the West, and long extracts were published in *Le Monde*, 22 February 1972.

5 Kovacs, J., *The New Elements of Socialist Constitutional Development* (in Hungarian), Budapest, 1962.

6 Tito later declared (at a meeting of trade-union leaders on 18 December 1971), that if firm action had not been taken against 'Croatian separatism', civil war and foreign intervention could have followed within six months.

Index of Persons

Names to which passing reference only is made in the text are excluded, as are the names of authors merely quoted or cited.

General Index

Matters relating to individual countries may be traced under an appropriate general heading, where references to more discursive passages appear. Places are indexed under country. Material in the Notes is excluded.

More about Penguins
and Pelicans

Penguinews, which appears every month, contains details of all the new books issued by Penguins as they are published. From time to time it is supplemented by *Penguins in Print*, which is our complete list of almost 5,000 titles.

A specimen copy of *Penguinews* will be sent to you free on request. Please write to Dept EP, Penguin Books Ltd, Harmondsworth, Middlesex, for your copy.

In the U.S.A.: For a complete list of books available from Penguins in the United States write to Dept CS, Penguin Books, 625 Madison Avenue, New York, New York 10022.

In Canada: For a complete list of books available from Penguins in Canada write to Penguin Books Canada Ltd, 2801 John Street, Markham, Ontario.

Books on European History published by
Penguin Books

Books on European History published by
Penguin Books

Machiavelli and Renaissance Italy   J. R. Hale
The European Mind 1680–1715   Paul Hazard
The Devils of Loudun   Aldous Huxley
Chronicles of the Crusades   Joinville and Villehardouin
The Pelican History of Medieval Europe   Maurice Keen
The Lords of Human Kind   V. G. Kiernan
The Making of Modern Russia   Lionel Kochan

Political Leaders of the Twentieth Century

Gomulka

Nicholas Bethell

Gomulka was the hero of post-war Europe, the man who stood up to Stalin in 1949 and Khrushchev in 1956. He became a national legend by bringing new political freedom to a humiliated Poland, and his stance against the Soviet leaders, it has been said, inspired the Hungarians to rise. Yet his growing inflexibility, coupled with his acute conception of Poland's political situation, made him the loudest voice urging invasion of Dubcek's Czechoslovakia in 1968.

Gomulka's full biography is known only to the Russian security police; he is also a reserved man and dislikes publicity. Lord Bethell has met the challenge, however, with this book, and succeeds brilliantly in making clear the complex life of a man whose activities and sympathies involve the complete history of modern Polish politics.

'... a political biography whose scholarly detail and unceasing effort to be fair will make it a book which anybody who wishes to know about Poland must read' – *Observer*

Political Leaders of the Twentieth Century

Stalin

Isaac Deutscher

During his life Stalin engendered the extremes of hatred and love: it was impossible to ignore him. Greater at his best, than Peter the Great; more brutal, at his worst, than Ivan the Terrible, the subject of this famous biography is himself sufficient explanation of the storm of controversy it aroused on publication. Some saw it as the rose-tinted apology of a former Communist, some as the bitter denunciation of a writer who had never subscribed to the Stalin cult. Deutscher's biography is, in reality, an unbiased appraisal of a revolutionary despot, and this Pelican edition contains a wholly new chapter covering Stalin's last years.

Fifty Years of Communism

THEORY AND PRACTICE 1917–1967

G. F. Hudson

What would Marx think of Marxism if he were alive today? Marxism, it could be said, has assumed strange shapes which would evoke his astonishment and often his indignation.

The development of communism, both in theory and practice, since the Bolshevik capture of power in Russia in 1917 is the subject of this remarkable work by G. F. Hudson of St Anthony's College, Oxford. *Fifty Years of Communism* begins with an account of the origins of Marxism and goes on to describe all the major events in the history of communism including Stalin's great purge, the rise of communism in China, Maoism, and communism in the Third World.

'. . . it forces one to re-examine one's views on the great issues with which it deals. And few will disagree with the author's searing account of the great purges in Russia in the thirties or with his criticism of the set-up there today' – George Aitken in *Tribune*

The Pelican Marx Library

Grundrisse

Introduction to the Critique of Political Economy

The *Grundrisse* throws light on many obscure corners of
Marx's thought and, in this light, the English reader can now
assess how far his economic and philosophic outlook changed
and how far it has simply been misinterpreted. For here is a
major part of Marx's work which was unknown even to Lenin.

The Revolutions of 1848

Political Writings Volume I

The bulk of this volume contains articles from the *Neue
Rheinische Zeitung*, a journal in which Marx (or occasionally
Engels) interpreted the risings in Vienna, Berlin and Prague.
In addition there are reviews, addresses, speeches on Poland
and the minute of the London meeting of 1850 when Schapper
and others finally left the Communist League.
At the head of these political writings is Marx's most famous
text – the *Manifesto of the Communist Party* (1848), in which
he outlines the class struggles of history.

Surveys from Exile

Political Writings Volume II

After perfecting his English Marx began to interpret, in a
series of articles for the American (and German) press, the
English political scene and British rule in India, and, on the
outbreak of the American Civil War, he wrote at length on
that conflict for a liberal paper in Vienna. Samples of these
extensive writings, by which Marx earned a scanty living,
appear in this volume, along with other reviews, speeches
and political statements.

The Pelican Marx Library includes

Early Writings
The First International and After
Capital (to be published in 3 vols.)

Published in association with *New Left Review*